Teaching Business and Human Rights

T0329766

Teaching Business and Human Rights

Edited by

Anthony Ewing

Lecturer in Law, Columbia Law School, USA and Co-Founder, Teaching Business and Human Rights Forum

ELGAR GUIDES TO TEACHING

Cheltenham, UK • Northampton, MA, USA

Cover image: © Detroit Institute of Arts / Gift of Edsel B. Ford / Bridgeman Images. North wall of a mural depicting Detroit Industry, 1932–33 (fresco). Creator: Rivera, Diego (1886–1957).

Published by
Edward Elgar Publishing Limited
The Lypiatts
15 Lansdown Road
Cheltenham
Glos GL50 2JA
UK

Edward Elgar Publishing, Inc.
William Pratt House
9 Dewey Court
Northampton
Massachusetts 01060
USA

Paperback edition 2023

A catalogue record for this book
is available from the British Library

Library of Congress Control Number: 2023933743

This book is available electronically in the **Elgar**online
Business subject collection
http://dx.doi.org/10.4337/9781802201130

ISBN 978 1 80220 112 3 (cased)
ISBN 978 1 80220 113 0 (eBook)
ISBN 978 1 0353 2919 9 (paperback)

For my students and teachers.

Contents

Figures

Tables

Exercises

Contributors

Christine Bader (Opinion Writing as a Teaching Tool) is the author of *The Evolution of a Corporate Idealist: When Girl Meets Oil*. From 2015 to 2017 she was Amazon's director of social responsibility. Prior to that she worked for BP in Indonesia, China, and the U.K., and served as adviser to the United Nations secretary-general's special representative for business and human rights. She has delivered talks around the world, including a TED talk; her writing has appeared in *The New York Times*, *The Atlantic*, and many other publications.

Dorothée Baumann-Pauly (Multistakeholder Human Rights Initiatives) is a professor at Geneva University's School of Economics and Management. She directs the Geneva Center for Business and Human Rights, the first human rights center at a business school in Europe. Since 2013, she has also been the research director at the Stern Center for Business and Human Rights at New York University.

Eric R. Biel (Trade and Human Rights) has been co-teaching a course on business and human rights with Meg Roggensack since 2009 at Georgetown University Law Center. Since 2018, he has served as senior adviser at the Fair Labor Association. From 2011 to 2017, he served in senior positions at the U.S. Department of Labor's Bureau of International Labor Affairs; earlier government service included high-level positions at the U.S. Department of Commerce and Trade Counsel at the Senate Finance Committee. He has spoken and written widely on trade and on business and human rights while working in both government and the private sector.

Claire Bright (Mandatory Human Rights Due Diligence) is an associate professor in private law as well as the founder and director of the NOVA Centre on Business, Human Rights, and the Environment at NOVA Law School in Lisbon. She has contributed to various expert studies and policy reports for non-governmental organizations and governments, as well as European and international organizations, including a study for the European Commission on Due Diligence Requirements through the Supply Chains that forms the basis for the Proposed Directive on Corporate Sustainability Due Diligence.

Nicolas Bueno (Mandatory Human Rights Due Diligence) is a professor in international and European law at UniDistance Suisse in Switzerland. His research focuses on law and economic globalization, business and human rights, and labor rights. He leads the research group on business and human rights at UniDistance Suisse. Professor Bueno also litigated as legal adviser in business and human rights at the European Center for Constitutional and Human Rights in Berlin and he advises stakeholders on drafting mandatory human rights and environmental due diligence legislation.

Humberto Cantú Rivera (Business and Human Rights in the Inter-American System) is a professor at the School of Law and Social Sciences of the University of Monterrey (Mexico) and director of its Human Rights and Business Institute. He holds an LL.D. from Université Panthéon-Assas Paris II. He has published widely on business and human rights and has extensive experience working with and advising states, international organizations, businesses, and civil society on business and human rights in international, regional, and domestic standard-setting processes and in the implementation of responsible business conduct standards.

Davis Chacon Hurtado (Engineering for Human Rights) is an assistant research professor in the Department of Civil and Environmental Engineering and the Human Rights Institute at the University of Connecticut. His research interests include transportation planning, equity, and human rights; economic resilience; environmental justice; and sustainable transportation. Davis completed his Ph.D. in Transportation and Infrastructure Systems at Purdue University. He also earned an M.S.C.E. from the University of Puerto Rico at Mayagüez and a B.Eng. from the University of San Antonio Abad of Cusco in Peru.

Dr. Rachel Chambers (Judicial Remedy) is an assistant professor of business law at the University of Connecticut, School of Business, where she researches and teaches on corporate accountability mechanisms. She is a codirector of the Teaching Business and Human Rights Forum (TeeachBHR.org). Rachel practiced in law as a barrister (England and Wales) for nearly a decade before moving into academia and she has worked as a consultant to the UN Global Compact and Amnesty International.

Angela B. Cornell (Labor Rights) is a clinical professor at Cornell Law School and founding director of the Labor Law Clinic. Her teaching, practice, and scholarship focus on domestic and international labor law and business and human rights. She is a coeditor of *The Cambridge Handbook of Labor and Democracy*. Her research has been published in a number of outlets and her opinions referenced by the media, including *The New York Times*, *The Economist*, the BBC, *Ms. Magazine*, *Washington Post*, and NPR.

Daria Davitti (Human Rights Due Diligence) is an associate professor in public international law at Lund University, Faculty of Law. Her research focuses on the intersection between international economic law and international human rights law and their implementation in complex contexts, such as situations of armed conflict, climate breakdown, and humanitarian and health emergencies. Prior to joining academia, Daria worked as a human rights officer for the UN Office of the High Commissioner for Human Rights and the UN Assistance Mission in Afghanistan.

Anthony Ewing (Introduction, Human Rights, The UN Guiding Principles on Business and Human Rights, The Alien Tort Statute, Complicity) is a lecturer at Columbia Law School where he has taught business and human rights since 2001. He cofounded the Teaching Business and Human Rights Forum and is a member of the Editorial Board of the *Business and Human Rights Journal*. Anthony is a business adviser, attorney, and teacher with two decades of experience counseling senior executives in the private and non-profit sectors on corporate responsibility, crisis management, and strategic communication. As a senior associate at Shift, the leading center of expertise on the UN Guiding Principles on Business and Human Rights, Anthony works with governments, business enterprises, and other partners to put the UN Guiding Principles into practice. He has also worked with the International Labour Organization, the Executive Office of the UN Global Compact, the International Secretariat of Religions for Peace, the International League for Human Rights, and the Inter-American Court of Human Rights; and taught English at the Colegio Técnico Profesional Agropecuario de Osa in Costa Rica. Anthony holds a B.A. in political science from Yale University and a law degree from Columbia University, where he was editor-in-chief of the *Columbia Human Rights Law Review*.

John Ferguson (Accounting for Human Rights) is a professor of accounting at the University of St Andrews and codirector of the Centre for Social and Environmental Accounting Research (CSEAR). He previously served as the editor of CSEAR's journal, *Social and Environmental Accountability Journal* (SEAJ). John has worked with the Scottish government to develop a National Baseline Assessment (NBA) on business and human rights and continues to provide input in the development of a Scottish National Action Plan.

Nina Luzatto Gardner (Memo to the Ambassador) is the director of Strategy International, a corporate sustainability advisory firm she founded in 2000. She works with companies to improve their commitment to sustainability and with investors to better understand environmental, social, and corporate governance risks in their portfolios. A lawyer by training, she has been teaching corporate sustainability, business, and human rights as an adjunct professor since

2008, and at the Johns Hopkins School of Advanced International Studies in Washington, D.C. since 2013. She has a B.A. from Harvard/Radcliffe and a J.D. from Columbia Law School.

Erika George (Finance, Investors, and Human Rights) is the Samuel D. Thurman professor of law in the S.J. Quinney College of Law and director of the Tanner Humanities Center. She teaches international human rights law and seminar courses on sustainability and corporate responsibility. Before entering the legal academy, she worked with Human Rights Watch and practiced corporate litigation. She serves on the boards of Earthjustice, the Fair Labor Association, and Shift. Her book *Incorporating Rights: Strategies to Advance Corporate Accountability* was published by Oxford University Press in 2021.

Dr. Daniela Heerdt (Mega-Sporting Events and Human Rights) is a researcher and consultant in sport and human rights at the T.M.C. Asser Institute in The Hague. She has a background in public international law and business and human rights and expertise in accountability for mega-sporting event-related human rights abuses. As a consultant she works for different civil society and intergovernmental organizations, such as the Centre for Sport and Human Rights and the European parliament, conducting research and providing legal advice.

Shareen Hertel (Engineering for Human Rights) is a professor of political science and human rights at the University of Connecticut, editor of *The Journal of Human Rights*, and coeditor of the Routledge International Studies Intensives series. She has authored *Tethered Fates: Companies, Communities and Rights at Stake* (Oxford University Press, 2019) and *Unexpected Power: Conflict and Change among Transnational Activists* (Cornell University Press, 2006) along with multiple edited volumes, articles, and book chapters. Hertel holds graduate degrees from Columbia University (2003, 2000, 1992) and a B.A. from The College of Wooster (1988).

Lisa J. Laplante (Right to Remedy) has been teaching business and human rights since 2013 when she joined New England Law, Boston. She also directs the Center for International Law and Policy (CILP), which includes programming focused on business and human rights, including the Operational Level Grievance Mechanism Research Project. Professor Laplante has published and presented on the theme of remedies and reparations for the past twenty years. She has a J.D. from the New York University School of Law.

Mina Manuchehri (Land Rights) is an attorney and associate director of corporate engagement at Landesa. Mina's work focuses on working with key stakeholders – including companies, investors, civil society organizations, communities, and governments – to achieve more responsible investments in land. Mina has over ten years of experience working on land tenure, human rights, and gender, and has extensive global experience working in the agriculture sector.

Jena Martin (Corporations) is a professor of law at West Virginia University, where her courses include business and human rights, business associations, and securities regulation. Her research focuses on the intersection of securities regulation and human rights. Professor Martin draws upon her extensive practice experience, including her work as a senior counsel at the United States Securities & Exchange Commission's Division of Enforcement and as a member of the Robert F. Kennedy's Center for Human Rights Global Advisory Team.

Robert McCorquodale (Human Rights Due Diligence) is a member of the United Nations Working Group on Business and Human Rights. He is also emeritus professor of international law and human rights at the University of Nottingham, UK, and a barrister and mediator at Brick Court Chambers, London. Robert has over thirty years of experience working in business and human rights with businesses of all sizes, governments around the world, and civil society. This has included capacity building, legislative proposals, and training, as well as being a legal practitioner in cases before domestic and international courts.

Roger McElrath (Technology and Human Rights) co-teaches business and human rights courses in the M.B.A. and undergraduate business programs at the Haas School of Business, University of California, Berkeley. Roger's work in human rights has included developing and implementing methodologies for calculating living wages in multiple countries, assisting in the development of a human rights assessment tools for the extractives and agricultural industries, conducting field-based human rights risk assessments, and providing detailed advice to companies on the content and implementation of supply chain codes of conduct.

Ariel Meyerstein (Finance, Investors, and Human Rights) has worked in the fields of human rights and sustainability for twenty years. He has advised global corporations on evolving human rights, sustainability, and sustainable finance standards and has engaged in various multistakeholder negotiations and advisory bodies. He has helped develop environmental and social risk standards across the financial sector, conducted human rights due diligence in client transactions, and contributed to overall sustainability and human rights strategy at a global bank. He has also published on sustainable finance and taught business and human rights at Fordham University Law School. Prior to his work in the sustainability field, Meyerstein practiced international dispute resolution at global law firms and in international tribunals.

Faris Natour (Technology and Human Rights) is an internationally recognized expert with over twenty years of experience working at the intersection of business and human rights. As cofounder and principal of Article One, a specialized consultancy with expertise in human rights, responsible innovation, and sustainability, Faris advises corporate and institutional clients across sectors and regions on human rights strategy and management with the aim of embedding human rights throughout business and institutional operations. He co-teaches business and human rights courses in the M.B.A. and undergraduate business programs at the Haas School of Business, University of California, Berkeley.

Justine Nolan (Modern Slavery in Supply Chains) is the director of the Australian Human Rights Institute and a professor in the Faculty of Law and Justice at UNSW Sydney. She has published widely on business and human rights, including *Addressing Modern Slavery* (2019) (with Martijn Boersma). She advises companies, non-governmental organizations, and governments and is a member of the Australian government's Expert Advisory Body on Modern Slavery. Justine has practiced as a private sector and international human rights lawyer. She is the executive editor of the *Australian Journal of Human Rights*, on the Editorial Board of the *Business and Human Rights Journal*, and a visiting scholar at the New York University Stern Center for Business and Human Rights.

Uché Ewelukwa Ofodile (The Right to Food, The Right to Water) holds the E. J. Ball Endowed Chair at the University of Arkansas School of Law and is currently a senior fellow of the Mossavar-Rahmani Center for Business and Government at Harvard University's Kennedy School of Government. As a member of the faculty of the LL.M. program in agricultural and food law, Professor Ofodile teaches and has taught a wide range of courses relating to food and agriculture, including "The Right to Food," "Intellectual Property Issues in Food and Agricultural Law," "Corporate Social Responsibility in Food and Agriculture," and "International Trade Law."

Michael Posner (Multistakeholder Human Rights Initiatives) is the Jerome Kohlberg Professor of Ethics and Finance and director of the Center for Business and Human Rights at the New York University Stern School of Business. Prior to coming to New York University, he was the assistant secretary of state for democracy, human rights, and labor in the Obama Administration from 2009 to 2013.

Beth Roberts (Land Rights) is the director of Landesa's Center for Women's Land Rights. She is a law, policy, and gender expert who works to strengthen gender-equal and socially inclusive rights to land and natural resources. Beth supports gender in practice across Landesa's programmatic work; leads

Landesa's work on human rights and the Stand for Her Land campaign; contributes to Landesa's climate action work; and collaborates with practitioners focused on gender and natural resource justice worldwide.

Margaret E. Roggensack (Trade and Human Rights) has been co-teaching a course on business and human rights with Eric Biel since 2009 (and Sarah Altschuller since 2013) at Georgetown University Law Center. Meg codirects the Teaching BHR Forum, a global network founded in 2011 to promote and strengthen business and human rights education worldwide. She practiced international trade law in Washington for nearly two decades and has played a leadership role with a range of human rights non-governmental organizations and multistakeholder initiatives to promote corporate respect for human rights in global supply chains.

Kendyl Salcito (Rights of Indigenous Peoples) is the executive director of NomoGaia and an adjunct professor at the University of Denver Law School. She holds an M.A. in Journalism and a Ph.D. in Epidemiology and has been developing, piloting, and validating methodologies for human rights due diligence since 2007. She has worked on Indigenous issues with affected populations on three continents and analyzed Indigenous safeguards at financial institutions, companies, and multistakeholder initiatives. She believes it is critically important that settler-descendant populations defer to Indigenous Peoples and amplify their voices in the teaching of business and human rights generally and Indigenous rights in particular.

Dr. Sara L. Seck (Human Rights and the Environment) is the Yogis & Keddy Chair in Human Rights Law at the Schulich School of Law, Dalhousie University, where she is a member of the Marine & Environmental Law Institute. She is a member of the Teaching Business and Human Rights Forum and a director at the Global Network for the Study of Human Rights and the Environment, and in 2019 she received a legal specialist award (Peace, Justice and Governance) from the Centre for International Sustainable Development Law.

Sandra Sirota (Engineering for Human Rights) is an assistant professor-in-residence in experiential global learning and human rights at the University of Connecticut, book review coeditor for *The Journal of Human Rights*, and faculty coordinator for the University of Connecticut's Early College Experience in Human Rights. Her recent articles have been published in *Comparative Education Review*, *The Journal of Human Rights*, and *Prospects*. Sirota earned her doctoral degree from Columbia University Teachers College, her M.A. in international human rights from the University of Denver, and her B.A. from Cornell University.

Salil Tripathi (Business and Conflict) is a senior adviser (global issues) at the Institute for Human Rights and Business. He has been a researcher at Amnesty International and a policy adviser at International Alert. He has written extensively on business and human rights through chapters in books, the media, and academic journals. He has also been involved with the formation of several multistakeholder initiatives. He obtained his M.B.A. from Tuck School at Dartmouth College. Born in India, he lives in the United States.

Elizabeth Umlas (The OECD National Contact Point Mechanism) is a lecturer at the University of Fribourg, an independent researcher and consultant in business and human rights, and a senior fellow at Croatan Institute. She also teaches business and human rights in the Master's program in international human rights law at the University of Oxford. Dr. Umlas holds a Ph.D. in political science from Yale University. She is currently a senior adviser to IndustriALL Global Union.

Florian Wettstein (Corporate Responsibility) is a professor and chair of business ethics and director of the Institute for Business Ethics at the University of St. Gallen in Switzerland. He has published widely on topics at the intersection of corporate responsibility, business ethics, and business and human rights and is editor-in-chief of the *Business and Human Rights Journal* (BHRJ) published by Cambridge University Press.

Mark Wielga (Human Rights Impacts Assessment, Non-Governmental Grievance Mechanisms) is a director of NomoGaia, a non-profit think tank devoted to business and human rights. He is a researcher specializing in fieldwork and has published scholarly articles on human rights impact assessment, human rights due diligence, and access to remedy. He has taught business and human rights in law, business, and international affairs school around the world. He was trained and practiced as a lawyer in the United States and has extensive experience with impact assessment.

Acknowledgments

I could not have assembled this volume without the collaboration and generosity of many people in the business and human rights (BHR) community.

I am grateful to each contributor for sharing their expertise and best teaching ideas. Alexandria Custodio provided invaluable research assistance.

Teaching Business and Human Rights builds on the work of the Teaching Business and Human Rights Forum, the platform for collaboration among BHR teachers I cofounded with Joanne Bauer in 2011. The BHR teachers, scholars, and practitioners who have supported the Teaching BHR Forum's efforts to promote and strengthen BHR education worldwide have shaped this teaching guide in innumerable ways. Thanks to my Columbia University colleague Joanne Bauer, Teaching BHR Forum codirectors Rachel Chambers and Meg Roggensack, and each Forum member who has served on its Governance Committee.

I am especially thankful for my students, from whom I have learned so much; for everyone who has inspired and supported my teaching over the years, a list that includes Fred Garcia, Elliot Schrage, and Louis Henkin; and for Elda, Samantha, Joshua, and Gabriela always.

Anthony Ewing

1.   Introduction to *Teaching Business and Human Rights*[1]

Anthony Ewing

BUSINESS AND HUMAN RIGHTS

As a law student in the 1990s, I found an intriguing course offered across Amsterdam Avenue at the Columbia University School of Business. "Transnational Business and International Human Rights," launched during a debate over corporate human rights responsibilities in China, was the first business and human rights course offered by a United States business school.[2] The course examined the impact on transnational business practices of international human rights standards and growing calls from human rights advocates for companies to accept responsibility for minimum labor standards in their global supply chains, and to consider the human rights conditions in the markets where they operate.[3]

"Business and human rights" (BHR) emerged as a discipline following the promulgation by states of universal human rights standards after World War II; recognition by the international community of the role of non-state actors in

---

[1]   Portions of this chapter originally appeared online in Anthony P. Ewing, "Teaching Business and Human Rights," in *Teaching Business and Human Rights Handbook* (Teaching Business and Human Rights Forum, 2016), https://teachbhr.org/resources/teaching-bhr-handbook/introduction-teaching-business-and-human-rights.
[2]   See Christopher L. Avery, *Business and Human Rights in a Time of Change* (November 1999), http://www.reports-and-materials.org/Chapter1.htm, citing P. Schwartz and B. Gibb, *When Good Companies Do Bad Things: Responsibility and Risk in an Age of Globalization* (New York: John Wiley & Sons, 1999), xi; Chris Marsden, "Human Rights Teaching in Business Schools," in *Human Rights and Business Matters* (Amnesty International UK Business Group Newsletter, spring 1999).
[3]   Elliot J. Schrage, "International Business B9501-33: Seminar in Corporate/International Relations, Transnational Business and International Human Rights" (Graduate School of Business, Columbia University, fall 1994), on file with the author. The course was developed and first taught in 1990 at Columbia University's Graduate School of Business by Diane F. Orentlicher, Eli Noam, Elliot Schrage, and Nadine Strossen.

the protection of human rights; and the globalization of business operations at a time when technological advances made information about corporate practices and human rights conditions worldwide immediately accessible. Over the past thirty years, BHR has become a distinct field of practice and study at the intersection of business, law, and public policy.[4]

The rapid development of this multidisciplinary field is remarkable.[5] When foreign companies operating in China adopted the first corporate human rights codes of conduct in the aftermath of the Tiananmen Square protests and military crackdown in 1989, business managers and human rights advocates could scarcely speak the same language.[6] The development of the United Nations Guiding Principles on Business and Human Rights (UNGPs)[7] between 2005 and 2011 forged a working consensus among diverse BHR actors, from governments to businesses to civil society organizations. By 2011, when Egyptian demonstrators filled Tahrir Square, executives and advocates alike framed the human rights issues at stake connected to business activity in the shared language of a corporate responsibility to respect human rights.[8] In just two decades, the field of BHR had come into its own.

The BHR movement has expanded in scope from an initial focus on labor conditions in global supply chains and corporate complicity with repressive states to examining the impacts of industries as diverse as agriculture, healthcare, and technology on the full range of internationally recognized human rights.[9] Tools for holding companies accountable for their human rights impacts and influencing business practice have multiplied, building on early

---

[4]   See Michael A. Santoro, "Business and Human Rights in Historical Perspective," *Journal of Human Rights* 14, no. 2 (2015): 155–161.

[5]   See "Preface," in *Business and Human Rights: From Principles to Practice*, eds. Dorothée Baumann-Pauly and Justine Nolan (London: Routledge, 2016), xix–x.

[6]   See, for example, Diane F. Orentlicher and Timothy A. Gelatt, "Public Law, Private Actors: The Impact of Human Rights on Business Investors in China," *Northwestern Journal of International Law & Business* 14 (1993–1994): 66–129, 96. ("[A]s one corporation after another seeks to meet its human rights responsibilities, there is a pressing need for clarity about what, precisely, those responsibilities are.")

[7]   United Nations Human Rights Council, *Guiding Principles on Business and Human Rights: Implementing the United Nations "Protect, Respect and Remedy" Framework*, Report of the Special Representative of the Secretary-General on the issue of human rights and transnational corporations and other business enterprises, UN doc. A/HRC/17/31 (March 21, 2011) (UN Guiding Principles).

[8]   See, for example, Salil Tripathi, "Commentary: How Businesses Have Responded in Egypt," Institute for Human Rights and Business (London, February 7, 2011), http://www.ihrb.org/commentary/how-businesses-responded-egypt.html.

[9]   See, for example, Justine Nolan, "Business and Human Rights in Context," in Dorothée Baumann-Pauly and Justine Nolan, eds., *Business and Human Rights: From Principles to Practice*, 2–11.

efforts to change business practice through consumer boycotts, shareholder activism, and civil litigation.[10]

After a decade of implementation, the UNGPs continue to shape state efforts to protect individuals from human rights abuses by business enterprises, expectations of responsible business conduct, and the remedies available to individuals affected by business activity. BHR concepts – human rights due diligence,[11] exercising leverage to address human rights impacts, and operational-level grievance mechanisms – are influencing conceptual developments in related disciplines of sustainability, accounting, and corporate governance.[12]

BHR practitioners today include advocates, policymakers, managers, and investors. Human rights defenders continue to shine a spotlight on corporate abuses in a wide range of industries, seek remedy for victims, and work to hold companies accountable for the human rights impacts of their operations worldwide.[13] States are addressing the human rights impacts of business through national legislation and regulation, such as mandatory corporate human rights reporting and due diligence. Companies are paying greater attention to the human rights risks connected to their businesses and contributing to a growing body of corporate human rights practice by adopting human rights policies, conducting human rights due diligence, and acting to prevent, mitigate, and remedy human rights impacts.

BUSINESS AND HUMAN RIGHTS EDUCATION

The UN Working Group on Business and Human Rights (UN Working Group), in its *Roadmap for the Next Decade of Business and Human Rights* (2021), points to the power and potential of BHR education.[14] BHR has been

---

[10] See Anita Ramasastry, "Corporate Social Responsibility versus Business and Human Rights: Bridging the Gap between Responsibility and Accountability," *Journal of Human Rights* 14, no. 2 (2015): 237–259, 248.

[11] John Gerard Ruggie, Caroline Rees, and Rachel Davis, "Ten Years After: From UN Guiding Principles to Multi-Fiduciary Obligations," *Business and Human Rights Journal* 6, no. 2 (2021): 179–197.

[12] Caroline Rees, *Transforming How Business Impacts People: Unlocking the Collective Power of Five Distinct Narratives* (November 2020), https://shiftproject.org/resource/unlocking-narratives.

[13] See "Business and Human Rights," in Erika George, Jena Martin, and Tara Van Ho, "Reckoning: A Dialogue About Racism, AntiRacists, and Business and Human Rights," *Washington International Law Journal* 30 (2021): 171–253, 187–196.

[14] United Nations Working Group on Business and Human Rights, *UNGPs 10+: A Roadmap for the Next Decade of Business and Human Rights* (November 2021), 41–42 (academic institutions are "uniquely placed to help scale up awareness on the UNGPs and the understanding that respect for human rights and environment should be at the core of business' role in society").

taught as an academic subject, in some form, since initial international efforts in the 1970s to apply international human rights standards to corporations as non-state actors[15] and the campaign seeking corporate divestment from Apartheid South Africa in the 1980s. The subject is now being taught at business schools, law schools, and schools of public policy worldwide. The Teaching Business and Human Rights Forum, for example, a platform for collaboration among individuals teaching BHR launched in 2011, has grown to include more than 350 individuals teaching BHR at over 200 institutions in some 45 countries.[16] BHR teaching is taking place in every region, from Africa and Asia to the Middle East and Latin America.[17] More than 100 universities have added BHR courses to their curricula in the past decade alone. Clinical BHR courses provide opportunities for students to research violations, advocate for victims, and advise companies and policymakers.[18] BHR is also being taught outside traditional university settings in training programs for both private and public sector professionals. As more and more individuals in the private sector, government, and civil society grapple with the human rights issues touching business operations, the community of BHR teachers and practitioners is expanding.

BHR is inherently multidisciplinary, drawing upon more established academic disciplines including law, management, business ethics, public policy, and international relations,[19] which has led to interdisciplinary approaches to

---

[15] See, for example, David Weissbrodt and Muria Kruger, "Norms on the Responsibilities of Transnational Corporations and Other Business Enterprises with Regard to Human Rights," *American Journal of International Law* 97 (2003), 901–922; Nadia Bernaz, *Business and Human Rights: History, Law and Policy – Bridging the Accountability Gap* (Oxford: Routledge, 2017), 163–208.

[16] Teaching Business and Human Rights Forum, https://teachbhr.org. The author cofounded the Teaching BHR Forum with Joanne Bauer, adjunct professor, School of International and Public Affairs, Columbia University, in 2011.

[17] Anthony P. Ewing, "Promoting Business and Human Rights Education: Lessons from Colombia, Ukraine, and Pakistan," *Business and Human Rights Journal* 6, no. 3 (2021): 607–615.

[18] See, for example, Joanne Bauer, "Equipping Professionals for the Next Challenges: The Design and Results of a Multidisciplinary Business and Human Rights Clinic," *Business and Human Rights Journal* 2, no. 2 (2017): 359–363.

[19] See, for example, Santoro, "Business and Human Rights in Historical Perspective," 155.

BHR teaching and scholarship.[20] Teachers have begun to apply a BHR lens to other disciplines, such as engineering and accounting.[21]

The scope and content of BHR courses vary widely, shaped by individual teachers and the faculties, geographies, and institutions in which the subject is taught. At law schools, BHR course content overlaps with human rights, international, labor, and corporate law curricula. BHR issues may also be covered in courses on corporate governance, trade law, and foreign investment. BHR courses commonly address competing definitions of corporate responsibility, the human rights responsibilities of business under international law, legal and policy tools to provide remedies to victims and hold companies accountable for human rights violations, and what companies are doing to manage the human rights impacts of their operations and business relationships. Law courses seek to equip students to understand international human rights standards, spot the human rights impacts of business operations, and advise both companies and advocates on best practice. Law teachers have also developed BHR courses on the human rights impacts of specific industries and of environmental issues.[22]

Policy courses seek to prepare students to "critically evaluate the responsibilities and actions of key actors in situations where corporate-related human rights abuses have occurred, including what prevention and/or mitigation steps could be effective."[23] BHR courses for students of public policy have considered how to incorporate international human rights standards in the design, implementation, and evaluation of multinational business activities, helping students to understand how managers make decisions about corporate responsibility, interact with policymakers and other stakeholders, and deal

---

[20]   See, for example, the *Business and Human Rights Journal* (accessed August 31, 2022, https://www.cambridge.org/core/journals/business-and-human-rights-journal) and the Global Business and Human Rights Scholars Association (accessed August 31, 2022, https://bhrscholarsassociation.org).

[21]   See Shareen Hertel and Allison MacKay, "Engineering and Human Rights: Teaching across the Divide," *Business and Human Rights Journal* 1 (2016): 159–164; Ken McPhail, "Human Rights Should Be on the MBA Curriculum," *Financial Times*, March 16, 2014.

[22]   See, for example, Andrea Shemberg, course handbook, "Business and Human Rights Law and Policy in Oil, Gas and Mining" (University of Dundee, Scotland, 2014), on file with the author; Rebecca Mackinnon and Cynthia Wong, course syllabus, "Research Seminar: Human Rights, Corporate Responsibility, and Information Communications Technology" (University of Pennsylvania Law School, 2013) (accessed August 31, 2022, https://pennlaw.instructure.com/courses/1092631/assignments/syllabus); Nadia Bernaz and Chiara Macchi, "Business, Human Rights and the Environment" (Wageningen University, 2020), on file with the author.

[23]   Joanne Bauer, syllabus, "Corporate Social Responsibility: A Human Rights Approach" (School of International and Public Affairs, Columbia University, fall 2014), on file with the author.

with complex policy issues.[24] Topics may include the history of corporate responsibility; legal, regulatory, and policy frameworks; specific cases and industries; and the BHR roles of different stakeholders.

While the uptake of BHR teaching and scholarship by business schools historically has lagged behind other faculties,[25] management programs have begun to add human rights to their curricula, preparing students to assess and manage the human rights impacts of business activity from within companies. BHR programs, for example, have been launched at the New York University Stern School of Business (2013), the Haas School of Business at the University of California, Berkeley (2016), and the University of Geneva School of Economics and Management (2019).[26] Initiatives including the Principles for Responsible Management Education and the Global Business School Network are promoting the addition of human rights to business school curricula.[27] At business schools, BHR topics may be addressed within an ethics course under the rubric of "corporate social responsibility," as a module in disciplines such as supply chain management, human resources, and business law, or in relation to a particular industry.

---

[24] See, for example, J. Paul Martin and Marcela Manubens, "Human Rights and International Business and the Global Economy" (Columbia University School of International and Public Affairs, Fall 2001), on file with the author; Nina Gardner and Katherine Gorove, syllabus, "International Business and Human Rights" (Johns Hopkins School of Advanced International Studies, spring 2013), on file with the author.

[25] Ken McPhail, "Human Rights Should Be on the MBA Curriculum" ("Most business school students are unfamiliar with human rights standards and their relevance for business.") Santoro, "Business and Human Rights in Historical Perspective," 157 ("It is unclear whether management scholars will embrace the BHR paradigm to reframe international business ethics issues.")

[26] Michael Posner, *Business Leaders Must Protect Human Rights* (Business School – Companies and Management Video, FT.com, accessed September 24, 2015, http://video.ft.com/4345313816001/Business-leaders-must-protect-human-rights/ Companies); Krysten Crawford, Haas School of Business, University of California Berkeley, "Berkeley-Haas Launches Human Rights and Business Initiative" (February 1, 2016, http://newsroom.haas.berkeley.edu/article/berkeley-haas-launches-human -rights-business-initiative); Geneva Center for Business and Human Rights, https:// gcbhr.org. See also Chris Jochnik and Louis Bickford, "The Role of Civil Society in Business and Human Rights," in Dorothée Baumann-Pauly and Justine Nolan, eds., *Business and Human Rights: From Principles to Practice* (2016), 181, n. 57 ("BHR-minded academic human rights centres and clinics have proliferated in the last two decades").

[27] See Principles for Responsible Management Education, "Business and Human Rights Working Group," https://www.unprme.org/prme-working-group-on-business -and-human-rights; The Global Business School Network for Business and Human Rights, https://gbsn.org.

TEACHING BUSINESS AND HUMAN RIGHTS

Teaching Business and Human Rights is a practical guide and resource for BHR teachers and students. Contributors explain common BHR topics, suggest teaching approaches that work in the classroom, and identify helpful teaching resources – those assembled here provide ample material to fill a BHR course syllabus. Each chapter provides a brief overview of the topic, describes teaching approaches, and includes learning objectives and key questions for students.

Chapters are organized in four parts: (1) foundational topics; (2) business practice; (3) corporate accountability; and (4) key issues.

In Part I, Florian Wettstein shares his approach for teaching corporate responsibility (Chapter 2) in an interdisciplinary BHR course, highlighting the conceptual foundations of corporate responsibility and the limitations of the shareholder value doctrine. I suggest ways to introduce human rights (Chapter 3) and the UN Guiding Principles on Business and Human Rights (Chapter 5) to BHR students who have not studied the topics previously. Angela B. Cornell situates international labor rights (Chapter 4) as a cornerstone of BHR, surveying their sources in international and regional human rights instruments and highlighting key labor right provisions in trade agreements and private codes of conduct. Lisa J. Laplante addresses the challenges of ensuring a right to remedy (Chapter 6) for individuals harmed by business activity through both judicial and non-judicial human rights grievance mechanisms – the "system of remedy" described in the UNGPs.

Part II includes topics to help BHR students understand business practice. Jena Martin offers an approach to teaching the purpose and structure of corporations (Chapter 7) to law students, noting the importance of translation in BHR: human rights advocates and business executives often clash over language. Robert McCorquodale and Daria Davitti contribute the chapter on the foundational BHR concept of human rights due diligence (Chapter 8), describing its origins, application in practice, and legal dimensions. Mark Wielga provides a practice-oriented approach to teaching both human rights impact assessment (Chapter 9), highlighting publicly available examples that can be used in the classroom, and non-governmental human rights grievance mechanisms (Chapter 10), including those administered by multistakeholder initiatives, development banks, and companies themselves.

Part III covers tools for seeking remedy and holding companies accountable for their human rights impacts. Claire Bright and Nicolas Bueno survey mandatory human rights due diligence legislation (Chapter 11), one of the most rapidly developing BHR topics, comparing their scope of application and enforcement mechanisms. Rachel Chambers shares her approach for teaching judicial remedy (Chapter 12) through home state civil litigation, a vital accountability tool for victims of human rights abuse, as well as for corporate accountability under domestic criminal law, highlighting recent case law developments in the United States, United Kingdom, Canada, and the Netherlands. I summarize the history of the Alien Tort Statute (Chapter 13) as a judicial remedy in the United States, tracing its increasingly narrow interpretation by the U.S. Supreme Court, and describe my approach to teaching complicity (Chapter 14) – the role that a business enterprise plays in human rights impacts caused by others. Elizabeth Umlas outlines the OECD National Contact Point (Chapter 15) complaints process, a state-based, non-judicial grievance mechanism with the potential for providing remedy to individuals harmed by business conduct. Dorothée Baumann-Pauly and Michael Posner emphasize the growing prominence and potential impact of multistakeholder human rights initiatives (Chapter 16). Finally, Humberto Cantú Rivera details the unique contributions of the Inter-American regional human rights system (Chapter 17) to BHR, addressing state responsibilities in relation to non-state actors and state duties to consult Indigenous Peoples.

Key topics included in many BHR courses appear in Part IV, which addresses specific rights and the human rights impacts of particular industries. Justine Nolan contributes the chapter on modern slavery in supply chains (Chapter 18), highlighting the regulatory developments that are "hardening" laws on corporate responsibility in key jurisdictions. Sara L. Seck provides an important environmental human rights framework (Chapter 19) for teaching BHR – an opportunity to explore the interconnection and interdependence of people and the planet and consider environmental and climate justice challenges. Mina Manuchehri and Beth Roberts place land rights (Chapter 20) at the nexus of BHR, emphasizing that businesses increasingly are expected to make responsible land-based investments. In her contribution, Kendyl Salcito suggests approaches to teaching BHR and the rights of Indigenous Peoples (Chapter 21), who are often harmed by business conduct. Uché Ewelukwa Ofodile provides an overview of the rights to adequate food (Chapter 22) and to safe drinking water (Chapter 23), which are instrumental for the enjoyment of other human rights, examining business impacts on these rights through the lens of the UNGPs.

Contributors also describe approaches to teaching the human rights impacts of particular industry sectors. Faris Natour and Roger McElrath take up the actual and potential human rights impacts of technology companies (Chapter 24), highlighting tools companies can deploy to mitigate the human rights risks of emerging technologies such as artificial intelligence. In their noteworthy approach to teaching engineering for human rights (Chapter 25), Shareen Hertel, Davis Chacon Hurtado, and Sandra Sirota apply a human rights lens across academic disciplines. Erika George and Ariel Meyerstein explore the intersection of finance, investors, and human rights (Chapter 26), emphasizing the need for BHR students to understand the roles played by the capital market actors that finance business enterprises and how investors and financial institutions can exercise leverage to respect human rights. John Ferguson surveys current developments in accounting for human rights (Chapter 27), an increasingly important role in the field of BHR due to the prevalence of sustainability reporting frameworks and the growing number of regulatory processes mandating business reporting on human rights performance. Daniela Heerdt shows how teaching the human rights impacts of mega-sporting events (Chapter 28) can illustrate key BHR issues, such as access to remedy, human rights due diligence, and supply chain management. Margaret E. Roggensack and Eric R. Biel describe how they have connected trade and business conduct to their BHR curriculum (Chapter 29). Finally, Salil Tripathi considers the heightened human risks of businesses operating in zones of conflict (Chapter 30), reflecting on lessons from the extractive industries with ongoing relevance for business activity connected to current conflicts, such as the Russian invasion of Ukraine.

There is something in this guide for anyone who has prepared to teach a BHR class, asking themselves, "How can I best convey the essentials of today's topic?" Methods for teaching BHR topics are as diverse as the individuals teaching the subject and the students studying it. The subject matter allows for creative pedagogy, such as simulations and role-playing exercises.[28] This volume includes suggestions for class discussions, for debate topics, and for student assignments, such as BHR Memos to the CEO or to the Ambassador (Exercises 5.2, 17.4) and opinion writing (Exercise 30.2). Contributors include exercises that they have used in the classroom, from outlining a corporate human rights policy (Exercise 3.1) to modeling human rights due diligence (Exercise 8.1) to addressing child labor and mine safety (Exercise 18.2).

My own students have benefited from BHR teaching approaches shared by others. Presentations by Michael Santoro (Leavey School of Business, Santa Clara University) and Nien-hê Hsieh (Harvard Business School) on using the business school case method in the classroom, for example, prompted me to begin using BHR teaching cases in my law classes. Contributor Mark Wielga (NomoGaia) has joined my class as a guest speaker to lead his excellent simulation on securing "free, prior, and informed consent" (see Exercise 21.3, "Colorado Petroleum"). I use a role play, based on an exercise developed by

---

[28] See, for example, Dorothée Baumann-Pauly, "Bridging Theory and Practice through Immersion: Innovations for Teaching Business and Human Rights at Business Schools," *Business and Human Rights Journal* 3, no. 1 (2018): 139–144.

a U.K.-based law firm,[29] to put students in corporate roles addressing hypothetical human rights issues.

The topics covered in this volume could fill a BHR course or curriculum, but they are not exhaustive. Approaches to teaching important BHR topics – human rights and inequality,[30] health and human rights,[31] the human rights responsibilities of state-owned enterprises,[32] the prospect for a binding BHR treaty,[33] human rights and investment treaties,[34] protecting the rights of vulnerable individuals,[35] and measuring the human rights performance of companies,[36] to name just a few topics that could be included in a comprehensive BHR curriculum – are missing. The next generation of BHR courses and curricula will cover many of these topics.

---

[29]   See Freshfields Bruckaus Deringer LLP, "UN Guiding Principles Exercise," Teaching Resources: Exercises (Teaching Business and Human Rights Forum), https://teachbhr.org/resources/teaching-bhr-handbook/teaching-resources-exercises.

[30]   See, for example, Business Fights Poverty, the University of Cambridge Institute for Sustainability Leadership (CISL), and Shift, *The Case for Living Wages: How Paying Living Wages Improves Business Performance and Tackles Poverty* (May 2022), https://shiftproject.org/resource/case-for-living-wages.

[31]   See, for example, Anthony Ewing, Jamie O'Connell, and Nina Gardner, "Teaching Note: Human Rights and the COVID-19 Pandemic," in *Teaching Business and Human Rights Handbook* (Teaching Business and Human Rights Forum, 2020), https://teachbhr.org/resources/teaching-bhr-handbook/teaching-notes/human-rights-and-the-COVID-19-pandemic.

[32]   See Larry Catá Backer, "Human Rights Responsibilities of State-Owned Enterprises," in *Research Handbook on Human Rights and Business*, eds. Surya Deva and David Birchall (Cheltenham: Edward Elgar Publishing, 2020), 223–244.

[33]   See, for example, Douglass Cassell and Anita Ramasastry, "White Paper: Options for a Treaty on Business and Human Rights," *Notre Dame Journal of International and Comparative Law* 6, no. 1 (2016): 9–13.

[34]   See, for example, Jesse Coleman, Kaitlin Y. Cordes, and Lise Johnson, "Human Rights Law and the Investment Treaty Regime," in *Research Handbook on Human Rights and Business*, eds. Surya Deva and David Birchall (Cheltenham: Edward Elgar Publishing, 2020), 290–314.

[35]   See, for example, United Nations Human Rights Council, "Report of the Working Group on the Issue of Human Rights and Transnational Corporations and Other Business Enterprises, Gender Dimensions of the Guiding Principles on Business and Human Rights," UN doc. A/HRC/41/43 (May 23, 2019); Business and Human Rights Resource Centre and International Service for Human Rights, *Shared Space under Pressure: Business Support for Civic Freedoms and Human Rights Defenders* (2018); Shift, *Beyond Pride: The Rights of LGBTI People and the Corporate Responsibility to Respect* (August 2021), https://shiftproject.org/resource/beyond-pride-series/beyond-pride.

[36]   Shift, *Leadership and Governance Indicators of a Rights Respecting Culture* (February 2021), https://shiftproject.org/resource/lg-indicators/about-lgis.

The UN Working Group called for "academic institutions – in particular business schools and law schools but also other relevant education programmes in economics and social sciences" to "include business and human rights in their curriculum" and "build on and expand existing initiatives for teaching and research on business and human rights."[37] Promoting BHR education everywhere, and teaching it effectively, has the potential to improve the protection of human rights.[38] Exposing future managers, advocates, and policymakers to BHR is a critical means to advance the corporate responsibility to respect human rights.

I hope *Teaching Business and Human Rights* strengthens BHR education by helping teachers to add BHR topics to their courses and curricula while inspiring creative BHR teaching.

---

[37] United Nations Working Group on Business and Human Rights, *UNGPs 10+: A Roadmap for the Next Decade of Business and Human Rights*, 41–42.

[38] "Local approaches will inevitably shape the coming decades of BHR teaching, scholarship, and practice." Anthony P. Ewing, "Promoting Business and Human Rights Education," 9.

PART I

Foundational topics

2. Corporate responsibility

Florian Wettstein

OVERVIEW

Business and human rights (BHR) sits at the intersection of two foundational disciplines: human rights and corporate responsibility. Most BHR courses address some of the foundations and core concepts underlying corporate responsibility directly or at least implicitly, such as when tying it to corporate purpose, the "business case" for human rights responsibility, or more generally the role of business in society. This chapter provides an overview of the conceptual foundations of corporate responsibility, takes a critical look at the limitations of some common corporate responsibility interpretations, and, finally, relates the concept of corporate social responsibility (CSR) in particular to the BHR discussion.

CORPORATIONS AND RESPONSIBILITY

The idea that corporations ought to have responsibility for human rights hinges on the view that (1) corporations can be bearers of responsibility in the first place; and (2) such responsibility reaches beyond merely maximizing their profits.

Whether corporations qualify as agents that can bear responsibility is not obvious, since it depends on certain abilities that are commonly ascribed only to humans such as reasoned decision-making, including the ability to assess the consequences of one's decision and to understand the implications of these consequences for those affected by them. Hence, whether corporations as collective agents can have responsibilities depends on whether a certain **moral personality** can be ascribed to them.

There has been a long-standing discussion, particularly in business ethics, on the moral stature of corporations. At the one end of the spectrum are those who argue that only individuals can bear responsibility, but not corporations.[1] At the other end of the spectrum are those who perceive corporations as full-fledged moral persons.[2] However, commonly, corporations are viewed as positioned in between the two extremes: while they are denied the status of moral persons, they are conceptualized as moral agents with certain capacities to acquire a limited set of rights and obligations.[3]

Law students may not commonly deal with the moral personality of companies; rather, it is their **legal personality** that enables corporations to acquire rights and obligations under the law. (See Corporations, Chapter 7.) A legal person is an artificial, non-human entity, which is recognized as a person under law. It is this status as a person that makes it possible for such an entity, for example, to enter into contracts, sue and be sued, or acquire property. Whether or not corporations have legal personality is controversial only with regard to international law. However, the discussion on whether corporations have international legal personality and, in fact, the whole distinction between subjects and objects of international law have lost significance in and for BHR in recent years.[4] Rather than starting with the assessment whether corporations can be subjects of international law as a presupposition for them to acquire international legal obligations, corporations are shown to already have acquired a variety of rights and obligations under international law, irrespective of their status.[5]

BEYOND PROFIT MAXIMIZATION

Establishing corporations as responsibility-bearing subjects or agents raises the second question: whether their responsibility reaches beyond profit maximization. One way to approach this question is to assess arguments that deny such responsibilities. The "classic" position against corporate responsibility beyond profit maximization was formulated by Milton Friedman in his 1962 book *Freedom and Capitalism* and later in his famous *New York Times*

---

[1]   Manuel Velasquez, "Why Corporations Are Not Morally Responsible for Anything They Do," *Business & Professional Ethics Journal* 2, no. 3 (Spring 1983): 1–18.
[2]   Peter A. French, "The Corporation as a Moral Person," *American Philosophical Quarterly* 16, no. 3 (July 1979): 207–215.
[3]   Thomas Donaldson, *Corporations and Morality* (Hoboken, NJ: Prentice Hall, 1982).
[4]   Andrew Clapham, *Human Rights Obligations of Non-State Actors* (Oxford: Oxford University Press, 2006).
[5]   Clapham, *Human Rights Obligations*; Nadia Bernaz, *Business and Human Rights. History, Law and Policy – Bridging the Accountability Gap* (Oxford: Routledge, 2017).

Magazine article of 1970, "The Social Responsibility of Business Is to Increase Its Profits."[6] In that article, Friedman famously argued that corporations ought not to consider any social responsibilities beyond maximizing their profits, as long as they are playing by the commonly accepted rules of the game and do not engage in deception or fraud. This position corresponds to what is now known as the shareholder value doctrine, which perceives the maximization of shareholder value as the ultimate and only goal of corporations.[7] For anyone interested in a larger justification of corporate human rights responsibility, it is essential to understand the arguments that are commonly used to defend such views and the reasons why they ultimately fail.

There are two bases on which shareholder value maximization is commonly defended. The first, utilitarian justification claims that by maximizing profits, corporations contribute to a growing economy, which ultimately benefits society as a whole. The second, libertarian justification perceives the "imposition" of corporate responsibility as an untenable infringement on personal freedom.

There are two sets of possible responses to this view, one pragmatic or instrumental and one normative.

COUNTERING THE "BUSINESS CASE"

Pragmatic or instrumental responses attempt to show that the goal of profit maximization itself requires that corporations adopt certain social responsibilities. This is what is commonly referred to as the "business case" for corporate responsibility.[8] A "positive" business case for corporate responsibility stresses the positive economic potential that emanates from responsible conduct; e.g., through reputational gains, more motivated and productive employees, or an expanding consumer base. A "negative" business case for corporate responsibility, on the other hand, emphasizes the economic risks that are attached to irresponsible business conduct, such as deteriorating image and reputation, consumer and investor boycotts, or increasing staff fluctuation.[9]

---

[6] Milton Friedman, *Capitalism and Freedom* (Chicago, IL: University of Chicago Press, 1962); Milton Friedman, "A Friedman Doctrine: The Social Responsibility of Business Is to Increase Its Profits," *The New York Times Magazine*, September 13, 1970.
[7] Michael Jensen and William H. Meckling, "Theory of the Firm: Managerial Behavior, Agency Cost and Ownership Structure," *Journal of Financial Economics* 3, no. 4 (October 1976): 305–360.
[8] Lynn S. Paine, "Does Ethics Pay?" *Business Ethics Quarterly* 10, no. 1 (January 2000): 319–330.
[9] Paine, "Does Ethics Pay?"

However, while such pragmatic arguments have been of critical importance to drive corporate responsibility into management practice, it is well established that they suffer from significant empirical and normative limitations and shortcomings.[10]

Therefore, it is important for BHR students to explore **normative responses** to the shareholder value doctrine beyond instrumental business case arguments. Normative responses to the utilitarian justification outlined above can explore to what extent economic growth indeed can and ought to serve as the primary, or even the only, objective for economic activity and to what extent its unequal distribution ought to matter to the economic process. Responses to the libertarian justification can propose a more holistic understanding of human freedom of which responsibility is not in opposition but an inherent part.[11] After all, it is the very essence of the freedom of intentional beings that they can pursue their actions with purpose and moderation.

STAKEHOLDER VERSUS SHAREHOLDER PRIMACY

Beyond such specific responses, it is important for students to adopt a more holistic understanding of corporations beyond a merely transactional view. Corporations are not merely economic but also social and political institutions with respective responsibilities. Corporations are not simply a function of supply and demand, an instrument to eliminate transaction costs, or a nexus of contracts, as some economic theories of the firm suggest.[12] Rather, they are communities consisting of countless social relations, producing and fostering unique cultures, purposes, and identities.[13] Introducing a relational rather than a transactional view on the corporation has been one of the key contributions

---

[10]   David Vogel, *The Market for Virtue: The Potential and Limits of Corporate Social Responsibility* (Washington, D.C.: Brookings Institution Press, 2005); Peter Ulrich, *Integrative Economic Ethics: Foundations of a Civilized Market Economy* (Cambridge: Cambridge University Press, 2008).

[11]   Florian Wettstein and Kenneth E. Goodpaster, "Freedom and Autonomy in the 21st Century: What Role for Corporations?", in *Markt, Mensch und Freiheit: Wirtschaftsethik in der Auseinandersetzung*, eds. Markus Breuer, Philipp Mastronardi, and Bernhard Waxenberger (Bern: Haupt, 2009); Ulrich, *Integrative Economic Ethics*.

[12]   E.g., Ronald Coase, "The Nature of the Firm," *Economica* 4, no. 16 (November 1937): 386–405.

[13]   Sandra Waddock and Neil Smith, "Relationships: The Real Challenge of Corporate Global Citizenship," *Business and Society Review* 105, no. 1 (2002): 47–62; Kenneth E. Goodpaster, *Conscience and Corporate Culture* (Oxford: Blackwell Publishing, 2007); Charles Handy, "What's a Business For?" *Harvard Business Review*, December 2002, 49–55.

of stakeholder theory.[14] Contrasting a narrow shareholder primacy view on the corporation with a stakeholder perspective can be an effective key to unlock the social dimension of business for students. However, while a stakeholder view on business allows us to confront the shortcomings of shareholder value primacy, it suffers from certain limitations and blind spots as well.[15] For one, it tends to lack a view on the larger political role and stature of corporations in society.[16]

BUSINESS IN SOCIETY

Corporations are profoundly engaged in shaping society, fulfilling various public, political, and governance functions, which a one-dimensional economic view of the firm cannot account for.[17] Dow Votaw, one of the early thinkers in corporate responsibility, already realized in the 1960s that a full understanding of corporate responsibility requires us to adopt a holistic view of corporations as economic, social, and political institutions:

> Only if we have a thorough familiarity with the corporation as a political institution, as well as an economic and social one, can we hope even to recognize the effects that it has had and will have on the rest of society.[18]

Accessing a deeper justification of corporate responsibility beyond maximizing profits as a foundation on which to discuss corporate human rights responsibility is equally important for business, public policy, and law students. For business students, such discussions provide a counter-narrative to the narrow accounts of the corporate role of the economic mainstream; for public policy

---

[14]   R. Edward Freeman, *Strategic Management: A Stakeholder Approach* (Boston, MA: Harper Collins, 1984); Thomas Donaldson and Lee E. Preston, "The Stakeholder Theory of the Corporation: Concepts, Evidence, and Implications," *Academy of Management Review* 20, no. 1 (1995): 65–91; Robert A. Phillips, ed., *Stakeholder Theory: Impact and Prospects* (Cheltenham: Edward Elgar, 2011).

[15]   Kenneth E. Goodpaster, "Business Ethics and Stakeholder Analysis," *Business Ethics Quarterly* 1, no. 1 (January 1991): 52–71; James P. Walsh, "Book Review Essay: Taking Stock of Stakeholder Management," *Academy of Management Review* 30, no. 2 (April 2005): 426–438.

[16]   Andreas G. Scherer and Guido Palazzo, "Toward a Political Conception of Corporate Responsibility: Business and Society Seen from a Habermasian Perspective," *Academy of Management Review* 32, no. 4 (October 2007): 1096–1120.

[17]   Dirk Matten and Andrew Crane, "Corporate Citizenship: Toward an Extended Theoretical Conceptualization," *Academy of Management Review* 30, no. 1 (January 2005): 166–179; Scherer and Palazzo, *Political Conception*.

[18]   Dow Votaw, "The Politics of a Changing Corporate Society," *California Management Review* 3, no. 3 (April 1961): 105–118.

students, political views on the corporation in particular can lead to a critical discussion on the adequacy of the state-centrism underlying traditional human rights thinking; for law students, it can help to fill in the blanks that the law has not sufficiently addressed in the BHR realm as of yet.

CORPORATE SOCIAL RESPONSIBILITY (CSR)

Of particular relevance to BHR is the concept of corporate social responsibility (CSR). CSR is the most influential discussion within the broader area of corporate responsibility. The discussion emerged in the 1950s and 1960s,[19] expanded throughout the 1970s and 1980s,[20] and became established in the management mainstream and broadly adopted in corporate practice in the 1990s and 2000s.[21]

Interestingly, CSR has rarely referred to human rights explicitly, despite certain overlaps with the BHR discussion. Some have argued that its focus on voluntary business engagement and its private and somewhat discretionary nature are at odds with a human rights focus that implies public and binding responsibilities.[22] The emergence of the BHR discussion can thus be seen as a response to these perceived shortcomings of CSR. Accordingly, rather than as a subset of CSR, BHR has emerged as an actual critique of it.[23] Against this background, it is important to point out to students that CSR and BHR are distinct discussions with different origins and trajectories.[24] Emanating from management studies, CSR has traditionally adopted a managerial perspective on corporate responsibility, often characterized by an instrumental outlook and

---

[19]   Howard R. Bowen, *The Social Responsibilities of the Businessman* (New York: Harper and Row, 1953); Keith Davis, "Can Business Afford to Ignore Corporate Social Responsibilities?" *California Management Review* 2 (April 1960): 70–76; Votaw, *Changing Corporate Society.*

[20]   Archie B. Carroll, ed., *Managing Corporate Social Responsibility* (Boston, MA: Little, Brown, 1977).

[21]   Dirk Matten and Jeremy Moon, "'Implicit' and 'Explicit' CSR: A Conceptual Framework for a Comparative Understanding of Corporate Social Responsibility," *Academy of Management Review* 33, no. 2 (April 2008): 404–424.

[22]   Florian Wettstein, "The History of 'Business and Human Rights' and Its Relationship with 'Corporate Social Responsibility'," in *Research Handbook on Human Rights and Business*, eds. Surya Deva and David Birchall (Cheltenham: Edward Elgar, 2020), 23–45.

[23]   Anita Ramasastry, "Corporate Social Responsibility Versus Business and Human Rights: Bridging the Gap between Responsibility and Accountability," *Journal of Human Rights* 14, no. 2 (2015): 237–259.

[24]   Florian Wettstein, "CSR and the Debate on Business and Human Rights: Bridging the Great Divide," *Business Ethics Quarterly* 22, no. 4 (October 2012): 739–770; Ramasastry, *Corporate Social Responsibility.*

a respective reliance on internal voluntary self-regulation. BHR, on the other hand, emanates from legal studies and thus adopts a much stronger focus on the role and shape of external accountability mechanisms.

TEACHING APPROACHES

My primary goal when teaching corporate responsibility in a BHR class is to clarify the conceptual foundations of extending human rights responsibility to corporations. The session is less about exploring solutions to practical dilemmas and cases. As such, it makes most sense at the beginning of the course as a foundational class. I commonly start my own BHR course with a general introduction to the history and general outlook of BHR in the first class, followed by a first foundational class on human rights and a second foundational class on corporate responsibility.[25] The remainder of the course is then about bringing the two foundations – human rights on the one hand and corporate responsibility on the other – together and exploring conceptual and practical issues and challenges at the intersection of the two. This seems to be an intuitive way to show students how the BHR discussion is situated at the intersection of these two larger discussions.

Learning objectives include:

- Enabling students to critically evaluate and confront common market-based justifications of corporate profit maximization and building sound arguments for corporate responsibility beyond narrow economic objectives.
- Understanding the key normative and conceptual foundations of assigning responsibility to corporations as a prerequisite of extending human rights responsibility to business later in the course.
- Knowing the different origins and trajectories of CSR and BHR and being able to discern the implications that derive from this distinction for corporate engagement for human rights both in theory and practice.

The question of whether corporations can be bearers of responsibility can be interesting to explore, particularly with students at the graduate level, since it allows for a deep conceptual discussion but also yields very practical implications. For example, the question can be explored whether the focus on corporations as bearers of collective responsibility has served to shield individuals within corporate structures from accountability. The global financial

---

[25] The course is a foundational course on BHR aiming at providing students with a general introduction to the BHR discussion. It is an interdisciplinary course covering legal and non-legal aspects of BHR, addressing students from various disciplines such as international law, management, finance, and international relations.

crisis of 2008 as an example is a case in point. Exploring the interplay between individual and collective responsibility seems particularly fruitful in interdisciplinary classrooms where both legal and ethical perspectives on the issue can be pondered. At a more general level, for law students in particular it can be a revelation to explore discussions that place the foundations of corporate human rights responsibility entirely outside of the law. However, embedded in a BHR class there is often little time to dive deep on this preliminary question. Therefore, depending on the focus of the course, it may make sense to simply presuppose that corporations can be bearers of responsibility and focus more on discussing why corporate responsibility ought to include more than maximizing profits.

EXERCISE 2.1

SHAREHOLDER VALUE DEBATE

A structured class debate tends to work well as an approach to teach and explore whether corporations do or do not have responsibilities beyond profit maximization and what such responsibilities ought to entail. I have applied both short and long formats for such debates, with the latter taking up a full 90-minute class session and shorter ones being integrated into a more comprehensive class on corporate responsibility.

In preparation, one or two texts can be assigned, which represent both arguments for and against the shareholder value doctrine. In class, students then get time to prepare a first round of arguments in favor of their respective positions. Ideally, students are assigned to one side of the issue without being able to choose which position they want to defend. In a second round, they focus on rebutting the other side's respective arguments. For the long format, a group of judges can be appointed who can ask clarifying questions during the delivery of the oral statements and engage in a "public" assessment and deliberation of the arguments at the end of the debate in order to determine which group provided the better case for their position.

Two other shorter exercises that I often make use of in corporate responsibility classes aim more at the exploration of corporate responsibility practices. The first one taps into students' own professional experience; the second one provides an opportunity to explore corporate responsibility approaches of well-known firms.

EXERCISE 2.2

EMPLOYER CORPORATE RESPONSIBILITY PRACTICES

For the first exercise, I hand out three questions at the very beginning of the class:

1. Can you think of best cases in corporate responsibility? What makes them best cases?
2. Can you think of worst cases in corporate responsibility? What makes them worst cases?
3. What corporate responsibility activities and initiatives does your own employer engage in? Do you consider your employer closer to the best or worst cases?

The students jot their answers down and hold on to them. At the end of the class, they revisit their answers in light of the classroom discussions and conceptual clarifications. This is followed by a class discussion on how the perspectives on best cases, worst cases, and the assessment of their employer's corporate responsibility may have changed or in what way the class content has confirmed some of their intuitions on corporate responsibility.

EXERCISE 2.3

CORPORATE RESPONSIBILITY STATEMENTS

For the second exercise, I confront the students with corporate responsibility statements of well-known firms (see Teaching Resources below) and ask them to reflect on them from a critical perspective:

- What strikes them as convincing about the statements?
- What do they perceive as odd, misleading, or inadequate?
- How does the company define responsibility for itself? What model of corporate responsibility is it adopting?

Public communications on corporate responsibility by businesses are often based on certain implicit assumptions whose exploration from a conceptual angle can be very enlightening for students. For example, statements that stress the economic potential of corporate responsibility offer an opportunity to critique such "business case" argumentation from both empirical and normative points of view. Statements that seemingly limit corporate responsibility to charitable projects of the company can be contrasted with a more holistic view of corporate responsibility as concerned with a company's core business processes. Showing the manifestation of such conceptual shortcomings in a company's official communications renders the critique tangible and practically relevant for students.

KEY QUESTIONS

A number of key questions can guide the discussions on the conceptual foundations of corporate responsibility in the classroom. The questions separated along disciplinary lines below can also provoke fruitful conversations in inter-disciplinary classroom settings.

General

- Some collective responsibility theorists have argued that corporations are moral persons akin to human beings. What would be the implications of this in terms of their rights and responsibilities? Is this a plausible position?
- Is there a business case for corporate responsibility? Generally, what are the strengths and what are the weaknesses of business case arguments?
- Stakeholder theory has been important and influential in countering shareholder value ideology. Is stakeholder theory adequate and sufficient also to frame human rights responsibilities of business? If not, how would you describe its limitations in this regard?
- CSR has often been criticized for being vague and undefined. Can you come up with a definition?
- The BHR discussion has evolved separately and in parallel to CSR. Should the two discussions be integrated more? Where do you see the potential of such an integration? What is the risk?

For Business Students

- What is the purpose of the corporation and how does this affect our view on corporate responsibility?
- What is the role of business culture for corporate responsibility (a) conceptually and (b) practically?
- CSR has often been criticized for a perceived lack of impact on the ground. In your opinion, what are the reasons for this lack of impact and what measures would you propose to make CSR more effective?
- Why have human rights traditionally not played much of a role for corporate responsibility both in practice and in theory? Can you make sense of this from a management perspective?

- "Greenwashing" is a big challenge in corporate responsibility.[26] How can we tell sincere commitment and engagement of companies from mere window dressing? What can be done to address the greenwashing problem?

For Law Students

- Legal rights and obligations derive from a corporation's legal personality. Why is it important for law students also to explore the moral personality of companies? How do the two concepts relate to each other?
- There is a risk that the focus on corporate responsibility can undermine efforts to hold individuals accountable. What can and should be done to prevent corporate decision makers from using the corporate structure as a shield to escape accountability?
- CSR tends to stress voluntary and proactive engagement of corporations and strives for a positive impact rather than "merely" harm avoidance. However, it is often criticized for a lack of binding force as a consequence. To what degree should CSR be legislated? What means do legislators have to mandate CSR and how far should they go in using them?
- In many countries company law mandates a narrow focus of corporate directors on maximizing return for investors. Do you see possibilities for companies to adopt corporate responsibility despite such laws? What are the limitations of such responsibility?
- Why have human rights traditionally not played much of a role for corporate responsibility both in practice and in theory? Can you make sense of this from a legal perspective?

For Policy Students

- How can states make use of the market mechanism to incentivize corporate responsibility? What are the limits of such market-based strategies?
- Dow Votaw mentioned in the 1960s that understanding the political dimension of corporations is key to fully grasp their responsibilities.[27] How would you describe this political dimension today and what implications does it have for corporate responsibility?
- States have traditionally been in charge of business regulation. However, increasingly, such regulatory tasks are outsourced to corporations them-

---

[26] Greenwashing means that a company embellishes its environmental or social performance; e.g., by communicating progressive policies while doing little to implement them on the ground. Thus, the company tries to gain and maintain a better social or environmental image than it actually deserves.

[27] Votaw, *Changing Corporate Society*.

selves, which advance corporate responsibility through self-regulation. What advantages do you see with such a division of the regulatory labor? What are the disadvantages?

- The policy reach of national governments is increasingly limited. What international mechanisms are needed to promote corporate responsibility?
- Why have human rights traditionally not played much of a role for corporate responsibility both in practice and in theory? Can you make sense of this from a policy/political science perspective?

TEACHING RESOURCES

Readings

Corporate (social) responsibility

- Carroll, Archie B., Kenneth J. Lipartito, James E. Post, Patricia H. Werhane, and Kenneth E. Goodpaster. *Corporate Responsibility: The American Experience*. Cambridge: Cambridge University Press, 2012.
- Crane, Andrew, Abagail McWilliams, Dirk Matten, Jeremy Moon, and Donald S. Siegel, eds. *The Oxford Handbook of Corporate Social Responsibility*. Oxford: Oxford University Press, 2008.
- Garriga, Elisabet, and Domènec Melé. "Corporate Social Responsibility Theories: Mapping the Territory." *Journal of Business Ethics* 53 (August 2004): 51–71.
- Wettstein, Florian. "Social Responsibility." In *The Routledge Companion to Business Ethics*, edited by Eugene Heath, Byron Kaldis, and Alexei Marcoux, 167–183. London: Routledge, 2018.
- Zadek, Simon. "The Path to Corporate Responsibility." *Harvard Business Review*, December 2004, 125–132.

Corporate social responsibility and human rights

- McCorquodale, Robert. "Corporate Social Responsibility and International Human Rights Law." *Journal of Business Ethics* 87 (December 2009): 385–400.
- Obara, Louise J., and Ken Peattie. 2018. "Bridging the Great Divide? Making Sense of the Human Rights-CSR Relationship in UK Multinational Companies." *Journal of World Business* 53, no. 6 (December 2018): 781–793.
- Werhane, Patricia. "Corporate Moral Agency and the Responsibility to Respect Human Rights in the UN Guiding Principles: Do Corporations

Have Moral Rights?" *Business and Human Rights Journal* 1, no. 1 (January 2016): 5–20.

- Wettstein, Florian. "From Side Show to Main Act: Can Business and Human Rights Save Corporate Responsibility?" In *Business and Human Rights: From Principles to Practice*, edited by Dorothee Baumann-Pauly and Justine Nolan, 78–87. London: Routledge, 2016.
- Wettstein, Florian. *Business and Human Rights: Ethical, Legal and Managerial Perspectives*. Cambridge: Cambridge University Press, 2022.

Representative corporate responsibility statements

The following are two concrete examples of CSR statements that represent (a) an instrumental position (i.e., the business case for corporate responsibility) and (b) a charitable position on corporate responsibility:

(a) "Being a sustainable business is about striking the balance between shareholder expectations and the needs and concerns of our employees, the workers in our supply chain and the environment. We truly believe that acting as a responsible business – one which is fully committed to respecting human rights – will contribute to lasting economic success."[28]

(b) "Our mission is to fill the world with emotion, through the power of creativity and technology, and to nurture innovation to enrich and improve people's lives. Through our partnerships with worthy causes, in-kind product donations and employee volunteerism, we strive to make a difference in our communities and the world around us."[29]

Videos

- Abbott, Jennifer and Joel Bakan. *The New Corporation: The Unfortunately Necessary Sequel*. Grant Street Productions and Screen Siren Pictures, 2021.
- Achbar, Mark, Jennifer Abbott, and Joel Bakan. "*The Corporation*." Big Picture Media Corporation, 2003, YouTube video, 2:24:40: https://www.youtube.com/watch?v=zpQYsk-8dWg.

---

[28] "Our Targets," Sustainability, Adidas, accessed June 30, 2022, https://www.adidas-group.com/en/sustainability/focus-sustainability/our-targets.

[29] "Corporate Social Responsibility," Sony, accessed January 13, 2022, https://www.sony.com/en_us/SCA/social-responsibility/overview.html.

3. Human rights

Anthony Ewing

OVERVIEW

Human rights are the central concern of business and human rights (BHR) for most BHR teachers and students. In over twenty years of teaching an elective BHR course to graduate students of law, business, and other disciplines, few students have prioritized business objectives over human rights outcomes. Effective BHR teaching introduces international human rights standards and illustrates the human rights impacts of business activity. Key topics for BHR courses include the sources of international human rights standards, the definition of specific human rights in international legal instruments, the human rights responsibilities of different actors under international law, and the evolution of the corporate responsibility to respect human rights.

This chapter provides a broad overview for introducing human rights to BHR students who have not studied the topic previously.

HUMAN RIGHTS

A foundational question is: What are human rights? While BHR courses typically do not have the time or scope to thoroughly cover the historical, philosophical, and moral definitions of human rights,[1] teachers can highlight key characteristics. Human rights are universal and inherent in human dignity and equality.[2] They are the rights of every individual without distinction of any kind. Human rights are claims against society that can be both "negative" – requiring actors to refrain from violating them, such as the right to freedom

---

[1] See, for example, "The Human Rights Idea," in *Human Rights*, eds. Louis Henkin, Gerald L. Neuman, Diane F. Orentlicher, and David W. Leebron (New York: Foundation Press, 1999), 2–72.

[2] Louis Henkin, *The Age of Rights* (New York: Columbia University Press, 1990), 1–5.

from torture or from discrimination, and "positive" – constituting a claim to be fulfilled, such as the right to equal pay for equal work, or to a fair trial.[3]

Human rights are fundamental, but not always absolute. International human rights instruments allow no derogation from basic rights to life, to freedom from torture and slavery, and to freedom of thought, conscience, and religion. Other rights, however, such as the right to privacy, may be restricted for reasons such as national security or public health.

INTERNATIONAL HUMAN RIGHTS STANDARDS

The development of international human rights law following World War II is a useful starting point for introducing the content of specific human rights. The creation of the United Nations and the promulgation by states of international human rights instruments established the cornerstones of modern international human rights law.[4] The Universal Declaration of Human Rights (1948) (UDHR)[5] and the two international Covenants (1966), on Civil and Political Rights (ICCPR) and Economic, Social, and Cultural Rights (ICESCR),[6] collectively the "International Bill of Rights," are sources of international human rights standards. Specific human rights enumerated in the UDHR include rights to life and physical security; to freedom of thought, expression, and religion; to freedom of association and of movement; to education and work; to family life and privacy; to freedom from torture, slavery, and forced labor (modern slavery); and to fair and decent work conditions. All human rights standards include the fundamental human rights principle of non-discrimination. These rights are elaborated in more detail in the legally binding treaties subsequently signed and ratified by states, such as the ICCPR and the ICESCR (UN Covenants).[7]

---

[3]   See generally Henry Shue, *Basic Rights: Subsistence, Affluence and U.S. Foreign Policy* (Princeton, NJ: Princeton University Press, 1980).

[4]   The human rights language in the UN Charter can also be helpful background for BHR discussions. United Nations, *Charter of the United Nations*, 1945, preamble, arts. 1 ("The purposes of the United Nations are ... To achieve international cooperation in ... promoting and encouraging respect for human rights ... for all without distinction"), 13, 55, 56.

[5]   UN General Assembly, Resolution 217A (III), *Universal Declaration of Human Rights*, A/RES/3/217A (December 10, 1948).

[6]   *International Covenant on Civil and Political Rights*, December 16, 1966, 999 U.N.T.S. 171 (entered into force March 23, 1976); *International Covenant on Economic, Social and Cultural Rights*, December 16, 1966, 993 U.N.T.S. 3 (entered into force January 3, 1976).

[7]   For the historical and ideological context (the Cold War) for the categorization of rights as either civil and political or economic, social, and cultural in two separate

Table 3.1   *Human rights in international standards*

Civil and political rights	Economic, social, and cultural rights
• Right to life, liberty, security	• Self-determination
• Freedom from slavery, torture	• Right to work
• Equality before the law	• Just and favorable conditions of work, including
• Protection from arbitrary arrest	equal pay for equal work
• Right to a fair trial	• Right to join and form trade unions
• Freedom of thought, opinion	• Right to social security
• Freedom of association	• Adequate standard of living
• Political participation	• Highest standard of health
	• Right to education

Listing and categorizing the full range of rights contained in international instruments is helpful for BHR students studying international human rights standards for the first time (see Table 3.1).

Rights affected by employment are often top of mind for BHR students. In BHR courses, it is helpful to highlight worker rights, such as the right to work, to an adequate standard of living, to workplace health and safety, and to freedom of association; and to emphasize that "labor rights" are human rights. BHR courses typically cover the rights defined and protected in International Labour Organization (ILO) Conventions and, in particular, the core international labor standards prohibiting forced labor and discrimination in employment, addressing child labor, and protecting freedom of association and the right to organize.[8] (See Labor Rights, Chapter 4.)

BHR courses may also reference additional international instruments that elaborate specific human rights, such as the conventions prohibiting geno-

---

UN Covenants, see Kenneth Roth, "Defending Economic, Social and Cultural Rights: Practical Issues Faced by an International Human Rights Organization," *Human Rights Quarterly* 26, no. 1 (February 2004): 63. Notably, the United States has signed but not ratified the ICESCR; the People's Republic of China has signed but not ratified the ICCPR.

[8]   International Labour Organization, *The International Labour Organization's Fundamental Conventions* (2003), https://www.ilo.org/wcmsp5/groups/public/---ed_norm/ ---declaration/documents/publication/wcms_095895.pdf. See also International Labour Organization, *Declaration of Fundamental Principles and Rights at Work* (1998). The ILO added a fifth fundamental principle and right at work – to a safe and healthy working environment – in June 2022.

cide,[9] racial discrimination,[10] torture,[11] and gender-based discrimination;[12] and the human rights of vulnerable groups, such as children[13] and Indigenous Peoples.[14] Internationally recognized human rights that are not yet defined in a specific international instrument, such as the rights to food, to water, and to a healthy environment, are also the subject of BHR teaching. (See The Right to Food, Chapter 22; The Right to Water, Chapter 23; Human Rights and the Environment, Chapter 19.)

BHR courses may also consider the definition of international crimes under international humanitarian law and their sources, such as the statute of the International Criminal Court (ICC).[15] International crimes include genocide, crimes against humanity, war crimes, and the crime of aggression.[16] It is important to note for BHR students that ICC jurisdiction extends only to "natural persons," not to corporations as "legal persons."[17] The exclusion of corporations from ICC jurisdiction, however, does not mean that companies are free from potential liability for international crimes under international law.[18] (See Complicity, Chapter 14; Corporate Accountability under Criminal Law in Chapter 12.)

[9] *Convention on the Prevention and Punishment of the Crime of Genocide*, December 9, 1948, 78 U.N.T.S. 277.

[10] *International Convention on the Elimination of All Forms of Racial Discrimination*, December 21, 1966, 660 U.N.T.S. 195 (entered into force January 4, 1969).

[11] *Convention against Torture and Other Cruel, Inhuman or Degrading Treatment or Punishment*, December 10, 1984, 1465 U.N.T.S. 85 (entered into force June 26, 1987).

[12] *Convention on the Elimination of All Forms of Discrimination Against Women*, December 18, 1979, 1249 U.N.T.S. 13 (entered into force September 3, 1981).

[13] *Convention on the Rights of the Child*, November 20, 1989, 1577 U.N.T.S. 3 (entered into force September 2, 1990).

[14] UN General Assembly, Resolution 61/295, United Nations Declaration on the Rights of Indigenous Peoples, A/RES/61/295 (13 September 2007), http://www.un.org/esa/socdev/unpfii/documents/DRIPS_en.pdf.

[15] *Rome Statute of the International Criminal Court*, July 17, 1998, 2187 U.N.T.S. 38544 (entered into force July 1, 2002). Additional sources are the Geneva Conventions (1949) and the jurisprudence of international criminal tribunals.

[16] See *Rome Statute*, Arts. 3–8bis. Crimes against humanity include, among other acts, slavery, torture, and sexual violence "when committed as part of a widespread or systematic attack directed against any civilian population." *Rome Statute*, Art. 7. War crimes include "grave breaches of the Geneva Conventions of 12 August 1949" and "[o]ther serious violations of the laws and customs applicable in international armed conflict." *Rome Statute*, Art. 8.

[17] *Rome Statute*, Art. 25 (1).

[18] See David Scheffer and Caroline Kaeb, "The Five Levels of CSR Compliance," *Berkeley Journal of International Law* 29, no. 1 (2011) 334: 357–361.

Customary international law – general state practice accepted as law – is another important source of human rights standards. Human rights violations so egregious that they are considered peremptory norms, or *"jus cogens"* – binding on all states regardless of treaty commitments – include genocide, slavery, disappearances, torture, prolonged arbitrary detention, systematic racial discrimination, crimes against humanity, and any consistent pattern of gross violations of other internationally recognized human rights.[19] The strongest argument for direct corporate responsibility for human rights violations under international law is for corporate acts that constitute international crimes and/or violate customary human rights standards.[20]

Regional human rights instruments are another source of international human rights standards and jurisprudence. The Inter-American Court of Human Rights, for example, has elaborated the responsibility of states to protect against violations of human rights by non-state actors, including business enterprises.[21] (See Business and Human Rights in the Inter-American System, Chapter 17.)

Covering the underlying sources of international human rights standards provides helpful context for introducing the United Nations Guiding Principles on Business and Human Rights (2011) (UNGPs), which under their second pillar define "the corporate responsibility to respect human rights" as referring to "internationally recognized human rights – understood, at a minimum, as those expressed in the International Bill of Human Rights and the principles concerning fundamental rights set out in the ILO's Declaration on Fundamental Principles and Rights at Work."[22] (See The UN Guiding Principles on Business and Human Rights, Chapter 5.)

---

[19]   See, for example, "Customary International Law of Human Rights," Restatement (Third) of the Foreign Relations Law of the United States, Sec. 702 (1987).

[20]   See, for example, John Ruggie, *Business and Human Rights: Mapping International Standards of Responsibility and Accountability for Corporate Acts*, Report of the Special Representative of the Secretary-General on the issue of human rights and transnational corporations and other business enterprises, UN doc. A/HRC/4/035 (February 9, 2007).

[21]   See Inter-American Court of Human Rights, Case of *Velásquez Rodríguez v. Honduras*, Merits, Judgment, Inter-Am. Ct. H.R. (ser. C) No. 4 (July 29, 1988).

[22]   United Nations Human Rights Council, *Guiding Principles on Business and Human Rights: Implementing the United Nations 'Protect, Respect and Remedy' Framework*, Report of the Special Representative of the Secretary-General on the issue of human rights and transnational corporations and other business enterprises, UN doc. A/HRC/17/31 (March 21, 2011) (UN Guiding Principles), Guiding Principle 12. Commentary to Guiding Principle 12 notes that business enterprises "can have an impact on virtually the entire spectrum of internationally recognized human rights" and may need to consider standards beyond these, including other UN instruments and the standards on international humanitarian law in situations of armed conflict.

HUMAN RIGHTS UNDER INTERNATIONAL LAW

Assigning and examining the text of the UDHR and each of the UN Covenants is a productive exercise for BHR students. Teachers can call attention to the explicit human rights responsibilities of states, as described in the UDHR:

- "to achieve ... the promotion of universal respect for and observance of" human rights (Preamble),

and defined in Article 2 of each UN Covenant:

- "to respect and to ensure to all individuals within its territory and subject to its jurisdiction" (ICCPR), and
- "to take steps ... to the maximum of its available resources, with a view to achieving progressively" (ICESCR), respectively.

Considering the meaning behind the different state responsibility language in each instrument sets the stage to discuss whether companies have similar human rights responsibilities.

The legal status of human rights under international law inevitably raises the issue of state versus non-state actors. States have direct human rights responsibilities. Business enterprises, as non-state actors and "legal persons," arguably, have no direct human rights responsibilities under international law.[23] Exploring arguments for direct corporate human rights responsibilities is a way to introduce international law concepts and encourage students to consider whether and how companies should define their human rights responsibilities.

United Nations bodies including the Human Rights Council and treaty mechanisms; and other multilateral international organizations, including the International Labour Organization[24] and the Organisation of Economic

---

[23] But see Andrew Clapham, *Human Rights Responsibilities of Non-State Actors* (Oxford: Oxford University Press, 2006), 251 ("Although the jurisdictional possibilities are limited under existing international tribunals, where national law allows for claims based on international law, it is becoming clear that international law obligates non-state actors"); Nadia Bernaz, *Business and Human Rights: History, Law and Policy – Bridging the Accountability Gap* (Oxford: Routledge, 2017), 81–117.

[24] The fact that businesses, through employer organizations, together with states and trade unions, play a role in the development of ILO Conventions through the "tripartite" governance of the ILO, an international organization that predates the establishment of the United Nations, is relevant for considering the role and responsibilities of business actors under international law.

Co-operation and Development (OECD), reference business enterprises as bearing responsibilities under international law.[25]

ENFORCING HUMAN RIGHTS

While international instruments and customary international law define international human rights standards, human rights enforcement is often left to states. With notable exceptions,[26] there are few supra-national mechanisms to enforce human rights standards, provide remedy to victims, or hold violators, including business enterprises, accountable. Human rights treaty commitments are implemented through national laws and institutions. BHR courses can highlight how international human rights standards are enforced domestically, through criminal and civil law and workplace health and safety regulations, for example, with particular attention to whether and how companies can be held liable for violations under national laws and regulations. (See Corporate Accountability under Criminal Law in Chapter 12; Mandatory Human Rights Due Diligence Legislation, Chapter 11.)

CORPORATE HUMAN RIGHTS RESPONSIBILITIES

The UDHR preamble states that "every organ of society ... shall strive ... to promote respect for these rights and freedoms and ... to secure their universal and effective recognition and observance." While not a binding treaty, the 193 member states of the United Nations commit to uphold the principles of the UDHR by virtue of their UN membership. According to Louis Henkin, "Every individual includes juridical persons. Every individual and every

---

[25] See, for example, John Ruggie, *Business and Human Rights: Mapping International Standards of Responsibility and Accountability for Corporate Acts*, Report of the Special Representative of the Secretary-General on the issue of human rights and transnational corporations and other business enterprises, UN doc. A/HRC/4/035 (February 19, 2007), ¶ 20; Committee on Economic, Social and Cultural Rights, "General Comment No. 24 on State Obligations under the International Covenant on Economic, Social and Cultural Rights in the Context of Business Activities" UN doc. E/C.12/GC/24 (June 23, 2017) ("Corporations are increasingly recognized as 'participants' at the international level, with the capacity to bear some rights and duties under international law"); Committee on Economic, Social and Cultural Rights, "General Comment No. 12: The Right to Adequate Food (Art. 11)" UN doc. E/C.12/1999/5 (May 12, 1999), ¶ 20 ("all members of society – individuals, families, local communities, non-governmental organizations, civil society organizations, as well as the private business sector – have responsibilities in the realization of the right to adequate food"); Clapham, *Human Rights Responsibilities of Non-State Actors*, 266–270.

[26] The International Criminal Court and regional human rights bodies such as the European Court of Human Rights and the Inter-American Court of Human Rights.

organ of society excludes no one, no company, no market, no cyberspace. The Universal Declaration applies to them all."[27]

An important issue for BHR students to consider is whether companies have any human rights responsibilities under international law. Considering this question allows for a discussion of public international law principles and the architecture of international human rights standards, institutions, and modes of enforcement. Key topics include:

- The role of states as both subjects and authors of international human rights standards.
- The development and definition of human rights standards under customary international law.
- The legally binding status of different international instruments, such as treaties versus declarations.
- The human rights obligations of non-state actors under international law.[28]
- The state duty to protect against human rights violations by non-state actors, including business enterprises.[29]
- "Hard law" versus "soft law."

Exploring whether corporations have any human rights responsibilities under international law and, if so, on what basis can frame discussion of any of these points. I encourage students to engage this debate along three lines of argument: (1) direct legal responsibility; (2) indirect legal responsibility; and (3) voluntary responsibility.[30]

Corporate human rights responsibility under international law can be direct, based on individual responsibility by virtue of corporations' status as "legal persons," as for international crimes. As international actors, companies may be directly responsible for committing international crimes and for complicity in human rights abuses committed by others. (See Complicity, Chapter 14.)

---

[27] Louis Henkin, "The Universal Declaration at 50 and the Challenge of Global Markets," *Brooklyn Journal of International Law* 25, no. 1 (April 1999): 25.

[28] See Clapham, *Human Rights Obligations of Non-State Actors*.

[29] Teachers can point to treaty body commentary emphasizing the state responsibility to protect against business actions that infringe rights. See, for example, ICESCR, General Comment No. 24 (2017) on State obligations under the International Covenant on Economic, Social and Cultural Rights in the context of business activities, UN Doc. E/C.12/GC/24 (August 10, 2017); ICCPR, General Comment No. 31, The Nature of the General Legal Obligation Imposed on States Parties to the Covenant, UN Doc. CCPR/C/21/Rev.1/Add. 13 (May 26, 2004), ¶ 8; Ruggie, *Mapping International Standards*, ¶¶ 10–18.

[30] See Ruggie, *Mapping International Standards*.

Second, companies can be held accountable for their human rights impacts indirectly via state duties under international law to protect against human rights violations by non-state actors.[31] Companies are subject to national laws that address their human rights impacts and states may regulate the extraterritorial conduct of actors over which they have jurisdiction. "Pillar I" of the UNGPs – the state duty to protect against human rights abuse by third parties, including business enterprises – captures this state responsibility. (See Mandatory Human Rights Due Diligence Legislation, Chapter 11; Judicial Remedy, Chapter 12.)

Finally, expectations for corporate conduct and human rights responsibility are also set by voluntary or "soft law" standards, such as the OECD Guidelines for Multinational Enterprises,[32] the UN Global Compact Principles,[33] and multistakeholder[34] or individual company codes of conduct. BHR teachers can distinguish the "hard law" nature of human rights responsibilities from "soft law" corporate responsibility initiatives.[35]

In my teaching, examining corporate human rights responsibility under international law leads into our consideration of the corporate responsibility to respect human rights under the UNGPs. (See The UN Guiding Principles on Business and Human Rights, Chapter 5.)

THE EVOLUTION OF INTERNATIONAL BHR STANDARDS

The history of BHR as an example of international standard-setting can be taught alongside the evolution of international human rights law. Teachers may reference the ILO Tripartite Declaration (1977, 2000),[36] the UN Draft Code of

[31] *Velásquez Rodríguez v. Honduras*, Merits, Inter-Am. Ct. H.R. (ser.C) No. 4 ¶ 172 (July 29, 1988).

[32] Organisation for Economic Co-operation and Development, *OECD Guidelines for Multinational Enterprises*, 2011 ed. (Paris: OECD Publishing, 2011).

[33] "The Ten Principles of the UN Global Compact," United Nations Global Compact, accessed August 8, 2022, https://www.unglobalcompact.org/what-is-gc/mission/principles.

[34] See, for example, "Fair Labor Code," Fair Labor Association, https://www.fairlabor.org/accountability/standards/manufacturing/mfg-code; "Principles on Freedom of Expression and Privacy," Global Network Initiative, https://globalnetworkinitiative.org/gni-principles.

[35] Anita Ramasastry, "Corporate Social Responsibility Versus Business and Human Rights: Bridging the Gap Between Responsibility and Accountability," *Journal of Human Rights* 14, no. 2 (2015): 237–259.

[36] ILO, *Tripartite Declaration of Principles Concerning Multinational Enterprises and Social Policy*, ILO Official Bulletin 1978, vol. LXI, Series A, no. 1 (amended ILO Official Bulletin 2000, vol. LXXXIII, Series A, no. 3).

Conduct on Transnational Corporations (1990),[37] the OECD Guidelines for Multinational Enterprises, the UN Global Compact, the draft UN Norms on the Responsibilities of Transnational Corporations and Other Business Enterprises with Regard to Human Rights (2003), and the UN Framework on Business and Human Rights (2008) as precursors to the UN Guiding Principles and the current BHR Treaty process.[38]

The UN Global Compact (UNGC), for example, the voluntary corporate responsibility initiative launched by UN Secretary General Kofi Annan in 2000, asks companies to "embrace, support and enact, within their sphere of influence, a set of core values in the areas of human rights, labour standards, the environment, and anti-corruption."[39] The explicit human rights principles are UNGC Principle 1: "Businesses should support and respect the protection of internationally proclaimed human rights" and Principle 2: "Make sure they are not complicit in human rights abuses." BHR students may be more familiar with the UNGC than the UNGPs. I often ask students to contrast the responsibility language aimed at UNGC participants with the state responsibility language in the legally binding UN Covenants.

CONNECTING HUMAN RIGHTS TO BUSINESS

Asking, "Which rights contained in the UDHR are relevant for business?" can lead to a productive discussion connecting potential human rights impacts to business activity. Distinct corporate functions, such as human resources, procurement, and security, can have both positive and negative human rights impacts. With respect to the rights to work, to an adequate standard of living, and to non-discrimination, for example, a global manufacturer's human resources operations have the potential to ensure employees are paid a living wage and to prevent discrimination in hiring based on gender or sexual orientation (see Figure 3.1).

---

[37] United Nations, *Draft Code of Conduct on Transnational Corporations*, UN Doc. E/1990/94 (June 12, 1990).

[38] For a succinct history, see Justine Nolan, "Mapping the Movement: The Business and Human Rights Regulatory Framework," in *Business and Human Rights: From Principles to Practice*, eds. Dorothée Baumann-Pauly and Justine Nolan (London: Routledge, 2016), 32–51.

[39] "The Ten Principles of the UN Global Compact," United Nations Global Compact, accessed August 8, 2022, https://www.unglobalcompact.org/what-is-gc/mission/principles.

Company function	Examples of relevant issues	Examples of human rights affected
Human resources	‣ Are our female and male staff hired, paid and promoted based solely on their relevant competences for the job? ‣ Are women and men paid the same wage for the same work? ‣ How is sexual harassment in the workplace dealt with?	‣ Freedom from discrimination ‣ Women's rights
Health and safety	‣ Are our workplaces safe when it comes to the mental and physical health of our staff?	‣ Right to just and favourable conditions of work ‣ Right to health
Procurement	‣ Do our suppliers adhere to core labour standards including on child labour, forced labour, freedom of association and collective bargaining?	‣ Right to form and join a trade union ‣ Right to bargain collectively ‣ Freedom from slavery ‣ Children's rights
Product safety	‣ Are any of our products potentially detrimental to our customers or end-users (for example, because they could harm their health or could involve the dissemination of sensitive personal information)?	‣ Right to health ‣ Right to privacy
Community relations	‣ Are local communities around our operations or facilities affected by what we do (for example, as a result of pollution, excess dust or noise)? ‣ Do any of our operations involve resettling people in a new location?	‣ Right to an adequate standard of living ‣ Rights to water and sanitation ‣ Right to health ‣ Indigenous peoples' rights including the right to free, prior and informed consent

Source: Global Compact Network Netherlands, Oxfam and Shift, "Doing Business with Respect for Human Rights: A Guidance Tool for Companies" (2016), https://www. businessrespecthumanrights.org. (Reprinted with permission.)

Figure 3.1   *Examples of the connection between a business and human rights*

TEACHING APPROACHES

I have taught an introductory, elective BHR course to law students since 2001.[40] While many law students are exposed to human rights and/or public

---

[40]   The course, "Transnational Business and Human Rights," originated at Columbia Business School in 1990, was offered jointly with Columbia Law School from 2001 to

international law in other coursework, there are no prerequisites for my BHR seminar. All BHR students, including business, policy, and undergraduate students, benefit from exposure to the normative foundations of BHR. When teaching human rights, BHR teachers can adjust the level of legal detail for students with different academic backgrounds and familiarity with the subject.

I devote approximately one two-hour class session to the underlying principles of international human rights law. BHR teachers can also introduce human rights through the text of the UNGPs or through sessions devoted to specific human rights, such as labor rights. For law students, I find that grounding the class in international human rights principles before introducing the UNGPs places the UNGPs and the field of BHR in the appropriate historical and legal context. Covering concepts like state responsibility under international law early in a BHR course can also make subsequent BHR topics, such as corporate complicity in human rights violations and the right to remedy for victims of human rights abuse connected to business activity, easier to understand.

Learning objectives for teaching human rights may include:

* Understanding the history, sources, and content of international human rights standards.
* Considering and contrasting the human responsibilities of states, non-state actors, individuals, and businesses.
* Assessing legal arguments for corporate human rights responsibilities.
* Connecting specific human rights to business activity.
* Translating the language of human rights into business terminology, and vice versa.
* Comparing the content of specific corporate human rights policies.

EXERCISE 3.1

OUTLINE A CORPORATE HUMAN RIGHTS POLICY

A brief in-class exercise allows students to apply international human rights standards by brainstorming a human rights policy for a hypothetical company. The goal of the exercise is for students to consider the appropriate scope and content of a company's human rights policy. I assign actual corporate

---

2004, and has resided at the Law School since 2007. Since 2019, I have also taught "Managing Human Rights," an elective seminar that explores BHR topics in greater detail, aimed at students already familiar with core BHR principles through professional experience or prior coursework.

human rights policies from different sectors as background reading in addition to the primary international human rights instruments.[41] This exercise works well when conducted before any in-class discussion of the content of the UDHR and UN Covenants. Students will look to the international texts for human rights definitions and language.

I present a brief description of a hypothetical company. Teachers can draw the details from actual companies and BHR cases, or simply invent a fact pattern that highlights relevant human rights issues for a company in a specific sector. For example:

• A Canadian mining company has acquired a gold mine in a part of a country where government control is being challenged by armed insurgents. Security for the mine is provided by government armed forces. State security forces have been accused of widespread human rights violations, including the forced disappearance of local villagers. The subsidiary that will manage the mine has no human rights policy.[42]

I typically divide the class into groups of three to five students. I then ask each group to outline a human rights policy for the hypothetical company. To guide their group discussions, I ask that each group outline a policy, in bulleted form, that:
(1) defines the company's human rights responsibilities;
(2) references relevant international standards; and
(3) identifies the specific human rights covered.
The first item connects the exercise to an earlier class session addressing definitions of corporate responsibility and to the corporate responsibility to respect human rights defined in the UNGPs.

Tip: Ask students to define the company's responsibilities in a single, complete sentence to force careful editing. The second item encourages students to look at the content of specific sources of international human

[41] For example: "Microsoft Global Human Rights Statement," Microsoft, accessed August 8, 2022, https://www.microsoft.com/en-us/corporate-responsibility/human-rights-statement; "The Coca-Cola Company Human Rights Policy," The Coca-Cola Company, accessed August 9, 2022, https://www.coca-colacompany.com/policies-and-practices/human-rights-principles; "GE Human Rights Statement of Principles," General Electric Company, accessed August 8, 2022, https://www.ge.com/sites/default/files/human_rights_statement_of_principles.pdf.
[42] This hypothetical case is distilled from a "buzz group case" in Chris Marsden, *Teaching Business and Human Rights: A Teaching Module for Business School Tutors* (Doughty Centre for Corporate Responsibility, Cranfield School of Management, 2012), https://www.cranfield.ac.uk/-/media/images-for-new-website/centres/school-of-management-centres/doughty-centre/pdfs/case-studies/business-and-human-rights-teaching-module.ashx.

rights standards, such as the UDHR, the UN Covenants, and core ILO Conventions. The third item requires students to identify and list specific human rights – e.g., rights to life, liberty, security; labor rights; land rights – connected to the hypothetical.

After a period of discussion, groups report back to the class, sharing their policy outlines.

Teachers can compare how different groups chose specific language – which verbs (protect, respect, ensure) in particular – to define the company's human rights responsibilities; which international standards they reference; and how they prioritize relevant rights. The exercise also allows students to analyze and critique the content of actual corporate human rights policies and can facilitate a discussion of the strengths and weaknesses of voluntary corporate standards.

KEY QUESTIONS

General

- What are human rights?
- What are the sources of international human rights standards?
- What international instruments comprise the "International Bill of Human Rights"?
- What human rights are contained in the Universal Declaration of Human Rights and the UN Covenants?
- What is meant by "negative" and "positive" rights?
- Which rights are instrumental for the enjoyment of other rights?
- Do businesses have any human rights responsibilities under international law? Why or why not?

For Business Students

- How do human rights relate to business activity? Which business functions can have human rights impacts?
- Which human rights should a company's human rights policy address?
- How should a company's business, operations, or sector shape which human rights are included?

For Law Students

- What are the human rights obligations of states under international law?
- What does the "duty to protect" mean under international law?

- What is the role of "non-state" actors under international law?
- How do state responsibilities differ under the ICCPR and the ICESCR? Which rights are contained in each instrument?
- What is the difference between "hard law" and so-called "soft law"?
- What is customary international law?
- What are international crimes? What are the sources of international humanitarian law?
- Which rights are considered *jus cogens* norms?
- What are the human rights responsibilities of individuals under international law?
- How are international human rights standards enforced?
- What role does domestic law play in human rights enforcement?

For Policy Students

- How have international human rights standards emerged and evolved since World War II?
- How have the UN Guiding Principles been operationalized in public policy and international standards?
- What policy tools are available to states to address the human rights impacts of business activity?
- Are voluntary or mandatory human rights standards for business enterprises most likely to improve human rights outcomes?

TEACHING RESOURCES

Readings

International human rights standards

- United Nations. *International Covenant on Civil and Political Rights*. 999 U.N.T.S. 171 (December 16, 1966, entered into force March 23, 1976).
- United Nations. *International Covenant on Economic, Social and Cultural Rights*. 993 U.N.T.S. 3 (December 16, 1966, entered into force January 3, 1976).
- United Nations. *Universal Declaration of Human Rights*. General Assembly Resolution 217A (III). A/RES/3/217A (10 December 1948), https://www.un.org/en/about-us/universal-declaration-of-human-rights.
- International Labour Organization. *Declaration of Fundamental Principles and Rights at Work* (1998), as amended in June 2022, https://www.ilo.org/global/lang--en/index.htm.

Commentary

- Nolan, Justine. "Mapping the Movement: The Business and Human Rights Regulatory Framework." In *Business and Human Rights: From Principles to Practice*, edited by Dorothée Baumann-Pauly and Justine Nolan, 32–51. London: Routledge, 2016.
- Simons, Penelope, "International Law's Invisible Hand and the Future of Corporate Accountability for Violations of Human Rights." In *Corporate Responsibility for Human Rights Impacts: New Expectations and Paradigms*, edited by Lara Blecher, Nancy Kaymar Stafford, and Gretchen C. Bellamy, 79–120. Chicago, IL: American Bar Association, 2014.
- Steinhardt, Ralph G. "Multinational Corporations and Their Responsibilities under International Law." In *Corporate Responsibility for Human Rights Impacts: New Expectations and Paradigms*, edited by Lara Blecher, Nancy Kaymar Stafford, and Gretchen C. Bellamy, 27–50. American Bar Association, 2014.

Reports

- Global Compact Network Netherlands, Oxfam and Shift. *Doing Business with Respect for Human Rights: A Guidance Tool for Companies*. 2nd ed., 2016. https://www.businessrespecthumanrights.org.
- International Council on Human Rights Policy, *Beyond Voluntarism: Human Rights and the Developing International Legal Obligations of Companies*. Geneva: International Council on Human Rights Policy, 2002.
- Monash University Castan Centre for Human Rights Law, UNHCHR and UN Global Compact. *Human Rights Translated 2.0: A Business Reference Guide*. 2016. http://www.ohchr.org/Documents/Issues/Business/Monash_HRT.pdf.
- Ruggie, John. *Business and Human Rights: Mapping International Standards of Responsibility and Accountability for Corporate Acts*, Report of the Special Representative of the Secretary-General on the issue of human rights and transnational corporations and other business enterprises, UN doc. A/HRC/4/035 (February 9, 2007).
- UN Global Compact. *A Guide for Business on How to Develop a Human Rights Policy*. 2010. http://www.unglobalcompact.org/docs/issues_doc/human_rights/Resources/How_to_Develop_a_Human_Rights_Policy.pdf.
- World Business Council for Sustainable Development, *CEO Guide to Human Rights*. 2nd ed., 2020. https://humanrights.wbcsd.org/ceo-guide-to-human-rights.

Websites

- Business and Human Rights Resource Centre, https://www.business -humanrights.org/en.

4.   Labor rights[1]

Angela B. Cornell

OVERVIEW

The rights of workers in the global economy are a fundamental cornerstone in the development of business and human rights (BHR) as a field of practice and study. Labor has not fared well under neoliberal economic restructuring where capital has few regulatory constraints and is highly mobile. More than 60 percent of workers throughout the world are in the informal economy, engaged in precarious work outside of the framework of legal protections and rights. Workers' freedom of association has been a formidable challenge in this context. Labor rights can be addressed in a BHR course together with human rights more broadly or through labor-related cases and topics. (See Human Rights, Chapter 3.)

This chapter is intended to help teachers provide students an overview of and introduction to the sources of international labor law. It highlights key provisions of both public and private international law that address labor rights.

INTERNATIONAL LABOR LAW

International labor rights are loosely regulated by an amalgam of public international and private law, binding and soft law norms, and a range of public–private global initiatives and transnational efforts. Few international human rights norms have enjoyed such widespread and historic recognition. Since 1919 when the International Labour Organization (ILO) was founded, labor rights have been identified as fundamental for a just society.

Recognized as both political and economic, labor rights hold the special status of being included in each of the core international instruments that comprise the International Bill of Human Rights: the Universal Declaration

---

[1]   An earlier version of this chapter appeared online in Angela B. Cornell, "Teaching Note: International Labor Rights," in *Teaching Business and Human Rights Handbook* (Teaching Business and Human Rights Forum, 2019), https://teachbhr.org/resources/teaching-bhr-handbook/teaching-notes/international-labor-rights.

of Human Rights (UDHR),[2] the International Covenant on Civil and Political Rights (ICCPR),[3] and the International Covenant on Economic, Social, and Cultural Rights (ICESCR).[4] Both United Nations Covenants are binding when ratified by states. All three instruments, UDHR, ICCPR, and ICESCR, recognize the significance of freedom of association and the right to form and join trade unions.[5]

Regional human rights instruments in the Americas, Europe, and Africa also recognize freedom of association and trade union rights.[6] There is a growing body of jurisprudence on labor rights from regional human rights courts.

Private agreements can also advance labor rights and many include dispute resolution mechanisms. These include collective bargaining agreements, multistakeholder agreements, codes of conduct that are incorporated into enforceable contracts, and global framework agreements.

PUBLIC INTERNATIONAL LAW

International Labour Organization

The ILO is the most significant global entity dealing with human rights in the workplace. The United Nations-related body is dedicated to the establishment and oversight of international labor standards. The ILO's tripartite governing structure is composed of governments, workers, and employers. It is the primary international body to address workplace rights in the global economy and has nearly universal membership of countries around the globe.[7] In 1944, the ILO established the fundamental principles that "labor is not a commodity"

---

[2]   UN General Assembly, Resolution 217A (III), *Universal Declaration of Human Rights*, A/RES/3/217A (December 10, 1948), art. 20(1); art. 23 (4).

[3]   *International Covenant on Civil and Political Rights*, December 16, 1966, 999 U.N.T.S. 17 (entered into force March 23, 1976), art. 22.

[4]   *International Covenant on Economic, Social and Cultural Rights*, December 16, 1966, 999 993 U.N.T.S 3 (entered into force January 3, 1976), art. 8.

[5]   For a helpful framing of labor rights in the broader human rights framework, see James A. Gross, ed., *Workers' Rights as Human Rights* (Ithaca, NY: Cornell University Press, 2003); John Gerald Ruggie, *Just Business: Multinational Corporations and Human Rights* (New York: W. W. Norton, 2013).

[6]   Franz Christian Ebert and Martin Oelz, *Bridging the Gap between Labour Rights and Human Rights: The Role of ILO Law in Regional Human Rights Courts* (Geneva: International Institute for Labour Studies, 2012).

[7]   One hundred and eighty-seven countries are now members of the ILO.

and that "freedom of expression and association are essential to sustained progress."[8]

The ILO has developed close to 200 conventions that set international labor standards and monitors state compliance with ratified conventions. ILO Conventions and Protocols are legally binding international treaties; recommendations supplement these with additional nonbinding guidelines. The supervisory process includes the Committee of Experts on the Application of Conventions and Recommendations (CEACR) and the Committee on the Application of Standards, which oversee compliance with ILO obligations. Member states submit reports on measures taken to implement ratified conventions, which are reviewed by CEACR.[9] Additional measures can be pursued with cases of noncompliance. Complaints alleging violations of the foundational Conventions 87 and 98 can be submitted to the Committee on Freedom of Association (CFA), even if the state has not ratified the Convention.[10] The CFA examines cases related to trade union rights, which can relate to collective bargaining, the right to strike, or related legislation. The Committee's action has led to the resolution of many issues, but some member states consistently fail to remedy violations.

Topics addressed in ILO Conventions include minimum wages, hours of work, occupational safety and health, violence and harassment in the workplace, as well as broader policies such as social security.[11] Core labor rights are contained in the ILO Declaration of Fundamental Principles and Rights at Work.

---

[8] *Philadelphia Declaration Concerning the Aims and Purposes of the International Labor Organization* (1944), incorporated into the ILO Constitution. International Labour Conference, 26th, Philadelphia, 1944 (The Declaration of Philadelphia).

[9] Committee on the Application of Standards of the International Labour Conference, *A Dynamic and Impact Built on Decades of Dialogue and Persuasion* (Geneva: ILO, 2011), https://www.ilo.org/wcmsp5/groups/public/---ed_norm/---normes/documents/publication/wcms_154192.pdf.

[10] International Labor Office, *Freedom of Association Compilation of Decisions of the Committee on Freedom of Association*, 6th ed. (Geneva: ILO, 2018).

[11] See, for example, ILO Convention No. 190, *Eliminating Violence and Harassment in the World of Work*, June 21, 2019 (entered into force June 25, 2021); ILO Convention No. 189, *Domestic Workers Convention*, June 16, 2011 (entered into force September 5, 2013).

Declaration of Fundamental Principles and Rights at Work (1998)
The ILO's Declaration on Fundamental Principles and Rights at Work[12] (ILO Declaration) represents the international consensus on the very core of workplace rights from eight ILO Conventions:

(1)   freedom of association and the effective recognition of the right to collective bargaining (Conventions 87 and 98);
(2)   the elimination of all forms of forced or compulsory labor (Conventions 29 and 105);
(3)   the effective elimination of child labor (Conventions 138 and 182);
(4)   the elimination of discrimination in respect to employment and occupation (Conventions 100 and 111); and
(5)   the right to a safe and healthy working environment.

All members of the ILO have an obligation to "respect, to promote, and to realize" these fundamental rights – even if they have not ratified the Conventions. The significance of the Declaration is seen in the extensive diffusion and incorporation into numerous public and private instruments, including the UN Guiding Principles on Business and Human Rights (UNGPs),[13] the OECD Guidelines for Multinational Enterprises,[14] the UN Global Compact,[15] bilateral and multilateral trade agreements, and global framework agreements, among others.

---

[12]   International Labour Organization, *Declaration of Fundamental Principles and Rights at Work* (1998), as amended in June 2022. The ILO added a fifth fundamental principle and right at work – to a safe and healthy working environment – in June 2022.
[13]   Business enterprises must respect internationally recognized human rights including the fundamental labor rights referenced in the instruments that comprise the International Bill of Human Rights, as well as the core rights contained in the ILO's Declaration on Fundamental Principles and Rights at Work. United Nations Human Rights Council, *Guiding Principles on Business and Human Rights: Implementing the United Nations "Protect, Respect and Remedy" Framework*, Report of the Special Representative of the Secretary-General on the issue of human rights and transnational corporations and other business enterprises, UN doc. A/HRC/17/31 (March 21, 2011), Principle 12.
[14]   Organisation for Economic Co-operation and Development, *OECD Guidelines for Multinational Enterprises* (Paris: OECD Publishing, 2011).
[15]   The UN Global Compact incorporates fundamental labor rights in its Principles 3–6. "The Ten Principles of the UN Global Compact," United Nations Global Compact, accessed August 8, 2022, https://www.unglobalcompact.org/what-is-gc/mission/principles.

Freedom of association, Conventions 87 and 98

Convention 87 provides that "[w]orkers and employers, without distinction whatsoever, shall have the right to establish and, subject only to the rules of the organization concerned, to join organizations of their own choosing."[16] The right to strike is considered to be part of this convention.[17]

Convention 98 promotes organizational rights, collective bargaining, and protection from anti-union discrimination and interference. Employer domination or control of a workers' organization is considered interference.[18]

Worst forms of child labor, Convention 182

Convention 182 seeks to eliminate the worst forms of child labor, including slavery, trafficking, sexual exploitation, and use of children in armed conflict or illicit or hazardous work that harms children's health, safety, or morals. Universal ratification of this convention was achieved in 2020, representing a milestone in ILO history as the only convention to do so.

The Universal Declaration of Human Rights (1948)

The UDHR states that "everyone has the right to freedom of peaceful assembly and association" (Art. 20(1)) and "everyone has the right to form and join trade unions for the protection of his interests" (Art. 23(4)).

International Covenant on Civil and Political Rights (1966)

The ICCPR recognizes that "[e]veryone shall have the right to freedom of association with others, including the right to form and join trade unions for the protection of his interests" (Art. 22).[19]

---

[16] International Labour Organization, *Convention concerning Freedom of Association and Protection of the Right to Organise*, July 9, 1948 (entered into force July 4, 1950), art. 2.

[17] Bernard Gernignon, Alberto Odero, and Horacio Guido, *ILO Principles Concerning the Right to Strike* (Geneva: ILO, 1998).

[18] ILO Convention No. 98, *Right to Organise and Collective Bargaining Convention*, July 1, 1949 (entered into force July 18, 1951).

[19] *International Covenant on Civil and Political Rights*, December 16, 1966, 999 U.N.T.S. 171 (entered into force March 23, 1976).

International Covenant on Economic, Social and Cultural Rights (1966)

The ICESCR requires governments to ensure: "the right of everyone to form trade unions and join the trade union of his choice, the right of unions to function freely and the right to strike" (Art. 8).[20]

Regional Human Rights Instruments

Inter-American human rights system

The American Convention on Human Rights states: "Everyone has the right to associate freely for ideological, religious, political, economic, labor, social, culture or other purposes."[21] Trade union rights are more explicitly advanced in the Additional Protocol to the American Convention on Human Rights in the Area of Economic, Social and Cultural Rights, the "Protocol of San Salvador,"[22] which recognizes "the rights of workers to organize trade unions and to join the trade union of their choice for the purpose of protecting and promoting their interests." The right of trade unions to form national federations, and confederations, to function freely without governmental interference, and the right to strike are also protected in the Protocol.

European human rights system

The European Convention for the Protection of Human Rights and Fundamental Freedoms states: "Everyone has the right to freedom of peaceful assembly and freedom of association with others for the protection of his interests."[23] The European Social Charter likewise recognizes the right to organize, bargain collectively, and engage in collective action.[24]

---

[20] *International Covenant on Economic, Social and Cultural Rights*, December 16, 1966, 993 U.N.T.S. 3 (entered into force January 3, 1976).

[21] *American Convention of Human Rights*, OAS Official Records, OEA/Ser.A/16 (English), T.S. No 36 (November 7–22, 1969), art. 16.

[22] November 17, 1988, O.A.S. Treaty Series No. 69 (entered into force November 16, 1999), OEA/Ser.L.V.II.82 doc.6 rev.1 at 67 (1992), art. 8(a)(1) & (2).

[23] *European Convention for the Protection of Human Rights and Fundamental Freedoms*, November 4, 1950, T.T.S. No. 5 (entered into force September 3, 1953), art. 11.

[24] Council of Europe, *European Social Charter (Revised)*, May 3, 1996, ETS 163 (entered into force July 1, 1999), art. 5 & 6.

African human rights system
The African Charter on Human and Peoples Rights provides that "Every individual shall have a right to free association."[25]

Trade Agreements

Fundamental labor rights have gained considerable traction in the new generation of trade agreements, which typically include a labor chapter with a dispute resolution mechanism. Since the US–Jordan Free Trade Agreement (FTA) in 2001, the U.S. has included a labor chapter as an integral part of the text of the agreement.[26] Commitments to the ILO's core labor rights contained in the ILO Declaration have been integrated into labor chapters in U.S. FTAs since 2007. While the inclusion of these rights in the body of the trade agreements has reinforced international labor standards, some commentators argue that there have been few gains in terms of remedies in either bilateral or multilateral trade agreements for labor violations using the dispute resolution mechanism contained in these agreements.[27]

The 2020 U.S.–Mexico–Canada Agreement (USMCA),[28] which replaced the North American Free Trade Agreement (NAFTA), contains additional mechanisms to bolster compliance with fundamental labor rights, including expedited enforcement of workers' freedom of association and bargaining rights at the facility level. There are also new provisions that require the parties to prohibit the importation of good produced through forced labor that address violence against workers exercising labor rights as well as language to protect migrant workers.

---

[25] Organization of African Unity (OAU), *African Charter on Human and Peoples' Rights ("Banjul Charter")*, June 27, 1981, CAB/LEG/67/3 rev. 5, 21 I.L.M. 58 (1982), art. 10.

[26] Jordan Free Trade Agreement, https://ustr.gov/trade-agreements/free-trade-agreements/jordan-fta. See, for example, Dominican Republic-Central America Free Trade Agreement, August 5, 4, Hein's No. KAV7157, https://ustr.gov/trade-agreements/free-trade-agreements/cafta-dr-dominican-republic-central-america-fta.

[27] "First Ever Labor Arbitration Ruling under CAFTA," Arbitration Info, University of Missouri, April 30, 2018, http://law.missouri.edu/arbitrationinfo/2018/04/30/first-ever-labor-arbitration-ruling-cafta. See Paula Church Albertson and Lance Compa, "Labour Rights and Trade Agreements in the Americas," in *Research Handbook on Transnational Labour Law*, eds. Adelle Blackett and Anne Trebilcock (Northampton, MA: Edward Elgar Publishing, 2015), 474.

[28] United States–Mexico–Canada Agreement (entered into force July 1, 2020), https://ustr.gov/trade-agreements/free-trade-agreements/united-states-mexico-canada-agreement.

There has been increased emphasis on forced labor as part of the U.S. trade policy. In 2021, the Uyghur Forced Labor Protection was signed by President Biden, which creates a presumption that goods produced in whole or part in the Xinjang Uyghur Autonomous Region of China are produced with forced labor and barred from importation.[29] Due diligence related to the supply chain will be required by importers and failure to comply could result in products being detained or seized under § 307 of the U.S. Tariff Act of 1930.[30]

PRIVATE INTERNATIONAL LAW

Global Collective Bargaining Agreements

Collective bargaining agreements that transcend national borders are rare, but one example applies in the maritime industry between the International Transport Workers Federation and the International Maritime Employers' Committee. Another, more limited, global agreement is between the United Steelworkers of America and ArcelorMittal (along with the European Metalworkers Federation and the International Metalworkers Federation), which addresses workplace health and safety. These agreements create enforceable workplace rights.

Global Framework Agreements

Global Framework Agreements[31] are bilateral contracts negotiated between a global union federation and transnational corporations that relate to working conditions at its facilities worldwide and frequently apply down the supply chain.[32] They are rights agreements that incorporate ILO core conventions, but do not generally include wages and terms and conditions of employment like a collective bargaining agreement. Thus far these agreements have not been enforceable legally, but typically have a dialogue-based dispute resolution mechanism.

---

[29] Pub.L.No. 117-78, §3(a), 135 Stat. 1529 (2001).

[30] 19 U.S.C. 1307. Additional statutes that seek to address supply chain forced labor and trafficking include: U.S. Trafficking Victims Protection Act, 22 U.S.C. §§ 7101-14 (2018), the California Transparency in Supply Chains Act, Cal. Civ. Code §1714.43, and UK Modern Slavery Act (2015).

[31] Also known as International Framework Agreements.

[32] Nikolaus Hammer, "International Framework Agreements in the Context of Global Production," in *Cross-Border Social Dialogue and Agreements: An Emerging Global Industrial Relations Framework*, ed. Konstantinos Papadakis (Geneva: International Institute for Labour Studies, 2008).

Codes of Conduct and Multistakeholder Agreements

Some public and private entities have codes of conduct that require compliance with labor rights for licensees or vendors. Codes of conduct can create a binding obligation for companies to abide by fundamental labor rights when they are integrated into contracts.[33] Violations can result in serious penalties, including the loss of licensing agreements and lucrative contracts. Egregious violations of labor rights can also become part of a campaign involving other civil society organizations. One example is the Russell Athletic Campaign when universities across the United States canceled their licensing agreements with the clothing manufacturer due to labor violations in the supply chain, which resulted in a successful and binding agreement that was tied to codes of conduct.[34]

Multistakeholder agreements are not always linked to codes of conduct. They can result from unrelated public campaigns denouncing labor violations by corporate entities, and this pressure can result in agreements to redress the violations or have corporations take a different course of action going forward. The parties to these agreements include civil society organizations, unions, and the corporation involved. Often a binding arbitration clause is part of the agreement. The Coalition of Immokalee Workers and the Campaign for Fair Food is an example of a successful campaign with agreements that have yielded tangible results.[35]

PUBLIC–PRIVATE INITIATIVES

OECD

The OECD Guidelines for Multinational Enterprises encourage corporations to comply with fundamental labor rights, including recognizing trade union rights and collective bargaining.[36] The Guidelines establish a complaint-based

---

[33] See, for example, Worker Rights Consortium Model Code of Conduct, "Model Code," Worker Rights Consortium, accessed August 8, 2022, https://www.workersrights.org/affiliates/model-code; Workers Rights Consortium, *The Designated Suppliers Program* (September 1, 2006), https://www.workersrights.org/wp-content/uploads/2019/08/Designated-Suppliers-Program-Revised.pdf.

[34] See Multistakeholder Human Rights Initiatives, Chapter 16.

[35] Joanne Bauer, "The Coalition of Immokalee Workers and the Campaign for Fair Food: The Evolution of a Business and Human Rights Campaign," in *Business and Human Rights: From Principles to Practice*, eds. Dorothée Baumann-Pauly and Justine Nolan (New York: Routledge, 2016), Section 4.7.

[36] Organisation for Economic Co-operation and Development, *OECD Guidelines for Multinational Enterprises* (Paris: OECD Publishing, 2011).

dispute resolution system using national contact points in OECD countries. Trade unions comprise an OECD Advisory Committee, TUAC, which has consultative status.

The UN Global Compact is another example of a public–private initiative that incorporates fundamental labor rights.[37]

TEACHING APPROACHES

In a BHR course, labor rights can be taught as an introductory lesson or a module.

Learning objectives for teaching labor rights may include:

- Becoming familiar with the principal sources of international labor norms.
- Understanding the significance of freedom of association in the international human rights framework.
- Understanding the role of business in compliance with freedom of association.
- Understanding different mechanisms to pursue redress for labor rights violations.
- Assessing the strengths and weaknesses of different mechanisms used to advance international labor law.

EXERCISE 4.1

RESEARCH AN ILO FREEDOM OF ASSOCIATION CASE

To engage students in the material on freedom of association, I assign them the task of researching a freedom of association case from the ILO website. It is easy for them to find labor standards, and then the link to the Committee on Freedom of Association. From there they can use NORMLEX[38] to find a case against a country you assign. I typically suggest the U.S., Turkey, or Chile, but give students the option of choosing any country. Each student gives a five-minute overview of the case in class. A range of violations, including the assassinations of trade unionists, barriers to union formation,

[37] "The Ten Principles of the UN Global Compact," United Nations Global Compact, accessed August 8, 2022, https://www.unglobalcompact.org/what-is-gc/mission/principles.

[38] International Labour Organization, "Information System on International Labour Standards," https://www.ilo.org/dyn/normlex/en/.

denial of collective bargaining rights, and strike-related terminations, typically surface.

Labor rights can also be introduced through specific cases involving efforts to ensure minimum standards in global supply chains.

EXERCISE 4.2

INTRODUCE A LABOR RIGHTS TOPIC

One approach to facilitate engagement is to have students introduce a topic that they select from a short list of options. I assign a five-page memo that enables students to dig deeper into the related material. The memos are shared electronically via a discussion board and students are required to post a comment or question. Students also do a classroom presentation on their BHR topic. Depending on the size of the group, the instructor can limit student presentation time to 10–12 minutes. Another approach is to cover one or two cases arising in different fora and divide up arguments and issues among groups of students.

Sample topics for business and policy students:

- Global Frameworks Agreements
- The OECD process involving a labor violation
- Inter-American Court Advisory Opinion OC/22/16 involving the standing of unions and corporations before the Court[39]
- Russell Athletic case involving codes of conduct.[40]
- The U.N. Special Rapporteur Maina Kiai's 2016 Report on the "Rights of Freedom of Peaceful Assembly and Association" would also provide rich material to facilitate student discussions about the most pressing labor issues in the world today and the broader implications of workers' rights in the global community.[41]

Sample topics for law students:

---

[39] Angela B. Cornell, "Inter-American Court Recognizes the Elevated Status of Trade Unions, Rejects Standing of Corporations," *International Labor Rights Case Law* 3, no. 1 (December 2017): 39–44.

[40] See, for example, Steven Greenhouse, "Michigan Is the Latest University to End a Licensing Deal with an Apparel Maker," *New York Times*, February 23, 2009.

[41] UN General Assembly, Report of the UN Special Rapporteur on Freedom of Peaceful Assembly and of Association, U.N. Doc. A/71/385 (September 14, 2016).

- An Inter-American Court decision involving freedom of association
- *Ricardo Baena et al. v. Panama* (February 2, 2001)
- *Huilca-Tecse v. Peru* (March 3, 2005) Inter-American Court decision related to the right to work, worst forms of child labor, work that involves high risk and imminent danger to workers, and access to justice
- *Case of the Workers of the Fireworks Factory in Santo Antonio De Jesus and Their Family Members v. Brazil* (July 15, 2020)[42]
- *Demir and Baykara v. Turkey* (2008)[43]
- The ILO's decision in Hoffman Plastic Compounds, involving an undocumented worker fired for organizing a union and the denial of backpay based on legal status, in violation of international norms.[44]

KEY QUESTIONS

General

- How do labor rights fit into the human rights framework?
- How is freedom of association related to labor rights?
- What specific rights form part of freedom of association in this context?
- How has globalization shifted the nature of compliance with labor norms?
- What does the corporate responsibility to respect human rights mean in the labor context?
- What mechanisms work best for holding corporations accountable for violations of international labor norms?

For Business Students

- How can corporations fulfill their responsibility to respect labor rights under the UN Guiding Principles?

---

[42] Inter-American Court of Human Rights, Case of the Workers of the Fireworks Factory in *Santo Antônio De Jesus and Their Families v. Brazil*, Preliminary Objections, Merits, Reparations and Costs, Judgment, Inter-Am. Ct. H.R. (ser. C) No. 407 (July 15, 2020).

[43] *Demir and Baykara v. Turkey*, App. No. 34503/97, 48 Eur. H.R. Rep. 54 (2008) (Landmark decision that recognized collective bargaining as "an essential" element of freedom of association under Article II of the European Convention of Human Rights and Fundamental Freedoms.

[44] ILO Normlex Report in which the Committee requests to be kept informed of development, Report No. 332, November 2003, Case No. 2227 (United States), https://www.ilo.org/dyn/normlex/en/f?p=1000:50002:0::NO:50002:P50002_COMPLAINT_TEXT_ID:2907332.

- What incentives exist for corporations to comply with international labor rights?
- Is it reasonable to hold corporations accountable for violations down the supply chain? Why or why not?
- What can transnational corporations do to exercise due diligence to avoid violating fundamental labor rights at contractor facilities?

For Law Students

- What are the sources of international labor rights?
- What are the "core" labor standards under international law?
- Do international labor law and corresponding enforcement mechanisms have sufficient teeth to provide meaningful remedies for violations of fundamental rights?
- What is the relationship between public and private law mechanisms to enforce labor standards?
- Many international labor norms rely on "soft law" instruments and mechanisms. What are the strengths and weaknesses of "soft law"?
- Does the state have a duty to protect against labor rights violations committed by corporate actors?
- Should corporations assume a greater role in complying with international labor law when domestic law is weak or not enforced?

For Policy Students

- What is the significance of collective rights?
- How can government actors collaborate with businesses and unions to advance compliance with international labor norms?
- Should the state be responsible under international law for violations committed by corporations?

TEACHING RESOURCES

Readings

Primary sources

- Atleson, James, Lance Compa, Kerry Rittich, Calvin William Sharpe, and Marley S. Weiss, eds. *International Labor Law: Cases and Materials on Workers' Rights in the Global Economy*. St. Paul, MN: Thomson/West, 2008.

- Cornell, Angela B. and Mark Barenberg, eds. *The Cambridge Handbook of Labor and Democracy*. New York: Cambridge University Press, 2022.
- International Labor Office. *Freedom of Association Compilation of Decisions of the Committee on Freedom of Association*. Geneva: ILO, 2018.
- International Labor Office. *The Committee on the Application of Standards of the International Labour Conference: A Dynamic and Impact Built on Decades of Dialogue and Persuasion*. Geneva: ILO, 2011.

Cases

- *Demir and Baykara v. Turkey*, App. No. 34503/97, 48 Eur. H.R. Rep. 54 (2008).
- *Ricardo Baena et al. v. Panama* (February 2, 2001). Inter-American Court of Human Rights, Case of *Baeuna-Ricardo et al. v. Panama*, Merits, Reparations and Costs, Judgment, Inter-Am. Ct. H.R. (ser. C) No. 72 (February 2, 2011).
- *Nestlé USA, Inc. v. Doe*, 141 S. Ct. 1931 (2021).

Commentary

- Fenwick, Colin and Tonia Novitz, eds. *Human Rights at Work: Perspectives on Law and Regulation*. Portland, RI: Hart Publishing, 2010.
- Locke, Richard M. "We Live in a World of Global Supply Chains." In *Business and Human Rights: From Principles to Practice*, edited by Dorothée Baumann-Pauly and J. Nolan, 299–316. London: Routledge, 2016.
- Sahan, Makbule. "The First International Standard on Violence and Harassment in the World of Work." *Business and Human Rights Journal* 5, no. 2 (July 2020): 289–295.

Reports

- UN General Assembly. *Report of the UN Special Rapporteur on Freedom of Peaceful Assembly and of Association*. U.N. Doc. A/71/385 (September 14, 2016), http://freeassembly.net/wp-content/uploads/2016/10/A.71.385_E.pdf.

Videos

- ENDEVR. "The True Cost: Who Pays the Real Price for Your Clothes? Investigatory Documentary." ENDEVR, 2015, YouTube video, 50:55: https://www.youtube.com/watch?v=5-0zHqYGnlo.

- Rainbow Collective and Openvizor. "Tears in the Fabric." 2014 documentary on the Rana Plaza disaster, YouTube video, 29:59: https://www.rainbowcollective.co.uk/tears-in-the-fabric.

Websites

- International Labor Organization. "Advancing Social Justice, Promoting Decent Work." https://www.ilo.org.
- International Trade Union Confederation. "International Trade Union Confederation. Building Workers' Power." https://www.ituc-csi.org.
- Trade Union Advisory Committee (TUAC) to the Organisation for Economic Co-operation and Development (OECD). https://tuac.org.

5. The United Nations Guiding Principles on Business and Human Rights

Anthony Ewing

OVERVIEW

The United Nations Guiding Principles on Business and Human Rights (2011)[1] (UNGPs) set an expectation that business enterprises will respect human rights, states will protect against human rights violations connected to business activity, and affected individuals will have access to effective remedy. A typical business and human rights (BHR) course covers most, if not all, of the principal issues addressed by the UNGPs.

The UNGPs detail how states and business enterprises can implement the "Protect, Respect and Remedy" Framework (2008) (UN Framework).[2] Both the UN Framework and UNGPs were authored by Professor John Ruggie, the Harvard University political scientist who served from 2005 to 2011 as the UN Secretary-General's special representative on business and human rights.[3]

---

[1] United Nations Human Rights Council, *Guiding Principles on Business and Human Rights: Implementing the United Nations "Protect, Respect and Remedy" Framework*, Report of the Special Representative of the Secretary-General on the issue of human rights and transnational corporations and other business enterprises, UN doc. A/HRC/17/31 (March 21, 2011) (UN Guiding Principles). The UNGPs were unanimously endorsed by state members of the UN Human Rights Council. Resolution adopted by the United Nations Human Rights Council, "Human Rights and Transnational Corporations and Other Business Enterprises," UN doc. A/HRC/RES/17/4 (July 6, 2011, adopted July 16, 2011).

[2] United Nations Human Rights Council, *Protect, Respect and Remedy: A Framework for Business and Human Rights*, Report of the Special Representative of the Secretary-General on the issue of human rights and transnational corporations and other business enterprises, UN doc. A/HRC/8/5 (April 7, 2008) (UN Framework).

[3] Professor Ruggie, an influential scholar of international relations, had advised UN Secretary-General Kofi Annan on the development of the Millennium Development Goals and the UN Global Compact as assistant secretary-general for strategic plan-

During his six-year mandate, Ruggie is credited with forging a working consensus among governments, companies, and human rights advocates on key issues surrounding the human rights responsibilities of business enterprises. For many stakeholders, the UNGPs have become the authoritative global standard on BHR, setting an expectation of all companies, regardless of size, sector, or location, to prevent and address adverse impacts on human rights linked to business activity.[4] Other international and regional standards have incorporated or refer to the UNGPs, and in particular the corporate responsibility to respect human rights.[5] Key aspects of the UNGPs, such as human rights due diligence, and reporting, have been adopted in national law and regulation. (See Mandatory Human Rights Due Diligence Legislation, Chapter 11.)

This chapter summarizes the history and provisions of the UNGPs, highlights key issues surrounding their implementation, and describes approaches for introducing the UNGPs to BHR students.

HISTORY

Ruggie's appointment as special representative followed an earlier UN effort to apply binding human rights standards to companies. The Norms on the Responsibilities of Transnational Corporations and Other Business Enterprises with Regard to Human Rights (2003),[6] which sought to hold companies directly responsible for human rights obligations under international law, while supported by civil society groups, met opposition from states and from the business sector, and were ultimately never acted upon by the UN Commission on Human Rights (now the Human Rights Council).[7]

---

ning from 1997 to 2001. See Stephen M. Walt, "A Realist Tribute to an Extraordinary Idealist," *Foreign Policy*, September 21, 2021, https://foreignpolicy.com/2021/09/21/a-realist-tribute-to-an-extraordinary-idealist.

[4]   See, for example, "Contribution of the United Nations System as a Whole to the Advancement of the Business and Human Rights Agenda and the Dissemination and Implementation of the Guiding Principles on Business and Human Rights, Report of the Secretary-General," U.N. Doc. A/HRC/21/21 (July 2, 2012), ¶ 2.

[5]   See, for example, Organisation for Economic Co-operation and Development, *OECD Guidelines for Multinational Enterprises* (Paris: OECD Publishing, 2011). (OECD Guidelines.)

[6]   UN Sub-Commission on the Promotion and Protection of Human Rights, *Norms on the Responsibilities of Transnational Corporations and Other Business Enterprises with Regard to Human Rights*, UN Doc. E/CN.4/Sub.2/2003/12/Rev.2 (August 26, 2003).

[7]   UN Commission on Human Rights, Decision 2004/116, UN Doc. E/CN.4/2004/L.73/Rev.1 (April 16, 2004).

In 2005, the Commission established the mandate for an individual expert to "identify and clarify" existing human rights standards for businesses; elaborate the role of states regulating business conduct in relation to human rights; and research key concepts such as corporate complicity in human rights abuses.[8] During his mandate, Ruggie sought to move "beyond the mandatory-vs.-voluntary dichotomy to devise a smart mix of reinforcing policy measures that are capable over time of generating cumulative change and achieving large-scale success – including in the law."[9] He described the approach that produced the UN Framework and UNGPs as "principled pragmatism."[10] The Special Representative conducted extensive global research, consulted with stakeholders, and piloted specific principles before submitting the UNGPs to the Human Rights Council in 2011.

THE "PROTECT, RESPECT AND REMEDY" FRAMEWORK (2008)

The UN Framework, contained in the special representative's 2008 report to the Human Rights Council,[11] has three "pillars":

(1) "The State duty to protect against human rights abuses by third parties, including business enterprises, through appropriate policies, regulation, and adjudication";
(2) "The corporate responsibility to respect human rights, which means that business enterprises should act with due diligence to avoid infringing on the rights of others and to address adverse impacts with which they are involved"; and
(3) "The need for greater access by victims to effective remedy, both judicial and non-judicial."[12]

The interrelated pillars of the "Protect, Respect and Remedy" Framework, which reflect Ruggie's view of the human rights responsibilities of both states and business enterprises under international law, highlight both the legal and policy dimensions of the state duty to prevent, investigate, and punish human rights abuses by non-state actors. The UN Framework defines the corporate responsibility to respect human rights as a responsibility that goes beyond

---

[8]   UN Commission on Human Rights, Resolution 2005/69 (2005).
[9]   John Gerard Ruggie, *Just Business: Multinational Corporations and Human Rights*, 1st edition (New York: W. W. Norton & Company, 2013), xxiii.
[10]   Ruggie, *Just Business*, xlii–xlvi.
[11]   UN Framework.
[12]   UN Guiding Principles, ¶ 6.

legal compliance, and that companies cannot satisfy through corporate philanthropy. This corporate responsibility is a social norm, or global expectation, that companies can meet by "knowing and showing" that they do not infringe on others' rights.

THE UN GUIDING PRINCIPLES ON BUSINESS AND HUMAN RIGHTS (2011)

The UNGPs build upon the topics introduced in the UN Framework by elaborating "the implications of existing standards and practices for states and businesses."[13] Thirty-one Guiding Principles, organized as "foundational" and "operational" principles for each of the three pillars, are accompanied by commentaries clarifying the meaning and implications of each Principle. More detailed interpretation of each Principle, approved by the Special Representative, was subsequently published by the UN Office of the High Commissioner for Human Rights.[14]

While the Guiding Principles are "universally applicable" to all states and to all business enterprises, the special representative emphasized that they are not an "off-the-shelf" toolkit;[15] means for their implementation will vary.

Protect

The state duty to protect against human rights abuse ("Pillar I," Principles 1–10) requires states to take "appropriate steps to prevent, investigate, punish and redress" abuses by business enterprises "within their territory and/or jurisdiction." While the UNGPs note that states are "not generally required under international human rights law" to regulate the extraterritorial activities of companies, they also emphasize that "nor are they generally prohibited from doing so." (See Judicial Remedy, Chapter 12.) The operational principles of Pillar I encourage states to: adopt a "smart mix of measures" to protect against abuses by business; address state-owned businesses and commercial business relationships; highlight the risks of human rights abuses in conflict-affected areas; and ensure policy coherence internally and externally.

---

[13]   UN Guiding Principles, ¶ 14.
[14]   UN Office of the High Commissioner for Human Rights, *The Corporate Responsibility to Respect Human Rights: An Interpretive Guide*, UN Doc. HR/ PUB/12/02, Sales No. E.13.XIV.4 (2012), http://www.ohchr.org/Documents/ Publications/HR.PUB.12.2_En.pdf.
[15]   UN Guiding Principles, ¶ 15.

Respect

Under the corporate responsibility to respect human rights ("Pillar II," Principles 11–24), the UNGPs expand upon the UN Framework by calling on companies to "avoid causing or contributing to adverse human rights impacts through their own activities" and to "seek to prevent or mitigate" those "directly linked to their operations, products or services by their business relationships." To meet their responsibility, companies must "know and show that they respect human rights." The scope of the responsibility to respect human rights includes all "internationally recognized human rights."[16] The Principles state that nothing in them creates new international law obligations.[17] The operational principles of Pillar II detail the steps companies should take to respect rights, including:

- Make a public commitment to respect human rights and embed that policy in business operations and through their business relationships;
- Implement an ongoing process of human rights due diligence that identifies and addresses actual and potential human rights impacts;
- Enable the remediation of human rights impacts; and
- Track and communicate what the company has done.

Remedy

"Pillar III" (Principles 25–31) describes ways that states must, and businesses should, ensure access to remedy for victims of human rights abuses, including judicial, non-judicial, and non-state-based grievance mechanisms; and provide effectiveness criteria for all non-judicial mechanisms.[18] (See Right to Remedy, Chapter 6; Non-Governmental Grievance Mechanisms, Chapter 10.)

Ruggie described the unanimous endorsement of the UNGPs by the UN Human Rights Council in 2011 as the "end of the beginning" – the UNGPs establish a "common global platform for action" by the stakeholders at the intersection of business and human rights.[19] In the decade since their publication, elements of the UNGPs have been incorporated or referenced in

---

[16] Internationally recognized human rights are understood, at a minimum, as those expressed in the International Bill of Human Rights and the International Labour Organization's Declaration of Fundamental Principles and Rights at Work. UN Guiding Principles, Principle 12 and Commentary.

[17] Nor are the Principles intended to limit the further development of international law.

[18] UN Guiding Principles, Principle 31.

[19] UN Guiding Principles, ¶ 13.

other international standards, such as the OECD Guidelines for Multinational Enterprises,[20] and in multistakeholder human rights initiatives; adopted by states in national law; referenced in National Action Plans on BHR;[21] and operationalized by companies seeking to demonstrate respect for human rights. (See Multistakeholder Human Rights Initiatives, Chapter 16; Mandatory Human Rights Due Diligence Legislation, Chapter 11.)

Upon the endorsement of the UNGPs and the expiration of the Special Representative's mandate in 2011, the UN Human Rights Council established a five-member UN Working Group on Business and Human Rights (UN Working Group) to foster dissemination and implementation of the UNGPs.[22] In the decade since, the UN Working Group has conducted country visits, elaborated key BHR issues and guidance on the UNGPs,[23] and convened an annual UN Forum on Business and Human Rights for affected individuals and stakeholders from civil society, business, government, and international organizations to take stock of implementation challenges and highlight ways to put the UNGPs into practice.[24]

CRITICISM OF THE UNGPs

The UNGPs, their conceptual foundations, the process that produced them, and implementation efforts since have also generated criticism from key BHR

---

[20]   OECD Guidelines.

[21]   See "National Action Plans on Business and Human Rights," Working Group on Business and Human Rights, Office of the UN High Commissioner for Human Rights, accessed August 9, 2022, https://www.ohchr.org/en/special-procedures/wg-business/national-action-plans-business-and-human-rights.

[22]   UN Human Rights Council, "Human Rights and Transnational Corporations and Other Business Enterprises," UN Doc. A/HRC/RES/17/4 (July 6, 2011). The three-year mandate of the UN Working Group, composed of five independent experts of balanced geographical representation, has been renewed by the Human Rights Council three times, most recently in 2020. UN Human Rights Council, "Business and Human Rights: The Working Group on the Issue of Human Rights and Transnational Corporations and Other Business Enterprises, and Improving Accountability and Access to Remedy," UN Doc. A/HRC/RES/44/15 (July 17, 2020).

[23]   The UN Working Group has issued thematic reports on, inter alia, conflict-affected regions, mandatory human rights due diligence, access to remedy, the gender dimensions the UN Guiding Principles, human rights defenders, and climate change and the UNGPs.

[24]   See generally, "About the Mandate," Working Group on Business and Human Rights, Office of the UN High Commissioner for Human Rights, accessed August 9, 2022, https://www.ohchr.org/en/special-procedures/wg-business; UN Working Group on Business and Human Rights, *UNGPs 10+: A Roadmap for the Next Decade of Business and Human Rights* (Geneva: UN Working Group on Business and Human Rights, 2021).

stakeholders. Critics, for example, consider legally binding standards to be the most effective means to challenge corporate abuses, and see the UNGPs as an impediment to true accountability; argue that the UNGPs inaccurately characterize corporate and state obligations under international law; question the ability of corporate human rights due diligence to prevent human rights abuses or improve human rights conditions on the ground; and challenge the notion that companies should play any role providing a meaningful remedy to victims of human rights abuses connected to business activity.[25] These criticisms have accompanied renewed efforts to draft an international business and human rights treaty via an Intergovernmental Working Group established by the UN Human Rights Council in 2014.[26]

Commentators have also pointed to perceived gaps in the UNGPs, such as their failure to address specific human rights impacts, to reference international standards protecting specific groups, or to focus attention on the human rights responsibilities of states.[27]

THE UNGPs IN PRACTICE

These criticisms notwithstanding, the UNGPs have influenced the conduct of companies that have made human rights commitments, conducted human rights due diligence, established grievance mechanisms, and communicated their human rights performance to stakeholders. The UNGPs have also influenced the efforts of governments, civil society, and other actors seeking to hold companies accountable for their human rights impacts and ensure access to remedy for those affected by business activity.

---

[25] See, for example, the articles collected in Surya Deva and David Bilchitz, eds., *Human Rights Obligations of Business: Beyond the Corporate Responsibility to Respect?* (Cambridge: Cambridge University Press, 2013); Tara Van Ho, "Business and Human Rights in Transitional Justice: Challenges for Complex Environments," in *Research Handbook on Human Rights and Business*, eds. Surya Deva and David Birchall (Cheltenham: Edward Elgar, 2020), 379–401.

[26] United Nations Human Rights Council, "Elaboration of an Internationally Legally Binding Instrument on Transnational Corporations and Other Business Enterprises with Respect to Human Rights," UN Doc. A/HRC/26/L.22/Rev.1 (June 25, 2014).

[27] See, for example, Erika George, "Racism as a Human Rights Risk: Reconsidering the Corporate 'Responsibility to Respect' Rights," *Business and Human Rights Journal* 6, no. 3 (October 2021): 576–583; Michael A. Santoro, "Why the United Nations Is Not the Ideal Forum for Business and Human Rights: The UNGPs and the Right to COVID-19 Vaccine Access in the Global South," *Business and Human Rights Journal* 6, no. 2 (June 2021): 326–335.

Business leaders and managers have implemented rights-respecting business practices aligned with the UNGPs. After a decade of implementation, key challenges for companies seeking to operationalize the UNGPs include:

- Translating the language of human rights into business terms;
- Building the capacity and expertise to identify and address human rights impacts across the enterprise; and
- Applying a human rights lens to all corporate functions, activities, and relationships.

Key issues embedded in the UNGPs that will occupy the creative energies of BHR practitioners for the next decade include:

- Exercising leverage to prevent, mitigate, and remedy the human rights impacts of other actors, especially through business relationships.
- Engaging the stakeholders affected by business activity and incorporating their perspectives in business decision-making.
- Providing meaningful access to remedy for individuals harmed by business activity.
- Measuring and tracking the human rights performance of business enterprises.
- Implementing the state responsibility to protect against human rights abuses connected to business activity through legislation and policymaking.[28]

BHR teachers can explore any of these topics, using specific examples, to teach the UNGPs and introduce students to their impact in practice.

TEACHING APPROACHES

Each pillar of the UNGPs – from state measures to prevent human rights abuses by business enterprises under Pillar I, to the practical meaning of corporate respect for human rights under Pillar II, to judicial and non-judicial approaches to provide effective remedy to victims under Pillar III – contains sufficient thematic material to fill a BHR course syllabus. Every topic in this volume touches the content of the UNGPs.

The UNGPs can be introduced as a brief module or elaborated in detail throughout a BHR course. Some instructors of stand-alone courses organize their entire course syllabus consistent with the three pillars of the UNGPs; others refer to the UNGPs in relation to specific topics. One classroom tech-

---

[28]   See, for example, Surya Deva, Anita Ramasastry, Florian Wettstein, and Michael Santoro. "Editorial: Business and Human Rights Scholarship – Past Trends and Future Directions," *Business and Human Rights Journal* 4, no. 2 (2019): 201–212.

nique, for example, when considering specific cases of companies connected to human rights impacts is to ask students whether the company's actions are consistent with the UNGPs. (For example: "Was Facebook's 2018 human rights impact assessment of its operations in Myanmar consistent with the UNGPs?"[29]) References to the UNGPs by civil society, by policymakers, and by businesses present opportunities to discuss the relevance of the UNGPs for various stakeholders. (For example: "Is the proposed European Union Directive on mandatory human rights due diligence aligned with the UNGPs? What are the gaps?"[30]) Teachers can apply the UNGPs to specific industrial sectors. (For example: "What do the UNGPs require of financial institutions or of professional service firms?"[31]) Each criticism of the UNGPs can also be an entry point to introduce and evaluate their content, impact, and gaps.

Because they cover so much ground, the UNGPs offer ample opportunities for an instructor to introduce both theoretical and practical BHR material in their teaching. After teaching an introductory BHR course for 18 years, I developed and began teaching an "advanced" seminar, "Managing Human Rights," that requires students to have prior BHR coursework or professional experience. I organized the course syllabus tracking the components of the corporate responsibility to respect in the UNGPs: adopt a human rights policy; identify human rights impacts; and prevent, mitigate, and remedy human rights impacts. With students already familiar with the basics of the UNGPs, we were able to explore challenging issues, such as exercising leverage in business relationships and providing access to remedy, in more depth, using more in-class exercises to apply concepts to specific examples.

Learning objectives for introducing the UNGPs may include:

* Understanding the historical context that led to the development of the UNGPs.
* Understanding the content and scope of the UNGPs.
* Applying the UNGPs to specific cases and actors.
* Critically assessing the strengths and weaknesses of the UNGPs.
* Explaining how both states and businesses can implement the UNGPs.

---

[29]   BSR, *Human Rights Impact Assessment: Facebook in Myanmar* (October 2018).

[30]   *Commission Proposal for a Directive of the European Parliament and of the Council on Corporate Sustainability Due Diligence and Amending Directive (EU)*, COM(2022) 71 final,2022/0051 (COD) (February 23, 2022).

[31]   See, for example, Shift, *Financial Institutions and Remedy: Myths and Misconceptions* (October 2021); Anita Ramasastry, "Advisors or Enablers? Bringing Professional Service Providers into the Guiding Principles Fold," *Business and Human Rights Journal* 6, no. 2 (June 2021): 1–19.

Law courses can use the UNGPs to explore the human rights responsibilities of states and of business enterprises under international law, to assess corporate efforts to meet the responsibility to respect human rights, to evaluate litigation strategies, and to consider their relevance in domestic corporate law. Research materials produced during the special representative's mandate, such as the reports on *Mapping International Standards of Responsibility and Accountability for Corporate Acts*[32] and *Human Rights and Corporate Law*,[33] are particularly useful for law teachers. The UNGPs are often contrasted with the Draft Norms that preceded them, or the renewed business and human rights treaty process that has followed them,[34] to prompt discussion of the merits of voluntary versus mandatory, or "hard law" versus "soft law," approaches to corporate human rights accountability.[35] The recent adoption in multiple jurisdictions of mandatory human rights reporting and due diligence for companies is an opportunity to assess how state legislation and regulatory approaches align with the UNGPs. (See Mandatory Human Right Due Diligence, Chapter 11.)

Business courses can consider the UNGPs' responsibility to respect human rights as one definition of "corporate responsibility" in discussions of corporate ethics and explore the practical implications for business managers of implementing rights-respecting practices in business operations. (See Corporate Responsibility, Chapter 2.) Specific disciplines, such as supply chain or human resource management, can use related elements of the UNGPs to illustrate particular topics or business practices. Contributors to this volume offer noteworthy examples for applying UNGPs in the fields of accounting, engineering, and finance.[36]

---

[32] John Ruggie, *Business and Human Rights: Mapping International Standards of Responsibility and Accountability for Corporate Acts*, Report of the Special Representative of the Secretary-General on the issue of human rights and transnational corporations and other business enterprises, UN doc. A/HRC/4/035 (February 9, 2007).

[33] "Human Rights and Corporate Law," UN doc. A/HRC/17/31/Add.2 (May 23, 2011).

[34] See Olivier De Schutter, "Toward a New Treaty on Business and Human Rights," *Business and Human Rights Journal* 1, no. 1 (January 2016): 41–67; "Open-Ended Intergovernmental Working Group on Transnational Corporations and Other Business Enterprises with Respect to Human Rights," UN Human Rights Council, accessed August 9, 2022, https://www.ohchr.org/en/hr-bodies/hrc/wg-trans-corp/igwg-on-tnc.

[35] See Anita Ramasastry, "Corporate Social Responsibility versus Business and Human Rights: Bridging the Gap between Responsibility and Accountability," *Journal of Human Rights* 14, no. 2 (2015): 237.

[36] See Accounting for Human Rights, Chapter 27; Engineering for Human Rights, Chapter 25; Finance, Investors, and Human Rights, Chapter 26.

Policy courses can consider state regulation of corporate conduct through the lens of the state duty to protect human rights in the first pillar of the UNGPs, assessing specific efforts to embed components of the UNGPs in national legislation and policy.

EXERCISE 5.1

MAP A COMPANY'S SALIENT HUMAN RIGHTS RISKS

A productive exercise for introducing the UNGPs is to designate a specific company – or a hypothetical company in a particular sector and geography – and ask students to "map" the company's "salient"[37] human risks consistent with the definitions and requirements in the text of the UNGPs. This exercise prompts students to define internationally recognized human rights; connect actual and potential adverse human rights impacts to business activity, operations, and relationships; and prioritize human rights impacts based on the severity of the impact to individuals. The "mapping" component helps students to correlate the full range of human rights impacts to all relevant business functions across a company's value chain, from suppliers to customers.

EXERCISE 5.2

MEMO TO THE CEO

A common challenge for many teachers is how to assess student comprehension of the varied, constantly evolving, and inherently multidisciplinary BHR course content. Since I began teaching BHR as an elective course to graduate students of law and business, I have never evaluated students via a traditional exam. At first, I assigned a research paper for which students could choose any BHR-related topic. For several years, I have assigned a "Memo to the CEO" that provides students a more structured final paper that encourages them to apply the specific topics covered in the syllabus in their assessment of an actual company's human rights performance. This assignment can be particularly helpful for ensuring that students can apply

---

[37] The human rights at risk of the most severe negative impact through the company's activities or business relationships. Shift and Mazars LLP, *UN Guiding Principles Reporting Framework* (2015); Caroline Rees and Rachel Davis, "Salient Human Rights Issues," in Dorothée Baumann-Pauly and Justine Nolan, eds., *Business and Human Rights: From Principles to Practice* (London: Routledge, 2016), 103–106.

the concepts contained in the UNGPs to a practical case.

Adopting the perspective of a corporate adviser (internal or external counsel for law students), students must prepare a memo to the CEO of a company managing human rights challenges.

I provide students with a representative list of companies that can be the subject of the memo. I try to ensure that the list includes a broad range of companies in different industries[38] and geographies. Additional criteria are whether the company is publicly traded, has made public human rights commitments, or is the subject of allegations of human rights abuse.

For the company they select, students must cover five topics in their memo:

(1) **Company and industry background:** A brief description of the relevant characteristics of the company and features of the industry.

(2) **Human rights at issue:** What are the three to five most significant human rights challenges facing this company? For these issues, what international human rights standards, from all sources, are implicated? How are adverse human right impacts linked to the company's operations, products, or relationships? Is the company causing or contributing to adverse human rights impacts?

(3) **Corporate human rights initiatives:** How is the company addressing actual or potential human rights issues connected to its operations? How does the company define and manage its human rights responsibilities? Does the company address human rights in a code of conduct? Does the company participate in any multistakeholder initiatives that address human rights? Does the company perform any form of human rights due diligence? How does the company track and communicate its efforts to manage human rights impacts?

(4) **Legal and business assessment:** What legal and business risks (actual and potential) arise from the human rights issues you identified as most significant? Do the company's human rights efforts meet the "responsibility to respect" human rights as defined by the UNGPs? Is the company at risk of complicity in human rights violations under international law? Is the company adequately managing these risks?

(5) **Recommendations:** Based on your legal and business assessment, what should the company do to better manage its human rights impacts? Given the company's activities and relationships, where should it focus its human rights efforts? What should the scope and content of any

---

[38]   Recent lists have included, for example, multinational companies in the consumer goods, extractives/utilities, financial and professional services, food/agriculture, healthcare, manufacturing/construction, media, and technology sectors.

human rights due diligence be? How can the company integrate human rights considerations into its existing policies and procedures? How can the company exercise leverage to manage human rights risks? What next steps do you recommend and how should the company prioritize them?

The length of the memo can be adjusted for different BHR courses and students. I typically give the greatest weight to the last two topics – their analysis of legal and business risks that arise from the human rights issues they identify and their recommendations for the company. Preparing the memo requires students to use a wide variety of research sources, including but not limited to the company's own public materials; to apply BHR concepts, including the UNGPs; and to make company-specific recommendations.

Students have produced many excellent memos, some of which have helped them when seeking BHR jobs.

KEY QUESTIONS

General

- What are the three pillars of the UNGPs?
- Which human rights must companies respect?
- What are the elements of the "corporate responsibility to respect human rights" under the UNGPs?
- Is the corporate responsibility to respect human rights dependent on whether states meet their duty to protect human rights?
- What are the strengths and weaknesses of the UNGPs?
- How are business enterprises implementing the UNGPs?
- How would you explain the UNGPs to a CEO?
- How do the UNGPs define corporate responsibility?
- What are a company's salient human rights risks?
- What are examples of the adverse human rights impacts of business enterprises?
- Which business functions are potentially connected to human rights impacts?
- How can a company meet its responsibility to respect human rights?
- What does effective human rights due diligence look like?
- How can a company create a rights-respecting culture?
- How should companies exercise leverage to prevent, mitigate, and remedy human rights impacts? How can a company increase its leverage to address human rights risks?
- How can a company measure and track its human rights performance?

For Law Students

- How would you explain the UNGPs to a corporate general counsel?
- Are the UNGPs an example of "hard" or "soft" law? Why?
- Do the UNGPs create any new legal obligations?
- What is the role of domestic law in implementing the UNGPs?
- How do the UNGPs treat complicity under international law?
- Must states regulate the extraterritorial conduct of businesses under the UNGPs?
- How could a binding treaty on business and human rights address gaps in the UNGPs?

For Policy Students

- What policy tools are available to states to protect against corporate human rights violations by business enterprises?
- How would you characterize the UNGPs as a model of global governance?
- What is "principled pragmatism"?
- How do the three pillars of the UNGPs interact?
- Do emerging mandatory human rights due diligence regulations align with the UNGPs?
- What is the potential of National Action Plans on BHR to advance human rights?

TEACHING RESOURCES

Readings

Primary sources

- United Nations Human Rights Council. *Guiding Principles on Business and Human Rights: Implementing the United Nations 'Protect, Respect and Remedy' Framework.* UN doc. A/HRC/17/31 (March 21, 2011). http://www.ohchr.org/Documents/Publications/GuidingPrinciplesBusinessHR_EN.pdf.
- United Nations Human Rights Council. *Protect, Respect and Remedy: A Framework for Business and Human Rights.* UN doc. A/HRC/8/5 (April 7, 2008). http://www.business-humanrights.org/SpecialRepPortal/Home/Protect-Respect-Remedy-Framework.
- United Nations Office of the High Commissioner for Human Rights. *The Corporate Responsibility to Respect Human Rights: An Interpretive Guide.*

UN Doc. HR/PUB/12/02 (2012). http://www.ohchr.org/Documents/
Publications/HR.PUB.12.2_En.pdf.
• United Nations Office of the High Commissioner for Human Rights.
*Frequently Asked Questions on the Guiding Principles on Business and
Human Rights.* UN Doc. HR/PUB/14/3 (2014). https://www.ohchr.org/en/
publications/special-issue-publications/frequently-asked-questions-about
-guiding-principles.

Commentary

• Deva, Surya and David Bilchitz, eds. *Human Rights Obligations of
Business: Beyond the Corporate Responsibility to Respect?* Cambridge:
Cambridge University Press, 2013.
• Newton, Alex. *The Business and Human Rights: Best Practice and the UN
Guiding Principles.* Abingdon: Routledge, 2019.
• Pitts, Chip. "The United Nations 'Protect, Respect, Remedy' Framework
and Guiding Principles." In *Business and Human Rights: From Principles
to Practice*, edited by Dorothée Baumann-Pauly and Justine Nolan, 51–63.
London: Routledge, 2016.
• Rodriguez-Garavito, César, ed. *Business and Human Rights: Beyond the
End of the Beginning.* Cambridge: Cambridge University Press, 2017.
• Ruggie, John Gerard. *Just Business: Multinational Corporations and
Human Rights.* New York: W. W. Norton & Company, 2013.
• Ruggie, John Gerard. "The Social Construction of the UN Guiding
Principles on Business and Human Rights." In *Research Handbook on
Human Rights and Business*, edited by Surya Deva and David Birchall,
379–401. Cheltenham: Edward Elgar Publishing Limited, 2020.
• Sherman, III, John F. "The Corporate General Counsel Who Respects
Human Rights." *Legal Ethics* 24, no. 1 (2021): 49–72. https://doi.org/10
.1080/1460728x.2021.1979731.

Teaching case

• Henderson, Rebecca and Nien-Hê Hsieh. *Putting the Guiding Principles
into Action: Human Rights at Barrick Gold.* Harvard Business School Case
No. 5-317-015, March 2015. Revised August 2020.

Videos

• Baab, Mike. "The UN Guiding Principles on Business and Human Rights:
An Introduction." January 2015. YouTube video, 3:36: http://youtu.be/
BCoL6JVZHrA.

- UNGP Reporting Framework. "Salient Human Rights Issues." Shift and Mazars. Video, 4:20: https://www.ungpreporting.org/resources/salient -human-rights-issues.

Websites

- Business and Human Rights Resource Centre. "UN Guiding Principles." https://www.business-humanrights.org/en/big-issues/un-guiding-principles-on-business-human-rights.
- Shift and Mazars. "UN Guiding Principles Reporting Framework." https://www.ungpreporting.org/framework-guidance.
- Shift Project. "UN Guiding Principles '101'." https://shiftproject.org/resources/ungps101.
- United Nations Office of the High Commissioner for Human Rights. "About Business and Human Rights." https://www.ohchr.org/EN/Issues/Business/Pages/BusinessIndex.aspx.
- United Nations Working Group on Business and Human Rights. "About the Mandate." https://www.ohchr.org/EN/Issues/Business/Pages/WGHRandtransnationalcorporationsandotherbusiness.aspx.
- UN Global Compact Academy. "Business and Human Rights: How Companies Can Operationalize the UN Guiding Principles." Online Course (free, registration required). https://academy.unglobalcompact.org/opencourses/learn/public/learning_plan/view/115/business-and-human-rights-how-companies-can-operationalize-the-un-guiding-principles.

6. Right to remedy

Lisa J. Laplante

OVERVIEW

The United Nations Guiding Principles (UNGPs) on Business and Human Rights recognize the right of all people and communities to a remedy when they suffer harms to their human rights that were caused or contributed to by businesses.[1] In doing so, the UNGPs incorporate the general right to a remedy that is recognized by international human rights law as embodied in most human rights treaties and as a part of international customary law.[2] This right forms an essential foundation to assuring that the whole human rights system works by enabling individuals and communities whose fundamental rights have been infringed upon to not only hold wrongdoers, such as companies, accountable but also to receive reparations for any harm they suffered.[3]

As recognized in Principle 1 of the UNGPs, states must not only protect fundamental rights but also provide a prompt and effective remedy when these rights are violated.[4] Importantly, this international legal obligation falls on

---

[1] United Nations Human Rights Council, *Guiding Principles on Business and Human Rights: Implementing the United Nations "Protect, Respect and Remedy" Framework*, Report of the Special Representative of the Secretary-General on the issue of human rights and transnational corporations and other business enterprises, UN doc. A/HRC/17/31 (UN Guiding Principles), http://www.ohchr.org/Documents/Publications/GuidingPrinciplesBusinessHR_EN.pdf.

[2] UN General Assembly, Resolution 60/97, *Basic Principles and Guidelines on the Right to a Remedy and Reparation for Victims of Gross Violations of International Human Rights Law and Serious Violations of International Humanitarian Law*, A/RES/60/147, preamble, ¶ 1 (March 21, 2006) (UN Basic Principles and Guidelines on the Right to a Remedy). For commentary, see Kelly McCracken, "Commentary on the Basic Principles and Guidelines on the Right to a Remedy and Reparation for Victims of Gross Violations of International Human Rights Law and Serious Violations of International Humanitarian Law," *Revue International de Droit Penal* 76, no. 1–2 (2005): 77–79.

[3] Dinah Shelton, *Remedies in International Human Rights Law* (Oxford: Oxford University Press, 2006), 21.

[4] UNGPs.

governments whether the infringement is caused by a state agent or a private, non-state actor such as companies.[5] The right to a remedy can be triggered by a wide range of scenarios where an individual or community experiences a grievance because a business directly causes or contributes to the violation of their rights.[6]

This chapter presents a general overview of the internationally recognized right to a remedy for human rights violations and offers approaches to teaching the right to remedy in the context of corporate accountability.

ACCESS TO REMEDY AND THE UNGPs

The right to remedy is recognized in the UNGPs. Specifically, the third pillar of the UNGPs, entitled "Access to Remedy," describes how states and businesses can ensure access to remedy for victims of human rights abuses, including "state-based judicial," "state-based non-judicial," and "non-state-based" grievance mechanisms.[7] The UNGPs incorporate most of the basic features of the right to remedy found in international law. In particular, the UNGPs reinforce, through Principle 25, that the state holds the primary duty of guaranteeing the right to remedy. The UNGPs also envision in Principle 22 that businesses should play an active role in providing or cooperating in remediation "through legitimate processes." Some of these processes entail non-judicial remedies that may be privately established through the company itself, as discussed below, thus expanding the traditional state-based notion of remedy as understood in human rights law. Principle 31 lists effectiveness criteria for all non-judicial mechanisms.[8]

SUBSTANTIVE AND PROCEDURAL REMEDY

Implementing the right to remedy requires an understanding of the two dimensions of the general concept of a remedy: the **procedural** dimension, which represents the means or mechanisms for seeking redress, as well as

---

[5]   Lisa J. Laplante, "Human Torts," *Cardozo Law Review* 39, no. 1 (October 2017): 251–258.

[6]   The UNGPs define a "grievance" as "a perceived injustice evoking an individual's or a group's sense of entitlement, which may be based on law, contract, explicit or implicit promises, customary practice, or general notions of fairness of aggrieved communities." UNGPs, Commentary to UNGP 25.

[7]   UNGPs, Principles 25–31.

[8]   Non-judicial grievance mechanisms should be legitimate, accessible, predictable, equitable, transparent, rights-compatible, and a source of continuous learning. Principle 31, UNGPs.

the **substantive** dimension, which represents the outcome of that procedure, namely some form of reparation. It is common to see the term "remedy" used to refer to both dimensions without distinction, leading to some confusion in how each aspect of the right functions in practice. A simple way to explain the difference is that a person has a right not only to bring a claim to a judicial or non-judicial mechanism to vindicate their violated right (procedural remedy) but also to receive adequate and effective reparations to redress any harms (substantive remedy) related to that infringement.[9] In this way, Courts strive to make a victim "whole" and return them to the *status quo ante*.[10]

Commentary to Guiding Principle 25 notes that remedies "generally speaking [aim to] to counteract or make good any human rights harms that have occurred."[11] Yet, it is a legal fiction to assume that reparations might make a person whole for the most egregious of human rights harms such as death or serious bodily injury. In response to this limitation, the Inter-American Court of Human Rights has developed the doctrine of *restitutio in integrum* to better approximate wholeness by recognizing a wide range of reparations beyond money.[12] Although the UNGPs never mention the term "reparation," commentary to Principle 25 names the most common types of reparations recognized in human rights law, such as apologies, restitution, rehabilitation, financial or non-financial compensation, and punitive sanctions (whether criminal or administrative, such as fines), as well as the prevention of harm through, for example, injunctions or guarantees of non-repetition.[13] The United Nations Working Group on Business and Human Rights (UN Working Group) also advocates for this "bouquet of remedies" to assure full redress.[14]

---

[9]   UN Basic Principles and Guidelines on the Right to a Remedy.

[10]   Lisa J. Laplante, "Bringing Effective Remedies Home: The Inter-American Human Rights System, Reparations, and the Duty of Prevention," *Netherlands Quarterly of Human Rights* 22, no. 3 (September 2004): 352 (hereafter cited as *Bringing Effective Remedies*).

[11]   UNGPs, Commentary to Principle 25.

[12]   Laplante, "Bringing Effective Remedies," 352; Thomas M. Antkowiak, "Remedial Approaches to Human Rights Violations: The Inter-American Court of Human Rights and Beyond," *Columbia Journal of Transnational Law* 46, no. 2 (2008): 351–419. Lisa J. Laplante, "Just Repair," *Cornell International Law Journal* 48, no. 3 (Fall 2015).

[13]   UNGPs, Commentary to Principle 25.

[14]   Report of the Working Group on the issue of Human Rights and Transnational Corporations and Other Business enterprises, transmitted by the Secretary-General to the General Assembly on its Seventy-Second Session, at 12, U.N. Doc. A/72/162 (July 18, 2017).

The right to a procedural remedy may be enforced through a range of governmental and non-governmental human rights grievance mechanisms.[15] (See Non-Governmental Human Rights Grievance Mechanisms, Chapter 10.) Table 6.1 distinguishes the different types of mechanisms available to victims.

Table 6.1   *Categories of human rights grievance mechanisms*

	Judicial	Non-judicial
State level	• Traditional courts.	• Ombudsmen. • Special commission or office to administer claims.
Company level (non-state)	*Not applicable* (A private company cannot establish a court.)	• Operational-level grievance mechanisms (OGMs). • Grievances associated with industry-wide voluntary initiatives.
International level	• International and regional human rights courts, commissions, and committees. • Bodies created by more than one state, usually through a treaty system.	• Independent Accountability Mechanisms (IAM) associated with financial and development institutions. • Examples include the World Bank's Compliance Advisor Ombudsman (CAO) and the OECD's National Contact Points.[a]

Note: [a] See The OECD National Contact Point Mechanism, Chapter 13.

"SYSTEM OF REMEDY"

The UNGPs view all of these different grievance mechanisms as a "system of remedy" in which state-based courts form the foundation,[16] since the duty to protect rights falls primarily on governments and, practically speaking, the threat of a lawsuit is what motivates many of the other avenues to stay effective. The first Guiding Principle reflects this hierarchical arrangement directing states to "protect against human rights abuse within their territory"

[15] Commentary to Principle 25 of the UNGPs defines the term grievance mechanism "to indicate any routinized, state-based or non-state-based, judicial or non-judicial process through which grievances concerning business-related human rights abuse can be raised and remedy can be sought." UNGPs, Commentary to Principle 25.

[16] UNGPs, Principle 25, Commentary to Principle 25.

and take "appropriate steps to … investigate, punish and redress such abuse."[17] Guiding Principle 25 reaffirms this duty with relation to remedies:

> As part of their duty to protect against business-related human rights abuse, States must take appropriate steps to ensure, through judicial, administrative, legislative or other appropriate means, that when such abuses occur within their territory and/or jurisdiction those affected have access to effective remedy.[18]

A system of remedy becomes especially important given that there are many legal, structural, and practical barriers to accessing state remedies.[19] For example, a state court may not have the capacity to handle all claims, may be situated far from where victims reside, may be limited by legal doctrines or jurisdiction that bars certain claims, or other situations that make them unable to serve the needs of victims.[20] Ultimately, one of the greatest hurdles comes down to social, cultural, and economic realities faced by victims. Thus, having other non-judicial routes serves an important purpose to ensuring the right to a remedy.

NON-JUDICIAL REMEDY

Guiding Principle 27 asserts that states may fulfill their international obligation to ensure access to an effective and appropriate remedy through non-judicial remedies.[21] If state-based, such alternative routes may appear in the form of a special administrative body located in any branch of government, such as

---

[17]   UNGPs, Principle 1.

[18]   *Id.*, Principle 25.

[19]   *Id.*, Commentary to Principle 25. ("[e]ven where judicial systems are effective and well-resourced, they cannot carry the burden of addressing all alleged abuses; judicial remedy is not always required; nor is it always the favoured approach for all claimants").

[20]   Jennifer Zerk, *Corporate Liability for Gross Human Rights Abuses: Towards a Fairer and More Effective System of Domestic Law Remedies. A Report Prepared for the Office of the UN High Commissioner for Human Rights* February 2014, www.ohchr.org/Documents/Issues/Business/DomesticLawRemedies/StudyDomesticeLawRemedies.pdf; Gwynne Skinner, "Beyond Kiobel: Providing Access to Judicial Remedies for Violations of International Human Rights Norms by Transnational Business in a New (Post-Kiobel) World," *Columbia Human Rights Law Review* 46, no. 1 (Fall 2014).

[21]   UNGPs. Commentary to Principle 27 ("gaps in the provision of remedy for business-related human rights abuses could be filled, where appropriate, by expanding the mandates of existing non-judicial mechanisms and/or by adding new mechanisms. These may be mediation-based, adjudicative or follow other culturally-appropriate and rights-compatible processes – or involve some combination of these – depending on the issues concerned, any public interest involved, and the potential needs of the parties").

through a minister's office or through the legislature.[22] Moving beyond the state, the UNGPs also place quite a bit of emphasis on non-state, non-judicial remedies. Two of the most prevalent non-governmental, non-judicial forms of remedy are:

- Human rights grievance mechanisms formed by inter-state, international, and regional agreements, often referred to as **Independent Accountability Mechanisms (IAMs)**. These grievance mechanisms are typically connected to international banks, inter-governmental banks, and other financial institutions that condition their loans on criteria that may include human rights norms and set up separate bodies to receive human rights claims when companies violate these norms.[23] Some examples include the Compliance Advisor Ombudsman of the International Finance Corporation and Multilateral Investment Guarantee Agency;[24] the Project Complaint Mechanism (PCM) of the European Bank for Reconstruction and Development (EBRD);[25] and the Independent Review Mechanism (IR M) of the African Development Bank (AfDB).[26] (See Non-Governmental Human Rights Grievance Mechanisms, Chapter 10.)
- Human rights grievance mechanisms set up by private companies, often referred to as **Operational-level Grievance Mechanisms (OGMs)**.[27] While OGMs are viewed as ideal for early response to grievances before they escalate, they also have increasingly been used to handle human rights claims.[28] OGMs can allow for a quicker and less expensive route to airing grievances while also offering businesses an opportunity to address

---

[22] Jonathan Drimmer and Lisa J. Laplante, "The Third Pillar: Remedies, Reparations and the Ruggie Principles," in *The Business and Human Rights Landscape: Moving Forward, Looking Back* (Cambridge: Cambridge University Press, 2015), 326–327.

[23] See Daniel D. Bradlow, "Private Complainants and International Organizations: A Comparative Study of the Independent Inspection Mechanisms in International Financial Institutions," *Georgetown Journal of International Law* 36, no. 2 (Winter 2005); Owen McIntyre and Suresh Nanwani, eds., *The Practice of Independent Accountability Mechanisms: Towards Good Governance in Development Finance* (Boston, MA: Brill/Nijhoff, 2020).

[24] See https://www.cao-ombudsman.org.

[25] See https://www.ebrd.com/pages/project/pcm.shtml.

[26] See https://www.afdb.org/en/independent-review-mechanism-irm.

[27] UNGPs, Principle 29 ("Business enterprises should establish or participate in effective operational-level grievance mechanisms for individuals and communities who may be adversely impacted").

[28] Lisa J. Laplante, "The Wild West of Company Level Grievance Mechanisms: Drawing Normative Borders to Patrol the Privatization of Human Rights Remedies," *Harvard International Law Journal* (forthcoming).

problems closer to the source.[29] These mechanisms may be "administered by enterprises, alone or in collaboration with others, including relevant stakeholders. They may also be provided through recourse to a mutually acceptable external expert or body."[30] Open to both employees and non-employees, these mechanisms may be better situated to engage and consult stakeholder groups through dialogue.[31]

Despite this wide range of mechanisms for bringing human rights grievances, providing effective remedies continues to be one of the most challenging aspects of ensuring human rights. On this subject, the Office of the High Commissioner for Human Rights initiated the Accountability and Remedy Project (ARP) in 2014 to study all of these mechanisms in order to recommend "practical actions for enhancing the effectiveness of the respective mechanism based upon good practice lessons observed during the ARP work."[32] ARP has since published multiple reports, which serve as important benchmarks for the development of the right to remedy for those negatively impacted by businesses and can be a rich resource for teaching remedies.

TEACHING APPROACHES

I teach the right to remedy for business-related harms, with particular emphasis on the role of non-judicial remedies, toward the end of the semester as part of a law school seminar that meets once a week for approximately two hours. The topic may involve several classes, although some years I emphasize only parts of this unit. I usually sequence coverage of non-judicial mechanisms after a discussion of judicial remedies (see Judicial Remedy, Chapter 12), during which time I highlight many of the practical limitations of accessing justice through the courts to help segue to other available means for vindicating the right to remedies.

---

[29] Office of the High Commissioner for Human Rights, The Corporate Responsibility to Respect Human Rights: An Interpretive Guide, at 68, U.N. Doc. HR/PUB/12/02, U.N. Sales No. E.13.XIV.4 (2012) ("operational-level grievance mechanism is a formalized means through which individuals or groups can raise concerns about the impact an enterprise has on them – including, but not exclusively, on their human rights – and can seek remedy").

[30] UNGPs, Commentary to Principle 29.

[31] *Id.*, Principle 31(h).

[32] "The Accountability and Remedy Project (ARP)," Office of the High Commissioner for Human Rights, accessed July 11, 2022, https://www.ohchr.org/en/business/ohchr-accountability-and-remedy-project.

Learning objectives include:

- Gaining familiarity with the sources of international human rights law that give rise to the right to remedy.
- Mastering the conceptual aspects of the right to remedy to understand how it is fully implemented.
- Learning how the right to remedy applies to claims against businesses in contrast to states.
- Understanding how the system of remedies functions to assure victims obtain satisfaction of their right to remedy.
- Appreciating the difficulties faced by victims in accessing all of the available remedies for vindicating their rights and many of the controversies surrounding different mechanisms.

I begin this unit with a general introduction to the right to remedy as recognized in international human rights law, using slides to present the universal and regional human rights systems and the most relevant treaties, and to introduce some of the basic concepts on the right to remedy. I build in an exercise in which students work in teams to review provisions from a range of treaties in order to discuss the similarities and differences, especially noting that more recent specialized treaties tend to understand the right to remedy more broadly. This lecture also includes a basic introduction to the UNGPs, highlighting access to remedy in Pillar III to clarify the obligations of states and companies and present "the system of remedies" the UNGPs promote.

EXERCISE 6.1

INTERNATIONAL ACCOUNTABILITY MECHANISMS

"ROUNDTABLE"

Turning to non-judicial remedies, I begin with a "roundtable" on Independent Accountability Mechanisms (IAMs). Each student signs up for one of the cases represented by Accountability Counsel, which I pre-select to assure a wide representation of regions and IAMs.[33] I provide students with a list of questions to help them digest not only the facts and legal developments in the case but also basic information about the IAM and how it works. In class, each student presents their case with the overall goal of sharing

---

[33] See "Our Work," Accountability Counsel, accessed July 12, 2022, https://www.accountabilitycounsel.org/community-cases.

knowledge about their assigned IAM, as well as opening up a general discussion on the strengths and weaknesses of these mechanisms. Teachers may choose to assign background reading that offers some critical assessments of the various IAMs. (See Teaching Resources below.)

EXERCISE 6.2

CASE STUDY: BARRICK GOLD

For the study of OGMs, I work with the case study of Barrick Gold, which is one of the most well-known examples of an OGM due to the controversy surrounding it. There are many excellent articles as well as UN documents that make it an especially rich case study to work with to tease out some of the issues surrounding purely private remedies. (See Teaching Resources below.)

Before class, I assign students one or two of the more well-known critical studies of Barrick Gold's Porgera Joint Venture (PJV) gold mine in Papua New Guinea (PNG).[34] These readings not only provide basic background on the case but also help to frame some of the issues we will discuss in class. I also assign the opinion issued by the Office of the High Commissioner of Human Rights regarding Barrick Gold.[35]

I begin class by showing a short video about the Barrick Gold mine. I recommend *Gold's Costly Dividend: The Porgera Joint Venture* created by Human Rights Watch or *Porgera Mine: An Inside Look at Barrick's Porgera Mine in Papua New Guinea* created by the French Cinétéve.

Students then work in small groups for ten minutes to identify the most serious human rights violations, using the Universal Declaration of Human Rights, based on the reporting in the video. Each group reports back the rights they selected, and I write the common ones on the board. Usually, students identify the right to a remedy among other civil and political, as well as economic and social rights violations. We then discuss how the obligation should fall on governments and private entities to resolve these possible claims.

We then begin to debrief on the experience of Barrick Gold's "Olgeta

---

[34]   See, for example, Sarah Knuckey and Eleanor Jenkin, "Company-Created Remedy Mechanisms for Serious Human Rights Abuses: A Promising New Frontier for the Right to Remedy?" *The International Journal of Human Rights* 19, no. 6 (2015).

[35]   Office of the High Commissioner for Human Rights, Letter regarding Allegations regarding the Porgera Joint Venture remedy framework (July 2013), accessed November 9, 2021, https://www.ohchr.org/Documents/Issues/Business/LetterPorgera.pdf.

Meri Igat Raits (All Women Have Rights)" remedy mechanism. Issues that can be discussed include: the use of waivers for reaching a settlement and the controversy surrounding a bar to judicial review; the question of what adequate reparations consist of and how you measure them; critiques of how the company engaged with communities and the difficulty of stakeholder engagement; the risks of relying on a purely private remedy without government oversight; and how to assess an OGM using Principle 31 of the UNGPs.

An alternative to a facilitated discussion is a role play in which students assume the role of the different stakeholders – victims, non-governmental organizations working with them, the company, the government, etc. – and discuss these issues, proposing amendments to the process to make it line up better with Principle 31. Teachers can develop a short role description to help the students anticipate the issues they will focus or have them rely on the assigned reading to improvise those positions. These exercises work best in small groups; for larger classes, teachers can create multiple small meetings with the same roles.

Teachers can conclude the class by setting up a debate that helps reveal the pros and cons of OGMs, with one part of the class arguing in favor and the other against. For this debate teachers can stick with the stakeholder roles or simply split the class in half and assign them the general role of pro or con. Students can then draw from the first exercise and readings to make their case in favor of or against an OGM.

After either of the above two exercises, teachers can ask students to work together in another role play in which they advise a company that has experienced alleged human rights claims (a real case[36] or a hypothetical one) on how to design an OGM that complies with Principle 31, avoiding some of the pitfalls experienced in the Barrick Gold case.

KEY QUESTIONS

General

- Why is the right to remedy important for the international human rights system to effectively protect the rights of people and individuals?
- What is the hierarchy of human rights grievance mechanisms within the "system of remedies" and how do they work together?

---

[36] New England Law's Operational Research Project is one source of possible cases to assign. Available at: https://www.nesl.edu/practical-experiences/centers/center-for-international-law-and-policy/projects/operational-grievance-mechanisms-project.

- What are some of the barriers to remedies faced by individuals and communities and why do they exist?
- How do the UNGPs address the right to remedy?

For Business Students

- What are the risks of a company engaging with IAMs or establishing OGMs?
- Where in the company should an OGM be situated? What background or expertise is needed by those who implement it?
- What level of transparency should OGMs have?
- How might an OGM contribute to a human rights due diligence process?
- How does an OGM contribute to creating a social license to operate?

For Law Students

- How should governments best assure the right to remedy is protected and fulfilled for human rights grievances related to private companies?
- What constitutes effective access to remedy in the third pillar of the UNGPs?
- What special considerations arise when vulnerable, disempowered communities engage with the different remedy mechanisms within the system of remedies presented by the UNGPs?
- Should OGMs be used to resolve serious human rights claims?

For Policy Students

- What type, if any, of government oversight should there be of operational-level human rights grievance mechanisms set up by companies?
- What, if any, limits should be placed on non-judicial grievance mechanisms?
- What are the approaches and tools for evaluating a non-judicial human rights grievance mechanism?

TEACHING RESOURCES

Readings

Commentary

- Coumans, Catherine. *Brief on Concerns Related to Project-Level Non-Judicial Grievance Mechanisms*. Ottawa: MiningWatch Canada, 2014.

- International Commission of Jurists. *Effective Operational-Level Grievance Mechanisms*. Geneva: International Commission of Jurists, 2019, https://www.icj.org/wp-content/uploads/2019/11/Universal-Grievance-Mechanisms-Publications-Reports-Thematic-reports-2019-ENG.pdf.
- International Federation for Human Rights. *Corporate Accountability for Human Rights Abuses: A Guide for Victims and NGOs on Recourse Mechanisms*. 3rd ed. Paris: International Federation for Human Rights, 2016.
- Knuckey, Sarah and Eleanor Jenkin. "Company-Created Remedy Mechanisms for Serious Human Rights Abuses: A Promising New Frontier for the Right to Remedy?" *The International Journal of Human Rights* 19, no. 6 (2015): 801–827.
- Rees, Caroline Rees. *Piloting Principles for Effective Company-Stakeholder Grievance Mechanisms: A Report of Lessons Learned, SRSG on the Issue of Human Rights and Transnational Corporations and Other Business Enterprises*. Cambridge: CSR Initiative, Harvard Kennedy School, 2014.
- Shift. *Remediation, Grievance Mechanisms and the Corporate Responsibility to Respect Human Rights*. New York: Shift, 2014.

Barrick Gold Case

- Aftab, Yousuf. *Pillar III on the Ground: An Independent Assessment of the Porgera Remedy Framework.* Enodo Rights, 2016.
- Amnesty International. *Undermining Rights: Forced Evictions and Police Brutality Around the Porgera Gold Mine, Papua New Guinea*. London: Amnesty International, 2010.
- Columbia Law School Human Rights Clinic and Harvard Law School International Human Rights Clinic. *Righting Wrongs? Barrick Gold's Remedy Mechanism for Sexual Violence in Papua New Guinea Key Concerns and Lessons Learned*. New York: Columbia Law School Human Rights Clinic, 2015.
- Office of the High Commissioner for Human Rights. Letter from the Office of the High Commissioner for Human Rights. *Allegations Regarding the Porgera Joint Venture Remedy Framework*. July 2013. http://www.ohchr.org/Documents/Issues/Business/LetterPorgera.pdf.

Teaching Cases

- Henderson, Rebecca and Nien-Hê Hsieh. *Putting the Guiding Principles into Action: Human Rights at Barrick Gold.* Harvard Business School Case No. 5-317-015, March 2015. Revised August 2020.

Videos

- Dozier, Marc and Daniel Vigne. "Porgera Mine: An Inside Look at Barrick's Porgera Mine in Papua New Guinea." Cinétéve, 2015, YouTube video, 13:10: https://www.youtube.com/watch?v=jFJ7KHcr15o.
- Human Rights Watch. "Gold's Costly Dividend: The Porgera Joint Venture." Human Rights Watch, 2011, YouTube video, 10:11: https://www.youtube.com/watch?v=Zbqe7TsJ7D4.

Websites

- Office of the UN High Commissioner for Human Rights. "Accountability and Remedy Project (ARP): Improving Accountability and Access to Remedy in Cases of Business Involvement in Human Rights Abuses." Accessed July 11, 2022. https://www.ohchr.org/EN/Issues/Business/Pages/OHCHRaccountabilityandremedyproject.aspx.

PART II

Business practice

7. Corporations[1]

Jena Martin

OVERVIEW

An understanding of corporate law and business entities is crucial to a student's grasp of business and human rights (BHR) issues. Too often, human rights advocates and business executives clash – not necessarily over ideology, but rather over language. Business and law students steeped in corporate law teachings often find it difficult to relate those concepts to the more amorphous field of international human rights law. Similarly, students who enter the BHR field as human rights advocates first are often outraged at concepts embedded in business and human rights, such as human rights due diligence and the business case for human rights.[2]

This chapter discusses the predominant business entity – the corporation – in a way that students in all disciplines can understand and contextualize within the larger BHR field. The chapter provides a basic understanding of corporations under U.S. law; addresses corporate structure, corporate purpose, and regulatory frameworks; and discusses how corporations' separate legal personality and purpose relate to corporate human rights impacts.[3]

STRUCTURE OF THE CORPORATION

Corporations come in a wide variety of shapes and sizes – from a small, one-person, closely held corporation to a large multi-million-dollar transna-

---

[1]   An earlier version of this chapter appeared online in Jena Martin, "Teaching Note: Corporations '101'," in *Teaching Business and Human Rights Handbook* (Teaching Business and Human Rights Forum, 2017), https://teachbhr.org/resources/teaching-bhr-handbook/teaching-notes/corporations-101-2.

[2]   The "business case" for human rights refers to attempts to justify spending money on non-financial social issues in a way that ultimately translates into corporate profitability.

[3]   For example, corporations could justify skimping on safety measures (that leads to negative human rights impacts) on the basis that installing these safety measures would reduce profitability.

tional corporation – however, the unifying feature of all these structures is that they have a separate legal personality from their owners and investors. To that end, teachers may find it helpful to analogize corporations to structures, providing students with a visual reference of the various stakeholders in a corporation and the role they play. It is also important to emphasize that, in a corporation, one person may have multiple roles. Knowing which role that person is playing when they undertake certain actions can have a significant impact on which legal rule is used to analyze any potential liability under state or federal law.

When corporations register their securities, a process known alternatively as going public or launching an initial public offering (IPO), they are subject to an additional regulatory framework in the United States – federal securities laws (primarily the Securities Act of 1933 and the Securities Exchange Act of 1934). (See Finance, Investors, and Human Rights, Chapter 26.) Students should understand that U.S. securities laws regulate corporations primarily by means of disclosure. Specifically, these laws require corporations to report on information that courts have found to be "material" to a reasonable investor.[4] As reporting companies, publicly traded corporations face additional pressure that often leads them to focus on short-term profits and gains rather than on long-term corporate value. Many social issues have arisen when the corporate value horizon is shortened in this way.

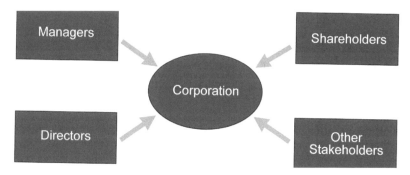

Figure 7.1   *The structure of a corporation*

---

[4]   See Securities Act of 1933, 17 CFR §230.405 (discussing materiality as whether "there is a substantial likelihood that a reasonable investor would attach importance in determining whether to purchase the security registered").

THE CORPORATION

While the corporate structure is in essence a legal fiction, corporations have certain rights under U.S. law (see Figure 7.1). For instance, a corporation can sue and be sued in its own name (in contrast with a partnership where it would be the individual partners that would be sued). A corporation can also own property, hold accounts in the corporation's name, and generally conduct many of the same legal actions that an individual may undertake. Instructors should highlight that, although it is a separate legal entity, the corporation still needs human intermediaries to effectuate its decisions. There are many potential landmines that can arise in those instances. (See Purpose of the Corporation below.) One of the most significant benefits of the corporate structure is that it generally provides limited liability for its investors – investor losses are typically limited to their initial investment. This is in stark contrast to other frameworks, such as sole proprietorships or partnerships, in which investors could be personally liable for *all* losses arising from the underlying structure.

Managers

Managers are the personnel responsible for the day-to-day operations of the corporation. They also manage the corporation and its policies. The highest-serving managers are also corporate officers. As officers, they have fiduciary duties to the corporation. Specifically, there are certain fiduciary duties under state corporate law that impact the relationships of officers to corporations and their shareholders. (See State Law below.) Officer positions include: (1) the chief executive officer (CEO); (2) the chief financial officer (CFO); (3) the chief operating officer (COO); (4) the corporation's general counsel; and (5) the corporate secretary.

The Board of Directors

The board largely functions as a single unit, approving all major decisions of the corporate officers. In addition, the directors serve in a monitoring role, monitoring all corporate activities for its shareholders. The directors are also bound by specific duties under state law. (See The Regulatory Framework below.)

SHAREHOLDERS

Shareholders are the owners of the corporation. Specifically, they are legal persons (either individuals or, increasingly, other entities) that invest in the corporation with the expectation of a profit, or a return on their investment (ROI). A key characteristic of shareholders, particularly shareholders of publicly traded corporations, is the "separation of ownership and control."[5] One way to illustrate the idea with students is a basic, colorful comparison between a shareholder of a corporation and an owner of a house:

> As the owner of the house, if one wanted to paint the structure pink, assuming there were no laws (or homeowner association rules) that prohibit it, one could do so. However, if an Apple shareholder made the decision to paint Apple's headquarters, they would likely be arrested (even if the shareholder only painted the representational value of their interest; i.e., if a 10 percent shareholder only painted 10 percent of Apple).

Instead, a shareholder's interest in a corporation generally entitles them to:

- Any dividends that a corporation may allocate;
- The right to vote on particularly important matters, usually the composition of the board of directors, the decision to merge with another company, and whether to change the corporate bylaws or articles of incorporation; and
- Have an ownership interest in the corporation – the right to receive the percentage of profits based on their shareholder interest if the company dissolves.

Other Stakeholders

It is also valuable to share with students other stakeholder groups that could affect the corporation's structure and its governance framework. Corporate stakeholders may include employees, suppliers, customers, and the communities where the corporation operates. While none of these stakeholders typically have formal representation within corporate law jurisprudence (officers and directors need not put stakeholder interest above shareholder profitability), these groups can influence corporate decision-making either through formal contracts, such as collective bargaining agreements for unions, or through softer, reputational influences, such as advocacy campaigns that target a business's negative human rights impacts. Stakeholder voices are particularly proficient at highlighting a corporation's negative human rights impacts, such as the corporate pollution of a community's water supply.

---

[5]   This concept was originally introduced by Adolf A. Berle and Gardiner C. Means in *The Modern Corporation and Private Property* (San Diego, CA: Harcourt, Brace & World, 1932) and cited in Harold Demsetz, "The Structure of Ownership and the Theory of the Firm," *Journal of Law & Economics* 26, no. 2 (June 1983).

PURPOSE OF THE CORPORATION

The number of corporations has grown exponentially in the last century. While originally designed as a way of pooling resources and acting within a very limited charter given by the state, the corporation has become the primary business organizational structure, crossing boundaries and (frequently) countries.[6]

Dodge v. Ford[7] is the seminal legal case for the enduring narrative of corporate purpose in the United States. Namely, the corporation is viewed as a vehicle "organized and carried on primarily for the profit of the stockholders."[8] This theme underlies subsequent legal cases and forms the basis of key principles in corporate jurisprudence.[9] One of the most important principles that has evolved, in part, from this narrative is the "business judgment rule" (BJR). The rule "protects directors from personal liability in certain situations"[10] where they are acting on behalf of the corporation.

The "shareholder profit" narrative also results in an inherent tension between the structure and purpose of a corporation. If a corporation can only act through its officers, and the officers are largely shielded from liability for their decisions, there is a danger that officers will make decisions largely for their own self-interest rather than on behalf of shareholders. To address this concern, state law has created fiduciary standards that officers must adhere to in order to receive legal protection. In short, BJR and fiduciary doctrines have evolved to try and balance the dual aims of: (1) allowing officers to take potentially beneficial corporate risks and (2) protecting shareholders.

There is, of course, significant room for discussion regarding whether the law has resolved these tensions. Shareholder primacy is a good starting point for discussing the role of the corporation in society or within a BHR framework.

---

[6]   The number of transnational corporations (TNCs) worldwide is well into the tens of thousands. James Zhan, "Covid-19 and Investment: An UNCTAD Research Round-Up of the International Pandemic's Effect on FDI Flows and Policy," *Transnational Corporations Investment and Development* 27, no. 1 (May 2020) (discussing the "top 5,000" TNCs).

[7]   *Dodge v. Ford Motor Co.*, 170 N.W. 668 (Mich. 1919) (shareholders brought a suit alleging that Ford was required to issue dividends instead of using corporate funds to build an automobile factory). The court noted that Ford's decision to forgo dividends went against the corporation's profit-making purpose.

[8]   *Id.*

[9]   Compare Lynn Stout, *The Shareholder Value Myth: How Putting Shareholders First Harms Investors, Corporations, and the Public* (San Francisco, CA: Berrett-Koehler, 2012).

[10]   Lori McMillan, "The Business Judgment Rule as an Immunity Doctrine," *William & Mary Business Law Review* 2, no. 2 (April 2013).

THE REGULATORY FRAMEWORK

Corporations are regulated simultaneously under two separate legal frameworks in the United States. First, there is the state law, which dictates the corporation's governance structure. Second, there is federal law, which regulates the corporation's sale of securities and, as such, its reporting and disclosure obligations. These two legal structures generally work synergistically.

State Law

State law dictates corporate governance rules – the *internal* rules of a corporation. The state of incorporation determines which state's law applies. For instance, Delaware law applies to all entities that are incorporated there, particularly for internal governance matters.[11] In fact, most publicly traded U.S. corporations are incorporated in Delaware, regardless of the company's headquarters.[12] As such, Delaware has significant corporate jurisprudence and expertise. Moreover, several jurisdictions rely on Delaware law for certain foundational principles. Law students who are studying U.S. corporate law should familiarize themselves with Delaware law on the subject.[13]

Fiduciary duties and the Business Judgment Rule
Generally, officers and directors owe two fiduciary duties to a corporation and, by extension, its shareholders: (1) a duty of loyalty and (2) a duty of care. If a corporate director is found to have violated either, then he or she may be personally liable in subsequent corporate litigation.[14]

Duty of care
The duty of care (DoC) provides that if officers and directors act with adequate care in formulating their decisions, they will be protected from personal liability, even for bad decisions. Specifically, the DoC applies to the board's

---

[11] There are some very limited exceptions, which are outside of the scope of this chapter.

[12] Many commentators argue that Delaware has a very corporate-friendly bench. William Jarblum and Bernard D. Bollinger, Jr., "Incorporation Issues: Why Delaware?" *American Bankruptcy Institute Journal* 18, no. 8 (October 1999): 6.

[13] The state law principles discussed here apply Delaware law. Teachers can also look to the Model Business Corporation Act (MBCA) for guidance.

[14] However, under Delaware's statutes corporate bylaws may waive personal liability for violations of the DoC (but not the duty of loyalty). Del. Code. Ann. Tit 8, § 102(b)(7).

decision-making procedures and not the decision itself.[15] If those procedures are informed, then the BJR applies and there is no DoC violation; the court will not examine the decision's merits. This requirement prevents shareholders and courts from critiquing a decision with the benefit of hindsight and, instead, defers to those with expertise. The standard varies by jurisdiction, but courts typically apply a gross negligence or recklessness standard to hold officers and directors liable for a breach of the DoC.[16] The DoC can also allow instructors to discuss whether corporate decisions should focus on potential human rights impacts even at the risk of shareholder profit. Under current Delaware law, officers and directors have the right to consider other stakeholders in determining whether to take a particular action. Therefore, if a corporate action would negatively impact a communities' human rights, under Delaware law corporate officers are allowed to consider that impact.[17]

Duty of loyalty

The duty of loyalty (DoL) provides that decisions must be made without self-dealing. Specifically, any transactions made with a board member who also has an interest in the underlying transaction may be subjected to a claim for the breach of the DoL. Litigation can also arise under the DoL if it is found that directors acted fraudulently or in bad faith.[18] Defendants can overcome this allegation if they prove that: (1) a majority of disinterested board members approved the transaction; (2) a majority of disinterested shareholders ratified the transaction; or (3) the overall transaction was fair.

Shareholder derivative suits

Shareholders can enforce these duties via a "derivative suit." This compels the corporation to sue its managers for fraud or breach of duty. The proceeds from any derivative actions go to the corporation.

---

[15] Similarly, the decision can be a decision to act or a decision to not act.

[16] Courts have also held that directors who *fail to make a decision* act without due care. In those cases, the Business Judgment Rule would not apply. *Francis v. United Jersey Bank*, 432 A.2d 814 (N.J. 1981).

[17] *Unocal Corp. v. Mesa Petroleum Co.*, 493 A.2d 946 (Del. 1985).

[18] Bad faith can arise in two situations: (1) intentional malice ("a subjective desire to do harm") or (2) an "intentional dereliction of duties" or "conscious disregard for one's responsibilities." In re Walt Disney Co. Derivative Litigation, 907 A.2d 693 (Del. 2005). Gross negligence, without more, is not considered to be bad faith.

Federal Securities Law

Publicly traded corporations in the United States also have an additional regulatory framework – federal securities laws. Generally, these laws do not affect private corporations.[19]

U.S. securities law requires corporations to disclose sufficient information for investors to make informed choices regarding whether to buy, hold, or sell their investment. Consequently, any publicly traded corporation must provide periodic public disclosures regarding numerous activities, usually relating to financial performance. Specific regulations require disclosures of non-financial issues, like conflict mineral transactions, or whether the corporation has a code of ethics.[20] In addition, more traditional laws like the Foreign Corrupt Practices Act[21] (prohibiting corporate bribery of foreign governments) and Rule 10b-5[22] (providing liability for fraudulent misstatements or omissions by a corporation or its executives) provide additional accountability for non-financial corporate activity.

TEACHING APPROACHES

Teaching this material allows BHR students to explore and deconstruct the corporate structure and discuss how its design (as a separate entity with limited personal shareholder liability) and its purpose (as a profit-making entity) relate to its responsibilities for human rights impacts. Many BHR courses address basic corporate law early in the syllabus, often in the context of defining "corporate responsibility." (See Corporate Responsibility, Chapter 2.)

Learning objectives may include:

• Explaining the purpose of the corporate form, basic corporate structure, and how corporations are regulated in the U.S.
• Identifying all corporate stakeholders and their effect on human rights impacts.
• Discussing how a corporation's separate legal personality may affect its human rights impacts.

---

[19]   Rule 10b-5 is a powerful exception. SEC Manipulative and Deceptive Devices and Contrivances, 17 C.F.R. § 240.10b-5 (2017). (See Exercise 7.2: Hiding Human Rights Impacts from Investors.)
[20]   Disclosure Required by Sections 406 and 407 of the Sarbanes-Oxley Act of 2022, 17 C.F.R. pts. 228, 229.
[21]   15 U.S.C. §§ 78dd-1 (2012).
[22]   17 C.F.R. § 240.10b-5 (2017).

Using Milton Friedman's classic article, which states the exclusive responsibility of a corporation is for shareholder profit,[23] highlights the inherent tension between the structure and design of the corporation. (See the Teaching Resources below for more recent counterexamples.)

Comparing public and private companies allows instructors to discuss the federal disclosure framework and explain the materiality standard. Instructors can use Congressional enactment of Sections 1502 and 1504 of the Dodd-Frank Act (relating to Conflict Minerals and Resource Extraction)[24] and the Securities and Exchange Commission's (SEC's) tortured path to promulgating rules around these issues[25] to illustrate how a corporation's human rights impacts may influence a shareholder's decision to buy, hold, or sell the company's stock.

EXERCISE 7.1

WEARING CORPORATE "HATS"

Law students, many of whom come from a non-business background, often have a particularly hard time discussing the different roles that one person can have in a corporation. Discussing these roles as "hats" that one may use and discard has been particularly effective in emphasizing the interchangeability of these roles.

BHR teachers can provide students with a scenario that depicts a corporate scandal involving specific human rights impacts (such as on the right to water or freedom from discrimination) and then discuss how liability standards could change depending on which "hat" someone within the corporate structure was wearing at the time.

---

[23] Milton Friedman, *Social Responsibility of Business* (*New York Times Magazine*, 1970). See also Becker Friedman Institute for Research in Economics: The University of Chicago, "Corporate Social Responsibility: Friedman's View," available at https://bfi.uchicago.edu/news/feature-story/corporate-social-responsibilty-friedmans-view.

[24] Pub. Law. 111-203 §§ 1502, 1504 124 Stat. 1376 (2010).

[25] See Jena Martin, "Hiding in the Light: The Misuse of Disclosure for Business and Human Rights Issues," *Columbia Journal of Transnational Law* 56 (2018).

EXERCISE 7.2

HIDING HUMAN RIGHTS IMPACTS FROM INVESTORS

Securities Exchange Act Rule 10b-5,[26] which applies to all corporations (public and private), allows instructors the opportunity to discuss potential litigation strategies that can be used against a corporation that has been accused of hiding negative human rights impacts from their investors. Rule 10b-5 is used by both the SEC and private litigants to establish corporate fraud. A successful action under 10b-5 must prove the following key elements: (1) a misstatement or omission; (2) with *scienter* (recklessness or knowing intent); (3) that was material; (4) that the plaintiff relied upon; and (5) that caused losses for the plaintiff.[27]

One possible exercise: a factual scenario in which a corporation made material misstatements regarding the use of forced labor in its supply chain. Instructors could discuss whether the allegations would be enough to survive a motion to dismiss.[28]

Business students can discuss the role corporate managers have in influencing corporate structure. Students can also consider the "separation of ownership and control" and its advantages and disadvantages. For instance, an advantage to divesting corporate decision-making from the hands of shareholders is more efficient and, potentially, more well-informed decision-making. One possible disadvantage arises from the concept of corporate managers playing with "other people's money."

For business students, instructors could also use a case study to compare the structure of closely held and publicly traded corporations, respectively, and analyze how each structure impacts a corporation's purpose. For instance, instructors could use the Body Shop example to highlight how the merger of a privately held corporation with a publicly traded corporation (with seemingly contradictory values) can affect the direction of a corporation and its owners.[29]

---

[26] *Id.*

[27] *Basic Inc. v. Levinson*, 485 U.S. 224 (1988). Plaintiffs are also required to show that the above elements were done "in connection with the purchase and sale of a security." *Blue Chips Stamps et al. v. Manor Drug Stores*, 421 U.S. 723 (1975).

[28] For one example, see Brett Murphy, "Rigged," *USA Today* (June 16, 2017) available at https://www.usatoday.com/pages/interactives/news/rigged-forced-into-debt-worked-past-exhaustion-left-with-nothing.

[29] See "A Brief History of the Body Shop," available at https://www.theguardian.com/fashion/fashion-blog/2011/nov/21/brief-history-of-body-shop; "The Body Shop: What Went Wrong?", available at http://www.bbc.com/news/business-38905530.

KEY QUESTIONS

General

- What is a corporation's purpose?
- Who are the various stakeholders of a corporation? How do their roles impact the corporate structure?

For Business Students

- What are the responsibilities of corporate managers to address other stakeholders' concerns?
- Do corporations have a role beyond generating profits for shareholders? Why or why not?

For Law Students

- Are corporations prohibited from pursuing social objectives?
- What possible claims can be brought under state law for officers and directors who make decisions that result in adverse human rights impacts?

For Policy Students

- What policy rationales underlie the premise of the corporation as a separate legal entity?
- What are the consequences of a corporation's purpose as a for-profit entity on larger societal values?

TEACHING RESOURCES

Readings

Commentary

- Cassell, Douglass. "Outlining the Case for a Common Law Duty of Care of Business to Exercise Human Rights Due Diligence." *Business and Human Right Journal* 1, no. 2 (July 2016).
- Martin, Jena. "Business and Human Rights: What's the Board Got to Do with It?": *University of Illinois Law Review* 2013, no. 3 (2013).

Videos

- Abbott, Jennifer, and Joel Bakan. "*The New Corporation: The Unfortunately Necessary Sequel.*" Grant Street Productions and Screen Siren Pictures, 2021.
- Achbar, Mark, Jennifer Abbott, and Joel Bakan. "The Corporation." Big Picture Media Corporation, 2003, YouTube video, 2:24:40: https://www.youtube.com/watch?v=zpQYsk-8dWg.

Websites

- Joel Bakan, accessed July 18, 2022, http://www.joelbakan.com.

8. Human rights due diligence

Robert McCorquodale and Daria Davitti

OVERVIEW

Understanding "human rights due diligence" (HRDD), and how it is applied, is a core element of business and human rights (BHR) courses. HRDD is a key component of the UN Guiding Principles on Business and Human Rights (UNGPs) and a foundational concept in BHR teaching. The recent adoption of mandatory HRDD requirements in a number of national jurisdictions makes HRDD a rapidly developing and highly relevant topic for BHR students. (See Mandatory Human Rights Due Diligence, Chapter 11.)

Over one-third of Pillar II of the UNGPs – the corporate responsibility to respect human rights – appears under the heading "Human Rights Due Diligence."[1] The UN Working Group on Business and Human Rights (UN Working Group) notes that "since the endorsement of the Guiding Principles by the Human Rights Council in 2011, corporate human rights due diligence has become a norm of expected conduct."[2] In addition, each international instrument that incorporates the UNGPs, such as the OECD Guidelines[3] and

---

[1] United Nations Human Rights Council, *Guiding Principles on Business and Human Rights: Implementing the United Nations "Protect, Respect and Remedy" Framework*, Report of the Special Representative of the Secretary-General on the issue of human rights and transnational corporations and other business enterprises, UN doc. A/HRC/17/31 (March 21, 2011) (UN Guiding Principles). See specifically UN Guiding Principles, Principles 17–21, which are also based on the reference to HRDD in Principle 15.

[2] Report of the Working Group on the issue of Human Rights and Transnational Corporations and Other Business Enterprises, transmitted by the Secretary-General to the General Assembly on its Seventy-Third Session, ¶ 20, U.N. Doc. A/73/163 (July 16, 2018).

[3] Organisation for Economic Co-operation and Development, *OECD Guidelines for Multinational Enterprises* (Paris: OECD Publishing, 2011). See also OECD, "Due Diligence Guidance for Responsible Business Conduct" (2018) 62, http://mneguidelines.oecd.org/OECD-Due-Diligence-Guidance-for-Responsible-Business-Conduct.pdf, accessed July 20, 2022).

the ILO Tripartite Declaration,[4] includes specific reference to HRDD, as do industry standards and national legislation.

DEFINING HUMAN RIGHTS DUE DILIGENCE

A key issue is how to define HRDD. While the term "due diligence" has been used before in other contexts, such as national securities legislation,[5] and in international human rights law, where it concerns the breadth of obligation of a state for actions of non-state actors,[6] it was new terminology in the context of BHR. HRDD has been summarized in the Office of the High Commissioner's Interpretive Guide to the UNGPs as: "an ongoing management process that a reasonable and prudent enterprise needs to undertake, in light of its circumstances (including sector, operating context, size and similar factors) to meet its responsibility to respect human rights."[7] Indeed, the use of the term "due diligence" in the UNGPs appears to be an innovative, clever, and deliberate tactic, as it is a term which is familiar both to business people and those

---

[4]   International Labour Organization, "ILO Tripartite Declaration of Principles concerning Multinational Enterprises and Social Policy 2017" (2017), https://www.ilo.org/empent/areas/mne-declaration/lang--en/index.htm (last accessed on February 9, 2022). See also Janelle Diller, "Social Conduct in Transnational Enterprise Operations: The Role of the International Labour Organization," in *Multinational Enterprises and The Social Challenges of the XXIst Century*, ed. Roger Blanpain (Alphen aan den Rijn: Kluwer, 2000).

[5]   See, for example, US Federal Securities Act 1933, 15 U.S.C. § 11 (1933), which enables a defense of "due diligence" if a defendant company has carried out a process of reasonable investigation and reasonably believed that the statements about a security were true and complete. There is also a long history of matters that can be seen as due diligence, which can be dated back to Roman law: see Jonathan Bonnitcha and Robert McCorquodale, "The Concept of 'Due Diligence' in the UN Guiding Principles on Business and Human Rights," *European Journal of International Law* 28, no. 3 (2017): 899–919.

[6]   The concept of due diligence as part of a state's human rights obligations was first expressed by the Inter-American Court of Human Rights in Case of Velasquez *Rodriguez v. Honduras*, Merits, Inter-Am. Ct. H.R. (ser.C) No. 4 ¶ 172 (July 29, 1988). For an overview on the use of this concept by the Inter-American System, see Inter-American Commission on Human Rights, "Business and Human Rights: Inter-American Standards" (November 1, 2019), OEA/Ser.L/V/II. Sections 2.I and 3.B.1, www.oas.org/en/iachr/reports/pdfs/Business_Human_Rights_Inte_American_Standards.pdf, accessed February 9, 2022.

[7]   UN Office of the High Commissioner for Human Rights, "The Corporate Responsibility to Respect Human Rights: An Interpretive Guide," HR/PUB/12/02 (2012) 6, www.ohchr.org/Documents/Publications/HR.PUB.12.2_En.pdf, accessed February 9, 2022.

involved with human rights and states, even though its meaning varies.[8] It is necessary, in particular, to distinguish between due diligence in business and how **human rights** due diligence is defined in the UNGPs. There are five main differences between business due diligence and HRDD under the UNGPs:[9]

(1)   Risk to the business versus risk to the rightsholder. The focus of the business human rights due diligence is about risk to the business itself, while human rights due diligence is about the risk to those humans who are or might be impacted by the business activities.[10]

(2)   One responsibility for each business versus many responsibilities to rightsholders. Business due diligence considers that each business has one responsibility – in relation to its own business activity. There are multiple responsibilities in human rights due diligence depending on the actions of the business. The latter includes responsibilities for a business enterprise's own adverse human rights impacts that it has caused or that it has contributed to, as well as responsibilities for the human rights impacts of third parties with which the business has relationships.[11]

(3)   Business due diligence requirements vary only as to product or financial matters, while HRDD requirements vary as to size, risk, and context of operations. While the level of business due diligence usually depends on the specific financial or product issues involved, the level of human rights due diligence expected will vary in complexity depending on the size of the business enterprise, the risk of severe human rights impacts, and the nature and context of its operations.[12]

---

[8]   See the debate in Jonathan Bonnitcha and Robert McCorquodale, "The Concept of 'Due Diligence' in the UN Guiding Principles on Business and Human Rights," *European Journal of International Law* 28, no. 3 (August 2017): 899–919; John Gerard Ruggie and John F. Sherrman, III, "The Concept of 'Due Diligence' in the UN Guiding Principles on Business and Human Rights: A Reply to Jonathan Bonnitcha and Robert McCorquodale," *European Journal of International Law* 28, no. 3 (August 2017): 921–928; and Jonathan Bonnitcha and Robert McCorquodale, "The Concept of 'Due Diligence' in the UN Guiding Principles on Business and Human Rights: A Rejoinder to John Gerard Ruggie and John F. Sherman, III," *European Journal of International Law* 28, no. 3 (August 2017): 929–933.

[9]   This is based on Robert McCorquodale, "Human Rights Due Diligence Instruments: Evaluating the Current Legislative Landscape," in *Research Handbook on Global Governance, Business and Human Rights* (London: Edward Elgar, 2022).

[10]   See Björn Fasterling, "Human Rights Due Diligence as Risk Management: Social Risk versus Human Rights Risk," *Business and Human Rights Journal* 2, no. 2 (July 2017): 225.

[11]   See UN Guiding Principles, Principle 13.

[12]   UN Guiding Principles, Principle 17.

(4)   One-off due diligence versus ongoing due diligence. Business due diligence is usually a one-off activity, such as for a merger or acquisition, while human rights due diligence is ongoing. The latter recognizes that the human rights risks may change over time as the business enterprise's operations and operating context evolve.[13]

(5)   Corporate social responsibility versus human rights law. Business due diligence can often be seen as part of corporate social responsibility with a tick-box approach, while HRDD has a human rights law foundation, which includes remediation responsibilities, and is often the responsibility of in-house legal counsel.[14]

Legislative developments have highlighted that environmental damage[15] and climate change impacts may also fall within the definition of HRDD.[16]
The key elements of HRDD are set out in Guiding Principle 17:

*   Assessing actual and potential human rights impacts;
*   Integrating and acting upon the findings;
*   Tracking responses; and
*   Communicating how impacts are addressed.

Clarifying these elements enables BHR students to see how HRDD processes are meant to operate. For example, a discussion of the assessment of actual and potential human rights impacts can examine the definition and scope of adverse human rights impacts under the UNGPs and how these impacts can be assessed, as well as what impacts are "salient" and should be prioritized.[17] This teaching approach links to BHR practice as it will show how a company must *first* determine its human rights impacts *before* it prioritizes its human rights-related remedial actions.

---

[13]   *Id.*

[14]   See Anita Ramasastry, "Corporate Social Responsibility versus Business and Human Rights: Bridging the Gap between Responsibility and Accountability," *Journal of Human Rights* 14, no. 2 (2015): 237.

[15]   OECD Guidelines, Section VI Environment.

[16]   Chiara Macchi, "The Climate Change Dimension of Business and Human Rights: The Gradual Consolidation of a Concept of Climate Due Diligence," *Business and Human Rights Journal* 6, no. 1 (February 2021): 93.

[17]   Salience is a "principled basis for sequencing how [company] resources [initially] get applied." Caroline Rees and Rachel Davis, "Salient Human Rights Issues: When Severe Risks to People Intersect with Risks to Business," in *Business and Human Rights: From Principles to Practice*, eds. Dorothée Baumann-Pauly and Justine Nolan (Oxford: Routledge, 2016), 104–115.

This leads to teaching about which businesses are meant to undertake HRDD, as GP 17(b) provides:

> [HRDD] will vary in complexity with the size of the business enterprise, the risk of severe human rights impacts, and the nature and context of its operations.

HUMAN RIGHTS DUE DILIGENCE IN PRACTICE

HRDD begins with a human rights impact assessment that is intended to identify and assess actual and potential human rights impacts across all the operations of a business, including in its value chain. (See Human Rights Impact Assessment, Chapter 9.) This includes full consultations with all relevant stakeholders. Then the business acts on the assessment by integrating the findings of the assessment into all its operations and tracks the outcomes and consequences as part of its ongoing process. Finally, a business reports on these outcomes both internally and externally, and begins the HRDD process again.

Applying HRDD requires BHR practitioners to consider issues such as a company's size, the severity of human rights impacts connected to the business, and the nature and context of a business enterprise's operations. These factors are relevant for the level of HRDD to be expected. Considering the nature and context of a business' operations can also give rise to discussions about different sectors;[18] on the particular impacts of business activities on vulnerable groups, such as Indigenous People, those with disabilities, and women; and on the importance of early and regular consultation by businesses with these groups and others. The UN Working Group, for example, has developed gender-sensitive guidance for implementing the UNGPs.[19]

Applying HRDD also raises additional issues, including that:

- HRDD is an ongoing and not a one-off process;

---

[18] See, for example, Radu Mares, "Corporate and State Responsibilities in Conflict-Affected Areas," *Nordic Journal of International Law* 83, no. 3 (August 2014): 293; Rolf Weber, "Human Rights Due Diligence as New Policy in Financial Institutions," in *Reconceptualising Global Finance and Its Regulation*, eds. Ross Buckley, Emilios Avgouleas, and Douglas Arner (Cambridge: Cambridge University Press, 2016), 419–441; and Alexander Kriebitz and Christoph Lütge, "Artificial Intelligence and Human Rights: A Business Ethical Assessment," *Business and Human Rights Journal* 5, no. 1 (January 2020): 84.

[19] United Nations Human Rights Council, "Report of the Working Group on the issue of human rights and transnational corporations and other business enterprises, Gender dimensions of the Guiding Principles on Business and Human Rights" (May 23, 2019), A/HRC/41/43, paras. 29 and 33.

- HRDD applies across the whole value chain, including the supply chain;[20]and
- Businesses have the responsibility to conduct HRDD even where they are acting in locations where domestic law seems to restrict what they can do.[21]

Raising these issues in a BHR class can lead to discussions with students about the reasons why businesses may want to conduct specific HRDD, such as risks to reputation, legal risks, and investor, employee, and consumer responses.[22]

LEGAL DIMENSIONS OF HUMAN RIGHTS DUE DILIGENCE

Teaching HRDD also allows teachers to link the topic to other areas within BHR, highlight the differences between international and national standards, and contrast many business and legal approaches to human rights matters.

One related topic is the link between HRDD and legal liability, as HRDD by itself does not give rise to legal liability without HRDD being made mandatory through domestic law and regulation. However, the Commentary to Guiding Principle 17 points out that "[c]onducting appropriate human rights due diligence should help business enterprises address the risk of legal claims against them by showing that they took every reasonable step to avoid involvement with an alleged human rights abuse."[23] This suggests that having conducted adequate and appropriate HRDD can serve as a viable defense against liability or as a mitigating circumstance in cases when company operations allegedly contributed to abuse.[24] The debate on the extent to which, and the circumstances under which, HRDD could be seen to serve as a defense against liability or to reduce remediation is an interesting one, with proposed national and

---

[20]   Justine Nolan and Nana Frishling, "Human Rights Due Diligence and the (Over) Reliance on Social Auditing in Supply Chains," in *Research Handbook on Human Rights and Business*, eds. Surya Deva and David Birchall (Cheltenham: Edward Elgar, 2020), 108–129.

[21]   A company's responsibility is "to honour the principles of internationally recognized human rights when faced with conflicting requirements." UN Guiding Principles, Principle 23. See also Arianne Griffith, Lise Smit, and Robert McCorquodale, "Responsible Business Conduct and State Laws: Addressing Human Rights Conflicts," *Human Rights Law Review* 20, no. 4 (December 2020): 641.

[22]   Hannes Hofmann, Martin Schleper, and Constantin Blome, "Conflict Minerals and Supply Chain Due Diligence: An Exploratory Study of Multi-tier Supply Chains," *Journal of Business Ethics* 147, no. 1 (January 2018): 115.

[23]   UN Guiding Principles, Commentary to Principle 17.

[24]   Robert McCorquodale, Lise Smit, Robin Brooks, and Stuart Neely, "Human Rights Due Diligence in Law and Practice: Good Practices and Challenges for Business Enterprises," *Business and Human Rights Journal* 2, no. 2 (July 2017): 195.

regional legislation and the draft BHR treaty being relevant to this debate.[25] This can also lead to discussion about directors' duties and senior management responsibilities,[26] as well as the links between HRDD and other areas of law.[27] It has also been argued that HRDD can be linked with a legal duty of care on business as part of the developments in this area by courts in cases such as *Vedanta v. Lungowe*[28] and *Four Nigerian Farmers v. Shell.*[29]

TEACHING APPROACHES

Thanks to its conceptual versatility, HRDD tends to be one of the most popular BHR class topics amongst students as it is suitable to various teaching and learning methods. Our experience has extended to students from diverse backgrounds who are studying for undergraduate law courses and Masters of Law courses around the world, as well as to legal practitioners, diplomats, and business leaders.

Representative **learning objectives** for teaching HRDD may include:

- Understanding the origin, content, and scope of HRDD.
- Understanding how HRDD works in practice and is applied in different contexts.
- Understanding the legal dimensions of HRDD and its relationship to legal liability.

These objectives can be easily adjusted to the specific cohort of students and the context within which a BHR course is taught, for instance by varying the emphasis on the practical and/or legal dimension of HRDD depending on whether the course is aimed at business students, law students, or working professionals. This is not to suggest that legal aspects should not be taught to

---

[25]   See, for example, Gabriela Quijano and Carlos Lopez, "Rise of Mandatory Human Rights Due Diligence: A Beacon of Hope or a Double-Edged Sword?" *Business and Human Rights Journal* 6, no. 2 (June 2021): 241.

[26]   See, for example, Robert McCorquodale and Stuart Neely, "Director's Duties and Human Rights Impacts: A Comparative Approach," *Journal of Corporate Law Studies* (February 7, 2022).

[27]   See, for example, Daria Davitti, *Investment and Human Rights in Armed Conflict: Charting an Elusive Intersection* (Oxford: Hart, 2019).

[28]   *Vedanta Resources Ltd v. Lungowe*, [2019] UKSC 20, before the UK Supreme Court. See, more generally, Douglass Cassel, "Outlining the Case for a Common Law Duty of Care of Business to Exercise Human Rights Due Diligence," *Business and Human Rights Journal* 1, no. 2 (July 2016): 179.

[29]   *Four Nigerian Farmers and Stichting Milieudefensie v. Royal Dutch Shell plc and another* [2021] ECLI:NL:GHDHA:2021:132 (Oruma), ECLI:NL:GHDHA:2021:133 (Goi), and ECLI:NL:GHDHA:2021:134 (Ikot Ada Udo) (Neth.).

business students or that practical aspects do not pertain to a legal education, but rather that the extent to which the class engages with specific aspects will always vary from situation to situation, depending, for instance, on the specific degree and qualification requirements of the broader program in which the course is situated.

The first learning objective, focusing on the **origin, content, and scope of HRDD**, is perhaps the one that is best suited to a more theoretical and, to a certain extent, philosophical approach to BHR. A helpful way for all students is to begin is with the definition of HRDD under the UNGPs and the OECD Guidelines, comparing HRDD with how due diligence is defined in a normal business sense (such as with a company acquisition) and in an international law sense (such as a state's responsibilities). Considering adverse and salient human rights impacts (with an emphasis on understanding what they are and the process through which they can be identified) and the challenges and implications of prioritization can be approached both theoretically and practically. These subtopics are ideal for students' presentations, group discussions, and interim written assignments. A successful way of teaching these topics, in our experience, is to adopt a sectoral case study that focuses, for instance, on the pharmaceutical, fashion, or extractive sector. This enables a more in-depth contextual examination of the potential adverse impacts characterizing a specific industry, as well as the most common HRDD practices adopted within the sector.

The second learning objective, dedicated to a deeper understanding of **HRDD in practice**, is particularly suited for including a certain level of interaction with invited speakers, for instance from companies, non-governmental organizations, think-tanks, and legal practice. These invited talks and class discussion provide students with the opportunity to engage with BHR experts and gain valuable insights on the everyday challenges of HRDD processes and their benefits and limitations. Engagement with external speakers also provides an opportunity to open up broader discussions on how HRDD intersects with other areas of law and policy, such as international investment law, climate change, and finance. External speakers can provide perspectives from other disciplines and help students to challenge their own assumptions and broaden their understanding of HRDD.

The third learning objective concerns the **legal dimension(s) of HRDD** and business responses to emerging legal liability for HRDD. Engaging with case law can help to map a clearer picture of the fast-paced legal and legislative developments, including ongoing debates whether HRDD should serve as a defense against liability or to reduce remediation. Discussing how HRDD is at the core of the drafting process for a binding instrument on business and human rights can be productive, given the attempts at closing some of the existing liability gaps through these negotiations. The prospects for a BHR treaty can be linked to developments in national and European Union law enacting mandatory human rights due diligence. (See Mandatory Human Rights Due Diligence, Chapter 11.) Teachers can address the interdisciplinary aspects of HRDD by considering how HRDD is used domestically (e.g. through a comparative study), regionally (e.g. with a focus on policy proposals for mandatory HRDD, as in the case of the European Union), or thematically (e.g. with a specific focus on environmental protection, food security, or Indigenous People's rights).

EXERCISE 8.1

MODELING HUMAN RIGHTS DUE DILIGENCE

HRDD is also an excellent topic to adopt alternative and creative teaching approaches that encourage students to think "outside of the box." We have set a creative partial assignment where the students are required to choose any of the HRDD topic covered in class and produce a 3D model or short music track in which they represented their chosen HRDD-related challenge or legal issue. Students are asked to introduce briefly the key aspects of their model in a short 3-minute video, followed by a 10-minute presentation to the class in which they presented the legal or policy reasoning underpinning their model. This assignment requires a time investment for both the teachers and the students involved, but it is an extremely rewarding exercise. The exercise engages different learning modalities (visual, auditory, kinesthetic, and tactile)[30] and strengthens the students' confidence by inviting them to step out of their comfort zone in a safe and collaborative environment. Once students are reassured that what is being tested is not their creativity or their artistic skills, but the reasoning that goes into their models and presentation, they are usually able to start thinking about their chosen topic differently. To encourage students' creativity, wherever possible, the best assessment format for this assignment is on a pass/fail basis. Throughout the years we have used this approach, students have represented different aspects of HRDD through jigsaw puzzles, board games, poems, music medleys, wire mazes, and playdough models. The assignment, which can be easily adapted for online teaching, is usually followed by a debriefing session in which the class reflect on the work produced and on how it may have helped them approach the chosen issue in a different way. To add some spark to the assignment, we often ask the students to vote

---

[30]   Norman Carroll and Michael O'Donnell, "Some Critical Factors in Student Learning" *International Journal of Education Research* 5, no. 1 (Winter 2010): 59.

for the best model and an informal prize is awarded to the student who re-ceives most votes, as a token of recognition for the effort and engagement. Winning models have included a board game explaining the HRDD process of an oil company (with cards that send you back to the starting point every time foreseeable adverse impacts are not avoided) and a song on the draft European Union corporate sustainability due diligence directive.

Other creative teaching approaches we have used effectively include role-plays, where various students take on roles such as a CEO, a consumer, a worker in a developing country, a representative of a local community, and a production manager to see the difference taking a corporate social responsibility and a BHR approach can make to the worker and community.

Assessments can also enhance the learning experience. We have used class participation and written a blog for different audiences about a BHR case or a current issue, as well as encouraging students to undertake case studies on HRDD.

KEY QUESTIONS

General

- Why is HRDD a core part of BHR?
- What are the key elements of HRDD?
- How is HRDD different from other forms of due diligence?
- HRDD considers the risks to whom?
- Why is HRDD not a one-off process?

For Business Students

- Which human rights must a company respect under the UNGPs?
- When carrying out HRDD in a state that has not ratified a specific human rights treaty, is a company required to respect the specific rights enshrined in that treaty?
- Does HRDD apply equally to all companies, including small or medium-sized enterprises?
- Why should companies have a HRDD policy and track its effectiveness?
- Who in a company should know about HRDD and human rights risks?
- How have companies launched HRDD processes internally? What are the potential obstacles?

For Law Students

- Does HRDD increase or decrease liability for a company? Why?
- What is needed in national legislation to ensure companies carry out HRDD?
- What is the difference between HRDD and legal duties of care?
- How can the UNGPs and the OECD Guidelines be used to help companies comply with HRDD?
- To what extent, and in what circumstances, can HRDD be seen to serve as a defense against liability or to reduce remediation?

For Policy Students

- How can a state's policies encourage business to implement HRDD effectively?
- What policy areas are relevant to HRDD?
- How can a business's behaviour be influenced so that it conducts HRDD appropriately?
- Whose interests should be considered when conducting HRDD?
- How can the effectiveness of HRDD processes be determined?

TEACHING RESOURCES

Readings

Tools

- Danish Institute for Human Rights. Human Rights Impact Assessment: Guidance and Toolbox, available at https://www.humanrights.dk/tools/human-rights-impact-assessment-guidance-toolbox.

For examples of corporate human rights impact assessments, see the Teaching Resources in Human Rights Impact Assessment, Chapter 9.

Reports

- BSR. *Conducting an Effective Human Rights Impact Assessment.* BSR, 2013. http://www.bsr.org/reports/BSR_Human_Rights_Impact_Assessments.pdf.
- Clean Clothes Campaign. *Fashioning Justice: A Call for Mandatory and Comprehensive Human Rights Due Diligence in the Garment Industry.* CCC, 2021. https://cleanclothes.org/news/2021/fashioning-justice.

- Shift. *Human Rights Reporting: Are Companies Telling Investors What They Need to Know?* New York: Shift, 2017. https://shiftproject.org/wp-content/uploads/2017/05/Shift_MaturityofHumanRightsReporting_May2017.pdf.

Commentary

- Buhmann, Karin. "Teaching Note: Human Rights Due Diligence." In *Teaching Business and Human Rights Handbook* (Teaching Business and Human Rights Forum, 2018), https://teachbhr.org/resources/teaching-bhr-handbook/teaching-notes/human-rights-due-diligence.
- Sherman, III, John F. "The Corporate General Counsel Who Respects Human Rights." *Legal Ethics* (2021), https://doi.org/10.1080/1460728x.2021.1979731.

Videos

- Baab, Mike. "Why Should Your Company Care About Human Rights?" 2017. YouTube video, 6:15: https://www.youtube.com/watch?v=mCtNx3hHZ08.
- Bader, Christine. "The Evolution of a Corporate Idealist." Filmed July 8, 2014 in New York. YouTube video, 7:17: https://www.youtube.com/watch?v=jAh7YJFxgLg&feature=youtu.be.
- Danish Institute for Human Rights. "Due Diligence – Business and Human Rights." Produced for Global Alliance of National Human Rights Institutions. 2018. YouTube video, 3:41: https://youtu.be/pQaW3ZqPizU.
- *The Economist.* "Conducting Human Rights Due Diligence in Times of Covid-19." March 25, 2021. YouTube video, 56:15: https://www.youtube.com/watch?v=34X2GDCyBBE.
- NOVA Business, Human Rights and the Environment, https://novabhre.novalaw.unl.pt. For videos and podcasts on HRDD, in both English and Portuguese.
- Strategy and Business. "The Challenges of Corporate Responsibility Inside a Big Company." 2015. YouTube video, 5:41: https://www.youtube.com/watch?v=qhqjQkETtio.

Websites

- Danish Institute for Human Rights. "Sustainable Development through Human Rights Due Diligence" (organized thematically per salient issue, linking the discussion to the relevant Sustainable Development Goals). Accessed July 20, 2022. https://biz.sdg.humanrights.dk.

- Poder. "Business and Human Rights." Accessed July 20, 2022. https:// poderlatam.org/en/category/projects/business-and-human-rights. In both Spanish and English: a civil society organization focusing on Latin America – useful for case studies and to discuss feminist advocacy on HRDD in the proposed binding treaty.
- World Benchmarking Alliance. "Corporate Human Rights Benchmark." Accessed July 20, 2022. https://www.worldbenchmarkingalliance.org/ corporate-human-rights-benchmark.

9. Human rights impact assessment

Mark Wielga

OVERVIEW

Why teach "human rights impact assessment" (HRIA) in a business and human rights (BHR) course? First, it can be an effective form of human rights due diligence that comes from an established field of practice. Second, there are publicly available HRIA examples that can be used for a variety of classroom purposes to see specific, detailed case studies of how businesses impact human rights. Third, there are careful, thoughtful methodologies that illuminate best practices for human rights due diligence. This chapter defines HRIA and suggests an approach for using HRIA examples in a BHR course.

DEFINING HUMAN RIGHTS IMPACT ASSESSMENT

Human rights impact assessment is a process of analyzing and describing the ways a policy or activity impacts human rights. When a HRIA is performed on behalf of, and directed toward, a business operation, it is one form of human rights due diligence as defined by the UN Guiding Principles on Business and Human Rights (UNGPs). (See Human Rights Due Diligence, Chapter 8 and The UN Guiding Principles on Business and Human Rights, Chapter 5.) HRIAs of planned, future business operations often consider potential negative impacts, referred to as "human rights risks." This term refers to risks to rightsholders that their rights may be violated, not risks to a company that could create liability or impair its business.

"Impact assessment" is its own field that predates, and intersects, contemporary business and human rights. "Impact assessment" is a term of art referring to a process for systematically identifying actual and potential impacts of a business operation, capital project, government policy, or inter-governmental agreement.[1] Environmental impact assessments of some business projects are

---

[1]   Frank Vanclay, "The Triple Bottom Line and Impact Assessment: How do TBL, EIA, SIA, SEA and EMS Relate to Each Other?" *Journal of Environmental Assessment Policy and Management* 6, no. 3 (September 2004): 265–288.

required by law in most countries.[2] Impact assessments focusing on health and social aspects of corporate actions are becoming increasingly common.[3] Impact assessment is a field with its own practitioners, theorists, organizations, and scholarly journals.[4] Human rights impact assessment is a relatively new and small part of that field.

HRIA has its roots in two separate fields: human rights policy and impact assessment. At least since 1995, donor agencies and development experts have sought to understand the effects of their programs on human rights.[5] Landman endeavored to link that analysis to firm indicators,[6] while Walker connected it to the practice and theory of impact assessment.[7] The field of "impact assessment" was established largely as part of environmental protection in the 1960s and 1970s.[8] Translating a tool for environmental measurement into a tool for human rights evaluation has been hindered by the fact that most human rights impacts are not as quantitatively measurable as, for example, contamination of soil, air, or water.[9] Nevertheless, advances have been made in both theory and practice of HRIA, with Harrison leading theoretical advancements in

---

[2]   William H. Rodgers Jr., "The Seven Statutory Wonders of U.S. Environmental Law: Origins and Morphology," *Loyola of Los Angeles Law Review* 27, no. 3 (Spring 1993): 1009–1022.

[3]   Henk A. Becker and Frank Vanclay, eds., *The International Handbook of Social Impact Assessment: Conceptual and Methodological Advances* (Cheltenham: Edward Elgar, 2003), 1–352.

[4]   See, for example, "IAIA," International Association for Impact Assessment, accessed July 20, 2022, https://www.iaia.org/index.php; "About the Journal," Environmental Impact Assessment Review, accessed July 20, 2022, https://www .sciencedirect.com/journal/environmental-impact-assessment-review; Becker and Vanclay, *The International Handbook of Social Impact Assessment.*

[5]   Todd Landman, *Studying Human Rights* (Oxford: Routledge, 2006), 1–188; Paul Portneyand and Robert Stavins, eds., *Public Policies for Environmental Protection*, 2nd ed. (Washington, DC: Resources for the Future Press, 2000), 1–9.

[6]   Todd Landman, "Measuring Human Rights: Principle, Practice and Policy," *Human Rights Quarterly* 26, no. 4 (November 2004): 906–931.

[7]   Simon Walker, *The Future of Human Rights Impact Assessments of Trade Agreements* (Cambridge: Intersentia, 2009), 1–252.

[8]   Portney and Stavins, *Public Policies for Environmental Protection.*

[9]   Kate Raworth, "Measuring Human Rights," *Ethics & International Affairs* 15, no. 1 (March 2001): 111–131.

evaluation of HRIA as a form of human rights "due diligence"[10] and Salcito producing tested mixed-method approaches to HRIA in practice.[11]

Human rights impact assessments originated as an evaluation mechanism for government policies, infrastructure, and trade agreements.[12] With the rise of the field of BHR, HRIAs have now been performed on business operations in an array of industries. Most of these have been on "large footprint" capital projects such as open-pit mines, oil and gas operations, large plantation agriculture, and factories. HRIAs have also been performed on tourism operations (hotels), mega-sporting events, and information and communications technology sector operations.[13]

HUMAN RIGHTS IMPACT ASSESSMENT VERSUS HUMAN RIGHTS DUE DILIGENCE

The UNGPs introduced the concept of human rights due diligence, a process by which a business investigates and responds to its own impacts on human rights.[14] While the UNGPs do not use the term "HRIA," they do refer to "assessing actual and potential human rights impacts."[15] When conducted by companies on business operations, human rights impact assessment is one form of human rights due diligence. The UNGPs have influenced HRIA practice so that HRIAs are now generally performed with the intention of falling within the UNGPs' definition of human rights due diligence. In accordance with John Ruggie's polycentric governance theories supporting the UNGPs, several soft

---

[10] James Harrison, "Establishing a Meaningful Human Rights Due Diligence Process for Corporations: Learning from Experience of Human Rights Impact Assessment," *Impact Assessment and Project Appraisal* 31, no. 2 (June 2013): 107–117.

[11] Kendyl Salcito et al., "Assessing Human Rights Impacts in Corporate Development Projects," *Environmental Impact Assessment Review* 42 (September 2013): 39–50.

[12] Walker, *The Future of Human Rights Impact Assessments of Trade Agreements.*

[13] Harrison, "Establishing a Meaningful Human Rights Due Diligence Process for Corporations." The ICT sector's Global Network Initiative Implementation Guidelines require its members to perform HRIAs when introducing new technologies, products, or services that may jeopardize freedom of expression or privacy. See "Implementation Guidelines," Global Network Initiative, accessed July 20, 2022, https://globalnetwork initiative.org/implementation-guidelines.

[14] United Nations Human Rights Council, *Guiding Principles on Business and Human Rights: Implementing the United Nations "Protect, Respect and Remedy" Framework*, Report of the Special Representative of the Secretary-General on the issue of human rights and transnational corporations and other business enterprises, UN doc. A/HRC/17/31 (March 21, 2011) (UN Guiding Principles).

[15] *Id.*

law and voluntary standards require companies to perform assessments of human rights impacts.[16] As there is still no agreed-upon terminology for different kinds of human rights due diligence, terms and processes have proliferated, including "human rights assessment," "human rights gap analysis," "human rights risk assessment," and "human rights impact assessment." These terms have not been clearly defined. In the resulting confusion, similar reports have quite different titles and wildly differing reports have similar titles.[17]

Human rights due diligence under the UNGPs requires action, not just investigation and analysis. The UNGPs require that the company act upon the findings, track its responses to them, and communicate how impacts are addressed.[18] The UNGPs also require that human rights due diligence must be ongoing, "recognizing that the human rights risks may change over time as the business enterprise's operations and operating context evolve."[19] None of these additional requirements are part of conventional impact assessment, and so an HRIA must include or lead to these actions in order to satisfy the UNGPs' requirements for human rights due diligence.

Normally, impact assessment considers a corporate project before it has been built. Its conclusions can help guide redesign of the project to reduce and mitigate negative impacts. If the likely impacts are severe and unavoidable, the government (or corporate entity) can decide that the project should not be built.[20] Some HRIAs take this prospective approach and consider a project that has been designed and planned, but not yet built. However, the UNGPs make it clear that human rights due diligence is an ongoing effort, and so a purely predictive analysis is not sufficient. Also, human rights issues are often fluid and unpredictable, so that a single, forward-looking analysis will almost never be accurate or complete.[21] Again, an HRIA that adopts the UNGPs' require-

---

[16]   See, for example, *The Equator Principles EP4 July 2020*, 9; Section 1.3.2 of the Initiative for Responsible Mining Assurance, *IRMA Standard for Responsible Mining IRMA-STD-001*, 2018, 26; and the Commentary on Human Rights, Organisation for Economic Co-operation and Development, *OECD Guidelines for Multinational Enterprises*, 2011 Edition, 34. This idea has been picked up in standards promulgated by multistakeholder initiatives as well; for example, Standard 2.5, Aluminum Stewardship Initiative, *ASI Performance Standard V3*, 2022, 11.

[17]   James Harrison, "Human Rights Measurement: Reflections on the Current Practice and Future Potential of Human Rights Impact Assessment," *Journal of Human Rights Practice* 3, no. 2 (July 2011): 162–187.

[18]   UN Guiding Principles.

[19]   UN Guiding Principles, Principle 17.

[20]   Leonard Ortolano, *Environmental Regulation and Impact Assessment* (New York: Wiley, 1997), 1–604.

[21]   Salcito, "Assessing Human Rights Impacts in Corporate Development Projects."

ment for due diligence must be part of an ongoing process, not a one-time, *ex ante* analysis.

CONDUCTING A HUMAN RIGHTS IMPACT ASSESSMENT

Because most corporations lack appropriate in-house human rights expertise, a HRIA, like most other impact assessments and some human rights due diligence, is usually conducted by expert consultants paid by the company. For all impact assessments, this presents the problem of bias, particularly when the consultants are dependent on companies for their livelihood.[22] Some consultants build reputations for independence and scientific rigor to rebut any implications of bias. In other circumstances, regulation, transparency, and the involvement of civil society commenting publicly on the assessment can protect against bias. For HRIA, in which reliable data is the basis for only a part of the analysis and subjective judgment is an unavoidable component, bias is a fundamental and critical problem. If HRIAs are performed with pro-company bias, they can be a form of human rights "greenwashing," hiding harmful actions behind the appearance of validated respect for human rights.

A company's human rights impacts are of interest to the local community, the government, and society generally. As such, there have been HRIAs performed by non-governmental organizations (NGOs) supporting local communities and by independent organizations.[23] Community- and NGO-led HRIAs are also subject to claims of bias, and anti-company sentiment embedded in a HRIA can have a delegitimizing effect. Companies frequently dismiss these HRIAs as baseless attacks.[24] Community- and NGO-led HRIAs often have the advantage of being public assessments that can open needed policy debates.[25]

---

[22] David Hulme, "Impact Assessment Methodologies for Microfinance: Theory, Experience and Better Practice," *World Development* 28, no. 1 (January 2000): 79–98.

[23] See, for example, "Community-Based Human Rights Impact Assessment Initiative," Oxfam America, accessed July 20, 2022, https://policy-practice .oxfamamerica.org/work/private-sector-engagement/community-based-human-rights -impact-assessment-initiative; "Work," NomoGaia, accessed July 20, 2022, http:// nomogaia.org/work.

[24] See, for example, the corporate responses to the Misereor-funded HRIA of the Tampakan Copper Mine in the Philippines, "Human Rights Impact Assessment of Tampakan Copper-Gold Project, Mindanao, Philippines," Business & Human Rights Resource Centre, accessed July 20, 2022, https://www.business-humanrights.org/ en/latest-news/human-rights-impact-assessment-of-tampakan-copper-gold-project -mindanao-philippines.

[25] Kaitlin Y. Cordes, Sam Szoke-Burke, and Tulika Bansal, "Collaborative and Participatory Approaches to HRIA: The Way Forward?" in *Handbook on Human*

HRIAs generally identify which human rights are considered in the assessment. Some include the full set of human rights (the International Bill of Rights plus the ILO core conventions, at a minimum) covered by the UNGPs.[26] Others explicitly limit themselves to specific rights.[27] For example, some HRIAs focus on the right to water, the right to security of person, or the right to health. HRIAs identify the rightsholders whose rights are being impacted. For example, the right to health may be affected by an unsafe work environment, where the employees are the rightsholders, or it may be affected by environmental pollution, in which case downstream water users are the affected rightsholders. HRIAs also articulate the degree and extent of the human rights impact. For example, a plantation that relocates a village impacts a variety of rights for the people relocated. The severity of those impacts depends on the provisions made for the relocated population. Some HRIAs consider positive impacts as well as negative ones. This is not required by the UNGPs for human rights due diligence but is considered by some to be necessary to fully understand the actual human rights impacts.[28] HRIAs also include concrete recommendations for changes in the design or management of the corporate project, as well as monitoring and follow-up to consider new impacts during the life of the project and to determine if the recommended actions have been carried out and are having the desired effect.

Rights Impact Assessment, ed. Nora Gotzman (Cheltenham: Edward Elgar, 2019), 66–83.

[26]   See, for example, Mark Wielga, Kendyl Salcito, and Elizabeth Wise, *Paladin Energy Human Rights Impact Assessment: Kayelekera Uranium Project of Karonga District, North Malawi* (Denver, CO: NomoGaia, 2010); LKL International Consulting Inc., *Human Rights Impact Assessment of the Bisha Mine in Eritrea* (Quebec: LKL International Consulting, 2014); Kuoni Travel Holding Ltd., TwentyFifty Ltd, and Tourism Concern, *Assessing Human Rights Impacts – Kenya Pilot Project Report*, November 2012 (Zurich: Kuoni, 2012).

[27]   Gillian MacNaughton and P. Hunt, "Health Impact Assessment: The Contribution of the Right to the Highest Attainable Standard of Health," *Public Health* 123, no. 4 (April 2009): 302–305; Gino Costa, *Comprehensive Review of Minera Yanacocha's Policies Based on the Voluntary Principles of Security and Human Rights* (Denver, CO: Newmont Mining, 2009).

[28]   Lloyd Lipsett and Mark Wielga, "Kick-Starting Human Rights Due Diligence: The Role of Human Rights Impact Assessment," *Mineral Law Series: Rocky Mountain Mineral Law Foundation Journal* no. 2 (2016).

HUMAN RIGHTS IMPACT ASSESSMENT METHODOLOGY

While no single, generally accepted methodology for HRIA exists, all the available methodologies include common elements.[29] First, there is a need to understand the human rights context in which the corporate project exists. A business operation in Myanmar will have completely different human rights impacts from an identical operation in Sweden. Issues particular to the place must be considered. This includes such topics as Indigenous Peoples' claims to a specific parcel of land or resource; whether the area is, or has recently been, a conflict zone; whether high HIV rates affect local populations; etc. Government repression and rights fulfillment must be considered along with the status of locally marginalized minorities. Labor plays a central role in business and human rights, and so labor issues, including salaries, working conditions, and the strength of unions, are considered. The environmental impacts of a corporate project may also have a bearing on the rightsholders' physical environment and health. Human rights impact assessments are interdisciplinary and require inputs from many different areas of expertise.[30] Methodologies differ in how the information is gathered and judgments are derived from various experts in specific disciplines. Good practice requires that rightsholders themselves are directly engaged, although many HRIAs fail to do this.[31]

TRANSPARENCY

Established impact assessments, particularly environmental impact assessments (EIAs), are often legally mandated and entirely public. A common component of EIA legislation is that the public is fully informed of the impacts and can comment. This was one method of identifying (or validating) the scope of impacts and generating strategies for reduction and mitigation of impacts.

The lack of transparency currently characterizing most HRIAs profoundly affects their credibility and effectiveness. Currently, no country's law requires an HRIA as such to be performed or mandates a public notice and comment process for them. Most companies keep confidential the human rights impact assessments prepared for them. This practice prohibits public scrutiny and

---

[29] Nora Gotzmann, *Handbook on Human Rights Impact Assessment*, 2–27.
[30] Nora Gotzmann, *Handbook on Human Rights Impact Assessment*, 319–335.
[31] Alejandro Gonzales, Tamar Aryrikyan, and Benjamin Cokelet, *Evaluating the Human Rights Impact of Investment Projects: Background, Best Practices, and Opportunities* (New York: Project Poder, 2014), 5–84.

exacerbates the claims of bias in their preparation. The HRIAs that have been made public are the exception rather than the rule. In some cases (for example, Nevsun's HRIA on its mine in Eritrea), the company intentionally made the HRIA public and claimed that its transparency was advantageous in a subsequent dispute and lawsuit. Other companies do not make their HRIAs public but publish summary descriptions of them (for example, Nestlé). (See Teaching Resources below.)

TEACHING APPROACHES

For teaching business and human rights, HRIAs are a useful a real-world source of BHR issues described in a detailed, comprehensive manner. To students, BHR can often seem theoretical. HRIAs can add detail to the concepts and the consideration of broad human rights principles applied to specific cases. This is usually the most effective use of HRIA in teaching. For more advanced students and courses, HRIA methods can be compared and critiqued to understand what effective human rights due diligence really means and does. Because of the variety of teaching uses described below, HRIA is a subject that can fit in a BHR course at various stages, but it most often comes in after introductory materials on the UNGPs and human rights due diligence. Some teachers use one or two HRIAs as examples that can be referred to repeatedly during the course. Others use an HRIA as a capstone summarizing the course as a whole and applying the ideas taught to a real setting. Still others have a standalone segment on HRIA methodology with a practical exercise attempting to prepare a simplified HRIA on a given set of facts or (role playing) informants. (See Exercise 9.2: Conducting a Human Rights Impact Assessment for a Mega-Sporting Event.)

The HRIA examples listed (see Teaching Resources below) vary in their usefulness for teachers. Some were early-stage, extremely general HRIAs performed when methodologies were not yet fully developed. Some are so lengthy and detailed that they may take too much class time to absorb. Teachers may pick one or two HRIAs to focus on.

How HRIAs are carried out goes to the heart of BHR. There may be questions of legitimacy regarding the company's influence over how they were performed and who prepared them. Community- and NGO-led HRIAs can be compared to the company-led HRIAs. Generally, governments and academia have not conducted HRIAs on their own, but the advantages of doing so can be discussed and debated. Bias is a fundamental problem for HRIAs. Classes can consider whether it is possible for HRIAs to be neutral, or whether they inevitably reflect a bias that undermines their conclusions.

HRIAs are useful for exploring the question of the practicality and efficacy of human rights due diligence. Are human rights too many and too complex to be adequately covered in one assessment? Can one analysis effectively cover issues as diverse as freedom of speech, the strength of unions, and health care? Can vague human rights standards be usefully applied to complex, nuanced conditions? What does the right to housing mean in an area where traditional homes are small, and made from forest materials? What does the right to a living wage mean in a location where most everyone is a subsistence farmer or petty trader living in extreme poverty by international standards? When does on-the-job training respect the right to education for employees who grew up during a conflict that effectively shut down the school system? Is a company respecting rights when no women even bother to apply for jobs? These concrete questions can lead to fruitful discussions in BHR classes often devoted to systems and theory.

Learning objectives may include:

- Engagement with a real-world example of businesses and human rights and what it really means in practice.
- Understanding human rights due diligence as required by the UNGPs.
- Appreciating the complexities and effort required to consider the full set of human rights as required by the UNGPs.
- Understanding the difficulties of applying human rights standard to actual situations.
- Recognizing the value of applying a "human rights lens" to business activity.
- Experiencing human rights enquiry on a well-developed fact situation.

EXERCISE 9.1

HUMAN RIGHTS IMPACT ASSESSMENT

Some BHR courses include segments in which the students perform their own human rights assessments. They are given materials, or conduct research, on corporate operations. To make these exercises feasible, a small group of students can be given one set of rights (labor rights, for example) and investigate how those rights apply to the operation.

One teaching technique is a **verbal group investigation**. This begins with the statement of a scenario – a corporate operation and a setting. The scenario can use a real project or a stylized amalgamation of real projects. The teacher or a guest speaker can act as a representative of the corporation with deep knowledge about the operation. The class then has an extensive question-and-answer session with the speaker trying to uncover and assess human rights issues. While some issues will be immediately apparent, the exercise can be designed so that other issues will only be apparent after thoughtful questioning and follow-up. A more elaborate version of this exercise has the class jointly interview a representative of the company, and then representatives of the community, the government, and an opposition NGO as well. In the mix of information, some of which is contradictory, the students can appreciate the challenge of conducting human rights assessments. This exercise can be based on an actual HRIA and, after it is completed, the students can be shown the HRIA.

KEY QUESTIONS

General

- What are the essential components of a HRIA?
- How are HRIAs different from human rights due diligence?
- Who should conduct a HRIA?
- How do companies use HRIAs?
- When should a HRIA be conducted?

For Business Students

- What should a company's human rights policy say about HRIAs?
- Should a company make its HRIAs public?
- What should a company say about its non-public HRIAs?
- Which corporate department should be responsible for commissioning and overseeing HRIAs?
- Which corporate department should be responsible for acting on the recommendations in an HRIA?
- How does HRIA relate to enterprise risk management?
- Should a lender commission, or require its borrower to commission, HRIAs?
- Should a project finance lender commission, or require its borrower to commission, HRIAs?
- Should HRIAs be performed in connection with a merger or acquisition?

For Law Students

- Why would a company have a HRIA performed?
- Can HRIAs create legal liability?
- How can HRIAs reduce legal liability?

- Should HRIAs be confidential and, if so, to what extent?
- Should HRIAs be covered by the attorney–client privilege?
- Does an HRIA fulfill the UNGPs' requirement of corporate human rights due diligence?

For Policy Students

- Should governments mandate HRIAs? If so, in what circumstances?
- Should government require HRIAs to be public?
- Should government shield companies from liability in order to promote public HRIAs?
- Is the traditional impact assessment model, where the government approves consultants who are then hired by the company, appropriate for HRIAs?
- Who are the sponsors of the most effective HRIAs, companies, governments, or NGOs/communities?
- Should governments perform HRIAs on corporate projects?

TEACHING RESOURCES

Readings

The best overall resource on this topic is:

- Gotzmann, Nora, ed. *Handbook on Human Rights Impact Assessment.* Cheltenham: Edward Elgar, 2019.

A short, clear summary of the HRIAs, written for businesspeople but useful as an introduction for students, is:

- Triponel Consulting *Human Right Impact Assessment: What, Why and How?* Accessed July 26, 2022. https://triponelconsulting.com/2017/11/28/human-rights-impact-assessments-what-why-and-how.

Methods

- Danish Institute for Human Rights. "Human Rights Impact Assessment Guidance and Toolbox." Accessed July 26, 2022. https://www.humanrights.dk/tools/human-rights-impact-assessment-guidance-toolbox. This resource contains a wealth of information on HRIA definitions, values, methodology and case studies for teachers and students.
- NomoGaia. "NomoGaia HRIA Methodology." NomoGaia HRIA Methodology Tool. Accessed July 26, 2022. http://nomogaia.org/human

-rights-impact-assessment-hria/methodology. This is an in-depth presentation of HRIA methods that have been applied in the field.

HRIAs

- Durex & Enfa (Reckitt Benckiser Brands) Value Chains (2020). *Human Rights Impact Assessment – Durex and Enfa Value Chains in Thailand.* Copenhagen: Danish Institute for Human Rights, 2020.
- Facebook (2018). BSR. *Human Rights Impact Assessment: Facebook in Myanmar.* 2018.
- FIFA for United Bid 2026 (2018). Ergon Associates. *Independent Report: Human Rights in Canada, Mexico and the USA in the context of a potential FIFA 2026 World Cup Competition.* 2018.
- Nestlé (2014). The Danish Institute for Human Rights. *Talking the Human Rights Walk: Nestlé's Experience in Assessing Human Rights Impacts in Its Business Activities.* Danish Institute for Human Rights, 2018.
- Nevsun Resources (2014). LKL International Consulting Inc. *Human Rights Impact Assessment of the Bisha Mine in Eritrea. Commissioned by Nevsun Resources Ltd.* 2014.
- Nevsun Resources (2015). LKL International Consulting Inc. *Human Rights Impact Assessment of the Bisha Mine in Eritrea 2015 Audit.* Commissioned by Nevsun Resources Ltd. and Eritrian National Mining Corporation. 2015.
- Total (2019). *Papua LNG Human Rights Impact Assessment: Focus on Gender, Security and Conflict.* Danish Institute for Human Rights, 2019.

Websites

- Nomogaia, http://nomogaia.org.
- Nomogaia."Community- or NGO-Led HRIAs." Accessed July 22, 2022, http://nomogaia.org/community-led-hrias. (Includes HRIAs performed by non-company actors as well as reviews and critiques of company-led assessments.)
- Nomogaia. "Corporate HRIAs." Accessed July 22, 2022, http://nomogaia.org/corporate-hrias. (A comprehensive and up-to-date list of HRIAs with links to the HRIAs themselves.)

EXERCISE 9.2

CONDUCTING A HUMAN RIGHTS IMPACT ASSESSMENT

FOR A MEGA-SPORTING EVENT

Anthony Ewing

BACKGROUND

This BHR exercise uses a well-known mega-sporting event – the FIFA World Cup – to illustrate and apply key considerations for conducting a human rights impact assessment from the perspective of different stake-holders. BHR teachers can prepare students for this in-class exercise by as-signing background readings on human rights due diligence, human rights impact assessments, and mega-sporting events generally.[32] While I used this fact pattern in the lead-up to the 2022 FIFA World Cup in Qatar, the exercise could be customized for any upcoming major sporting event.

EXERCISE

Ask students to consider the components for a human rights impact as-sessment of the 2022 FIFA World Cup in Qatar. Distribute the following background information (the timeframe for this **hypothetical** exercise was originally 2017):

- In 2010, FIFA awarded the 2022 World Cup (the quadrennial inter-national men's football championship of at least 32 national teams) to Qatar. The tournament will be played from 21 November to 18 December 2022 (to avoid the summer heat between May and September); 86,000 fans are expected to attend the opening ceremony at the Lusail Stadium, and billions will watch the tournament worldwide.
- Major FIFA sponsors include the multinational companies Adidas, Visa, Hyundai, and Coca-Cola. The last World Cup (Russia, 2018) generated an estimated $6 billion in revenue.
- Seven new stadiums have been built for the tournament. Additional construction projects include a new airport, roads, and hotels.

---

[32] See the Teaching Resources for the chapters on Human Rights Due Diligence, Human Rights Impact Assessment, and Sports and Human Rights.

- Amnesty International has accused Qatar of widespread labor abuses, including the use of forced labor and restrictions on freedom of movement. Human rights advocates have highlighted the persistence of Qatar's "Kafala" system of sponsorship-based employment, which legally binds foreign workers to their employers, restricting all workers' ability to change jobs and preventing many from leaving the country without their employers' permission.[33]
- FIFA adopted a Human Rights Policy in 2017.[34] (I have provided excerpts of the Policy and/or encouraged students to refer to it during the exercise.)
- According to the U.S. Department of State's 2017 Human Rights Report on Qatar: "The most significant human rights issues included restrictions on freedoms of speech and press, including criminalization of libel; restrictions on assembly and association, including prohibitions on political parties and labor unions; restrictions on the freedom of movement for migrant workers' travel abroad; limits on the ability of citizens to choose their government in free and fair elections; and criminalization of male same sex sexual activity. There were reports of forced labor that the government made efforts to eliminate."[35]
- *The Guardian* reported in 2021 that more than 6,500 migrant workers have died in Qatar since 2010.[36]
- The Government of Qatar has expressed a commitment to align its laws and practices with international labor standards and fundamental principles and rights at work. Qatar has recently ratified the International Covenant on Civil and Political Rights (ICCPR) and the International Covenant on Economic, Social and Cultural Rights (ICESCR), albeit with reservations – refusing to fully recognize equal rights for women

---

[33]   Amnesty International, "Reality Check: Migrant Worker Rights with Four Years to Qatar 2022 World Cup," (February 2019), https://www.amnesty.org/en/latest/campaigns/2019/02/reality-check-migrant-workers-rights-with-four-years-to-qatar-2022-world-cup. Other civil society organizations have made similar allegations. In October 2019, the Qatari Labour Ministry committed to abolish the kafala (sponsorship) system.

[34]   Fédération Internationale de Football Association, *FIFA's Human Rights Policy* (Zurich, May 2017), https://digitalhub.fifa.com/m/1a876c66a3f0498d/original/kr05dqyhwr1uhqy2lh6r-pdf.pdf.

[35]   U.S. Department of State, "Qatar," Country Human Rights Reports (2017), https://www.state.gov/documents/organization/277505.pdf.

[36]   "Revealed: 6,500 Migrant Workers Have Died in Qatar Since World Cup Awarded," *The Guardian*, February 23, 2021), https://www.theguardian.com/global-development/2021/feb/23/revealed-migrant-worker-deaths-qatar-fifa-world-cup-2022.

(in matters of personal laws such as inheritance); interpreting the term "punishment" in line with the Islamic Sharia (maintaining the death penalty and corporal punishment for crimes including murder, banditry, and adultery); and allowing only Qatari nationals to form associations and trade unions.

Divide the class into groups and assign each group one of the following stakeholder groups:
(1) Fans and athletes;
(2) Workers;
(3) Local communities;
(4) Journalists; and
(5) Human rights defenders.

Ask each group to consider the following questions from the perspective of their assigned stakeholder group:
(1) **What are the actual or potential human rights impacts of the event?**
(2) **How can due diligence be carried out to identify impacts on rightsholders? What would due diligence look like?**
(3) **Based on the results of a human rights impacts assessment, what actions can be taken by FIFA (alone or together with other actors) to prevent, mitigate, or remedy human rights impacts?**

I typically ask each group to record their answers to these questions in the form of a chart with three columns. By mapping human rights impacts to what due diligence looks like, and to what the organization might do as a result, students can build a full picture of a hypothetical human rights impact assessment focused on one rightsholder group.

Rightsholder group: [ ]

Human rights impacts	Due diligence/indicators	Potential actions
• [List]		

Each group can share their resulting chart with the full class. For example:
Rightsholder group: *Human rights defenders*

Human rights impacts	Due diligence/indicators	Potential actions
• Physical safety • Criminal prosecutions • Harassment • Freedom of speech • Freedom of movement/assembly • Forced disappearance/deportation	• Mapping historic human rights issues • Identifying stakeholders and rightsholders • Stakeholder engagement (interviews with international human rights groups, government officials, etc.) • Identify partnership opportunities (e.g. with sponsor brands in ensuring human rights are respected)	• Engage host country government • Leverage the willingness of the host government to align their laws and practices with international standards • Work with human rights defenders on when and how to advocate based on these risks • Education/training on potential issues • Establish a mechanism to handle grievances • Consider increasing security • Conduct an after-action human rights impact assessment

Teachers can ask each group to report on the discussion that led to their identification of specific human rights impacts, which impacts they consider to be the most "salient,"[37] and how they would prioritize next steps.

After each group has shared their chart, a productive exercise that mirrors the challenges faced by BHR practitioners is to ask the full class: "You have limited resources (financial, human, time) to conduct this impact assessment and act on it. Given all the potential human rights impacts identified for all rightsholder groups, which **three** (but only three) would you prioritize for action? Why?"

---

[37]   The human rights at risk of the most severe negative impact through the company's activities or business relationships. Shift and Mazars LLP, *UN Guiding Principles Reporting Framework* (2015); Caroline Rees and Rachel Davis, "Salient Human Rights Issues," in Dorothée Baumann-Pauly and Justine Nolan, eds., *Business and Human Rights: From Principles to Practice* (London: Routledge, 2016), 103–106.

10. Non-governmental human rights grievance mechanisms

Mark Wielga

OVERVIEW

How does a rightsholder remedy a human rights violation resulting from corporate action? The answer should address government processes, such as court systems. (See Judicial Remedy, Chapter 12.) But there are also complaint mechanisms that do not rely on governments and purport to provide rightsholders with remedies. An analysis of these is necessary for business and human rights (BHR) students to understand whether, when, and to what extent rightsholders obtain remedies for human rights infringements they experience. (See Right to Remedy, Chapter 6.)

The third pillar of the UN Guiding Principles on Business and Human Rights (UNGPs) addresses "Access to Remedy,"[1] requiring companies, individually and in collaborative initiatives, to establish or participate in effective grievance mechanisms to provide access to remedies for violation of human rights related to business activities.[2] (See The UN Guiding Principles on Business and Human Rights, Chapter 5.)

Mechanisms that provide access to remedy can be:

(1) Governmental/judicial (laws enforced by courts or administrative bodies);
(2) Governmental/non-judicial (bodies or processes created by agreement among nation states or by a non-judicial government entity within a state); or

---

[1] United Nations Human Rights Council, *Guiding Principles on Business and Human Rights: Implementing the United Nations "Protect, Respect and Remedy" Framework*, Report of the Special Representative of the Secretary-General on the issue of human rights and transnational corporations and other business enterprises, UN doc. A/HRC/17/31 (March 21, 2011) (UN Guiding Principles).
[2] *Id.*

(3)   Non-governmental (private mechanisms in which companies participate voluntarily).

This chapter focuses on teaching non-governmental human rights grievance mechanisms, the third category that includes grievance mechanisms administered by multistakeholder initiatives (MSIs), in which corporations are members. (See Multistakeholder Human Rights Initiatives, Chapter 16.) Development banks' complaint mechanisms are also included in this category recognizing them as separate from government-run mechanisms, despite the fact they are created by governments.[3] The last main component in this group are company-run complaint mechanisms, which accept internal claims by employees and external claims by communities either company-wide or at an operational level, as well as those in the company's supply chain.

Principle 31 of the UNGPs seeks to "provide a benchmark for designing, revising or assessing a non-judicial grievance mechanism to help ensure that it is effective in practice."[4] According to these criteria, non-judicial grievance mechanisms should be legitimate, accessible, predictable, equitable, transparent, rights-compatible, and a source of continuous learning. These procedural characteristics have been a focus for evaluating whether non-governmental grievance mechanisms are providing effective remedies.[5]

MULTISTAKEHOLDER INITIATIVE GRIEVANCE MECHANISMS[6]

MSI Integrity's Multi-Stakeholder Initiative Database found only a few MSIs that have complaint mechanisms that publicly report specific information

---

[3]   The Office of the High Commissioner for Human Rights has a multi-phase Accountability and Remedy Project. Phase III of that work addresses non-state-based grievance mechanisms in cases of business-related human rights abuse. It includes development finance accountability mechanisms. See "OHCHR Accountability and Remedy Project III: Enhancing Effectiveness of Non-State-Based Grievance Mechanisms in Cases of Business-Related Human Rights Abuse," accessed July 26, 2022, Office of the High Commissioner for Human Rights, https://www.ohchr.org/EN/Issues/Business/Pages/ARP_III.aspx#:~:text=The%20OHCHR%20Accountability%20and%20Remedy,on%20each%20phase%20of%20ARP.

[4]   UN Guiding Principles, Commentary to Principle 31.

[5]   In the discussion below, "claimants" refers to the people or entities who bring the claim and "respondents" refers to the parties (here, usually a company) that are the subject of the claim and against whom the claim is brought. "Claim" and "complaint" are used interchangeably.

[6]   Multistakeholder human rights initiatives are discussed in more detail in Chapter 16.

on the claims.[7] Almost all published claims are reported by the Fair Labor Association (FLA) (apparel supply chains), Fair Wear Foundation (apparel supply chains), Bangladesh Accord (apparel manufacturing in Bangladesh), Forest Stewardship Council (lumber), or Roundtable for Sustainable Palm Oil (palm oil) (RSPO).[8] (See Teaching Resources below.) Obviously, these cover only a few industries and are far from representing a comprehensive system. There are also a number of MSIs with complaint mechanisms that have yet to take a claim to conclusion (for example, Bonsurco (sugarcane supply chain) and the Aluminum Stewardship Initiative (aluminum supply chain)).[9]

The number of human rights claims differ greatly for these MSIs, from fewer than a dozen for the Forest Stewardship Council to fewer than a hundred for the RSPO and FLA, and to fewer than a thousand handled by the Fair Wear Foundation and the Bangladesh Accord. But a "claim" is not a unit of standard size: multiple large communities involving thousands of people can file one claim, as can a single worker who was denied one bonus payment.

Claims handled by MSIs must be tied to the industry involved and must address violations of their standards. So, the complaints addressed by the FLA, Bangladesh Accord, and Fair Wear Foundation deal with labor rights in apparel factories, such as coerced excessive overtime and barriers to unionization, while the RSPO can deal with rights to land used for plantations or pollution from mills. MSI mechanisms handle some kinds of human rights claims as well as other non-human rights issues, such as the improper use of certification marks.

DEVELOPMENT BANK GRIEVANCE MECHANISMS

Like MSIs, many development finance institutions have complaint mechanisms that sometimes consider human rights claims. Development finance institutions are normally funded by governments and provide loans and other investments and financial instruments to promote the development of

---

[7]   MSI Integrity and Duke Human Rights Center, *The New Regulators? Assessing the Landscape of Multi-Stakeholder Initiatives* (2017). See "The MSI Database," MSI Integrity, accessed July 26, 2022, https://msi-database.org/database.

[8]   James Harrison and Mark Wielga, "Grievance Mechanisms in Multi-Stakeholder Initiatives: Providing Effective Remedy for Human Rights Violations?" *Business and Human Rights Journal* (2023): 1–23.

[9]   "Bonsucro Grievance Mechanism," Bonsucro, accessed July 20, 2022, https://www.bonsucro.com/complaints-and-grievances/bonsucro-grievance-mechanism/#:~:text=The%20Bonsucro%20Grievance%20Mechanism%20is,with%20the%20Bonsucro%20Grievance%20Mechanism; "ASI Complaints Mechanism," Aluminium Stewardship Initiative, accessed July 20, 2022, https://aluminium-stewardship.org/asi-certification/asi-complaints-mechanism.

the beneficiary country. They often have an entity that provides financing to governments and a separate entity that provides loans to private businesses, but with the goal of developing the economy. The largest development finance institution is the World Bank, which supports governments, while its affiliate the International Finance Corporation (IFC) funds private companies. There are currently twenty-two so-called independent accountability mechanisms (IAMs),[10] which are mostly run by development banks (e.g., IFC, European Investment Bank, FMO (Dutch Development Bank), African Development Bank), along with other financial entities (e.g., JBIC (Japan's Import Export Bank), Green Climate Fund). Some of these mechanisms are government-based and others do not deal with business and human rights claims, so not all are non-governmental human rights grievance mechanisms. Available information about claims to these systems varies wildly, from the IFC's Compliance Advisor/Ombudsman (CAO) having a vast, detailed library of information to others that provide virtually no information. (See Teaching Resources below.)

Claims can be made to the IAMs alleging that the lending institutions standards have not been carried out by the company-borrower or which simply "raise social or environmental issues."[11] Generally, these mechanisms are rather flexible as to the type of claim brought, as long as harm is alleged to have resulted from their financing of a corporate project. Many, but not all, of the claims made to IAMs allege human rights violations.

Following the lead of the IFC's CAO, most of the IAMs have a form of mediation with the claimant, bank, and borrower, to try to resolve the complaint. In the IFC's own words: "CAO does not make a judgment about the merits of a complaint, nor does it impose solutions or find fault. Its objective is to help the parties play a lead role in identifying and implementing their own solutions."[12] If that is successful, the claimant can receive some form of remediation agreed upon by the borrower company. If it is not successful, the bank investigates whether and how the bank failed to police its standards. The result of this can be a useful critique of the bank's process with the potential for future improvement, a result that may help the bank but provides no remedy for the aggrieved rightsholders.

The Dutch (FMO), German (DEG), and French (Proparco) development banks share a complaint mechanism (the Independent Complaints

---

[10]   See IAMnet (Independent Accountability Mechanisms Network), https://lnadbg5 .adb.org/ocrp002p.nsf.

[11]   "Compliance Advisor Ombudsman." Office of the Compliance Advisor Ombudsman, last modified in 2009. http://www.cao-ombudsman.org/howwework/ ombudsman.

[12]   *Id.*

Mechanism), which can be used by any party adversely affected by a project financed by any of these institutions. This process was pioneered by FMO and includes an expert panel empowered to investigate claims in depth. Independent Complaints Mechanism detailed reports are a rich source of case study materials. (See Teaching Resources below.) This is one of the most elaborate development bank complaint mechanisms, but, as with all these systems, its effectiveness in providing remedy to claimants is open to debate.

COMPANY-RUN GRIEVANCE MECHANISMS

This type of complaint system breaks down into three general groups: "company-wide" complaint mechanisms, local "operational-level" complaint mechanisms, and mechanisms that cover the company's "supply chain." Company-wide mechanisms often consider complaints that include ethics, bribery, labor, and violations of a corporation's code of conduct. Some of these will be human rights violations but may not be stated in human rights terms. Claimants are normally employees or contractors. For example, there can be alleged violations of anti-discrimination and anti-sexual harassment (human rights) standards, but they may be labeled "human resources" claims with no explicit reference to human rights. Large, multinational companies often have standards (often called "codes of conduct") that apply company-wide and so extend across national boundaries. These standards can be enforced through complaints filed with the company's compliance, legal, or human resources departments.

Operational-level complaint mechanisms often consider claims from communities living near a corporate operation, such as a large refinery, plantation, or open-pit mine. They can include tort claims ("your Land Rover ran over my goat"), environmental claims ("dust from your trucks is blanketing our market"), or misconduct ("your security personnel threaten and intimidate us"). Many such systems have long been part of the community relations function of the local business operation but were not generally called human rights grievance mechanisms until recognized and prioritized as such by the UNGPs.[13] Private security employees or contractors responsible for protecting company personnel and property can be the subject of community complaints, which may be serious. The Voluntary Principles on Security and Human Rights and the International Code of Conduct for Private Security Service

---

[13] Operational-level grievance mechanisms are specially addressed in Principle 29. UN Guiding Principles, Principle 29.

Providers, which are the leading voluntary standards in this area, both require complaint mechanisms that cover human rights violations.[14]

Supply chain complaint mechanisms permit both complainants and respondents to be outside of the company. The company has the role of running the complaint mechanism and pressuring its suppliers to be responsive to it. The classic case would be that of an international brand receiving the claim of a worker in a supplier's factory. The brand has committed to labor standards throughout its supply chain so that it can claim that the products it sells are free from human rights violations. It then must manage a complaint system directed at labor violations in factories it does not own or run, but over which it may have significant leverage as an important buyer.

While company-led mechanisms are the most numerous and widespread type of non-governmental business and human rights complaint mechanism, there is an almost universal failure of transparency on the details of these claims, making them extremely difficult to uncover and to study.[15] Two have been made public and repeatedly studied. They were both created by one company (Barrick Gold, an international mining company) in Papua New Guinea and Tanzania in response to credible allegations of gross human rights violations. (See Teaching Resources below.) Occasionally, information about other complaint systems has become available, either through carefully controlled and edited corporate statements or in general accountants by researchers using limited public information, or aggregated data presented by consultants who worked on and in the system.[16]

There is one final non-governmental grievance mechanism that does not fit into any of the categories discussed above – complaint systems created by global framework agreements (also called "transnational framework agree-

[14]   "The Voluntary Principles," Voluntary Principles on Security and Human Rights, January 13, 2020. https://www.voluntaryprinciples.org/the-principles. "The Code – ICoCA – International Code of Conduct Association," ICoCA, accessed July 26, 2022, https://icoca.ch/the-code.
[15]   Ben Grama, "Company-Administered Grievance Processes for External Stakeholders: A Means for Effective Remedy, Community Relations, or Private Power?" *Wisconsin International Law Journal* 39, no. 1 (2022): 71.
[16]   An example of the first is Unilever's Palm Oil Grievance Tracker. See "First Half 2022 Results," Unilever, accessed July 26, 2022, https://www.unilever.com/Images/Unilever-Palm-Oil-Grievance-Tracker_tcm244-530071.pdf. An example of the second is chapter 4, "Company Mechanisms" (Adidas, Hewlett Packard, Goldcorp.), in *Corporate Accountability: The Role and Impact of Non-Judicial Grievance Mechanisms*, eds. Karin Lukas et al. (Cheltenham: Edward Elgar, 2014), 260–325. An example of the third is Laura Curtze and Steve Gibbons, *Access to Remedy: Operational Grievance Mechanisms. An Issues Paper for ETI. 2017*, https://www.ethicaltrade.org/sites/default/files/shared_resources/ergon_-_issues_paper_on_access_to_remedy_and_operational_grievance_mechanims_-_revised_draft.pdf.

ments"). These are agreements between multinational companies and multinational labor organizations to cover claims involving labor rights. These have mostly appeared in the European Union. It is not yet clear what role they will play as non-governmental human rights grievance mechanisms,[17] and so they will not be treated further in this chapter.

TEACHING APPROACHES

One goal of BHR courses is to locate non-governmental grievance mechanisms within the applicable governance systems (see Table 10.1). Grievance mechanisms are part of the UNGPs "Pillar III" (Access to Remedy). They are also part of the governance systems that create them, whether MSIs, development banks, or companies. There is a potential tension between these separate systems so that a grievance mechanism can police an MSI's standards or a corporation's code of conduct, yet completely fail to satisfy the substantive or procedural requirements of the UNGPs.

Another goal is to describe them accurately. Non-governmental human rights grievance mechanisms have a few essential elements:

(1) **Parties.** Who can bring a claim, who must respond to a claim, and what other parties must be involved in what capacity?

(2) **Scope.** What are the standards that have been violated? What kinds of claims can be brought?

(3) **Process.** Who determines what facts are true? How do they do that? Who determines whether the facts found to be true violate the applicable standards? How do they do that? What responsibility do the claimant and respondent have in the process? Is there an appeal process? What are the timelines for each step?

(4) **Remedy.** What are the kinds of remedies the mechanism can order? How does it effectuate its orders? Are the remedies provided sufficient to satisfy the claimants/rightsholders?

Non-governmental grievance mechanisms differ in all these elements. For example, a claim brought under the Roundtable for Sustainable Palm Oil, an MSI:

(1)   Can be brought by anyone harmed against a member company;

(2)   Must involve the violation of the RSPO Standards;

---

[17]   Hans-Wolfgang Platzer and Stefan Rüb, *International Framework Agreements: An Instrument for Enforcing Human Rights* (Berlin: Friedrich-Ebert-Stiftung, 2014).

Table 10.1   Elements of non-governmental grievance mechanisms

	Roundtable on Sustainable Palm Oil (RSPO)	International Finance Corporation (IFC)	Fair Labor Association (FLA)
Parties Claimants: Respondents:	• Anyone harmed by RSPO member company • Member company	• Anyone harmed by IFC finance project • IFC and borrower	• Any person or union harmed in a factory producing goods for a FLA member brand • The factory
Scope	Labor, environmental, community land, security forces	Any IFC Performance Standard, including labor, Indigenous rights	Labor
Process	Claim investigated and adjudicated by an RSPO committee. Party can supply detailed evidence and a third-party investigator can be appointed.	Mediation with IFC, borrower and claimant. If no agreement, detailed investigation by IFC and final report noting failures and making recommendations.	FLA member brand either does the investigation or hires a third-party investigator. Brand then monitors remediation. FLA monitors process and can intervene if needed.
Remedy	Actions to be performed by member companies, including stopping plantations from expanding onto community land, improving work conditions.	No remedy ordered, but claimant made obtain benefits through negotiations with borrower.	Actions to be performed by factory, including paying money owed, improving conditions, and rehiring workers.

(3)   Requires the parties to present facts to a Board selected from the members. (The Board can also send an investigator to determine the facts.)

(4)   Renders a formal decision determining if and how the RSPO standards have or have not been violated; and

(5)   Can result in a remedy being ordered. The remedies can include ordering the member company not to enter on and plant oil palms on a parcel of land or remedy labor abuses but cannot include ordering compensatory payments.

In contrast, for a claim to the IFC's CAO:

(1)   It can be brought by anyone harmed by financing, with the involvement of the company receiving the financing in a mediation run by the CAO;

(2)   It can be brought for any harm alleged to be caused by the financing;

(3)   There is a mediation discussion between the company financed and the claimants facilitated by the CAO to attempt to resolve the claim by set-

tlement. If that fails, the CAO does an investigation of whether the IFC has failed to follow its own standards;

(4)   If it has, the CAO makes recommendations to the IFC on how it can perform better in the future; and

(5)   No remedy is ordered to benefit the claimant.

Similar analyses can be done comparing different non-governmental grievance mechanisms to each other as well as to government-based grievance mechanisms.

Students, understandably, want to know "Do non-governmental grievance mechanisms work?" Answering this question should be a key goal for BHR teachers. Describing and placing them within the BHR context should not imply that they are effective. What it means for a complaint system to "work" (or "fail," in whole or in part) is a useful topic of discussion and analysis. Grievance mechanisms work in different ways for different ends. The Forest Stewardship Council, for example, puts a lot of effort into its complaint system, but the goal is to police its membership – it does not want members who are failing to live up to its standards and so a valid claim can result in a company losing its membership – not to provide remedy to rightsholders for past wrongs. The Fair Labor Association's system tends to deal with large-scale and systematic issues in claims brought by labor unions. The Fair Wear Foundation often deals with claims by individual workers for something as granular as one late paycheck (though it can also manage larger-scale claims). Each of these grievance mechanisms has a role to play but differs in what it is trying to achieve.

The "Do they work?" question involves component questions, such as:

(1)   What kind of claims from what kinds of claimants do the systems address (and which are left out)?

(2)   Are many legitimate claims never filed? Why?

(3)   Did rightsholders receive an effective remedy?

(4)   Are these grievance systems fair?

Finally, there is the structural question of the inherent limitations of human rights grievance mechanisms. These are all systems that companies participate in voluntarily. Under what circumstances will a company decide that the benefits of the system are outweighed by its disadvantages? For MSIs, the benefits of membership may be one way to measure the value of the worst possible sanction. The Roundtable on Sustainable Palm Oil complaint system had several cases in which the respondent company was found to have violated a standard, for example the duty to obtain community consent before incorporating community land into a palm oil plantation. Rather than comply with the remedy ordered, respondent companies left the RSPO (or sold the subject planation to a non-member company) and so entirely evaded the complaint system.[18] Presumably, the companies decided the benefits of membership and certification of their products were outweighed by the costs of providing a remedy in the case they lost.

The most obvious limitations exist for company-run complaint mechanisms. These systems are perceived by management to benefit the company, perhaps by making the company's code of conduct enforceable, perhaps by the early warning and investigation function a complaint mechanism can provide. For example, repeated claims of sexual harassment may indicate a toxic work environment, or a whistleblower reporting a bribe may be the first sign of a corrupt manager. Many rightsholder claimants, however, do not trust these systems, considering them rigged. The company is the defendant, the judge, the jury, and the enforcer. Such a system violates the most basic principles of justice. (See Right to Remedy, Chapter 6.) It is worth considering when and how such a system could be beneficial to rightsholders and when it would be incompatible with human rights values.

EXERCISE 10.1

INDIVIDUAL CLAIMS TO NON-GOVERNMENTAL

GRIEVANCE MECHANISMS

For teaching purposes, it can be a rich experience to look at individual claims made to these mechanisms and discuss the outcome, benefits, and frustrations. The Roundtable on Sustainable Palm Oil, for example, has an adversarial-type system (one in which the claimant and respondent submit facts and arguments). This makes for a ready-made, real case study and can be turned into a class exercise by assigning an individual or small group to play the role of the claimant, respondent, and decision-making body. The development banks' Independent Complaints Mechanism is inquisitorial, with the expert panel investigating how it wishes to find a reliable account of what occurred. This approach opens the possibility of allowing a group investigation with documents or data to request and review and (mock) witnesses to interview.

Another classroom role-playing exercise would involve creating a hy-

---

[18] Mark Wielga and James Harrison, "Assessing the Effectiveness of Non-State-Based Grievance Mechanisms in Providing Access to Remedy for Rightsholders: A Case Study of the Roundtable on Sustainable Palm Oil," *Business and Human Rights Journal* 6, no. 1 (February 2021): 80–82.

pothetical scenario and applying one of the complaint mechanisms to it. An individual or small group would play the part of the claimant, the respondent, and the decision maker within the complaint mechanism. The difficulty may be in determining who is right on the facts, applying the facts to the applicable standard, fashioning a meaningful remedy, or all of these. If time allows, the same claim with the same fact pattern can be made using the procedures of a different system and the two can be compared. This can reveal the stark differences between, for example, a company's operational-level complaint system and that of a development bank or MSI.

KEY QUESTIONS

General

- What kind of claims from what kinds of claimants do the systems address (and which are left out)?
- For the cases we can study, did rightsholders receive a remedy?
- What are the inherent limitations of these systems?
- Are these systems fair?
- Are the requirements of the UNGPs with respect to non-governmental remedy currently being fulfilled?

For Business Students

- In what circumstances should a company join an MSI with a complaint mechanism?
- Should a company have a company-wide complaint system for its code of conduct? If so, how should it be structured?
- Should a company create operational-level complaint mechanisms? If so, how should they be run? How would it differ by type of industry?
- Should a company participate in a supply chain complaint mechanism?

For Law Students

- Do non-governmental complaint mechanisms comply with due process?
- For a given non-governmental complaint mechanism, are the procedures more like an inquisitorial system or an adversarial system?
- What basic elements should a non-governmental complaint mechanism have?
- Do the rulings made by non-governmental complaint systems create liability?

- Can mediation systems provide remedy, or is an adjudicatory system needed for that?

For Policy Students

- Do the UNGPs give sufficient guidance to create rights respectful non-governmental complaint mechanisms? If not, how should that be remedied?
- Should the development bank complaint mechanisms be considered state-based, non-state-based, or a hybrid? What are the policy implications of that categorization?
- When and why can multiple complaint systems that overlap as to claimants and claims type be counterproductive?

TEACHING RESOURCES

Readings

- Office of the UN High Commissioner for Human Rights. "Accountability and Remedy Project, Phase III: Enhancing Effectiveness of Non-State-Based Grievance Mechanisms in Cases of Business-Related Human Rights Abuse." https://www.ohchr.org/EN/Issues/Business/Pages/ARP_III.aspx.

MSI grievance mechanism cases and documents

- Accord on Fire and Building Safety in Bangladesh. "Complaints filed with the Accord." https://bangladeshaccord.org/safety-complaints.
- Corporate Accountability Research. "Non-Judicial Redress Mechanisms Project Publications." https://corporateaccountabilityresearch.net/njm -project-publications.
- Fair Labor Association. "Third Party Complaint Tracking Chart." Updated June 15, 2022. https://www.fairlabor.org/third-party-complaint-tracking -chart.
- Fair Wear Foundation. "Complaints." https://fairwear.force.com/public/s/ complaints.
- Forest Stewardship Council. "Current Cases." https://fsc.org/en/ unacceptable-activities/cases.
- MSI Integrity. "Not Fit for Purpose: The Grand Experiment of Multi-Stakeholder Initiatives in Corporate Accountability, Human Rights and Global Governance." https://www.msi-integrity.org/not-fit-for -purpose.

- Roundtable for Sustainable Palm Oil. "Status of Complaints." https://askrspo.force.com/Complaint/s/casetracker.

Development bank grievance mechanisms

- Database: Claims Submitted to the Multilateral Development Bank Accountability Mechanism 1994–2022. https://susanmpark.com/database-multilateral-development-banks-accountability-mechanisms.
- DEG. "Independent Complaints Mechanism DEG." January 1, 2017. https://www.deginvest.de/DEG-Documents-in-English/About-us/Responsibility/170101_Independent-Complaints-Mechanism_DEG.pdf.
- IAMnet (Independent Accountability Mechanisms Network), https://lnadbg5.adb.org/ocrp002p.nsf. A central resource for all these mechanisms.
- IFC, Compliance Advisor Ombudsman. "Welcome to Cases Center." https://www.cao-ombudsman.org/cases. The IFC Compliance Advisor/Ombudsman has a searchable database of all its cases and makes all documents public. This is a massive resource.
- Independent Complaint Mechanism (used by the Dutch (FMO), German (DEG), and French (Proparco) Development Banks) and annual reports from the Independent Complaints Mechanism. FMO. "Independent Complaints Mechanism." https://www.fmo.nl/independent-complaints-mechanism.
- Proparco. "Environmental and Social Independent Complaints Mechanism." ICM. https://www.proparco.fr/en/icm.

Company grievance mechanisms

- Aftab, Yousuf. *Pillar III on the Ground: An Independent Assessment of the Porgera remedy Framework.* Enodo Rights, 2016. https://www.enodorights.com/assets/pdf/pillar-III-on-the-ground.pdf.
- Columbia Law School Human Rights Clinic and Harvard Law School International Human Rights Clinic. *Righting Wrongs? Barrick Gold's Remedy Mechanism for Sexual Violence in Papua New Guinea: Key Concerns and Lessons Learned.* 2015. http://www.rightingwrongsporgera.com.
- Grama, Ben. "Company-Administered Grievance Processes for External Stakeholders: A Means for Effective Remedy, Community Relations, or Private Power?" *Wisconsin International Law Journal* 39, no. 1 (January 2022): 71.
- International Commission of Jurists. *Effective Operational-Level Grievance Mechanisms.* Geneva: International Commission of Jurists, 2019.

https://www.icj.org/wp-content/uploads/2019/11/Universal-Grievance
-Mechanisms-Publications-Reports-Thematic-reports-2019-ENG.pdf.
- New England Law School, Center for International Law & Policy,
  "Operational-Level Grievance Mechanism Research Project." https://www
  .nesl.edu/practical-experiences/centers/center-for-international-law-and
  -policy/projects/operational-grievance-mechanisms-project.
- Rights and Accountability in Development. "Tanzanian Victims
  Commence Legal Action in UK against Barrick." *RAID*, February 10,
  2020.   https://www.raid-uk.org/blog/tanzanian-victims-commence-legal
  -action-uk-against-barrick.
- Rights and Accountability in Development. *Human Rights Violations
  Under Private Control: Acacia Mining's Grievance Mechanism and the
  Denial of Rights*. London: RAID, 2019. http://www.raid-uk.org/sites/
  default/files/raid_report_on_private_grievance_mechanisms_final_12_june
  _2019.pdf.

Teaching Cases

- Henderson, Rebecca and Nien-Hê Hsieh, *Putting the Guiding Principles
  into Action: Human Rights at Barrick Gold* (Harvard Business School Case
  No. 5-317-015, March 2015. Revised August 2020.

PART III

Corporate accountability

11. Mandatory human rights due diligence
Claire Bright and Nicolas Bueno

OVERVIEW

Since the United Nations Guiding Principles on Business and Human Rights (UNGPs) were unanimously endorsed by the UN Human Rights Council in 2011,[1] a growing number of laws seeking to implement them have been adopted at the domestic, regional, and international level. In particular, legislation requiring companies to exercise human rights due diligence (HRDD) has been proposed or adopted in multiple jurisdictions since 2017.

The study of mandatory HRDD legislation is particularly relevant in a business and human rights (BHR) course because it underlines the progressive move from soft law to hard law that the BHR field has undergone over the past decade. Originally framed as a moral or ethical responsibility arising out of social expectations, the corporate responsibility to respect human rights and the correlated responsibility for companies to exercise HRDD set out in the UNGPs is being crystallized into legislation, creating legally binding obligations for companies. Emerging legislation is also extending similar due diligence requirements to fields other than human rights, most notably through environmental due diligence. (See Human Rights Due Diligence, Chapter 8; Human Rights and the Environment, Chapter 19.)

This chapter surveys categories of HRDD legislation, highlights key HRDD laws and their features, and suggests approaches to teaching the topic.

---

[1] United Nations Human Rights Council, *Guiding Principles on Business and Human Rights: Implementing the United Nations "Protect, Respect and Remedy" Framework*, Report of the Special Representative of the Secretary-General on the issue of human rights and transnational corporations and other business enterprises, UN doc. A/HRC/17/31 (March 21, 2011) (UN Guiding Principles).

TYPES OF HUMAN RIGHTS DUE DILIGENCE LEGISLATION

As described in the UNGPs, HRDD refers to a continuous process that companies are expected to put in place in order to identify, prevent, mitigate, and account for how they address their impacts on human rights.[2] (See The UN Guiding Principles on Business and Human Rights, Chapter 5; Human Rights Due Diligence, Chapter 8.) It is helpful for BHR students to compare and contrast the different types of HRDD legislation. This chapter distinguishes mandatory human rights disclosure legislation (laws only requiring the disclosure of information relating to human rights) from mandatory HRDD legislation (laws requiring companies to exercise substantive human rights due diligence).

Mandatory Human Rights Disclosure Legislation

Several domestic laws require companies to disclose information concerning (or including) issues of human rights. Examples include the California Transparency in Supply Chains Act (2010), Section 1502 of the Dodd-Frank Act (2010), the European Union Directive 2014/95 on Disclosure of Non-Financial Information (2014), the U.K. Modern Slavery Act (2015), and the Australian Modern Slavery Act (2018).[3] The obligations prescribed by these laws are limited to corporate disclosure. Although they may contribute to spurring companies to conduct HRDD, mandatory disclosure laws are generally criticized for "lacking teeth." In addition, they only address one of the steps of the HRDD process as defined in the UNGPs, namely the communication element, by requiring companies to communicate externally on how they address their human rights impacts.[4] When teaching mandatory HRDD, it is therefore important to distinguish mandatory disclosure from HRDD.

---

[2]   UN Guiding Principles, Principle 17.
[3]   *California Transparency in Supply Chains Act*, CAL.CIV. CODE §1714.43; *The Dodd-Frank Wall Street Reform and Consumer Protection Act*, Pub. L. No. 111-203, 124 Stat. 1376 (United States, 2010); EU Directive 2014/95/EU of the European Parliament and of the Council of October 22, 2014 amending Directive 2013/34/EU as regards disclosure of non-financial and diversity information by certain large undertakings and groups, OJ 2014 No. L 330 (entered into force December 6, 2014); United Kingdom, *Modern Slavery Act 2015*, 30, cl. 54; Australia, *Modern Slavery Act 2018*, No. 153, 2018.
[4]   UN Guiding Principles, Principle 21.

Mandatory Human Rights Due Diligence Legislation

Several laws require corporations to exercise substantive human rights due diligence that goes beyond mere disclosure requirements. As presented in Table 11.1, mandatory HRDD laws vary in terms of scope of application (the companies covered and issues or sectors covered), due diligence requirements (how due diligence is defined and the reach of the obligation down the supply/ value chain), and enforcement mechanisms. There are two main categories of enforcement mechanisms: (1) public enforcement mechanisms and (2) judicial enforcement through a civil liability provision.[5] The distinction is important because in the first category, administrative or criminal sanctions are in place to ensure that companies comply with their HRDD obligations. However, public enforcement mechanisms do not ensure that affected individuals have access to effective remedy, which, in turn, fails to align with the third pillar of the UNGPs calling, inter alia, for state-based judicial mechanisms. (See Right to Remedy, Chapter 6.)

This section presents mandatory HRDD laws that have been adopted since the UNGPs in chronological order. It also includes the recent European Union (EU) Commission Proposal for a Directive on Corporate Sustainability Due Diligence that aims to create a standard on mandatory HRDD at the EU level.[6] When adopted, each EU Member State will have to adopt or revise its existing national legislation in order to implement it.

- The French Duty of Vigilance Law adopted in 2017 was the first legislation in the world to impose mandatory human rights due diligence obligations, crystallizing the UNGPs' expectations into hard law.[7] The law's purpose is twofold: (1) to enhance corporate accountability and (2) to provide access to remedy for individuals and communities whose human rights have been adversely affected by the activities of French companies or suppliers in their global supply chains.[8] The law requires large French companies to put in place, effectively implement, and publish a "vigilance plan" in order

---

[5]   Nicolas Bueno and Claire Bright, "Implementing Human Rights Due Diligence through Corporate Civil Liability," *International & Comparative Law Quarterly* 69, no 4 (2021): 789–818, https://doi.org/10.1017/S0020589320000305.

[6]   *Commission Proposal for a Directive of the European Parliament and of the Council on Corporate Sustainability Due Diligence and amending Directive (EU) 2019/1937*, COM(2022) 71 final (February 23, 2022).

[7]   French Duty of Vigilance Law 2017. See Sandra Cossart, Jérôme Chaplier, and Tiphaine Beau de Lomenie, "The French Law on Duty of Care: A Historic Step Towards Making Globalization Work for All," *Business and Human Rights Journal* 2, no. 2 (July 2017): 317–323.

[8]   Bueno and Bright, "Mapping Human Rights Due Diligence Regulations," 88.

to identify the risks and prevent severe violations of human rights and fundamental freedoms, health and safety, and the environment, including climate change.[9] Due diligence obligations apply with regard to the company's operations, operations of the companies it controls, and operations of subcontractors or suppliers with whom it maintains an established commercial relationship. The law provides for two judicial enforcement mechanisms. First, interested parties may seek an injunction with a French court (after having first addressed a formal notice to the company) to order the company to comply with the law, with periodic penalty payments in case of continued non-compliance. Second, the law expressly establishes civil liability mechanism whereby the company's failure to comply with its obligations gives rise to a damage on the basis of the general tort of negligence.[10] Unlike the mandatory human rights disclosure laws in the previous section that rely on a public enforcement mechanism, the French law offers a remediation mechanism for affected individuals seeking remedy. A number of cases have been brought on this basis and are currently pending before the French courts even though none have yet reached the merits stage.

- In 2017, the EU adopted the Conflict Minerals Regulation that contains specific supply chain due diligence obligations for importers of certain conflict minerals.[11] The Regulation expressly refers to the UNGPs. It sets specific obligations regarding management system, risk management, and third-party audits, as well as disclosure requirements.[12] The Regulation provides that each EU Member State shall designate a competent authority responsible for the applicable of the Regulation and carry out ex-post checks on EU importers.[13]

- The Dutch Child Labour Due Diligence Act was adopted in 2019.[14] The law is framed in terms of consumer protection, as its objective is to ensure consumers' "peace of mind."[15] To that end, the law requires companies selling goods or providing services to Dutch end-users to exercise human

---

[9] French Duty of Vigilance Law 2017, Art. 1 (French Commercial Code, Article L. 225-102-4).

[10] *Id.*, Art. 2 (French Commercial Code, Article L. 225-102-5).

[11] EU Regulation 2017/821 of May 17, 2017 (establishes supply chain due diligence obligations for EU importers of tin, tantalum, and tungsten; their ores; and gold originating from conflict-affected and high-risk areas).

[12] French Duty of Vigilance Law 2017, Arts. 4–7.

[13] *Id.*, Arts. 10 and 11.

[14] Dutch Child Labour Due Diligence Act 2019.

[15] Claire Bright, "Mapping Human Rights Due Diligence Regulations and Evaluating Their Contribution in Upholding Labour Standards in Global Supply Chains," in *Decent Work in Globalised Economy: Lessons from Public and Private*

rights due diligence in relation to child labor. More specifically, companies must investigate whether there is a "reasonable suspicion" that the goods that they sell or services that they provide have been produced with child labor. If so, a company must draw up and implement an action plan.[16] The Dutch law provides for a public supervising authority to monitor compliance that may issue administrative fines in cases of non-compliance. Criminal sanctions are also in place for repeat offenses.[17] Yet the law itself does not contain a specific corporate civil or criminal liability provision for the use of child labor. The Dutch Act has not yet entered into force.[18] After its adoption and following EU developments, the Dutch government has discussed a new Bill for Responsible and Sustainable International Business Conduct which would extend the due diligence obligations to cover all human rights, labor rights and environmental standards.[19] If adopted, the new law would repeal the Child Labour Due Diligence Act.

- In Switzerland, due diligence obligations for corporations relating to child labor and conflict minerals have been incorporated into the Swiss Code of Obligations[20] after the Swiss Responsible Business Initiative was rejected in November 2020.[21] The due diligence obligations apply to companies that import or process certain conflict minerals in Switzerland and to large companies that sell goods or services for which there exists a founded suspicion of child labor for their production. Companies must have in place a management system and adopt a supply chain policy as well as a tracing system in their supply chains. They must identify risks, elaborate a plan to manage risks, and take measures to reduce identified risks to the minimum. In terms of enforcement, the law requires companies to annually report on the implementation of their due diligence duties. Criminal sanctions are in place to ensure reporting on due diligence obligations.[22] In addition,

---

Initiatives, eds. Guillaume Delautre, Elizabeth Echeverría Manrique, and Colin Fenwick (Geneva: ILO, 2021), 85.

[16] Dutch Child Labour Due Diligence Act 2019, Arts. 3.1 and 5.1.

[17] *Id.*, Arts. 7 and 9.

[18] As of March 2022.

[19] Dutch Bill for Responsible and Sustainable International Business, unofficial translation available at https://www.mvoplatform.nl/en/wp-content/uploads/sites/6/2021/03/Bill-for-Responsible-and-Sustainable-International-Business-Conduct-unofficial-translation-MVO-Platform.pdf.

[20] Swiss Code of Obligations, Art. 964j to 964l, for the detail.

[21] Nicolas Bueno, "The Swiss Popular Initiative on Responsible Business: From Responsibility to Liability," in *Accountability, International Business Operations, and the Law*, eds. Liesbeth Enneking et al. (London: Routledge 2019), 239–258, https://doi.org/10.4324/9781351127165-12.

[22] Swiss Criminal Code, Art. 325.

an independent expert must verify that the company complies with its obligations in relation to conflict minerals. This obligation does not exist in relation to child labor. Enforcement mechanisms in this law have been criticized for being too weak by comparison of other existing laws.[23]

- In Germany, a baseline assessment revealed that only 13–17 percent of large companies exercised human rights due diligence in line with the German National Action Plan for Business and Human Rights.[24] As a result, the German government decided to put forward the Act on Corporate Due Diligence in Supply Chains, which was adopted in June 2021. The law requires large companies in Germany to exercise human rights due diligence and, to some extent, environmental due diligence. The due diligence obligation covers a list of human rights and environmental issues defined in the law.[25] The exercise of due diligence is limited to the company's own operations and to the activities of "direct" suppliers. With respect to "indirect" suppliers, a due diligence obligation exists only to the extent that the company obtains "substantiated knowledge" of a possible violation or is otherwise prompted by other circumstances.[26] In terms of enforcement, the law provides that the German Federal Office for Economic Affairs and Export Control is responsible for enforcing the law. Public authorities can investigate cases of non-compliance and issue fines.

- In June 2021, Norway adopted the Transparency Act.[27] The law places on large companies domiciled in Norway, as well as on companies selling goods and services into Norway, a duty to exercise due diligence in relation

---

[23] Nicolas Bueno and Christine Kaufmann, "The Swiss Human Rights Due Diligence Legislation: Between Law and Politics," *Business and Human Rights Journal* 6, no. 3 (October 2021): 542–549, https://doi.org/10.1017/bhj.2021.42.

[24] German Federal Foreign Office, *Monitoring the Status of Implementation of the Human Rights Due Diligence Obligations of Enterprises Set Out in the National Action Plan for Business and Human Rights 2016–2020 Final Report*, October 13, 2020, https://www.auswaertiges-amt.de/blob/2417212/9c8158fe4c737426fa4d721 7436accc7/201013-nap-monitoring-abschlussbericht-data.pdf.

[25] German Act on Supply Chain Due Diligence 2021, § 2. See Markus Krajewski, Kristel Tonstad, and Franziska Wohltmann, "Mandatory Human Rights Due Diligence in Germany and Norway: Stepping, or Striding, in the Same Direction?" *Business and Human Rights Journal* 6, no. 2 (2021): 550–558.

[26] German Act on Supply Chain Due Diligence 2021, § 9.

[27] Norwegian Transparency Act, 2022. Act on business transparency and work with fundamental human rights and decent work, Proposition 150 L (2020-2021), available (in Norwegian) at: https://www.regjeringen.no/contentassets/c33c3faf34044 1faa7388331a735f9d9/no/pdfs/prp202020210150000dddpdfs.pdf. For an unofficial English translation, see Lovdata, "Act Relating to Enterprises' Transparency and Work on Fundamental Human Rights and Decent Working Conditions (Transparency Act)," accessed July 26, 2022, https://lovdata.no/dokument/NLE/lov/2021-06-18-99.

to human rights and decent work, and to document the steps that they are taking. The draft law provides that the national consumer authority shall be responsible for providing guidance and monitoring compliance with the law and may impose penalties in case of non-compliance.

- In February 2022, the European Commission released its much-awaited Draft Directive on Sustainable Corporate Due Diligence.[28] According to the Draft Directive, Member States shall ensure that very large companies and large companies in "high-impact sectors" (defined as textile, agriculture, and minerals) that are established in the EU, or in third-country companies but operating in the EU,[29] conduct human rights and environmental due diligence.[30] The due diligence obligations cover the companies' own operations, the operations of their subsidiaries, and the operations of entities with whom they have an "established business relationships" within their value chain.[31] In terms of enforcement, EU Member States are required to establish supervisory authorities that have notably the power to carry out investigations and impose pecuniary sanctions.[32] In addition, the Draft Directive contains a civil liability provision under which EU Member States must ensure that companies are liable for damages if they fail to comply with their due diligence obligations and, as a result of this failure, an adverse impact occurs and leads to damage.[33] This is a fault-based regime and the burden of proof will normally fall on the claimant(s) to prove that they suffered a damage as a result of a breach of due diligence obligations by the company. In practice, this is likely to cause practical difficulties for affected individuals to access effective remedies. The provision also excludes liability for damages caused by *indirect* business partners when the company has sought contractual assurances unless it was unreasonable to expect that the action actually taken would be adequate to prevent, mitigate, bring to an end, or minimize the extent of the adverse impact.

---

[28] *Commission Proposal for a Directive of the European Parliament and of the Council on Corporate Sustainability Due Diligence and Amending Directive (EU) 2019/1937*, COM(2022) 71 final (February 23, 2022) (*EU Draft Directive*). The *EU Draft Directive* follows a March 2021 European Parliament resolution with recommendations to the European Commission on corporate due diligence and corporate accountability. European Parliament, Resolution of March 10, 2021 with recommendations to the Commission on corporate due diligence and corporate accountability.

[29] *EU Draft Directive*, Art. 2.

[30] *Id.*, Annex, for the specific list human rights and environmental obligations.

[31] *Id.*, Arts. 1 and 5–11, for the material elements of the due diligence obligation.

[32] *Id.*, Arts. 18 and 20.

[33] *Id.*, Art. 22.

Table 11.1   Mandatory human rights due diligence legislation (in chronological order)

Scope of application	Scope of due diligence			Enforcement	
Companies covered	Overarching issue/sector	Due diligence requirements	Scope of due diligence along the supply/value chain	Public enforcement	Civil liability
		FRENCH DUTY OF VIGILANCE LAW, 2017			
Large companies [incorporated or registered in France] >5000 employees in France or >10000 worldwide (art. 1)	Violations of human rights and fundamental freedoms, serious bodily injury or environmental damage or health risks (art. 1)	Establish, effectively implement, and publish a vigilance plan setting out the vigilance measures to identify risks and prevent serious violations. The vigilance plan must include: (1) a mapping of the risks involved; (2) procedures to regularly assess risks; (3) actions to mitigate risks and prevent serious harm; (4) a whistleblowing mechanism collecting reports of potential and actual risks and effects, drawn up in consultation with the company's representative trade unions; and (5) a mechanism to monitor measures that have been implemented and evaluate their effectiveness	Own operations and operations of controlled subsidiaries and of the subcontractors or suppliers with whom the company maintains an established commercial relationship (art. 1)		X (Art. 2)

	Scope of application		Scope of due diligence		Enforcement	
	Companies covered	Overarching issue/sector	Due diligence requirements	Scope of due diligence along the supply/value chain	Public enforcement	Civil liability
EU CONFLICT MINERALS REGULATION, 2017						
	EU importers of tin, tantalum, and tungsten, their ores, and gold originating from conflict-affected and high-risk areas	Conflict minerals	Adopt and clearly communicate on supply chain policy; identify and assess the risks of adverse impacts in their mineral supply chain; implement a strategy to respond to the identified risks carry out audits via an independent third party (arts. 4–9)	Entire supply chain covered	X (Arts. 10–13)	
DUTCH CHILD LABOUR DUE DILIGENCE LAW, 2019						
	Companies selling goods or services to Dutch consumers (art. 4)	Child labor (art. 2)	Investigate whether there is a reasonable suspicion that the goods or services to be supplied have been produced using child labor; if so, put in place and implement an action plan; issue a statement declaring that they exercised due diligence (arts. 4–5)	Entire supply chain covered	X (Arts. 3 and 7–9)	

Scope of application		Scope of due diligence		Enforcement	
Companies covered	Overarching issue/sector	Due diligence requirements	Scope of due diligence along the supply/value chain	Public enforcement	Civil liability
SWISS CODE OF OBLIGATIONS (ART 964j ff) and ORDINANCE ON DUE DILIGENCE AND TRANSPARENCY, 2020					
Companies placing or processing minerals containing tin, tantalum, tungsten, gold, or metals; large companies offering products with reasonable suspicion of child labor (art. 6 Ordinance)	Conflict minerals and metals; child labor	Maintain a management system stipulating a supply chain policy and a system by which the supply chain can be traced; identify and assess the risks of harmful impacts in their supply chain; draw up a risk management plan and take measures to minimize the risks identified (art. 964k CO; sc 5 Ordinance)	Entire supply chain covered	X (Art. 16 Ord; 964l CO)	
GERMAN ACT ON CORPORATE DUE DILIGENCE IN SUPPLY CHAINS, 2021					
Large companies (sc 1 (1))	Human rights risks (as defined in sc 2(2)); environment-related risks (as defined in sc 2(3))	Establish a risk management system (c 4(1)); designate a responsible person or persons within the enterprise (sc 4(3)); perform regular risk analyses (sc 5); issue a policy statement (sc 6 (2)); lay down preventative measures (sc 6); take remedial action (sc 7 (1) to (3)); establish a complaints procedure (sc 8); implement due diligence obligations with regard to risks at indirect suppliers in certain circumstances (sc 9); document (sc 10 (1)) and report (sc 10 (2))	Own activities and activities of "direct" suppliers. Extension to the activities of indirect suppliers only where the company obtains "substantiated knowledge" of a possible violation or is otherwise prompted by other circumstances. (sc 9)	sc 12–21	

NORWEGIAN ACT RELATING TO ENTERPRISES' TRANSPARENCY AND WORK ON FUNDAMENTAL HUMAN RIGHTS AND DECENT WORKING CONDITIONS ('TRANSPARENCY ACT'), 2021

Scope of application		Scope of due diligence		Enforcement	
Companies covered	Overarching issue/sector	Due diligence requirements	Scope of due diligence along the supply/value chain	Public enforcement	Civil liability
Large companies (defined as exceeding 2 or three conditions: 50 employees/NOK 35 million balance sheet/ NOK 7 million turnover) (sc 2)	Human rights and decent working conditions (sc 3(b–c))	(a) Embed responsible business conduct into the enterprise's policies; (b) identify and assess actual and potential adverse impacts on fundamental human rights and decent working conditions that the enterprise has either caused or contributed to, or that are directly linked to the enterprise's own operations, products, or services via the supply chain or business partners; (c) implement suitable measures to cease, prevent, or mitigate adverse impacts based on the enterprise's prioritizations and assessments; (d) track the implementation and results of measures taken; (e) communicate with affected stakeholders and rightsholders regarding how adverse impacts are addressed; (f) provide for or cooperate in remediation and compensation where this is required (sc 4). Duty to account for due diligence (sc 5) and to provide information to stakeholders (sc 6)	Entire supply chain covered	X (sc 9–10)	

Scope of application	Scope of due diligence			Enforcement	
Companies covered	Overarching issue/sector	Due diligence requirements	Scope of due diligence along the supply/value chain	Public enforcement	Civil liability
DRAFT DIRECTIVE OF THE EUROPEAN COMMISSION ON CORPORATE SUSTAINABILITY DUE DILIGENCE					
Very large companies (art. 2(1)(a)); large companies in high-impact sectors (art. 2(1)(b)); very large third-country companies (art 2(2)(a)); large third-country companies in high-impact sector (art 2(2)(b))	Human rights adverse impacts (as defined in Annex I, Part I); environmental adverse impacts (as defined in Annex I, Part II); climate change (art. 15)	Integrate due diligence into policies (art. 5); identify actual or potential adverse impacts (art. 6); prevent and mitigating potential adverse impacts (art. 7); bring actual adverse impacts to an end and minimize their extent (art. 8); establishing and maintain a complaints procedure (art. 9); monitor the effectiveness of the due diligence policy and measures (art. 10); publicly communicate on due diligence (art. 11)	Own operations and operations in the value chain carried out by established business relationships (arts. 1 and 3(f))	X (arts. 17–21)	X (art. 22)

TEACHING APPROACHES

Learning objectives for teaching mandatory HRDD may include:

• Understanding the range of existing and proposed mandatory HRDD laws.
• Examining the differences among mandatory HRDD provisions.
• Considering how mandatory HRDD can shape corporate behaviour.
• Considering whether mandatory HRDD provisions align with the UNGPs and provide access to remedy for affected individuals.

Teachers can compare legislation in different countries with regard to their purpose, scope, and requirements. BHR legislation may be divided in categories, such as mandatory human rights disclosure and mandatory human rights due diligence, and among the latter teachers can compare and contrast the various building blocks of each law (aim, scope, content of the due diligence requirements, reach down the supply/value chain, and enforcement mechanisms).

Using such categories offers a practical way to discuss sometimes complex domestic laws for policy and business students. Policy students, for example, may focus on the practical and political context for differences in scope of the legislation or why some countries are passing laws while others do not. Business students may analyze more carefully the practical and expected impacts as well as the cost of each kind of legislation for corporate behaviour.

Instructors in law may wish to present legislation in more detail, for example by examining legal texts. Some mandatory disclosure laws require a report, while in others the company must only provide a clear and reasoned explanation for not doing so. The scope of due diligence duties varies considerably from one law to another. Instructors in law as well as in business ethics can use practical examples to discuss the extent to which HRDD would apply in a practical case. Such an approach helps students to understand the conduct that is expected from a company with regard to its own operations, within a corporate group, as well as in its supply chain. BHR teachers can compare corporate liability mechanisms distinguishing different types of criminal and tort liability, such as strict liability or fault-based liability.

EXERCISE 11.1

MANDATORY DUE DILIGENCE CASE STUDY

A practical exercise is to assign a case study that involves a company domiciled in one of the countries that has enacted a mandatory due diligence law (France, for example) and is selling goods in a country that has adopted a law with a wide scope of application (for example, the Netherlands with the Dutch Child Labour Due Diligence Act that applies to all companies that sell goods or provide services to Dutch end-users). The case study may provide that the company in question has received allegations of child labor or other types of human rights harms from non-governmental organizations in relation to some of its products supplied by a subsidiary and/or business partner domiciled in a third country. Students must identify the human rights issues involved and the responsibility of each company in relation to these issues, and decide whether relevant laws (the French Duty of Vigilance Law and the Dutch Child Labour Due Diligence Act, respectively) are applicable or would be applicable had they entered into force (in the case of the Dutch Child Labour Due Diligence Act). If so, what are the obligations of the parent company under that law, and what actions would they advise the company to take in relation to the alleged harms?

KEY QUESTIONS

General

- Which domestic laws, adopted or proposed, make BHR mandatory for companies?
- What is the purpose of these laws?
- What is the scope and type of obligations prescribed by each?
- What are the differences between mandatory human rights disclosure laws and mandatory HRDD laws?
- To what extent do these laws align with the UNGPs? Where are the gaps?
- How is mandatory HRDD enforced?

For Business Students

- What are the elements of HRDD, consistent with the UNGPs?
- What do mandatory human rights disclosure laws require a company to do?
- What do mandatory HRDD laws require a company to do?

- Which category of laws may have the greatest impact on business conduct and why?
- How is "due diligence" defined in mandatory HRDD laws?
- What does mandatory HRDD mean in practice for covered companies?
- What organizational measures must a company adopt with regard to subsidiaries and suppliers according to these different laws? Are they precise enough for corporations?
- Do companies support or oppose mandatory HRDD? What are the arguments?

For Law Students

- What are the differences among existing/proposed mandatory HRDD legislation in different jurisdictions?
- What is the reach of various mandatory HRDD laws across the supply/value chain?
- How is mandatory HRDD enforced?
- How can companies be held liable under mandatory HRDD provisions?
- If you were drafting mandatory human rights due diligence legislation, what provisions would you include? Which existing laws would you use as a model?
- How should corporate counsel advise companies based on where the company operates?

For Policy Students

- Why do some countries regulate the conduct of their multinational enterprises and others do not?
- How do these laws reinforce or undermine the international non-binding standards set by the UNGPs?
- How does the adoption of such laws in one country affect policy in other countries?
- What are the advantages and disadvantages of adopting laws covering specific issues and commodities only, such as modern slavery or the use of conflict minerals?
- How does the prospect of an EU corporate due diligence standard affect existing national laws in EU member states, and vice versa?

TEACHING RESOURCES

Readings

Commentary

- Bright, Claire. "Mapping Human Rights Due Diligence Regulations and Evaluating their Contribution in Upholding Labour Standards in Global Supply Chains." In *Decent Work in Globalized Economy: Lessons from Public and Private Initiatives*, edited by Guillaume Delautre, Elizabeth Echeverría Manrique, and Colin Fenwick, 75–108. Geneva: ILO, 2021. https://novabhre.novalaw.unl.pt/wp-content/uploads/2021/02/DecentWor kGlobalizedEconomy_ClaireBright.pdf.
- Chambers, Rachel and Anil Yilmaz Vastardis. "Human Rights Disclosure and Due Diligence Laws: The Role of Regulatory Oversight in Ensuring Corporate Accountability." *Chicago Journal of International Law* 21, no. 2 (2021): 323–366. https://chicagounbound.uchicago.edu/cjil/vol21/iss2/4.
- Ewing, Anthony P. "Mandatory Human Rights Reporting." In *Business and Human Rights: From Principles to Practice*, edited by Dorothée Baumann-Pauly and Justine Nolan, 284–298. London: Routledge, 2006.

Reports

- Shift, *Human Rights Due Diligence: The State of Play in Europe* (March 2021), https://shiftproject.org/resource/mhrdd-europe-map.
- Shift, *The EU Commission's Proposal for a Corporate Sustainability Due Diligence Directive: Shift's Analysis* (March 2022), https://shiftproject .org/resource/eu-csdd-proposal/shifts-analysis.
- Shift and Office of the UN High Commissioner for Human Rights, *Enforcement of Mandatory Due Diligence: Key Design Considerations for Administrative Supervision*. 2021. https://www.ohchr.org/Documents/ Issues/Business/ohchr-shift-enforcement-of-mhrdd.pdf.

Websites

- Business and Human Rights Resource Centre. "Mandatory Due Diligence." Accessed July 25, 2022. https://www.business-humanrights.org/en/big -issues/mandatory-due-diligence.
- Sherpa, Terre Solidaire and Business and Human Rights Resource Centre. "Duty of Vigilance Radar." Accessed July 25, 2022. https://vigilance-plan .org.

12. Judicial remedy

Rachel Chambers

OVERVIEW

Judicial remedy is a central topic in a business and human rights (BHR) course because it is the cornerstone of corporate accountability, the key underpinning of the BHR movement. Judicial mechanisms can represent rightsholders' most promising option for accessing remedy. While new human rights due diligence laws are being enacted that require companies to put measures in place to prevent and mitigate their human rights impacts, judicial remedy through civil litigation remains a vital means of remedying past human rights violations and, in addition, can serve as a deterrent to harmful business conduct. Furthermore, "litigation puts enforcement in the hands of those with the greatest incentive to enforce compliance – the victims – and targets the costs of non-compliance to those with the greatest ability to police their own actions – corporations."[1]

This chapter takes so-called home state litigation – litigation that takes place in the state that is home to the parent or lead company rather than the state where the harm has occurred – as its focus. Home state litigation in the BHR field has gradually increased in volume over the past thirty to forty years as plaintiffs have pursued judicial remedies to hold companies accountable for human rights violations committed abroad. Bringing such cases is fraught with difficulties for plaintiffs, however, and the vast majority are unable to access remedy through this route. Home state litigation reached a highpoint with cases brought before U.S. courts by foreign plaintiffs under the *Alien Tort Statute*.[2] (See Alien Tort Statute, Chapter 13.) As recent U.S. Supreme Court

---

[1]   EarthRights International, *Cancel Corporate Abuse: How the United States can Lead on Business and Human Rights* (EarthRights International, 2020), 18, https://earthrights.org/wp-content/uploads/EarthRights-How-the-US-can-lead-on-business-human-rights-2020.pdf.

[2]   Rachel Chambers, "Parent Company Direct Liability for Overseas Human Rights Violations: Lessons from the UK Supreme Court," *University of Pennsylvania Journal of International Law* 42, no. 3 (2021): 519.

rulings have decisively narrowed this path for plaintiffs, other home state jurisdictions have taken the baton and opened their courts to this type of claim.[3]

Teaching judicial remedy through home state litigation begins with examining the jurisprudence which has evolved first in the United States, then in several European jurisdictions and Canada, scrutinizing decisions such as the courts' rulings on jurisdiction, applicable law, and substantive liability. The aim is to enable students to develop an understanding of how a plaintiff brings a case against a company in its home state and about the prospects for holding that company accountable in its home state courts for human rights violations abroad. This knowledge equips students with the ability to assess judicial remedy as a means of providing access to remedy in BHR cases, the litigation risk for companies in the BHR field, and the inevitable gaps.

The subject of litigation can be divided into two major topics: (1) case law developments in different jurisdictions demonstrating the evolving strategies and prospects for plaintiffs in such cases and (2) the role and limitations of litigation in providing access to remedy for business-related human rights abuses. These two topics are discussed below, followed by a section on key issues and debates.

CASE LAW

The focus here is on civil litigation (litigation between private parties). Civil litigation for the most part comprises claims in tort law alleging intentional or, more commonly, negligent infliction of harm. Judicial remedy for victims of corporate-related human rights harms may also be available under domestic criminal law. (See Corporate Accountability under Criminal Law below.)

Teachers can cover key civil litigation trends. These trends include the volume of cases; relevant legal developments, such as legislation and case law precedent; other developments that affect the prospects of success for plaintiffs, such as arrangements for funding of litigation; the availability of suitable lawyers; and the outcome of cases, whether through court decisions or settlements.

While the focus here is on litigation in home states, teachers can also address host state litigation – bringing claims in the courts of the country where the harm has occurred. They can interrogate why access to remedy may be denied in the host state – looking at the cost of litigation, corruption, weak rule of law, under-resources courts, lack of suitable lawyers, etc. – but also share positive

---

[3]   Rachel Chambers and Gerlinde Berger-Walliser, "The Future of International Corporate Human Rights Litigation: A Transatlantic Comparison," *American Journal of Business Law* 58, no. 3 (Fall 2021): 579.

examples of innovative case law developments in host states that may offer untapped or underexplored potential for access to remedy for plaintiffs.

Key home state jurisdictions for civil litigation are:

United States: The Alien Tort Statute (ATS) provides a federal cause of action for plaintiffs, distinct from tort litigation under state law, for alleged breaches of customary international law, such as an egregious human rights violation. With the demise of the ATS due to decisions of the U.S. Supreme Court, some scholars have predicted there will be a rise in ordinary tort cases for BHR claims.[4]

United Kingdom: With no equivalent to the ATS, BHR cases have been brought as ordinary tort claims. Plaintiffs have used a theory of parent company direct liability to overcome the legal separation between the U.K.-based parent company and the foreign subsidiary and attribute liability to the parent company. This theory has been endorsed by the U.K. Supreme Court, opening the U.K. courts to BHR litigation. Changes to rules relating to jurisdiction and extraterritoriality brought about due to Brexit, however, may curtail plaintiffs' ability to access the U.K. courts.[5]

Canada: Canadian courts have accepted a theory of parent company liability for human rights harms, like the U.K. courts. More radically, in a recent case the Canadian Supreme Court allowed litigation to proceed in which allegations of breaches of customary international law formed part of the plaintiffs' case.[6] Thus, Canada holds promise for plaintiffs in BHR cases.

The Netherlands: This is a key site for litigation as it is the only home state jurisdiction in which a direct parent company liability case has gone to trial and the plaintiffs were successful.[7] Other Dutch cases – e.g., regarding climate change – suggest a willingness on the part of the courts to censure harmful corporate conduct.

---

[4]   See, for example, Beth Stephens, "The Rise and Fall of the Alien Tort Statute," in *Research Handbook on Human Rights and Business*, eds. Surya Deva and David Birchall (Cheltenham: Edward Elgar, 2020), 46–62.

[5]   Ekaterina Aristova, "The Future of Tort Litigation against Transnational Corporations in the English Courts: Is Forum [Non] Conveniens Back?" *Business and Human Rights Journal* 6, no. 3 (October 2021): 399–422.

[6]   *Nevsun Resources Ltd. v. Araya*, 2020 SCC 5.

[7]   *Four Nigerian Farmers and Stichting Milieudefensie v. Royal Dutch Shell plc and another* [2021] ECLI:NL:GHDHA:2021:132 (Oruma), ECLI:NL:GHDHA:2021:133 (Goi) and ECLI:NL:GHDHA:2021:134 (Ikot Ada Udo) (Neth.).

LITIGATION AS REMEDY

The role of litigation in providing access to remedy connects the subject to the UN Guiding Principles on Business and Human Rights (UNGPs)[8] and the three types of remedial mechanism that are referenced in Pillar III of the UNGPs – judicial mechanisms, non-judicial (state-based) grievance mechanisms, and operational-level/non-state-based grievance mechanisms. (See Right to Remedy, Chapter 6; Non-Governmental Grievance Mechanisms, Chapter 10.) The limitations of litigation in providing access to remedy are viewed from the perspective of rightsholders: the hurdles they experience in accessing the courts, bringing and succeeding in their claims, and the limitations of court-ordered sanctions in remedying the harm they have suffered.

In the absence of binding international rules, backed up by judicial enforcement, requiring companies to respect human rights throughout their global operations, the role of home state litigation both in providing access to remedy for business-related human rights abuses and in setting standards for business conduct is an important one. But whether states are required under international law to provide access to remedy in extraterritorial situations is debated.[9] The state obligation that is a foundational principle from Pillar III of the UNGPs is to provide access to effective remedy where abuses occur in the state's territory or jurisdiction.[10] For cross-border cases, where the harm occurs overseas, the UNGPs provide in its operational principle on state-based judicial mechanisms that:

> States *should* take appropriate steps to ensure the effectiveness of domestic judicial mechanisms when addressing business-related human rights abuses, including considering ways to reduce legal, practical and other relevant barriers that could lead to a denial of access to remedy.[11] (emphasis added)

---

[8] United Nations Human Rights Council, *Guiding Principles on Business and Human Rights: Implementing the United Nations "Protect, Respect and Remedy" Framework*, Report of the Special Representative of the Secretary-General on the issue of human rights and transnational corporations and other business enterprises, UN doc. A/HRC/17/31 (March 21, 2011) (UN Guiding Principles).

[9] Claire Methven O'Brien, "The Home State Duty to Regulate the Human Rights Impacts of TNCs Abroad: A Rebuttal," *Business and Human Rights Journal* 3, no. 1 (January 2018): 47–73.

[10] UN Guiding Principles, Principle 25.

[11] UN Guiding Principles, Principle 26.

The commentary gives examples of the legal barriers that can prevent legitimate cases involving business-related human rights abuse from being addressed in court, including:

> where claimants face a denial of justice in a host State and cannot access home State courts regardless of the merits of the claim.[12]

Certain UN treaty bodies have taken a more demanding approach to extraterritoriality, articulating home state obligations under international human rights law to take steps to prevent and redress infringements of human rights due to the activities of business entities over which they can exercise control.[13] In practice, however, states do not appear to accept this as a binding obligation, and despite the positive case law developments outlined above, access to remedy in extraterritorial cases remains patchy.

Although there are two remedial mechanisms set out in Pillar III of the UNGPs, judicial remedy is the cornerstone. The role of courts and judicial mechanisms is a key operational branch for implementing the principles, as the UNGPs state that "[e]ffective judicial mechanisms are at the core of ensuring access to remedy."[14] The UN Office of the High Commissioner for Human Rights has issued guidance on enhancing the effectiveness of judicial mechanisms.[15]

In practice, it is through litigation that we have seen the legal articulation and judicial examination of some of the thorniest BHR issues such as aiding and abetting, parent company liability, and supply chain supervision. But the serious challenges plaintiffs face in achieving corporate accountability through litigation means that, rather than offering a solution to the widely discussed business and human rights governance gap, judicial remedy is arguably one aspect of the governance gap.

---

[12]   UN Guiding Principles, Commentary to Principle 26.

[13]   Committee on Economic, Social and Cultural Rights, *General Comment No. 24: State Obligations under the International Covenant on Economic, Social and Cultural Rights in the Context of Business Activities* (2017) UN Doc, E/C12/GC/24, ¶ 30: States must "take steps to prevent and redress infringements of Covenant rights that occur outside their territories due to the activities of business entities over which they can exercise control, especially in cases where the remedies available to victims before the domestic courts of the State where the harm occurs are unavailable or ineffective."

[14]   UN Guiding Principles, Commentary to Principle 26.

[15]   UN Office of the High Commissioner for Human Rights, "Accountability and Remedy Project I: Enhancing effectiveness of judicial mechanisms in cases of business-related human rights abuse" (2016) A/HRC/32/19.

KEY ISSUES AND DEBATES

Litigation and the UNGPs

One of the key debates concerning litigation is its role in providing access to remedy in cases of business-related human rights abuse. How does litigation fit with the other methods of getting access to remedy, namely state-based and non-state-based grievance mechanisms? Underpinning this is a fundamental question: does litigation or the risk of litigation serve as a prompt to improve corporate behavior? Should advocacy organizations devote campaigning time and resources to bringing or funding litigation as a strategy for seeking corporate accountability? Are certain types of cases more amenable to different methods of accessing remedy? How does the settlement of cases affect access to remedy and corporate performance moving forward?

Extraterritoriality

Home state litigation engages questions related to sovereignty: Should these cases be litigated in the courts of the home state? What does this mean for host states, which are typically the site of the harm that has occurred, and the opportunity for their courts to adjudicate the dispute in question and thereby establish and apply norms for corporate conduct?

From the perspective of plaintiffs, there are also dilemmas raised by home state litigation. What is the impact on plaintiffs of having to seek access to remedy in another jurisdiction, which may be a country far away where a different language is spoken? With access to remedy such a remote prospect in cases of business-related human rights abuse, there may be no alternative to home state litigation.

From the business perspective, there are also debates about how companies can defend cases against them responsibly and in line with the UNGPs, given the adversarial nature of the litigation process.

Obstacles Facing Plaintiffs

There are additional legal questions pertaining to the feasibility of such litigation – what the cause of action is, what the legal issues are, and what are the plaintiffs' likely prospects of success. There are also practical questions relating to the cost and availability of legal representation and the plaintiffs' personal safety if they bring such a case.

TEACHING APPROACHES

I teach judicial remedy as part of an undergraduate course called "Corporate Social Responsibility and Accountability." This is a seminar class of approximately thirty undergraduate students, typically in their final year of study. There are no prerequisites for the class, but seats are reserved for students with a major in business or in human rights. Sequentially, judicial remedy fits in the syllabus after subjects that establish foundational knowledge of the field, such as an introduction to human rights law and the UNGPs.

Law classes can devote more space in a BHR syllabus to judicial remedies and to the substantive and procedural legal issues surrounding civil litigation as a tool for corporate accountability. Lectures can explore the legal questions that are at stake in BHR litigation in different jurisdictions, including: how home state courts take jurisdiction over cases concerning foreign events; different causes of action; how plaintiffs surmount the hurdles of the "corporate veil" (the legal separation between parent and subsidiary company) and the "contractual veil" (the legal separation between the lead company and supplier company); evidential hurdles (can plaintiffs access internal corporate documents that evidence, for instance, the role of the parent company in managing or supervising the subsidiary?); funding hurdles; damages calculation; whether any other form of remedy apart from damage is available to the plaintiffs; and, relatedly, the role of settlement of such cases.

These legal questions would also be covered in a class for non-law students at an appropriate level of detail. Certain introductory concepts may require explanation, including what a tort claim is and how courts decide if they can take jurisdiction in a particular case.

Learning objectives may include:

- Considering the strengths and weaknesses of judicial remedy for business-related human rights harms.
- Assessing why access to remedy in host states can be problematic.
- Comparing the legal foundations of home state litigation in different jurisdictions.
- Drawing conclusions on current trends in BHR litigation.
- Assessing the dilemmas raised by home state litigation for plaintiffs, host states, and companies.

One approach to teaching judicial remedy is to use a mix of lecture, class discussion, and presentations.

EXERCISE 12.1

PRESENT A KEY LEGAL BHR CASE

Instructors may assign key legal cases against companies to students to present in class. Doing so provides an opportunity to examine the factual allegations that form the basis of claims, as well as the various legal issues at play, and the outcome of the litigation. This approach provides students with insight into the nature of allegations against companies; the viability of the mechanism; and how litigation fits into the larger picture of access to remedy.

In a class focused on home state litigation, students may be assigned to present one of the following key BHR cases:

United States

* *Kiobel v. Royal Dutch Petroleum* (2013)
* *Jesner v. Arab Bank* (2018)
* *Nestlé USA, Inc. v. Doe* (2021)

Key U.S. Supreme Court decisions on the scope of the Alien Tort Statute. (See Alien Tort Statute, Chapter 13.)

United Kingdom

* *Vedanta Resources v. Lungowe* (2019)
* *Okpabi v. Royal Dutch Shell* (2021)

Recent decisions of the U.K. Supreme Court that make it easier for plaintiffs to establish the liability of parent companies in tort litigation.

Canada

* *Choc v. Hudbay Minerals Inc.* (2013). The court holds that a parent company could be held directly liable for its role in wrongdoing by its subsidiary and the subsidiary's security provider.
* *Nevsun Resources Ltd. v. Araya* (2020). Key precedent in which the Canadian Supreme Court holds that alleged breaches of customary international law are actionable in a tort claim.

The Netherlands

• *Four Nigerian Farmers and Milieudefensie v. Shell* (2021). Dutch Court of Appeal decision that represents the only example of home state litigation that has been won by the plaintiffs following a full trial of the facts.

Germany

• *Jabir and others v. KiK Textilien und Non-Food GmbH* (2019). An attempt to establish direct parent company liability before the German courts in a supply chain case, which was ultimately unsuccessful.

(See Teaching Resources below for full citations. Secondary sources describing these cases can be assigned instead of the judicial decisions themselves.)

BHR students may be tasked with preparing a short presentation summarizing the facts, the law, the outcome in their assigned case, and how the case fits into litigation trends. Depending on the length of the class, this preparation work can be done prior to the class or in breakout groups during the class. The instructor can circulate among the breakout groups, speaking with students about their case and answering any questions about the case and about the lecture.

Judicial remedy can also be taught as part of an overview of mechanisms intended to offer access to remedy or in a session that compares and contrasts either state-based and non-state-based grievance mechanisms, or judicial and non-judicial mechanisms.

Films such as *Crude: The Price of Oil* (see Teaching Resources below) can be used to introduce students to the question of why it may be difficult for plaintiffs to get access to remedy in host states; and to begin to explore some of the reasons why home state litigation may also present dilemmas for plaintiffs. Although an extreme example of prolonged and acrimonious litigation –described as "lawfare" in the case in question, which concerned Texaco/Chevron's operations in Ecuador – the film highlights non-legal factors such as the risks to lawyers as human rights defenders, the experience for plaintiffs traveling to a foreign country to bring their case, and the challenges of litigating in the host state including corruption and delay. These subjects can be captured in a discussion, either as a whole class or in small groups.

Considering the hurdles for plaintiffs and the dilemmas raised by home state litigation leads into discussion of the role and limitations of litigation in providing access to remedy for business-related human rights abuses. This subject lends itself well to class discussion. Depending on what topics have been covered already in the course, students may be able to consider different options for plaintiffs seeking access to remedy and to situate litigation within these. They may also consider how, if at all, the UNGPs and other international policy and soft law developments, have affected decisions in cases and how states can use policy and legislation to enable access to remedy in business and human rights cases.

KEY QUESTIONS

General

- Which litigation strategies have proven successful for plaintiffs?
- What are the legal bases for different types of home state civil litigation? (Alien Tort Statute, tort law, contract law, etc.)
- What are the hurdles plaintiffs face when pursuing home state litigation?
- What outcomes do plaintiffs seek from home state litigation?
- How convincing is the argument that the cases brought as home state litigation should be litigated in the host state, the site of where the harm occurred?
- How does litigation fit into Pillar III of the UNGPs?

For Business Students

- What home state litigation risks do businesses face in different jurisdictions?
- What measures can companies put in place to identify and prevent human rights impacts, thus helping to avoid litigation?
- What measures can companies put in place to address rightsholder grievances in such a way that litigation may be avoided?
- If a company is sued, how can it defend itself in a human rights case responsibly and in line with the UNGPs?
- What can companies learn from judicial remedy and how might it help the company improve its human rights performance?

For Law Students

- What judicial remedies are available to business and human rights plaintiffs?
- How is jurisdiction established over business-related human rights abuse that took place overseas? What are common jurisdictional obstacles for plaintiffs?

- What is the role of legal doctrines such as *forum non conveniens* and *forum necessitates* in preventing or enabling litigation to proceed before home state courts?
- How do choice of law rules determine the applicable law for home state litigation and what are the implications for the prospects of success for plaintiffs?
- How do the "corporate veil" and the "contractual veil" act to prevent plaintiffs from suing parent corporations for human rights violations that occurred through the operations of their subsidiaries?
- How do the "corporate veil" and the "contractual veil" act to prevent plaintiffs from suing lead corporations for human rights violations that occurred through the operations of their suppliers?
- How does the settlement of litigation in business and human rights cases affect access to remedy?

For Policy Students

- How might governments use policy or legislation to facilitate access to domestic judicial mechanisms for addressing business-related human rights abuses?
- How have international and multilateral organizations sought to improve access to judicial remedy?
- What are policy rationales for governments to incorporate civil liability into human rights due diligence laws?
- How might judgments from business and human rights litigation be used to affect policy decisions in other parts of government; e.g., procurement decisions?
- How does litigation fit among other policy initiatives to provide access to remedy under Pillar III of the UNGPs?
- How does the proposed international treaty on business and human rights address civil litigation as a remedy?

TEACHING RESOURCES

Readings

Policy documents

- Committee on Economic, Social and Cultural Rights. *General Comment No. 24: State Obligations under the International Covenant on Economic, Social and Cultural Rights in the Context of Business Activities*, UN Doc, E/C12/GC/24 (2017), ¶ 26.

- United Nations Human Rights Council. *Guiding Principles for Business and Human Rights: Implementing the United Nations "Protect, Respect and Remedy" Framework*. UN doc. A/HRC/17/31 (March 21, 2011), Principles 25–26 and Commentary. http://www.ohchr.org/Documents/Publications/GuidingPrinciplesBusinessHR_EN.pdf.

Books

- Joseph, Sarah. *Transnational Corporations and Human Rights*. Oxford: Hart Publishing, 2004.
- Meeran, Richard, ed. *Human Rights Litigation against Multinationals in Practice*. Oxford: Oxford University Press, 2021.
- Rouas, Virginie. *Achieving Access to Justice in a Business and Human Rights Context: An Assessment of Litigation and Regulatory Responses in European Civil-Law Countries*. London: University of London Press, 2022.
- Skinner, Gwynne L. with Rachel Chambers and Sarah McGrath, *Transnational Corporations and Human Rights: Overcoming Barriers to Judicial Remedy*. Cambridge: Cambridge University Press, 2020.

Commentary

- Cassel, Doug. "Outlining the Case for a Common Law Duty of Care of Business to Exercise Human Rights Due Diligence." *Business and Human Rights Journal* 1 (July 2016): 179.
- Dodge, William "Business and Human Rights Litigation in US Courts Before and After Kiobel." In *Business and Human Rights: From Principles to Practice*, edited by Dorothée Baumann and Justine Nolan (London: Routledge, 2016), 244–251.
- Kaufmann, Christine. "Holding Multinational Corporations Accountable for Human Rights Violations: Litigation Outside the United States." In *Business and Human Rights: From Principles to Practice*, edited by Dorothée Baumann and Justine Nolan (London: Routledge, 2016), 253–264.
- Lindt, Angela. "Transnational Human Rights Litigation: A Means of Obtaining Effective Remedy Abroad?" *Journal of Legal Anthropology* 40, no. 2 (Winter 2020): 57.
- Riley, Christopher and Oludara Akanmidu, "Explaining and Evaluating Transnational Tortious Actions against Parent Companies: Lessons from Shell and Nigeria." *African Journal of International and Comparative Law* 30, no. 2 (May 2022): 229.

- Schrempf-Stirling, Judith and Florien Wettstein. "Beyond Guilty Verdicts: Human Rights Litigation and Its Impact on Corporations' Human Rights Policies." *Journal of Business Ethics* 145, no. 3 (2017): 545.
- Stephens, Beth. "The Curious History of the Alien Tort Statute." *Notre Dame L. Rev.* 89, no. 4 (2014): 1467.

Legal cases

United States

- *Kiobel v. Royal Dutch Petroleum*, 569 U.S. 108 (2013), https://www.supremecourt.gov/opinions/12pdf/10-1491_l6gn.pdf.
- *Jesner v. Arab Bank*, 138 S. Ct. 1386 (2018), https://www.supremecourt.gov/opinions/17pdf/16-499_1a7d.pdf.
- *Nestlé USA, Inc. v. Doe*, 141 S. Ct. 1931 (2021), https://www.supremecourt.gov/opinions/20pdf/19-416_i4dj.pdf.

United Kingdom

- *Vedanta Resources v. Lungowe*, [2019] UKSC 20, https://www.supremecourt.uk/cases/docs/uksc-2017-0185-judgment.pdf.
- *Okpabi v. Royal Dutch Shell*, [2021] UKSC 3, https://www.supremecourt.uk/cases/docs/uksc-2018-0068-judgment.pdf.

Canada

- *Choc v. Hudbay Minerals Inc.*, 2013 ONSC 1414 [2013], https://www.americanbar.org/content/dam/aba/administrative/environment_energy_resources/Events/Summit/course_materials/1_choc_v_hudbay-minerals-inc.pdf.
- *Nevsun Resources Ltd. v. Araya*, 2020 SCC 5 [2020], https://decisions.scc-csc.ca/scc-csc/scc-csc/en/item/18169/index.do.

The Netherlands

- *Four Nigerian Farmers and Stichting Milieudefensie v Royal Dutch Shell plc and another* [2021] ECLI:NL:GHDHA:2021:132 (Oruma), ECLI:NL:GHDHA:2021:133 (Goi) and ECLI:NL:GHDHA:2021:134 (Ikot Ada Udo). (Neth.). https://uitspraken.rechtspraak.nl/inziendocument?id=ECLI:NL:GHDHA:2021:1825.

Germany

- *Jabir and others v. KiK Textilien und Non-Food GmbH*, Case No. 7 O 95/15 (2019).

Videos

- Berlinger, Joe, Crude: The Real Price of Oil. Red Envelope Entertainment of an Entendre Films Production, 2009. Video, 1:44. https://watchdocumentaries.com/crude-the-real-price-of-oil.
- Sparrow, Claudia, dir. *Maxima*. 2019. https://www.standwithmaxima.com.

Websites

- Business and Human Rights Resource Centre. "Lawsuits Database." https://www.business-humanrights.org/en/from-us/lawsuits-database.
- Human Rights Insights. "Ongoing Lawsuits against Multinational Companies." https://humanrightsinsightshome.wpcomstaging.com/2021/04/19/on-going-lawsuits-against-multinational-companies.
- *Opinio Juris* (blog), http://opiniojuris.org, and Just Security (blog), https://www.justsecurity.org, provide up-to-date commentary on case law.

CORPORATE ACCOUNTABILITY UNDER CRIMINAL LAW

Where corporations are subject to domestic criminal law – in the United States, England, Japan, and India, for instance – key questions for BHR teachers and students include:

(1) For which domestic law offences that correspond to human rights violations can a company be prosecuted?[16] Do any of these offences cover extraterritorial actions/omissions?[17]

(2) Can a company be prosecuted in a particular national court for international crimes? (Note that companies are not prosecuted for such crimes at the international level – International Criminal Court (ICC) jurisdiction extends only to "natural persons," not to corporations as "legal persons."[18])

(3) How is criminal liability attributed to the corporation? (In the United States, for example, "*respondeat superior*" is used to attribute criminal liability to corporate bodies,[19] while in the United Kingdom it is through the "identification principle."[20])

(4) What criminal sanctions may be applied to companies and, relatedly, how effective are these at punishing companies and deterring criminal

---

[16] In England, for example, a corporation may be held liable just as a natural person may be held liable and may be convicted of common law and statutory offences. Exceptions to this general rule exist, including perjury, bigamy, rape (which cannot be committed by a company), and murder (excluding corporate manslaughter or homicide). Companies of course cannot be imprisoned, so a company cannot be convicted of any offence for which the only sentence is imprisonment (rather than a fine *or* imprisonment) – see *R v. ICR Haulage Ltd.* [1944] K.B. 551.

[17] As a general rule, English criminal courts only have jurisdiction over acts performed within the territory of England and Wales, unless specified otherwise by an Act of Parliament. In the United States, certain statutes have potential criminal liability for companies for extraterritorial acts. For instance, in 2018, the U.S. Department of Justice gained the ability to prosecute U.S. companies for some forced labor crimes that occur outside the United States through amendments to the Trafficking Victims Protection Act.

[18] *Rome Statute of the International Criminal Court*, July 17, 1998, 2187 U.N.T.S. 38544 (entered into force July 1, 2002), Art. 25 (1).

[19] This is vicarious liability. Criminal activity may be attributed to a corporation if and only if an employee or agent of that corporation committed each element of the crime, while within the scope of their employment and in order to advance the corporation's interest.

[20] Where a mental state is a required element of the offence, only the mental state of a senior person representing the "directing mind and will" of an organization can be attributed to a corporation.

behavior? This touches on theories of organizational (as opposed to individual) culpability and responsibility.

Domestic law offences vary from state to state, although there is likely some commonality between states in terms of corporate conduct that is criminalized. International criminal law offences, on the other hand, are defined through customary international law and treaties such as the Rome Statute of the ICC. As a general rule, international crimes must be prosecuted at the domestic level first.[21]

Teachers covering corporate accountability under criminal law in a BHR course will likely want to demonstrate global trends with regard to criminal prosecution of corporate human rights violations. In practice, there are very few cases in which corporations have been investigated for international crimes at the domestic level,[22] and fewer still in which corporations have been prosecuted. Two key examples of such criminal investigations and prosecutions are ongoing in France[23] and Sweden[24] – both civil law countries. Common law countries seem to lag behind. For instance, there has been a complete failure to date to hold U.K. companies that are complicit in human rights abuses abroad criminally to account.[25] There is also the possibility of bringing

---

[21]   The preamble to the Rome Statute states that the court will "complement the jurisdictions of national criminal courts" and that "National courts have the primary responsibility for trying international crimes: the ICC only steps in when local courts cannot or will not act." International crimes form part of domestic law, for example in England through the International Criminal Court Act 2001.

[22]   The Dutch courts have established jurisdiction over corporate executives accused of foreign human rights abuses, for example Guus Kouwenhoven, head of the Oriental Timber Corporation, who was convicted by the Dutch Appeal Court in 2017 for war crimes and arms smuggling during the height of Liberia's brutal civil war.

[23]   See "Lafarge Lawsuit (re Complicity in Crimes Against Humanity in Syria," Lawsuit, Business & Human Rights Resource Centre, accessed August 10, 2022, https://www.business-humanrights.org/en/latest-news/lafarge-lawsuit-re-complicity-in -crimes-against-humanity-in-syria.

[24]   See "Lundin Energy Lawsuit (re Complicity in War Crimes, Sudan," Lawsuit, Business & Human Rights Resource Centre, accessed August 10, 2022, https://www .business-humanrights.org/en/latest-news/lundin-petroleum-lawsuit-re-complicity-war -crimes-sudan.

[25]   For example, the attempts by Amnesty International to persuade the U.K. prosecutorial authorities to investigate/prosecute the company Trafigura for its documented role in the dumping of highly toxic waste in Cote d'Ivoire, West Africa. "Trafigura: A Toxic Journey," Amnesty International, accessed August 10, 2022, https://www .amnesty.org/en/latest/news/2016/04/trafigura-a-toxic-journey.

civil claims for reparations at the same time as a criminal prosecution in civil law countries such as France, but not in common law countries.[26]

International human rights law has long recognized the role of criminal law in ensuring accountability for human rights abuses, and this applies no less to companies than it does to individual perpetrators of human rights abuses.[27] Despite some promising examples of criminal investigations and prosecutions, this role has been largely unrealized.

---

[26] A civil action may be brought by anyone who "personally suffered the harm directly caused by the offense." Code Civil [C. Civ.] [Civil Code] art. 2 (Fr.).

[27] Shane Darcy, "The Potential Role of Criminal Law in a Business and Human Rights Treaty," in *Building a Treaty on Business and Human Rights*, eds. Surya Deva and David Bilchitz (Cambridge: Cambridge University Press, 2017), 439–471.

13. The Alien Tort Statute

Anthony Ewing

OVERVIEW

Civil litigation is a form of state-based judicial remedy under the third pillar of the UN Guiding Principles on Business and Human Rights (UNGPs).[1] For many years, the Alien Tort Statute (ATS) in the United States was the judicial mechanism most often used by plaintiffs harmed by extraterritorial business conduct seeking financial compensation and to hold companies accountable for their human rights impacts.

This chapter summarizes the history of this judicial remedy mechanism and ATS claims against companies, describes the increasingly narrow interpretation of the scope of the ATS by the U.S. Supreme Court, and offers an approach for teaching the ATS in a business and human rights (BHR) course.

HISTORY OF THE ALIEN TORT STATUTE

A single sentence in the First Judiciary Act of 1789, the ATS provides that:

> The District Courts shall have original jurisdiction of any civil action by an alien for a tort only, committed in violation of the law of nations or a treaty of the United States.[2]

The ATS was barely used before its first modern application by enterprising human rights advocates to hold a former Paraguayan police officer residing in the U.S. responsible for the torture and death of a 17-year-old Paraguayan citi-

---

[1]   United Nations Human Rights Council, *Guiding Principles on Business and Human Rights: Implementing the United Nations "Protect, Respect and Remedy" Framework*, Report of the Special Representative of the Secretary-General on the issue of human rights and transnational corporations and other business enterprises, UN doc. A/HRC/17/31 (March 21, 2011) (UN Guiding Principles).
[2]   Alien Tort Statute, 28 USC §1350 (1976).

zen.[3] Since then, U.S. Federal courts have interpreted the sparse ATS language to expand recognized causes of action that violate "well-established, universally recognized norms on international law"[4] and extended its application to companies as legal persons,[5] and have grappled with issues including permissible defenses to ATS claims and whether the ATS recognizes liability for corporate complicity under international law. (See Complicity, Chapter 14.)

ATS CLAIMS

To bring an ATS claim against a company in a U.S. District Court, the plaintiff must be a noncitizen ("alien"), establish personal jurisdiction over the defendant corporation, and plead a cause of action that constitutes a violation of international law ("law of nations") or a treaty to which the United States is a party.

An approach to analyzing ATS cases, the likelihood of plaintiffs prevailing, and potential corporate legal exposure, is to:

(1) Identify the specific violation of international law that gives rise to a cause of action.

(2) Determine whether that violation requires state action under ATS cases or can be violated by an individual or corporation ("a legal person").

(3) Consider the relationship of the company to the violation – as either committing the violation directly or indirectly through complicity with another actor.

(4) Consider available defenses.[6]

---

[3]   *Filártiga v. Peña-Irala*, 630 F. 2d. 876 (2d. Cir., 1980). The case, litigated by attorneys from the Center for Constitutional Rights, resulted in a $10.4-million-dollar verdict for the victim's family. Before Filártiga, the ATS was cited by fewer than two dozen reported cases. Beth Stephens, "The Rise and Fall of the Alien Tort Statute," in *Research Handbook on Human Rights and Business*, eds. Surya Deva and David Birchall (Cheltenham: Edward Elgar, 2020), 46–62, 48, n. 17.

[4]   *Filártiga*; *Kadic v. Karadžić,* 70 F. 3d. 232 (2d. Cir., 1995).

[5]   *Wiwa v. Royal Dutch Petroleum Co.*, 226 F. 3d. 88 (2d Cir. 2000); *Doe v. Unocal,* 395 F. 3d. 932 (9th Cir., 2002), vacated 395 F 3d 978 (9th Cir., 2003).

[6]   Common defenses to ATS claims include: a lack of personal jurisdiction over the defendant, the doctrine of *forum non conveniens*, no exhaustion of domestic remedies, the case raises a political question or issues of international comity, the defendant enjoys sovereign immunity or is protected by the act of state doctrine, a parent company is not responsible for the actions of a subsidiary (cannot "pierce the corporate veil"), and tolling of the statute of limitations for the underlying violation.

Causes of action against corporations allowed to proceed in ATS cases include allegations of human rights violations, or complicity in violations by others, including:

- Genocide;
- Crimes against humanity;
- Slavery;
- Forced labor;
- Torture;
- Cruel, inhuman, or degrading treatment; and
- Summary execution.

Sources of international law standards giving rise to a cause of action under the ATS include international human rights instruments, international criminal law instruments and case law, and customary international law, including evidence of state practice. (See Human Rights, Chapter 3.)

Most ATS cases against corporations have alleged companies aided and abetted violations committed by other actors, such as state security forces. Some U.S. courts have allowed ATS claims of torture, genocide, forced labor, and other violations of customary international law to proceed directly against individuals, as well as against corporations.[7]

While ATS cases against companies have resulted in a few notable financial settlements with plaintiffs,[8] most have been dismissed by U.S. courts.

DEFINING THE SCOPE OF THE ALIEN TORT STATUTE

In a series of ATS cases that have reached the U.S. Supreme Court, the Court's decisions have dramatically narrowed the scope of the ATS and limited its utility as a mechanism for holding companies accountable or for providing remedy to plaintiffs.

The Court has defined, and redefined, the scope of the ATS in four major decisions since 2004. The descriptions below provide the key takeaways from each case that a BHR teacher can highlight for students. Many aspects of each case, and much legal nuance, is necessarily omitted. Teachers can assign the text of the decisions themselves or widely available commentary. (See Teaching Resources below.) A benefit of assigning legal opinions is their succinct recitation of facts and comprehensive reference of prior decisions. In my BHR courses aimed at law students, for example, I have typically assigned

---

[7]   See, for example, *Kadic v. Karadžić; Doe v. Unocal.*
[8]   Unocal, Shell, and Yahoo! have settled ATS cases, for example.

only the most recent Supreme Court ATS decision. I tell the story of ATS jurisprudence in four parts.

Part I: The Door is Ajar

- *Sosa* (2004)[9]

The first ATS case to reach the Supreme Court did not involve a corporation, but rather U.S. drug enforcement agents who kidnapped a Mexican physician (Alvarez-Machain) in Mexico with the assistance of a Mexican citizen (Sosa) and brought the individual to the United States to stand trial. Alvarez-Machain brought an ATS suit alleging transborder abduction and arbitrary arrest. The claims against the U.S. agents were dismissed due to their immunity under the Federal Tort Claims Act. The Court of Appeals for the Ninth Circuit had affirmed an ATS judgment against Sosa for arbitrary arrest and detention. The Supreme Court overturned the judgment, holding that the prohibition of arbitrary arrest, in the majority's view, was not binding customary international law and did not meet the standard for a cause of action under the ATS. The Court gave weight to a limited set of customary international law norms and emphasized international practice. The Court established a test for any modern violations to meet the threshold for an ATS cause of action: acts must violate a "specific, universal, and obligatory international norm" with no "less definite content and acceptance" than the original violations of the law of nations alleged in 18th-century ATS cases – piracy, violations of safe conducts extended to aliens, and interference with ambassadors.[10] In its decision, the Court stated that the "door is still ajar" to ATS litigation but "subject to vigilant doorkeeping."[11]

Part II: The Door is Only Open for Activity in the U.S.

- *Kiobel* (2013)[12]

The second ATS case to reach the Supreme Court for review involved claims that the Anglo-Dutch energy company Royal Dutch Petroleum had aided and abetted the Nigerian government in committing abuses in the Niger Delta, including arbitrary arrest, torture, and crimes against humanity. A three-judge panel of the Court of Appeals for the Second Circuit had dismissed the case

---

[9]   *Sosa v. Alvarez-Machain*, 542 U.S. 692 (2004).
[10] *Id.*, at 732.
[11] *Id.*, at 729.
[12] *Kiobel v. Royal Dutch Petroleum*, 569 U.S. 108 (2013).

against the company holding that corporate liability is not a universally recognized norm of customary law and therefore corporations could not be sued under the ATS. The Supreme Court asked the parties to address two questions: (1) does the ATS apply to corporations; and after the first oral argument, (2) whether and under what circumstances the ATS allows causes of action for violation within the territory of another sovereign. In its ultimate decision upholding the dismissal of the case against Royal Dutch Petroleum, the Court ignored the first question and held more narrowly that a "presumption against extraterritoriality" applies to ATS claims.[13] Even where claims "touch and concern the territory of the U.S.," they must do so with sufficient force to displace the presumption. The majority opinion noted that all relevant activity in this case took place outside the United States and that mere corporate presence in the U.S. is insufficient to sustain an ATS claim. Concerned that the U.S. provides no safe harbor for any "torturer or other common enemy of mankind," four justices concurred in the result of the case, but offered an alternate test to determine ATS jurisdiction: (1) that the actions occur on U.S. soil; (2) that the defendant is a U.S. national; or the (3) that the defendant's conduct "substantially and adversely affects important national interest."[14] In the view of the four concurring justices, the defendants' actions did not trigger the third prong of their alternate test for overcoming the presumption against extraterritoriality.

Part III: The Door Protects Foreign Defendants

• *Jesner* (2018)[15]

The third opportunity for the Supreme Court to interpret the ATS involved a claim brought on behalf of individuals injured or killed by terrorist acts committed abroad alleging a Jordanian bank, through its New York branch, provided financing to terrorist organizations that caused or facilitated those acts. The dismissal of the claim on the basis that corporations could not be sued under the ATS had been affirmed by the Court of Appeals for the Second Circuit. The Supreme Court's majority opinion held that *foreign* corporations may not be defendants in suits brought under the ATS, reasoning that doing so raised separation-of-powers and foreign policy concerns. Justice Sotomayor's dissent argued forcefully that the majority opinion "absolves corporations

---

[13] *Id.*

[14] Justice Breyer's concurrence stated that the basic purpose of the ATS is "to provide compensation for those injured by today's pirates" and asked, "Who are today's pirates? Certainly today's pirates include torturers and perpetrators of genocide."

[15] *Jesner v. Arab Bank*, PLC, 138 S. Ct. 1386 (2018).

from responsibility under the ATS for conscience-shocking behavior"; nothing about the corporate form "raises foreign-policy concerns that require the Court … to immunize all foreign corporations from liability"; and the result allows corporations to "take advantage of the significant benefits of the corporate form and enjoy fundamental rights … without having to shoulder attendant fundamental responsibilities."[16]

Part IV: The Door Slams Shut

- *Nestlé* (2021)[17]

The most recent of the U.S. Supreme Court decisions defining the scope of the ATS addressed a case alleging complicity by two U.S.-based companies – Nestlé USA and Cargill – in forced labor present in their West African cocoa supply chain. The plaintiffs are former enslaved children who were kidnapped in Mali and forced to work on cocoa farms in Ivory Coast. The Court of Appeals for the Ninth Circuit, in two prior decisions, had allowed claims of aiding and abetting child slavery to proceed against the companies because of the "universal and absolute" prohibition of child slavery under international law[18] and held that the domestic conduct alleged – major operational decisions regarding its cocoa supply chain – does not require extraterritorial application of the ATS.[19]

In a plurality decision, the Supreme Court reversed the Circuit Court decision, affirming that corporations can still be sued under the ATS, but holding that "general corporate activity," like decision-making, in the United States is insufficient to meet the "touches and concerns" test of *Kiobel*.[20] The decision held that financing decisions alone by companies in the United States, when all injuries occurred overseas, made the suit an impermissible extraterritorial application of the ATS. While concurring in the case dismissal because plaintiffs failed to allege a domestic application of the ATS, three justices again emphasized the importance of allowing ATS claims for the most egregious violations of specific, universal, and obligatory norms of international law:

[16] *Id.*
[17] *Nestlé USA, Inc. v. Doe*, 141 S. Ct. 1931 (2021).
[18] *Doe v. Nestlé*, S.A., 929 F. 3d. 623 (9th Cir., 2018).
[19] *Id.* The foreign corporate defendants in the lawsuits were dismissed following the *Jesner* decision.
[20] *Nestlé USA, Inc. v. Doe*, 141 S. Ct. 1931 (2021) ("Nearly all the conduct that they say aided and abetted forced labor – providing training, fertilizer, tools, and cash to overseas farms – occurred in Ivory Coast").

"Like pirates of the 18th Century, today's torturers, slave traders, and perpetrators of genocide are *hostis humani generis*, an enemy of all mankind."[21]

THE ATS AND CORPORATE ACCOUNTABILITY

The Supreme Court's ATS decisions have dramatically narrowed the Statute's scope and utility as a remedy for individuals harmed by corporate conduct.

What remains of the ATS as a tool for corporate accountability? A noncitizen who can establish personal jurisdiction over a U.S. corporation may bring an ATS claim in a U.S. District Court alleging that the corporation violated a "specific, universal, and obligatory international norm" with "definite content" and widespread acceptance, if the corporate action "touches and concerns" the United States in ways more substantial than "mere corporate presence" or corporate decision-making. The fact patterns meeting these thresholds are now limited to egregious violations by U.S. companies taking place in the United States – corporate acts that constitute or assist[22] forced labor, torture, genocide, or similar violations of international law.

The legacy of the ATS as a tool for corporate accountability is decidedly mixed. Individual ATS cases brought against companies and the legal battles fought through ATS jurisprudence in the United States have shined a spotlight on corporate human rights abuses, forced companies to address their risks of complicity in human rights violations, and served as a model for emerging forms of judicial remedy in other jurisdictions for victims of human rights violations connected to corporate conduct.[23]

Plaintiffs seeking remedy for the extraterritorial acts of companies, however, have a greater likelihood of success pursuing civil claims under other legal theories and in other jurisdictions. A consequence of the "rise and fall" [24] of

---

[21] *Nestlé USA, Inc. v. Doe*, Concurrence of Justice Sotomayor (citing *Sosa v. Alvarez-Machain* at 732).

[22] In *Nestlé*, the U.S. Supreme Court declined to address whether aiding and abetting a violation of international law can be the basis of a cause of action under the ATS. Compare the definitions of aiding and abetting in *Doe v. Unocal* (9th Cir., 2002) and *Presbyterian Church of Sudan v. Talisman Energy* (2nd Cir., 2009). See Rachel Chambers and Jena Martin, "United States: Potential Paths Forward after the Demise of the Alien Tort Statute," in *Civil Remedies and Human Rights in Flux: Key Legal Developments in Selected Jurisdictions*, eds. Ekaterina Aristova and Ugljesa Grusic (London: Bloomsbury Publishing, 2022), 351–369, 357.

[23] See Beth Stephens, "The Rise and Fall of the Alien Tort Statute," 46–62. See also Judith Schrempf-Stirling and Florian Wettstein, "Beyond Guilty Verdicts: Human Rights Litigation and its Impact on Corporations' Human Rights Policies," *Journal of Business Ethics* 145, no. 3 (October 2017).

[24] Stephens, "The Rise and Fall of the Alien Tort Statute," 46–62.

the ATS is that plaintiffs are pursuing civil litigation in U.S. state courts as tort law claims. Plaintiffs are also seeking remedy in other jurisdictions, such as the United Kingdom, Canada, and the Netherlands, where courts are allowing civil cases alleging human rights harms caused by companies to proceed under different legal theories. (See Judicial Remedy, Chapter 12.)

The ATS as written in 1789 was not designed to bear the weight of corporate accountability for human rights violations and has collapsed under the burden of conservative Supreme Court interpretation coupled with well-resourced corporate defendants. "What is left of the ATS is of only limited value as a tool to hold corporations accountable for human rights violation."[25] Legislative action by the United States Congress could explicitly provide access to judicial remedy, clarify causes of action based on international law, define corporate accountability for extraterritorial acts, and encourage companies to respect human rights consistent with international standards, such as the UNGPs.[26] The Torture Victim Protection Act (1991),[27] for example, provides a cause of action, against natural persons only, for torture and extrajudicial killing under color of foreign law. The Trafficking Victims Protection Reauthorization Act (2008), which applies extraterritorially, provides a civil cause of action against both individuals and corporations for victims of slavery, forced labor, and human trafficking.[28]

TEACHING APPROACHES

I have included ATS cases in my BHR course since I began teaching the subject over twenty years ago. The legal pleadings and decisions themselves provide succinct factual descriptions of some of the most notable BHR allegations against multinational companies during this period, including claims against Unocal, Texaco, Chevron, Exxon Mobil, Chiquita, Del Monte, Coca-Cola, Ford, IBM, Pfizer, Firestone, Yahoo!, Cisco, Wal-Mart, Nestlé, and Cargill.[29]

---

[25] Stephens, "The Rise and Fall of the Alien Tort Statute," 61.
[26] See, for example, Pierre-Hugues Verdier and Paul Stephan, "After ATS Litigation: A FCPA for Human Rights?" *Lawfare* (blog), May 7, 2018, https://www.lawfareblog.com/after-ats-litigation-fcpa-human-rights; William S. Dodge and Oona Hathaway, "Answering the Supreme Court's Call for Guidance on the Alien Tort Statute," *Just Security*, June 2, 2022, https://www.justsecurity.org/81730/answering-the-supreme-courts-call-for-guidance-on-the-alien-tort-statute.
[27] 106 Stat. 73, note following 28 U.S.C. §1350.
[28] 122 Stat. 5044.
[29] See *Doe v. Unocal*; *Aguinda v. Texaco*, 303 F. 3d. 470 (2d. Cir., 2002); *Bowoto v. Chevron Texaco Corp.*, 312 F. Supp. 2d. 1229 (N.D. Cal., 2004); *Doe VIII v. Exxon Mobil Corp.*, 654 F. 3d. 57 (D.C. Cir., 2011); re Chiquita Brands (11th); *Aldana v. Del Monte Fresh Produce N.A., Inc.*, 578 F. 3d. 1283 (11th Cir., 2009); *Sinaltrainal v.*

Law students can explore in depth the legal issues and reasoning in ATS decisions. Business students can use the case fact patterns to consider what measures companies can put in place to reduce the risk of human rights impacts and of legal exposure. Policy students can assess the utility of civil litigation as a form of judicial remedy and the policy tools available for states to protect the human rights of individuals harmed by corporate conduct.

Teaching ATS jurisprudence in a BHR course can advance a number of **learning objectives**, including:

* Understanding the intellectual history of the BHR movement and efforts to hold companies accountable for extraterritorial conduct.
* Exploring the challenges of achieving meaningful remedy for corporate human rights abuses, and the obstacles facing plaintiffs seeking judicial remedy through civil litigation.
* Serving as a point of comparison for judicial remedy in other jurisdictions and for the enforcement of emerging forms of mandatory human rights disclosure and human rights due diligence.
* Assessing the distinct interpretation of international law by U.S. Federal courts and the avenues for incorporating international human rights standards in U.S. law.[30]
* Introducing the U.S. legal system, federal courts, and common law approaches to judicial review to students trained in other jurisdictions.

(The last two objectives consistently engage LL.M. candidates taking my BHR course, providing a unique window into the U.S. legal system.)

KEY QUESTIONS

* What is required to bring a claim under the Alien Tort Statute (ATS)?
* What violations of international law have been the basis for causes of action against corporations under the ATS?
* How has the U.S. Supreme Court interpreted the scope of the ATS?
* Are the Supreme Court's ATS decisions consistent with international law?
* How has the ATS been used as to achieve corporate accountability?

Coca-Cola, 578 F. 3d. 1252 (11th. Cir., 2009); *Abdullahi v. Pfizer, Inc.*, 562 F. 3d. 163 (2nd. Cir., 2009); *In re S. African Apartheid Litig.*, 56 F. Supp. 3d 331 (S.D.N.Y. 2014); *Flomo et al v. Firestone*, 643 F. 3d. 1013 (7th Cir., 2011); *Xiaoning v. Yahoo!, Inc.*, No. C 07-2151 CW (N.D. Cal., 2007); *Doe I v. Cisco Systems, Inc.*, 66 F. Supp. 3d. 1239 (N.D. Cal., 2014); *Wal-Mart* (9th); *Doe v. Nestlé, S. A.*
[30] See, for example, "Brief of International Law Scholars as Amici Curiae in Support of the Petition for Writ of Certiorari," *Jesner v. Arab Bank*, S. Ct. No. 16-499 (November 14, 2016).

- How should companies manage their exposure to ATS litigation?[31]
- How does a company's litigation strategy relate to its responsibility to respect human rights?
- What other policy tools could advance corporate accountability and judicial remedy for corporate human rights abuses in the United States?
- What state-based judicial mechanisms offer the best prospect of meaningful remedy for victims of corporate human rights abuses?

TEACHING RESOURCES

Readings

Alien Tort Statute Cases (U.S. Supreme Court)

- *Sosa v. Alvarez-Machain*, 542 U.S. 692 (2004), https://www.supremecourt.gov/opinions/03pdf/03-339.pdf.
- *Kiobel v. Royal Dutch Petroleum*, 569 U.S. 108 (2013), https://www.supremecourt.gov/opinions/12pdf/10-1491_l6gn.pdf.
- *Jesner v. Arab Bank*, 138 S. Ct. 1386 (2018), https://www.supremecourt.gov/opinions/17pdf/16-499_1a7d.pdf.
- *Nestlé USA, Inc. v. Doe*, 141 S. Ct. 1931 (2021), https://www.supremecourt.gov/opinions/20pdf/19-416_i4dj.pdf.

Commentary

- Chambers, Rachel and Jena Martin. "United States: Potential Paths Forward after the Demise of the Alien Tort Statute." In *Civil Remedies and Human Rights in Flux: Key Legal Developments in Selected Jurisdictions*, edited by Ekaterina Aristova and Ugljesa Grusic (London: Bloomsbury Publishing, 2022), 351–369.
- Congressional Research Service. *The Alien Tort Statute: A Primer.* Updated January 11, 2022. https://sgp.fas.org/crs/misc/R44947.pdf.
- Dodge, William S. "Business and Human Rights Litigation in US Courts Before and After *Kiobel.*" *Business and Human Rights: From Principles to Practice*, edited by Dorothée Baumann-Pauly and Justine Nolan (London: Routledge, 2016), 244–252.
- Ruggie, John. "Kiobel and Corporate Social Responsibility," Harvard Kennedy School, September 4, 2012. https://www.hks.harvard.edu/sites/default/files/

---

[31] See, for example, Jonathan Drimmer, "Five Tips to Avoid the Human Rights Litigation Trap," *Corporate Counsel*, March 26, 2009.

centers/mrcbg/programs/cri/files/KIOBEL_AND_CORPORATE_SOCIAL _RESPONSIBILITY%20(3).pdf.

- Scheffer, David J. "U.S. Supreme Court Assesses Corporate Complicity in Child Slavery." *Foreign Affairs*, December 9, 2020. https://www.cfr.org/ article/us-supreme-court-assesses-corporate-complicity-child-slavery.
- Sherman, III, John F. "*Jesner v. Arab Bank* and the UN Guiding Principles on Business and Human Rights." *The Clarion* 3, no. 1 (2017).
- Skinner, Gwynne L. with Rachel Chambers and Sarah McGrath. *Transnational Corporations and Human Rights: Overcoming Barriers to Judicial Remedy*. Cambridge: Cambridge University Press, 2020.
- Stephens, Beth. "The Curious History of the Alien Tort Statute." *Notre Dame Law Review* 89, no. 4 (2014): 1467.
- Stephens, Beth. "The Rise and Fall of the Alien Tort Statute." In *Research Handbook on Human Rights and Business*, edited by Surya Deva and David Birchall, 46–62. Cheltenham: Edward Elgar, 2020.

Videos

- C-Span, "Oral Argument," *Nestlé USA, Inc. v. Doe* (December 1, 2020) (audio recording only), https://www.c-span.org/video/?477430-1/nestle -usa-inc-v-doe-i-oral-argument.
- *The Alien Tort Statute: In Pursuit of Corporate Accountability*, Harvard Law School (2014), https://www.youtube.com/watch?v=szJg74x5Qgo.

Websites

- Business and Human Rights Resource Centre. "Corporate Legal Accountability," https://www.business-humanrights.org/en/big-issues/ corporate-legal-accountability.
- Center for Constitutional Rights. "The Alien Tort Statute: Protecting the Law that Protects Human Rights." April 17, 2013. https://ccrjustice.org/ home/get-involved/tools-resources/fact-sheets-and-faqs/alien-tort-statute -protecting-law-protects.
- Just Security. "Alien Tort Statute." https://www.justsecurity.org/tag/alien -tort-statute.

14. Complicity

Anthony Ewing

OVERVIEW

The role that a business enterprise plays in human rights impacts caused by others – complicity – is a thread running through most topics covered in a typical business and human rights (BHR) course. Through the lens of complicity, BHR teachers can explore human rights standards under international law, the ways companies are connected to human rights impacts, and tools for holding companies accountable and providing remedy to individuals affected by business activity.

Cases in which a company violates human rights directly, by using forced labor to produce goods for example, are relatively easy to analyze within a BHR framework. Defining a company's responsibility is straightforward. Business enterprises should stop causing human rights harms, provide remediation to victims,[1] and may be held legally responsible for acts that violate national law or that constitute international crimes.

Corporate complicity scenarios can be less obvious, more difficult to identify as having human rights impacts connected to a business enterprise, and more challenging to address consistent with international standards and stakeholder expectations for responsible business conduct. The risk of corporate complicity with other actors who are violating human rights is a more common concern for most companies than that of direct human rights violations. State security forces threaten or arbitrarily arrest workers seeking to unionize a factory supplying international apparel brands. Private security forces harass or abuse individuals living near a mine operated by a multinational extractives company. A consumer goods company sells chocolate made

---

[1]   See United Nations Human Rights Council, *Guiding Principles on Business and Human Rights: Implementing the United Nations "Protect, Respect and Remedy" Framework*, Report of the Special Representative of the Secretary-General on the issue of human rights and transnational corporations and other business enterprises, UN doc. A/HRC/17/31 (March 21, 2011) (UN Guiding Principles), Guiding Principles 11, 13, 19.

with cocoa sourced in a region known to have widespread forced or child labor in agriculture. A telecommunications company turns over user information in response to a government request. Hate speech on a social media platform incites violence. These are the kinds of real-life corporate complicity scenarios that occupy BHR practitioners, advocates, and policymakers.

This chapter outlines the legal elements and sources of complicity, considers complicity in the context of the corporate responsibility to respect human rights, surveys common corporate complicity scenarios in different sectors, and describes an approach to teaching complicity in a BHR course.

ELEMENTS OF COMPLICITY

Complicity is both a legal and a non-legal concept. Criminal law concepts, such as "aiding and abetting" and conspiracy, define criminal corporate complicity in jurisdictions where companies are subject to domestic criminal law, such as in the United States, England, Japan, and India.[2] (See Corporate Accountability under Criminal Law in Chapter 12.) To establish a crime, criminal law typically requires both a criminal act and the intent to commit a crime. Companies, as legal persons, may be subject to liability for complicity in international crimes in some jurisdictions.[3] A criminal complaint, for example, has been filed in French courts charging Lafarge, a cement company, with complicity in war crimes, crimes against humanity, financing of a terrorist enterprise, and forced labor based on the actions of its subsidiary in Syria.[4] Wrongs, or "torts" that harm people, which do not rise to the level of international crimes, such as restrictions on freedom of expression, can also be the basis for holding companies responsible for "international torts" under domestic law.[5]

Business enterprises may also be subject to civil liability for complicity in human rights abuses. (See Judicial Remedy, Chapter 12.) A business enterprise may be responsible for negligent harm if it breaches a duty of care to an individ-

---

[2] John Ruggie, *Business and Human Rights: Mapping International Standards of Responsibility and Accountability for Corporate Acts*, Report of the Special Representative of the Secretary-General on the issue of human rights and transnational corporations and other business enterprises, UN doc. A/HRC/4/035 (February 9, 2007) (Mapping International Standards), ¶ 27.

[3] John Ruggie, *Mapping International Standards*, ¶¶ 19–32.

[4] "French Court Upholds Syria 'Complicity in Crimes against Humanity' Charge against Lafarge," *Agence France Presse*, May 8, 2022, https://www.france24.com/en/live-news/20220518-paris-court-upholds-charges-of-complicity-in-crimes-against-humanity-linked-to-lafarge-s-cement-plant-in-syria.

[5] See Andrew Clapham, *Human Rights Obligations of Non-State Actors* (Oxford: Oxford University Press, 2006), 261–263.

ual causing (proximate cause) foreseeable harm to that person.[6] For example, a class action on behalf of Rohingya refugees from Burma (Myanmar) residing in the United States has been filed against Facebook's parent company alleging the company negligently designed its algorithms to fill Burmese users' news feeds with hate speech and misinformation that resulted in ethnic violence against the Rohingya by the Myanmar military.[7] Corporate complicity may also be established through a joint venture with the principal actor. Key questions for establishing civil liability for corporate complicity include: Did the company exercise reasonable care to avoid causing harm? Was the harm reasonably foreseeable? Did the company know, or should it have known, that its action would likely contribute to a harm? Would the harm have occurred without the corporate action (or omission)?

Individual corporate executives, as natural persons, may be subject to both civil and criminal liability for complicity.[8]

Legal elements of complicity from criminal and civil law can be synthesized as three factors: (1) causation, (2) knowledge, and (3) proximity.[9]

In the absence of any domestic legal liability, business enterprises may still be seen as complicit in abuses by others.[10] The International Commission of Jurists has noted that

> [t]here are company acts and omissions that may be currently beyond legal sanction, but that may nonetheless be criticised publicly by different actors as unacceptable behaviour as a matter of morality or ethics, or that may give rise to market-place or public image implications for companies.[11]

---

[6]   See, for example, American Law Institute. Restatement of the Law, Second, Torts 2d. (St. Paul, MN: American Law Institute Publishers, 1965), § 282.

[7]   Dan Milmo, "Rohingya Sue Facebook for £150bn over Myanmar Genocide," *The Guardian*, December 6, 2021; *Doe v. Meta*, Class Action Complaint (Cal. Super. Ct., December 6, 2021), https://digitalcommons.law.scu.edu/cgi/viewcontent.cgi?article=3596&context=historical (the suit seeks $150 billion in compensatory damages under theories of strict product liability and negligence).

[8]   See, for example, "Human Rights Coalition Calls on ICC to Investigate Role of Chiquita Executives in Contributing to Crimes against Humanity," International Federation for Human Rights, May 18, 2017, https://www.fidh.org/en/region/americas/colombia/human-rights-coalition-calls-on-icc-to-investigate-role-of-chiquita.

[9]   See International Commission of Jurists, *Corporate Complicity and Legal Accountability*, vol. 1, *Facing the Facts and Charting a Legal Path, Report of the ICJ Expert Legal Panel on Corporate Complicity in International Crimes* (Geneva: ICJ, 2008).

[10]   UN Guiding Principles, Commentary to Guiding Principle 17.

[11]   International Commission of Jurists, *Corporate Complicity and Legal Accountability*, 7.

The voluntary UN Global Compact Principles, for example, emphasize that businesses should "[m]ake sure that they are not complicit in human rights abuses."[12]

COMPLICITY UNDER INTERNATIONAL LAW

The risk of legal complicity is greatest for companies if the underlying violation committed by a third party rises to the level of an international crime – genocide, slavery, disappearances, torture, prolonged arbitrary detention, systematic racial discrimination, crimes against humanity, war crimes, and any consistent pattern of gross violations of other internationally recognized human rights.[13]

Complicity for individuals is defined under international criminal law, which establishes responsibility for "aiding and abetting," or for engaging in a joint criminal enterprise to commit, an international crime. Aiding and abetting means "knowingly" providing "practical assistance, encouragement, or moral support, which has a substantial effect on the persecution of the crime."[14] The individual need not share the intent of the principal actor to commit the crime. A joint criminal enterprise means agreeing to participate in an illegal act with another actor, which can be established "even if the act, while outside common design, was nevertheless a natural and foreseeable consequence of the effecting of that purpose."[15] Individual industrialists and bankers, for example, were prosecuted "for their involvement with the crimes committed by the Nazis," a precedent "of great relevance to contemporary students and observers of the field of business and human rights."[16]

---

[12] UN Global Compact, available at https://www.unglobalcompact.org/what-is-gc/mission/principles, Principle 2.

[13] War crimes include "grave breaches of the Geneva Conventions of 12 August 1949" and "[o]ther serious violations of the laws and customs applicable in international armed conflict." *Rome Statute of the International Criminal Court*, 2187 U.N.T.S. 38544, July 17, 1998 (entered into force July 1, 2002) (Rome Statute), Art. 8. Crimes against humanity include slavery, torture, and sexual violence "when committed as part of a widespread or systematic attack directed against any civilian population." Rome Statute, Art. 7. See also "Customary International Law of Human Rights," Restatement (Third) of the Foreign Relations Law of the United States, Sec. 702 (1987).

[14] *Prosecutor v. Furundžija*, Trial Chamber, Judgment (Int'l Crim. Trib. for the Former Yugoslavia (December 10, 1998). Compare Rome Statute, Art. 25(3)(c).

[15] International Criminal Tribunal for the former Yugoslavia, *Prosecutor v. Tadić*, Appeals Chamber, Judgment of July 15, 1999. See also Genocide Convention (1948), Art. 3(b); Charter of the International Military Tribunal (IMT) in Nuremberg, Art. 6(a).

[16] Nadia Bernaz, *Business and Human Rights: History, Law and Policy – Bridging the Accountability Gap* (London: Routledge, 2017), 76. The International Military

The same principles can be applied to companies as legal "persons." While the jurisdiction of the International Criminal Court (ICC) extends only to "natural persons,"[17] the exclusion of corporations from ICC jurisdiction does not mean that companies are free from potential liability for international crimes under international law.[18]

COMPLICITY UNDER THE ALIEN TORT STATUTE IN THE UNITED STATES

Alien Tort Statute (ATS) jurisprudence in the United States illustrates competing legal definitions of complicity. (See The Alien Tort Statute, Chapter 13.) Before the first U.S. Supreme Court decision (*Sosa*) addressing the scope of the ATS, a U.S. circuit court, in *Doe v. Unocal*, held that the relevant standard for determining whether Unocal had "aided and abetted" Burmese security forces in human rights violations, including forced labor, rape, torture, and summary execution, is "knowing practical assistance or encouragement that has a substantial effect on the perpetration of the crime" with "reasonable knowledge that the accomplice's actions will assist the perpetrator in the commission of the crime." The Court, looking to the international criminal law definition of aiding and abetting, held that it was not necessary for Unocal to have shared the intent of the security forces to commit the violations.[19] After *Sosa*, in which the U.S. Supreme Court held that international law violations recognized as ATS causes of action must have "definite content and widespread acceptance,"[20] a different U.S. circuit court set a higher standard for aiding and abetting, requiring practical assistance with both knowledge and the intent to facilitate the actor's commission of the crime.[21] The circuit court split on the definition of aiding and abetting under international law to be applied by U.S. courts remains unresolved. The U.S. Supreme Court, in its most recent

---

Tribunal at Nuremberg indicted a German corporate executive (Krupp) for war crimes and the U.S. Military Tribunals tried individual German industrialists and bankers (Flick, I.G. Farben, Krupp and Ministries trials) for actively helping the Nazi regime to commit war crimes; inter alia, suppling poisonous gas to concentration camps knowing it would be used to exterminate human beings; actively seeking slave labor to work in their factories; acquiescing or helping in the deportation, murder, and ill-treatment of slave workers; donating money to support the criminal Nazi party; and plundering property in occupied Europe. *Id.*, 62–78.

[17]   *Rome Statute*, Art. 25 (1).

[18]   See David Scheffer and Caroline Kaeb, "The Five Levels of CSR Compliance," *Berkeley Journal of International Law* 29, no. 1, (2019): 357–361.

[19]   *Doe v. Unocal* (9th Cir., 2002).

[20]   *Sosa v. Alvarez-Machain*, 542 U.S. 692 (2004), 732.

[21]   *Presbyterian Church of Sudan v. Talisman Energy* (2nd Cir., 2009).

ATS decision (*Nestlé*), declined to address whether aiding and abetting a violation of international law can be the basis of a cause of action under the ATS.[22]

COMPLICITY AND THE UNGPs

Avoiding complicity is part of the corporate responsibility to respect human rights defined in the UN Framework for Business and Human Rights[23] and the UN Guiding Principles. The UN Framework emphasizes the responsibility of companies to "avoid complicity in human rights abuses by others" [24] and that companies can avoid complicity by employing due diligence.[25] Under the UNGPs, business enterprises are required to "avoid causing *or contributing to* adverse human rights impacts through their own activities"[26] and should "treat the risk of causing *or contributing* to gross human rights abuses as a legal compliance issue wherever they operate"[27] (emphasis added). While the UN Framework notes that "it is not possible to specify definitive tests for what constitutes complicity in any given context,"[28] the UNGPs identify "knowingly providing practical assistance or encouragement that has a substantial effect on the commission of a crime" as the relevant standard under international criminal law.[29]

The UNGPs also require companies to "seek to prevent or mitigate adverse human rights impacts *that are directly* linked to their operations, product or service by their business relationships, even *if they have not contributed to* those impacts"[30] (emphasis added). Aligning the UNGPs' "causing or contributing" and "directly linked" language of Principle 13 with international legal concepts of complicity can be a challenge for BHR teachers. Does contributing to a human rights impact capture all forms of legal complicity? Can being

---

[22] *Nestlé USA, Inc. v. Doe*, 141 S. Ct. 1931 (2021). See concurrence of Justice Sotomayor at 11 (citing *Khulumani v. Barclay Nat. Bank Ltd.*, 504 F. 3d 254, 268–277 (CA2 2007) (Katzmann, J., concurring) (surveying aiding-and- abetting liability under international law).

[23] United Nations Human Rights Council, *Protect, Respect and Remedy: A Framework for Business and Human Rights*, Report of the Special Representative of the Secretary-General on the issue of human rights and transnational corporations and other business enterprises, UN doc. A/HRC/8/5 (April 7, 2008) (UN Framework).

[24] "[T]he relationship between complicity and due diligence is clear and compelling: companies can avoid complicity by employing … due diligence." UN Framework, ¶ 81.

[25] See UN Framework, ¶¶ 73–81.

[26] UN Guiding Principles, Principle 13(a).

[27] UN Guiding Principles, Principle 23(c).

[28] UN Framework, ¶ 76.

[29] UN Guiding Principles, Commentary to Principle 17.

[30] UN Guiding Principles, Principle 13(b).

directly linked to a human rights impact, without contributing to it, constitute complicity under aiding and abetting, negligence, or other legal definitions? I often frame this discussion for students as an example of a BHR concept without fixed boundaries between legal and non-legal requirements, but one that companies nonetheless must address to meet stakeholder expectations. Corporate stakeholders, including employees and investors, increasingly expect companies to respond to all forms of actual, potential, or perceived complicity. Rights-respecting companies will identify and address any business relationships that present a risk of complicity with human rights impacts, whether legally enforceable under existing mechanisms or not.

Specific responsibilities under the UNGPs flow from how a company is connected to human rights impacts. The scope of a company's responsibility to respect human rights varies based on its degree on involvement – whether the company has "caused or contributed to" the human rights impact, or if adverse human rights impacts are "directly linked to their operations, products or services by their business relationships, even if they have not contributed to those impacts."[31] If a company has contributed or may contribute to an impact, it should prevent or mitigate its contribution to the impact and contribute to remediating any harm to the extent of its contribution. If it is not "contributing" to an impact, but is nonetheless "linked" through its relationships, the company should use its leverage to seek to prevent or mitigate the adverse human rights impacts and may seek to enable or take a role in remedy.

Figure 14.1 helps to explain these concepts.

ASSESSING COMPLICITY

To illustrate these concepts, I encourage students to apply both legal and non-legal criteria to the fact pattern when assessing potential corporate complicity in the actions of others affecting human rights. This "complicity analysis" asks:

• What is the underlying human right at issue?
• Who is causing the human rights harm?
• Who are the affected rightsholders?
• How is the company connected to the human rights impact?
• Is the company complicit in the human rights harm caused by another actor?
• How is the company contributing to the human rights impact?

---

[31]   UN Guiding Principles, Principle 13.

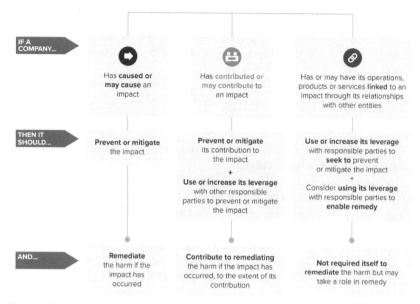

Source: Shift Project (reprinted with permission).

*Figure 14.1   Cause, contribution, and linkage under the UN Guiding
                Principles*

- What must the company do to avoid complicity and meet its responsibility
  to respect human rights?

Assessing the complicity of a business enterprise in specific circumstances
begins by understanding the human rights violation or impact at issue. For
example, when a telecommunications company turns off cell phone service at
the request of a government seeking to crack down on anti-government protests,[32] what are the actual or potential adverse human rights impacts? Impacts
may include violations of freedom of expression and freedom of association,
for example. The government crackdown may involve arbitrary arrests and
abuse of detainees. Cell customers without service may be unable to access
healthcare or emergency services.

---

[32]   This discussion draws on the example of Vodaphone's actions in Egypt in 2011
during the popular protests against the Mubarak government and the crackdown by
Egyptian security forces against protesters, political opposition, and Egyptian citizens.
See, for example, Rebecca MacKinnon, *Consent of the Networked* (New York: Basic
Books, 2012), 51–71.

The next step is identifying the actor committing the human rights violation or causing the harm. Is the cell phone company or the government violating the freedom of expression of cell phone customers? Who is arbitrarily detaining protesters? Who are the perpetrators with respect to each potential human rights impact?

For each right at issue, who are the affected rightsholders? Are only the cell phone company's customers affected by the cell service shut down? How are the cell company's employees, anti-government protesters, or the general public affected by the company's actions?

Based on the answers to the first three questions, how is the company connected to each human rights impact?

To assess potential legal complicity, students consider the synthesized elements from both criminal and civil law: (1) causation, (2) knowledge, and (3) proximity.[33] Considering *causation* means asking whether a company has enabled, exacerbated, or facilitated a violation by another actor. Would the human rights impact have occurred without the company's action or omission? Did the company's actions make the impact worse or easier? If the answer to any of these questions is yes, the company could be in a "zone of legal risk" for complicity.[34]

The second factor, knowledge, means either the intent to enable, exacerbate, or facilitate an abuse; or that a company knew or should have known (foreseeability) of the risk that its conduct would contribute to the abuse. The former standard is drawn from criminal law and both the criminal act and the intent to commit a crime are required; the latter is drawn from civil liability or "tort" law, with a reasonableness standard of "constructive knowledge." Was it reasonably foreseeable that shutting off cell service would contribute to human rights abuses? Should the company have known of the potential human rights impacts? Evidence of knowledge may include information provided by a company's own due diligence, provided to the company by others, or that is publicly available. The information may be about actual or potential human rights abuses or conditions, or the likelihood that a company's actions would contribute to human rights impacts.

The third element, proximity, considers the relationship of the company to principal actors or the victims of human rights abuse. Proximity may be considered a "certain level of closeness" to the underlying abuses, perpetrators, or

---

[33]   See International Commission of Jurists, *Corporate Complicity and Legal Accountability*.

[34]   The ICJ analysis "describes the kind of conduct that a company should avoid if it is to ensure that it does not become complicit in gross human rights abuses, and as a result find itself in a zone of legal risk." International Commission of Jurists, *Corporate Complicity and Legal Accountability*, 6.

victims that supports a company's contribution and knowledge.[35] This prong of the ICJ's synthesis is the most problematic to align with the standard in the UNGPs, which does not consider a company's influence but rather its connection to adverse human rights impacts when determining its responsibility. The UN Framework and Guiding Principles explicitly separate "responsibility" from the notion of a company's "sphere of influence."[36]

Common defenses raised by companies in the face of complicity allegations include:

- Our actions were legitimate business activity and/or legal under national law.
- If we had not provided the assistance, another company would have.
- We had no control over the perpetrator.[37]

Each of these excuses will fail if the facts of the case meet the causation and knowledge factors above. Willful blindness to the risk of human rights impacts, by choosing not to conduct human rights due diligence, for example, is also an insufficient corporate defense. A company may plead the defense of duress or necessity, arguing that it was compelled to provide the assistance. To succeed, this defense generally must show that corporate actors faced physical threats for failure to carry out an order to help commit human rights abuses.[38]

Finally, BHR teachers can ask students how the company should respond and what the business consequences could be for any action taken. If the cell phone company decides not to turn off cell service, for example, how should it

---

[35] International Commission of Jurists, *Corporate Complicity and Legal Accountability*, 24–26. A company may be sufficiently close to the violation, perpetrator, or victim through geographic closeness; or through economic, political, legal, or business relationships. "[A] prudent company should be aware that the closer it is to the principal perpetrator of gross human rights abuses or the victims of abuses, the more likely it is to face allegations of complicity, and the closer it will be to a zone of legal risk wherein its conduct may have enabled, exacerbated or facilitated the abuses. Furthermore, it will be more likely that the law will consider that the company knew of the abuses, or that it should have known."

[36] UN Framework, ¶¶ 65–72; United Nations Human Rights Council, *Clarifying the Concepts of "Sphere of Influence" and "Complicity,"* Report of the Special Representative of the Secretary-General on the Issue of Human Rights and Transnational Corporations and other Business Enterprises, John Ruggie, UN doc. A/HRC/8/16 (May 15, 2008).

[37] International Commission of Jurists, *Corporate Complicity and Legal Accountability*, 16–18.

[38] See Nadia Bernaz, *Business and Human Rights: History, Law and Policy – Bridging the Accountability Gap* (Oxford: Routledge, 2017), 72–75.

proceed to refuse the government's request? Could local employees be at risk of harm as a result?

CORPORATE COMPLICITY – COMMON SCENARIOS

Common corporate complicity scenarios include active assistance to security forces committing human rights violations; providing goods or services used to commit abuses; hiring security for company operations that results in human rights violations; and being connected to abuses through the company's supply chain or other business relationships.

Common scenarios that may not rise to the level of legal complicity, yet may still call for a corporate response, include "silent presence" – a company operates where human rights abuses are taking place (e.g., in a country where freedom of association is restricted or where gender-based discrimination in employment is permitted under national law); "economic benefit" – a company gains an economic benefit from human rights abuses committed by others (e.g., by using infrastructure produced through government violations or manufacturing in an export zone where union activity is outlawed); and paying general purpose taxes to a government committing abuses (as opposed to taxes specifically funding abuses). The UN Framework notes that "[m]ere presence in a country, paying taxes, or silence in the face of abuses is unlikely to amount to the practical assistance required for legal liability. However, acts of omission in narrow contexts have led to legal liability of individuals when the omission legitimized or encouraged the abuse."[39] Each of these scenarios may be perceived as moral complicity in the underlying violations and create an expectation that the company act to prevent them or to distance itself from the geography or perpetrator.[40]

TEACHING APPROACHES

In the BHR courses I teach at a law school, I cover legal definitions of complicity, derived both from criminal and civil law, and give students the opportunity to apply a "complicity analysis" to a range of fact patterns reflecting the variety

---

[39]   UN Framework, ¶ 77 (citing, for example, Trial Chamber judgement Kvocka et al., Case No. IT-98-30/1-T (Int'l Crim. Trib. For the former Yugoslavia, November 2, 2001), ¶¶ 257–261).

[40]   The South African Truth and Reconciliation Commission, for example, recognized three orders of corporate involvement with the Apartheid regime: (1) actively helped; (2) products used for repression; and (3) ordinary business activities that benefited indirectly by operating in Apartheid society. See United Nations Human Rights Council, *Clarifying the Concepts of "Sphere of influence" and "Complicity,"* n. 23.

of business relationships that present the risk of complicity in human rights violations by others, particularly state actors. I emphasize that considering the potential complicity of a company has both legal and non-legal dimensions.

Learning objectives for teaching complicity in a BHR course may include:

- Understanding the elements of complicity under civil and criminal law.
- Understanding how the UNGPs treat corporate complicity.
- Applying a "complicity analysis" to specific cases in different industry sectors.
- Surveying the ways companies can assess their business relationships for the risk of complicity in human rights abuses.

EXERCISE 14.1

IS THE COMPANY COMPLICIT?

Applying complicity criteria to the actions of specific companies engages students with real-life cases and allows BHR teachers to explore different approaches to defining and addressing corporate complicity in the actions of third parties. A simple exercise is to divide a class into groups, provide each with a specific case, and ask each group to assess whether the company is at risk of complicity in human rights violations. Cases can be clustered in the same industry or across diverse sectors. Groups report back, allowing students to ask follow-up questions. Representative cases in the information and communications technology (ICT) sector, for example, include:

- Yahoo! provides personally identifiable information of an e-mail user at the request of the Chinese government.[41]
- Google agrees to censor search terms internet users in China.[42]
- Cisco sells routers to the Chinese government.[43]

---

[41] As a result, journalist Shi Tao was arrested and sentenced to ten years in jail for emailing to a foreign website information about Chinese government warnings to domestic media organizations about covering the anniversary of Tiananmen Square. MacKinnon, *Consent of the Networked*, 133–139. See also John Gerard Ruggie, *Just Business: Multinational Corporations and Human Rights*, 1st edition (New York: W. W. Norton & Company, 2013), 14–18; Sandra J. Sucher and Daniel Baer, *Yahoo! in China*, Harvard Business School Case No. 609051 (revised April 25, 2011).
[42] MacKinnon, *Consent of the Networked*, 35–40; David Drummond, "A New Approach to China: An Update," *The Official Google Blog*, March 22, 2010.
[43] MacKinnon, *Consent of the Networked*, 169–171.

- Safaricom transmits texts inciting violence against ethnic groups during elections in Kenya.[44]
- Facebook allows fake accounts on its platform to target voters with disinformation in the United States,[45] profits off data collection that violates the privacy rights of its users,[46] and allows users in Myanmar to post hate speech and misinformation that contributes ethnic violence against the Rohingya minority persecuted by the government.[47]
- Apple and Google offer in their online "app" stores a Saudi application that facilitates gender discrimination in the provision of government services.[48]
- Apple refuses an FBI request in the United States to unlock an iPhone.[49]
- Twitter suspends the account of a U.S. political figure due to the "risk of further incitement of violence."[50]
- European technology companies sell facial recognition software to Chinese security agencies.[51]

[44] Institute for Human Rights and Business, *Corporate Responses to Hate Speech in the 2013 Kenya Presidential Elections: Case Study: Safaricom* (November 2013), https://www.ihrb.org/uploads/reports/DD-Safaricom-Case-Study.pdf.
[45] See, for example, "Facebook, in Cross Hairs After Election, Is Said to Question Its Influence," *The New York Times*, November 12, 2016.
[46] See, for example, "Facebook's Role in Data Misuse Sets Off Storms on Two Continents," *The New York Times*, March 18, 2018.
[47] See Office of the High Commissioner for Human Rights, *Report of the Independent International Fact-Finding Mission on Myanmar*, UN Doc. A/HRC/39/64 (September 12, 2018), ¶ 74 ("The extent to which Facebook posts and messages have led to real-world discrimination and violence must be independently and thoroughly examined"); BSR, *Human Rights Impact Assessment: Facebook in Myanmar* (October 2018), 25.
[48] Sara Boboltz, "Saudi Arabia's Women-Tracking App Has Critics Coming for Google and Apple," *Huffpost*, February 12, 2019, https://www.huffpost.com/entry/saudi-women-tracking-app-google-apple_n_5c62e51be4b00ba63e4abf62.
[49] Tim Cook, "A Message to Our Customers," Apple, February 16, 2016, https://www.apple.com/customer-letter.
[50] Twitter, Inc., "Permanent suspension of @realDonaldTrump," *Company* (blog), January 8, 2021, https://blog.twitter.com/en_us/topics/company/2020/suspension.
[51] See Amnesty International, *Out of Control: Failing EU Laws for Digital Surveillance Export* (London: Amnesty International, 2020), 24–32.

EXERCISE 14.2

CASE STUDY: VODAPHONE IN EGYPT

Vodaphone's actions in Egypt provide a useful fact pattern to explore the meaning of complicity and apply it to a real-life situation.

During the January 2011 mass protests in Egypt opposing the thirty-year-old Mubarak regime, government officials ordered private telecommunications companies to shut down the country's cellular phone network. In response, the Egyptian subsidiary of U.K.-based Vodaphone suspended and ultimately blocked cell service for its customers. Vodaphone also transmitted pro-government texts authored by Egyptian authorities to its customers.[52] After public criticism of its actions, Vodaphone defended its actions, arguing that the company had "no choice but to obey Egyptian authorities" and that the interests of Vodaphone's employees and customers in Egypt were "least badly served" by its actions at the time.[53]

After describing the facts at the time, a BHR teacher can ask students, "You are the CEO of Vodaphone Egypt. Do you take down the network? Do you transmit the government-authored text messages?" A productive follow-up question is: "What additional information would you want before you make a decision?" Issues that arise in the subsequent discussion include:

- What are the actual or potential human right impacts of each Vodaphone action?
- Who is violating the rights at issue?
- Who are the affected individuals?
- Is Vodaphone complicit in these human rights impacts?
- Is Vodaphone causing, contributing, or linked to each human rights impact?
- How should Vodaphone define its responsibility to employees, to customers, and to Egyptian citizens?
- What steps can the company take before following the government requests? What are the business and human rights implications of each step?
- How should Vodaphone communicate its actions?

---

[52] Raphael G. Satter, "Vodaphone: Egypt Forced Us to Send Text Messages," *Salon*, February 3, 2011.

[53] Vodaphone Group Plc, "Response on Issues Relating to Mobile Network Operations in Egypt," February 22, 2011.

- How could the company have been better prepared to address this situation before it arose?
- How can the company prevent or mitigate its contribution to the human rights violations committed by the Egyptian government?

KEY QUESTIONS

General

- What are the legal elements of complicity?
- How do the UNGPs treat corporate complicity?
- How can companies be connected to human rights impacts through business relationships? Which relationships?
- How can human rights due diligence address complicity?
- What is "silent complicity"?

For Business Students

- How can a company enable, exacerbate, or facilitate a human rights violation?
- How can companies avoid complicity in human rights violations?
- What business functions are best positioned to identify actual or potential complicity in human rights violations by others?
- What are the particular complicity risks in specific industry sectors?
- What business relationships present the greatest risk of complicity for a specific company or industry?

For Law Students

- How do legal definitions of complicity differ in criminal law and in tort law?
- What is the definition of aiding/abetting under international criminal law?
- What defenses are available to rebut an allegation of aiding/abetting?
- Is "willful blindness" a defense?
- What evidence can establish reasonable knowledge of potential human rights impacts?
- What tools are available to hold companies accountable for complicity in human rights violations? To provide remedy to victims?
- What do the terms "cause, contribute, or directly linked" mean in the UNGPs?

- How do the underlying human rights at issue change the analysis of corporate complicity?

For Policy Students

- Are companies complicit in state human rights violations when they pay taxes?
- How should the proposed binding business and human rights treaty define corporate complicity in human rights impacts?

TEACHING RESOURCES

Readings

- International Commission of Jurists. *Report of the ICJ Expert Legal Panel on Corporate Complicity in International Crimes.* Vols. I, II and III, 2008.
- Ruggie, John. *Business and Human Rights: Mapping International Standards of Responsibility and Accountability for Corporate Acts*, Report of the Special Representative of the Secretary-General on the issue of human rights and transnational corporations and other business enterprises, UN doc. A/HRC/4/035 (February 9, 2007).
- Ruggie, John. "Complicity." In *Protect, Respect and Remedy: A Framework for Business and Human Rights*, UN doc. A/HRC/8/5 (April 7, 2008), paras. 73–81.
- Shift Project. *Using Leverage in Business Relationships to Reduce Human Rights Risks.* November 2013. https://www.shiftproject.org/media/ resources/docs/Shift_leverageUNGPs_2013.pdf.
- United Nations Human Rights Council. "Responsibilities of Intermediaries." *Report of the Special Rapporteur on the Promotion and Protection of the Right to Freedom of Opinion and Expression*, U.N. doc. A/HRC/17/27 (May 16, 2011).

Videos

- Kaneva, Milena. *Total Denial* (2001) (includes Court of Appeals for the 9th Circuit hearing in *Doe v. Unocal*), https://www.youtube.com/watch?v =13IrUvZdDVA.

15. The OECD National Contact Point Mechanism[1]

Elizabeth Umlas

OVERVIEW

Over a decade after the unanimous endorsement of the United Nations Guiding Principles on Business and Human Rights (UNGPs),[2] the lack of progress on their third pillar – achieving meaningful access to remedy for corporate-related human rights abuses – remains a major concern. Given the obstacles to judicial and non-judicial grievance mechanisms worldwide, having a range of remedies is necessary. Improving access to and strengthening each type of mechanism is a key goal of survivors, their advocates, and scholars alike. A focus of both practitioners and academics has been exploring the range of accountability mechanisms available for survivors and addressing barriers to using them. (See Right to Remedy, Chapter 6.)

The Organisation for Economic Co-operation and Development (OECD) National Contact Point (NCP) complaints process is one such accountability mechanism, but its potential remains unrealized. In discussions of corporate accountability, the NCP mechanism provides a key illustration of a state-based, non-judicial grievance mechanism under the UNGPs. The NCP process has been the subject of significant critical analysis and offers a rich set of case studies across an increasing range of subjects, sectors, and contexts. It is therefore an important part of teaching business and human rights (BHR).

---

[1]   An earlier version of this chapter appeared as Elizabeth Umlas, "Teaching Note: OECD National Contact Point Complaints," in *Teaching Business and Human Rights Handbook* (Teaching Business and Human Rights Forum, 2016), https://teachbhr.org/resources/teaching-bhr-handbook/teaching-notes/oecd-ncp-complaints.

[2]   United Nations Human Rights Council, *Guiding Principles on Business and Human Rights: Implementing the United Nations "Protect, Respect and Remedy" Framework,* Report of the Special Representative of the Secretary-General on the issue of human rights and transnational corporations and other business enterprises," UN doc. A/HRC/17/31 (March 21, 2011) (UN Guiding Principles).

This chapter begins with an overview of NCPs (their structure, the complaints process, noteworthy complaints), explores various criticisms of the NCPs as an accountability mechanism, and offers teaching approaches to the NCP complaint process for law, business, and policy courses.

NATIONAL CONTACT POINTS

The OECD first adopted its Guidelines for Multinational Enterprises (Guidelines) in 1976. The Guidelines are binding on OECD member states and provide recommendations by governments to corporations on business ethics, legal compliance, and observation of international standards and "other societal expectations." The most recent update of the Guidelines in 2011 brought them in line with the UNGPs and added a chapter on human rights.[3]

All governments adhering to the Guidelines must establish an NCP.[4] NCPs are tasked with promoting the Guidelines and serve as a mediation and dispute resolution platform for problems arising in relation to their implementation.[5] NCPs are responsible for helping, through dialogue and mediation, to address allegations of non-observance of the Guidelines through a complaints process called "specific instances." As NCPs are created by governments, and their actions do not have the force of law, they are an example of what the UNGPs classify as a "state-based, non-judicial grievance mechanism" (NJGM).[6]

NJGMs are not a substitute for judicial remedies, such as litigation. (See Judicial Remedy, Chapter 12.) They can, however, complement such remedies, which might not always be effective or accessible in a particular situation. Based in mediation, the specific instance process could, in principle, be less costly and antagonistic – and lead to a quicker resolution – than litigation. Notably, NCPs provide a forum for extraterritorial cases, or ones in which the country where alleged violations occurred differs from the home country of the company in question. Because NCPs are the grievance mechanism of the

---

[3]   Organisation for Economic Co-operation and Development (OECD), *OECD Guidelines for Multinational Enterprises* (Paris: OECD Publishing, 2011) (OECD Guidelines).

[4]   OECD, *OECD Guidelines*, 18. As of 2022, 50 governments had NCPs: a list of NCPs of governments adhering to the OECD Guidelines can be found at "What Are National Contact Points for RBC?" OECD, accessed August 3, 2022, https://mneguidelines.oecd.org/ncps.

[5]   "What Are National Contact Points for RBC?" OECD, accessed August 3, 2022, https://mneguidelines.oecd.org/ncps.

[6]   NCPs were created in 1984 and became NJGMs in 2000. OECD, *Implementing the OECD Guidelines for Multinational Enterprises: The National Contact Points from 2000 to 2015: Key Findings* (Paris: OECD, 2016), 1 https://mneguidelines.oecd.org/15-Years-of-the-National-Contact-Points-Highlights.pdf.

Guidelines, and the Guidelines are aligned with the UNGPs, it has been said that "through the vehicle of NCPs, the Guidelines are a *de facto* implementation mechanism of the UNGPs."[7]

NCP STRUCTURE AND COMPLAINTS PROCESS[8]

States may set up their NCPs as they choose, and the structure of NCPs has evolved over time. The OECD has noted, for example, that some governments are no longer housing an NCP in a single ministry.[9] NCPs can also be based in one ministry "but involve other [m]inistries and other stakeholders," or can consist of "an office with independent experts and a supporting secretariat attached to a [m]inistry."[10] Still others might be inter-ministerial, and some are tripartite or quadripartite, involving representatives of government, employees, business, or civil society.

Any "interested party" – individuals, communities, non-governmental organizations (NGOs), trade unions, employers' organizations – can file a "specific instance" with an NCP. If the alleged violation(s) took place in an adhering country, complainants should file the complaint with that state's NCP, but can also file it with the NCP of the home country of the entity in question.[11] Most often, NGOs, communities, or trade unions file specific instances against multinational enterprises. Complaints can, however, be filed

---

[7] Roel Nieuwenkamp, "OECD's Human Rights Grievance Mechanism as a Competitive Advantage," Institute for Human Rights and Business, November 4, 2014, http://www.ihrb.org/other/governments-role/oecds-human-rights-grievance-mechanism-as-a-competitive-advantage.

[8] On how to file a complaint, see "6. Filing a Complaint at the NCP: the 'Specific Instances' Procedures," *Corporate Accountability for Human Rights Abuses: A Guide for Victims and NGOs on Recourse Mechanisms*, FIDH, updated 2021, https://corporateaccountability.fidh.org/the-guide/mediation-mechanisms/oecd-guidelines-for-multinational-enterprises/filing-a-complaint-at-the-ncp-the-specific-instances-procedures.

[9] OECD, *Implementing the OECD Guidelines*, 6.

[10] OECD, *Implementing the OECD Guidelines*, 6.

[11] As FIDH notes, "NGOs have sought to highlight the issue of parent company responsibility by simultaneously filing cases before the host and home country NCPs and calling on both NCPs to collaborate." FIDH, "Corporate Accountability."

against other entities.[12] According to the OECD, as of 2022 NCPs had handled over 600 cases (see Table 15.1).[13]

The Guidelines provide Procedural Guidance on the NCP process.[14] NCPs must operate according to "core criteria of visibility, accessibility, transparency and accountability."[15] Their functions include making an initial assessment of the allegations. If the issue calls for further examination, the NCP is expected to "offer good offices" to resolve the issue. After the procedure, the NCP should publicize the results by issuing a final statement or report and, if relevant, recommendations on implementation of the Guidelines. Where the parties fail to reach an agreement, or if one party refuses to participate, the NCP should publish a statement identifying the parties and issues and any recommendations and observations on why the process did not yield an agreement. The Procedural Guidance lays out an "indicative timeframe" for these steps, saying NCPs should "strive to conclude the procedure within 12 months from receipt of the specific instance."[16]

CRITICISMS OF THE NCP MECHANISM

The NCP system has received significant criticism from scholars and practitioners, and any discussion of the mechanism will benefit from examining some of its weaknesses. Regarding performance, OECD Watch[17] found in 2020 that, while "NCP functioning" had "improved significantly" since 2000, the Guidelines mechanism was marred by barriers to access, a high rate of case rejection, and perceived conflicts of interest at NCPs.[18] The organization's

---

[12] For example, specific instances have been filed against the football federation, FIFA; the NGO WWF International; and the multistakeholder Roundtable for Responsible Palm Oil (RSPO). See OECD, *National Contact Points for Responsible Business Conduct: Providing Access to Remedy: 20 Years and the Road Ahead* (2020), 17, https://mneguidelines.oecd.org/NCPs-for-RBC-providing-access-to-remedy-20 -years-and-the-road-ahead.pdf.

[13] OECD, *Stocktaking Report on the OECD Guidelines for Multinational Enterprises* (2022), 3, https://mneguidelines.oecd.org/stocktaking-report-on-the-oecd -guidelines-for-multinational-enterprises.pdf.

[14] See OECD, *OECD Guidelines*, 71–74 (and Commentary, 78–87) for Procedural Guidance relating to NCPs.

[15] OECD, *OECD Guidelines*, Procedural Guidance, Part I, 71.

[16] OECD, *OECD Guidelines*, 87.

[17] OECD Watch, a global network of civil society organizations, is "the official representative of civil society at the OECD Investment Committee" and "Policy & Advocacy," OECD Watch, accessed August 3, 2022, https://www.oecdwatch.org/ about-us/our-work/advocacy.

[18] OECD Watch, *The State of Remedy under the OECD Guidelines* (Amsterdam: OECD Watch, 2020), 1, https://www.oecdwatch.org/wp-content/uploads/sites/8/2020/ 06/State-of-Remedy-2020.pdf.

Table 15.1   Noteworthy OECD National Contact Point complaints

Complaint	NCP	Year
Society for Threatened Peoples vs. Credit Suisse Risks associated with North Dakota Access Pipeline in the USA	Switzerland	2019
EC and IDI vs. Australia and New Zealand Banking Group ANZ's role in displacing and dispossessing Cambodian families[1]	Australia	2018
Former employees vs. Heineken Unlawful dismissals by Heineken's subsidiary in eastern DRC	Netherlands	2017
Bart Stapert vs. Mylan Mylan's export of drugs used for death penalty in the USA	Netherlands	2016
Lok Shakti et al. vs. POSCO (S. Korea), ABP/APG (Netherlands) and NBIM (Norway) POSCO's involvement in human rights and environmental impact in India	Norway	2012

Note: 1   See also "Cambodia: Securing Compensation for ANZ-Backed Land Grab," Inclusive Development International, accessed August 3, 2022,https://www.inclusivedevelopment.net/cases/cambodia-sugarcane-land-grabs/?__cf_chl_tk=hLYVEDn8QBznI8jm8Jj7RN5e3eP3P5DyeIlrmhe9Lcg-1650632241-0-gaNycGzNCP0.

(See Teaching Resources below for full citations.)

2015 analysis concluded that NCPs could be a "valuable tool" for access to remedy, but that they were "not meeting that potential," with only 14 percent of cases having "some beneficial results that may have provided some measure of remedy."[19]

While NCPs are supposed to be functionally equivalent, in practice some are much weaker than others.[20] The resources and powers states devote to NCPs vary greatly, which in turn has an impact on their effectiveness. OECD Watch has pointed out that some NCP structures, as well as where the NCP is located in government, "contribute to a (perceived) lack of independence."[21] Placing an NCP in the Ministry of Trade, for example, could raise questions about how

---

[19]   Caitlin Daniel et al., *Remedy Remains Rare* (Amsterdam: OECD Watch, 2015), 5 and 19. Note that OECD Watch studied only cases filed by NGOs, individuals, and communities, not those brought by trade unions, which are monitored separately by the OECD's Trade Union Advisory Committee (TUAC). See Resources regarding searchable specific instance databases maintained by OECD Watch, TUAC and the OECD.

[20]   See, for example, OECD Watch's evaluations of NCP performance, "NCP Evaluations," OECD Watch, accessed August 3, 2022, https://www.oecdwatch.org/indicator. Functional equivalence, per the OECD Guidelines' Procedural Guidance, means all NCPs are expected to "operate in accordance with core criteria of visibility, accessibility, transparency and accountability." OECD, *OECD Guidelines*, Procedural Guidance, Part I, 71.

[21]   Daniel et al., *Remedy Remains Rare*, 33–34.

objectively it would assess allegations of corporate wrongdoing if it reports to a ministry that fosters commercial opportunities for multinationals. Likewise, OECD Watch found some correlation between effective outcomes and NCPs with independent expertise, multistakeholder oversight, or "a balanced tripartite structure."[22] Underscoring the unevenness of NCP performance, Macchi notes EU-based NCPs have done "relatively better" in terms of impact and that "most of these success stories" have come from a handful of European NCPs.[23]

Two fundamental problems with the process are the fact that NCPs are not required to issue findings on whether the Guidelines have been violated;[24] and the lack of consequences, legal, financial, or otherwise, for the few companies that have been found by an NCP to have breached the Guidelines or that refuse to participate in the process altogether. Claimants have little recourse if a company ignores an NCP's recommendations to address allegations, or the NCP fails to make a public statement on a case. These weaknesses have significantly diminished the mechanism's credibility.

Governments can choose to build consequences into specific instance outcomes. In 2015, for example, the Canadian NCP became the first (and as of 2022 the only) NCP to impose sanctions when it did so on China Gold, a Canada-based mining company, for failing to engage in a complaint against it by the Canada Tibet Committee. The NCP's response included withdrawing certain government services and support abroad.[25]

An adhering country, OECD Watch, or the OECD advisory committees for trade unions and business (TUAC and BIAC, respectively) can submit a com-

---

[22] Daniel et al., 34–35.

[23] Chiara Macchi, "The Role of the OECD National Contact Points in Improving Access to Justice for Victims of Human Rights Violations in the EU Member States," in *La Implementación de los Principios Rectores de las Naciones Unidas Sobre Empresas y los Derechos Humanos por la Unión Europea y sus Estados Miembros*, eds. Maria del Carmen Márquez Carrasco and Inmaculada Vivas Tesón (Aranzadi Thomson Reuters, 2017), 145–165. According to OECD Watch, only five NCPs have placed consequences on companies that fail to engage in a Specific Instance. All of these are in Europe. See "Consequences," Procedures, OECD Watch, accessed August 3, 2022, https://www.oecdwatch.org/indicator/consequences.

[24] OECD Watch, *OECD Watch Statement on the Update of the OECD Guidelines for MNEs* (May 25, 2011), https://www.oecdwatch.org/wp-content/uploads/sites/8/2011/05/OECD-Watch-statement-on-the-update-of-the-OECD-Guidelines-for-Multinational-Enterprises.pdf, noting this is "a minimum requirement for any credible complaint mechanism." OECD Watch reports that just over one-quarter of NCPs issue determinations. For a list of these, see "Determinations," Procedures, OECD Watch, accessed August 3, 2022, https://www.oecdwatch.org/indicator/determinations.

[25] Daniel et al., *Remedy Remains Rare*, 46. See also 28n and OECD Watch's NCP Evaluations: "Consequences," Procedures, OECD Watch, accessed August 3, 2022, https://www.oecdwatch.org/indicator/consequences.

plaint to the OECD Investment Committee about an individual NCP's han-dling of specific instances.[26] As of 2022, this procedure, too, was rarely used.

One way the OECD has sought to strengthen NCPs is through peer reviews. The Guidelines merely "encourage" such reviews,[27] though NGOs have called for them to be mandatory.[28] The OECD itself has noted lack of skills and leverage at NCPs; lack of visibility and accessibility; and failure to guarantee safe proceedings as some of the challenges facing this mechanism. Among other things, the OECD has called for an increase in resources to NCPs, more stakeholder involvement in the Guidelines process, better coordination among NCPs, and a more consistent approach by governments to procedural aspects and Guidelines interpretation.[29]

On the positive side, OECD Watch's 2020 study found recent cases had widened the mechanism's scope to include both new issues (e.g., climate change, the digital economy) and entities that had mostly escaped earlier scru-tiny under the Guidelines process (e.g., multistakeholder initiatives, banks, and other financial institutions).[30]

OECD GUIDELINES STOCKTAKING PROCESS

In 2020–21, the OECD conducted a "stocktaking" of the Guidelines to deter-mine whether they were still "fit for purpose." The review took place in the face of concerns that, as OECD Watch put it, the NCPs "and the Guidelines themselves are at risk of becoming obsolete," given the emergence of laws mandating corporate human rights due diligence and stakeholders' growing frustration with "non-binding measures."[31]

The stocktaking was based on extensive consultation, including an NCP survey, public commentary, and stakeholder input.[32] It revealed "significant

---

[26]   OECD, *OECD Guidelines*, 74.

[27]   OECD, *OECD Guidelines*, 81.

[28]   See, for example, Daniel et al., *Remedy Remains Rare*, 51.

[29]   OECD, "National Contact Points," chap. 5.

[30]   OECD Watch, *State of Remedy*. For a critical view of a specific instance against a bank in relation to its responsibility for passive investments and as a nominee share-holder, see BankTrack and OECD Watch, "Swiss NCP Misses the Mark on UBS Links to Mass Surveillance of Uighurs," BankTrack, March 3, 2021, https://www.banktrack.org/article/swiss_ncp_misses_the_mark_on_nominee_shareholdings_in_ubs_case.

[31]   OECD Watch, *State of Remedy*, 3. See also, Marian Ingrams, Joseph Wilde-Ramsing, and Janna Fleuren, *Get Fit: Closing Gaps in the OECD Guidelines to Make Them Fit for Purpose* (Amsterdam: OECD Watch, June 2021), https://www.oecdwatch.org/wp-content/uploads/sites/8/2021/06/OECD-Watch-Get-Fit-Closing-gaps-in-the-OECD-Guidelines-to-make-them-fit-for-purpose-1.pdf.

[32]   OECD, *Stocktaking Report*, 11.

gaps" in reaching NCP functional equivalence, due in part to lack of resources and "weak monitoring and oversight mechanisms."[33] It also underscored the need for the Guidelines to be strengthened in areas such as climate change, digitalization, protection of at-risk groups, and application of the Guidelines to business models beyond traditional corporations.[34] As of May 2022, it remains to be seen whether the review will lead to strengthening the NCP process as a remedy mechanism.

TEACHING APPROACHES

In a BHR course, the NCP complaint process can be taught as part of an overview of remedy mechanisms. It is useful to have students review Pillar III of the UNGPs, "Access to Remedy." Instructors can situate NCPs and specific instances in a broader discussion of corporate accountability. This could involve introducing examples of state judicial; state non-judicial; and non-state, non-judicial grievance mechanisms, and encouraging critical and strategic thinking about how to improve access to remedy in each case, including which mechanisms might work best in various contexts. An essential message for students is that multiple tools are often necessary in each situation. Instructors might point students toward OECD's thematic and sectoral due diligence guidance as part of the framework on corporate accountability.[35] NCPs can also be discussed as "fill[ing] a gap" left by other grievance mechanisms, in that they can provide mediation, "public accountability as a result of final statements," and potentially even remedy and prevention.[36]

There is easily enough material for an entire session on NCPs. The strengths and weaknesses of the NCP process represent a rich topic, covered in detail by a growing critical literature.[37]

---

[33] OECD, *Stocktaking Report*, 9.

[34] OECD, *Stocktaking Report*, 7 and 17.

[35] OECD has published general due diligence guidance for responsible business conduct as well as guidance on extractives, garments and footwear, institutional investment, agriculture, and other sectors. See OECD, *OECD Due Diligence Guidance for Responsible Business Conduct* (OECD, 2018), http://mneguidelines.oecd.org/OECD -Due-Diligence-Guidance-for-Responsible-Business-Conduct.pdf.

[36] Karin Buhmann, "National Contact Points under OECD's Guidelines for Multinational Enterprises: Institutional Diversity Affecting Assessments of the Delivery of Access to Remedy," in *Accountability, International Business Operations and the Law: Providing Justice for Corporate Human Rights Violations in Global Value Chains*, eds. Liesbeth Enneking et al. (London: Routledge, 2019).

[37] For a listing of numerous scholarly articles on the Guidelines and the NCPs, see n. 172 in OECD, *Draft Report for the Stocktaking of the OECD Guidelines for Multinational Enterprises* (Paris: OECD, June 2021).

Learning objectives in courses covering the NCP complaints process may include:

- Gaining a detailed understanding of a key state-based, non-judicial grievance mechanism.
- Learning how this mechanism fits into the larger picture of access to remedy.
- Critically assessing the strengths and weaknesses of NCPs.
- Understanding the connection between the Guidelines and the UNGPs via the NCP mechanism.
- Gaining insight, through case studies of specific instances, into how NCPs function, as well as differences across countries

Law instructors might ask students to compare NCPs from various countries and discuss the legal parameters of the powers with which they are endowed. For example, the Danish NCP has the power to investigate allegations and determine if a party has breached the Guidelines.[38] In contrast, the US NCP has stated that, "consistent with the voluntary nature of the Guidelines," it "does not make a determination whether a violation of the Guidelines has occurred."[39] Law students can discuss the advantages and disadvantages of pursuing a non-judicial route, such as a specific instance, in comparison to a judicial route in particular situations. The NCP mechanism can also be used as an entrée to the complexities (legal and otherwise) of cases involving extraterritorial human rights abuses.

Law students might also benefit from assessing the value of the diverse non-judicial remedies that specific instances can (in principle) yield, such as a formal apology, a change in company policy, promises of non-repetition, reparation, and so forth.[40]

---

[38] "OECD Watch Welcomes Denmark's Strengthened NCP," OECD Watch, October 5, 2012, https://www.oecdwatch.org/oecd-watch-welcomes-denmarks -strengthened-ncp-the-new-mediation-and-complaints-mechanism-with-a-mandate-to -investigate-allegations-and-make-recommendations.

[39] US NCP, *U.S. NCP Final Assessment: Communications Workers of America (AFL-CIO, CWA)/ver.di and Deutsche Telekom AG* (Bureau of Economic and Business Affairs, July 9, 2013), https://2009-2017.state.gov/e/eb/oecd/usncp/links/rls/211646 .htm. For more on the "fundamentally different conceptions" various NCPs have of their functions, see Juan Carlos Ochoa Sanchez, "The Roles and Powers of the OECD National Contact Points Regarding Complaints on an Alleged Breach of the OECD Guidelines for Multinational Enterprises by a Transnational Corporation," *Nordic Journal of International Law* 84, no. 1 (February 2015): 89–126.

[40] Buhmann notes: "NCPs cannot make determinations on compensation, but they can make recommendations in their final statements, and they can facilitate agreements between parties, which may include reparations." Buhmann, "National Contact Points."

Business courses can explore how various companies have reacted to specific instances (for this, OECD Watch's *Remedy Remains Rare* offers a useful range of short cases that can foster discussion). The same students might want to explore the above-mentioned China Gold case – the business implications of a government denying certain services and support abroad to a company that refused to participate in an NCP process.

Policy courses can emphasize the fact that, per the Guidelines, NCPs are "encouraged" to inform other government agencies of their statements and reports where the NCP knows them "to be relevant to a specific agency's policies and programmes."[41] This provision is interesting to discuss with policy students, given OECD Watch's assertion that "policy incoherence between the NCP and other government departments" is common.[42] It is also worth underscoring the "voluntary nature" of this provision,[43] which provides an entry to discussing voluntary versus mandatory instruments.

Policy students can explore the different tools with which governments might reinforce the work of NCPs – requiring NCPs to make compliance determinations, or instituting sanctions for corporate non-compliance with the Guidelines, such as tying export credit and other government services to NCP findings and recommendations; discuss the policy implications of a state's granting more power and resources to its NCP; and consider how NCPs fit into National Action Plans (NAPs) on business and human rights.

EXERCISE 15.1

OECD NATIONAL CONTACT POINT CASE STUDIES

Teachers can assign students specific NCP cases to present. NCP case studies allows students to examine the variations in how states approach NCPs, as well as the reasons why complainants choose this route over others. Ultimately, students will gain insight into the mechanism's viability and how NCPs fit into the larger picture of access to remedy.

• **Heineken**

The Dutch NCP brokered an agreement in 2017 between former Congolese workers and Heineken for its subsidiary's alleged human rights abuses in 1999–2003. The agreement included financial compensation for the work-

---

41 OECD, *OECD Guidelines*, 85.
42 OECD Watch, *State of Remedy*, 15.
43 OECD, *OECD Guidelines*, 85.

ers, an unusual outcome, as was the fact that the Dutch NCP did not apply a statute of limitations.[44]

• **Mylan**

Law students might be particularly interested in the Mylan case, which involved a US pharmaceutical company that moved its headquarters to the Netherlands. A specific instance was filed with the Dutch NCP against Mylan over the company's alleged breach of the Guidelines due to its sale of a drug used in lethal injection executions in US prisons.[45] The case touches on several interesting legal issues – company involvement in, or connection to, the death penalty; the implications of a relocated business being subject to a different set of laws and social norms (on the death penalty, for example) than those in its original home country; and the extent of a company's responsibility with regard to the distribution of its products.

• **POSCO**

The POSCO case provides an excellent example of how the Guidelines can be applied to institutional investors, and thus an entrée into discussing the broadening scope of the mechanism. Several NGOs filed a specific instance with multiple NCPs against both POSCO (a Korean multinational steel company), over its proposed operations in India, and two of its institutional investors. Each investor reacted differently, with one cooperating and accepting the NCP's findings and recommendations and the other not engaging in the process and eventually arguing that the Guidelines did not apply to it as a minority shareholder. The case led to a confirmation by the UN Office of the High Commission for Human Rights that the UNGPs and the Guidelines (and therefore the NCP process) apply to institutional investors, including minority shareholders, as forms of business enterprise.[46]

---

[44]   See "Six Secrets to Success: Analysis of Key Success Factors for Remedy in the Case of DRC workers vs. Heineken at the Dutch NCP," December 3, 2017, OECD Watch, https://www.oecdwatch.org/six-secrets-to-success-analysis-of-key-success-factors-for-remedy-in-the-case-of-drc-workers-vs-heineken-at-the-dutch-ncp.

[45]   See Dutch NCP, *Final Statement, Bart Stapert, attorney, vs. Mylan* (The Hague: Ministry of Foreign Affairs, April 11, 2016), https://www.oecdguidelines.nl/documents/publication/2016/4/11/bart-stapert-attorney-vs-mylan.

[46]   This position was confirmed in 2013 by the UN Office of the High Commission for Human Rights: see Craig Mokhiber to Joris Oldenziel, "Subject: The Issue of the Applicability of the Guiding Principles on Business and Human Rights to Minority Shareholders," April 26, 2013, https://www.ohchr.org/Documents/Issues/Business/LetterSOMO.pdf; and in the same year by the Norwegian and Dutch NCPs. Norwegian NCP, *Final Statement, Complaint from Lok Shakti Abhiyan, Korean Transnational*

Discussing it allows students to explore what investor responsibility under the Guidelines means for portfolio management (e.g., what is investor "human rights due diligence"? How might specific instances against investors affect their behavior?).[47] Students can also examine more recent investor-related cases emerging from the Guidelines process.[48]

KEY QUESTIONS

General

- What are OECD National Contact Points and how do they function?
- Who can file a "specific instance"?
- When would someone file one, and what outcome might they hope for?
- What are the strengths and weaknesses of the specific instance process?
- Overall, is this mechanism promising in relation to the "access to remedy" pillar of the UNGPs?

Corporations Watch, Fair Green and Global Alliance and Forum for the Environment and Development vs. Posco (South Korea), ABP/APG (Netherlands) and NBIM (Norway) (Oslo, May 27, 2013), https://www.oecdwatch.org/wp-content/uploads/sites/8/dlm_uploads/2021/03/final%20statement%20norwegian%20NCP.pdf, 21–23. For more on the case, see John G. Ruggie and Tamaryn Nelson, "Human Rights and the OECD Guidelines for Multinational Enterprises: Normative Innovations and Implementation Challenges," *Brown Journal of World Affairs* 22, no. 1 (Fall/Winter 2015), 119–120.

[47] On this point, see generally OECD, *Responsible Business Conduct for Institutional Investors: Key Considerations for Due Diligence under the OECD Guidelines for Multinational Enterprises* (2017), https://mneguidelines.oecd.org/RBC-for-Institutional-Investors.pdf.

[48] For example, "Society for Threatened Peoples Switzerland and UBS Group," OECD, accessed August 3, 2022, http://mneguidelines.oecd.org/database/instances/ch0021.htm. Further, in 2021 the Dutch, Norwegian and US NCPs accepted a case filed against McDonald's for gender-based violence and harassment at its operations in multiple countries, and against two of its investors, APG and NBIM, for alleged failure to conduct due diligence in relation to the allegations. Netherlands National Contact Point for Responsible Business Conduct, *Initial Assessment of the Notification of 4 Trade Unions vs. APG Asset Management* (The Hague: Ministry of Foreign Affairs, May 20, 2021), https://www.oecdguidelines.nl/notifications/documents/publication/2021/05/20/initial-assessment-of-the-notification-of-4-trade-unions-vs-apg-asset-management.

For Business Students

- What are the implications of applying the Guidelines – and thus the NCP complaint procedure – to institutional investors as "business enterprises" like any other?
- What about the implications of applying the procedure to banks?
- Are there fundamental differences in how the Guidelines should be applied to one industry versus another?
- What incentives do businesses have to participate in the voluntary specific instance process?
- What are the implications for business of governments' attaching sanctions to non-compliance with the Guidelines?

For Law Students

- How does the OECD NCP mechanism complement judicial mechanisms for survivors of corporate-related human rights abuses?
- How does the process compare with other accountability mechanisms addressing extraterritorial corporate activities?
- Is it inconsistent with the non-binding (on companies) nature of the OECD Guidelines for NCPs to make a public determination of whether a company breached the Guidelines?
- What recourse do governments have when a company refuses to participate in NCP mediation?
- How might governments, through regulatory measures, address NCP weaknesses?

For Policy Students

- How might governments use policy to address weaknesses of the NCP mechanism? Must the Guidelines themselves be changed to do so?
- How might NAPs strengthen the work of NCPs?
- What are the implications of placing an NCP in the Foreign Ministry? The Trade Ministry? The Ministry of Justice? What might be the policy reasons for placing an NCP in each?
- What might be the rationale of using a particular NCP structure?
- How might NCP decisions be used to influence policy decisions in other parts of government?

TEACHING RESOURCES

Readings

Primary sources

- Organisation for Economic Co-operation and Development, OECD Guidelines for Multinational Enterprises (OECD Publishing, 2011).

NCP statements

- **Australian** National Contact Point. *Final Statement: EC and IDI vs. Australia and New Zealand Banking Group.* June 27, 2018. https://www.oecdwatch.org/download/28899.
- **Norwegian** National Contact Point. *Final Statement: Complaint from Lok Shakti Abhiyan, Korean Transnational Corporations Watch, FairGreen and Global Alliance and Forum for Environment and Development vs. Posco (South Korea), ABP/APG (Netherlands) and NBIM (Norway).* May 27, 2013. https://www.oecdwatch.org/wp-content/uploads/sites/8/dlm_uploads/2021/03/final%20statement%20norwegian%20NCP.pdf.
- **Netherlands** National Contact Point. *Final Statement: Former employees vs. Heineken.* August 18, 2017, https://www.oecdwatch.org/download/29241.
- **Netherlands** National Contact Point. *Final Statement: Bart Stapert, attorney, vs. Mylan.* The Hague: Ministry of Foreign Affairs, April 11, 2016, https://www.oecdguidelines.nl/documents/publication/2016/4/11/bart-stapert-attorney-vs-mylan.
- National Contact Point of **Switzerland**. *Final Statement: Specific Instance Regarding Credit Suisse Submitted by the Society for Threatened Peoples Switzerland.* October 16, 2019. https://www.oecdwatch.org/wp-.content/uploads/sites/8/dlm_uploads/2021/03/Abschlusserklarung%20CS.pdf.
- **UK** National Contact Point. *Final Statement Following Agreement Reached in Complaint from WWF International Against SOCO International PLC.* July 2014. https://www.oecdwatch.org/wp-content/uploads/sites/8/dlm_uploads/2021/03/WWF%20SOCO%20final%20statement.pdf.

Commentary

- Amnesty International. *Obstacle Course: How the UK's National Contact Point Handles Human Rights Complaints under the OECD Guidelines for Multinational Enterprises.* London: Amnesty International UK,

2016. https://www.amnesty.org.uk/sites/default/files/uk_ncp_complaints _handling_full_report_lores_0.pdf.
- OECD Watch. "Second Evaluation of NCPs Shows Persistent Gaps in Performance." November 25, 2021. https://www.oecdwatch.org/second -evaluation-of-ncps-shows-persistent-gaps-in-performance.

Websites

- Business at OECD (BIAC). "Business Advocacy at the OECD." https:// www.businessatoecd.org.
- OECD. "OECD Home." https://www.oecd.org.
- OECD Guidelines for Multinational Enterprises. "Database of Specific Instances." http://mneguidelines.oecd.org/database.
- OECD Watch. "Complaints Database." https://www.oecdwatch.org/ complaints-database. This database contains specific instances filed by civil society organizations.
- OECD Watch. "Holding Corporations and Governments Accountable Using the OECD Guidelines for Multinational Enterprises." https://www .oecdwatch.org.
- Trade Union Advisory Committee. "TUAC MNE Guidelines and Complaints." https://tuac.org/mne-guidelines-complaints-by-trade-union. This database contains specific instances filed by workers' organizations. It is only partially publicly available; the full database is accessible only to TUAC affiliates and its partners.
- Trade Union Advisory Committee to the OECD. https://tuac.org.

16. Multistakeholder human rights initiatives

Dorothée Baumann-Pauly and Michael Posner

OVERVIEW

The first multistakeholder initiatives (MSIs) addressing human rights were created in the 1990s in response to high-profile controversies in the apparel, manufacturing, forestry, and mining industries.[1] MSIs emerged as large multinational companies felt the need to address human rights challenges that had become more obvious in a globalizing economy. Participants recognized that these challenges were too big for any one company to take on alone.[2] They also were responding to consumer and public demands for change.

Over the past three decades, MSIs have established themselves as a new governance form that combines the efforts of civil society, business, academia, and sometimes governments. Together, these actors are able to define human rights standards, metrics, and means of evaluation in the many places around the world where local governments are unable or unwilling to protect the basic human rights of their own people. MSIs have emerged as important avenues to address such governance gaps. They develop so-called "soft law" requirements that regulate transnational company conduct.[3] MSIs can also serve as

---

[1] Key examples of early MSIs are the Fair Labor Association in the apparel industry or the Forest Stewardship Council in the forestry sector and the Voluntary Principles on Security and Human Rights in the mining sector.

[2] Dorothée Baumann-Pauly, Justine Nolan, Sarah Labowitz, and Auret van Heerden, "Setting and Enforcing Industry-Specific Standards for Human Rights: The Role of Multi-stakeholder Initiatives in Regulating Corporate Conduct," in *Business and Human Rights: From Principles to Practice*, ed. Dorothée Baumann-Pauly and Justine Nolan (New York: Routledge, 2016).

[3] Sébastien Mena and Guido Palazzo, "Input and Output Legitimacy of Multi-Stakeholder Initiatives," *Business Ethics Quarterly* (2012).

platforms for companies to conduct human rights due diligence, presenting necessary complements to emerging human rights due diligence legislation.[4]

The role of MSIs is an important part of business and human rights (BHR) teaching due to their potential impact and growing prominence among businesses.[5]

This chapter describes how MSIs emerged, under what conditions they serve to advance human rights in corporate practice, and how they can complement human rights due diligence legislation.

HUMAN RIGHTS MSIs

MSIs addressing human rights have been formed in a range of industries – garments, toys, electronics, oil and mining, information and communications technology, and private security. Some focus on specific human rights issues, such as trafficking, corruption, or privacy; some focus on the human rights impacts of specific commodities, such as palm oil or cocoa.

Prominent MSIs include the Fair Labor Association (1996), the Voluntary Principles on Security and Human Rights (2000), the Roundtable on Sustainable Palm Oil (2004),[6] the Global Network Initiative (2008), the International Code of Conduct for Private Security Providers (2010), and the Accord on Fire and Building Safety in Bangladesh (2013).[7]

There is no comprehensive directory for human rights MSIs but an initial mapping effort in 2017 by MSI Integrity, an independent civil society organization, identified 45 transnational, standard-setting organizations for corruption, human rights, and environmental challenges. According to this mapping study, 45 MSIs engage over 50 national governments and regulate over 9,000 companies, including "65 Fortune Global 500" businesses with combined annual revenues of more than $5.4 trillion dollars.[8]

---

[4]   Dorothée Baumann-Pauly and Lilach Trabelsi, "Complementing Mandatory Human Rights Due Diligence: Using Multi-Stakeholder Initiatives to Define Human Rights Standards," *NYU Stern School of Business*, January 2021. Available at SSRN: https://ssrn.com/abstract=3810689.

[5]   Dorothée Baumann-Pauly and Justine Nolan, "Mapping the Landscape of Multi-Stakeholder Initiatives – Few MSIs Are Equipped to Address Governance Gaps," *NYU Stern Center for Business and Human Rights*, July 5, 2017, https://bhr.stern.nyu.edu/blogs/few-msis-are-equipped-to-address-gaps.

[6]   Roundtable for Sustainable Palm Oil, https://rspo.org.

[7]   Accord on Fire and Building Safety in Bangladesh, https://bangladeshaccord.org.

[8]   MSI Integrity, *Not Fit-for-Purpose: The Grand Experiment of Multi-Stakeholder Initiatives in Corporate Accountability, Human Rights and Global Governance* (San Francisco, CA: MSI Integrity, 2020).

Not all MSIs are created equal. They vary significantly in terms of their ambition, structure, and effectiveness. It is important to discuss what constitutes an MSI and what are the key characteristics to make MSIs effective in regulating corporate conduct. While participation in MSIs is voluntary, the most advanced MSIs set concrete standards and metrics that are monitored by independent third parties, and that are compulsory for member companies. It is helpful to discuss possible MSI typologies and highlight the criteria that differentiate human rights governance MSIs from corporate dominated trade associations, learning platforms, and certification bodies. It is also useful to discuss and distinguish certification schemes, which certify products and measure corporate governance and management systems, and MSI assessment or accreditation systems, which involve periodic independent reviews of company performance measured against industry standards and metrics.[9]

In a June 2021 white paper entitled "Seeking a 'Smart Mix': Multistakeholder Initiatives and Mandatory Human Rights Due Diligence," Dorothée Baumann-Pauly and Isabelle Glimcher further develop criteria for strong human rights governance MSIs:[10]

• Governance: Each stakeholder group forming part of the MSI should have an equal role in the governance of the organization – equal representation on the board and an equal role in decision-making.
• Rigorous standards: The MSI's standards should be aligned with international law as well as any other relevant established international standards with the focus on always adhering to the highest standard should a conflict arise.
• Independent monitoring: Compliance with the MSI's standards should be evaluated independently rather than self-reported. In addition, the MSI should facilitate verification of any remediation done on non-compliances reported through the monitoring process.
• Transparency: Public transparency regarding a company's performance against standards is an important element to maintaining accountability of the MSI's members.

---

[9] Dorothée Baumann-Pauly, Justine Nolan, Auret Van Heerden, and Michael Samway, "Industry-Specific Multi-Stakeholder Initiatives That Govern Corporate Human Rights Standards: Legitimacy Assessments of the Fair Labor Association and the Global Network Initiative," *Journal of Business Ethics* 143, no. 4 (2017).
[10] Baumann-Pauly and Glimcher, "Seeking a Smart Mix: Multistakeholder Initiatives and Mandatory Human Rights Due Diligence." 2021. Available at https://gcbhr.org/backoffice/resources/white-paper-msis-24p.pdf.

- Remedy: The MSI should have meaningful ways in which it can enforce compliance, including through providing members and affected parties access to remedy such as an operational-level grievance mechanism.

If these criteria are met, MSIs are equipped to address governance gaps by setting and enforcing industry-specific human rights standards.

MSIs AND MANDATORY HUMAN RIGHTS DUE DILIGENCE

A key question is how MSIs will fit into the emerging landscape of mandatory human rights due diligence. (See Mandatory Human Rights Due Diligence, Chapter 11.) MSIs are positioned at the intersection of voluntary and mandatory human rights initiatives, in a polarized and rapidly evolving BHR space. It remains an open question as to what role they can or should play as mandatory requirements for human rights due diligence are adopted and begin to be implemented.

With the emergence of mandatory human rights due diligence laws in Europe and elsewhere, some commentators are suggesting that MSIs will be rendered obsolete. In fact, the opposite may be true.[11] Policymakers face the daunting prospect of turning a very broad "due diligence" requirements into a legally enforceable standard. Companies can cite their internal efforts and assert that they are indeed exercising due diligence. Courts and regulators will need to find ways to put meat on these bones, and to develop practical ways to determine what actually constitutes compliance with a due diligence requirement. MSI standards can serve as a point of reference for regulators and judges.

In each specific industry, MSI codes of conduct create a level playing field for industry participants. In the private security industry, for example, the International Code of Conduct for Private Security Service Providers Association (ICoCA) has developed indicators for companies, such as on the use of firearms, detention, and measures companies must undertake to prevent violence against women.

MSIs can help to clarify human rights commitments of companies and make them real in daily business operations. The US representative to the UN Human Rights Council has highlighted that "one key factor of the wide acceptance of the UN Guiding Principles on Business and Human Rights (UNGPs) has been the multistakeholder dialogue that has led to their development and

---

[11] Bennett Freeman, "Rethinking MSIs: Time to Bury MSIs? – Not So Fast," Human Rights@Harvard Law, last modified October 1, 2020, https://hrp.law.harvard .edu/corporate-accountability/rethinking-msis-time-to-bury-msis-not-so-fast.

has characterized their implementation. The success of efforts to build upon them in the next decade will depend on maintaining this approach."[12] The UN Working Group for BHR has been using MSIs like ICoCA as examples for how to implement human rights due diligence.[13] In its "Next Decade of Action," the UN Working Group continues to stress the importance of multistakeholder approaches to implementation of business and human rights. In their 2021 stocktaking report, they highlight that the "Guiding Principles to date have enabled broader levels of participation from a wider range of stakeholders, challenging them but also bringing them together to learn from each other and to generate the diversity of responses that the complex nature of business and human rights requires."[14]

MSI CHALLENGES

Some civil society critics of the MSI model argue that MSIs as institutions have failed to deliver on their promises.[15] While this is a fair criticism of certain MSIs, it is too sweeping an indictment to be applied across the board. Each MSI needs to be evaluated and judged separately. Many critics dismiss MSI as being irrelevant because they are "voluntary." In Germany, for example, advocates of the new German Supply Chain Act[16] made the case that the law was needed because companies did not adequately self-regulate and report on their social and environmental risks.[17] While the German law is a welcome development, an essential next step is for the German government and courts to determine how they will apply this law, and whether standards and metrics developed by MSIs can help their implementation.

---

[12] US representative, "12th Meeting, 47th Regular Session on the UN Human Rights Council," UN Web TV, June 28, 2021, video, 02:16:46 to 02:17:15, https://media.un.org/en/asset/k1b/k1bpousf71.

[13] See Anita Ramasastry's comment in ICoCA, "Ten Years of the UN Guiding Principles on Business and Human Rights – The Case of Private Security," recorded June 30, 2021, video, 1:05:04, https://www.youtube.com/watch?v=Bf1HJy6L8JE.

[14] UN Working Group on Business and Human Rights, *Guiding Principles for Business and Human Rights at 10: Taking Stock of the First Decade*, UN doc. A/HRC/47/39 (June 2021), para. 114.

[15] MSI Integrity, *Not Fit-for-Purpose*.

[16] Federal Ministry of Labour and Social Affairs, "Act on Corporate Due Diligence Obligations in Supply Chains of July 16 2021," *Federal Law Gazette* Part I no. 46 (July 22, 2021). https://www.bmas.de/EN/Services/Press/recent-publications/2021/act-on-corporate-due-diligence-in-supply-chains.html.

[17] Andrew Green, "In Germany, Voluntary Monitoring of Supply Chain Abuses 'Has Failed'," *Devex*, July 27, 2020, https://www.devex.com/news/in-germany-voluntary-monitoring-of-supply-chain-abuses-has-failed-97790.

It is important to understand the practical challenges facing existing MSIs and what needs to change for them to reach their full potential.

Typically, MSIs come with a built-in set of internal governance challenges caused by power differences between representatives of large corporations, big governments, and smaller civil society groups. There is a constant tension to make these organizations real and not simply a vehicle for legitimizing corporate or governmental interests.[18]

MSIs often have difficulties ensuring strong civil society representation. Non-governmental organizations (NGOs) in particular have time and resource constraints. Negotiations to develop and agree on a common industry code of conduct are time-consuming and can often be contentious. Developing an effective, credible system to assess company compliance is even harder. It requires companies to yield a measure of control, which they are reluctant to do. It requires NGOs to stand behind a process that gives public credit to companies that are deemed to be compliant. The most effective MSIs combine a shared learning model with effective accountability mechanisms, which is a hard balance to strike. Reaching consensus on all of these elements requires compromises, which many NGOs, companies, and other participants are unwilling to make. It can be much easier for certain NGOs to report on corporate violations rather than to sit in the room with companies who may be engaged in violative conduct. Participating in an MSI can be a risk to the reputation of advocacy NGOs. It also requires an arm's-length relationship with companies, one that does not come with remunerative benefits.

Most MSIs still face severe budgetary constraints that limit their operational capacity. In a small survey conducted in 2016, the NYU Stern Center for Business and Human Rights found that only a couple of MSIs had adequate funding to staff their operations. From experience working with MSIs we know that very large companies fight to limit corporate dues to some of these organizations not simply as a budgetary measure but to limit their capacity to function effectively. There is a great disparity between MSIs in terms of their resources and capacity. For example, the 20-year-old Fair Labor Association (FLA), which addresses labor practices in apparel manufacturing and agriculture, has an annual budget of over $8 million US dollars and a staff of 40. By contrast, the Voluntary Principles on Security and Human Rights (VPs), which addresses security issues in the extractive industries, founded at the same time as the FLA, currently has seven staff members and in 2016 a budget of 700,000 US dollars. The Global Network Initiative (GNI), founded in 2006 to address

[18] Barbara Gray, Jill Purdy, and Ansari Shahzad (2022), *Confronting Power Asymmetries in Partnerships to Address Grand Challenges. Organization Theory*, April 2022.

privacy and free expression issues in the information technology sector, currently has a staff of seven and in 2016 a budget of 733,295 US dollars.[19]

There is a pressing need to address the weaknesses in some of these smaller MSIs for them to be effective. Key questions facing MSI participants include: Can adapted discourse facilitation or an organizational governance model that provides equal decision-making rights to all stakeholder groups be applied, and what will be the incentives for companies or governments to accept this model? How can additional corporate funding be generated to strengthen the operations of MSIs with very small staffs?[20]

TEACHING APPROACHES

Teaching BHR should equip students with skills and tools to identify, analyze, and resolve human rights challenges in business. Corporate engagement in MSIs is one avenue through which companies can develop a practical framework for their internal human rights due diligence efforts and implement their human rights commitments. MSIs help to define industry-specific standards and they can help companies to develop practical ways to resolve human rights challenges.

Learning objectives for teaching multistakeholder human rights initiatives may include:

- Being able to explain what an MSI is and being familiar with the most prominent examples of human rights MSIs.
- Understanding how MSIs emerged and what needs they address in global governance.
- Explaining the value and the challenges of MSIs.
- Being able to describe the conditions for human rights governance MSIs that can define and enforce industry-specific standards.
- Understanding the complementarity of MSI standards with mandatory human rights due diligence requirements.

Based on our experience teaching BHR at business schools, clearly most business school students today understand the need to address human rights risks in various types of business operations. They are most interested in learning about tools that they can deploy that will help companies improve outcomes in ways that are both publicly credible and affordable. Typically, businesses

---

[19] Baumann-Pauly, Nolan, Labowitz, and van Heerden, "Setting and Enforcing Industry-Specific Standards."

[20] Green, "Voluntary Monitoring."

face chronic challenges, which can never be completely resolved. MSIs offer practical ways to confront these challenges and significantly reduce the risks of human rights impacts for business and rightsholders. We present MSIs as platforms that can (1) define and implement industry-specific standards aimed at reducing these risks, (2) provide assessment systems to measure compliance with these standards, and (3) help companies adopt remedial measures when problems are identified. As such, MSIs are critical collaborations for resolving BHR challenges that individual companies cannot solve on their own.

In our classes at NYU Stern and the Geneva School for Economics and Management we dedicate at least one full session in our BHR courses to multistakeholder human rights initiatives. To prepare students, we assign background readings that discuss the MSI model. We also assign the websites of human rights MSIs for students to see how this model can look in practice.

It is important to put the MSI model into context. We present MSIs as the middle ground in the polarized BHR debate between voluntary and mandatory BHR, and as a complement to emerging mandatory human rights due diligence laws.

To highlight the relevance of MSIs to students, we often identify a guest speaker from a corporation that explains the value that the participation in an MSI brings to their human rights work. A guest speaker can talk about the company's motivations to join an MSI, how they selected an initiative, and discuss the challenges of working through an MSI and its limitations. Similarly, it can be very useful to identify a guest speaker from a civil society organization that is actively involved in a human rights MSI. A governmental perspective, from a participant in the VPs or ICoCA, for example, also would be valuable to discuss the benefits and liabilities of formal governmental participation in these organizations.

One type of exercise that we regularly conduct in our courses are student debates in which student groups take on different stakeholder roles. Based on a concrete case scenario that we create, each group is asked to present arguments from their specific stakeholder perspective with the objective to find solutions to the given dilemma. The cases are drafted based on real and recent BHR challenges that companies have experienced. A role-play type of exercise highlights the value of broad stakeholder involvement and the need for concrete human rights standards to clarify expectations and resolve human rights issues. (See Exercise 18.2: Addressing Child Labor and Mine Safety in the Democratic Republic of the Congo (DRC) for an example of a BHR role play we have used in the classroom.)

One way to assess whether students have understood the valuable role that MSIs can play for the advancement of human rights in corporate practice is to assign student papers that require students to identify, analyze, and resolve a specific BHR challenge. In the resolution part of the paper, we invite students to discuss the role that existing MSIs could play, or if the company could lead in the creation of a new MSI to address the human rights issue(s) in question.

KEY QUESTIONS

General

- What are the key features of an MSI?
- Why did MSIs emerge?
- What type of challenges do MSIs tackle?
- What challenges do MSIs face as organizations?
- What opportunities arise for MSIs with the emergence of mandatory human rights due diligence requirements in Europe?

For Business Students

- How can standards set by MSIs help companies to align profits and principles?
- How have companies used MSIs to advance human rights in corporate practice?
- What should companies consider before joining an MSI?
- What are the advantages for companies working on BHR challenges through an MSI?
- What are the disadvantages and limitations?

For Law Students

- How can MSIs complement the emerging mandatory human rights due diligence requirements?
- MSIs can be considered as "soft law" instruments for hard issues. In what ways are MSIs better positioned than regulators to define concrete industry standards?
- What are the tools of meaningful accountability for companies that participate in MSIs? How do MSIs enforce compliance with its rules?
- What role should lawmakers assign to MSIs in developing emerging mandatory human rights due diligence regulations and laws? Can MSIs be safe havens that give participating companies a free pass for additional due diligence?
- What criteria should regulators adopt to distinguish meaningful MSIs?

For Policy Students

- Why do MSIs represent a new governance form that is well positioned to solve human rights issues in a globalized economy?
- Under what conditions are MSIs legitimate rule-setters?
- How could governments incentivize the development of industry-specific BHR standards?
- How could governments integrate MSIs in emerging human rights due diligence legislation?
- How can governments strengthen existing MSIs?

TEACHING RESOURCES

Readings

White paper

- Baumann-Pauly, Dorothée and Isabelle Glimcher. "Seeking a Smart Mix: Multistakeholder Initiatives and Mandatory Human Rights Due Diligence." 2021. https://gcbhr.org/backoffice/resources/white-paper-msis-24p.pdf

Commentary

- Baumann-Pauly, Dorothée, Justine Nolan, Sarah Labowitz, and Auret van Heerden. "Setting and Enforcing Industry-Specific Standards for Human Rights: The Role of Multistakeholder Initiatives in Regulating Corporate Conduct." In *Business and Human Rights: From Principles to Practice*, edited by Dorothée Baumann-Pauly and Justine Nolan, 170–191. New York: Routledge, 2016.
- Utting, Peter. "Multistakeholder Regulation of Business: Assessing the Pros and Cons." In *International Business and Sustainable Development*, edited by Rob Van Tulder, Alain Verbeke, and Roger Strange, 425–446. Bingley: Emerald Group Publishing Limited, 2014.

Videos

- World Business Council of Sustainable Development (WBCSD), the International Chamber of Commerce (ICC), and the Geneva Center for Business and Human Rights (GCBHR), "The Role of Voluntary, Collaborative Human Rights Due Diligence Initiatives," recorded April 29, 2021, video, 1:29:00, https://gcbhr.org/insights/2021/04/the-role-of-voluntary-collaborative-human-rights-due-diligence-initiatives.

Websites

- Fair Labor Association, https://www.fairlabor.org.
- Global Network Initiative, https://globalnetworkinitiative.org.
- International Code of Conduct for Private Security Service Providers, https://icoca.ch.

17. Business and human rights in the Inter-American System

Humberto Cantú Rivera

OVERVIEW

The issue of business impacts on human rights is not new for the Inter-American Human Rights System (IAHRS).[1] Early cases reviewed by the Inter-American Commission on Human Rights (IACHR), for example, analyzed the participation of global companies in situations that imperiled democracy and human rights in Latin American countries, such as Coca-Cola in Guatemala.[2]

Since the adoption by the United Nations (UN) Human Rights Council in 2011 of the UN Guiding Principles on Business and Human Rights (UNGPs),[3] as the topic of business and human rights has been mainstreamed, the IAHRS has developed a renewed, more specific approach. The focus of the IACHR has become much more centered on the duties of states in the context of business activities, such as the involvement of national and foreign oil companies in Ecuador,[4] and the existing state duties in the context of mining and logging operations.[5] However, the original and unique contribution of the IAHRS is the determination that a state's international responsibility may derive not just

---

[1] The IAHRS comprises both the Inter-American Commission on Human Rights and the Inter-American Court of Human Rights.

[2] *Marcelino Santos Chajón et al. v. Guatemala*, Case 7383, Inter-Am. Comm'n H.R., Report No. 32/81 (1981); *De Sus Afiliados, Edgar René Aldana et al. v. Guatemala*, Case 7403, Inter-Am. Comm'n H.R., Report No. 33/81, OEA/Ser.L/V/II.54 (1981).

[3] United Nations Human Rights Council, *Guiding Principles on Business and Human Rights: Implementing the United Nations "Protect, Respect and Remedy" Framework*, Report of the Special Representative of the Secretary-General on the issue of human rights and transnational corporations and other business enterprises, UN Doc A/HRC/17/31 (March 21, 2011) (UN Guiding Principles).

[4] Inter-American Commission Human Rights, *Report of the Situation of Human Rights in Ecuador*, OAS/Ser.L/V/II.96 Doc. 10 rev. 1 (April 24, 1997).

[5] See Teaching Resources in this chapter.

from its actions but also from omissions to prevent harmful conducts from non-state actors.[6]

The Inter-American System is the regional human rights system that has most extensively engaged with the general question of state responsibilities in relation to non-state actors – such as business enterprises – in the field of human rights, while elaborating with important nuances the different functions that the state must perform to ensure human rights in the context of business activities. The IAHRS has tested, explained, and interpreted the contours of the state duty to *ensure* human rights, an approach that goes beyond the restricted focus on protection under the first pillar of the UNGPs (see The UN Guiding Principles on Business and Human Rights, Chapter 5), and has allowed the IAHRS to explain the importance for the state to fulfill its different roles and use the different tools available in the context of business activities for the realization of human rights.

As a regional human rights system, the focus of the IAHRS is not on corporate conduct *per se*, but rather on the state obligations to respect and ensure human rights recognized under the American Convention on Human Rights[7] and other Inter-American treaties. In that regard, a state's responsibility may be compromised as a result of its failure to prevent, investigate, sanction, and remedy abuses by non-state actors,[8] including business enterprises. The IACHR and the Inter-American Court of Human Rights (IACtHR) have established that a state can be held responsible for the violation of individual or collective rights for its failure to protect against human rights abuses committed by companies. Both the IACHR and the IACtHR have made important contributions relevant for business and human rights. These include clarifying the scope and content of the state duty to *ensure* human rights and addressing the ways in which states should discharge their duties to consult Indigenous Peoples.

After briefly presenting the IAHRS, this chapter addresses the scope and content of the state duty to ensure human rights, which is the main legal basis on which the business and human rights agenda has evolved; it then proceeds to analyze the two strands in which the topic has evolved in the regional system, namely Indigenous Peoples' rights and other specific business and human rights issues. Finally, the chapter addresses different teaching approaches of

---

[6]   Inter-American Court of Human Rights, Case of *Velásquez Rodríguez v. Honduras*, Merits, Judgment, Inter-Am. Ct. H.R. (ser. C) No. 4, ¶ 172 (July 29, 1988).
[7]   American Convention on Human Rights, November 22, 1969, 1144 U.N.T.S. 132 (entered into force July 18, 1978) (ACHR).
[8]   See generally Dinah Shelton and Ariel Gould, "Positive and Negative Obligations," in *The Oxford Handbook of International Human Rights Law*, ed. Dinah Shelton (Oxford: Oxford University Press, 2013).

business and human rights in the context of the IAHRS, through exercises, key questions, and relevant resources on the topic.

THE INTER-AMERICAN HUMAN RIGHTS SYSTEM

The IAHRS is the regional human rights system for the Americas and is composed of two main bodies: the IACHR and the IACtHR.[9] While the Court is a judicial organ that adjudicates contentious cases and issues advisory opinions, much in line with the regular functions of other international tribunals, the Commission plays several important roles for the promotion and protection of human rights in the Americas.

One such role is its *interpretation and dissemination* of human rights standards, most notably through thematic reports that serve to illustrate how states should implement their obligations to respect and ensure human rights. Through such tools, the Commission has the possibility of expanding the meaning of the duties under the American Convention on Human Rights in light of specific contexts or new developments, while facilitating its understanding by state authorities and other actors. Another role relates to the *protection* of human rights through its petition system. Individuals whose rights have been affected by state actions or omissions can present a petition before the Commission, who must decide on its admissibility under article 46 of the ACHR and other regulations. Where a petition is declared admissible, a contentious procedure allows the state, the Commission, and the representative of victims to present their arguments and views, on the basis of which the IACHR must issue a merits report. If the state fails to comply with the recommendations issued by the IACHR, the petition may then be sent to the IACtHR.

In general terms, the roles of the Commission and the Court are complementary and have made important contributions to the understanding and development of international human rights standards. A recent focus has particularly been on business and human rights, where both bodies have issued reports and judgments explaining in detail the scope of state obligations in the context of business activities.

---

[9]   For a general explanation of the functioning of the IAHRS, see Olivier De Schutter, *International Human Rights Law: Cases, Materials, Commentary*, 3rd ed. (Cambridge: Cambridge University Press, 2019), chapter 11.2.

THE SCOPE AND CONTENT OF THE STATE DUTY TO ENSURE HUMAN RIGHTS

Both the IACHR and the IACtHR have explored the scope and content – the contours – of the state duty to ensure human rights, covering the duties to adopt measures and to put into place mechanisms and procedures to regulate and enforce obligations of non-state actors in the field of human rights. Several judgments by the IACtHR stand out for introducing different elements of the state duty defined in Article 1.1 of the American Convention of Human Rights.[10] For example, in several cases against Paraguay, the Inter-American Court considered that Paraguay had a duty to consult Indigenous Peoples who may be affected by development projects. Such an approach was followed years later in cases against Surinam and Ecuador, where the IACtHR detailed that state duties included undertaking environmental and social impact assessments, in order to be aware of the actual and potential risks that an extractive or development project may entail for the human rights of people in close proximity to those projects, and to adopt prevention or mitigation measures in that regard.

Beyond these examples, the Inter-American Court has dealt with cases notoriously involving forced labor and dangerous activities, in both cases highlighting the relevant role that the state must play in monitoring and regulating business enterprises within those contexts. Through both judgments, the Inter-American Court has held that the state duty to ensure human rights involves not just an obligation to have an adequate legal framework in place but also explicit duties to regulate and monitor the performance of business activities, a duty that is heightened whenever the state is aware of the fact that they are of a dangerous nature. In that regard, both duties are part of the more general duty to prevent human rights violations, and thus coincide with the due diligence obligation that the Inter-American Court has assigned to states in the context of activities of non-state actors.[11] For the Court, the due diligence obligation of states implies that they will not necessarily be held accountable for the actions of private actors, but will be held to account for their failure to

---

[10] ACHR, art. 1.1: "1. The States Parties to this Convention undertake to respect the rights and freedoms recognized herein and to ensure to all persons subject to their jurisdiction the free and full exercise of those rights and freedoms, without any discrimination for reasons of race, color, sex, language, religion, political or other opinion, national or social origin, economic status, birth, or any other social condition."

[11] Inter-American Court of Human Rights, Case of *Velásquez Rodríguez v. Honduras*, Merits, Judgment. of Inter-Am. Ct. H.R. (ser. C) No. 4, ¶ 172 (July 29, 1988).

take adequate measures to prevent human rights violations by private actors, and where impossible, to investigate, sanction, or redress said violations.[12]

From a different standpoint, the Inter-American Commission has also elaborated the content of state obligations in the context of business activities. In its seminal 2019 thematic report on Inter-American business and human rights standards,[13] the IACHR stipulated that the state duty implies a need to monitor compliance and respect of rights in private relationships; an obligation to regulate the activities of non-state actors, even extraterritorially; and finally, a duty to adopt measures to regulate business enterprises in relation to human rights. The IACHR supports the adoption of national action plans on business and human rights as a step in the right direction, but challenges the apathy of states in the region to adopt other measures, including legislative measures.

INDIGENOUS PEOPLES' RIGHTS AND THE ROLE OF THE STATE

The IAHRS has notably contributed to the elucidation and elaboration of Indigenous Peoples' rights through its proactive interpretation of their rights on the basis of ILO Convention 169, the UN Declaration on the Rights of Indigenous Peoples, and other reports and instruments.[14] (See Rights of Indigenous Peoples, Chapter 21.) The Inter-American Court has particularly elaborated upon the content of the rights to consultation and to consent, highlighting the need for an active participation of the state in that regard.[15] Of note is the explanation that "free, prior and informed consultation" requires the timely performance of environmental and social impact assessments, where the results must be presented in a culturally adequate and timely manner to Indigenous communities to ensure that they have adequate information about any given project that may impact their rights, allowing them to freely express their preferences regarding the realization of any given project.

---

[12] *Id.*

[13] IACHR and Special Rapporteur on Economic, Social, Cultural and Environmental Rights Soledad García Muñoz, *Business and Human Rights: Inter-American Standards*, OEA/Ser.L/V/II, CIDH/REDESCA/INF.1/19 (November 1, 2019).

[14] See, for example, Luis Rodríguez-Piñero, "The Inter-American System and the UN Declaration on the Rights of Indigenous Peoples: Mutual Reinforcement," in *Reflections on the UN Declaration on the Rights of Indigenous Peoples*, eds. Stephen Allen and Alexandra Xanthaki (Oxford: Hart, 2011).

[15] Humberto Cantú Rivera, "Towards a Global Framework on Business and Human Rights, Indigenous Peoples, and Their Right to Consultation and Free, Prior, and Informed Consent," in *The Prior Consultation of Indigenous Peoples in Latin America: Inside the Implementation Gap*, eds. Claire Wright and Alexandra Tomaselli (London: Routledge, 2018).

OTHER BUSINESS AND HUMAN RIGHTS ISSUES

Beyond the more general elements described above, the IACHR has addressed other important questions relevant for business and human rights. For example, the Commission has addressed the topic of extraterritoriality, highlighting that home states of transnational businesses have a particular duty to regulate their activities in foreign countries, as well as to ensure access to remedy for transnational harms. Furthermore, the Commission has addressed to some extent other relevant topics connected to the business and human rights agenda, including climate change and the role of business enterprises; transitional justice and the role of companies in the determination of truth, justice, reparation, and non-repetition; and privatization and state-owned enterprises.[16] In general, however, the IACHR's emphasis still lies on the powerful reminder of the nature of international human rights law, which imposes state duties to monitor human rights compliance by non-state actors, and to adopt different types of measures to ensure that business enterprises respect human rights.

TEACHING APPROACHES

Teaching the Inter-American Human Rights System in general can be a straightforward task. Teachers can follow a very traditional international law approach, covering the basic elements and postulates of public international law, including state responsibility, due diligence, and reparation. However, the Inter-American Human Rights System may prove challenging due to its progressiveness, the far-reaching and imaginative orders for reparation it issues, and the *pro persona*[17] interpretation that may go beyond other more orthodox approaches and legal systems. This, of course, adds to the interest and potential of teaching business and human rights in the Inter-American System.

I have taught this topic in undergraduate, Master's, and Doctoral courses, most often at law schools in Latin America. In several of these courses, participants have included students of education, sociology, criminology, international relations, and business, which may lead to very different results in the understanding of the specific nuances of the topic. Law and policy stu-

---

[16] IACHR, *Business and Human Rights: Inter-American Standards.*

[17] See Hayde Rodarte Berbera, "The Pro Personae Principle and Its Application by Mexican Courts," *QMHRR* 4, no. 1 (2017): 9, where the author explains: "According to [the *pro homine* or *pro personae* principle], human rights norms should be interpreted as extensively as possible when recognizing individuals' rights and, by contrast, as restrictively as possible when the norm imposes limited on the enjoyment of human rights. At the same time, the principle commands that in case of conflicts between human rights norms, the norm that better protects the individual's rights should prevail."

dents with a public law or international law background may be familiar with the logic of the Inter-American System and its approach to legal reform, legal interpretation, and the adoption of policy measures to comply with recommendations and judgments. Using analogies to other disciplines, such as civil or tort law, can be useful for students who are more familiar with corporate law and business students.

Learning objectives may include:

- Understanding the legal perspectives of different parties (government, IACHR, representative of victims) to an Inter-American case.
- Analyzing and framing legal arguments.

The following exercises can complement the more classic approach to the role of the Inter-American Human Rights System that is usually provided in readings.

EXERCISE 17.1

MOCK TRIAL IN THE INTER-AMERICAN SYSTEM

A classic type of exercise is a mock trial. Teachers can prepare a hypothetical case and divide students into two or three groups, representing the state, representatives of victims, and the Inter-American Commission. All parties are asked to prepare briefs and oral presentations, with the intention of simulating a real-life case taking place before the IACHR in Washington, DC or the IACtHR in San José, Costa Rica. Several business and human rights cases have already been litigated before the Inter-American Court, notably on privatization and its impact on human rights; on extractive industries (particularly mining and oil) or development projects; on dangerous activities; and in relation to forced labor. Other topics that have yet to be addressed in the case law of the Inter-American Court include state-owned enterprises, public procurement, and trade and investment agreements vis-à-vis human rights.

EXERCISE 17.2

LEGAL ANALYSIS OF ADMISSIBILITY OR MERITS OF

A COMPLAINT IN THE INTER-AMERICAN SYSTEM

This type of exercise can be done individually or in groups. As in the mock trial, students are required to analyze the admissibility or merits of a hypothetical case from different perspectives, as an official from the Inter-American Commission drafting the basis of the decision to admit the case or determine the responsibility of the state, or, on the other hand, as a government official that has to prepare a legal brief arguing for or against state responsibility in the given case. Two elements stand out: (1) the need to clearly stipulate the nexus between the action or omission by the state that is linked to business activities and (2) the basic procedural elements to be considered when deciding on the admissibility or merits of a complaint in the Inter-American System.

EXERCISE 17.3

PREPARING A STATE RESPONSE TO AN ALLEGATION

OF BUSINESS-RELATED HUMAN RIGHTS ABUSES IN THE

INTER-AMERICAN SYSTEM

This exercise, generally completed in groups, requires greater preparation by the teacher. The hypothetical case is framed in the context of a litigation before the Inter-American Court, which implies providing a larger factual and legal framework that includes several stages of Inter-American procedure. However, the exercise can facilitate a more pronounced understanding by students of the challenges for governments to litigate these types of cases, especially when they arise from allegations of gross human rights violations.

Each group addresses one of the arguments being litigated before the IACtHR. One important challenge is how to frame the factual context in a way that presents an analytical challenge regarding when a state is responsible – or not – for business activities. Cases involving the state-business nexus (privatization, state-owned enterprises, or public procurement) can provide important elements to challenge students in their understanding, analysis, and framing of the response to the legal questions presented.

KEY QUESTIONS

General

- In your opinion, what have been the most relevant advances on business and human rights in the Inter-American System?
- How can the Inter-American System address the state-business nexus?
- How can the Inter-American System further advance the business and human rights agenda in the region?
- How are the Inter-American System and the universal human rights system similar in their approach to business and human rights? How do they differ?

For Business Students

- How are decisions and reports produced by the organs of the Inter-American System relevant to a company's operations and decision-making?
- What is the best way to integrate the Inter-American concept of due diligence into corporate due diligence processes?
- Should sustainability reports use benchmarks from the Inter-American System? Which ones?
- How could Inter-American approaches to BHR be useful for ESG criteria?

For Law Students

- How can states fulfill their duties to respect and to ensure human rights in the context of business activities, as interpreted by Inter-American human rights bodies?
- How does the Inter-American approach to business and human rights differ from the approach in the UN Guiding Principles?
- What has been the approach of the Inter-American Court of Human Rights to the question of competing international obligations (i.e., international investment and trade agreements vs. human rights treaties)?
- What are the legal and practical complexities of the implementation of environmental and social impact assessments?
- What is the role of the state in the context of privatization?
- What type of legislative measures should states adopt to regulate the activities of business enterprises?

For Policy Students

- Should states take into consideration their obligations under the American Convention on Human Rights when drafting business and human rights policies?
- What elements of Inter-American case law should be considered by states when drafting business and human rights policies?
- What is the main difficulty in ensuring horizontal and vertical state policy coherence on business and human rights?
- How do National Action Plans (NAPs) in the region address the Inter-American approach to business and human rights?
- What is the best way to address urgent social issues through a business and human rights policy?
- Should there be an effort (and would it be feasible) to develop regional business and human rights policies beyond Europe?

TEACHING RESOURCES

Readings

Judgments of the Inter-American Court of Human Rights

- Inter-Am. Ct. H.R., Case of the Employees of the Fireworks Factory of Santo Antônio de Jesus and their families v. Brazil. Preliminary Objections, Merits, Reparations and Costs. Judgment of July 15, 2020. Series C No. 407.
- Inter-Am. Ct. H.R., Case of the Hacienda Brasil Verde Workers v. Brazil. Preliminary Objections, Merits, Reparations and Costs. Judgment of October 20, 2016. Series C No. 318.
- Inter-Am. Ct. H.R., Case of Ximenes Lopes v. Brazil. Merits, Reparations and Costs. Judgment of July 4, 2006. Series C No. 149.
- Inter-Am. Ct. H.R., Case of Kichwa Indigenous People of Sarayaku v. Ecuador. Merits and Reparations. Judgment of June 27, 2012. Series C No. 245.
- Inter-Am. Ct. H.R., Case of the Kaliña and Lokono Peoples v. Suriname. Merits, Reparations and Costs. Judgment of November 25, 2015. Series C No. 309.
- Inter-Am. Ct. H.R., Case of the Saramaka People v. Suriname. Preliminary Objections, Merits, Reparations, and Costs. Judgment of November 28, 2007. Series C No. 172.

- Inter-Am. Ct. H.R., Case of the Sawhoyamaxa Indigenous Community v. Paraguay. Merits, Reparations and Costs. Judgment of March 29, 2006. Series C No. 146.
- Inter-Am. Ct. H.R., Case of the Yakye Axa Indigenous Community v. Paraguay. Merits, Reparations and Costs. Judgment of June 17, 2005. Series C No. 125.

Reports by the Inter-American Commission on Human Rights

- Inter-American Commission on Human Rights. Business and Human Rights: Inter-American Standards. OEA/Ser.L/V/II. CIDH/REDESCA/INF.1/19 (November 1, 2019).
- Inter-American Commission on Human Rights. Indigenous Peoples, Afro-Descendent Communities, and Natural Resources: Human Rights Protection in the Context of Extraction, Exploitation, and Development Activities. OEA/Ser.L/V/II. Doc. 47/15 (December 31, 2015).

Reports from the Organization of American States

- Inter-American Juridical Committee. *Corporate Social Responsibility in the Area of Human Rights and the Environment in the Americas*. CJI/doc.449/14 rev. 1 (2014).
- Inter-American Juridical Committee. *Incorporation of the United Nations Guiding Principles on Business and Human Rights* (August 2022).

Commentary

- Cantú Rivera, Humberto. "Business and Human Rights in the Americas: Defining a Latin American Route to Corporate Responsibility." In *The Future of Business and Human Rights: Theoretical and Practical Considerations for a UN Treaty*, edited by Jernej Letnar Černič and Nicolás Carrillo Santarelli. Cambridge: Intersentia, 2018.
- Carrillo Santarelli, Nicolás. "La promoción y el desarrollo de la protección de los derechos humanos frente a abusos empresariales en el sistema interamericano." In *Derechos humanos y empresas: Reflexiones desde América Latina*, edited by Humberto Cantú Rivera. San José: IIDH, 2017.
- Gonza, Alejandra. "Integrating Business and Human Rights in the Inter-American Human Rights System." *Business and Human Rights Journal* 1, no. 2 (2016).
- Iglesias Márquez, Daniel. "Estándares interamericanos sobre empresas y derechos humanos: Nuevas perspectivas para la conducta empresarial responsable en las Américas." *Anuario de Derechos Humanos* 16, no. 2, 2020.

- Londoño Lázaro, María Carmelina, Thoene, Ulf, and Pereira-Villa, Catherine. "The Inter-American Court of Human Rights and Multinational Enterprises: Toward Business and Human Rights in the Americas?" *The Law and Practice of International Courts and Tribunals* 16 (2017).
- Salazar, Katya. "Business and Human Rights: A New Challenge for the OAS?" *Blog de la Fundación para el Debido Proceso Legal.* October 14, 2015. http://dplfblog.com/2015/10/14/business-and-human-rights-a-new-challenge-for-the-oas.

Websites

- Inter-American Commission on Human Rights. http://www.cidh.org.
- Inter-American Court of Human Rights. http://www.corteidh.or.cr.

EXERCISE 17.4

MEMO TO THE AMBASSADOR

Nina Luzatto Gardner

BACKGROUND

As governments seek to expand trade and investment globally, they are increasingly conscious of the impact companies have on local communities. When companies are complicit in human rights abuses, it reflects poorly on the host government, where the company's operations are located, and the government in which the company is headquartered (home government). Both host and home governments have a unique role to play in fulfilling their duty to protect and facilitating businesses' responsibility to respect human rights.

To better understand the interplay of these actors and issues, I ask my graduate students in public policy in my "Corporate Sustainability, Business and Human Rights" course to write a two-page policy memo analyzing a timely business and human rights (BHR) challenge – implicating allegations of corporate misconduct and providing recommendations for how a home government could mitigate the human rights impacts.

The purpose of this assignment is three-fold:

- To strengthen student understanding of the role of governments in advancing the UN Guiding Principles on Business and Human Rights (UNGPs) and how governments work with other stakeholders to advance BHR.
- To strengthen student ability to analyze a BHR issue in the broader economic, social, and political context of the country and explore potential mechanisms to affect change.
- To strengthen student ability to write clearly and concisely, a skill that is highly valued by employers, and to develop a practical writing sample for their job search.

EXERCISE

Write a policy memo from the perspective of a diplomat in a foreign mission – most likely as economic or legal counsellor – to your boss, the Ambassador, regarding a business impact that would fall under the UNGP framework and BHR in general. You are free to represent any country you wish, but your primary concern must be about negative human rights impacts of a multinational from your country doing business in the country where you are posted (if you represent France in a foreign mission, you must write about the behavior of a French company in the host country – though if other country multinationals are also misbehaving, you may consider reaching out to your counterpart/s to consider a coordinated strategy). You will inform the Ambassador about the BHR issue and provide two to three recommendations for how your government could address it. Given the multistakeholder nature of BHR, students are encouraged to include a multistakeholder component in their recommendations, which would involve, for example, assessing a company's impacts to the local community. When making the case for addressing this issue, students are advised to consider the social, economic, and political ramifications of inaction. While the officer writing the memo may be attuned to BHR as a field, you should assume the Ambassador is *not* an expert in BHR and may need further elucidation as to what the UNGPs represent and concrete information on how taking action aligns with the strategic priorities delineated in your country's National Action Plan (NAP),[18] if there is one, and what improvements might be made to future revisions of the NAP.

When exploring potential solutions, students are encouraged to consider:

- Why would the home government become involved in this particular issue?
- What tools does a home government have to advance BHR?
- How could a home government work with other stakeholders to advance BHR?
- How do you identify the right champions on the ground to leverage to address this issue?
- What might an appropriate remedy look like in this context?

---

[18] See United Nations Office of the High Commissioner for Human Rights, "National Action Plans on Business and Human Rights," Working Group on Business and Human Rights, https://www.ohchr.org/en/special-procedures/wg-business/national-action-plans-business-and-human-rights.

PART IV

Key issues

18. Modern slavery in supply chains

Justine Nolan

OVERVIEW

Businesses rely on vast global supply chains that connect consumers to goods and labor. Supply chains permeate our lives and dominate modern business operations, but they have also become synonymous with human rights abuses. The scale and complexity of global supply chains means they can be difficult to regulate and exploitative practices, such as modern slavery, can be difficult to detect. Modern slavery is a global problem. It is estimated that 50 million people are trapped in modern slavery.[1] The International Labour Organization (ILO) estimates that forced labor (a form of modern slavery) in the private economy generates US$150 billion in illegal profits each year.[2] Regular revelations about modern slavery show that this practice can reach into every aspect of a company's operations and supply chains, as well as into consumers' lives through our daily consumption, and it poses uncomfortable truths for businesses and individuals.[3]

This chapter first discusses the definition of modern slavery and the various exploitative practices that fall within the broad definition. It then provides an overview of the pervasive impact of supply chains in the global economy and how they are often tainted by modern slavery. The discussion that follows highlights the different regulatory tactics that are emerging to address modern slavery and the challenges of regulating global supply chains. Finally, the

---

[1] International Labour Organization (ILO) and Walk Free Foundation, Global Estimates of Modern Slavery: Forced Labor and Forced Marriage (Geneva: ILO and Walk Free Foundation, 2021).

[2] "ILO Says Forced Labor Generates Annual Profits of US$150 billion," International Labour Organization, May 20, 2014, https://www.ilo.org/global/about -the-ilo/newsroom/news/WCMS_243201/lang--en/index.htm.

[3] Justine Nolan and Martijn Boersma, *Addressing Modern Slavery* (Sydney: University of New South Wales Press, 2019); Monti Narayan Datta and Kevin Bales, "Slavery Is Bad for Business: Analyzing the Impact of Slavery on National Economies," The Brown Journal of World Affairs 19, no. 2 (Spring/Summer 2013): 205–223.

chapter offers some suggestions for how this subject can be taught to business and human rights (BHR) students, including relevant case studies and questions to provoke discussion.

DEFINING MODERN SLAVERY

Modern slavery is a term that has contemporary resonance and is of increasing concern to governments, business, trade unions, civil society, investors, and consumers. The United Nations Sustainable Development Goals, for example, include the aim of ending modern slavery by 2030 as one of its global targets.[4] Yet there is no globally recognized definition. Modern slavery is an umbrella term that incorporates a range of serious exploitative practices including: trafficking in persons; slavery; servitude; forced marriage; forced labor; forced marriage; debt bondage; deceptive recruiting for labor or services; and the worst forms of child labor.[5] Each of these terms is defined in treaties and documents of the United Nations and the International Labour Organization.[6] (See Human Rights, Chapter 3; Labor Rights, Chapter 4.)

Several exploitative practices associated with modern slavery are specifically associated with working conditions in global supply chains: forced labor, which refers to work performed against people's will under the threat of punishment;[7] bonded or indebted labor, when individuals work to pay off

---

[4]　"Indicators and a Monitoring Framework: Launching a Data Revolution for the Sustainable Development Goal 8.7," Sustainable Development Solutions Network, accessed August 3, 2022, https://indicators.report/targets/8-7.

[5]　International Labour Organization and Walk Free Foundation, *Global Estimates of Modern Slavery: Forced Labour and Forced Marriage* (Geneva: ILO and Walk Free Foundation, 2017), https://www.ilo.org/wcmsp5/groups/public/---dgreports/---dcomm/documents/publication/wcms_575479.pdf.

[6]　See, for example, *ILO Forced Labour Convention, 1930 (No. 29)*, June 28, 1930, 39 U.N.T.S. 55 (entered into force May 1, 1932), Art. 1(1); Protocol of 2014 to the Forced Labour Convention, 1930; *Protocol to Prevent, Suppress and Punish Trafficking in Persons, Especially Women and Children, Supplementing the United Nations Convention against Transnational Organized Crime*, Art. 3, November 15, 2000, 2237 U.N.T.S. 319 (entered into force December 25, 2003) (also known as the Palermo Protocol); *International Covenant on Civil and Political Rights*, December 16, 1966, 999 U.N.T.S. 171 (entered into force March 23, 1976); *International Covenant on Economic, Social and Cultural Rights*, December 16, 1966, 993 U.N.T.S. 3 (entered into force January 3, 1976); *Convention on the Rights of the Child*, November 20, 1989, 1577 U.N.T.S. 3 (entered into force September 2, 1990); and Slavery Convention, September 25, 1926, 60 L.N.T.S. 253 (entered into force March 9, 1927).

[7]　*Forced Labour Convention, 1930 (No. 29)*, Art. 2(2). Also see *Abolition of Forced Labour Convention, 1957 (No. 105)*, June 5, 1957, 320 U.N.T.S. 291 (entered into force January 17, 1959) and Protocol P029 – Protocol of 2014 to the Forced Labour Convention, 1930.

a debt while losing control over working conditions and repayments; human trafficking, which concerns the recruitment, transportation, transfer, harboring, or receipt of people through force, fraud, or deception with the intent to exploit them;[8] and child slavery, which is distinct from child labor as children not only work but are also exploited by a third party.

Modern slavery should be understood as existing on a continuum of exploitation.[9] Such an outlook recognizes that people can be exposed to working conditions that gradually worsen, sometimes leading to modern slavery.[10] Research shows that if labor abuses such as "non-payment of minimum wage, unfair dismissals, forced and unpaid overtime, denial of benefits, and denial of the rights of freedom of association and collective bargaining are prevalent and left unchecked, more severe exploitation often develops."[11] For example, the deterioration of labor standards and the absence of legal recourse may result in workers being at the mercy of their employer, leaving them no other option than to do as they are told.

There are clear indicators of what makes workers more vulnerable to modern slavery: limited language skills and knowledge of rights, gender (women are vastly overrepresented), and migration status, as well as factors such as financial hardship or a history of unemployment. Exploitation does not always have to be premeditated or involve human trafficking or captivity (which is the traditional view of slavery). The distinctive feature in many cases is the control exercised by employers, who by means of threats, coercion, or manipulation dictate exploitative working conditions and limit workers' alternatives to find new work or to seek improvements or recourse for their current working conditions.

---

[8] *Protocol to Prevent, Suppress and Punish Trafficking in Persons, Especially Women and Children, Supplementing the United Nations Convention against Transnational Crime*, November 15, 2000, 2237 U.N.T.S. 319 (entered into force December 25, 2003).

[9] Nolan and Boersma, 3n, 10.

[10] Hannah Lewis, Peter Dwyer, Stuart Hodkinson, and Louise Waite, *Precarious Lives: Forced Labour, Exploitation and Asylum* (Bristol: Policy Press, 2015), 152–153.

[11] Labour Exploitation Advisory Group, "Labour Compliance to Exploitation and the Abuses in-Between" (FLEX-LEAG Position Paper, April 2016), https://www.laborexploitation.org/publications/labor-exploitation-advisory-group-leag-position-paper-labor-compliance-exploitation; Klara Skrivankova, *Between Decent Work and Forced Labor: Examining the Continuum of Exploitation* (JRF, 2010), http://www.gla.gov.uk/media/1585/jrf-between-decent-work-and-forced-labor.pdf.; Ethical Trading Initiative, *Managing Risks Associated with Modern Slavery: A Good Practice Note for the Private Sector* (Ergon and ETI, 2018), https://www.ethicaltrade.org/sites/default/files/shared_resources/Managing%20risks%20associated%20with%20modern%20slavery.pdf.

It is useful to understand the scope and scale of modern slavery. It occurs in every region of the world, in both developing and developed countries, affecting women disproportionately. Women account for 71 percent of the estimated 40 million victims.[12] Of the 28 million people estimated to be working as forced laborers, 86 percent are working in the private economy.[13] Modern slavery is found in all industries but is notably prevalent in domestic work, manufacturing, construction, mining, agriculture, and fishing.[14]

GLOBAL SUPPLY CHAINS

Trade, production, investment, employment relations, and labor itself have drastically changed with the growth of supply chains. The United Nations Conference on Trade and Development estimates that approximately 80 percent of international trade is linked to the global production networks of multinational enterprises.[15] Supply chains impact every aspect of our lives. For example:

> [F]rom the moment you get out of bed in the morning to the time you go to sleep, the products you use and the services you rely on have a good chance of being linked to modern slavery. You wake up in the morning and take a shower. Palm oil is a common ingredient in household soap and is probably in the one you just used. The vast majority of the world's palm oil supply, nearly 85%, is grown in Indonesia and Malaysia and to meet the growing global demand for cheaply produced palm oil, some producers are relying on modern slavery. On your way to work, you stop for a cappuccino with a sprinkling of chocolate on top. Your coffee may contain beans that were harvested and cultivated by slaves in Côte d'Ivoire and Côte d'Ivoire, together with Ghana, is responsible for producing 60% of the world's cocoa. From the cocoa bean to the chocolate that sits on a supermarket shelf, the cocoa supply chain is difficult to trace and it is often not clear how the cocoa in any particular product was sourced. An estimated 95% of retail chocolate today is not certified to be free from child or forced labour ... Your day has only just begun, and you are already intimately connected with modern slavery.[16]

In the 40 countries that make up 85 percent of the global gross domestic product and account for around two-thirds of the labor force around the world,

---

[12] ILO and Walk Free, 1n.
[13] ILO and Walk Free, 1n.
[14] Andrew Crane, Genevieve LeBaron, Jean Allain, and Laya Behbahani, "Governance Gaps in Eradicating Forced Labor: From Global to Domestic Supply Chains," *Regulation and Governance* 13, no. 1 (2019): 86–106.
[15] United Nations Conference on Trade and Development, World Investment Report 2013: Global Value Chains: Investment and Trade for Development, New York: United Nations, U.N. Sales No. Sales No. E.13.II.D. (2013).
[16] Nolan and Boersma, 3n, 113.

the employment linked to supply chains has increased by 53 percent since 1995, culminating in 453 million formal jobs in supply chains in 2013.[17] The International Trade Union Confederation estimates that 60 percent of global trade in the real economy depends on the supply chains of 50 corporations, which employ only 6 percent of workers directly and rely on a hidden workforce of 116 million people.[18] These facts demonstrate the influence of global supply chains, the international fragmentation of production, the changing nature of employment relations, the unprecedented power of a few large corporations, and the potential extent of labor exploitation around the world. Together these factors raise several challenges. While many companies have seized the economic opportunities in burgeoning markets – creating local jobs and contributing to regional economic prosperity – outsourcing production and sourcing from low-cost regions creates an opaque network of global suppliers with negative side effects.[19] While the supply chain has become an intrinsic part of a company's operations, it generally comprises separate legal entities, thus limiting legal liability along the supply chain and making legal regulation challenging.

ADDRESSING MODERN SLAVERY

States and other stakeholders have pursued a range of emerging responses to address modern slavery in supply chains. While tackling modern slavery in supply chains is the primary duty of states, the fragmented nature of supply chains can be an obstacle to cross-border regulation. Business is increasingly called on to play a part in reducing the incidence of slavery.

Some governments have focused on the need to increase visibility in supply chains and have mandated that companies must report on the risks of modern slavery in supply chains. For example, social disclosure laws in California (Transparency in Supply Chains Act, 2010), the United Kingdom (Modern Slavery Act, 2015), and Australia (Modern Slavery Act, 2018) specifically

---

[17] International Labour Organization, *World Employment and Social Outlook 2015: The Changing Nature of Jobs* (Geneva: ILO, 2015), http://www.ilo.org/global/research/global-reports/weso/2015-changing-nature-of-jobs/WCMS_368626/lang--en/index.htm.

[18] International Trade Union Confederation (ITUC), *ITUC Frontlines Report 2016: Inside the Global Supply Chains of 50 Top Companies*, 2016, https://www.ituc-csi.org/IMG/pdf/pdffrontlines_scandal_en-2.pdf.

[19] Thomas Clarke and Martijn Boersma, "Global Corporations and Global Value Chains: The Disaggregation of Corporations?" in *The Oxford Handbook of the Corporation*, eds. Thomas Clarke, Justin O'Brien, and Charles R. T. O'Kelley (Oxford: Oxford University Press, 2019), 318–365.

target modern slavery in supply chains by requiring companies to identify and report on such risks.

These legislative measures impose corporate social reporting requirements that operate beyond national borders by asking companies to report on risks in their entire supply chain. However, the effectiveness of such mandated social disclosures is inconclusive. Early analysis of statements issued by companies in these jurisdictions raises questions about the superficiality of some corporate responses and the ineffective enforcement of these laws.[20] While mandatory reporting laws harden the expectation that business will address modern slavery, they are ultimately founded on an enforcement approach that is largely outsourced to the market.[21] Legislative efforts in France, the Netherlands, Germany, Norway, and the European Union have built upon this concept of social disclosure to incorporate an additional requirement for business to conduct human rights due diligence to strengthen the approach to both identifying and responding to risk. (See Mandatory Human Rights Due Diligence Legislation, Chapter 11.)

Other jurisdictions have adopted different approaches to addressing modern slavery in supply chains. The United States' Tariff Act of 1930,[22] which applies to all U.S. importers, allows the government to apply a temporary withholding or conclusive ban of goods that are suspected to be the result of forced or child labor.[23] In December 2021, the United States passed the Uyghur Forced Labor Prevention Act, which is designed to ensure that goods made with forced labor in the Xinjiang Uyghur Autonomous Region of China are prohibited from entering the U.S. market. The U.S. Federal Acquisition Regulations[24] require qualifying government contractors and subcontractors to certify that they have made efforts to ensure their supply chain is free from forced labor and human trafficking. Failure to comply may result in a termination of the procurement

---

[20]   Radu Mares, "Corporate Transparency Laws: A 'Hollow Victory?'" *Netherlands Quarterly of Human Rights* 36, no. 3 (July 2018): 189–213; Human Rights Law Centre et al., "Paper Promises: Evaluating the Early Impact of Australia's Modern Slavery Act," February 2022, video, 56:01, https://www.humanrights.unsw.edu.au/events/evaluating-early-impact-australias-modern-slavery-act.

[21]   Peter Grabosky, "Meta-regulation," in *Regulatory Theory: Foundations and Applications*, ed. Peter Drahos (Canberra: Australian National University Press, 2017).

[22]   Tariff Act of 1930, 19 U.S.C. §1307, §307 (2016).

[23]   "Forced Labor," U.S. Customs and Border Protection, accessed August 3, 2022, https://www.cbp.gov/trade/programs-administration/forced-labor.

[24]   Federal Acquisition Regulations for National Aeronautics and Space Administration 80 Fed. Reg. 4967 (January 29, 2015), subpart 22.17.

contract. The U.S. Department of Labor publishes a list of products it believes are produced by forced and child labor.[25]

Since 2004, Brazil has published a "dirty list" disclosing companies who have engaged in illicit labor practices who are then banned from accessing any public financing.[26] The list is a public register of companies found by governmental inspectors to have forced labor in their supply chains. Companies named on the list are monitored for two years and are also potentially subject to fines. The "dirty list" is reinforced by a further governmental decree,[27] which recommends that financial bodies refrain from granting financial assistance to companies on the list.

Litigation in national courts has also been used sporadically to attempt to hold companies accountable for modern slavery but the potential for civil litigation to secure extraterritorial accountability remains unclear and is heavily dependent on the jurisdiction in which accountability is sought.[28]

Several multistakeholder initiatives, including the Ethical Trading Initiative and the Fair Labor Association (FLA), have developed specific programs to combat forced labor in supply chains. In December 2020, for example, because of the high risk of forced labor, the FLA prohibited its members from sourcing and production from Xinjiang, China.[29] (See Multistakeholder Human Rights Initiatives, Chapter 16.)

These examples highlight the variety of tactics that are emerging to address modern slavery in supply chains, utilizing a combination of hard and soft laws to establish relevant standards that companies strive to achieve. The source of such hard law is generally international and national legislation focused on defining consistent workplace standards. Soft law standards are more nebulous, including instruments as diverse as the United Nations Guiding Principles on Business and Human Rights that contain "principles, norms, standards or other statements of expected behaviour,"[30] and widely accepted

---

[25] "List of Goods Produced by Child Labor or Forced Labor," Bureau of International Labor Affairs, accessed August 3, 2022, https://www.dol.gov/agencies/ilab/reports/child-labor/list-of-goods#:~:text=The%20most%20common%20agricultural%20goods,and%20diamonds%20are%20most%20common.

[26] Ministry of Labor and Employment Decree No. 540/2004.

[27] Decree No. 1 150.

[28] See, for example, *Nestlé USA, Inc. v. Doe*, 141 S. Ct. 1931 (2021) under the Alien Tort Statute in the United States and *Nevsun Resources Ltd. v. Araya*, 2020 SCC 5 under Canadian common law.

[29] "FLA Statement on Sourcing from China," Fair Labor Association, December 3, 2020, https://www.fairlabor.org/blog/entry/fla-statement-sourcing-china.

[30] Dinah Shelton, "Normative Hierarchy in International Law," *American Journal of International Law* 100, no. 2 (April 2006): 319. Also see Jaye Ellis, "Shades of Grey: Soft Law and the Validity of Public International Law," *Leiden Journal of*

multistakeholder codes of conduct. When viewed holistically, these regulatory approaches reflect a growing consensus that corporate actors have a clear and expected role to play in addressing the human rights impacts of business and that the state also has a complementary regulatory responsibility to prevent and redress those abuses. Modern slavery disclosure laws have the potential to harden responsible business conduct principles that have traditionally been cast as voluntary, but in order to do so greater attention needs to be paid to crafting an effective enforcement framework.

It is unlikely that laws alone will reform exploitative supply chain practices. There has long been a tug of war among scholars, activists, companies, unions, governments, and other actors about the value of "law" as a mechanism to cross-pollinate business with human rights. Law is but one way to influence behaviour and not all laws are created or implemented equally. What is clear is that calls for companies to adopt a more purposeful approach to business, including greater transparency and assuming responsibility over working conditions in their supply chains, are growing. As the concept and expectation that business should conduct human rights due diligence in supply chains gains further traction, such pressures on business will only increase. (See Mandatory Human Rights Due Diligence Legislation, Chapter 11.)

TEACHING APPROACHES

Modern slavery in supply chains can be taught as a single module within a broader BHR course or it can be a standalone course. At UNSW Sydney, this topic is enveloped into a broader BHR course taught in the Faculty of Law and Justice. The class on modern slavery focuses first on the definitional challenges stakeholders face in understanding the different forms of modern slavery and understanding what differentiates an unsafe workplace from one that has modern slavery. It uses case studies (currently garment production in Xinjiang, China; rubber gloves from Malaysia; fruit picking in Australia; and seafood from Thailand) to illustrate contemporary examples of modern slavery. The class then delves into the regulatory landscape and examines the modern slavery laws from the United Kingdom, California, and Australia, and analyzes the utility of social disclosure. It adopts a comparative approach that analyzes the effectiveness of social disclosure laws against import bans and other tactics such as litigation to determine which, if any, mechanisms will

---

International Law 25, no. 2 (June 2012): 313–334 and David Vogel, "Private Global Business Regulation," *Annual Review of Political Science* 11 (June 2008): 262, who refers to civil regulation as soft law and defines it as "socially focused voluntary global business regulations."

combat modern slavery. The class is followed by another module on human rights due diligence and the emerging laws and practices in this area.

If taught as a standalone course, more time could be devoted to in-depth case studies including debt bondage and forced labor in the United States.[31] It could also examine the role of multistakeholder initiatives, litigation, and corporate law (for example, the role of directors) in addressing the problem.

Learning objectives may include:

* Understanding the historical context of slavery and how modern slavery is now conceptualized.
* Understanding the role of global supply chains in business operations.
* Analyzing the content, scope, and efficacy of national and international laws to address modern slavery.
* Utilizing case studies to relate examples of modern slavery to students' everyday life.
* Critically assessing the efficacy of emerging measures to reduce modern slavery.
* Considering how the developing area of human rights due diligence may be relevant for identifying and addressing modern slavery in supply chains.

There are several ways to approach teaching modern slavery in supply chains in BHR courses.

Legal courses may adopt a framework that first considers the role of international human rights and labor law in defining and regulating modern slavery, and the difficulties of addressing issues embedded in cross-jurisdictional supply chains under international law. It can be particularly relevant to focus on the efficacy of current regulatory frameworks. Legal courses may consider the role of "hard versus soft law" approaches, and the value of mandated disclosures versus trade measures versus domestic criminal or civil regulation for tackling modern slavery. For example, transparency does not necessarily equate to accountability. Modern slavery disclosure models currently embody an "accountability deficit"[32] that could potentially be overcome with the support of state regulation.

---

[31] Kara Siddharth, *Modern Slavery: A Global Perspective* (New York: Columbia University Press, 2017); Daffodil Altan and Andrés Cediel, "Trafficked in America," *PBS Frontline*, April 24, 2018, video, 54:47, https://www.pbs.org/wgbh/frontline/film/trafficked-in-america.

[32] Hannah Harris and Justine Nolan, "Outsourcing the Enforcement of Modern Slavery: Overcoming the limitations of a Market-Based Disclosure Model," *Journal of Industrial Relations* 64, no. 2 (April 2022): 223–247.

Business courses may choose to focus on the supply chain as an area of potential commercial, and reputational, risk for companies. It is increasingly recognized that "one of the most significant and growing liabilities from which firms are attempting to distance themselves is that of forced labor."[33] Specific business disciplines, such as supply chain or human resource management, can approach the "regulation" of modern slavery with a focus that is broader than a legalistic approach and also takes into account the role and purpose of corporations in addressing "social" issues.[34] The role of investors is also particularly important to consider given their potential leverage in driving improvements in corporate respect for human rights and for more substantive reporting on modern slavery.[35]

Policy courses may consider the broader regulatory and societal framework in which modern slavery exists and the system of global governance more broadly. Teachers can discuss the role of state and non-state actors in addressing modern slavery and what a "smart mix"[36] of regulatory strategies is to reduce the exploitation. Policy students may also dive into other issues such as the use of technology in perpetuating modern slavery[37] or the broad challenge

---

[33] Genevieve LeBaron, "Subcontracting Is Not Illegal, but Is It Unethical? Business Ethics, Forced Labor and Economic Success," *The Brown Journal of World Affairs* 20, no. 2 (Spring/Summer 2014): 237–249.

[34] For example, the campaign to establish a new modern slavery law in Australia was championed by a prominent Australian businessman and philanthropist, Andrew Forrest (of Fortescue Metals Group), whose public support for the law helped to garner government attention and action. Andrew Forrest, "I Found Slaves in Our Supply Chain," *Sydney Morning Herald*, July 2, 2018, www.smh.com.au/national/i-found -slaves-in-our-supply-chain-20180701-p4zow9.html.

[35] Finance Against Slavery and Trafficking, "Mobilizing the Financial Sector Against Modern Slavery and Human Trafficking," accessed August 3, 2022 https:// www.fastinitiative.org.

[36] Commentary to UN Guiding Principle 3 notes that states "should consider a smart mix of measures – national, international, mandatory and voluntary – to foster business respect for human rights." United Nations Human Rights Council, *Guiding Principles on Business and Human Rights: Implementing the United Nations "Protect, Respect and Remedy" Framework*, Report of the Special Representative of the Secretary-General on the issue of human rights and transnational corporations and other business enterprises, UN doc. A/HRC/17/31 (March 21, 2011). Also see Shift, *Fulfilling the State Duty to Protect: A Statement on the Role of Mandatory Measures in a "Smart Mix,"* February 2019, https://shiftproject.org/fulfilling-the-state-duty-to -protect-a-statement-on-the-role-of-mandatory-measures-in-a-smart-mix.

[37] Owen Pinnell and Jess Kelly, "Slave Markets Found on Instagram and Other Apps," *BBC News Arabic*, October 31, 2019, https://www.bbc.com/news/technology -50228549.

of examining how modern slavery and workplace exploitation is argued to find its roots in capitalism.[38]

EXERCISE 18.1

MODERN SLAVERY CASE STUDIES

There is a plethora of case studies available from popular media sources and civil society reports that BHR teachers can use in the classroom. Many case studies provide an opportunity to explore the challenges and solutions relevant to a particular sector. For example, class exercises could be set that focus on the alleged use of forced labor to pick cotton in Xinjiang, or on the production of rubber gloves in factories in Malaysia; or on the use of forced child labor on in cobalt mines in the DRC.[39] (See Exercise 18.2: Addressing Child Labor and Mine Safety in the Democratic Republic of the Congo (DRC).) The Associated Press has developed an in-depth series on "Seafood from Slaves," which explores the abusive practices of the fishing industry in South East Asia.[40] Human Rights Watch has published a series of reports examining the plight of migrant workers and risk of forced labor.[41] Another interesting case study could examine the intersection of modern slavery and major sporting events such as the FIFA World Cup or the Olympics.[42] There are also case studies of trafficked workers in Ireland, England, Australia, and the United States across different industries.[43] Each of these cases provides compelling stories that students can relate to and can then be used to set the scene for examining the broader framework in which governments, business, unions, civil society, and international institutions are all trying to address these challenges. It is useful to provide BHR stu-

---

[38]   William Dalrymple, *The Anarchy: The Relentless Rise of the East India Company* (London: Bloomsbury, 2019).
[39]   See, for example, Michael Davie, "Blood Cobalt," *ABC*, February 24, 2022, https://www.abc.net.au/news/2022-02-24/cobalt-mining-in-the-congo-green-energy/100802588.
[40]   "Seafood from Slaves," Associated Press, accessed August 3, 2022, https://www.ap.org/explore/seafood-from-slaves.
[41]   "Exploitation, Forced Labor and Trafficking" Human Rights Watch, accessed August 3, 2022, https://www.hrw.org/topic/refugees-and-migrants/exploitation-forced-labor-trafficking.
[42]   "Qatar World Cup of Shame," Amnesty International, accessed August 3, 2022, https://www.amnesty.org/en/latest/campaigns/2016/03/qatar-world-cup-of-shame and International Trade Union Confederation, *China: A Gold Medal for Repression* (ITUC, 2022), https://www.ituc-csi.org/china-a-gold-medal-for-repression.
[43]   Nolan and Boersma, 3n.

dents with a variety of examples that demonstrate the breadth in which such practices are embedded in global supply chains.

KEY QUESTIONS

General

- What is modern slavery?
- Do we need one definitive definition of modern slavery?
- What is the difference between forced labor and human trafficking?
- What is an example of bonded or indentured labor?
- When do work practices move from bad working conditions to modern slavery?
- How are different countries regulating modern slavery?

For Law Students

- How should modern slavery laws be enforced?
- How might law be shaped to both incentivize and sanction business to avoid non-compliance?
- Is mandatory transparency likely to lead to a reduction in modern slavery in supply chains?
- Do the modern slavery disclosure laws of California, the UK and Australia strike an effective balance between hard law standards and "soft law" enforcement?
- What is a "smart mix" of legal regulation to address this issue? Should mandated disclosures be complemented by trade bans to prohibit the importation of goods tainted by modern slavery?
- What are the challenges of devising a regime of legal liability for modern slavery that reaches up and down the supply chain?
- What is the most effective way of enforcing mandatory disclosure laws? Should enforcement be left to the market or should the state sanction non-compliance?

For Business Students

- Can business be trusted with the business of addressing modern slavery?
- Does motivation matter? Should business focus on results or is it important why and how companies address human rights issues such as modern slavery?
- What is the role of investors in addressing modern slavery?

- Can modern slavery be reduced without radically reforming global supply chains?
- Should brands at the top of supply chains be responsible for working conditions at the bottom?
- Should brands be held legally liable for modern slavery in their supply chain at any level?

For Policy Students

- What policy tools are available to states to address modern slavery?
- Which actors among governments, business, non-governmental organizations, unions, and consumers should lead the "accountability challenge" to reduce modern slavery?
- What is the role and ability of multilateral institutions such as the UN, ILO, or OECD to tackle modern slavery?
- Can supply chains be reformed without destroying or replacing capitalism?

TEACHING RESOURCES

Readings

Books

- Bales, Kevin. *Understanding Global Slavery*. Berkeley: University of California Press, 2005.
- LeBaron, Genevieve. *Combatting Modern Slavery: Why Labour Governance is Failing and What We Can Do About It*. Cambridge: Polity Press, 2020.
- Nolan, Justine and Martijn Boersma. *Addressing Modern Slavery*. Sydney: University of New South Wales Press, 2019.

Reports

- Associated Press. *Seafood from Slaves*. Associated Press, 2015–2016. https://www.ap.org/explore/seafood-from-slaves.
- Carrier, Patricia. *Modern Slavery Act: Five Years of Reporting*. Business and Human Rights Resource Centre, 2021. https://media.business-humanrights.org/media/documents/Modern_Slavery_Act_2021.pdf.
- Field, Frank, Maria Mille, and Baroness Butler-Sloss GBE. Independent Review of the Modern Slavery Act*, Second Interim Report: Transparency in Supply Chains*. London: UK Home Office, 2019.

- Human Rights Law Centre, *Paper Promises: Evaluating the Early Impact of Australia's Modern Slavery Act* (2022), https://www.hrlc.org.au/reports/2022/2/3/paper-promises-evaluating-the-early-impact-of-australias-modern-slavery-act.
- International Labour Office. *Indicators of Forced Labour.* https://www.ilo.org/wcmsp5/groups/public/---ed_norm/---declaration/documents/publication/wcms_203832.pdf.
- Xu, Vicky Xiuzhong, Danielle Cave, James Leibold, Kelsey Munro, and Nathan Ruser. *Uyghurs for Sale.* Policy Brief Report No. 26/2020. Australian Strategic Policy Institute, 2020. https://www.aspi.org.au/report/uyghurs-sale.

Videos

- Associated Press. "Seafood from Slaves." Collection of articles, photos, and videos. 2015–2016. https://www.ap.org/explore/seafood-from-slaves.
- Bales, Kevin. "How to Combat Modern Slavery." 2010. TED video, 17.45. https://www.ted.com/talks/kevin_bales_how_to_combat_modern_slavery?language=en.
- Davie, Michael. "Blood Cobalt." Updated February 25, 2022. https://www.abc.net.au/news/2022-02-24/cobalt-mining-in-the-congo-green-energy/100802588.
- Nolan, Justine. "Addressing Modern Slavery." 2021. Video, 16:27. https://drive.google.com/file/d/1hPnB9s9C4PAnMAm04XScaxCEHwPQ-qv_/view?usp=sharing.

Websites

- Anti-Slavery International. "What Is Modern Slavery?" https://www.antislavery.org/slavery-today/modern-slavery.
- Walk Free. "Global Slavery Index. Modern Slavery: A Hidden, Every Day Problem." https://www.globalslaveryindex.org.
- Yale University. "Modern Slavery Working Group." https://modernslavery.yale.edu.

EXERCISE 18.2

ADDRESSING CHILD LABOR AND MINE SAFETY IN THE

DEMOCRATIC REPUBLIC OF THE CONGO (DRC)

Michael Posner and Dorothée Baumann-Pauly

BACKGROUND

Cobalt is the key ingredient in the rechargeable lithium-ion batteries needed to power everything from Apple gadgets to Tesla's electronic cars. Two-thirds of the world's cobalt comes from the Democratic Republic of the Congo (DRC), and 15–30 percent of it is mined by hand in "artisanal mines" (ASM) (small informal mining operations run by the local population). Most of the cobalt mined in the DRC goes to a Chinese processing company in China called Huayou Cobalt, whose products then end up in the batteries that are used to power electronics and electric vehicles.

Rising demand led cobalt prices to quadruple from 2016 to 2018, trading near decade highs above $90,000 a ton. Although the price has dropped somewhat in recent years, in 2022 the price climbed back to $82,000.[44]

About a quarter of global cobalt production is used in smartphones. Electric cars contain about 10 kilograms of cobalt, more than 1,000 times the amount used in an iPhone. Elon Musk, the CEO of Tesla, has announced that Tesla aims to manufacture 20 million electric cars by 2030.[45] California Governor Gavin Newsom recently announced his plan for California to require that all new cars and trucks sold there must be non-fossil fuel powered by 2035.

Even though international standards are clear, cobalt artisanal mining is linked to the worst forms of child labor and serious gaps in mine safety including the use of very dangerous and unstable makeshift tunnels. An Amnesty International investigation in 2016 found that "cobalt mined by children and adults in horrendous conditions in the DRC is entering the supply chains of some of the world's biggest brands."[46] When Amnesty

---

[44] "Cobalt," Summary, Trading Economics, accessed August 14, 2022, https://tradingeconomics.com/commodity/cobalt.

[45] Michael Posner, "How Tesla Should Combat Child Labor in the Democratic Republic of the Congo," *Forbes*, October 7, 2020.

[46] Amnesty International and Afrewatch, *"This is What We Die For": Human Rights Abuses in the Democratic Republic of the Congo Power the Global Trade in*

International approached these companies, they were alarmed to find out that many were failing to ask basic questions about where their cobalt comes from. According to the U.S. Department of Labor, as many as 35,000 children are working in ASM cobalt mines in the DRC.[47]

Tesla has developed a Human Rights and Conflict Minerals policy that outlines the company's expectations to all suppliers and partners that work with them.[48] Tesla suppliers are required to provide evidence of the existence of policies that address social, environmental, and sustainability issues as well as responsible sourcing. While Tesla has sought to gain greater transparency at the level of refiners in the DRC, they have very little visibility into their supply chain in the mining sites where human rights risks are the greatest.

In 2019, a lawsuit was filed by a human rights firm, International Rights Advocates, on behalf of 14 parents and children from the DRC against the world's largest tech companies including Apple, Google, Dell, Microsoft, and Tesla.[49] The families claimed that their children were killed or maimed while mining for cobalt used to power smartphones, laptops, and electric cars.[50] The families and injured children seek damages for forced labor and further compensation for unjust enrichment, negligent supervision, and intentional infliction of emotional distress. It was the first time that any of the tech companies have faced such a legal challenge. The lawsuit argues that Apple, Google, Dell, Microsoft, and Tesla all aided and abetted the mining companies that profited from the labor of children who were forced to work in dangerous conditions – conditions that ultimately led to death and serious injury.[51] The families argue that their children were working illegally at mines owned by UK mining company Glencore. The court papers allege that cobalt from the Glencore-owned mines is sold to Umicore, a Brussels-based metal and mining trader, which then sells battery-grade cobalt to Apple, Google, Tesla, Microsoft, and Dell.

Cobalt, London: Amnesty International, January 2016, https://www.amnesty.org/download/Documents/AFR6231832016ENGLISH.PDF.

[47]   "Child Labor and Forced Labor Reports," Bureau of International Labor Affairs, U.S. Department of Labor, accessed August 14, 2022, https://www.dol.gov/agencies/ilab/resources/reports/child-labor/congo-democratic-republic-drc.

[48]   *Tesla Conflict Minerals Report*, December 31, 2018, https://www.tesla.com/sites/default/files/about/legal/2018-conflict-minerals-report.pdf.

[49]   Sabastian Klovig Skelton, "Major Tech Companies Respond to Lawsuit over Mining Deaths," *Computer Weekly*, October 9, 2020.

[50]   Annie Kelly, "Apple and Google Named in US Lawsuit over Congolese Child Cobalt Mining Deaths," *Guardian*, December 16, 2019.

[51]   Siddharth Kara, "I Saw the Unbearable Grief Inflicted on Families by Cobalt Mining, I Pray for Change," *Guardian*, December 16, 2019.

On August 25, 2020, the five companies named in the lawsuit filed a motion to dismiss the case, claiming that the "expansive theories alleged in the complaint are not supported by law."[52] In November 2021, a Washington, DC court dismissed the lawsuit, but the victims have announced that they will appeal. This will draw further attention to the human rights challenges in the cobalt supply chain.[53]

On March 31, 2021, the *Entreprise Générale du Cobalt* (EGC), a new state entity that was created to support the commercialization of artisanal cobalt in the DRC, launched its Responsible Sourcing Standards[54] for artisanal cobalt production. The EGC has the monopoly for buying and selling artisanal cobalt and only artisanal cobalt in compliance with the standard is accepted. Artisanal cobalt from non-compliant mine sites will be illegal in the future. The EGC is working with Trafigura, a privately held Swiss-based commodity trading firm in developing a standard for ASM mining. But to date neither Tesla nor other major cobalt buyers have joined this effort. Adding to the uncertainty, in the last two months there have been rumors that the EGC management team will be replaced because of political changes in the DRC. One year after the launch of the EGC standard, there are still no ASM sites that have been reformed to comply with the standard.

GROUP EXERCISE

BHR teachers can divide a class into groups, provide additional background for each of the following roles, and ask students to respond to the prompts below from the perspective of their assigned role.

Role: Tesla Sourcing Team

*   Elon Musk ambitiously aims at producing 20 million electric vehicles a year by 2030 to fulfill the company's mission "to accelerate the advent

---

[52]   Skelton, "Major Tech Companies Respond to Lawsuit over Mining Deaths."

[53]   "USA: Washington DC Court Dismisses Cobalt Mining Deaths' Case Against Five Major Technology Companies," Business and Human Rights Centre, accessed August 14, 2022, https://www.business-humanrights.org/en/latest-news/usa-washington-dc-court-dismissed-cobalt-mining-deaths-case-against-five-major-technology-companies.

[54]   Enterprise Générale du Cobalt (EGC), *EGC Responsible Sourcing Standard*, March 2021, https://www.trafigura.com/media/3098/2021_trafigura_egc_responsible_sourcing_standards_english.pdf.

of sustainable transport by bringing compelling mass market electric cars to market as soon as possible."

- At one point Musk pledged to source all cobalt from North America as it ramps up its electric car production. "It will enable us to establish a supply chain that is local and focused on minimizing environmental impact while significantly reducing battery cost," said Liz Jarvis-Shean. Yet Canada and the U.S. together produce roughly 4 percent of the world's supply, nowhere near Tesla's needs for just one of its models.
- You are responsible for setting and executing the strategy to ensure the smooth and cost-effective operation of the Tesla supply chain. You are also responsible for briefing the investor relations team before their upcoming call with investors. If the company meets its product projections, there is simply not enough cobalt in North America to meet this demand.
- Tesla recently joined forces with Glencore and the Fair Cobalt Alliance to address human rights issues in ASM. They are also now participating in the Global Battery Alliance (GBA), a multistakeholder platform that started at the World Economic Forum.

Prompt:

Tesla is expecting questions regarding Amnesty International's reporting on child labor and other human rights risks in Tesla's cobalt supply chain. What is your sourcing strategy for meeting production needs and at the same time mitigating these risks in your supply chain?

Role: Tesla Investor Relations Team

- You are the primary liaison to Tesla's investors and charged with preparing the CEO for quarterly earnings calls. Given the recent combative earnings call that made headlines, you feel extra pressure to productively engage with your investors.
- In reaction to the Amnesty International report, students are organizing on college campuses demanding action on child labor used to create "sustainable electronic vehicles."
- One of your main investors is a large European sovereign wealth fund. They have a stated policy on child labor, and you are expecting tough questions.
- Moreover, emerging human rights due diligence legislation in Europe forces you to start looking systematically into human rights risks in your supply chain, up to the production of raw materials.

Prompt:

You have been asked by the "C-Suite" to develop a response for investors to give them assurance that your cobalt supply chain is developing standards and metrics to address effectively child labor and ensure mine safety.

Role: Large European Sovereign Wealth Fund

- You are a very large sovereign wealth fund, based in Sweden, with more than $500 billion in assets. You have a sustainability mandate that includes strong prohibitions against investments in the worst forms of child and forced labor. You have significant investments in Tesla.
- You've just read several articles and the Amnesty International reports alleging child labor and lapses in mine safety in Tesla's supply chains. There's an active discussion within your team about the strategy that Tesla is pursuing to clean up their supply chains. In anticipation of emerging human rights due diligence legislation in Europe, you are wondering if Tesla is conducting "adequate" due diligence for its cobalt supply chain.
- The ethics council of your fund is meeting in early May and will expect a recommendation on whether or not to endorse Tesla's strategy on this issue.

Prompt:
You need to evaluate Tesla's strategy with respect to cobalt procurement and decide whether your fund should endorse its actions as meaningful, keep them under review pending further engagement, or divest from the company altogether. What should your fund do?

Role: International Rights Activist

- You understand that lawyers representing the five companies you have sued may be preparing a settlement offer. Rumor has it that they may be interested in settling the case and would offer a significant cash settlement if your clients are willing to drop the suit. The eight-figure sum they are considering proposing would reward each of your 14 clients quite handsomely. Some of the plaintiffs have told you that they want to settle the case and would take these funds. Others are reluctant to do so because the five companies are not offering to make any changes in their sourcing of cobalt in the DRC.
- If such a settlement is offered and accepted, International Rights Advocates would receive 25 percent of the settlement funds. This would

make available badly needed resources because you are operating your non-profit organization on a shoestring. If a settlement is offered and your clients accept it, you have been thinking of using this to set up a multi-year litigation fund with your portion of the settlement.

- You need to decide how to reconcile these varying interests, both among your clients and in making recommendations to them about whether to accept a possible settlement. You are worried that none of the companies are making meaningful commitments to address child labor and mine safety, and by settling you give up the leverage in pushing them to do so.
- You are also struggling to balance the interests of your various clients and trying to figure out how to address their different perspectives if you have an opportunity to settle the case. In the back of your mind, you realize that settling the case now would provide International Rights Advocates much-needed funding to continue its work.

Prompt:

How should you advise your clients and reconcile their different interests and perspectives? Does the possible settlement make sense to you?

19. Human rights and the environment[1]

Sara L. Seck

OVERVIEW

The environment has long been a subject of responsible business conduct (RBC) guidance tools. The UN Global Compact (2000), for example, dedicates three of its ten principles to environment and only two explicitly to human rights.[2] The OECD Guidelines for Multinational Enterprises added a chapter on the environment in 1991, long before introducing its human rights chapter in 2011.[3] Yet while the environment has been a common theme, it has generally been treated – and taught – as distinct from human rights. An environmental human rights approach to teaching business and human rights (BHR) provides an opportunity to explore with students the interconnection and interdependence of humans (people) and the environment (planet), while also drawing attention to differential impacts of environmental harms in line with understandings of environmental justice and environmental racism.[4] It also provides an opportunity to grapple with the human rights implications of what the United Nations Environment Programme (UNEP) describes as a triple planetary crisis of climate change, biodiversity loss, and pollution.[5]

---

[1] An original version of this chapter appeared as Sara L. Seck, "Teaching Note: Human Rights and the Environment," in *Teaching Business and Human Rights Handbook* (Teaching Business and Human Rights Forum, 2020), https://teachbhr.org/resources/teaching-bhr-handbook/teaching-notes/human-rights-and-the-environment.

[2] "The Ten Principles of the UN Global Compact," United Nations Global Compact, accessed August 20, 2022, https://www.unglobalcompact.org/what-is-gc/mission/principles.

[3] Organisation for Economic Co-operation and Development (OECD), *OECD Guidelines for Multinational Enterprises* (Paris: OECD Publishing, 2011).

[4] See, for example, Sumudu Atapattu, Carmen Gonzalez, and Sara L. Seck, eds., *Cambridge Handbook of Environmental Justice and Sustainable Development* (Cambridge: Cambridge University Press, 2021).

[5] United Nations Environment Programme (UNEP), *Making Peace with Nature: A Scientific Blueprint to Tackle the Climate, Biodiversity and Pollution Emergencies* (Nairobi: UNEP, 2021), https://www.unep.org/resources/making-peace-nature.

The Covid-19 pandemic has brought into focus the importance of an environmental human rights approach to BHR. This is because the health of people and the health of our planet are intimately connected. For example, those with health problems arising from exposure to pollution are more vulnerable to diseases like Covid-19, while those who lack access to clean water are less able to protect themselves by complying with public health guidelines such as handwashing.[6] Yet, some governments and industries treat the economic challenges arising from Covid-19 as a reason to reduce environmental protection, by lowering environmental standards, suspending environmental monitoring requirements, reducing environmental enforcement, and restricting public participation, viewing it as a luxury.[7] These actions also have adverse impacts on the work of environmental human rights defenders (EHRDs).[8]

Old arguments about the tension between environment and development or environment and economy present false choices. The real question is who pays (suffers) the environmental and climate costs (harms) externalized by industry and governments. The answer is those most vulnerable to environmental and climate harms. These are environmental and climate justice problems that involve violations of human rights.

At a time of "building back better,"[9] it is important that the environment and human rights are not treated as separate silos as has been commonplace in RBC guidance, industry practice, state law, policy, and education. The environment must be understood as the floor from which a healthy society and healthy economy may grow, as well as a ceiling that limits development within planetary boundaries.[10]

---

[6]   UNEP, UN COVID-19 Response, and Office of the High Commissioner for Human Rights (OHCHR), *Human Rights, the Environment and COVID-19: Key Messages* (2020), https://www.ohchr.org/sites/default/files/Documents/Issues/ClimateChange/HR-environment-COVID19.pdf (COVID-19 Key Messages).

[7]   COVID-19 Key Messages; "Global Conservation Rollbacks Tracker," Conservation International, last updated March 11, 2021, https://www.conservation.org/projects/global-conservation-rollbacks-tracker.

[8]   COVID-19 Key Messages; see, for example, UNEP, *COVID-19 and Impacts on Environmental Human Rights Defenders and Environmental Protection in Southeast Asia* (2022), https://wedocs.unep.org/20.500.11822/39602.

[9]   "Building Back Better: A Sustainable, Resilient Recovery after COVID-19," Policy Responses to Coronavirus (COVID-19), OECD, June 5, 2020, http://www.oecd.org/coronavirus/policy-responses/building-back-better-a-sustainable-resilient-recovery-after-covid-19-52b869f5/#section-d1e45.

[10]   Stockholm Resilience Centre, *Planetary Boundaries A Safe Operating Space for Humanity*, https://www.stockholmresilience.org/download/18.6d8f5d4d14b3 2b2493577/1459560273797/SOS+for+Business+2015.pdf. The nine boundaries are: climate change, loss of biosphere integrity, changes to biogeochemical flows, land use

This chapter introduces an environmental human rights framework for teaching BHR and reflects on environmental and climate justice challenges, then explores different approaches to teaching BHR and environment for law, business, and policy students with sample exercises and key questions for discussion.

UNDERSTANDING ENVIRONMENTAL HUMAN RIGHTS

Many sources of international and regional human rights and environmental law clarify the nature of existing environmental human rights.[11] Notably, in October 2021, the UN Human Rights Council adopted a resolution recognizing the "right to a clean, healthy, and sustainable environment as a human right that is important for the enjoyment of human rights" and that is "related to other human rights and existing international law."[12]

The 2018 Framework Principles for Human Rights and the Environment consist of sixteen Principles largely aimed at clarifying state obligations.[13] The commentary to the first and second Framework Principles clarifies the interdependence of environment and human rights: without a clean, healthy, and sustainable environment, it is impossible to fully enjoy a vast range of human rights, including rights to life, health, food, water, and development; yet in order to protect the environment, it is vital to exercise human rights including rights to information, freedom of expression and association, participation, and remedy.[14] Principle 12 confirms "States should ensure environmental standards are effectively enforced against both public and private actors." Paragraph 35 clarifies that the business responsibility to respect human rights in accordance with the United Nations Guiding Principles on Business and Human

---

change, release of novel entities, atmospheric aerosol loading, freshwater abstraction, ocean acidification, and loss of stratospheric ozone.

[11] UN General Assembly, *Human Rights Obligations relating to the enjoyment of a Safe, Clean, Healthy and Sustainable Environment*, Report of the Special Rapporteur on the issue of human rights obligations relating to the enjoyment of a safe, clean, healthy and sustainable environment, UN Doc. A/73/188 (July 19, 2018) (HR Obligations).

[12] UN Human Rights Council, Resolution 48/13, The human right to a clean, healthy, and sustainable environment, UN Doc. A/HRC/RES/48/13 (October 8, 2021). The resolution invites the UN General Assembly to consider the issue.

[13] UN Human Rights Council, *Framework Principles on Human Rights and the Environment*, Report of the Special Rapporteur on the issue of human rights obligations relating to the enjoyment of a safe, clean, healthy and sustainable environment, UN doc. A/HRC/37/59 (January 24, 2018), Annex (Framework Principles), Principles 1-16.

[14] Framework Principles, para 4.

Rights (UNGPs)[15] applies to adverse human rights impacts that arise through environmental harm, and that beyond compliance with environmental laws, businesses should respect human rights through environmental protection and remediation of adverse environmental human rights impacts they cause or to which they contribute.[16]

The Framework Principles reflect concepts and issues that are well known by those who study environmental rights, but often less well known by many in the BHR field. Fulsome implementation of an environmental human rights approach requires understanding the essential elements of the right to a clean, healthy, and sustainable environment, including both procedural and substantive environmental rights, with cross-cutting attention to non-discrimination.[17]

PROCEDURAL ENVIRONMENTAL RIGHTS[18]

Procedural environmental rights include:

- Access to information on environmental matters that may undermine rights.
- Prior assessment of possible environmental impacts of proposed projects and policies including effects on human rights.
- Freedom of expression, peaceful assembly, and association with regard to environmental matters, as well as a safe space for environmental human rights defenders that is free from harassment, intimidation, and violence.
- Effective public participation in environmental decision-making for all.
- Access to effective remedies for violations of environmental human rights, including both violations of procedural rights and substantive rights.

[15] UN Human Rights Council, *Guiding Principles on Business and Human Rights: Implementing the United Nations "Protect, Respect and Remedy" Framework*, Report of the Special Representative of the Secretary-General on the issue of human rights and transnational corporations and other business enterprises, UN Doc. A/HRC/17/31 (March 21, 2011) (UN Guiding Principles).

[16] Framework Principles, ¶ 35.

[17] OHCHR, *The Right to a Safe, Clean, Healthy, and Sustainable Environment: Factsheet*, https://www.ohchr.org/sites/default/files/2022-05/Recognition-Factsheet-FINAL.pdf.

[18] Framework Principles, Principles 4–10.

SUBSTANTIVE ENVIRONMENTAL RIGHTS

The overarching substantive right to a clean, healthy, and sustainable environment may be subdivided into the following smaller issue areas:

* the right to breathe clean air;[19]
* the right to a safe climate;[20]
* the right to safe, sufficient water;[21]
* the right to healthy and sustainably produced food;[22]
* the right to non-toxic environments in which to live, work, or play;[23] and
* the right to healthy biodiversity and ecosystems.[24]

While substantive environmental standards should be established by states, if national standards do not sufficiently protect the full realization of human rights dependent on the environment, then business compliance with state law will not be sufficient to "do no harm" in accordance with the independent

---

[19] UN Human Rights Council, *The Right to Breathe Clean Air*, Report of the Special Rapporteur on the issue of human rights obligations relating to the enjoyment of a safe, clean, healthy and sustainable environment, UN doc. A/HRC/40/55 (January 8, 2019).

[20] UN General Assembly, *A Safe Climate*, Report of the Special Rapporteur on the issue of human rights obligations relating to the enjoyment of a safe, clean, healthy and sustainable environment, UN Doc. A/74/161 (July 15, 2019) (Safe Climate); OHCHR, *Human Rights, Climate Change, and Business: Key Messages*, https://www.ohchr.org/Documents/Issues/ClimateChange/materials/KMBusiness.pdf.

[21] UN Human Rights Council, *Human Rights and the Global Water Crisis: Water Scarcity, Water Pollution and Water-Related Disasters*, Report of the Special Rapporteur on the issue of human rights obligations relating to the enjoyment of a safe, clean, healthy and sustainable environment, UN Doc. A/HRC/46/28 (January 19, 2021).

[22] UN General Assembly, *Healthy and Sustainable Food*, Report of the Special Rapporteur on the issue of human rights obligations relating to the enjoyment of a safe, clean, healthy and sustainable environment, UN Doc. A/76/179 (July 19, 2021).

[23] UN Human Rights Council, *The Right to a Non-Toxic Environment*, Report of the Special Rapporteur on the issue of human rights obligations relating to the enjoyment of a safe, clean, healthy and sustainable environment, UN Doc. A/HRC/49/53 (January 12, 2022) (Non-Toxic Environment); UNEP and OHCHR, *Human Rights and Hazardous Substances: Key Messages*, https://www.ohchr.org/Documents/Issues/ClimateChange/materials/KMHazardousSubstances25febLight.pdf.

[24] UN General Assembly, *Human Rights Depend on a Healthy Biosphere*, Report of the Special Rapporteur on the issue of human rights obligations relating to the enjoyment of a safe, clean, and sustainable environment, UN doc. A/75/161 (July 15, 2020); UNEP and OHCHR, *Human Rights and Biodiversity: Key Messages*, https://wedocs.unep.org/bitstream/handle/20.500.11822/35407/KMBio.pdf.

responsibility to respect rights under the UNGPs.[25] Even in the absence of a substantive constitutional protection of a right to a clean, healthy, and sustainable environment, environmental human rights protections equally arise through the "greening" of other human rights – the recognition that without adequate environmental protection, these human rights are impossible to fully enjoy, including the right to life.[26]

NON-DISCRIMINATION AND ATTENTION TO VULNERABILITY

The Framework Principles treat non-discrimination as a cross-cutting theme while Principle 14 elaborates upon the need for additional measures in relation to "those who are most vulnerable to, or at particular risk from, environmental harm." Vulnerability may arise due to the unusual susceptibility of some individuals to environmental harm, or due to a denial of their human rights, or both. Those most vulnerable or at risk include women and gender-diverse persons, older persons, the disabled, those living in poverty, racialized minorities, displaced persons, and children. Principle 15 elaborates particular obligations in relation to Indigenous Peoples and other traditional communities, including: recognition and protection of their traditional territories, lands, and resources; respect for rights of consultation and free, prior, and informed consent before decisions are made; respect for and protection of traditional knowledge regarding sustainable use and conservation practices; and fair and equitable benefit sharing from activities involving their resources, lands, or territories.

ENVIRONMENTAL AND CLIMATE JUSTICE

Compounding the triple planetary crisis is the fact that solutions to one crisis may undermine another crisis while creating environmental and climate justice challenges and raising human rights concerns. For example, the impacts of climate change are disproportionately felt by those who have contributed least to the problem yet are unable to adapt due to a lack of capacity or access to finance, combined with the impossibility of preventing harms resulting from sea-level rise, drought, and melting ice, as well as sudden-onset weather events like tsunamis, among others.[27] A BHR and climate justice lens illuminates the responsibility of business enterprises to prevent and remedy climate-related

---

[25]   UN Guiding Principles, Principles 11 and 23.
[26]   HR Obligations, ¶¶ 12–13.
[27]   Safe Climate.

harms as appropriate for the degree of involvement.[28] Yet the move away from fossil fuels to green energy solutions must at the same time be undertaken while respecting human rights. Environmental justice concerns arise at each stage of the life cycle of green energy solutions, from mining of rare earth minerals to refining, manufacturing, and production, through siting of wind turbines or hydro-dams, to waste management and disposal when use of technology has run its course.[29]

TEACHING APPROACHES

Teaching about business responsibilities for environmental human rights can be integrated into many different courses beyond courses that are dedicated to BHR. For example, in the law school context, the Framework Principles together with the UNGPs can be taught as elements of a domestic Environmental Law class and offer an opportunity to consider the relationship between environmental impact assessment laws, human rights due diligence, and human rights impact assessment.[30] Both case law and legislation raising transnational environmental human rights issues including access to justice fit well within a course on private international law. This offers an opportunity to compare important BHR cases such as the Netherlands decision in *Four Nigerian Farmers*[31] and Canadian cases like *Chevron*[32] and *Nevsun*.[33]

---

[28] Sara L. Seck, "A Relational Analysis of Enterprise Obligations and Carbon Majors for Climate Justice," *Oñati Socio-Legal Series: Climate Justice in the Anthropocene* 11, no. 1 (2021): 254–284; Commission on Human Rights of the Philippines, *National Inquiry on Climate Change* Report (2022), https://chr.gov.ph/wp-content/uploads/2022/05/CHRP-NICC-Report-2022.pdf (Philippines *National Inquiry*).

[29] Non-Toxic Environment; United Nations Framework Convention on Climate Change (UNFCCC), OECD, UNEP, *Responsible Business Conduct and Climate Change*, https://mneguidelines.oecd.org/responsible-business-conduct-and-climate -change.pdf.

[30] See, for example, "Responsible Business Conduct and Impact Assessment Law," Schulich Law Scholars, Dalhousie University Schulich School of Law, accessed August 20, 2022, https://digitalcommons.schulichlaw.dal.ca/ialawrbc.

[31] *Four Nigerian Farmers and Milieudefensie v. Royal Dutch Shell* [2021] 200.126.804 and 200.126.834 (parent company breaches duty of care and Nigerian subsidiary is liable in relation to oil pollution from pipeline leak).

[32] *Chevron Corporation v. Yaiguaje*, 2015 SCC 42, [2015] 3 S.C.R. 69 (Can.) (to seek recognition and enforcement of a foreign environmental liability judgment there is no requirement of a real and substantial connection between the enforcing court and the foreign parent company defendant or action).

[33] *Nevsun Resources Ltd. v. Araya*, 2020 SCC 5, 1443 D.L.R. (4th) 183 (Can.) (claims for breaches of customary international law against a corporation in relation to foreign human rights abuses may proceed to trial).

Similarly, in a BHR course, a class on corporate accountability for environmental injustice represents an important opportunity to link learning on access to justice with environmental human rights, drawing upon the wide range of case studies involving extractive industries.[34] BHR teachers can also cover new developments connecting corporate climate litigation and human rights including in particular the recent Dutch decision in *Mileudefensie*[35] as well as recent developments in mandatory human rights and environmental due diligence.[36] (See Mandatory Human Rights Due Diligence Legislation, Chapter 11.)

Learning objectives when integrating environmental human rights into a more traditional BHR course might include:

- Explaining foundational concepts underpinning the relationship between human rights and the environment, and evaluating the implications of these concepts for BHR.
- Distinguishing between a procedural environmental rights approach and a substantive environmental rights approach, and understanding the relationship between the two.
- Identifying and evaluating international, domestic, and transnational law sources that support an environmental human rights approach to BHR.
- Understanding and explaining cross-cutting issues of non-discrimination, vulnerability, and risk in relation to environmental harms, and the potential of an environmental human rights approach to BHR to address concerns of environmental and climate justice.

Additional learning objectives might include:

- Debating the difference between a human rights due diligence approach and an environmental management approach to supply and value chain responsibility.
- Considering the relationship between human rights impact assessment (HRIA), environmental impact assessment, and other forms, such as social and sustainability impact assessments.

---

[34] See, for example, *Amnesty International, Injustice Incorporated: Corporate Abuses and the Human Right to Remedy* (London: Amnesty International Ltd., March 7, 2014), https://www.amnesty.org/download/Documents/8000/pol300012014en.pdf.

[35] *Mileudefensie v. Royal Dutch Shell* [2021] C/09/571932 / HA ZA 19-379 (by 2030 RDS must reduce greenhouse gas emissions across its own operations and from the oil it produces by 45 percent).

[36] See, for example, *Commission Proposal for a Directive of the European Parliament and of the Council on Corporate Sustainability, Due Diligence and amending Directive (EU) 2019/1937*, COM(2022) 71 final (February 23, 2022), 2022/0051 (COD).

- Explaining the difference between rights of nature[37] and environmental impacts on human rights, and their application to BHR.

Additional issue areas also deserve attention in BHR classes. For example, climate change has given rise to many responsible business guidance initiatives, but it is questionable how many fully integrate a BHR approach. It is important to distinguish between an approach to climate change that accounts for risks to the business and investors and a BHR approach that accounts for risks to those vulnerable to climate harms.[38] Students could be asked to design a model climate change and human rights policy for corporate clients, or to develop arguments for plaintiffs seeking to sue greenhouse gas emitters to prevent and remedy climate harms.[39] Other rarely explored but tremendously important issues include BHR and climate migration, as well as remedy for climate loss and damage.

Another way to explicitly link BHR and the environment is to consider issues that arise under the mandate of the UN Special Rapporteur on hazardous substances.[40] Previous reports have considered business responsibilities in relation to the protection of workers from toxic substances[41] as well as good practices for the disposal of toxics.[42] An emerging issue area considers the implications of the global plastic waste problem on human rights.[43] These reports provide a particularly useful opportunity to consider the relationship between workers' rights, BHR, and the environment, as well as intersections with circular economy. Another important issue is the relationship between

---

[37] David Boyd, *Rights of Nature: A Legal Revolution That Could Save the World* (Toronto: ECW Press, 2017).

[38] Seck, "A Relational Analysis".

[39] Philippines, *National Inquiry.*

[40] "Special Rapporteur on the Implications for Human Rights of the Environmentally Sound Management and Disposal of Hazardous Substances and Wastes," OHCHR, accessed August 20, 2022, https://www.ohchr.org/en/special-procedures/sr-toxics-and -human-rights.

[41] UN Human Rights Council, *Guidelines for Good Practices*, Report of the Special Rapporteur on the implications for human rights of the environmentally sound management and disposal of hazardous substances and wastes, UN doc. A/HRC/36/41 (July 20, 2017).

[42] UN Human Rights Council, *Principles on Human Rights and the Protection of Workers from Exposure to Toxic Substances*, Report of the Special Rapporteur on the implications for human rights of the environmentally sound management and disposal of hazardous substances and wastes, UN doc. A/HRC/42/41 (July 17, 2019).

[43] UN General Assembly, *The Stages of the Plastics Cycle and Their Impacts on Human Rights*, Report of the Special Rapporteur on the implications for human rights of the environmentally sound management and disposal of hazardous substances and wastes, UN Doc. A/76/207 (July 22, 2021).

land rights and EHRDs.[44] The International Service for Human Rights (ISHR) has developed a defender's toolkit that considers the specific challenges faced by EHRDs with reference to procedural environmental rights, as well as the particular issues confronting Indigenous Peoples and women who defend the environment.[45] However, rather than adopting a "do no harm" approach in line with the UNGPs, the ISHR defender's toolkit suggests that businesses have a "discretionary opportunity to act" that goes beyond the "normative responsibility to act."

A different area of learning might be an analysis of the duties of corporate boards in relation to the environment and climate change. Several jurisdictions, including Canada and the United Kingdom, specifically list the environment as a "stakeholder" that should be considered by boards of directors.[46] Policy directions put forward by securities regulators on disclosure in relation to climate risks are being updated and formalized[47] to accord with the work of the Task Force on Climate-Related Financial Disclosures.[48] Yet it is not clear how all of these initiatives align with a true environmental human rights approach to BHR. These issues can be discussed when teaching about the roles and responsibilities of institutional investors; fiduciary duties; and environmental, social, and governance (ESG) factors. (See Finance, Investors, and Human Rights, Chapter 26.)

---

[44]   John Knox, *Policy Brief: Environmental Human Rights Defenders – A Global Crisis* (Universal Rights Group, February 2017), https://www.universal-rights.org/wp-content/uploads/2017/03/EHRDs.pdf.

[45]   International Service for Human Rights, A Human Rights Defender Toolkit For Promoting Business Respect for Human Rights (2015), http://www.ishr.ch/sites/default/files/article/files/ishr_hrd_toolkit_english_web.pdf.

[46]   UK Companies Act, 2006, c. 46, s. 172(1)(d); Canada Business Corporations Act, R.S.C. 1985, c. C-44, s. 122(1.1)(b).

[47]   "Canadian Securities Regulators Seek Comment on Climate-Related Disclosure Requirements," Canadian Securities Administrators, October 18, 2021, https://www.securities-administrators.ca/news/canadian-securities-regulators-seek-comment-on-climate-related-disclosure-requirements; U.S. Securities and Exchange Commission, "SEC Proposes Rules to Enhance and Standardize Climate-Related Disclosures for Investors," press release, March 21, 2022, https://www.sec.gov/news/press-release/2022-46.

[48]   "Publications," Task Force on Climate-Related Financial Disclosures, accessed 26 June 2022, https://www.fsb-tcfd.org/publications.

EXERCISE 19.1

COMPARING HUMAN RIGHTS AND ENVIRONMENTAL

APPROACHES

A useful exercise is comparing the approach taken to human rights and environment in common responsible business conduct guidance tools and in dispute resolution. For example, ask students to compare the human rights and environment chapters in the OECD Guidelines for Multinational Enterprises. Then consider how these issues are treated in the OECD's new Due Diligence guidance,[49] as well as other sector-specific guidance tools, such as the OECD–FAO Guidance for Responsible Agricultural Supply Chains.[50] Similarly, consider how OECD National Contact Points mechanisms have treated specific instance complaints that raise both human rights and environmental issues.[51] (See The OECD National Contact Mechanism, Chapter 15.)

KEY QUESTIONS

General

- Which human rights are affected by environmental impacts?
- How do environmental harms cause or contribute to adverse human rights impacts?
- Could an environmental human rights approach to BHR help to address problems of overproduction and overconsumption, or are more radical

---

[49] OECD, *OECD Due Diligence Guidance for Responsible Business Conduct* (OECD, 2018), https://mneguidelines.oecd.org/OECD-Due-Diligence-Guidance-for-Responsible-Business-Conduct.pdf.

[50] OECD and Food and Agriculture Organization of the United Nations, *OECD-FAO Guidance for Responsible Agricultural Supply Chains* (Paris: OECD Publishing, 2016).

[51] See OECD, "Database of Specific Instances," accessed 26 June 2022, https://mneguidelines.oecd.org/database and OECD Watch, "National Contact Points," accessed 26 June 2022, https://www.oecdwatch.org/oecd-ncps/national-contact-points-ncps. See further OECD, "The Role of OECD Instruments on Responsible Business Conduct in Progressing Environmental Objectives" (2021), https://mneguidelines.oecd.org/The-role-of-OECD-instruments-on-responsible-business-conduct-in-progressing-environmental-objectives.pdf.

solutions required, such as fundamental changes to corporate laws and governance? What about the concept of the "circular economy"?[52]

- Does the adoption of an environmental human rights approach have implications for how we understand the human who holds rights,[53] as well as how we should understand the interests of directors and shareholders?[54]
- How does environmental harm affect members of vulnerable populations disproportionately?

For Business Students

- What business functions are connected to potential environmental harms?
- How might a business approach its responsibility to remedy environmental human rights harms that it has caused or to which it has contributed even in the absence of laws mandating environmental remediation?
- How could a responsibility to prevent and remedy environmental human rights harms be built into business strategy?
- BHR is often seen as an issue of business ethics, whereas sustainability raises questions of business strategy, including how time factors into decision-making. Could an environmental human rights approach to climate change, with particular attention to the rights of children, help to link business ethics with business sustainability strategy?
- How can/should human rights due diligence address environmental impacts?

For Law Students

- How is the right to a safe, clean, healthy, and sustainable environment defined under international law?
- What are the sources and content of state obligations to protect individuals from environmental harm?
- Given the global ecological crisis, could some environmental human rights meet the threshold of customary international law *jus cogens* norms so as to ground a cause of action as in the *Nevsun* (Canada) case?

---

[52] Anne Velenturf and Phil Purnell, "What a Sustainable Circular Economy Would Look Like," *The Conversation*, May 6, 2020, https://theconversation.com/what-a-sustainable-circular-economy-would-look-like-133808.

[53] Sara L. Seck, "Transnational Labour Law and the Environment: Beyond the Bounded Autonomous Worker," *Canadian Journal of Law and Society* 33, no. 2 (2018): 137–157.

[54] Seck, "A Relational Analysis".

- As more governments consider adoption of mandatory due diligence legislation modeled on France's Droit de Vigilance,[55] how can an environmental human rights approach help to align business conduct of human rights and environmental due diligence?
- What lessons could be learned from (environmental) impact assessment legislation in your jurisdiction?

For Policy Students

- Could an environmental human rights approach to implementation of the 2030 Sustainable Development Goals help both business and government actors to better integrate the economic, social, and environmental pillars within safe planetary boundaries?
- As governments adopt National Action Plans (NAPs) for BHR, how can they better integrate environmental dimensions into BHR, rather than as a separate consideration?
- Could BHR NAPs be aligned with nationally determined climate actions on mitigation and adaptation under the Paris Agreement? What about climate loss and damage?
- Governments are increasingly adopting action plans on other issues such as plastic pollution that adopt a circular economy approach. How can BHR be integrated into circular economy approaches?
- How do you conceptualize the "human" who holds rights: as an individual whose rights are independent from their relationships with family, community, and nature, or as an individual whose relationships, including with the natural world and earth systems, are integral to their understanding of self, and so their wellbeing and rights?

TEACHING RESOURCES

Readings

Commentary

- Bright, Claire and Karin Buhmann. "Risk-Based Due Diligence, Climate Change, Human Rights and the Just Transition." *Sustainability* 13, no. 18 (2021): 10454. https://doi.org/10.3390/su131810454.

---

[55] France, "Loi relative au devoir de vigilance des sociétés mères et des entreprises donneuses d'ordre," 2017, http://www.assemblee-nationale.fr/14/ta/ta0924.asp.

- Macchi, Chiara. *Business, Human Rights and the Environment: The Evolving Agenda* (Springer, 2022). https://link.springer.com/book/10.1007/978-94-6265-479-2.
- Martin-Ortega, Olga, Fatimazahra Dehbi, Valerie Nelson, and Renginee Pillay. "Towards a Business, Human Rights and the Environment Framework." *Sustainability* 14, no. 11 (2022): 6596. https://doi.org/10.3390/su14116596.
- Schilling-Vacaflor, Almut. "Integrating Human Rights and the Environment in Supply Chain Regulation." *Sustainability* 13, no. 17 (2021): 9666. https://doi.org/10.3390/su13179666.
- Seck, Sara L. "Indigenous Rights, Environmental Rights, or Stakeholder Engagement? Comparing IFC and OECD Approaches to the Implementation of the Business Responsibility to Respect Human Rights." *McGill Journal of Sustainable Development Law* 12, no. 1 (2016): 48–91.
- Seck, Sara L. "Revisiting Transnational Corporations and Extractive Industries: Climate Justice, Feminism, and State Sovereignty." *Transnational Law & Contemporary Problems* 26, no. 2 (2017): 1–28.
- Toft, Kristian Hoyer. "Climate Change as a Business and Human Rights Issue: A Proposal for a Moral Typology." *Business and Human Rights Journal* 5, no. 1 (2020): 1–27.
- Varvastian, Sam and Felicity Kalunga. "Transnational Corporate Liability for Environmental Damage and Climate Change: Reassessing Access to Justice after *Vedanta v Lungowe*." *Transnational Environmental Law* 9, no. 2 (2020): 323–345.

UN materials

- UN Human Rights Council. Resolution 48/13. The human right to a clean, healthy and sustainable environment. UN Doc. A/HRC/RES/48/13 (October 8, 2021). https://digitallibrary.un.org/record/3945636?ln=en.
- UN Human Rights Council. *Framework Principles on Human Rights and the Environment*, Report of the Special Rapporteur on the issue of human rights obligations relating to the enjoyment of a safe, clean, healthy and sustainable environment. UN Doc. A/HRC/37/59 (January 24, 2018), Annex (Framework Principles). https://undocs.org/A/HRC/37/59.

Podcast

- Seck, Sara L. and Siobhan Quigg. *4: Corporate Climate Responsibility*. Dalhousie Law Journal Podcast. Recorded January 2020 at Dalhousie University for *Dal Law Journal*. https://digitalcommons.schulichlaw.dal.ca/dlj_podcast/4.

Video

- Seck, Sara L. (Instructor) with Surya Deva (Discussant). "Business, Human Rights, and the Environment." Recorded June 2021 for Global Network for Human Rights and the Environment (GNHRE) and United Nations Environment Programme (UNEP), Critical Perspectives in Human Rights and the Environment: The Summer/Winter School 2021. YouTube video: 1:31:17. https://gnhre.org/critical-perspectives-on-human-rights -and-the-environment-the-2021-gnhre-unep-summer-winter-school/2021 -summer-winter-school-business-human-rights-and-the-environment.

Websites

- Children's Environmental Rights Initiative. https://www.childrenvironment .org.
- Environment-Rights.Org. "Who We Are." https://environment-rights.org/ about-us-2.
- Kuncak, Baskut. UN Special Rapporteur 2014–2020. "Human Rights and Toxic Substances." http://www.srtoxics.org.
- Office of the High Commissioner for Human Rights. "UN Special Rapporteur on Human Rights and the Environment." https://www.ohchr .org/en/special-procedures/sr-environment and UN Special Rapporteur on Human Rights and the Environment. http://www.srenvironment.org.
- Office of the High Commissioner for Human Rights. "UN Special Rapporteur on Toxics and Human Rights." https://www.ohchr.org/en/ special-procedures/sr-toxics-and-human-rights.
- The Permanent Peoples' Tribunal on Human Rights, Fracking and Climate Change. https://www.tribunalonfracking.org.

20. Land rights[1]

Mina Manuchehri and Beth Roberts

OVERVIEW

Land sits at the nexus of business and human rights (BHR). Businesses frequently cannot avoid questions of land tenure rights and governance (and the human rights implications of these questions) within their operations. Land is increasingly recognized as a standalone human right, and land rights are fundamental to numerous other internationally recognized human rights: equality, an adequate standard of living, housing, food security, cultural life, freedom from violence, self-determination – even the right to life. Secure land rights can reduce poverty and conflict, increase economic activity, empower women, strengthen food security, and improve environmental sustainability.

This chapter defines land rights in the context of BHR, provides an overview of international human rights guidance on land rights relevant to business actors, outlines incentives and challenges for companies in respecting land rights, and provides approaches and key questions for teaching land rights.

DEFINING LAND RIGHTS

Globally, land use and access are subject to a broad range of legal and customary land tenure arrangements. Tenure types are complex and varied (formal vs. customary, urban vs. rural, market-based vs. family or community-based). Understanding land rights goes beyond an analysis of formal legal frameworks to account for the *quality, legality and effective implementation, par-*

---

[1]   An original version of this chapter appeared as Chris Jochnick, Mina Manuchehri, and Beth Roberts, "Teaching Note: Land Rights," in *Teaching Business and Human Rights Handbook* (Teaching Business and Human Rights Forum, 2017), https:// teachbhr.org/resources/teaching-bhr-handbook/teaching-notes/land-rights.

ticipation, and *enforceability* of land rights, applying a gender-equality and social-inclusion lens to each element.[2]

- *Quality* means land rights are clearly defined and scoped, and include all forms of tenure exercised by women and men (ownership, access, use, lease, transfer, inherit, rent, occupy). Rights are granted for a clear, ideally extended, duration.
- *Legality and effective implementation* means land rights are legally recognized. Customary law is acknowledged by formal laws and administrative structures. Women's land rights are guaranteed by law regardless of customary, religious, community, or familial recognition. Rights to land are equitable, regardless of sex, gender, age, ethnicity, religion, socioeconomic status, and other identities.
- *Participation* requires the inclusion of rural women and men, youth, other minority groups, and civil society in policymaking bodies regarding land ownership and use, and in processes related to land acquisition or to land use decisions within a community or affecting a community's use of land.
- *Enforceability* requires women and men to be fully informed of their land rights and have non-discriminatory and equitable access to justice in relevant formal and customary dispute resolution bodies.

LAND RIGHTS: A FOUNDATIONAL OPPORTUNITY FOR FULFILLING HUMAN RIGHTS

Individuals and communities affected by business activities in developing-country settings often depend on agriculture for their livelihoods. Understanding land rights can help BHR students conceptualize how human rights can be both distinct and interrelated. For instance, Indigenous Peoples' right to self-determination under the International Covenant on Civil and Political Rights[3] is recognized apart from the right to an adequate standard

---

[2] Office of the High Commissioner for Human Rights Working Group on Discrimination Against Women and Girls, *Insecure Land Rights for Women: a Threat to Progress on Gender Equality and Sustainable Development* (July 2017), https://www.ohchr.org/en/special-procedures/wg-women-and-girls/insecure-land-rights-women-threat-progress-gender-equality-and-sustainable-development.

[3] *International Covenant on Civil and Political Rights* (ICCPR), December 16, 1966, 999 U.N.T.S. 171 (entered into force March 23, 1976), Article 1, https://www.ohchr.org/en/instruments-mechanisms/instruments/international-covenant-civil-and-political-rights; see also *International Covenant on Economic, Social and Cultural Rights* (ICESCR), December 16, 1966, 993 U.N.T.S. 3 (entered into force January 3, 1976), Article 1, https://www.ohchr.org/en/instruments-mechanisms/instruments/international-covenant-economic-social-and-cultural-rights.

of living under the International Covenant on Economic, Social and Cultural Rights.[4] But for many Indigenous communities, secure rights to the land on which they depend for a livelihood and from which their cultural identity is derived may be necessary to realize these formally recognized rights. (See Rights of Indigenous Peoples, Chapter 21.) Likewise, women have the right under international law to equal enjoyment and non-discrimination of economic, social, and cultural rights.[5] But unequal rights to land under formal and customary systems in many countries hinder women's equal enjoyment of land as a primary source of livelihood. This inequality is often exacerbated in the context of an investment, as women are often excluded from decisions about land, employment opportunities, and compensation.

According to a 2016 Land Matrix Initiative report, a large majority of the 1,204 concluded land deals recorded in low- and middle-income countries targeted prime agricultural land.[6] Governments have seized land from communities to make it available to investors and business. They have also granted concessions to private sector actors, failed to effectively regulate land speculation that deprived communities and individuals of just compensation, widened inequalities between rural communities and domestic elites,[7] and fed corruption by land administration officials. Acquisition of land, and land administration more generally, is marked globally by a high level of corruption.[8]

An estimated 65 percent of the world's land is held under customary or communal tenure but is rarely recognized by formal law. This legal gap renders the populations who live and depend on such land bereft of protections in the context of business activities affecting such lands.[9] Customary tenure systems

---

[4]   ICESCR, Article 11.

[5]   ICESCR, Articles 2, 3.

[6]   Kerstin Nolte, Wytske Chamberlain, and Markus Giger, *International Land Deals for Agriculture: Fresh Insights from the Land Matrix – Analytical Report II* (Bern: Centre for Development and Environment, 2016), https://landmatrix.org/documents/47/Analytical_Report_II_LMI_English_2016.pdf.

[7]   Anni Arial et al., Transparency International and FAO, "Corruption in the Land Sector" (working paper, 04/2011, 2011, Transparency International and the UN Food and Agricultural Organization), 5, http://www.transparency.org/whatwedo/publication/working_paper_04_2011_corruption_in_the_land_sector.

[8]   Transparency International, *Global Corruption Report: Climate Change*, eds. Gareth Sweeney, Rebecca Dobson, Krina Despota, and Dieter Zinnbauer (London: Earthscan, 2011), http://www.transparency.org/whatwedo/publication/global_corruption_report_climate_change.

[9]   Rights and Resources Initiative, *Who Owns the World's Land: A Global Baseline of Formally Recognized Indigenous and Community Land Rights* (Washington, DC: Rights and Resources Initiative, 2015), vii, http://www.rightsandresources.org/wp-content/uploads/GlobalBaseline_web.pdf. (This lack of alignment between formal and customary land rights makes it imperative that states parties consider customary

can support the power imbalance that frequently favors interests of traditional authorities and domestic elites over land users' interests in acquisitions for large-scale land-based investments. This dynamic has implications for women's rights, as men typically hold rights within customary tenure systems.

In response to increasing criticism of business practices that affect land rights, the international community – including civil society organizations, governments, and companies – has identified a critical need for more responsible investments in land. Companies have been censured for failing to: identify legitimate rights holders and users; perform impact assessments to help avoid or mitigate the adverse effects of land transfers and use changes; carry out consultations with communities and individuals who will be affected by land transfers or use changes; obtain free, prior, and informed consent (FPIC) consistent with international law;[10] and ensure access to remedy. Corporate practices that fail to address land rights have the potential to cause or exacerbate social, economic, political, and gender inequalities. The risk of human rights violations related to land has also been identified in other sectors, including renewable energy.[11]

GUIDELINES AND STANDARDS FOR RESPONSIBLE LAND-BASED INVESTMENT

Best practices for responsible land-based investment are detailed in numerous international guidelines and standards, such as the Voluntary Guidelines on the Responsible Governance of Tenure of Land, Fisheries and Forests in the Context of National Food Security (VGGT),[12] the FPIC provision of the UN

---

tenure rights when they are drafting legislation or creating other formal requirements for investors, including due diligence requirements or guidelines.) Julia Behrman, Ruth Meinzen-Dick, and Agnes Quisumbing, "The Gender Implications of Large-Scale Land Deals" (International Food Policy Research Institute Discussion Paper, 2011), 6, https://ebrary.ifpri.org/utils/getfile/collection/p15738coll2/id/124877/filename/124878 .pdf.

[10] UN Food and Agriculture Organization (FAO), "Respecting Free, Prior and Informed Consent: Practical Guidance for Governments, Companies, NGOs, Indigenous Peoples and Local Communities in Relation to Land Acquisition," Governance of Tenure Technical Guide No. 3 (Rome: FAO, 2014), http://www.fao.org/3/a-i3496e .pdf.

[11] See, e.g., USAID, "Issue Brief: Land Tenure and Energy Infrastructure," released March 15, 2016, https://land-links.org/issue-brief/land-tenure-and-energy -infrastructure.

[12] FAO Committee on Food Security (CFS), *Voluntary Guidelines on the Responsible Governance of Tenure of Land, Fisheries, and Forests in the Context of National Food Security* (VGGT) (Rome: FAO, 2022), http://www.fao.org/docrep/016/ i2801e/i2801e.pdf.

Declaration on the Rights of Indigenous Peoples (UNDRIP),[13] and the Principles for Responsible Investment in Agriculture and Food Systems.[14] These guidelines call on governments and companies to:

• Identify and map legitimate land rights.
• Assess and mitigate social and environmental impacts, including impacts on women and other marginalized groups.
• Consult with legitimate land rightsholders, including women and men.
• Obtain the FPIC of Indigenous Peoples and local communities.
• Provide just and fair compensation to communities.
• Ensure access to remedy.
• Monitor and evaluate project implementation.

These international standards tend to lack clarity regarding the roles and responsibilities of companies versus governments. This gap has spawned the development of implementation guidance, such as the UN Food and Agriculture Organization's (FAO's) Responsible Governance of Tenure: A Technical Guide,[15] USAID's *Operational Guidelines for Responsible Land-Based Investment*,[16] and the Landesa's Responsible Investments in Property and Land (RIPL) Online Platform.[17]

Instruments relating more broadly to BHR are also relevant and useful, such as the United Nations Guiding Principles on Business and Human

---

[13]   UN General Assembly, Resolution 61/295, United Nations Declaration on the Rights of Indigenous Peoples (UNDRIP), A/RES/61/295, Articles 10, 11, 19, 28, 29 (September 13, 2007), http://www.un.org/esa/socdev/unpfii/documents/DRIPS_en .pdf.

[14]   FAO CFS, *Principles for Responsible Investment in Agriculture and Food Systems* (2014), http://www.fao.org/fileadmin/templates/cfs/Docs1314/rai/CFS _Principles_Oct_2014_EN.pdf.

[15]   Darrly Vhugen, "Responsible Governance of Tenure: A Technical Guide for Investors," Governance of Tenure Technical Guide No. 7 (Rome: FAO, 2016), http:// www.fao.org/3/a-i5147e.pdf.

[16]   USAID, *Operational Guidelines for Responsible Land-Based Investment* (2015), https://www.land-links.org/wp-content/uploads/2016/09/USAID_Operational _Guidelines_updated.pdf.

[17]   Landesa, "Resource Platform for Responsible Investments in Property and Land," accessed August 3, 2022, https://ripl.landesa.org.

Rights (UNGPs)[18] and the United Nations Global Compact.[19] The UNGPs include land as an example of states' duty to protect both rightsholders and business interests,[20] and the UN Global Compact has authored several resources and hosted events to map land rights to their principles, human rights frameworks broadly, and the Sustainable Development Goals (SDGs).[21]

RESPECTING LAND RIGHTS – INCENTIVES

Civil society advocacy has been a catalyst for resources related to land-based investment. For example, the Oxfam campaign "Behind the Brands" applied pressure to the ten largest food and beverage companies by scoring each company on seven different human rights categories, including land rights.[22] The campaign resulted in significant consumer pressure and several companies adopted land rights policies and committed to compliance with guidelines like the VGGTs and FPIC.[23]

Companies may also view respecting land rights as a means to mitigate business risk. Recent studies estimate that land tenure conflict can increase the cost of a project by up to 29 times due to project delays, brand reputation harm, and loss of financing.[24] Respecting land rights can also help to strengthen relations with communities and preserve companies' "social license" to operate.[25]

---

[18] United Nations Human Rights Council, *Guiding Principles on Business and Human Rights: Implementing the United Nations "Protect, Respect and Remedy" Framework*, Report of the Special Representative of the Secretary-General on the issue of human rights and transnational corporations and other business enterprises, UN doc. A/HRC/17/31 (March 21, 2011) (UN Guiding Principles).

[19] United Nations Global Compact, "Promote Sustainable Food and Agriculture Systems," *Food and Agriculture*, accessed August 3, 2022, https://www.unglobalcompact.org/what-is-gc/our-work/environment/food-agriculture.

[20] UN Guiding Principles, Commentary to Principle 3.

[21] See, for example, Royal Institute of Chartered Surveyors and United Nations Global Compact, *Advancing Responsible Business Practices in Land, Construction, Real Estate Use, and Investment* (2015), https://www.unglobalcompact.org/library/1361.

[22] Beth Hoffman, *Behind the Brands* (Oxfam International, 2013), https://s3.amazonaws.com/oxfam-us/www/static/media/files/Behind_the_Brands_Briefing_Paper_Final.pdf.

[23] Numerous companies, such as PepsiCo, AB InBev, Illovo Sugar, and Unilever, have made land-related commitments. See generally Interlaken Group, "About the Interlaken Group," accessed August 3, 2022, https://www.interlakengroup.org/about.

[24] TMP Systems, *IAN: Managing Tenure Risk* (TMPS, 2016), https://teachbhr.files.wordpress.com/2017/10/d9880-ian_managingtenurerisk_final_.pdf.

[25] TMP Systems, *IAN: Managing Tenure Risk*.

RESPECTING LAND RIGHTS – CHALLENGES FOR COMPANIES

Numerous challenges can make implementation of land rights commitments difficult for companies. These include:

- The concept of "respecting land rights" is a relatively new area of corporate responsibility and BHR. Consequently, companies and other relevant stakeholders (e.g., auditors) may not know how to identify and address land rights issues or may lack familiarity with distinctions and interrelationships between land rights and human rights instruments.
- How a company implements its commitments varies depending on where it is located in the supply chain. For example, a producer company that owns or leases land or directly contracts with smallholder farmers may be able to more easily identify land issues "on the ground" versus a buyer company that may not own or lease land or directly source from farmers.
- There is limited guidance on "legacy land issues" – land rights issues that date back to the actions of a company that previous owned or used the land, or to government expropriation – particularly regarding who should be responsible for remedying harms.
- Despite the lack of clarity regarding the role of companies versus governments, companies may need to fill gaps in countries' land governance frameworks where there is limited government capacity and will to implement and enforce laws and policies.

TEACHING APPROACHES

Learning objectives for teaching land rights may include:

- Becoming familiar with international, regional, and domestic guidelines, standards, and guidance on responsible land-based investment.
- Understanding how secure land tenure relates to human rights enshrined in international instruments.
- Understanding the types and scope of international human rights and sector-based guidance related to land rights and business activities.
- Identifying human rights issues associated with different land tenure types and different modes of accessing land.
- Recognizing gendered aspects of land rights in all settings and implications for BHR.
- Understanding the challenges for companies navigating legal frameworks in developing countries, community engagement, supply chain sustainability, and traceability.

• Understanding the tensions between land rights as a governance challenge that requires a lengthy time horizon and land rights as a challenge for businesses' need for efficiency and return on investment.

Law students should understand international, regional, and domestic laws, policies, guidelines, standards, and guidance on responsible land-based investment. Students should also understand major human rights instruments related to land and business activities, including the International Covenants and the work of UN treaty monitoring bodies,[26] guidance documents like the UNGPs, and how domestic and international law can interact in the context of investments. Additionally, law courses can introduce comparative law with a focus on investment treaties and domestic, corporate, and land law frameworks, and the potential impacts on human rights that result from inadequate legal protections in these bodies of law.

Policy courses can address how land rights fit into a larger administrative picture for the host state of an investment. Efficient and equitable land administration requires long-term and strategic investment and implementation; this creates significant challenges for companies who want to comply with human rights requirements in countries where land governance is weak, and challenges for governments in developing-country contexts as they try to put these long-term solutions in place in the context of pressure to welcome investments. Policy students can consider the challenges associated with creating an enabling environment so that companies profit, land governance is strengthened (or at least not weakened through corruption or bypassed), and communities benefit.

Business courses can consider the business case for human rights and land rights, issues like corruption, host state versus home state obligations for businesses, and supply chain management issues related to land rights. Business students will also benefit from understanding how land rights relate to the mitigation of risks (e.g., costs, delays, reputational harm) and can help to unlock opportunities (e.g., agricultural productivity, climate adaptation and mitigation, livelihoods).

---

[26] The Committee on Economic, Social and Cultural Rights recently issued a draft General Comment on business activities that references land and investment issues related to land. "Day of General Discussion on Draft General Comment on State Obligations under the International Covenant on Economic, Social and Cultural Rights in the Context of Business Activities," Meetings and Events, UN Office of the High Commissioner for Human Rights, accessed August 3, 2022, http://www.ohchr.org/EN/HRBodies/CESCR/Pages/Discussion2017.aspx.

The approaches below could be used for an introductory lesson or module on land rights in the context of a BHR course, or as elements of a course focused on land rights and business activities.

TOPICAL APPROACHES

Each of the following topics allows teachers to provide concrete examples of the intersection between human rights, business activities, and land.

- **The global land rush.** While the acquisition of land from communities by government or the private sector for private use or development is not a recent phenomenon, the food and fuel crisis in 2007–2008 led to international media coverage of the adverse consequences of large-scale land acquisitions. This period included global shocks related to food prices and a series of high-profile acquisitions for biofuel production. Teachers can highlight the links between business activities, international law and trade, and land rights, and how the phenomenon of land-based investments can lead to human rights impacts on food security and livelihoods. These trends around demand for land have also been found in other sectors, including extractives, renewable energy, and conservation.
- **Supply chain issues.** Multinational companies often find themselves embroiled in land tenure issues that are a complex mixture of customary law, weak land governance in host countries, and other factors affecting agricultural productivity. This means that companies must account for all these factors when estimating their operation costs and developing strategies for growth and sustainability. Land tenure issues related to supply chains can include agricultural productivity (which can increase with greater tenure security), labor availability (as people age out of agriculture or migrate to cities in search of more lucrative work), lack of clarity of land ownership (as users of land – especially women – may not have formal rights, and formal owners may not reside on or near the land they own), climate action (secure land tenure is linked to increased investment in climate adaptation and mitigation), and other issues that can impact business operations.
- **Elite capture.** Transactions for land-based investments often take place between government officials and multinational corporations, or between expatriates who own land and investors. Examining this phenomenon can illustrate challenges in human rights advocacy, policy and legislative development, and business compliance with human rights norms in contexts with endemic corruption and significant governance gaps.
- **Gender and land-based investment.** Women are likely to be disproportionately harmed in the context of land investments. Relative to men,

women are less likely to be included in negotiation processes by both company and community representatives, and their rights and uses of land are less likely to be recognized. They are less likely to receive compensation or other benefits stemming from projects (e.g., employment), are disadvantaged in livelihood replacement and resettlement, and are less likely to be able to access justice in both informal and formal settings. These dynamics and others contribute to severe human rights infringements and violations for women.

- **Community engagement.** Guidelines and standards for responsible land-based investment address the process of community engagement in order to assist companies in respecting human rights. Outlining the process of community engagement can assist students in understanding land rights-related challenges in the context of business activities from the perspective of communities affected by these investments and the civil society actors that often serve as representatives for communities. (See Exercise 21.3: Securing Free, Prior, and Informed Consent – "Colorado Petroleum.")
- **Industry and commodity-based effects.** The industry (e.g., agriculture, extractives, infrastructure, energy), commodity type (e.g., high-value vs. low-value crops), and types of actors involved (e.g., commercial farmers vs. smallholder farmers) in land-based investment all create different conditions and challenges for protecting human rights. Legal frameworks particular to extractives can limit communities' ability to negotiate directly with investors. Supply chains with smallholders present complex and unique land tenure-related challenges; multinational corporations may only or predominantly have contact with government officials and lack awareness of how customary rules or ground-level conditions affect productivity or the livelihoods of women and men in communities. Examining land-based investment by industry and commodity can provide comparative geographical perspective as well, helping students understand BHR challenges for one industry or commodity across different regional and national human rights, land governance, and corporate legal frameworks.

EXERCISE 20.1

CASE STUDY: LAND RIGHTS AND PHATA COOPERATIVE

Case studies, such as the Phata Cooperative,[27] can help students identify how to approach specific challenges. For example: What conditions should be present in an outgrower scheme to ensure land rights are identified and respected? For an interactive approach, students can be divided into three groups (business, government, and civil society) and identify interests and challenges from the perspective of their group, comparing results. This allows students to grasp some of the complexities and competing interests that arise in a land rights and business context.

KEY QUESTIONS

General

- What are land rights?
- How are land rights related to human rights?
- What standards, guidelines, guidance, and tools are available to help companies make responsible land-based investments?
- What are best practices for responsible land-based investments?
- What factors have incentivized companies to commit to respecting land rights?
- What issues do companies face in implementing commitments to respecting land rights?
- What gap-filling role should companies serve when operating in countries with weak land governance systems?

For Business Students

- Is there a business case for respecting land rights?
- How can a company practically implement land rights-related commitments? How do implementation strategies vary depending on a company's role in the supply chain (e.g., buyers, suppliers, investors)?
- How can companies develop realistic strategies for implementing land rights policies?

---

[27]   Landesa et al., *Phata Cooperative Case Study* (2019), https://cdn.landesa.org/wp-content/uploads/Phata-Case-Study-9.6.19-FINAL.pdf.

- How can companies monitor whether they are complying with best practices?
- What corporate functions should be involved in implementing land rights policies?
- What third parties will companies potentially need to consult to ensure compliance with their land-related commitments?
- How are companies in different industries addressing responsible land-based investment?

For Law Students

- What are the international human rights laws and standards most relevant to ensuring responsible investment in land? How can these instruments be used in conjunction with land rights standards and guidance?
- Should non-state actors assume greater roles under international legal frameworks when domestic legal frameworks are weak or unenforced?
- What legal or regulatory mechanisms can governments put in place to ensure companies respect land rights and comply with best practices?
- What gaps in international human rights and national legal frameworks contribute to adverse human rights impacts?
- What do landmark cases[28] from human rights bodies and international courts indicate about business activities and land-related human rights?

For Policy Students

- What legal or regulatory frameworks have the greatest impact on land rights and use?
- How can government actors collaborate with civil society to promote and ensure responsible investments in land?
- How could home states promote responsible land-related investment requirements with host state representatives?
- What incentives can civil society in home states create for companies to conduct responsible land-related investments? In host states?

---

[28] See, for example, African Commission on Human and Peoples' Rights, *The Social and Economic Rights Action Center for Economic and Social Rights v. Nigeria*, Comm. No. 155/96, (2001); African Commission on Human and Peoples' Rights, *Endorois v. Kenya*, 276/2003; Federal Court of Australia, *Griffiths v. Northern Territory of Australia* [No. 3] (2016) FCA 900 (Austl.); Inter-American Court of Human Rights, *Case of the Kichwa Indigenous People of Sarayaku v. Ecuador*, Merits and Reparations, Judgment, Inter-Am. Ct. H.R. (June 27, 2012).

- How can host state government agencies coordinate to ensure responsible investments in land?
- What data (types and methods) should host state government entities collect to make accurate information that promotes human rights available to investors?

TEACHING RESOURCES

Readings

International standards

- International Finance Corporation. *Performance Standards on Environmental and Social Sustainability*. Washington, DC: IFC 2012. https://www.ifc.org/wps/wcm/connect/topics_ext_content/ifc_external_corporate_site/sustainability-at-ifc/publications/publications_handbook_pps. Standards 3, 5, and 7 are most relevant.
- New Alliance for Food Security & Nutrition and Grow Africa. *Analytical Framework for Land-based Investments in African Agriculture*. 2015. https://www.growafrica.com/sites/default/files/Analytical-framework-for-land-based-investments-in-African-agriculture_0.pdf.
- UN Office of the High Commissioner for Human Rights. *Land and Human Rights: Standards and Applications*. UN Doc. HR/PUB/15/5/Add.1 (2015). https://www.ohchr.org/sites/default/files/Documents/Publications/Land_HR-StandardsApplications.pdf.

Guidance

- Interlaken Group and Rights and Resources Initiative. Land Legacy Issues: Guidance on Corporate Responsibility. Washington, DC: Interlaken Group and RRI, 2017. https://assets.website-files.com/5d819417269ec78 97f93e67a/5dcb5578c74abf5dc2f80f18_Interlaken_Group_Land_Legacy _Guidance.pdf.
- Namati, Community Land Protectors: Facilitators Guide (2016), https:// namati.org/wp-content/uploads/2016/02/Namati-Community-Land-Protection -Facilitators-Guide-Ed.1-2016-LR.pdf.
- UN Food and Agriculture Organization. *Governance of Tenure Technical Guide No. 1. Governing Land for Women and Men: A Technical Guide to Support the Achievement of Responsible Gender-Equitable Governance*

Land Tenure. Rome: FAO, 2013. http://www.fao.org/docrep/017/i3114e/
i3114e.pdf.

Commentary

• Columbia Center on Sustainable Investment and Open Contracting
  Partnership. *Transparency in Land-Based Investment: Key Questions and
  Next Steps*. March 2016. https://academiccommons.columbia.edu/catalog/
  ac:206373.
• Cotula, Lorenzo, Sonja Vermeulen, Rebeca Leonard, and James
  Keeley. *Land Grab or Development Opportunity? Agricultural Investment
  and International Land Deals in Africa*. London: IIED, FAO and IFAD,
  2009. http://www.fao.org/3/a-ak241e.pdf.
• De Schutter, Olivier. "The Green Rush: The Race for Farmland and
  the Rights of Land Users," Harvard International Law Journal 52, no. 2
  (Summer 2011): 504–559. https://harvardilj.org/wp-content/uploads/sites/
  15/2011/07/HILJ_52-2_De-Schutter1.pdf.

Case Studies

• USAID, "Responsible Land-Based Investment Project in Ghana," https://
  land-links.org/case-study/responsible-land-based-investment-project-in
  -ghana.
• USAID, "Responsible Land-Based Investment Project in Kenya," https://
  land-links.org/case-study/responsible-land-based-investment-project-in
  -kenya.
• USAID, "Responsible Land-Based Investment Project in Mozambique,"
  https://land-links.org/case-study/responsible-land-based-investment-
  project-in-mozambique.

Websites

• Interlaken Group (multistakeholder group focused on responsible
  investment in land). Interlaken Group. "Private Sector Action to Secure
  Community Land Rights." https://www.interlakengroup.org.

- Landesa, RIPL Online Platform (includes guidebooks for companies, government, and communities; and topical primers on FPIC, grievance mechanisms, compensation, gender, vulnerable groups, and monitoring and evaluation). Landesa Rural Development Institute. "Resource Platform for Responsible Investments in Property and Land." https://ripl.landesa.org.
- Responsible Land-Based Investment Navigator (resource platform for guidelines, guidance, and tools on responsible land-based investment). "The Responsible Land-Based Investment Navigator." https://landinvestments.org.

21. Rights of Indigenous Peoples

Kendyl Salcito[1]

OVERVIEW

This chapter focuses on the rights of Indigenous Peoples as they intersect with business entities. Throughout history, business interests have caused harms to Indigenous populations, from enslavement for plantation labor; to eviction for transportation networks; to extraction of timber, ore, and other economic goods. Business interests have disregarded the spiritual and ancestral value of resources, as well as the legitimate Indigenous claims to profit-sharing from extraction of such resources. Both risks to and remedies for abuses against Indigenous Peoples require private sector participation, making Indigenous issues important in a business and human rights (BHR) course. This chapter suggests approaches for teaching BHR and the rights of Indigenous Peoples.

RIGHTS OF INDIGENOUS PEOPLES UNDER INTERNATIONAL LAW

The term "Indigenous Peoples" has no universally accepted definition. It broadly applies to communities that (1) self-identify as members of a distinct cultural group, (2) hold collective attachment to ancestral territories and/or natural resources, (3) retain customary governance systems distinct from the nation-state, and/or (4) speak a distinct language from the nation-state where they reside.

These populations hold communal and individual rights[2] under two dominant frameworks within international law: International Labour Organization

---

[1]   This chapter was peer reviewed by Kate Finn, the Executive Director of First Peoples Worldwide. Her expertise is in researching, evaluating, and minimizing the impacts of development on indigenous communities in the US and worldwide. She is an enrolled member of the Osage Nation.

[2]   Indigenous Peoples' individual rights are safeguarded under universal protections. See United Nations Department of Economic and Social Affairs, *State of the World's Indigenous Peoples*, vol. 5 (Geneva: UN, 2021), 49, https://www.un.org/

(ILO) Convention 169 on the Rights of Indigenous and Tribal Peoples, entered into force in 1990,[3] and the United Nations Declaration on the Rights of Indigenous Peoples (UNDRIP), adopted in 2007.[4] While efforts to safeguard Indigenous Peoples predated these seminal instruments, those efforts were framed either in the context of legal jurisprudence or in assimilationist terms, making them unfit for broader application.[5]

Both ILO 169 and UNDRIP establish state, not corporate, responsibilities to protect, promote, and fulfill Indigenous rights and freedoms. However, the instruments explicitly acknowledge the role of corporate actors in violating Indigenous rights. ILO 169 provides safeguards against forced labor, forced recruitment, workplace discrimination, labor trafficking, and other conditions endemic to agricultural or industrial expansion onto Indigenous lands and territories (Articles 11, 20, 21, and 22). It also explicitly references the displacement of Indigenous Peoples for "exploration or exploitation" of natural resources (Article 15). UNDRIP reaffirms these protections (see Article 32(2)) and carves out additional, specific protections against the deposition of hazardous materials on Indigenous lands (Article 29(1)). On a global scale, these impacts are disproportionately contributed by business.

Despite the fulsome articulation of Indigenous protections in these instruments, implementation has been limited. Three decades after its drafting, only 23 countries have ratified ILO 169. While UNDRIP has broad endorsement, it is non-binding and has no enforcement mechanism. Practical gaps affect both instruments, including that neither one mandates that states, corporations, or other decision-makers conduct research to help locate and identify Indigenous communities under the criteria provided above. Likewise, neither articulates how sovereign-to-sovereign relationships should be managed with Indigenous groups, or how structural discrimination should be tackled, leaving states

---

development/desa/indigenouspeoples/wp-content/uploads/sites/19/2021/03/State-of
-Worlds-Indigenous-Peoples-Vol-V-Final.pdf.

[3]   ILO Convention No. 169, *Indigenous and Tribal Peoples Convention*, 1989 (June 27, 1989).

[4]   United Nations General Assembly, Resolution 61/295, *United Nations Declaration on the Rights of Indigenous Peoples* (UNDRIP), A/RES/61/295 (13 September 2007).

[5]   The ILO's first Indigenous Peoples convention (in 1957) safeguarded labor protections but considered assimilation inevitable and desirable. ILO Convention No. 107, *Indigenous and Tribal Peoples Convention*, 1957 (June 26, 1957). Additionally, the International Court of Justice concluded that the Article 1 protections for "self-determination" outlined in the UN Charter should apply to the Indigenous Western Saharawi Peoples, but no enforcement mechanisms or Charter amendments accompanied the ruling. Western Sahara, Advisory Opinion, 1957 I.C.J. Rep. (separate opinion by Dillard, J.), 108–118.

unwilling or unable to safeguard Indigenous Peoples. As such, even countries that have ratified ILO 169 and codified UNDRIP in law have left many Indigenous communities unprotected.[6]

INDIGENOUS RIGHTS AND THE UN GUIDING PRINCIPLES

Government failures to protect, promote, and fulfill Indigenous rights do not absolve companies of their responsibility to "respect" Indigenous rights. On the contrary, state failures to implement and enforce the content of these instruments generate risks for companies – both that they might inadvertently (or advertently) adversely impact Indigenous rights and that they might jeopardize their licenses, permits, and value chain relationships if adverse impacts occur.

The UN Guiding Principles on Business and Human Rights (UNGPs) expressly identify Indigenous Peoples as requiring special protections in the context of corporate impacts,[7] the corporate responsibility to respect human rights,[8] and access to remedy.[9] Under Pillar II, "respect" is directed to "specific groups or populations that require particular attention," such as "Indigenous Peoples" as well as "ethnic, religious and linguistic minorities."

The active duty to "respect" the rights of Indigenous Peoples is implemented through "due diligence."[10] A duly diligent business will know, for example, what processes states use for identifying Indigenous and Tribal Peoples' territories and whether that is consistent with ILO 169. It will know whether government authorities have recognized Indigenous Peoples' relationships to natural resources, and whether functional mechanisms enable affected Indigenous communities to participate in agreement-making, benefit-sharing, and compensation rate-setting. Companies can be expected to conduct "capacity-building" to secure communities the legal protections and negotiating competency they need to interact with the company from a position of

---

[6] Sarah Sax and Mauricio Angelo, "'We Are Invisible': Brazilian Cerrado Quilombos Fight for Land and Lives." Mongabay, April 30, 2020.

[7] United Nations Human Rights Council, *Guiding Principles on Business and Human Rights: Implementing the United Nations "Protect, Respect and Remedy" Framework*, Report of the Special Representative of the Secretary-General on the issue of human rights and transnational corporations and other business enterprises, U.N. Doc. A/HRC/17/31 (March 21, 2011) (UN Guiding Principles). See UN Guiding Principles, Pillar I, B. 3 Commentary, ¶ 5, 5.

[8] UN Guiding Principles, Pillar II, A. 12 Commentary, ¶ 3, 14.

[9] See UN Guiding Principles, Pillar III, B. 26 Commentary, 29.

[10] See UN Guiding Principles, Pillar II, A. 15(b).

power.[11] The vast majority of public and private sector development finance banks have now codified these expectations through Environmental and Social Performance Standards.[12]

FREE, PRIOR, AND INFORMED CONSENT (FPIC)

From a business perspective, the most substantive development in Indigenous protections since the passage of UNDRIP was the commitment by development finance institutions to require clients to safeguard the Indigenous right to free, prior, and informed consent (FPIC). FPIC has roots in ILO 169 and crises triggered occasional corporate commitments to Indigenous rights, but uptake of FPIC by corporate actors drastically accelerated after its inclusion in lending standards.[13] In 2012, both the private lending arm of the World Bank (the International Finance Corporation, IFC) and the private sector consortium of project finance banks known as the Equator Principles Financial Institutions committed to require clients to "obtain" FPIC from all Indigenous communities whose lands, livelihoods, and cultures would be affected by operations they financed.[14]

---

[11]   International Finance Corporation (IFC), *ILO Convention 169 and the Private Sector* (IFC, 2007).

[12]   IFC, *Performance Standard 7: Indigenous Peoples* (Washington, DC: IFC, 2012); Equator Principles Association, *The Equator Principles EP 4 July 2020*, https:// equator-principles.com/app/uploads/The-Equator-Principles_EP4_July2020.pdf.

[13]   One such crisis was the James Bay Cree asserting their rights against Hydro Quebec. Amy Lehr and Gare Smith, *Implementing a Corporate Free, Prior, and Informed Consent Policy: Benefits and Challenges* (Washington, DC: Foley Hoag, July 2010), https://justice-project.org/wp-content/uploads/2017/07/foley-hoag-for-talisman .pdf; Rebecca Adamson, *Investors and Indigenous Peoples: Trends in Sustainable and Responsible Investment and Free, Prior, and Informed Consent* (Fredericksburg, VA: First Peoples Worldwide, 2013).

[14]   IFC, Performance Standard 7; Equator Principles Association, The Equator Principles EP 4. The European Investment Bank, the European Bank for Reconstruction and Development, the Inter-American Development Bank, and the African Development Bank all share similar commitments and explicitly require clients to obtain FPIC when impacting Indigenous Peoples.

However, each component of the FPIC acronym poses challenges of oversight for lenders, alongside challenges for communities and companies. Non-exhaustive examples are below.

Free: Consent issued without coercion is difficult to discern in contexts characterized by power imbalances or where laws give the nation-state authority over Indigenous lands.
Prior: FPIC processes commenced prior to construction but after permit processes, feasibility studies, and planning occurs is not "prior" to impacts. Indigenous groups often identify the mere presence of outsiders on their lands as an impact that necessitates consent.
Informed: Information provided in a mode, language, or level of technicality that communities cannot understand does not sufficiently inform them.
Consent: "Obtaining" consent prior to a specific impact may not imply consent for cumulative impacts. Consent may be revoked as a result of changing conditions, or it may be illegitimate if not secured through communal processes.

CHALLENGES FOR EFFECTIVE FPIC PROCESSES

Private sector actors have conceptualized FPIC differently than Indigenous communities and their international advocates, while relying on the same core framework.[15] Indigenous groups conceptualize FPIC as a safeguard for "their control over the future development of their territories," while Western actors conceptualize it as "evidence of an agreement."[16] The distinction differentiates Indigenous expectations that FPIC safeguards their self-determination rights, from industry actors' expectations that FPIC safeguards their social license to control the resources they seek to exploit. This explains why private sector actors see FPIC as something that can be "obtained," while Indigenous People and their advocates see it as a condition for the realization of the full suite of rights.[17] The tension has been captured in compendia of conflicts between Indigenous Peoples and settler entities, whereby contractual agreements prove to be a source of conflict rather than agreement.[18]

---

[15] Ishita Petkar, *The Need for Conceptual Guidance on FPIC*. Submitted to the UN Expert Mechanism on the Rights of Indigenous Peoples (February 28, 2018), https://www.ohchr.org/Documents/Issues/IPeoples/EMRIP/FPIC/PetkarIshita.pdf.
[16] Some operators have sought to "document" agreement ceremonially with communities that have no culture of written agreements. This advancement in corporate understanding of consent processes is not an assured indication of FPIC.
[17] Dan Mullins and Justus Wambayi. *Testing Community Consent* (Nairobi: Oxfam America, 2018), https://www.oxfamamerica.org/explore/research-publications/testing-community-consent.
[18] Elsa Stamatopoulou, ed., *Indigenous Peoples' Rights and Unreported Struggles: Conflict and Peace* (New York: Columbia University Institute for the Study of Human Rights, 2017), https://doi.org/10.7916/D82R5095.

Compounding the fundamental divergence of perspectives on FPIC, there are regulatory and oversight limitations of FPIC for the companies that seek to "obtain" FPIC from communities. Some of these result from definitions that equate consultation with "consent" in national legislation.[19] Others result from the implementation, monitoring, and evaluation of these processes by government agencies or development finance institutions that have no Indigenous expertise on staff. The IFC, for example, has benchmarked FPIC based on individual residents' acceptance of cash settlements, when individual payouts are used as tools to divide communities and coerce consent.[20]

Soliciting consent is vastly different from garnering FPIC. The FPIC process involves relationship-building, ensuring equitable participation and fair decision-making abilities. This requires incisive investigation into systemic inequities baked into corporate, legal, or regulatory regimes. Absent such investigation, corporate entities may rely on domestic regulatory processes as the full "FPIC process" without recognizing, for example, that most legal processes are predicated on Indigenous marginalization. Corporate language and processes around FPIC that are imported from domestic regimes can replicate inadequate systems of engagement. When the *process* is inadequate, the *human rights* at stake cannot be understood as adequately respected or protected.

Community governance structures have been fragmented overtly and passively, weakening their ability to drive consensuses in a society. Companies and governments have frequently cited the lack of community cohesion to bypass robust consent-seeking process. One common "bypass" is to scope impact evaluation to a very specific and localized environment or sub-population. These processes find very little information on wider impacts, such as whether the project affects ancestral or treaty territories that are no longer inhabited, or whether the resource is linked to cultural heritage. However, in practice, impacts from development are not cabined but are wide-ranging and cumulative over time. Myopic impact evaluation is common when large companies develop pipelines and other projects that cross vast areas and find that there are numerous divergent views about the project. Today's companies may lament that the community is "divided" or celebrate that they have "strong support" among a certain sub-group.

Students can identify this mentality as harmful and exploitative through simulations and real-world case studies, which demonstrate the discrimina-

---

[19]   FIP, *¿Qué es la Consulta Previa y el CLPI?* (Bogota: FIP, 2018), https://www.ideaspaz.org/publications/posts/1667.

[20]   Kendyl Salcito, *Indigenous Peoples and the IFC – How Development Finance Can Better Safeguard Indigenous Rights* (Denver, CO: NomoGaia, October 2020).

tory attacks on human dignity incumbent with an inadequate process. This is a moment to teach students to recognize the difference between the process (FPIC) and the rights safeguarded by the process. Just as human rights conditions are fluid, so is consent. Any instance of potential human rights harm is sufficient to trigger reconsideration of the project itself.

FPIC AND INDIGENOUS PROTECTIONS IN PRACTICE

FPIC has not safeguarded self-determination, because nation-states, companies, and investors retain oversight of FPIC implementation.[21] A 2021 study of IFC's investment portfolio found that 70 percent of investments made under the 2012 performance standards were in countries with Indigenous Peoples but less than 1 percent applied the Indigenous Peoples Performance Standard, and only 0.1 percent documented an FPIC process.[22] Follow-up research found dozens of Indigenous communities that were bypassed for Indigenous protections for political and economic reasons.[23] The problem is not unique to IFC. The European Investment Bank, for example, has only ever acknowledged the presence of Indigenous Peoples at three of its investments,[24] and all three of those acknowledgments resulted from direct complaints by communities assisted by international non-governmental organizations. The proliferation of failed FPIC casts doubt on its legitimacy as a process.[25]

Private sector actors have a vested interest in defining FPIC as agreement-making. But it is difficult to know whether an agreement will endure without a fulsome understanding of the community structure. Companies that interface only with community leaders may be surprised to learn that leadership roles may be term-limited. Likewise, company processes that involve case-by-case, individual approvals from members may generate a majority of members "consenting" to the project individually without actually securing

---

[21] Cathal Doyle and Jill Cariño, *Making Free Prior and Informed Consent a Reality: Indigenous Peoples and the Extractive Sector* (London: Indigenous Peoples Links, Middlesex University, and ECCR, 2013).

[22] Salcito, *Indigenous Peoples and the IFC.*

[23] Kendyl Salcito, *Missing Peoples – IFC Projects That Did Not Apply PS7* (Denver, CO: NomoGaia, May 2021).

[24] North Pole Onshore Windfarm (Sweden), Power System Expansion Project (Nepal), and Nenskra hydroelectric project (Georgia).

[25] Terry Mitchell, Courtney Arseneau, Darren Thomas, and Peggy Smith, "Towards an Indigenous-Informed Relational Approach to Free, Prior, and Informed Consent (FPIC)," *The International Indigenous Policy Journal* 10, no. 4 (October 2019): 1–30; Aimée Craft et al., *UNDRIP Implementation: More Reflections on the Braiding of International, Domestic and Indigenous Laws* (International Governance Innovation, October 2018), 1–156.

a communal acceptance of impacts to shared resources. Companies may perceive revoked consent as bad faith in such contexts, when Indigenous Peoples may, likewise, see efforts to secure individual consent as a violation of their communal agreement-making practices.

TEACHING APPROACHES

I teach Indigenous Peoples rights within a broader course on human rights and non-state actors, introducing Indigenous rights after students strongly grasp the human rights framework, the processes involved in human rights due diligence, and concepts of vulnerability to corporate impacts. Once students understand why companies take on Indigenous rights commitments, they can be challenged to think about what forces in the company might resist implementing those commitments.[26]

A full-term course on this subject can take stock of the limitations on the effectiveness of Indigenous protections and explore ways forward. Such a course would have BHR course prerequisites, as baseline familiarity with business and human rights is a precursor for analyzing collective rights.

There are no internal structures in firms, businesses, banks, or, often, governments to prioritize Indigenous rights. The goal of a course or module on Indigenous rights is to demonstrate the importance of Indigenous worldviews (and the hazards of ignoring them) to future lawyers, CEOs, policymakers, activists, and bankers, so that they can prepare their future workplaces to engage on topics that are broadly unfamiliar. Because a core issue for Indigenous Peoples is the failure of businesses to recognize and acknowledge them, my approaches place students in the role of corporate actors trying to meet business interests as they are confronted with Indigenous interests.

Learning objectives may include:

- Learning the history of Indigenous protections under international, tribal, and domestic law, from antiquities protections to environmental regulations.
- Understanding how historic and ongoing structural discrimination can fragment Indigenous societies and complicate engagement and consent processes.

---

[26] Deanna Kemp and John Owen, "Corporate Readiness and the Human Rights Risks of Applying FPIC in the Global Mining Industry," *Business and Human Rights Journal* 2, no. 1 (January 2017): 163–170.

- Drawing the links between Indigenous rights instruments (UNDRIP), business and human rights instruments (UNGPs), and the human rights framework more broadly.
- Recognizing conflicting interpretations of both indigeneity and of FPIC held by diverse Indigenous groups, as well as by states, companies, and investors.
- Experiencing an interaction between an affected Indigenous group and a company that seeks to advance a project.
- Learning what compromises companies and Indigenous groups must make to achieve ongoing consensus about the company's presence on Indigenous land.
- Understanding the difficulties of achieving FPIC.
- Witnessing what "successful" FPIC looks like as a multifaceted and ongoing engagement.
- Engaging with real-world examples of FPIC processes and agreements, including iterative agreements revised over time as project designs and local conditions shift.

EXERCISE 21.1

FPIC AGREEMENTS

Provide students four separate consent agreements (see Teaching Resources below) and work collaboratively to articulate (1) the community's role in dictating protocols for engaging, (2) the extent and nature of engagement with a diverse array of community members, and (3) the basis of their consent; i.e., the terms under which they have agreed that an impact may occur.

A simulation can be conducted as a single-class exercise or carried out over several weeks, emulating the ongoing nature of engagement for Indigenous recognition and FPIC, highlighting key points of interaction where relationships with Indigenous Peoples can be secured or derailed. Simulations can also emulate the interactions between a financial institution, a corporate client, and an Indigenous community when state agents begin issuing threats and committing reprisals against Indigenous populations.

In real life, Indigenous issues often only become apparent to companies after environmental harms or personal security violations occur. As such, I have successfully introduced the concept of Indigenous self-identification to students during simulations where they are already evaluating whether human rights violations have occurred. Asking them to additionally evaluate whether *communal* rights violations compound individual rights violations challenges them to contemplate the identification of "Indigenous Peoples" and determine what rights-respectful next steps look like for businesses.

(For a simulation regarding FPIC processes, see Exercise 21.3: Securing Free, Prior, and Informed Consent – "Colorado Petroleum.")

EXERCISE 21.2

IFC PERFORMANCE STANDARDS

Evaluate the adequacy of project documents to meet IFC Performance Standard 7 on Indigenous Peoples for a project whose context can be studied at a desktop level (for example, a wind power project in rural Pakistan, a mining project in Andean Peru, an agriculture project in Inner Mongolia, China). Students use public reports to re-evaluate state definitions of indigeneity and discover that carrying out such an investigation during the Environmental and Social Impact Assessment of the permitting process runs afoul of national law.

Potential follow-on simulation: Conduct a consultation with the affected community (represented by the educator or a guest speaker) and learn that consultation protocols under tribal rules differ from what national law permits. Learn also that population subsets (women, for example) are excluded from these protocols. Evaluate the implications for respecting rights under the UNGPs and UNDRIP.

KEY QUESTIONS

General

- What is FPIC?
- Why aren't non-Indigenous Peoples entitled to FPIC rights?
- Who determines indigeneity?
- How do Indigenous Peoples get "identified"?
- Who determines when FPIC is needed?
- Who within a business or financial institution evaluates whether the FPIC process is adequate?
- What are hallmarks of "consent" that is freely given with complete information prior to an impact occurring?

For Business Students

- What do you need to know about affected Indigenous Peoples to run a business operation in/near Indigenous Peoples? To secure development bank financing?
- What should a corporate policy on Indigenous Peoples say? What are the pitfalls and opportunities in developing/adopting such a policy?
- Why do consent agreements fail/succeed?
- What should a company do if it cannot get consent?

For Law Students

- What are the legal drivers for FPIC processes?
- Can there be legal clarity on "consent"?
- What are confidentiality expectations around consent agreements – from both the corporate and tribal sides?
- Are FPIC agreements legally binding?
- What do international court rulings mean for Indigenous Peoples, on the ground?

For Policy Students

- Should FPIC be applied only to Indigenous Peoples?
- Can states be relied on to uphold Indigenous rights?
- Who should oversee enforcement of FPIC agreements? What accountability mechanisms are available?
- Who should conduct FPIC evaluations? Who should draft FPIC agreements?

TEACHING RESOURCES

Readings

Consultation protocols and FPIC agreements
Real-world Indigenous protocols for engaging with outsiders about impacts, and real-world FPIC agreements, are useful for studying both varying approaches for establishing communal consent, and stronger/weaker (legitimate/illegitimate) determinations of consent by corporate actors.

Consultation protocols
Canada

- Government of Ontario. Webequie Terms of Reference for Consultation and for the resulting Land Use Plan. *Webequie Supply Road Environmental Assessment terms of Reference.* August 2020. https://www.supplyroad.ca/wp-content/uploads/2020/08/WSR-ToR-Sections-10-11.pdf and https://www.ontario.ca/page/webequie-terms-reference) (useful for depicting inter-tribal conflicts, as the Webquie-Ontario agreement angered other tribes).
- The Squamish Consent Process. https://www.squamish.net/woodfibre-lng.

Brazil

- Protocolo de Consulta Gibrié de São Lourenço (Portuguese only). https://fase.org.br/wp-content/uploads/2018/07/ACOQUIGSAL-Protocolo-de-Consulta-Oficial-1.pdf.

Colombia

- Protocolo Autonomo del Pueblo Arhuaco (Spanish only).http://www.hchr.org.co/files/eventos/2017/PROTOCOLO-AUTONOMO-PUEBLO-ARHUACO.pdf

FPIC agreements

- Celsia Solar Valledupar Consent Agreement, Colombia (Spanish Only). Ministerio Del Interior. Certifcacion Numero 1356. October 31, 2016. https://www.mininterior.gov.co/sites/default/files/documentos/ConsultaPrevia/CERTIFICACIONES2016/1356.pdf.
- First Peoples Worldwide. *Free Prior and Informed Consent Due Diligence Questionnaire.* https://www.colorado.edu/program/fpw/sites/default/files/attached-files/fpic_due_diligence_questionnaire-2.pdf).
- Gumatj Clan FPIC agreements, Australia. Australian Trade and Investment Commission. "Gyumatj Corporation." https://www.austrade.gov.au/land-tenure/engagement-guide/how-do-i-engage-with-traditional-owners/gumatj-corporation.
- The Squamish Nation Consent Agreement and 25 Conditions and the Environmental Assessment Office inclusion of Squamish Nation demands in permitting process (In the matter of the Environmental Assessment Act S.B.C. 2022, c.43 by Woodfibre LND Ltd. for the Woodfibre LNG Project, Reasons for Ministers' Decision (October 26, 2015)).
- Upper Trishuli Consent Agreement, Nepal, facilitated by IFC. Nepal Warer and Energy Development Company and International Finance Corporation.

Upper Trishuli-1 Hydropower Porject Updated Non-Technical ESIA Addenda. March 2019. https://drive.google.com/file/d/1RVFjySYdBvDGy jJxPjwVpHXziGHpXUPY/view?usp=sharing.

Commentary
The review of FPIC agreements can lead to follow-on lessons about when a consent agreement must be revisited, what factors drive communities to rescind their consent, and what actions are needed to maintain consent.

*   Anaya, James. *Indigenous Peoples in International Law.* 2nd ed. Oxford: Oxford University Press, 2004.
*   Dunlap, Alexander. "'A Bureaucratic Trap': Free, Prior and Informed Consent (FPIC) and Wind Energy Development in Juchitán, Mexico." *Capitalism Nature Socialism* 29, no. 4 (2017): 88–108. https://www .tandfonline.com/doi/full/10.1080/10455752.2017.1334219.
*   Kemp, Deanna and John Owen. "Corporate Readiness and the Human Rights Risks of Applying FPIC in the Global Mining Industry." *Business and Human Rights Journal* 2, no. 1 (January 2017): 163.
*   Kemp, Deanna, James Anaya, and Jessica Evans. *Lessons Learned from the Merian Mine. Expert Advisory Panel.* Boulder, CO: Resolve, 2017. https://www.resolve.ngo/docs/merian-expert-advisory-panel_final -report636870303537629126.pdf.
*   Papillon, Martin and Thierry Rodon. "The Transformative Potential of Indigenous-Driven Approaches to Implementing Free, Prior and Informed Consent: Lessons from Two Canadian Cases." *International Journal on Minority and Group Rights* 27, no. 2 (2020): 314–335.
*   Tomlinson, Kathryn. "Indigenous Rights and Extractive Resource Projects: Negotiations over the Policy and Implementation of FPIC." *The International Journal of Human Rights* 23, no. 5 (2019): 880–897. https:// www.tandfonline.com/doi/abs/10.1080/13642987.2017.1314648.

Court Cases

*   *Kaliña and Lokono Peoples v. Suriname*, Inter-Am Ct. H.R., (Ser. C) No. 309 (2015).
*   *Moiwana Village v. Suriname*, Inter-Am Ct. H.R., (Ser. C) No. 124 (2005).
*   *Northern Territory v. Arnhem Land Aboriginal Land Trust*, Australian High Court 236 CLR 24 (2008).
*   *Saramaka People v. Suriname*, Inter-Am Ct. H.R., (Ser. C) No. 172 (2007).

Videos and Podcasts

- *America Reframed*. Season 8, episode 8, "The Blessing." Aired on November 24, 2020, on PBS. https://www.pbs.org/video/the-blessing -zjq1a8 (Season 8, Episode 8, Navajos and coal mining).
- Reel, Monte. *Blood River*. Produced by Bloomberg. Podcast. https:// podcasts.apple.com/us/podcast/blood-river/id1523301867 (indigeneity in Honduras and the murder of Berta Caceres).
- *This Land*. Crooked Media. Podcast. https://crooked.com/podcast-series/ this-land (Season 2, oil and gas interests and adoption laws).

Websites

- Cultural Survival. www.culturalsurvival.org.
- Equitable Origin FPIC 360. www.FPIC360.org.
- Forest Peoples Programme. www.forestpeoples.org.
- University of Colorado Boulder. First Peoples Worldwide. https://www .colorado.edu/program/fpw.

EXERCISE 21.3

SECURING FREE, PRIOR, AND INFORMED CONSENT – "COLORADO PETROLEUM"

Kendyl Salcito and Mark Wielga

BACKGROUND

The hypothetical fact pattern below can serve as the basis for a classroom exercise that explores, *inter alia*: (1) the corporate responsibility to respect land rights and the rights of Indigenous Peoples in the extractive sector; (2) what human rights due diligence looks like in practice; and (3) the challenges of engaging affected rightsholders and securing "free, prior, and informed consent." After presenting the hypothetical case, the teacher can lead a discussion of these issues and/or use the suggested prompts to ask students, individually or in groups, to adopt the role of legal advisor to the company and prepare the requested responses.

HYPOTHETICAL CASE

"Colorado Petroleum" (CP) is an integrated, multinational oil and gas company. It has exploration, production, transmission, and retail operations on four continents. CP's "El Alto Project" is a large production-transmissio n-liquefaction-export operation in the "Republic of Bolivar." The project begins with a largely natural gas production field in the El Alto Plateau high in the Andes. It feeds a 180-km gas pipeline that descends to the Pacific coast. CP is the operator of the project and the leader of the consortium that owns it. El Alto cost over $3 billion to construct. It is a centerpiece of CP's Latin American strategy and is on the cover of this year's Annual Report to Shareholders.

The "Republic of Bolivar" stretches from the Andes to the Pacific coast of South America. It is a low- to middle-income country with a wide disparity of incomes, including large rural and urban segments of the population which has been left behind in last commodities boom. Mining and oil and gas are the two largest segments of the economy. Bolivar is a stable democracy with a strong central government and executive. Its national government has promised to return Bolivar's mineral wealth to the people.

Bolivar has a large Indigenous population that is mostly concentrated in the highlands. As a group, they have not participated in the growth in the middle class and have a sense of being left behind. Various Indigenous groups have reasserted their separate and special identity.

The "Korubi Indigenous Peoples" (KIP) have occupied the El Alto Plateau as long as records have been kept. The KIP are in the bottom quintile of the Bolivarian population for income, educational achievement, life expectancy, and infant mortality. Over 70 percent of El Alto's production fields are in an area predominantly occupied by KIP. There have been many roads built, some temporary, some permanent, to reach exploration and production sites. The local people have benefited from the use of these roads. There have also been increased sales from roadside stalls of food and small trade goods. Hired lodging has been in short supply and local owners have both charged exorbitant prices and multiplied the units available. Bars, prostitution, and drug sales have flourished. These economic impacts have been pronounced.

But most people are herders and have not benefited from these impacts. For them, local prices have risen and their income from herding has stagnated. Some of the roads have made transportation easier, but there have also been disruptions. Trucks and drill rigs cross pastures. A waste oil "accident" contaminated a water well. Noise and lights frighten animals and bother people. There were incessant invasions of their land. Social disruption also came with the strangers and their money, bringing drug gangs and crime. There is an overwhelming sense that great wealth is being made off their land, but not by them.

A Community Benefits Agreement was signed by the leader of a significant Korubi group and CP. It provides a detailed schedule of payments in the form of clinic upgrades and equipment, the building of two new elementary schools, and provision of grain and cooking oil to be distributed to the community and a recurring payment into the Community Development Fund managed by the Ekoi Korubi Tribal Counsel. The Community Benefits Agreement was signed with great fanfare.

The Community Benefits Agreement includes the following language, drafted by the CP Legal Department: "We the Korubi People, having been fully informed of all relevant matters, and recognizing the sufficiency of the goods received, as described above, on our behalf and on behalf of our brethren and children and their children forever, do hereby freely give our consent to the recovery of hydrocarbons within our traditional lands by CP, its affiliates and assigns."

Under Bolivarian law, all subsurface valuable minerals, including hydrocarbons, belong to the nation. Private owners and users of the surface estate are required to make way and accommodate "use of the surface reasonably needed to extract the value of the subsurface minerals." CP has obtained all permits and licenses needed for its operations under Bolivarian law and regulations. CP has an Opinion Letter from a very well-respected Bolivarian law firm that it has legal rights supporting all its surface and subsurface operations on the El Alto Plateau.

The Constitution of Bolivar states that "The Bolivarian People are one. They are each and every one equal. There shall be no gradations or distinctions among the People." No Indigenous groups are recognized as legal entities. The status of being "Indigenous" is not recognized in Bolivarian law. There has been a long-standing legal position in Bolivar that the Indigenous population has been entirely accepted into the legal status of a citizen.

STUDENT PROMPTS

• CP Headquarters has received the following email and registered letter from a prominent international human rights organization:

"Dear Colorado Petroleum,
We represent the Korubi Peoples Coalition. As you know, Colorado Petroleum's El Alto Project has oil and gas wells on the traditional lands of the Korubi. Under the UN Declaration of the Rights of Indigenous Peoples, no exploitation of the carbon values contained in these traditional lands can take place without the free, prior, and informed consent of the Korubi. As you know, Colorado Petroleum has recently publicized its Human Rights Policy that adopts the United Nations Guiding Principles on Business and Human Rights. Those Principles require Colorado Petroleum to *respect* the Korubis' rights.
We demand that any and all effort to take the Korubis' oil and gas cease immediately. These actions must stop until you have obtained the requisite free, prior, and informed consent. If no such consent is obtained, the El Alto Project must be abandoned in its entirety and payment required for all hydrocarbons extracted and damage inflicted.
Respond to this demand in seven days or we will begin to take action."

You are in CP's legal department. Your supervisor has never heard of the Korubi Peoples Coalition and all she knows about the situation is in terms of the Community Benefits Agreement. She gives you a copy of that agreement, which was intended to be evidence of the Korubi's free, prior, and informed consent. Your supervisor asks you to write a response and send a copy of the Community Benefits Agreement to the human rights organization. Unfortunately, it is already six days since the email was received, so you have to respond immediately.

- The international human rights organization has posted your response to their website, along with their follow-up response:

"Dear Colorado Petroleum,
Thank you for your letter in response to our request.
We were frankly astonished that you had the audacity to send us the Community Benefits Agreement. We represent the Korubi Peoples Coalition. Your agreement was signed by the leader of the Ekoi Korubi. The Ekoi Korubi are the West Korubi, one of five main Korubi subgroups. The Ekoi Korubi have no right to speak for the Korubi People. Their leader is a well-known abuser of his position. As you know, he was deposed from his position and imprisoned for corruption. He has publicly admitted receiving the construction materials for a house, a Toyota Land Cruiser and 200 kilos of rice in return for signing the Community Benefits Agreement.
There was no free, prior, and informed consent of the Korubi people to the El Alto Project. We demand that any and all efforts to take the Korubi's oil and gas cease immediately."

The website and social media already have dozens of comments viciously mocking Colorado Petroleum. You take this to your supervisor. She is not happy with you or the situation. She returns and gives you the email address of the CP Regional Counsel in Bolivar. She directs you to send him an email asking all the information you need to respond to this threat and to advise the company what to do.

- **The CP Regional Counsel replies:**

"I have investigated the situation and can give you the following reliable information:
The Eoka Korubi are the largest and best organized of the Korubi peoples. They are by far the largest sub-group and make up almost 55 percent of the recognized Korubi population still in the area. They have had a coherent political structure longer than any of the other groups and so were the only real, existing entity we could deal with at the time.
Their leader was later found to have somewhat abused certain aspects of his position, none of which was proven at the time the Community Benefits Agreement was signed. But he does care for his people and was an excellent advocate for them. As is customary and expected, gifts were given in connection with the Community Benefits Agreement.
I don't know how we could have handled this differently."

Now your supervisor is really upset. She orders you to develop an action plan for the company based on CP's Human Rights Policy (which explicitly recognizes the UN Guiding Principles on Business and Human Rights) and to justify the actions recommended as consistent with that policy and with CP's general business goals.

- **Before you begin, your supervisor tells you to speak to the El Alto Community Relations Chief, who happens to be visiting the home office. He is a longtime CP employee, respected by senior management. "He is a Bolivar 'hand,' ask him anything!" What questions do you ask?**

22. The right to food

Uché Ewelukwa Ofodile

OVERVIEW

Despite decades of global action to address hunger and malnutrition, the number of people in the world facing chronic food deprivation continues to rise. According to *The State of Food Security and Nutrition in the World 2020*, nearly 690 million people or 8.9 percent of the world population were hungry in 2018 (up by 10 million people in one year and up by nearly 60 million in five years). Furthermore, the number of people affected by severe food insecurity continues to trend upward. In 2019, close to 750 million – or nearly one in ten people in the world – were exposed to severe levels of food insecurity.[1] Counting the number of people affected by moderate or severe levels of food insecurity, an estimated 2 billion people in the world did not have regular access to safe, nutritious, and sufficient food in 2019.[2] The COVID-19 pandemic and associated containment measures increased food insecurity in almost every country in the world. Between 720 and 811 million people in the world faced hunger in 2020 – as many as 161 million more than in 2019, and nearly 2.37 billion people did not have access to adequate food in 2020 – an increase of 320 million people in just one year.[3]

There are a number of reasons to address the right to adequate food when teaching business and human rights (BHR). First, the right to adequate food is directly linked to the inherent dignity of the human person and is absolutely

---

[1] Food and Agriculture Organization (FAO), International Fund for Agricultural Development (IFAD), United Nations Children's Fund (UNICEF), World Food Programme (WFP), and World Health Organization (WHO), *The State of Food Security and Nutrition in the World 2020: Transforming Food Systems for Affordable Healthy Diets* (Rome: FAO, 2020).

[2] FAO et al., *The State of the Food Security and Nutrition in the World 2020*.

[3] FAO, IFAD, UNICEF, WFP, and WHO, *The State of the Food Security and Nutrition in the World 2021: Transforming Food Systems for Food Security, Improved Nutrition and Affordable Healthy Diets for All* (Rome: FAO, 2021).

indispensable for the fulfillment of every other human right.[4] Second, the right to adequate food is inseparable from social justice. Lack of access to food is frequently linked to inequality, marginalization, and exclusion, issues that are exacerbated by market concentration in the agricultural sector. Third, there is a growing call for policymakers to examine the industrial food system's impact on small-scale farmers, agricultural workers, individuals, and local communities.

This chapter provides BHR teachers with an overview of the right to adequate food and examines the business impacts on the right to food through the "Protect-Respect-Remedy" framework of the United Nations Guiding Principles on Business and Human Rights (UNGPs). (See The UN Guiding Principles on Business and Human Rights, Chapter 5.)

THE RIGHT TO FOOD UNDER INTERNATIONAL LAW

The right to food is recognized in numerous international treaties. The principal international legal instrument that addresses food and hunger is the International Covenant on Economic, Social and Cultural Rights (ICESCR).[5] The ICESCR recognizes the right to adequate food as part of the right to an adequate standard of living. Article 11(1) guarantees "the right of everyone to an adequate standard of living for himself and his family, including adequate food." Furthermore, the ICESCR explicitly recognizes "the fundamental right of everyone to be free from hunger" (Art. 11(2)).

Variations of the right to adequate food are now enshrined in several other treaties including, the Convention on the Elimination of All Forms of Discrimination against Women (1979), the Convention on the Rights of the Child (1989), and the Convention on the Rights of Persons with Disabilities (2006). The right to adequate food is also recognized in regional human rights instruments such as the African Charter on the Rights and Welfare of the Child (1990) and the Additional Protocol to the American Convention on Human Rights in the Area of Economic, Social and Cultural Rights (1988).[6] In the

---

[4] All human rights are "universal, indivisible and interdependent and interrelated." World Conference on Human Rights, *Vienna Declaration and Programme of Action*, June 25, 1993.

[5] *International Covenant on Economic, Social and Cultural Rights*, December 16, 1966, 993 U.N.T.S. 3 (entered into force January 3, 1976).

[6] *Additional Protocol to the American Convention on Human Rights in the Area of Economic, Social and Cultural Rights "Protocol of San Salvador,"* November 17, 1988, O.A.S.T.S. No. 69 (entered into force November 16, 1999), https://www.oas .org/dil/1988%20Additional%20Protocol%20to%20the%20American%20Convention %20on%20Human%20Rights%20in%20the%20Area%20of%20Economic,%20Social %20and%20Cultural%20Rights%20(Protocol%20of%20San%20Salvador).pdf.

case of *SERAC and CESR v. Nigeria* that centers around massive oil spills in the Niger Delta region of Nigeria, the African Commission on Human and Peoples' Rights (African Commission) affirmed that "[t]he right to food is inseparably linked to the dignity of human beings and is therefore essential for the enjoyment and fulfilment of such other rights as health, education, work and political participation."[7]

Non-binding international instruments, so-called "soft law," contribute to the development of customary international law. A growing number of soft-law instruments explicitly address the right to food. These include: the Universal Declaration of Human Rights (1948),[8] the Rome Declaration on World Food Security (1996), and the Voluntary Guidelines on the Responsible Governance of Tenure of Land, Fisheries and Forests in the Context of National Food Systems (2012). As with all human rights, the right to food is best advanced when it is enshrined in the domestic legal framework of a state. In many jurisdictions, internationally guaranteed human rights cannot be directly enforced in domestic courts unless they are first incorporated into the domestic legal framework. The right to food is expressly mentioned in the constitutions of Brazil (Article 227), Columbia (Article 34), Guatemala (Article 51 and 99), and South Africa (Article 27), to mention a few.

Numerous UN bodies address issues relating to hunger, food insecurity, and the right to food. However, the Committee on Economic, Social and Cultural Rights (ESCR Committee) and the Special Rapporteur on the Right to Adequate Food (Special Rapporteur)[9] are particularly involved in implementing the right to food.

DEFINING THE RIGHT TO ADEQUATE FOOD

In 1999, the ESCR Committee published *General Comment No. 12 on the Right to Adequate Food* to clarify the content and scope of the right to food.[10] According to the ESCR Committee, the right to adequate food "is realized when every man, woman and child, alone or in community with others, has

---

[7]   *Social and Economic Rights Action Center and the Center for Economic and Social Rights* v. Nigeria, Communication No. 155/96, African Commission on Human and Peoples' Rights, ¶ 65.

[8]   UN General Assembly, Resolution 217A (III), *Universal Declaration of Human Rights*, A/RES/3/217A (December 10, 1948), Art. 25.

[9]   "Special Rapporteur on the Right to Food," Purpose of the Mandate, UN Office of the High Commissioner for Human Rights, accessed August 13, 2022, https://www.ohchr.org/en/issues/food/pages/foodindex.aspx.

[10]   Committee on Economic, Social and Cultural Rights, *General Comment No. 12: Right to Adequate Food (Art. 11)*, U.N. Doc. E/C.12/1999/5 (May 12, 1999) (GC 12).

physical and economic access at all times to adequate food or means for its procurement."[11] The core content of the right to adequate food implies the following:

> The availability of food in a quantity and quality sufficient to satisfy the dietary needs of individuals, free from adverse substances, and acceptable within a given culture.
> The accessibility of such food in ways that are sustainable and that do not interfere with the enjoyment of other human rights.[12]

The right to adequate food entails five components: availability, accessibility, acceptability, sustainability, and stability.

• Availability

Availability "refers to the possibilities either for feeding oneself directly from productive land or other natural resources, or for well-functioning distribution, processing and market systems that can move food from the site of production to where it is needed in accordance with demand."[13] Availability is about quantity as well as the quality of food. This means diets must as a whole "contain a mix of nutrients for physical and mental growth, development and maintenance, and physical activity that are in compliance with human physi-ological needs at all stages throughout the life cycle and according to gender and occupation."[14]

• Accessibility

Accessibility of food has two dimensions: economic accessibility and physical accessibility. Economic accessibility "implies that personal or household financial costs associated with the acquisition of food for an adequate diet should be at a level such that the attainment and satisfaction of other basic needs are not threatened or compromised."[15] Physical accessibility "implies that adequate food must be accessible to everyone, including physically vul-nerable individuals."[16]

• Acceptability

---

[11] GC 12, ¶ 6.
[12] GC 12, ¶ 8; emphasis added.
[13] GC 12, ¶ 12.
[14] GC 12, ¶ 9.
[15] GC 12, ¶ 13.
[16] *Id.*

Cultural or consumer acceptability focuses on perceived non-nutrient-based values attached to food and food consumption. State parties to the ICESCR are obliged, as far as possible, to take cultural and/or consumer acceptability into account in meeting their obligations.

• Sustainability and Stability

Sustainability is a forward-looking concept that incorporates the notion of long-term availability and accessibility. Sustainability asks a very crucial question: Will food be available and accessible for both present and future generations?

STATE RESPONSIBILITIES

The right to adequate food imposes three obligations on states parties: to respect, to protect, and to fulfill. The obligation to respect existing access to adequate food "requires States parties not to take any measures that result in preventing such access."[17] The obligation to protect "requires measures by the State to ensure that enterprises or individuals do not deprive individuals of their access to adequate food."[18] The obligation to fulfill has two dimensions – the obligation to facilitate and the obligation to provide.

THE RIGHT TO FOOD AND THE UNGPs

The UNGPs do not explicitly mention the right to food. However, under the UNGPs, businesses have a responsibility to respect "internationally recognized human rights" (GP 11). This means businesses "should avoid infringing on the human rights of others and should address adverse human rights impacts with which they are involved" (GP 11). The business responsibility to respect the right to food requires that business enterprises have in place appropriate policies and processes including: (a) a policy commitment to meet their responsibility to respect the right to food; (b) a human rights due diligence process to identify, prevent, mitigate, and account for how they address their impacts on the right to food; and (c) processes to enable the remediation of any adverse impacts on the right to food that they cause or to which they contribute (GP 13).

---

[17]   GC 12, ¶ 15.
[18]   *Id.*

BUSINESS IMPACTS ON THE RIGHT TO ADEQUATE FOOD

Business activity is inextricable linked to the right to adequate food. Beyond legal compliance and the responsibility to respect rights, there are additional reasons for businesses to care about the right to adequate food. First, stakeholders including consumers and institutional investors are demanding better sustainability in relation to food and agricultural production. Second, civil society and grassroots organizations are pushing businesses to consider the impact of their operations on the global food system and to implement significant reforms. Third, studies suggest that for all businesses, doing well by doing good can affect a company's bottom line positively. Finally, environmental changes, particularly climate change, are forcing businesses to consider the full impact of their business operations on the planet.

Businesses can both promote and undermine the right to adequate food. Business impact on the right to food is not limited to enterprises in the food and agricultural sector. The negative impacts of business activities on the right to food often arise when states fail to put in place the necessary legal, policy and regulatory frameworks, typically by failing to recognize the right to food in domestic law, failing to adequately enforce relevant laws, or failing to provide appropriate and effective remedies when rights are breached. Negative impacts also arise when states prioritize the interests of business enterprises over other considerations, or deliberately pursue policies that negatively affects human rights.[19]

• Availability

Businesses can adversely affect the availability of food in many ways. The availability of food can be compromised in situations where large businesses enjoy a disproportionate advantage in the competition over land, resources, or market access to the detriment of small-scale farmers who today comprise a vast majority of the world's hungry.[20] (See Land Rights, Chapter 20.) Food availability can be adversely affected when businesses make excessive use of groundwater to the disadvantage of farmers and other stakeholders. In rural Pakistan and in the Six Nations of the Grand River Indigenous reserve in

---

[19] Kari Hamerschlag, Anna Lappé, and Stacy Malkan, *Spinning Food: How Food Industry Front Groups and Covert Communications are Shaping the Story of Food* (London: Friends of the Earth, 2015).

[20] See, for example, Oxfam, *Divide and Purchase: How Land Ownership Is Being Concentrated in Colombia* (2013), https://www-cdn.oxfam.org/s3fs-public/file _attachments/rr-divide-and-purchase-land-concentration-colombia-270913-en_0.pdf.

Ontario, for example, Nestlé is accused of bottling and selling groundwater near villages that cannot afford clean water.[21] Food availability is also compromised when businesses sell unsafe food or produce and distribute products with excessively high levels of pesticides.[22] Food availability is undermined when industrial activities lead to pollution of surrounding water, soil, and environment and make it impossible for local populations to grow their own food. (See Human Rights and the Environment, Chapter 19.) In South Africa, for example, unbridled expansion of mining in Mpumalanga eroded arable land in the region and raised major concern regarding the impact of mining on agricultural production and food security.[23]

• Accessibility

Businesses can undermine access to food through poor, exploitive, or discriminatory working conditions.[24] In this regard, the more than 450 million men and women working as waged workers in agriculture are the hardest hit. According to Oxfam, over 60 percent of agricultural workers live in poverty. Poor labor and working conditions in India's tea plantations has been linked to starvation of plantation workers.[25] Businesses adversely affect the accessibility of food when they engage in practices that price land and other agricultural inputs out of the reach of subsistence farmers.[26] Infrastructure (e.g., roads, dams, pipelines, and bridges) constructed without adequate consultation with the local population can cut off access to food for whole communities. Food accessibility is implicated when foreign investment in agricultural land leads to forced eviction of local inhabitants.

• Acceptability

---

[21] Alexandra Shimo, "While Nestle Extracts Millions of Litres from Their Land, Residents Have No Drinking Water," *Guardian*, October 4, 2018, https://www.theguardian.com/global/2018/oct/04/ontario-six-nations-nestle-running-water.

[22] United Nations Human Rights Council, Report of the Special Rapporteur on the right to food, UN doc. A/HRC/34/48 (January 14, 2017), ¶106 (according to the Special Rapporteur, pesticides "are a global human rights concern" and "can have very detrimental consequences on the enjoyment of the right to food").

[23] Lindi van Rooyen, "Agriculture Is Losing the Battle against Mines – BFAP," *Farmers Weekly*, May 31, 2012, http://www.farmersweekly.co.za/news.aspx?id=22654&h=Agriculture-is-losing-the-battle-against-mines-%E2%80%93-BFAP.

[24] Connor Yearsley, "Tainted Tea: The Abysmal Conditions on Assam's Tea Estates," *HerbalGram*, no. 109 (Spring 2016), https://www.herbalgram.org/resources/herbalgram/issues/109/table-of-contents/hg109-feat-assamtea.

[25] Columbia Law School Human Rights Institute, *"The More Things Change… The World Bank, Tata and Enduring Abuses on India's Tea Plantations"* (January 2014).

[26] Beth Hoffman, *Behind the Brands* (Oxford: Oxfam GB, 2013).

Businesses can undermine the acceptability of food through industrial pollution that compromise local water sources and soil. Although all business sectors can potentially pollute grounds water, the food sector is reportedly responsible for more than 50 percent of organic water pollutant. Acceptability is also in issue with the production and sale of genetically modified food and crops, the use of hormones in food production, and the increasing application of controversial technology in the production of food.

• Sustainability and Stability

Sustainability of food sources is compromised when business activity contaminates land and water sources, or adversely affects local farmers and makes it impossible for them to safely produce food. Sustainability is also implicated when businesses or states evict farming, fishing, or nomadic communities from communal lands and water sources. (See Rights of Indigenous Peoples, Chapter 21.)

TEACHING APPROACHES

For over ten years, I have taught "The Right to Food" to law students at the University of Arkansas School of Law, including students enrolled in the school's Master of Laws (LL.M.) Program in Agricultural and Food Law. The target students are law students interested in a general overview of the interaction of business and human rights, students from other disciplines interested in understanding the role and limits of law in shaping corporate behavior, and individuals (practicing attorneys, corporate executives, and other mid-career professionals) who have already earned a law degree and wish to pursue intensive study in food and agricultural law.

Learning objectives for teaching the right to food may include:

• Introducing students to emerging issues in the food and agricultural sector.
• Introducing students to international and regional human rights instruments relevant to BHR and the right to food.
• Helping students see how businesses in all economic sectors potentially affect the right to food.
• Exposing students to ongoing debates about the responsibilities of food companies and agribusiness to human rights abuses in their value chains.

My goals in law classes include exposing students to comparative legal approaches to the right to food and judicial and non-judicial mechanisms used to vindicate the right to food; helping them assess progress and shortcomings in the response of states and businesses to the remedy pillar of the UNGPs;

and getting students to grasp the normative content of the right to food and the different ways businesses can violate and/or strengthen the right to food.

Objectives for business students may include introducing the business case for the right to food and discussing the cost and benefits of businesses respecting the right to food. Classes for policy students can introduce students to the myriad of public policy issues and questions that impinge on the right to food; and expose students to the enormous challenges associated with implementing the right to food in poorly resourced or politically charged settings.

I tend to employ a multiplicity of classroom techniques when teaching this course including case studies, approaching the topic from different perspectives, debates, documentaries, and reflection essays.

Case Studies

• Grassroots Movements and Campaigns

I often introduce case studies of past and ongoing campaigns and protests. Oxfam, for example, launched the "Behind the Brands" campaign in 2013 to influence the sourcing policies of the world's ten biggest food and beverage companies,[27] and it launched the "Behind the Barcodes" campaign in 2018 to examine policies and practices of supermarket chains around the world – and to pressure them to do better. In the U.S., protests over a controversial pipeline, Line 3, is a helpful case. When completed, Line 3 would reportedly carry 760,000 barrels of oil a day across 200 bodies of water and areas that are home to traditional wild rice harvesting.

• Vulnerable Groups

Sometimes I teach this course with a focus on a specific vulnerable group such as women, Indigenous Peoples, or agricultural workers. Teachers can focus on agricultural workers – a group comprising approximately one third of the world's workforce, or 1.3 billion people – to underscore business impact on the right to food. Although agricultural workers play a critical role in fulfilling the universal human rights to food, studies show that they are among the most food insecure in the world, work under very dangerous conditions, and do not have labor and employment protections.[28]

• Specific Sectors

---

[27] "Behind the Brands," Oxfam, accessed August 14, 2022, https://www.behindthebrands.org.

[28] UN General Assembly, "Right to Food," *Interim Report of the Special Rapporteur on the Right to Food*, A/73/164 (July 16, 2018).

The right to food can be taught with a focus on a particular sector such as agriculture, extractives, or infrastructure. The extractive industry offers many case studies. In the Philippines, for example, Canadian-Australian OceanaGold Corporation is accused of contaminating the Didipio River with damaging results for agriculture. According to a 2017 report, local farmers in barangay Didipio observed that agricultural activity drastically reduced by as much as 30 percent and has attributed the low yield to the effects of air pollution, river pollution, and water shortage due to the large-scale mining operations in their barangay.

Different Perspectives

• Financial Institutions

Another teaching approach is to focus on a specific actor. I often focus on the role of international financial institutions (IFIs) in promoting or undermining the right to food. (See Finance, Investors, and Human Rights, Chapter 26.) IFIs lend money to corporations and through these corporations finance a wide range of projects – dam projects, rural development projects, electrification projects, and even agricultural projects – that can affect the availability and accessibility of food. In *Jam v. International Financial Corporation*, for example, fishing communities and farmers from Gujarat, India filed a lawsuit against the International Finance Corporation seeking damages and injunctive relief for property damage, environmental destruction, loss of livelihoods, and threats to human health arising from the Tata Mundra Plant that was developed with a $450 million loan from the IFC.[29]

• Remedies

Sometimes I teach this course through the lens of the UNGPs' Pillar III (Access to Remedy). A growing number of complaints and cases relating to business and the right to food have come before domestic, regional, and international judicial and quasi-judicial bodies. Teaching through cases before different judicial and non-judicial mechanisms (1) helps to underscore the rights-based approach to the right to food affirmed in Article 11 of the ICESCR[30] and (2) helps students evaluate progress and challenges in meeting the goals of Pillar III of the UNGPs.

---

[29] *Jam v. International Finance Corp.*, No. 16-7051; *Jam v. International Finance Corp.*, No. 16-7051 (D.C. Cir. 2017).
[30] "Do Not Confuse Food Charity with 'Right to Food,' UN Expert Tells Italians, Labelling Food System Exploitative," UN News, United Nations, January 31, 2020, https://news.un.org/en/story/2020/01/1056402.

Victims of abuse are also using international and regional quasi-judicial bodies to assert their rights. In *Länsman et al. v. Finland*, reindeers herders of Sami ethnic origin filed a complaint against Finland with the UN Human Rights Committee alleging that a contract permitting a private company to quarry stone affected their livelihood.[31] In the case of *SERAC and CESR v. Nigeria*, the African Commission interpreted the right to food as being implicitly protected under the African Charter through the right to life (Article 4), the right to health (Article 16), and the right to economic, social and cultural development (Article 21).[32]

In the United States, class actions targeting the food and beverage industry have alleged false and misleading advertising, as well as other unfair practices. Lawsuits are increasingly filed regarding the origin of the ingredients, the use of sweeteners, the number of servings in packaged goods, and environmental impacts, and sourcing and sustainability claims.[33]

Debates

Debates are a great tool for getting students to think critically about controversial issues and allows students to see issues from every angle. Right to food topics for debate include:

- Do large agribusinesses harm smallholder farmers?[34]
- Will agribusiness save our food system and deliver on food security?
- Does corporate control of farm and food systems compromise the right to food?

KEY QUESTIONS

General

- What does the right to food mean to you?
- What are the key elements of the right to food?

---

[31] Human Rights Committee, *Länsman et al. v. Finland*, Communication No. 511/1992 (November 8, 1994).

[32] *Social and Economic Rights Action Center and the Center for Economic and Social Rights* v. Nigeria, Communication No. 155/96, African Commission on Human and Peoples' Rights, ¶ 65.

[33] See, for example, *McCoy v. Nestlé USA*, No. 3: 2015cv04451 (N.D. Cal. March 29, 2016).

[34] "Large Agribusiness Hurting Small Landholders, Says UN Rights Expert," UN News, United Nations, March 10, 2010, https://news.un.org/en/story/2010/03/331552 -large-agribusiness-hurting-small-landholders-says-un-rights-expert.

- How do businesses impact the right to food?
- Which business sectors can affect access to and availability of adequate food?

For Law Students

- How is the right to adequate food defined under international law?
- What are the main international instruments that recognize the right to food?
- What is the content of state obligation with respect to the right to adequate food?
- Is there a difference between the right to adequate food and the right to be free from hunger?
- What is the status of General Comment 12 of the CESCR under international law? Is General Comment No. 12 binding on State parties to the ICESCR?
- What legal and regulatory mechanism can governments use to promote/implement the right to food?
- How do the UNGPs relate to the right to food?

For Business Students

- What are the different ways that businesses can violate the five components of the right to food: availability, stability, accessibility, sustainability, and acceptability?
- Can a business respect the right to food and still be profitable?
- How can/should businesses strengthen their due diligence to ensure that they are respecting the right to food in their operations and throughout their supply chain?

For Policy Students

- What policy and regulatory frameworks impact the right to food?
- What is the relationship between weak laws, policies, and institutions, and violations of the right to food?
- How do businesses abuse the right to food in poor countries? In rich countries?

TEACHING RESOURCES

Readings

Primary sources

- United Nations. *International Covenant on Economic, Social and Cultural Rights*. 993 U.N.T.S. 3 (December 16, 1966, entered into force January 3, 1976), art. 11.
- United Nations. *International Covenant on Civil and Political Rights*. 999 U.N.T.S. 171 (December 16, 1966, entered into force March 23, 1976).
- United Nations General Assembly. *Convention on the Rights of the Child* (CRC). 1577 U.N.T.S. 3, U.N. Doc. A/Res/44/25 (November 20, 1989, entered into force September 2, 1990).
- United Nations General Assembly. *Convention on the Elimination of All Forms of Discrimination Against Women*. 1249 U.N.T.S 13, U.N. Doc. A/RES/34/180 (December 18, 1979, entered into force September 3, 1981).

Secondary sources (non-binding instruments)

- Committee on Food Security (CFS) and Food and Agriculture Organization (FAO). Principles for Responsible Investment in Agriculture and Food Systems. 2014. http://www.fao.org/fileadmin/templates/cfs/Docs1314/rai/CFS_Principles_Oct_2014_EN.pdf.
- Committee on Food Security (CFS) and Food and Agriculture Organization (FAO). Voluntary Guidelines on the Responsible Governance of Tenure of Land, Fisheries, and Forests in the Context of National Food Security. Revised version. Rome: FAO, 2022. http://www.fao.org/docrep/016/i2801e/i2801e.pdf.
- United Nations. *United Nations Declaration on the Rights of Indigenous Peoples (UNDRIP)*. General Assembly Resolution 61/295 (September 13, 2007), Articles 10, 11, 19, 28, 29, http://www.un.org/esa/socdev/unpfii/documents/DRIPS_en.pdf.
- United Nations Commission on Economic, Social and Cultural Rights (CESCR). *General Comment 3: The Nature of States Parties' Obligations (Art. 2, Para. 1, of the Covenant)*. U.N. Doc. HRI\GEN\1\Rev.1 (1 December 1990).
- U.N. Food and Agriculture Organization (FAO). *Voluntary Guidelines to Support the Progressive Realization of the Right to Adequate Food in the Context of National Food Security*. Rome: FAO, 2004. http://www.fao.org/righttofood/common/ecg/51596_en_VGS_eng_web.pdf.

Cases

- *Company Secretary of Arcelormittal South Africa v. Vaal Environmental Justice Alliance* (69/2014) [2014] ZASCA 184.
- Human Rights Committee. *Länsman v. Finland*, Communications Nos. 511/1992 and 1023/2001. Views adopted on October 26, 1994 and April 15, 2005, respectively.
- *Nevsun Resources Ltd. v. Araya*, 2020 SCC 5, [2020] S.C.J. No. 5 (Can.).
- *Vedanta Resources PLC and another (Appellants) v. Lungowe and others (Respondents)*, [2019] UKSC 20.
- *Yaiguaje v. Chevron Corporation*, 2018 ONCA 472, [2018] O.J. 2698 (Can.).

Videos

- Rasool, Zahra, dir. *Oil in Our Creeks*. Screened at Vancouver International Film Festival, Festival de Rio, Change Ville, Cape Town International Animation Festival, and Rio Creative Conference. AJ Contrast, 2018, http://contrastvr.com/oilinourcreeks.

23. The right to water

Uché Ewelukwa Ofodile

OVERVIEW

According to a 2016 study published in *Science Advances*, about 4 billion people worldwide experience severe water scarcity during at least one month of the year.[1] Furthermore, some 884 million people worldwide lack access to safe drinking water.[2] By all accounts, the world is entering an era of water scarcity.[3] Studies attribute the growing water scarcity to a mix of natural and human-made causes including population growth, rapid urbanization, competing land uses, declining biodiversity, new and intensifying industrial uses, and climate change. Problems arise because water is a finite resource that is vital for virtually every aspect of human activity and existence. As the famed British poet W. H. Auden once noted, "Thousands have lived without love, not one without water."[4]

Why should businesses care about the right to water? First, the use of water by businesses can affect a local community significantly and can undermine a business' social license to operate in such a community. Second, in its growing role as a water provider, the private sector has immense power to affect the availability of water; presently, the global water market represents several billion dollars. Third, as part of the global community, businesses are expected to help ensure the sustainability of our planet. Fourth, there is a busi-

---

[1]   Mesfin M. Mekonnen and Arjen Y. Hoekstra, "Four Billion People Facing Severe Water Scarcity," *Science Advances* 2, no. 2 (February 2016), https://advances.sciencemag.org/content/2/2/e1500323/tab-figures-data.

[2]   World Health Organization (WHO) and United Nations Children's Fund (UNICEF), *Progress on Household Drinking Water, Sanitation and Hygiene 2000–2017. Special Focus on Inequalities* (New York: UNICEF and WHO, 2019).

[3]   UN-Water and FAO, "Coping with Water Scarcity: Challenge of the Twenty-First Century" (World Water Day 2007, March 22, 2007), https://www.fao.org/3/aq444e/aq444e.pdf.

[4]   W. H. Auden, "First Things First" (1057) in *Oxford Essential Quotations*, ed. Susan Ratcliff, 4th ed. (Oxford: Oxford University Press, 2016).

ness case for why businesses should take water risks seriously.[5] Consumers are changing their spending habits in favor of companies with better environmental credentials and investors are demanding better environmental performance. Furthermore, a growing number of jurisdictions are imposing mandatory environmental, social, and governance (ESG) reporting requirements, standards, and regulations. (See Mandatory Human Rights Due Diligence Legislation, Chapter 11.) Finally, experts agree that "[w]ater risks like scarcity, floods and droughts can cause operational and supplier disruptions, higher operational costs, brand damage and heightened regulatory uncertainty."[6]

This chapter provides business and human rights (BHR) teachers with an overview of the right to safe drinking water, it outlines the actual and potential impacts of business operations on this right, and it explains implications of the United Nations Guiding Principles (UNGPs) for businesses in relation to the right to safe drinking water. The chapter examines the private sector's impacts on the right to water through the "Protect-Respect-Remedy" framework of the UNGPs and especially through Pillar II – the corporate responsibility to respect human rights. (See The UN Guiding Principles on Business and Human Rights, Chapter 5.) The chapter focuses primarily on the right to water and not on the right to sanitation; although closely related, water and sanitation do not enjoy the same status under international law.[7]

THE RIGHT TO WATER IN INTERNATIONAL LAW

The right to water is not explicitly recognized as a human right in any international human rights treaty. However, there is consensus that international human rights law entails specific obligations related to access to safe drinking water. Numerous treaties contain obligations related to safe drinking water including the International Covenant on Economic, Social and Cultural Rights (ICESCR), the Convention on the Elimination of All Forms of Discrimination against Women (article 14(2)), the Convention on the Rights of the Child (Article 24 and 27(3)), and the Convention on the Rights of Persons with Disabilities (Article 28).

Under the ICESCR, the right to safe drinking water is derived from the right to an adequate standard of living. Article 11, paragraph 1 of the ICESCR pro-

---

[5]   Arjen Y. Hoekstra, "Water Scarcity Challenges to Business," *Nature Climate Change* 4 (May 2014): 318–320.

[6]   "Corporate Water Stewardship," Word Resources Institute, accessed August 15, 2022, https://www.wri.org/initiatives/corporate-water-stewardship.

[7]   The right to sanitation is found in non-binding international legal instruments but is yet to be enshrined in a binding treaty. The ICESCR does not explicitly reference the right to sanitation.

vides: "The States Parties to the present Covenant recognize the right of every-one to an adequate standard of living for himself and his family, including adequate food, clothing and housing." The ESCR Committee has stated that the right to safe drinking water "clearly falls within the category of guarantees essential for securing an adequate standard of living, particularly since it is one of the most fundamental conditions for survival."[8]

Some regional human rights bodies have also recognized the right to safe drinking water. In a 2020 decision, the Inter-American Court of Human Rights, for the first time in a contentious case, found a violation of the right to water based on Article 26 of the American Convention on Human Rights which obliges state parties to "achiev[e] progressively ... the full realization of the rights implicit in the economic, social, educational, scientific, and cultural standards set forth in the Charter of the Organization of American States."[9] Non-binding international legal instruments containing obligations related to safe drinking water include: the UN Guidelines for the Realisation of the Right to Drinking Water and Sanitation (2006), the Dublin Statement on Water and Sustainable Development (1992),[10] and the ILO Recommendation No. 115 of 1965 on Workers' Housing. In 2010, the United Nations General Assembly recognized the right to safe drinking water as a universal human right (Resolution 64/292). In September 2010, the Human Rights Council affirmed the right to safe drinking water (Resolution 15/9).

Several UN bodies play a significant role in monitoring the implementation of the right to safe drinking water including the Committee on Economic, Social and Cultural Rights (ESCR Committee) and the Special Rapporteur on the human rights to safe drinking water and sanitation (Special Rapporteur).[11] From time to time the ESCR Committee issues "General Comments" to elaborate on the meaning and scope of the provisions of the ICESCR. In 2002, the ESCR Committee adopted *General Comment No. 15 on the Right to Water* (GC 15).[12]

---

[8]   UN Committee on Economic, Social and Cultural Rights, *General Comment No. 15: The Right to Water (Arts. 11 and 12 of the International Covenant on Economic, Social and Cultural Rights)*, UN. Doc E/C.12/2002/11 (January 20, 2003) (GC 15), ¶ 3.

[9]   *American Convention on Human Rights*, 1144 U.N.T.S. 123, November 22, 1969 (entered into force July 18, 1978), Art. 26.

[10]   International Conference on Water and the Environment, *The Dublin Statement on Water and Sustainable Development* (A/CONF.151/PC/112), Principle 3.

[11]   UN Human Rights Council, Report of the Independent Expert on the issue of human rights obligations related to access to safe drinking water and sanitation, Catarina de Albuquerque, Addendum, U.N. Doc. A/HRC/15/31/Add.1 (July 1, 2010).

[12]   GC 15, ¶ 12(b).

DEFINING THE RIGHT TO WATER

The human right to water "entitles everyone to sufficient, safe, acceptable, physically accessible and affordable water for personal and domestic uses." The ESCR Committee considers the right to water a broad right that contains both freedoms (e.g., freedom from discrimination) and entitlements (e.g., minimum access to safe drinking water to sustain life and health). The right to water entitles everyone, without discrimination, to have access water that is *adequate* for human dignity. The adequacy of water is not measured by mere reference to volumetric quantities and technologies but rather entails five factors: availability, accessibility, quality and safety, affordability, and acceptability.[13]

* Availability

Availability means that the water supply for each person must be sufficient and continuous for personal and domestic uses. This is understood to ordinarily include drinking, personal sanitation, washing of clothes, food preparation, and personal and household hygiene; but not activities such as swimming and gardening.[14] Water for agriculture or pastoralism is not covered but GC 15 encourages states to give priority to "the water resources required to prevent starvation and disease."

* Accessibility

Accessibility has four overlapping dimensions: *physical accessibility, economic accessibility, information accessibility*, and *non-discrimination.* Essentially, water and water facilities and services must be accessible to everyone within the territory and/or jurisdiction of a state party without discrimination. Physical accessibility requires that water must be within safe physical reach for all sections of the population. Non-discrimination requires that water, water facilities, and water services be accessible to all, in law and in fact, without discrimination. Finally, information accessibility includes the right to seek, receive, and impart information concerning water issues.[15]

* Quality and Safety

Quality and safety mean that the water required for personal or domestic use must be free from micro-organisms, chemical substances, and radiological

---

[13]   *Id.*
[14]   GC 15, ¶ 12(a).
[15]   *Id.*

hazards that constitute a threat to a person's health. It also means that water should be of an acceptable color, odor, and taste for each personal or domestic use. The World Health Organization has set minimum requirements for safe drinking water. Safe drinking water is water that "does not represent any significant risk to health over a lifetime of consumption, including different sensitivities that may occur between life stages."[16]

• Affordability

Although human rights law does not guarantee a right to free water, it requires that cost recovery not be a barrier to access to water and that no person be denied access to water because of an inability to pay. Essentially, the direct and indirect costs and charges associated with securing water must be affordable, and must not compromise or threaten the realization of other rights.

• Acceptability

Acceptability is the final component of the right to safe drinking water. According to the World Health Organization, "[t]he provision of drinking-water that is not only safe but also acceptable in appearance, taste and odour is of high priority."[17] Water that is aesthetically unacceptable is likely to undermine the confidence of consumers and often force consumers to use water from sources that are less safe. It is important that water and water facilities meet social and cultural norms from the perspective of a user.

BUSINESS AND THE RIGHT TO WATER

Applying a human rights lens to water management means "focusing on water-related *risks to people* rather than water-related *risks to the business*."[18] Pursuant to the UNGPs, all businesses have a responsibility to respect the right to safe water in their operations and in their supply chains. This means that they must proactively develop relevant policies, carry out relevant due diligence and risk assessments, avoid negative impacts on water quality, and address such impacts when they occur. Businesses can be connected to adverse impacts on the right to water in multiple ways, including through water privatization processes, through mega projects such dam construction, and through

---

[16] WHO, *Guidelines for Drinking-Water Quality: Fourth Edition Incorporating the First Addendum* (Geneva: WHO, 2017), 1.
[17] WHO, *Guidelines for Drinking-Water Quality,* 219.
[18] CEO Water Mandate, *Guidance for Companies on Respecting the Human Rights to Water and Sanitation: Bringing a Human Rights Lens to Corporate Water Stewardship* (January 2015), 18.

normal business operations. A single enterprise or business operation can impact all five dimensions of the right to water. "Virtually every industry and business sector is directly or indirectly linked to the production, use, release or disposal of hazardous substances and wastes, up and down supply and value chains, that may result in water contamination."[19]

• Availability

Businesses can limit the water available to local communities in a variety of ways including through: (1) intensive industrial water use without corresponding water management or stewardship programs; (2) projects that compromise water sources; and (3) failure to provide access to safe drinking water for all employees in the workplace.[20] In their role as water service providers businesses can also operate in such a manner that water is not available to certain groups and communities.

Intensive industrial water use can undermine availability of water for individuals and groups in surrounding communities and severely limit the water available for local food production. In 2020, for example, the Special Rapporteur raised concern about the impact of Chile's Alto Maipo Hydroelectric Project on the right to water. "The Chilean Government would not be fulfilling its international human rights obligations if it prioritises economic development projects over the human rights to water and health," the Special Rapporteur warned.[21] Beverage giants – Coca-Cola and PepsiCo – have, in the past, been accused of over-exploiting and misusing groundwater to the detriment of surrounding communities in Kerala, India. One study found that PepsiCo held 53 acres of land in a 750-acre industrial park and extracted 48 percent of the groundwater in Palakkad district.[22] Chile's booming avocado business and

[19] Sam Geall and Mohamad Mova Al'Afghani, *The Right to Safe Water in Southeast Asia* (London: China Dialogue and Raoul Wallenberg Institute of Human Rights and Humanitarian Law), https://cdn.chinadialogue.net/content/uploads/2020/07/07131910/The-right-to-safe-water-in-Southeast-Asia_2020-01_28_web.pdf.

[20] UNICEF and WHO, *Progress on drinking Water, Sanitation and Hygiene in Schools: Special Focus on COVID-19* (New York: UNICEF and WHO, 2020), https://washdata.org/sites/default/files/2020-08/jmp-2020-wash-schools.pdf.

[21] "Chile Must Prioritise Water and Health Rights over Economic Interests, Says UN Expert," Office of the High Commissioner for Human Rights, August 20, 2020, https://www.ohchr.org/en/NewsEvents/Pages/DisplayNews.aspx?NewsID=26177&LangID=E.

[22] "Kerala: Cola Giant Pepsi Exploiting Ground Water?" NDTV, March 18, 2020, https://www.ndtv.com/india-news/kerala-cola-giant-pepsi-exploiting-ground-water-413001.

associated avocado irrigation is blamed for the shortage of water in Chile's Valparaiso region.[23]

• Accessibility

Access to safe drinking water is compromised when communities are displaced to make room for business operations. Questions about access also arise in the context of water privatization. The right to adequate drinking water does not require states to utilize any particular model of service provision and risks to human rights exist within both privately and publicly provided water services.[24] However, the ESCR Committee has stressed that "[w]here water services … are operated or controlled by third parties, States parties must prevent them from compromising equal, affordable, and physical access to sufficient, safe and acceptable water."[25] To prevent abuses by businesses, it is incumbent on States parties to the ICESCR to establish an "effective regulatory system … which includes independent monitoring, genuine public participation and imposition of penalties for non-compliance."[26]

• Quality and Safety

Businesses can impact the quality of water through ineffective waste management and through pollution of water sources.[27] In Bangladesh, the textile industry has long been accused of disposing billions of litters of untreated effluent into surrounding rivers and streams.[28] In 2011, a court in Ecuador fined Chevron Corporation $8.6bn (£5.3bn) for, among other things, polluting a large part of the country's Amazon region.[29] In 2010, Hungary declared a state of emergency when sludge – a mixture of water and mining waste containing heavy metals – leaked from an alumina plant, polluted the Marcal

[23] Nicky Milne, "Chile's Booming Avocado Business Blamed for Water Shortages," *Global Citizen*, June 4, 2019, https://www.globalcitizen.org/en/content/chile-avocado-business-water-shortages/?template=next.

[24] UN Human Rights Council, Report of the Independent Expert on the issue of human rights obligations related to access to safe drinking water and sanitation, Catarina de Albuquerque, U.N. Doc. A/HRC/15/31 (29 June 2010).

[25] *Id.*

[26] *Id.*

[27] Riana Cermak, "COVID-19 and the Right to Water: The Crucial Role of Business During and After the Pandemic," *COVID-19* (blog), GBI, April 14, 2020, https://gbihr.org/updates/covid-19-and-the-right-to-water-the-crucial-role-of-business-during-and-aft.

[28] Human Rights Watch, *Toxic Tanneries: The Health Repercussions of Bangladesh's Hazaribagh Leather* (2012).

[29] "Chevron Fined for Amazon Pollution by Ecuador Court," *BBC News*, February 15, 2011, https://www.bbc.com/news/world-latin-america-12460333.

River, and endangered the Danube River.[30] A 2015 spill by a Guatemalan palm oil company, Reforestadora de Palmas del Petén, S.A., dumped toxic palm oil effluent into the Pasión River, which runs through the municipality of Sayaxché in Guatemala's Peten region.[31] In the Democratic Republic of Congo, Plantations et huileries du Congo owned by Feronia Inc. has been accused of consistently dumping untreated waste into the Congo River and polluting the only drinking water source for villagers.[32] Industrial agriculture is a leading cause of water pollution in many countries. In the U.S., agricultural pollution "is the top source of contamination in rivers and streams, the second-biggest source in wetlands, and the third main source in lakes," according to the National Resource Defense Council.[33]

- Affordability

The affordability of water comes up frequently in the context of privatization. Increasingly, private companies are operating or controlling water services such as piped water networks, water tankers, and access to rivers and wells. Studies suggest that water privatization, when not properly managed and regulated, can result in poor outcomes in terms of quality and affordability.

- Acceptability

Businesses adversely affect the acceptability of water when they: (i) dispose waste in a manner that does not respect the cultural rights of surrounding communities or groups within that community; (ii) establish development projects through sacred lands without the free prior and informed consent of affected communities; or (iii) introduce water treatment plans without engaging with and researching the views of their customers. As more and more municipalities turn to alternative water sources such as recycled and desalinated water, issues relating to acceptability will grow.

---

[30]   Mark Tran and agencies, "Hungary Toxic Sludge Spill and 'Ecological Catastrophe' Says Government," *Guardian*, October 5, 2010, https://www.theguardian .com/world/2010/oct/05/hungary-toxic-sludge-spill.
[31]   Jeff Conant, "Palm Oil's Toxic Legacy in Guatemala," *Medium*, September 7, 2016, https://medium.com/invironment/palm-oils-toxic-legacy-in-guatemala -df12d58e9f50.
[32]   Human Rights Watch, *A Dirty Investment* (Human Rights Watch, 2019).
[33]   Melissa Denchak, "Water Pollution: Everything You Need to Know," NRDC, April 18, 2022, https://www.nrdc.org/stories/water-pollution-everything-you-need -know.

TEACHING APPROACHES

I have taught the right to water as part of my law school "Right to Food" course (See The Right to Food, Chapter 22.) and as a segment of my "Public International Law" course. The target students are law students interested in a general overview of the interaction of business and human rights, students from other disciplines interested in understanding the role and limits of law in shaping corporate behavior, and individuals (practicing attorneys, corporate executives, and other mid-career professionals) who already earned a law degree and wish to pursue intensive study in food and agricultural law.

Learning objectives for teaching the right to water may include:

- Introducing students to the concept of BHR, to the right to water, and to the interaction between businesses and the right to water.
- Introducing students to international and regional human rights instruments relating to the right to water.
- Introducing students to a growing number of water stewardship standards and principles.
- Exposing students to a host of complex and thorny issues at the intersection of business profitability and the right to water.

I employ multiple classroom techniques when teaching the right to water, including debates, case studies, critical and/or reflection essays, lectures, and documentaries.

Debates

Debate is a useful approach to teaching the right to water. Debate can center around "hot button" issues such as the privatization and "re-municipalization" of water[34] and the tension between the right to water and other rights.[35] Regarding privatization, over the last three decades, many governments transferred the management and control of water and sanitation services to the private sector. However, in the face of massive protests, a growing number of

---

[34] Human rights and the privatization of water and sanitation services. UN General Assembly. *Human Rights and the Privatization of Water and Sanitation* Services, Report of the Special Rapporteur on the human rights to safe drinking water and sanitation, Léo Heller, U.N. Doc. A/75/208 (July 21, 2020), https://undocs.org/en/A/75/208.

[35] The impact of mega-projects on the human rights to water and sanitation. UN General Assembly, Report of the Special Rapporteur on the human rights to safe drinking water and sanitation, U.N. Doc. A/74/197 (July 19, 2019), https://undocs.org/A/74/197.

governments are terminating unsatisfactory privatization arrangements and are embarking on the process of remunicipalization, a term that refers to "the return of previously privatised water supply and sanitation services to public service delivery."[36]

Case Studies

- Indivisibility, Interrelatedness and Interdependence of Rights; Intersectionality

Human rights are indivisible, interrelated, and interdependent in the sense that violation of one right frequently affects the enjoyment of related rights and that one right cannot be realized without realization of related rights. The right to safe drinking water is closely connected to several other rights including the rights to life, work, the highest attainable standard of health, safe and nutritious food, and education. I have often taught this course through the lens of indivisibility by examining how violation of the right to water affects a host of related rights. The relationship between the right to water and right to health could be the focus of a full course. From the gold mines in South Africa to oil wells in Ecuador, water contamination has been associated with diseases, learning disabilities, behavioral disorders, and even death, particularly among children.

- Sectoral Focus

A sectoral focus is also a good way to teach the right to water. Many sectors, including the extractive industries,[37] the agricultural sector, the textile sector, and the infrastructure sector, have a long history of water pollution. From the oil spills in Nigeria's Niger Delta to heavy metal contamination in the Didipio river in the Philippines, the extractive industry provides rich materials for a course on the right to water. In the Philippines, local communities and Indigenous groups accuse Canadian-Australian OceanaGold Corporation of "depleting and contaminating the water around the mine, and damaging the watershed downstream leading into the Cagayan River."[38] In a scathing report

---

[36] Satoko Kishimoto, Emanuele Lobina, and Olivier Petitjean, eds., *Our Public Water Future: The Global Experience with Remunicipalisation* (Amsterdam: Transnational Institute, Public Services International Research Unit, Multinationals Observatory, Municipal Services Project, and the European Federation of Public Service Unions, 2015), 7.

[37] Heather Whitney, "Vietnam: Water Pollution and Mining in an Emerging Economy," *Asian-Pacific Law & Policy Journal* 15, no. 1 (2013).

[38] Robin Broad et al., *OceanaGold in the Philippines: Ten Violations that Should Prompt Its Removal* (Institute for Policy Studies and MiningWatch Canada, 2018), 9.

released in 2016, the South African Human Rights Commission noted that "the mining sector is riddled with challenges related to land, housing, water, [and] the environment."[39]

Pillar III: Access to Remedy

The growing number of lawsuits, petitions, and complaints relating to water filed with domestic, regional, and international judicial and non-judicial grievance mechanisms can be drawn on to teach a BHR course on the right to water. The goal would be to help students understand the third pillar of the UNGPs (access to remedy) as it applies to the right to water and to identify gaps in state and business response to Pillar III.

The bad news is that for most victims of abuse, access to remedy is limited or non-existent. The good news is that in a handful of countries, specialized courts providing specialized justice are beginning to appear. The first court dedicated to prosecuting crimes against the environment was inaugurated Guatemala in 2015.[40] Also in 2015, Judge Karla Hernandez, Guatemala's first environmental judge, ruled that effluent spills constituted "ecocide" and ordered relevant agencies to temporarily cease operations in order to undertake an investigation.[41] Notable cases that directly or indirectly touch on the right to water include, *Okapi v. Shell*[42] (oil spills in the context of oil exploration and extraction), *Lungowe v. Vedanta*[43] (pollution in the context of copper mining), *Kiobel v. Royal Dutch Petroleum Co.*[44] (oil spill in the Niger Delta region of Nigeria), and *Poma v. Peru* (diversion of water away from pastoral lands).[45]

---

[39] South African Human Rights Commission, *National Hearing on the Underlying Socio-economic Challenges of Mining-affected Communities in South Africa* (2016), https://www.sahrc.org.za/home/21/files/SAHRC%20Mining%20communities%20report%20FINAL.pdf.

[40] "Guatemala's Environmental Crimes Court Hears First Case," https://www.sustainablebusiness.com/2016/01/guatemalas-environmental-crimes-court-hears-first-case-55448.

[41] This decision was subsequently overturned and the presiding judge forced to step down.

[42] *Okpabi and others v. Royal Dutch Shell Plc and another* [2018] EWCA Civ 191, 196.

[43] *Lungowe and Ors. v. Vedanta Resources Plc and Konkola Copper Mines Plc.* [2019] UKSC 20.

[44] *Kiobel v. Royal Dutch Petroleum*, 569 U.S. 108 (2013).

[45] *Ángela Poma Poma v. Peru*, CCPR/C/95/D/1457/2006, https://juris.ohchr.org/Search/Details/1495.

Corporate Policies, Multistakeholder Initiatives, and Emerging Best Practices

I sometimes teach the right to water by examining evolving best practices of businesses and industries. A course could evaluate the compatibility of evolving best practices and initiatives with the spirit and letter of the UNGPs. Business can be proactive about the right to safe drinking water by, *inter alia*:

- Supporting the promulgation of regulations and policies to control pollution of water resources including surveillance, disincentives, and pollution penalties
- Identifying and assessing adverse impacts on water quality arising out of their operations
- Preventing and mitigating adverse impacts by applying relevant impact assessment findings to their operations
- Respecting the right to water even when states fail to enact and enforce an enabling legal framework.

Over the past decade, some of the world's leading multinational companies announced notable new water policies and commitments. Companies that have announced water commitments include Coca-Cola, PepsiCo, Cargill,[46] McDonalds,[47] Starbucks,[48] and General Mills.[49] In 2021, three agricultural giants – Danone North America, Ingredion, and Mars, Inc. – announced new commitments to improve water stewardship.[50] Multistakeholder initiatives related to the right to water are also emerging. Three prominent examples

---

[46] "Cargill Commits to Restoring 600 Billion Liters of Water by 2030," Cargill, July 21, 2020, https://www.cargill.com/2020/cargill-commits-to-restoring-600-billion -liters-of-water-by-2030.

[47] "Nature, Forests & Water," McDonalds, accessed August 16, 2022, https:// corporate.mcdonalds.com/corpmcd/our-purpose-and-impact/our-planet/water -stewardship.html.

[48] "A Message from Starbucks CEO Kevin Johnson: Starbucks New Sustainability Commitment," Starbucks Stories, January 21, 2020, https://stories.starbucks.com/ stories/2020/message-from-starbucks-ceo-kevin-johnson-starbucks-new-sustainability -commitment.

[49] Amanda Best, "The Kansas City Mill Celebrated 100 Years," News & Stories, General Mills, August 15, 2022, https://www.generalmills.com/en/News/Issues/water -policy.

[50] "Three major companies announce new AgWater Challenge Commitments improve water stewardship and sustainable agriculture," Ceres, updated March 22, 2021, https://www.ceres.org/news-center/press-releases/three-major-companies-announce -new-agwater-challenge-commitments-improve.

are the Alliance for Water Stewardship,[51] the 2030 Water Resource Group,[52] and the CEO Water Mandate.[53] Global standards around water stewardship are beginning to emerge as well. In 2015, the CEO Water Mandate published *Guidance for Companies on Respecting the Human Rights to Water and Sanitation* (Guidance) that is influenced by the UNGPs.[54]

KEY QUESTIONS

General

- Should the right to adequate drinking water be recognized as a human right?
- What are the arguments for and against private sector involvement in the provision of water services?
- How might privatization of water affect water availability, affordability, acceptability, accessibility, and quality? Are there real-life examples where privatization resulted in the abuse of the right to adequate drinking water?
- How might privatization actually support the realization of the right to adequate water? Are there real-life examples where privatization of water enhanced water availability, accessibility, affordability, acceptability, and/ or quality?

For Law Students

- What international law instruments recognize the right to water?
- What legal framework in a state enable or exacerbate human rights risks when the private sector is involved in water provision?
- When states privatize water services, what types of laws and regulation might be necessary to ensure the respect and realization of human rights by private sector actors that are involved in water service provision?

---

[51] "A Global Standard for Water Stewardship: Download the AWS Standard V2.0 and Guidance," Alliance for Water Stewardship, accessed August 15, 2022, https://a4ws.org.

[52] "2030 WRG: Collective Action on Water Security for People, Environment, and Economy," 2030 Water Resources group, accessed August 15, 2022, https://www.2030wrg.org.

[53] "Six Commitment Areas," CEO Water Mandate, accessed August 15, 2022, https://ceowatermandate.org/about/six-commitment-areas.

[54] "New Guidance for Companies on How to Respect the Human Rights to Water and Sanitation," News, Shift, January 2015, https://shiftproject.org/new-guidance-for-companies-on-how-to-respect-the-human-rights-to-water-and-sanitation.

- Do international human rights instruments, in particular the ICESCR, encourage or discourage the privatization of water services?

For Business Students

- How should businesses balance competing rights and navigate trade-offs between the right to water and other rights?
- What are the trends with regards to private sector participation in the water sector in rich countries, in poor countries, and in emerging market economies?
- Does the privatization of water serve the public interest?

For Policy Students

- Is the current international legal and regulatory framework sufficient to address human rights gaps that arise when water privatization occurs?
- How can states compel private water companies to respect human rights? Are there any examples of innovative policies in this regard?

TEACHING RESOURCES

Readings

Primary Sources

- United Nations. *International Covenant on Economic, Social and Cultural Rights* (ICESCR), 993 U.N.T.S. 3 (December 16, 1966, entered into force January 3, 1976).
- United Nations General Assembly. *Convention on the Elimination of All Forms of Discrimination against Women* (CEDAW), 1249 U.N.T.S 13, U.N. Doc. A/34/180 (December 18, 1979, entered into force September 3, 1981).
- United Nations General Assembly. *Convention on the Rights of the Child* (CRC), 1577 U.N.T.S. 3, U.N. Doc. A/44/45 (November 20, 1989, entered into force September 2, 1990).
- United Nations General Assembly. *United Nations Declaration on the Rights of Indigenous Peoples* (UNDRIP), G.A. Res. 61/295, U.N. Doc. A/61/L.67 and Add.1 (2007).

Secondary Sources (non-binding instruments)

- United Nations General Assembly. "The Human Rights to Safe Drinking Water and Sanitation," Resolution 70/169, U.N. Doc. A/RES/70/169 (February 22, 2016).
- United Nations General Assembly. Resolution 72 (b), *The Human Rights to Safe Drinking Water and Sanitation*, U.N. Doc. A/RES/72/178 (January 29, 2018).
- United Nations Human Rights Council. Resolution 15/9, *Human Rights and Access to Safe Drinking Water and Sanitation*, U.N. Doc. A/HRC/RES/15/9 (October 6, 2010). https://undocs.org/A/HRC/RES/15/9.
- United Nations Human Rights Council. Resolution 16/2, *The Human Right to Safe Drinking Water and Sanitation*, U.N. Doc. A/HRC/ RES/16/2 (April 8, 2011). https://undocs.org/en/A/HRC/RES/16/2.
- United Nations Committee on Economic, Social and Cultural Rights (CESCR). *General Comment No. 15: The Right to Water (Arts. 11 and 12 of the International Covenant on Economic, Social and Cultural Rights)*. UN. Doc E/C.12/2002/11 (January 20, 2003). https://www.undocs.org/e/c.12/2002/11.
- UN Committee on Economic, Social and Cultural Rights. *General Comment No. 24: State obligations under the International Covenant on Economic, Social and Cultural Rights in the context of business activities.* UN Doc. E/C.12/GC/24 (June 23, 2017). https://undocs.org/E/C.12/GC/24.

Cases

- Inter-American Court of Human Rights. Case of the Indigenous Communities Members of the Lhaka Honhat Association v. Argentina or Comunidades Indígenas Miembros de la Asociación Lhaka Honhat (Nuestra Tierra) v. Argentina, Merits, Reparations and Costs. Judgment. Inter-Am. Ct. H.R. (ser. C) No. 400 (February 6, 2020).

Videos

- Friends of the Earth. "Palm Oil's Toxic Legacy in Sayaxché, Guatemala." September 3, 2016. YouTube video, 6:14: https://www.youtube.com/watch?v=-XKXvHrL-GY.
- Salina, Irena, dir. *Flow: For Love of Water*. Oscilloscope Laboratories. 2008.
- Snitow, Alan and Deborah Kaufman, dirs. *Thirst*. Snitow-Kaufman Productions. 2004.

24. Technology and human rights

Faris Natour and Roger McElrath

OVERVIEW

Many of today's most high-profile business and human rights (BHR) challenges involve technology companies. From U.S. technology company Apple pushing back against orders by the FBI to unlock the phones of suspected mass shooters[1] to social media giant Facebook acknowledging misuse of its platform to incite violence in Myanmar,[2] it is hard to open the newspaper and not find a story at the intersection of technology and BHR.

Advancements in emerging technologies such as artificial intelligence (AI), machine learning, 5G communication networks, and the "internet of things"[3] bring new human rights risks that are just beginning to be understood, allowing students to apply basic BHR frameworks and concepts to new and emerging issues. At the same time, the COVID-19 pandemic has brought into stark relief the potential human rights benefits of technology, for example by enabling remote learning for many students whose schools closed for in-person instruction, thereby advancing their human right to education.

These same emerging technologies and their increasingly broad adoption in sectors as varied as manufacturing, mining, transportation, and retail mean that companies in virtually all industries face technology-related human rights risks. This makes it essential that students planning to work in the BHR field

---

[1] Lily Hay Newman, "This Apple-FBI Fight Is Different from the Last One," *Wired*, January 16, 2020, https://www.wired.com/story/apple-fbi-iphone-encryption-pensacola.

[2] Alexandra Stevenson, "Facebook Admits It Was Used to Incite Violence in Myanmar," *New York Times*, November 6, 2018, https://www.nytimes.com/2018/11/06/technology/myanmar-facebook.html.

[3] The "internet of things" (IoT) is broadly defined as the network of physical objects that are embedded with technological devices (sensors, cameras, software, etc.) designed to connect and exchange information and data with other devices and systems over the internet. Such objects range from basic household objects to complex industrial tools.

understand the technology sector's salient human rights risks[4] and opportunities, as well as the tools and approaches that technology companies can deploy to mitigate risks and maximizing the opportunities for positive human rights impacts.

This chapter provides an overview of the technology sector and its human rights impacts, the most effective approach to teaching the details around the actual and potential impacts on human rights of technology companies, and the efforts technology companies are making to respect human rights in managing those impacts and risks.

THE TECHNOLOGY SECTOR

To teach the intersection of technology and BHR effectively, it is critical to introduce the unique operating context of the technology sector relative to other industries. This includes the speed of innovation, the immense scale of users – and therefore rightsholders – of certain technology platforms, as well as the deployment and use of many technology platforms across multiple jurisdictions and almost all industries. In addition, the corporate culture at some technology companies emphasizes speed to market and celebrates disruption, which can make human rights protections difficult to implement through integration into product development and understanding of how products are being used. This operating context significantly impacts both the human rights risk profile of many technology companies and their ability to effectively mitigate these risks.

DOWNSTREAM HUMAN RIGHTS IMPACTS

When designing a course module on technology and human rights, teachers should primarily focus on downstream human rights impacts, specifically the potential adverse impacts of technology products and services on users, data subjects, and other individuals or communities. While the technology sector faces human rights risks across the value chain, including significant upstream supply chain risks related to conflict minerals and working conditions in the manufacturing supply chain, and risks related to diversity and inclusion and the human rights of contract workers in companies' own operations, we focus the technology and human rights module in our courses on downstream human

---

[4]   Salient human rights impacts and risks are those that have the greatest impact with respect to: severity – the seriousness of the impacts or risks of impacts on rightsholders; scope – the number of rightsholders impacted or potential impacted; and remediability – the potential for the negative human rights impacts to be remediated.

rights risks, specifically risks related to the use and misuse of technology products, services, and platforms.

The reason to focus on downstream risks is threefold. First, the prevalence and saliency of these risks are particularly high in the technology sector, which makes it particularly important to cover these risks in limited time focused on the sector in a broader BHR course. Second, the exploration of these downstream risks raises significant and challenging questions, including on the scope of responsibility, effective risk mitigation, and the identification and implementation of effective remedies, the analysis of which contributes significantly to the course's overall learning objectives. Third, the upstream human rights risks and associated management systems can typically be covered elsewhere in broader BHR courses, such as in modules focused on supply chain risks or specific sectors such as apparel, footwear, toys, or other consumer products.

Salient downstream human rights risks include adverse impacts on the right to privacy as well as the follow-on human rights abuses that may be triggered by a privacy infringement, such as arbitrary arrest, torture, infringements on the right to life and personal security, and the right to work and an adequate standard of living. It should also include impacts on freedom of expression and access to information, as well as impacts related to artificial intelligence, machine learning, augmented and virtual reality, surveillance mechanisms, and other emerging technologies. Potential human rights impacts associated with emerging technologies, for example, include discrimination from algorithmic bias, violation of the right to equality before the law, or loss of work and livelihood due to automation.

A discussion of salient risks should reference upstream impacts related to working conditions in the supply chain and for employees and contractors, as well as diversity, equity, and inclusion in the technology sector.

RIGHTSHOLDERS

Rightsholders that should be considered by the technology sector include users of products, services, and platforms, data subjects, employees and contractors, workers in the supply chain, and others. Additional rightsholders are vulnerable or marginalized groups whose rights are at greater risk and thus should be given special consideration, including children and youth, low-wage workers, ethnic minorities, human rights defenders, and members of economically disadvantaged, politically persecuted, and other vulnerable groups.

For example, contracted workers employed by third-party vendors hired by social media companies to moderate online content are often based in countries with high risk for substandard working conditions and may face barriers to accessing benefits such as mental health counseling.[5] Impacts on the users of technology products can include adverse impacts on their right to privacy and personal security, for example through mass surveillance systems, such as those allegedly deployed in China to surveil the Uyghur community.[6]

DEFINING RESPONSIBILITY AND REMEDY

The scope of responsibility for technology companies and, in particular, technology platforms for human rights impacts related to the use or misuse of technology products, services, and platforms can be challenging to define. Many technology solutions involve products and services from multiple providers working together to enable the use case, and with it potential adverse human rights impacts. For example, a facial recognition technology solution may be misused in ways that adversely impact the right to privacy of data subjects. This solution relies on a camera and storage solutions from hardware providers, software and data services from various technology companies, and an internet service provider to provide connectivity. To determine the responsibility of each company requires assessment of whether each actor is causing, contributing, or is directly linked to the adverse impact, using the methodology of the UN Guiding Principles on Business and Human Rights (UNGPs). (See The UN Guiding Principles on Business and Human Rights, Chapter 5.)

Similarly, providing remedy can be difficult in a context in which the scope of impact could be enormous and the identification of appropriate remedies is challenging. For example, harmful content spread on social media may be viewed by millions of users, potentially impacting their human rights to non-discrimination, dignity and personal security, and exposure to the content cannot be undone.

For both defining the scope of responsibility and the need for and adequacy of remedial actions, the UNGPs provide guidance to support a company's assessment of these key aspects of managing human rights. Specifically, the UNGPs set forth a three-level framework and specific criteria for assessing the scope of responsibility: did a company cause (level 1), contribute to (level 2), or is it linked (level 3) to the human rights impact? The UNGPs mandate that companies provide remedy for human rights impacts that they have "caused" and/or "contributed" to; and for situations in which a company is "directly linked" to human rights impacts, it should consider collaborating with actors

---

[5] Anna Drootin, "Community Guidelines: The Legal Implications of Workplace Conditions for Internet Content Moderators," *Fordham Law Review* 90 (2021): 1197–1244.
[6] Johana Bhuiyan, "'There's Cameras Everywhere': Testimonies Detail Far-Reaching Surveillance of Uyghurs in China," *Guardian*, September 30, 2021.

that are directly involved in human rights impacts in order to identify the nature of appropriate remedies and when possible to participate in the provision of those remedies.

MANAGING HUMAN RIGHTS RISKS

Risk mitigation tools and approaches deployed by technology companies include human rights policies, responsible AI principles, product and country-specific human rights impact assessments, customer due diligence frameworks, responsible innovation processes, and multistakeholder initiatives such as the Global Network Initiative.[7] Companies, including Microsoft, HPE, and Google, have adopted responsible AI principles guiding the development and deployment of AI and other emerging technologies. Responsible AI toolkits provide engineers and developers inside and beyond the company with the tools and guidance to apply the responsible AI principles.[8]

In our experience advising technology companies on mitigating human rights risks, a growing number of technology companies are developing and implementing customer due diligence frameworks that seek to identify potentially high-risk transactions based on inherent human rights risk at the country or sector level and initiating more in-depth assessments of those potential transactions to identify and address human rights risks.

Issues informing corporate approaches include: the role of technology in society, specifically the tradeoffs and tensions between the human rights risks and societal benefits of technology development and use; emerging human rights risks related to new and emerging technologies; and evolving standards, norms, and principles, and government demands, such as the concept of meaningful consent to data collection and use in the age of hyperconnectivity.

TEACHING APPROACHES

A module on technology and human rights should use the unique human rights context of the technology sector to build students' understanding of human rights impacts involving technology and the management challenges in addressing these impacts. It should also introduce students to practical tools and approaches deployed by technology companies to overcome these challenges.

---

[7] "Protecting and Advancing Freedom of Expression and Privacy in the ICT Sector," About, Global Network Initiative, accessed August 16, 2022, https://globalnetworkinitiative.org.

[8] See, for example, "Responsible AI," Microsoft, accessed August 16, 2022, https://www.microsoft.com/en-us/ai/responsible-ai?activetab=pivot1:primaryr6.

Learning objectives may include:

- Understanding the ways in which the technology sector can impact human rights both positively and adversely.
- Understanding the unique operating context and resulting challenges for addressing human rights impacts in the ICT sector, including the scale of users, the breadth of technological applications across industries and governments, the speed of innovation, and prevailing tech company cultures encouraging disruption rather than diligence.
- Applying the UNGPs to determine the scope of responsibility for digital platforms and other technology companies for human rights impacts involving their products and services.
- Critically assessing the degree to which technology companies today are meeting the human rights impacts within their scope of responsibility.
- Providing an overview of the mitigation measures technology companies can deploy in addressing human rights risks and the unique challenges that make risk mitigation in the sector difficult.
- Empowering students to shape their perspective on emerging human rights risks and evolving standards and norms related to emerging technology.

We teach business students at the MBA and undergraduate business level. While our courses at both levels are also attended by students in other disciplines, our teaching approaches are geared primarily toward engaging business students. Below we describe teaching approaches and methods that have worked for us in achieving the learning objectives described above. In some of our broader BHR courses, we have been able to devote multiple sessions to the technology sector. In those instances, we focused the first session on the more practice-oriented learning objectives, including salient risks, scope of responsibility, and risk mitigation and integration, while the second session focused more on broader philosophical discussion of the role of technology in society and emerging standards and norms.

Overview Lecture

While our course is primarily based on group discussion and interactive exercises, we do include an overview lecture to set the context for the technology module. The lecture provides a broad overview of the technology sector and the landscape of different actors involved in bringing a technology solution to market. Following a brief Q&A with students to confirm their understanding of the technology sector, we then go into further detail on the unique operating context of the technology sector, such as the immense scope of potential impacts and the speed of technology innovation, which can eclipse the adoption of corresponding regulatory standards. We discuss the challenges the unique operating context presents for the identification of human rights risks and impacts, the determination of scope of responsibility, and the steps necessary to mitigate human rights risk. We involve the students through questions, before providing the answers by showing them our slides.

Practitioner Guest Lecturers

Throughout our course, we make extensive use of guest lectures from practitioners who bring different practical experiences and perspectives into the classroom. Learning directly from practitioners exposes students to the operational reality and complexity in managing human rights in dynamic and often very large companies. In no sector is this more relevant than in the technology sector, where the human rights risks are significant and still evolving, and where company culture can play a significant role in whether internal human rights champions succeed or fail in advancing human rights. In addition to bringing our own experiences as business and human rights consultants at Article One and BSR into the classroom, our students have been able to hear from human rights managers at companies such as Facebook, Microsoft, Google, Twitter, and Intel, as well as from technology experts at human rights organizations such as Amnesty International.

Case Studies

Case studies can help students learn and practice applying the UNGPs to the technology sector and stimulate critical analysis. These can be longer, more complex case studies providing students with significant detail, or shorter case studies that enable brief in-class exercises, which allows for multiple case studies. In our course we have used case studies such as Facebook's role in Myanmar, the use of facial recognition technology in so-called "smart city" applications, the decision by Twitter and other social media companies to ban former US President Donald Trump, and Airbnb's decision to delist, and then relist, rental listings in Israeli settlements in the Palestinian territories deemed illegal under international law. (See Teaching Resources below.)

In-class Discussions

Our course is primarily discussion based, which is particularly helpful in teaching the technology module. As most students will be heavy users of technology, teachers could start this module with a discussion about their experiences and expectations for the technology products, services, and platforms that they use and addressing the fundamental issue of whether or not access to technology should be a "human right." What is their expectation of privacy? Do they understand how their data is used? Do they feel like they have control over their data? From there, we often use the case studies described above to stimulate in-class discussion. Using simplified versions of the cases described above, we seek to stimulate debate and discussion on the scope of the company's responsibility and collaboration on surfacing potential pathways to risk mitigation.

News Review

In all our class sessions, including the module on technology and human rights, we include a segment in which students share news stories that caught their eye over the previous week. This is particularly helpful in the technology module given that many of the salient human rights risks are live and evolving issues covered extensively in the news. The news review segment allows us to connect the frameworks and standards we teach in class to real-world events. It enables students to apply what they have learned to an ongoing human rights issue, often illustrating the complexity and difficulty involved in applying theoretical standards in the "real world." Most importantly, the news segment is a way to teach students to look at the world through a business and human rights lens and that BHR is no longer a niche topic, but that BHR considerations can be relevant in a diverse and growing range of domestic and international contexts. Finally, the segment is a great way for us to inform our course's student participation grade.

EXERCISE 24.1

IDENTIFY HUMAN RIGHTS RISKS FOR A TECHNOLOGY COMPANY OR PRODUCT

To help students identify salient risks and opportunities in the tech sector and to critically examine the role of technology in society, we assign a range of technology focused exercises either as in-class, individual, or group assignments, or as take-home graded assignments. For example, the teachers may break up students into small groups and assign each group a specific technology company, for which the students then should identify the most salient human rights risks, the scope of responsibility of the company for those risks applying the UNGPs' "cause/contribute/linked" framework, and the groups of rightsholders that are particularly vulnerable to adverse human rights impacts. The same exercise can be designed for a shorter in-class assignment, by focusing not on the company's entire operations but on a specific technology product, such as a smart camera, virtual reality gaming console, or feature such as facial recognition or synthetic speech.

KEY QUESTIONS

Given the broad scope of technology-related human rights impacts, key questions for in-class discussions and case studies, as well as for mid-term and final exams, touch on a wide range of topics, including salient risks, business operations, scope of responsibility, national and international laws and standards, stakeholder relations, and engagement with multistakeholder initiatives.

General

- What makes the technology sector unique in the way it may impact human rights and in the way those impacts can be addressed?
- What are the internationally recognized human rights that are most salient for technology companies and their value chains?
- What is the scope of responsibility of social media and other technology platforms for impacts related to the use or misuse of their platforms? What factors influence the level of responsibility?
- What is the responsibility of consumers/users of technology for technology-related human rights impacts?
- Numerous examples exist of governments using technology to violate human rights (for example, for overbroad surveillance), but are there examples of where governments have used technology from the private sector to protect human rights? How can we maximize these opportunities for positive impact while minimizing the risks of adverse impacts of technology?
- How much leverage does a technology company have over how its customers use its products, services, and platforms? How does leverage change when the customer is a government entity? What opportunities exist for a company to increase and use its leverage?
- How is the technology sector similar and different to other industries in terms of its commitment to implementing the UNGPs?
- What is the most important business case for technology companies adopting and implementing the UNGPs?

For Business Students

- What are the human rights risks or impacts associated with emerging technologies such as artificial intelligence, machine learning, augmented and virtual reality, and others?
- What would effective and scalable human rights due diligence look like for technology companies with millions or billions of users? What role could technology play in scaling human rights due diligence responsibly and effectively?
- What formal and informal measures could be deployed to ensure that product developers and engineers consider human rights in the design and development of technology?
- If you start a new technology company, how would you build respect for human rights in from the ground up?
- For companies in the technology sector, what is the general scope of responsibility for negative human rights impacts in their supply chains and those that are generated through the use or misuse of their products by other companies and/or governments (for example, surveillance technology, artificial intelligence, social media)?
- Is there potential for technology companies to play a positive role in ensuring respect for human rights by other businesses both directly and indirectly?
- How can technology companies more effectively engage users on their right to privacy? What would effective terms and conditions look like that users would actually read and understand?

For Law Students

- How do the legal risks that technology companies are exposed to with respect to human rights differ from those for companies in other industries?
- Are these legal risks likely to increase in the future, and if yes, then what will be the primary factors driving the increasing legal risks?
- For globally available social media and technology platforms, how can companies ensure respect for human rights while complying with legal and regulatory requirements in different jurisdictions, including on data localization and law enforcement requests for user data?
- How should a technology company respond to a law enforcement request for user data in a country with a poor human rights record? How should a social media platform respond to a government request to take down content critical of the government? How should a network operator respond to a government order of an internet shutdown to quell anti-government protests?

- Does the "business case" for adopting the UNGPs in order to reduce legal risk apply equally to technology companies, or is there something unique about their products and services that magnifies or minimizes the risks?
- Does the trend of increasingly "mandatory" human rights due diligence pose a greater burden on and/or risk to technology companies than companies in other sectors?
- How can a company determine the need for and deliver effective remedy in the case of a human rights violations associated with a technology-based product or service that could impact millions of rightsholders?

For Policy Students

- What tools are available to policymakers seeking to improve the human rights performance of technology companies?
- Given the potential scope and scale of impact on human rights of technology companies' products and services, is there a need to modify and/or reinforce current international standards on how companies manage human rights to ensure respect for human rights?

TEACHING RESOURCES

Readings

Commentary

- Donahoe, Eileen and Megan MacDuffee Metzger. "Artificial Intelligence and Human Rights." *Journal of Democracy* 30, no. 2 (April 2019): 115–126.
- McCorquodale, Robert, Lise Smit, Stuart Neely, and Robin Brooks. "Human Rights Due Diligence in Law and Practice: Good Practices and Challenges for Business Enterprises." *Business and Human Rights Journal* 2, no. 2 (July 2017).

Reports

- Fjeld, Jessica, Nele Achten, Hannah Hilligoss, Adam Chritopher Nagy, and Madhulika Srikumar. *Principled Artificial Intelligence: Mapping Consensus in Ethical and Rights-Based Approaches to Principles for AI.* Cambridge, MA: Berkman Klein Center for Internet and Society, January 15, 2020. http://dx.doi.org/10.2139/ssrn.3518482.
- Hope, Dunstan Allison, Faris Natour, and Farid Baddache. *Applying the Guiding Principles on Business and Human Rights to the ICT*

Industry. BSR, September 2012. https://www.bsr.org/reports/BSR_Guiding
_Principles_and_ICT_2.0.pdf.
- World Economic Forum and BSR. *Responsible Use of Technology*.
Geneva: World Economic Forum, August 2019. https://www3.weforum
.org/docs/WEF_Responsible_Use_of_Technology.pdf.

Case studies

Facebook in Myanmar

- Taub, Amanda and Max Fisher. "Where Countries Are Tinderboxes and
Facebook Is a Match." *New York Times*, April 21, 2018.
- Warofka, Alex. "An Independent Assessment of the Human Rights Impact
of Facebook in Myanmar." Updated August 26, 2020. https://about.fb
.com/news/2018/11/myanmar-hria.

Bias and discrimination in facial recognition technology

- Dastin, Jeffrey and Munsif Vengattil. "Microsoft bans face-recognition sales
to police as Big Tech reacts to protests." *Reuters*, June 12, 2020. https://
www.reuters.com/article/us-microsoft-facial-recognition/microsoft-bans-face
-recognition-sales-to-police-as-big-tech-reacts-to-protests-idUSKBN23I2T6.
- Najibi, Alex. "Racial Discrimination in Face Recognition Technology."
Special Edition: Science Policy and Social Justice (blog), October 24,
2020. https://sitn.hms.harvard.edu/flash/2020/racial-discrimination-in-face
-recognition-technology.

Twitter and Facebook ban of former US President Donald Trump

- Issac, Mike and Sheera Frenkel. "Facebook Says Trump's Ban Will Last at
Least 2 Years." *New York Times*, June 4, 2021. https://www.nytimes.com/
2021/06/04/technology/facebook-trump-ban.html.
- Twitter's announcement of the decision. Twitter, Inc. "Permanent
Suspension of @realDonaldTrump." *Company* (blog). January 8, 2021.
https://blog.twitter.com/en_us/topics/company/2020/suspension.

Videos

- In Lieu of Fun. "In Lieu of Fun, Episode 531: Brittan Heller on Augmented
Reality." Podcast. October 18, 2021. YouTube video, 1:02:00: https://
www.youtube.com/watch?v=U6MYtxn2w38&t=274s.

- Institute for Human Rights and Business. "Deep Dive: Miranda Sissons on Facebook's New Human Rights Policy." March 29, 2021. YouTube video, 52:44 https://www.youtube.com/watch?v=HR6kkAuCG00.

Websites

- Freedom House. "Freedom on the Net." https://freedomhouse.org/report/freedom-net.
- Ranking Digital Rights. The 2020 RDR Index. https://rankingdigitalrights.org/index2020.

25. Engineering for human rights

Shareen Hertel, Davis Chacon Hurtado, and Sandra Sirota

OVERVIEW

This chapter focuses on the emergence of "engineering for human rights" as a new area of teaching, scholarship, and professional practice. Faculty at the University of Connecticut (UConn) have collaborated to draw students from multiple fields together within interdisciplinary courses that bridge the science, technology, engineering, and math (STEM) and non-STEM fields. Since the early 2000s, we and other faculty have developed team-taught courses that are cross-listed between our School of Engineering and College of Liberal Arts and Sciences. These courses focus on a range of topics – from human and environmental impact of global supply chains to the politics of sustainable energy transitions. They broaden the range of students in our undergraduate Human Rights Major/Minor[1] and have paved the way for the creation of a new Bachelor of Science in Multidisciplinary Engineering with a thematic focus on Human Rights and Sustainability that was launched in 2021–2022.[2]

"Every discipline works together to come up with solutions."[3]

At UConn, we have built a lively research and teaching community centered around six core areas: (1) Engineering Substance and Process Sustainability; (2) Cybersecurity, Privacy, and Human Vulnerability; (3) Engineering Education

---

[1]   Shareen Hertel and Allison MacKay, "Engineering and Human Rights: Teaching across the Divide," *Business and Human Rights Journal* 1, no. 1 (2016): 159–164.

[2]   For details, see "About the Multidisciplinary Engineering Major," University of Connecticut School of Engineering, accessed December 29, 2021, https://mde.engr.uconn.edu.

[3]   Susan Fourtané, "Engineers without Borders: Inspiring the Next Generation of Engineers," Interesting Engineering blog, February 4, 2020, accessed December 29, 2020, https://interestingengineering.com/engineers-without-borders-inspiring-the-next-generation-of-engineers.

and Accessibility Rights; (4) Product Design, Manufacturing, and Supply Chain Management; (5) Community Planning, Resilience, and Justice for a Changing Environment; and (6) Water, Health, and Food Security.[4] Courses cutting across these themed areas build the capacity of all students (engineering and non-engineering students alike) to think systematically and holistically about the role of technology in society and the challenges of protecting and promoting human rights in the context of business practice.

Indeed, these courses not only equip engineers with unique skills but also develop the abilities of human rights students in other fields to go on to careers as practitioners with exposure to engineering concepts – putting those types of knowledge to work in careers within corporations or government entities, where they may oversee the promotion of human rights auditing, compliance, or stakeholder engagement. Or they may pursue careers in civil society organizations in which their engineering education strengthens their ability to advocate for rights in the context of engineering projects.

Equipping students to take stock of the good, the bad, and the indeterminate in a course like ours is only half the challenge. The other half is inspiring them to take action in whatever field they may ultimately work in, whether as an engineer or not. Alumni of our courses take on a range of professional roles. Some work in auditing and compliance organizations; others work in corporations with global reach. Some apply their engineering or social and environmental impact assessment skills in public policy settings. Others gravitate toward laboratory settings where they conduct bench research. Still others seek out non-governmental organizations (NGOs) involved in science education and public outreach or focused on human rights in business. Individual instructors or institutions, in turn, can adapt these approaches in order to teach engineering for human rights in business and human rights (BHR) courses, and create curricula to bridge the STEM/human rights divide.

ENGINEERING ROLES AND EDUCATION

The conceptual framework and practical implementation of "engineering for human rights" overlap with the main sectors central to BHR itself, namely business, government, and civil society. In both fields, the common curricular touchstones are integrative: students learn how to manage challenges within and across each sector. For engineering students, the interdisciplinarity of our

---

[4] For details, see "Engineering for Human Rights Initiative," University of Connecticut School of Engineering, accessed December 29, 2021, https://engin eeringforhumanrights.initiative.uconn.edu.

engineering for human rights course offerings is often novel, revealing new professional and research pathways.

Engineers can work in for-profit corporations, designing new products and processes. Or they may use their skills in government-run entities, designing and building infrastructure, monitoring risks and hazards, or setting standards. Or they may be employed by civil society-based organizations that use inclusive and sustainable design as a vehicle for promoting equity and inclusion, or that use science-based information to protect people at risk.

In any of these arenas, engineers as professionals are responsible for upholding basic codes of ethics in the context of their work – codes that stipulate how to avoid harm and how to determine individual responsibility when it occurs.[5] Because they are trained within different subfields (for example, chemical, mechanical, biomedical, civil, electrical), practicing engineers are subject not only to an overarching code of professional practice by a national certifying body but also to sub-field specific codes that regulate activity within specific industries.

Scholars who study technology and social change have urged engineering educators to more holistically take on the positive and negative dimensions of the field's impact on society and the environment.[6] This would mean developing pedagogical tools that equip students to recognize historicized patterns of inequality integral to how technology has evolved, and to recognize ecological limits and the impact that today's design, production, and consumption choices have on future generations.

Historically, from the revolt of engineers in the 1920s[7] to the adoption of Sen's Capabilities approach,[8] progressive engineers have invoked a greater

---

[5]   See, for example, "National Society of Professional Engineers (NSPE) Code of Ethics for Engineers," NSPE, accessed January 11, 2022, https://www.nspe.org/resources/ethics/code-ethics; "American Society of Civil Engineers (ASCE) Code of Ethics," ASCE, accessed January 11, 2022, https://www.asce.org/career-growth/ethics/code-of-ethics; "Institute of Electrical and Electronics Engineers (IEEE) Code of Ethics," IEEE, accessed January 11, 2022, https://www.ieee.org/about/corporate/governance/p7-8.html.

[6]   Erin Cech, "Great Problems of Grand Challenges: Problematizing Engineering's Understandings of Its Role in Society," *International Journal of Engineering, Social Justice, and Peace* 1, no. 2 (2012): 85–94.

[7]   Edwin T. Layton, Jr., *The Revolt of Engineers: Social Responsibility and the American Engineering Profession* (Baltimore, MD: The Johns Hopkins University Press, 1986).

[8]   Amartya Sen, *Development as Freedom* (New York: Anchor, 2000, reprint edition); see also Jon A. Leydens and Juan C. Lucena, *Engineering Justice: Transforming Engineering Education and Practice* (Hoboken, NJ: Wiley-IEEE Press, 1st edition). See also E.T. Oosterlaken, "Taking a Capability Approach to Technology and Its Design: A Philosophical Exploration" (Ph.D. diss., TU Delft, 2013), accessed

purpose of engineering for society to promote change in engineering practice and education. However, many of these efforts have the limitation of not having a universal baseline (a standard that applies to all peoples) to guide the work of engineers toward that greater purpose and that could serve as a framework for accountability by overarching local and international agencies. A human rights-based approach, on the other hand, provides an internationally recognized framework focused on human dignity to which every individual in any nation is entitled.[9] "Engineering for human rights" offers a springboard for this type of teaching practice.

ALIGNING THE ETHICAL FOUNDATIONS OF ENGINEERING AND HUMAN RIGHTS

Human rights lay out basic standards that engineers can use to evaluate the past, present, or potential future impact of their work in relation to society and the environment. The hybrid teaching approach explored in this chapter focuses on courses that explore human rights in relation to other complementary frameworks shaping contemporary engineering practice – such as the US-based National Academy of Engineering's "Grand Challenges" framework for the 21st century, or the UN Sustainable Development Goals (SDGs).[10] These courses explicitly align the ethical obligations of engineers (as individuals and the field as a whole, framed as micro and macro ethics)[11] with internationally based human rights norms derived from universal processes of negotiation and implementation. The UN human rights system is now over 70 years old. While there are lively debates over the relevance, timeliness, inclusiveness, effectiveness, and/or appropriateness of human rights norms,[12] we nevertheless use universal human rights as our ethical anchor because it grounds engineering ethics in an understanding of people as rightsholders and governments and

December 29, 2021, https://repository.tudelft.nl/islandora/object/uuid%3Adf91501f -655f-4c92-803a-4e1340bcd29f.

[9] United Nations, *Universal Declaration of Human Rights*, General Assembly Resolution 217A (III), U.N. Doc. A/810 (1948).

[10] National Academy of Engineering, "NAE Grand Challenges for Engineering," accessed December 29, 2021, http://www.engineeringchallenges.org/challenges.aspx; see also United Nations, Department of Economic and Social Affairs, "Sustainable Development – The 17 Goals," accessed December 29, 2021, https://sdgs.un.org/goals.

[11] Joseph R. Herkert, "Future Directions in Engineering Ethics Research: Microethics, Macroethics and the Role of Professional Societies," *Science and Engineering Ethics* 7, no. 3 (2001): 403–414. https://doi.org/10.1007/s11948-001-0062 -2.

[12] Sen, *Development as Freedom*.

other powerful actors in society and corporations as duty bearers and in which engineers have active participation.

TEACHING APPROACHES

Foundational Concepts

Engineering for human rights addresses five foundational principles: distributive justice, participation, consideration of duty bearers, accountability, and indivisibility of rights (see Figure 25.1).[13] Each of these principles is grounded in a rich, interdisciplinary literature full of its own internal debates.[14]

Figure 25.1   Five principles of engineering for human rights

---

[13]   Davis Chacon Hurtado, Kazem Kazerounian, Shareen Hertel, Jonathan Mellor, Jack Barry, and Tulasi Ravindran, "Engineering for Human Rights: The Theory and Practice of a Human Rights-Based Approach to Engineering" (Storrs, CT: University of Connecticut, undated manuscript).
[14]   On distributive justice, see Michael Goodhart, *Injustice: Political Theory for the Real World* (Oxford: Oxford University Press, 2018). On participation, see Shareen

In our courses, we start by centering people who work in relation to engineered processes or are affected by such processes, and we center the natural environment in which they live and work. We introduce each of the five foundational principles by explicitly (often in a Socratic manner), helping students position themselves as individual consumers, employees, or stakeholders in relation to each of the principles. When we introduce the idea of **distributive justice**, for example, we use case studies of engineering firms that create product(s) or service(s) to explore who wins or loses in relation to those productive processes and to identify associated positive and negative externalities. We teach students how to measure the outcomes of productive processes in terms of safety, economic gain/loss, or environmental sustainability against concrete baselines. We examine pre-existing factors that affect distributive outcomes. We explicitly lengthen the timeline to analyze the potential impact of engineered products and processes on the social and environmental prospects of future generations.

To do this, we introduce students to international human rights treaty law as well as specific industry standards such as the International Standards Organization/ISO 9000 or 14000 standards, or the Social Accountability/ SA8000 standard on labor rights.[15] These laws and standards provide a baseline for measuring distributive impacts of engineering. To help students understand the dynamics of **participation**, we explore how different firms, government entities, or other organizations where the work of engineering happens either

---

Hertel, *Tethered Fates: Companies, Communities, and Rights at Stake* (Oxford: Oxford University Press, 2019), especially 15–35 and 133–162; or Tara J. Melish, "Putting 'Human Right' Back into the UN Guiding Principles on Business and Human Rights: Shifting Frames and Embedding Participation Rights," in *Business and Human Rights: Beyond the End of the Beginning*, ed. César Rodríguez-Garavito (New York: Cambridge University Press, 2017), 76–96. On duty bearers, see Joanne Bauer, "Business and Human Rights: A New Approach to Advancing Environmental Justice in the United States," in *Human Rights in the United States: Beyond Exceptionalism*, eds. Shareen Hertel and Kathryn Libal (New York: Cambridge University Press, 2011), 175–196. On accountability, see Radhika Balakrishnan, James Heintz, and Diane Elson, *Rethinking Economic Policy for Social Justice: The Radical Potential of Human Rights* (Abingdon: Routledge, 2016). On indivisibility, see Philip Alston, Report of the Special Rapporteur on extreme poverty and human rights, to the Human Rights Council 32nd Session, Agenda item 3 (A/HRC/32/31), accessed December 29, 2021, https:// chrgj.org/wp-content/uploads/2016/06/A_HRC_32_31_AEV.pdf. Given space constraints, this chapter offers a somewhat stylized overview of each principle as it relates to our efforts in teaching engineering for human rights.

[15] International Organization for Standardization (ISO), "ISO 9000 Family Quality Management," accessed December 29, 2021, https://www.iso.org/iso-9001-quality -management.html. See also Social Accountability International. "SA8000 Standard," accessed December 29, 2021, https://sa-intl.org/programs/sa8000.

engage people impacted by engineered processes in mitigating harms or, ideally, prevent such harms through dialogue and inclusive design up front. In the US context, the implications of Title VI of the Civil Rights Act[16] and environmental justice mandates in engineering work are explored. Case studies offer a vehicle for exploring different mechanisms of participation in the context of work sites, at multiple nodes along the sourcing, production, and distribution chain, or in communities proximate to manufacturing sites.

Some treaties explicitly require community participation to obtain free, prior, and informed consent for mining and extractive industrial activity, such as the International Labour Organization's Indigenous and Tribal Peoples Convention (ILO 169).[17] (See Rights of Indigenous Peoples, Chapter 21.) Similarly, some voluntary standards require worker consultation as part of the process of shaping the content of such standards: the Fair Food Program developed by the Coalition of Immokalee Workers, which covers large-scale agricultural practices in the tomato industry, is one example.[18] Other standards do not require any such participation. Our students learn to distinguish between and among such benchmarks and to discern when and how key principles are evident (or not) in engineering processes and practices.

Similarly, we introduce the idea of **consideration of duty bearers** and **accountability** for wellbeing by using the notion of chain of custody in management of hazardous substances. Our chemical engineering students and others who have worked in university or industry laboratories are personally familiar with the idea of chain of custody, which lays out an interlocking set of relationships of parties responsible (duty-bound) to prevent harm and obliged to remedy it (accountable) if a spill, leak, or other industrial accident occurs. We widen the lens from the individual lab to the industry or economic sector, and then to the nation-state, exploring distinctions in how the "precautionary principle" is interpreted (forestalling action until the scope of potential hazards is fully understood, or moving ahead and then assessing damages after the

---

[16]   US Department of Justice. "Title VI of the Civil Rights Act of 1964," accessed December 29, 2021, https://www.justice.gov/crt/fcs/TitleVI-Overview.

[17]   ILO 169 has only been ratified by 23 of the ILO member states since being opened for signature in 1989; over half those states are in Latin America. For details, see https://www.ilo.org/global/topics/indigenous-tribal/lang--en/index.htm (accessed December 29, 2021).

[18]   Becca Berkey, "An In-Depth Look at the Coalition of Immokalee Workers," *Journal of Agriculture, Food Systems, and Community Development* 8, no. 1 (2018): 197–199. For broader discussion of the "worker-driven social responsibility" framework as it relates to contemporary supply chain management, see Hertel, *Tethered Fates*, 133–162; see also Juliane Reinecke and Jimmy Donaghey, "Towards Worker-Driven Supply Chain Governance: Developing Decent Work through Democratic Worker Participation," *Journal of Supply Chain Management* 57, no. 2 (2021): 14–28.

fact).[19] We compare the effects of these differing interpretations on actual people or communities impacted by engineering activity in different contexts.

Finally, we routinely invite guest speakers to take part in our classes because their on-the-ground perspective often illustrates the **indivisibility of human rights** in the context of engineering better than any academic case study could. A representative of a major industrial gas company, for example, can explain how chain of custody issues are integral to plant safety, while also discussing how the truck drivers who move her company's gasses across the USA and Brazil have become point people in anti-human trafficking efforts. By partnering with NGO-led networks that report child sexual abuse along trucking routes, truckers involved in the firm's supply chain address multiple dimensions of safety and wellbeing. Similarly, the director of a major botanical garden may speak to our students about LEED (Leadership in Energy and Environmental Design) certification of curatorial buildings but may also take the time to reflect on the challenge of shoring up food security in urban areas by promoting community gardening in neighborhoods historically marginalized by racial and economic segregation in the same city.

Pedagogy

Our syllabi are structured around core readings that introduce students to the central concepts discussed above. Engineering for human rights-related courses at UConn typically blend classic lectures (that aim to drive home core concepts) with more interactive group problem-based learning (that serves the purpose of reinforcing the concepts while also equipping students to work with peers from other disciplines).[20] Public student-led presentations (such as poster sessions) or in-class mini-conferences offer vehicles for professionalizing students' engagement with each other and members of the wider academic community. Crucially, these dynamic pedagogical approaches align with the aims of human rights education as stated in the United Nations Declaration on Human Rights Education and Training (UNDHRET).[21] In teaching human rights, the Declaration calls for educators to not only instill knowledge and

---

[19] Timothy O'Riordan and James Cameron, *Interpreting the Precautionary Principle* (London: Routledge, 2013).

[20] Karl A. Smith, Sheri D Sheppard, David W. Johnson, and Roger T. Johnson, "Pedagogies of Engagement: Classroom-Based Practices," *Journal of Engineering Education* 94, no. 1 (2005): 87–101.

[21] United Nations, General Assembly Resolution A/RES/66/137 adopted December 19, 2011. *Declaration on Human Rights Education and Training.* Accessed December 29, 2021. https://www.ohchr.org/EN/Issues/Education/Training/Compilation/Pages/UnitedNationsDeclarationonHumanRightsEducationandTraining(2011).aspx.

cultivate advocacy skills, but to also create a classroom environment that empowers students and "respects the rights of both educators and learners."[22]

Because UConn's School of Engineering has a highly developed "Senior Design" capstone for undergraduate engineering majors,[23] many of our cross-listed courses include engineering students who are already socialized to working with industry, government, or NGO "partners" on a year-long "real-world" problem. Our semester-long courses thus benefit from this cultural disposition among engineering students – and expand the practical, hands-on orientation to other students who may come from across the College of Liberal Arts and Sciences, School of Business, School of Education, School of Fine Arts, or College of Agriculture, Health and Natural Resource, for example.

Group Projects

By carefully curating the composition of small-group work to include students from across multiple subfields and student levels within engineering and by integrating students from other schools and colleges into each group, we create the types of mixed-skills professional cohorts that students will likely encounter in their work lives following graduation. We are also particularly attuned to creating groups with gender balance since engineering and other STEM fields have historically been skewed toward students who self-identify as male whereas students in the Human Rights program at UConn have been proportionately more weighted toward those identifying as female.

This interactive, project-based learning is a crucial part of the semester-long experience in our Engineering for Human Rights courses. Group projects involve students in preparing assessments of specific industries' approaches to supply chain management or engineering projects, for example, or in assessing the social and environmental impact reports produced by specific companies or environmental impact studies. By setting aside time weekly for groups to meet even briefly and by using class-based websites for online exchange of working documents, we create a safe and natural space within which students can build working relationships, and often friendships. Our student evaluations consistently attest to the powerful experience of learning how to work with others in a productive, deliberately structured manner and to the benefits of learning how to apply concepts concretely.

---

[22]   *UN Declaration on Human Rights Education and Training.*
[23]   For details on UConn Engineering Senior Design, see: https://seniordesignday .engr.uconn.edu/about (accessed December 29, 2021).

We allocate two to three class sessions to develop a guided case study that students will use as an example for their final project. In the process, we familiarize students with practice-based organizations such as the UN Global Compact or publicly available databases such as the Business and Human Rights Resource Centre[24] and then train students to use those sources to conduct industry-specific as well as firm-specific research. Students focus on engineering-intensive sectors in manufacturing as well as social and environmental dilemmas central to contemporary extractive industries, agricultural production, or service delivery in new sectors such as e-commerce. They learn to use publicly disclosed data from companies to evaluate reported actions against performance rubrics central to international law and/or voluntary standards such as process-based auditing standards (e.g., Global Emissions Systems Inc/GeSI; Electronics Industry Citizenship Coalition/EICC Code of Conduct; Responsible Recycling/R2 program; or the e-Stewards electronics recycling standard created by the Basel Action Network).

Links to all of these auditing standards and corresponding monitoring programs along with related publicly available company or NGO reporting are curated on the class website for each team's use and for all students' review. Students use the materials as a starting point for further research and we provide a rubric for reporting in written form and later, for corresponding group presentations of their findings.

Learning objectives for our students include:

- Identifying and applying each principle (distributive justice, participation, consideration of duty bearers, accountability, indivisibility of human rights) to engineering case studies.
- Evaluating engineering performance over time in relation to social and environmental criteria.
- Comparing and contrasting rival performance frameworks.
- Analyzing change in the social and environmental context of sector innovation, focusing particularly on factors that influence variation in how corporate or government entities adapt engineered processes over time to new constraints.

KEY QUESTIONS

- What are the five core principles of the engineering for human rights paradigm?

---

[24] Business and Human Rights Resource Centre, accessed August 10, 2022, https://www.business-humanrights.org.

- How does the human rights framework both unify professional codes of ethics for engineers and provide a frame for accountability?
- Give two examples of the types of reporting frameworks and/or impact assessment standards that companies can use attest to attest to performance integrity.
- How does education in engineering for human rights benefit: (1) future engineers; (2) future human rights professionals; (3) professionals in other fields?
- How does participation (by community members, corporate actors, government, etc.) figure into the practice of engineering for human rights?

TEACHING RESOURCES

Our courses have been taught in multiple formats, both in-person and online synchronously, in small-group style (under 20 students) and larger lecture-based format (with a course cap of 40 students). Regardless of the mode of delivery, each course relies on a highly developed course website to curate a range of teaching materials, often organized by modules that track closely with each course syllabus.

Readings

Because there is no standard textbook at the intersection of engineering and human rights, we integrate a range of peer-reviewed journal articles, scholarly book chapters, and United Nations reports, industry-specific materials (e.g., corporate reports or reports produced by standard-setting and certification bodies) along with documentation produced by NGOs into our syllabi. A few key examples:

Commentary

- Arjen Y. Hoekstra and Thomas O. Wiedmann, "Humanity's Unsustainable Environmental Footprint," *Science*, June 6, 2014, issue 6188, 1114–1117. https://doi.org/10.1126/science.1248365.

Reports

- Report of the World Commission on Environment and Development: Our Common Future ("Brundtland Report"). New York: Oxford University Press, for the United Nations, 1987. https://archive.org/details/ourcommonfuture00worl.

Videos

We integrate film and video clips at multiple points in the semester, interspersing them to add the immediacy of a first-hand view to the themes addressed in our own lectures.

* Annie Leonard, *The Story of Stuff* (2007), https://www.storyofstuff.org/movies/story-of-stuff.[25] (In a week on planetary boundaries, to illustrate environmental limits and social impact of consumption choices.)
* Interactive sites on Life Cycle Analysis such as "Life Cycle Assessment (LCA) Example of Hand Dryer Options in SimaPro by PRé Sustainability," https://www.youtube.com/watch?v=_VdfKd-8M3M.
* Johan Rockström, *Let the Environment Guide Our Development* (July 2010), https://www.ted.com/talks/johan_rockstrom_let_the_environment _guide_our_development.[26] (In the same assessment and supply chains course.)

Websites

* Business and Human Rights Resource Centre, https://www.business -humanrights.org/en.
* Better Biomass/NTA 8080, https://www.betterbiomass.com (certification site).
* International Labour Organization Decent Work Initiative, https://www.ilo .org/global/topics/decent-work/lang--en/index.htm.
* World Resources Institute, "About Eutrophication," https://www.wri.org/ our-work/project/eutrophication-and-hypoxia/about-eutrophication.

---

[25] Annie Leonard's video has been viewed 50 million times online. Accessed December 29, 2021.
[26] The Ted Talk by the Swedish environmental scientist Johan Rockström has been similarly influential; it has been viewed over 1.5 million times. Accessed December 29, 2021.

26. Finance, investors, and human rights[1]

Erika George and Ariel Meyerstein

OVERVIEW

Capital is the life blood of businesses, making investors that finance business enterprises critical players in their growth and strategic direction. It is important to study the role investors can play in shaping the way companies carry out their responsibilities to respect human rights. For larger companies seeking growth through public or private capital markets, financial institutions play the essential role of facilitating investment and advising businesses on their strategic growth, so understanding their role as it relates to human rights is equally important.[2] Moreover, financial institutions, as business enterprises themselves, are also expected to respect human rights in their own operations.[3]

This chapter provides teachers of business and human rights (BHR) with an approach to teaching about the intersection of finance, investors, and human rights. The basic content assembled here introduces students to the high-level architecture of the value chain of capital flows connecting investors, financial institutions, and companies, and describes ways the investment community can influence corporate human rights performance. Key concepts for understanding various actors' roles are "fiduciary duty" which determines a level of care owed between a financial actor and those for whom they are transacting or investing and "materiality," which broadly refers to the set of issues that could be relevant to investors as they evaluate companies for investments

---

[1]   The authors acknowledge with appreciation the research assistance of Hannah Picket in the preparation of this chapter.

[2]   Small- and medium-sized enterprises (SMEs) and private corporations are beyond the scope of this chapter, as is the large literature on human rights obligations and practices of development finance and multilateral institutions. We focus on large publicly traded corporations and financial institutions in the private sector.

[3]   United Nations Human Rights Council, *Guiding Principles on Business and Human Rights: Implementing the United Nations "Protect, Respect and Remedy" Framework*, Report of the Special Representative of the Secretary-General on the issue of human rights and transnational corporations and other business enterprises, UN doc. A/HRC/17/31 (March 21, 2011) (UN Guiding Principles).

and how these issues contribute to or detract from the value of a company. Understanding these concepts equips BHR students to appreciate the leverage financiers and investors can exert and when these actors should exercise influence to avoid and address human rights risks.

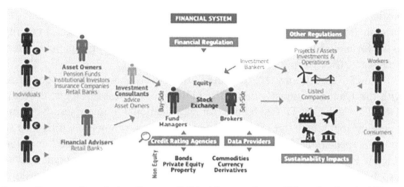

Source: European Commission, European Political Strategy Centre, "Financing Sustainability: Triggering Investments for the Clean Economy," 25 (June 8, 2017), https://gsgii.org/wp-content/uploads/2017/10/strategic_note_issue_25.pdf. Reprinted with permission.

Figure 26.1   Financial system actors

MAPPING THE FINANCIAL MARKETS

Since the advent of the corporation, investors have financed business enterprises that can have both positive and negative impacts on the enjoyment of human rights. The Dutch East India Company, the first company to issue equity shares of its business to the public, secured capital to finance its operations in global trade, with tremendous impacts on human rights (facilitating the slave trade and colonial expansion), as well as on the growth and fragility of global economic markets (the first stock exchange – the Amsterdam Stock Exchange – and the first stock market bubble and crash – Tulipmania).[4]

Today, a range of actors play different roles in economic markets and have varying responsibilities to each other and the marketplace (Figure 26.1). All capital market actors have a responsibility to understand and address their human rights impacts. To appreciate the human rights roles and responsibilities of different actors in the financial system it is useful to understand who the key players are and what their relationship is to a corporation.

---

[4]   Nick Robins, *The Corporation That Changed the World: How the East India Company Shaped the Modern Corporation* (London: Pluto Press, 2006).

Corporations

Businesses seek capital from investors when operations are too costly for the enterprise to finance without additional assistance. In exchange, businesses can offer investors equity – a share in the ownership of the business and its profits provided in the form of shares. A corporation can finance its activities through debt – bonds bought by investors or credit issued by banks – or equity, in the form of shares, whether privately placed or offered through public stock exchanges. (See Corporations, Chapter 7.)

Financial institutions are expected to respect human rights, consistent with the United Nations Guiding Principles on Business and Human Rights (UNGPs) and OECD Guidelines for Multinational Enterprises. New and emerging regulations on modern slavery and human rights due diligence set similar expectations for companies and financial institutions.[5] (See Mandatory Human Rights Due Diligence, Chapter 11.) Publicly traded companies are also bound by national laws to disclose material information to investors.[6] Companies are also subject to legal expectations to not mislead investors. What information should be disclosed will turn on questions of "materiality" of the information to the nature of capital (equity vs. debt, short-term vs. long-term) provided. For example, institutional investors like public pension funds (universal owners that invest broadly in the economy through purchasing shares (i.e. equity) in public companies, seeking to grow assets for multi-generational beneficiaries), often take a longer-term and more holistic view of the potential materiality of issues to the value of a company, including the impact of such issues on intangible value like brand reputation. By contrast, a fixed-income investment like a bond has a fixed and likely shorter duration of several years to a decade, so investors are more focused on the impact of human rights issues on credit risk, or the company's revenues and profit and therefore its ability to pay investors their promised returns in the short term.

---

[5] For a survey of BHR regulatory developments, see, for example, Clare Bartram et al., *The Rapidly Changing World of Human Rights Regulation: A Resource for Investors* (ISS ESG, June 24, 2022), https://www.issgovernance.com/file/publications/iss-esg-the-rapidly-changing-world-of-human-rights-regulation.pdf; "Around the Globe: Business Human Rights Update," Norton Rose Fulbright, April 2022, https://www.nortonrosefulbright.com/en-gb/knowledge/publications/0ed8097a/around-the-globe-business-human-rights-update.

[6] See discussion of materiality below.

Investment Banks

Investment banks raise capital on behalf of their clients (corporate issuers) in the form of equity or debt from investors in public or private markets. Investment banking involves taking companies public through initial public offerings (IPOs) and other strategic deals, such as mergers and acquisitions (M&A). The process by which investment banks help corporations issue securities is called "underwriting."[7] When underwriting, an investment bank assesses the risk and determines the appropriate price of a particular security. Based on the bank's analysis, the corporate issuer seeks to sell the securities to investors. The underwriting process is a crucial vetting exercise that aims to ensure the securities offering will raise the amount of capital the company needs to grow. In this context, the bank acts as an advisor to the company and may, depending on the scope and nature of the relationship, have a fiduciary duty to their clients.[8] Soft law standards and emerging regulations on modern slavery and mandatory human rights due diligence set expectations that banks also take into account their responsibility to respect human rights by conducting thorough due diligence into the human rights risks associated with transactions and, by trying to use their leverage with their clients to encourage the clients to do appropriate due diligence, addressing any actual or potential impacts.[9] Human rights due diligence may lead banks to recommend to their clients that certain risks and efforts to mitigate them are disclosed along with other risk information provided to investors in public securities offering memoranda.

---

[7]   Underwriting is the process through which an individual or institution takes on financial risk for a fee. This risk most typically involves loans, insurance, or investments. See Adam Hayes, "Financial Risk," Investopedia, June 4, 2022, https://www.investopedia.com/terms/f/financialrisk.asp; Julia Kagan, "Loan," Investopedia, April 19, 2021, https://www.investopedia.com/terms/l/loan.asp.

[8]   The topic of fiduciary duty as it applies to banks is broad and nuanced. For an in-depth review, see Andrew F. Tuch, "Fiduciary Principles in Banking," *The Oxford Handbook of Fiduciary Law*, eds. Evan J. Criddle, Paul B. Miller, and Robert H. Sitkoff (New York: Oxford University Press, 2019), 130–138.

[9]   See, for example, Organisation for Economic Co-operation and Development (OECD), *Responsible Business Conduct for Institutional Investors: Key Considerations for Due Diligence under the OECD Guidelines for Multinational Enterprises* (2017); OECD, *Due Diligence for Responsible Corporate Lending and Securities Underwriting: Key Considerations for Banks Implementing the OECD Guidelines for Multinational Enterprises* (2019).

Institutional Investors

Institutional investors buy and sell stocks, bonds, or other securities on behalf of clients, customers, members, or shareholders. Institutional investors may be public entities, such as public pension funds; or private entities, like mutual funds or commercial banks.[10] Public pension funds have a fiduciary duty to their members and often view their role as preserving assets for multiple generations, and therefore often take a long-term and broad perspective on the drivers of financial performance and value creation.

Retail Investors

The average person investing in the stock market, with or without the assistance of an investment advisor, for personal or family purposes, is a retail investor.[11]

Asset Managers

Asset managers invest on behalf of others. Managers owe their clients – institutional investors and retail investors – a fiduciary duty to invest prudently.

MATERIALITY

Materiality is a much-debated concept in national and international regulatory frameworks and voluntary standard-setting initiatives. The traditional view of materiality established in the U.S. Securities and Exchange Act[12] and elaborated over time by the U.S. Supreme Court is narrowly focused on financial materiality – how information impacts a company's value, and therefore, what information a company must disclose to investors. This requirement was originally created by the U.S. Congress to protect investors in response to fraudulent misrepresentation in the stock exchanges leading to the 1929 stock market crash.[13] The Supreme Court has stated that information is material if

---

[10]   Private institutional investors include endowment funds, insurance companies, mutual funds, hedge funds, private equity funds, and private pension funds.

[11]   The U.S. Securities Exchange Act (1934), rule 151-1(b)(1), defines a retail customer as a "natural person" who receives a recommendation of any securities transaction or investment strategy involving securities from a broker or dealer and uses the recommendation primarily for personal, family, or household purposes. 17 C.F.R. § 240.151-1.

[12]   Securities Exchange Act of 1934, 15 U.S.C. § 78a et seq.

[13]   https://www.investopedia.com/terms/s/securitiesact1933.asp.

its exclusion would have altered the "total mix" of information considered by a reasonable investor in making an investment decision.[14] The total-mix concept suggests that material information is not defined by whether it would have changed an investor's decision. Rather, information is deemed to be material if it is significantly likely *to be considered* by a reasonable investor in investment decisions – a higher threshold than if it "might" be considered – by such an investor. In a subsequent case, the U.S. Supreme Court expanded on the definition of "materiality" by indicating that materiality can be assessed by two factors: the probability that an event may take place and the magnitude of impact of the event on the company.[15]

By contrast, global corporate sustainability standard-setters, such as the Global Reporting Initiative (GRI), have long embraced a broader concept of materiality – "double materiality" that considers not only a narrow definition of financial materiality but a broader view of the impacts of a company on people and the environment informed by the views not only of shareholders, but also other stakeholders. The European Union's (EU's) *Non-Financial Reporting Directive* (2014) embraced this broader notion of materiality.[16] The EU's non-binding Guidelines (2017) also encouraged companies to take a long-term and comprehensive view of materiality,[17] particularly its Guidelines around climate change (2019), which contrasted this view with the more limited financial materiality approach taken by the Taskforce on Climate-Related Financial Disclosures.[18]

The evolving notion of materiality was further elaborated in the concept of "dynamic materiality" introduced by the World Economic Forum (WEF) in early 2020 and has subsequently been endorsed by all five leading global sustainability reporting standards – CDP,[19] Climate Disclosure Standards Board (CDSB), the Global Reporting Initiative (GRI), the International Integrated

---

[14] See *TSC v. Northway*, 426 U.S. 439 (1976).

[15] *Basic v. Levinson*, 485 U.S. 224 (1988).

[16] EU Directive 2014/95/EU of the European Parliament and of the Council of 22 October 2014 amending Directive 2013/34/EU as regards disclosure of non-financial and diversity information by certain large undertakings and groups, OJ 2014 No. L 330 (entered into force December 6, 2014).

[17] See European Commission, Guidelines on non-financial reporting (methodology for reporting non-financial information) (June 5, 2017) OJ C 215/01, https://eur-lex.europa.eu/legal-content/EN/TXT/HTML/?uri=CELEX:52017XC0705(01)&from=EN.

[18] See Financial Stability Board, European Commission, Guidelines on Non-Financial Reporting: Supplement on Reporting Climate-Related Information (June 20, 2019) C 209/01, 4-8, https://eur-lex.europa.eu/legal-content/EN/TXT/PDF/?uri=CELEX:52019XC0620(01)&from=EN.

[19] CDP, accessed August 18, 2022, https://www.cdp.net/en.

Reporting Council (IIRC), and the Sustainability Accounting Standards Board (SASB). Dynamic materiality asserts that sustainability topics can become financially material over time. According to WEF, "the ability to anticipate stakeholder reactions to emerging sustainability issues and how they could affect a business and its performance is therefore critical."[20]

The creation of the International Sustainability Standards Board (ISSB) in 2021 under the auspices of the International Financial Reporting Standards (IFRS) Foundation (already responsible for the IFRS Accounting Standards required by more than 140 jurisdictions around the world) means that new global Sustainability Disclosure Standards will be developed that will have to address how to reconcile the competing concepts of materiality.[21]

EVOLVING NOTIONS OF FIDUCIARY DUTY

A common concept affecting most capital markets actors is fiduciary duty, which effectively means an obligation to act placing another actor's best interests at the center of decision-making. Although there is variation across common law and civil law jurisdictions and specific countries, there is a common understanding that the duty consists of two correlated obligations:

(1)   the duty of loyalty – fiduciaries should act honestly and in good faith in the interests of their beneficiaries, should impartially balance the conflicting interests of different beneficiaries, should avoid conflicts of interest, and should not act for the benefit of themselves or a third party; and

(2)   the duty of prudence – fiduciaries must act with due care, skill, and diligence.[22]

---

[20]   See "Materiality: Traditional New, Double or Dynamic," PracticalESG.com, April 21, 2021, https://practicalesg.com/2021/04/materiality-traditional-new-double-or-dynamic; Charlotte Bancilhon and Jacob Park, "Dynamic Materiality: How Companies Can Future-Proof Materiality Assessments," *Materiality* (blog), *BSR*, July 22, 2021, https://www.bsr.org/en/our-insights/blog-view/dynamic-materiality-how-companies-can-future-proof-materiality-assessments.

[21]   See "ISSB: Frequently Asked Questions," IFRS, accessed August 17, 2022, https://www.ifrs.org/groups/international-sustainability-standards-board/issb-frequently-asked-questions; see also IFRS Sustainability, *Exposure Draft IFRS Sustainability Disclosure Standard: [Draft] IFRS S1 General Requirements for Disclosure of Sustainability-related Financial Information* (March 2022), which sets out the overall requirements for an entity to disclose sustainability-related financial information about all its significant sustainability-related risks and opportunities.

[22]   United Nations Environment Programme Finance Initiative (UNEP FI) and Principles for Responsible Investment (PRI), *Fiduciary Duty in the 21st Century*

Officers and directors of public companies have a fiduciary duty to the company's stockholders to disclose material information and investors investing on behalf of clients, have a fiduciary duty to consider all material information. All institutional investors or asset managers have a fiduciary duty to their clients, beneficiaries, or shareholders to invest prudently in the interests of those whose assets they are investing.

Whether fiduciary duty allows or requires consideration of historically non-financial issues, such as environmental and social governance (ESG) issues, including human rights impacts, has been vigorously debated over the last quarter century. A key question is whether a specific ESG issue related to a particular company is "material" – information that investors would want to know before making an investment decision.[23] Failure to consider material information would constitute a breach of fiduciary duty.

In the early 2000s, with the growth of socially responsible investing, notions of investor fiduciary duty were being reexamined, including through the publication in 2005 of the "Freshfields Report" commissioned by the UN Environment Programme's Finance Initiative (UNEPFI). The report examined the legal responsibilities of institutional investors in nine capital markets, concluding that taking environmental and social issues into account when investing assets is "clearly permissible and is arguably required" and that failure to do so "will often be a breach of legal duties."[24] Laws in Australia, France, Germany, and the U.K. required "investment decision-makers" for private and public pension funds and other investors to disclose the extent to which they take ESG considerations into account.[25] In the other countries there was no impediment to investors doing so.[26]

Building on this momentum, UNEPFI helped birth a new initiative to help shape investors' approach to this expanded view of fiduciary duty – the UN

(October 2019), 11–12, https://www.unepfi.org/publications/investment-publications/fiduciary-duty-in-the-21st-century-final-report.

[23] See UNEP FI and PRI, *Fiduciary Duty in the 21st Century*.

[24] Freshfields Bruckhaus Deringer, *A Legal Framework for the Integration of Environmental, Social and Governance into Institutional Investment (Produced for the Asset Management Working Group of the UNEP Finance Initiative)* (October 2005), https://www.unepfi.org/fileadmin/documents/freshfields_legal_resp_20051123.pdf. A follow-up project has further expanded understandings of fiduciary duty of investors in other jurisdictions. See UNEP FI and PRI, *Fiduciary Duty in the 21st Century*.

[25] Similar legislation was pending in Italy.

[26] Under the Employee Retirement Income Security Act of 1974 (ERISA), 29 U.S.C. 1001 et seq., in the U.S. for example, plan fiduciaries have a duty of loyalty and prudence to plan beneficiaries.

Principles for Responsible Investment (PRIs), which states in their preamble that investor signatories:

> have a duty to act in the best long-term interests of our beneficiaries. In this fiduciary role, we believe that environmental, social, and corporate governance issues can affect the performance of investment portfolios (to varying degrees across companies, sectors, regions, asset classes and through time). We also recognize that applying these Principles may better align investors with broader objectives of society.[27]

The commitment to act in the best long-term interests of beneficiaries captures the practical concern that social and environmental issues have implications for investment performance. The Principles for Responsible Investment (PRI) set forth steps to be taken by investors to advance both the long-term interests of beneficiaries and broader societal interests, including incorporating ESG issues into investment analysis; engaging in "active" ownership; and seeking disclosure and reporting on ESG issues. PRI grew to include thousands of signatories across the investment landscape. By 2010, stewardship codes were introduced, first in U.K. law, that formalized this enhanced expectation of investors' role in corporate governance, based on the logic of fiduciary duty.

Key milestones demonstrate how investor sentiment has shifted on these issues, increasingly shaping companies' understanding of their role in creating value and for whom that value is created. The annual letters to CEOs by Larry Fink, the CEO of BlackRock, the world's largest asset manager, signal the growing importance of "non-financial" issues to investors. In these letters, Fink writes that "as a fiduciary for our clients who entrust us to manage their assets – to highlight the themes that I believe are vital to driving durable long-term returns and to helping them reach their goals." In his 2020 letter, Fink acknowledged that climate risk is investment risk, and in his 2021 letter he noted that shareholders will benefit if CEOs "can create enduring, sustainable value for *all* of your stakeholders."[28] In the last five years, the total assets under management focused on ESG strategies has grown exponentially to approximately $40 trillion in 2020, or 40 percent of total managed assets

---

[27] "What Are the Principles for Responsible Investment?" About Us, United Nations Principles on Responsible Investment, accessed August 17, 2022, https://www.unpri.org/about/the-six-principles.

[28] "A Fundamental Reshaping of Finance," Larry Fink's 2020 Letter to CEOs, BlackRock, accessed August 17, 2022, https://www.blackrock.com/corporate/investor-relations/2020-larry-fink-ceo-letter; "Larry Fink's 2021 Letter to CEOs," BlackRock, accessed August 17, 2022, https://www.blackrock.com/us/individual/2021-larry-fink-ceo-letter.

globally,[29] and other qualitative research points to major shifts in investor sentiment on key issues.[30] Companies, in turn, have internalized some of these messages, with corporate reporting on ESG issues growing exponentially in recent years.[31] In addition, the mainstream Business Roundtable, a trade association of the 181+ largest U.S. companies, updated its views on corporate governance in 2020 in a "Statement on the Purpose of a Corporation," which acknowledged that all companies "share a fundamental commitment to all of our stakeholders" beyond just shareholders.[32]

The contemporary expansive notion of fiduciary duty that recognizes the relevance of non-financial issues of interest to stakeholders beyond just shareholders often reinforces and aligns with the responsibility to respect human rights set forth in the UNGPs to avoid causing or contributing to rights abuses.

INVESTOR RESPONSIBILITY TO RESPECT HUMAN RIGHTS

Since being unanimously endorsed by the UN Human Rights Council in 2011, the UNGPs have come to provide an "authoritative focal point" around which to address issues of business and human rights.[33] (See The UN Guiding Principles on Business and Human Rights, Chapter 5.) In order to meet the "responsibility to respect human rights," companies must at a minimum avoid involvement in rights abuses and address abuses and adverse impacts that occur. To do this, businesses must identify and understand the impacts of their business operations on human rights, including through its business

---

[29]   See "Global Asset Manager AUM Tops US$100 Trillion for the First Time," Thinking Ahead Institute, accessed August 17, 2022, https://www.thinkingahea dinstitute.org/news/article/global-asset-manager-aum-tops-us100-trillion-for-the-first -time.

[30]   See Robert G. Eccles and Svetlana Klimenko, "The Investor Revolution: Shareholders Are Getting Serious about Sustainability," *Harvard Business Review*, June 2019, https://hbr.org/2019/05/the-investor-revolution (reporting on interviews with 70 senior executives at 43 global institutional investing firms).

[31]   In 2020, 92 percent of S&P 500 companies published sustainability reports or disclosures, compared to just 20 percent in 2011. See Governance and Accountability Institute, Inc., *Sustainability Reporting in Focus: S&P 500 + Russell 1000* (2021), https://www.ga-institute.com/fileadmin/ga_institute/images/FlashReports/2021/ Russell-1000/G_A-Russell-Report-2021-Final.pdf?vgo_ee=s64Dstpxhr%2BUa 57KJOE4zufUqaWO5j4IGC9dfRtqdQY%3D.

[32]   "Business Roundtable Redefines the Purpose of a Corporation to Promote 'An Economy That Serves All Americans," Corporate Governance, Business Roundtable, August 19, 2019, https://www.businessroundtable.org/business-roundtable-redefines -the-purpose-of-a-corporation-to-promote-an-economy-that-serves-all-americans.

[33]   UN Guiding Principles.

relationships. Companies can best meet their responsibility to respect rights by conducting human rights due diligence and assessing human rights impacts of its business activities and relationships. The UNGPs – and specifically the concept of human rights due diligence – have been incorporated into many regulatory requirements, soft law standards, and industry guidelines across sectors and are increasingly used by investors and financial institutions.[34]

The UNGPs urge business enterprises to leverage relationships to ensure respect for human rights. According to the commentary interpreting Guiding Principle 19: "Leverage is considered to exist where the enterprise has the ability to effect change in the wrongful practices of an entity that causes a harm. … If the business enterprise has leverage to prevent or mitigate the adverse impact, it should exercise it." Financial institutions and investors are uniquely situated to exercise leverage, although not all relationships between corporates and financial institutions of different kinds are equivalent.

LEVERAGING INVESTOR INFLUENCE TO PROMOTE RESPECT FOR HUMAN RIGHTS

Shareholder Resolutions

Shareholder resolutions are one of the key ways that investors act on their fiduciary duty and exhibit "active ownership" consistent with the PRI and the notion of exercising leverage under the UNGPs.[35] In the United States, the Securities and Exchange Commission regulates the shareholder resolution submission process for publicly traded companies.[36] Shareholders seeking to make proposals must meet certain eligibility and procedural requirements.[37] A company must include all qualifying shareholder proposals in the proxy materials it distributes to shareholders. If a shareholder's proposal meets the SEC requirements, a company cannot refuse to include the resolution in its proxy materials and the matter must be put to a vote at an annual or other meeting of the company. In this way, proposals can bring human rights issues to the attention of the investing public.

---

[34] See UN Working Group on Business and Human Rights, *Taking Stock of Investor Implementation of the UN Guiding Principles on Business and Human Rights*, U.N. Doc. A/HRC/47/39/Add.2 (June 2021).

[35] Proposals, or resolutions, are requests to vote on a particular policy at a company's annual meeting submitted by eligible individuals or institutions that own shares in the company.

[36] Securities and Exchange Act of 1934, § 14(a).

[37] 17 CFR 240.14a-8.

Corporate management usually opposes shareholder resolutions. Companies can seek to exclude shareholder proposals by appealing to the SEC's Division of Corporation Finance Staff to issue a "no-action letter." SEC rules allow corporations to exclude proposals and statements in support of proposals that are materially false or misleading.[38] The SEC has allowed proposals regarded as socially or politically significant, so company requests to exclude must explain why a proposal is not significant to the company.[39]

Support for ESG-related resolutions has grown consistently in recent years.[40] While environmental and climate change matters have driven much of the growth, social issues (including human rights concerns) have also recently gained traction, driven by the SEC's adoption of new rules on the disclosure of material human capital metrics, the COVID-19 pandemic's exacerbation of workforce welfare and equality concerns, and the rising focus on racial justice fueled by the murder of George Floyd. Figure 26.2 shows examples of human rights-related shareholder proposals.[41]

As shareholder resolutions are often a means of engaging with senior management, they can open the door to non-binding, negotiated reforms with investors. Shareholder resolution withdrawal rates have also reached all-time highs, suggesting that companies are being more receptive to investor demands, most likely given the increased focus on ESG issues and increased odds that resolutions will garner large support if put on the proxy ballot.[42] Resolutions have also increasingly focused on disclosure, risk assessment, and oversight rather than demanding that management enact certain policies or practices

---

[38] See 17 CFR 240.14 a-8(i)(3); 17 CFR 240.14a-9; Staff Legal Bulletin No. 14B explaining when it would be inappropriate to exclude proposals and supporting statement in certain circumstances. Securities and Exchange uDivision of Corporation Finance, Staff Legal Bulletin No. 14B, September 15, 2004.

[39] *Id.*; see, for example, *Amalgamated Clothing and Textile Workers Union v. Wal-Mart Stores, Inc.* 821 F. Supp. 877 (S.D.N.Y. 1993) (ruling in favor of proponent shareholders of a resolution seeking disclosure of Walmart's anti-discrimination policies over company objection).

[40] Jackie Cook and John Hale, "2019 ESG Proxy Voting Trends by 50 U.S. Fund Families," March 23, 2020, https://corpgov.law.harvard.edu/2020/03/23/2019-esg-proxy-voting-trends-by-50-u-s-fund-families.

[41] See Matteo Tonello, "2021 Proxy Season Preview and Shareholder Voting Trends (2017–2020)," Harvard Law School Forum on Corporate Governance, February 11, 2021, https://corpgov.law.harvard.edu/2021/02/11/2021-proxy-season-preview-and-shareholder-voting-trends-2017-2020.

[42] Kosmas Papadopoulos, "The Long View: US Proxy Voting Trends on E&S Issues from 2000 to 2018," Harvard Law School Forum on Corporate Governance, January 31, 2019, https://corpgov.law.harvard.edu/2019/01/31/the-long-view-us-proxy-voting-trends-on-es-issues-from-2000-to-2018.

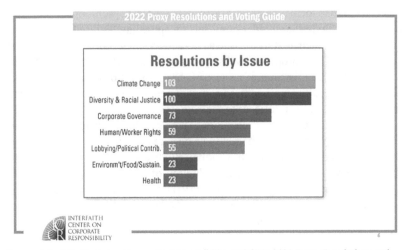

Source: Interfaith Center on Corporate Responsibility, "ICCR's 2022 Proxy Resolutions and Voting Guide" (Presentation, February 16, 2022), https://www.iccr.org/sites/default/files/_2022_ proxybook_webinar_ppt_final.pdf. Reprinted with permission.

Figure 26.2   Proxy resolutions by issue

(which can more easily be excluded by the SEC's advisory "no-action" letters as "micromanagement").

Despite being non-binding and frequently defeated in votes, shareholder resolutions play an important role in corporate governance and have the potential to lead to improvements in corporate policies and serve to increase public awareness about issues related to corporate practices. To that end, shareholder proposals are becoming an increasingly important part of environmental and human rights advocacy.

Investor Advocacy

Investors also engage in direct advocacy with companies via ongoing steward-ship activities that do not necessarily escalate to shareholder proposals but are still forms of exercising leverage.[43] For example, BlackRock and other asset managers now increasingly disclose their engagement with companies on

---

[43]   See "An Introduction to Responsible Investment – Stewardship," PRI, February 19, 2021,   https://www.unpri.org/an-introduction-to-responsible-investment/an-introduction -to-responsible-investment-stewardship/7228.article.

issues of climate change, diversity, and human rights.[44] The Investor Alliance for Human Rights has organized smaller faith-based and responsible investment firms, as well as public pension funds for a total of $10 trillion in assets under management (AUM),[45] in calls for better practices among large companies across sectors whose performance on human rights integration and due diligence was scored as poor by third-party benchmarks, such as the Corporate Human Rights Benchmark.[46]

Financing Standards

Corporate and investment banks can also exercise leverage by adopting financing standards for clients with related due diligence and engagement.[47] Similarly, for project-related transactions, 134 financial institutions (mostly banks) in 38 countries have adopted the Equator Principles (2003), a set of best practices for environment and social risk review and mitigation that incorporates the IFC Performance Standards and UNGPs. Implementation of the Equator Principles is reinforced by binding loan covenants to ensure borrower compliance, a built-in engagement process for banks to work with clients on

---

[44] See, for example, BlackRock, *BlackRock Investment Stewardship Report January 1–December 31, 2021*, https://www.blackrock.com/corporate/literature/publication/annual-stewardship-report-2021.pdf (noting that in 2021, across all ESG issues, the stewardship team "held more than 3,600 engagements with more than 2,300 unique companies across 57 markets, covering 68% of our clients' equity assets under management (AUM)." The Climate Action 100+ is a significant investor initiative of over 700 investors with $68 trillion AUM focused on encouraging the public companies with the most GHG emissions to take climate action. See "Global Investors Driving Business Transition," Climate Action 100+, accessed August 17, 2022, https://www.climateaction100.org.

[45] See "Members," Investor Alliance for Human Rights, accessed August 17, 2022, https://investorsforhumanrights.org/members.

[46] See "Investors with Nearly US$7 Trillion in Assets Call Out Leading Companies over Human Rights Performance," Join the Alliance, Investor Alliance for Human Rights, accessed August 17, 2022, https://investorsforhumanrights.org/cross-sectoral/investors-over-us45-trillion-assets-call-out-leading-companies-over-human-rights.

[47] See, for example, Standard Chartered Sector Policy Framework, "Our Framework," Standard Chartered, accessed August 17, 2022, https://www.sc.com/en/sustainability/position-statements/#sectorstatements; ING, *Human Rights Review 2021/22*, 46–50, https://www.ing.com/Sustainability/Sustainable-business/Human-rights.htm (bank due diligence and engagement on human rights). For an overview of bank efforts to integrate human rights due diligence specifically, see BankTrack, *The BankTrack Human Rights Benchmark 2019*, 3rd ed. (to be updated in 2022), https://www.banktrack.org/news/4_out_of_5_banks_failing_on_human_rights_report_shows.

remedial actions to bring client performance back into compliance, and the potential for penalties when other engagement fails.[48]

TEACHING APPROACHES

We have taught this topic in law school courses on business and human rights and sustainability. This topic would also be well suited to a business school strategy course. "Finance, investors, and human rights" could be introduced in class sessions dedicated to exploring the use of market strategies to improve the human rights performance of publicly traded corporations after outlining the elements of the business responsibility to respect human rights and basic corporate governance.

We recommend that instructors approach this content in phases:

• Phase I: presentation and explanation

Determine the knowledge base of students and tailor the presentation and explanation of information accordingly. When teaching business school students, consider spending more time on the regulatory framework of securities law and the legal obligation of fiduciary duties. When teaching law school students, consider devoting time to negotiating trade-offs between competing stakeholder concerns and risk assessment.

• Phase II: problem solving and guided practice

After explaining basic concepts, develop activities for students to apply the information. We have found lectures followed by discussions and small-group exercises to be an effective format for presenting content.

• Phase III: participation and collaboration

Invite students to collaborate in developing some work product (e.g., a strategy pitch to senior management surveying a company's or sector's human rights issues, benchmarking performance and proposing organizational change to

---

[48]   See "Members and Reporting," Equator Principles, accessed August 17, 2022, https://equator-principles.com/members-reporting. Under the Equator Principles, banks categorize project risks (Principle 1), require clients to assess project risks, including human rights impacts (Principle 2), and create a management system and action plan to mitigate risks (Principle 4), among other requirements consistent with the expectations under the UNGPs related to stakeholder engagement and grievance mechanisms, which all become embedded into loan covenants (Principle 8). See *The Equator Principles EP4 July 2020*, https://equator-principles.com/app/uploads/The-Equator-Principles_EP4_July2020.pdf.

mitigate impacts and respond to investor pressure) that connects the content presented to a contemporary human rights challenge.

Learning objectives may include:

- Identifying different capital markets actors and their roles in the financial value chain.
- Explaining the human rights responsibilities of each actor as detailed in international standards.
- Explaining the concepts of fiduciary duty and materiality, and how they relate to human rights.
- Articulating the relationship between fiduciary duty and human rights due diligence.
- Assessing how financial actors can respect human rights and influence businesses to demonstrate respect for human rights.
- Understanding how investors can exercise leverage to promote respect for human rights.

EXERCISE 26.1

INVESTORS ASSESS HUMAN RIGHTS RISK –

"ACME ACTIVE APPAREL"

This exercise is intended to illustrate how capital markets and investors assess human rights risks, exercise leverage, and play a critical role in human rights due diligence.

Consider the following fact pattern:

- Angela is an outstanding athlete. She is also outraged. She recently learned that the athletic apparel brand (Acme Active Apparel) that she's worn on soccer fields around the world is linked to sourcing material from cotton fields where enslaved children have been worked to death. As a children's rights activist with a significant youth fan following, she believes that she's suffered reputational injury from representing the brand, wearing the brand, and being an Acme investor. She's called for her fans to boycott the brand. Her coach has suggested that a better course could be putting together a shareholder proposal to push the brand to do better.

What do you recommend Angela do were she to pursue this course of action? Draft a shareholder resolution to present at an Acme annual

meeting.

- Angela decided she could do better. She's now planning to bring her own brand of athletic apparel to market focused on sustainable sourcing. The private label company she founded is flourishing and attracting new customers. A few consumers have questioned the labor conditions at the factories where the products are manufactured, but for the most part Angela trusts that she's received good advice from her advisors, and she knows she's not as bad as the brand she's left behind. She understands that the brand sources from 20 different countries and serious labor rights violations have been documented in five of the 20 countries by international experts. Approximately 20 percent of her products are sourced primarily from these five countries. She's decided to have an initial public offering.

You lead the investment banking team advising Angela. Consider the following questions:

- How should the bank advise Angela on her company's human rights responsibilities?
- What are the investment bank's human rights responsibilities in this engagement?
- What human rights are at risk?
- Who can avoid or address the risks presented?
- How do you decide which risks to prioritize?
- How do you place a value on the impact of these issues to the brands? Acme's brand? Angela's brand?
- How do you determine what disclosures to the public about human rights risks would be warranted?
- Where might there be opportunities to exert influence to improve human rights policies and practices?

TEACHING RESOURCES

Readings

Books

- Behar, Andrew. *The Shareholder Action Guide: Unleash Your Hidden Powers to Hold Corporations Accountable*. Oakland, CA: Berrett-Koehler Publishes, 2016.

Commentary

- Lee, Allison Herren. *Living in a Material World: Myths and Misconceptions about "Materiality."* Keynote Remarks at the 2021 ESG Disclosure Priorities Event, Washington, D.C. https://www.sec.gov/news/speech/lee-living-material-world-052421.
- Lopez, David, Jared Gerber. and Jonathan Povilonis. "The Materiality Debate and ESG Disclosure: Investors May Have the Last Word." Harvard Law School Forum on Corporate Governance. January 31, 2022. https://corpgov.law.harvard.edu/2022/01/31/the-materiality-debate-and-esg-disclosure-investors-may-have-the-last-word/#4.
- Mandyck, John. "What if Banks Had to Disclose the Climate Impact of Their Investments?" *Harvard Business Review.* May 20, 2022.
- Mishra, Subodh. "The Rapidly Changing World of Human Rights Regulation: A Resource for Investors." Harvard Law School Forum on Corporate Governance. July 18, 2022. https://corpgov.law.harvard.edu/2022/07/18/the-rapidly-changing-world-of-human-rights-regulation-a-resource-for-investors.

Reports

- *Dutch Banking Sector Agreement on International Responsible Business Conduct Regarding Human Rights.* Final Monitoring and Progress Report, July 13, 2020. https://www.imvoconvenanten.nl/-/media/imvo/files/banking/banking-final-report-2020.pdf?la=en&hash=DCBBC9C81C44E934344D51E88DD6189C.
- Institute for Human Rights and Business. *Investing the Rights Way: A Guide for Investors on Business and Human Rights.* London: IHRB, 2013. https://www.ihrb.org/pdf/Investing-the-Rights-Way/Investing-the-Rights-Way.pdf.
- Reinboth, Bettina and Nikolaj Halkjaer Pedersen. *Why and How Investors Should Act on Human Rights.* UN Principles for Responsible Investing, 2020. https://www.unpri.org/human-rights/why-and-how-investors-should-act-on-human-rights/6636.article.
- UN Working Group on Business and Human Rights. *Taking Stock of Investor Implementation of the UN Guiding Principles on Business and Human Rights.* U.N. Doc. A/HRC/47/39/Add.2. Geneva: June 2021.

Teaching Cases

- Wielga, Mark and John Richardson. *Teaching Note: Banks and Human Rights.* In Teaching Business and Human Rights Handbook (Teaching

Business and Human Rights Forum, 2017). https://teachbhr.org/resources/
teaching-bhr-handbook/teaching-notes/banks-and-human-rights.

Videos

- Bakan, Joel and Jennifer Abbott, dirs. *The New Corporation: The Unfortunately Necessary Sequel.* Grant Street with Screen Siren Pictures, 2020. https://thenewcorporation.movie.
- UNGP Reporting Framework. "UNGPs Reporting Framework: Salient Human Rights Issues." Shift and Mazars. Video, 4:20: https://vimeo.com/154834462.

Websites

- Interfaith Center on Corporate Responsibility. https://www.iccr.org.
- Investor Alliance for Human Rights. https://investorsforhumanrights.org.
- Principles for Responsible Investment. https://www.unpri.org.
- United Nations Environment Program Finance Initiative. "Human Rights Guidance Tool for the Financial Sector." https://www.unepfi.org/humanrightstoolkit/finance.php.
- United Nations Office of the High Commissioner for Human Rights. "Human Rights and the Finance Sector," Working Group on the issue of human rights and transnational corporations and other business enterprises. https://www.ohchr.org/en/special-procedures/wg-business/financial-sector-and-human-rights.

27. Accounting for human rights

John Ferguson

OVERVIEW

Accounting plays an increasingly important role in the field of business and human rights (BHR). In particular, accounting, reporting, and assurance processes are central to the implementation by companies of their responsibility to respect human rights under the United Nations Guiding Principles on Business and Human Rights (UNGPs). Further, the prevalence of sustainability reporting frameworks, such as the Global Reporting Initiative (GRI), along with the growing number of regulatory processes mandating business reporting on human rights performance, make accounting, auditing, and reporting processes fundamental to the emerging legal, organizational, and institutional field of business and human rights.

This chapter provides an overview of current developments in BHR that have an accounting dimension. In doing so, the chapter provides an assessment of the challenges of accounting for BHR, along with a consideration of possible approaches to teaching these issues to different cohorts of students. The following section, which is primarily aimed at teachers from a non-accounting background, provides a brief description of the different strands of accounting practice. Specifically, this section provides an overview of the different types of accounting information, along with the intended audiences associated with each strand of practice. This is followed by a discussion of the role of accounting envisioned in the UNGPs and its wider implementation; in particular, this section draws attention to the accounting and reporting requirements associated with human rights due diligence (HRDD).

Other key attempts to develop corporate human rights reporting and indicators are discussed in the subsequent section, which is followed by a discussion of the challenges associated with accounting for human rights. The final sections of the chapter provide guidance on approaches to teaching accounting for human rights.

ACCOUNTING, REPORTING, AND ASSURANCE

There are a number of distinct strands to accounting practice, depending on the purpose and intended users of accounting information. The management accounting is primarily concerned with the provision of financial and non-financial information for managers, for the purpose of informing management decision making. Financial accounting and reporting is primarily concerned with the recording of an entity's financial transactions for the purposes of preparing financial statements for external users (in particular, stockholders and providers of capital) in order for these external users to assess managerial performance and to inform investment decisions. Financial accounting is closely linked to audit practice – i.e., the provision of independent, third-party assurance to users of financial statements that the financial statements are accurate and free from misstatement. In addition to management and financial accounting, accounting is often broadly considered to include the provision of non-financial information to external users. Non-financial reporting (NFR) provides a form of corporate accountability to a wider range of stakeholders and often includes information about the social and environmental performance of the reporting entity. As with financial reporting, NFR is often subject to third-party assurance. However, while financial reporting and audit are a legal requirement for listed companies, conducted in accordance with international standards, NFR and associated assurance practice tends to be undertaken on a voluntary basis.

Each of these distinct strands of accounting are relevant, in different ways, to the practice of accounting for human rights – as will be outlined in the proceeding discussion.

ACCOUNTING AND THE UNGPs

The UNGPs[1] have engendered a "significant shift [to] the organizational and institutional context within which accounting operates,"[2] with important implications for the related practices of reporting, auditing, and assurance. For example, the commentary to Guiding Principle 3 states that "financial report-

---

[1]   United Nations Human Rights Council, *Guiding Principles on Business and Human Rights: Implementing the United Nations "Protect, Respect and Remedy" Framework*, Report of the Special Representative of the Secretary-General on the issue of human rights and transnational corporations and other business enterprises, UN doc. A/HRC/17/31 (March 21, 2011) (UN Guiding Principles).

[2]   Kenneth McPhail and John Ferguson, "The Past, Present and Future of Accounting for Human Rights," *Accounting, Auditing and Accountability Journal* 29, no. 4 (2016): 527.

ing requirements should clarify that human rights impacts in some instances may be 'material' or 'significant' to the economic performance of the business enterprise."[3] In some respects, this commentary signals the need for a reassessment of the traditional corporate reporting model, a widening of the definition of materiality, and broader disclosure requirements.

A central tenet of Pillar II of the UNGPs is that business enterprises have a responsibility to undertake HRDD in order to "identify, prevent, mitigate and *account* for how they address their impacts on human rights."[4] (See The UN Guiding Principles on Business and Human Rights, Chapter 5.) Such "accounting" for human rights impacts requires that business enterprises collect, manage, and disclose "appropriate qualitative and quantitative indicators"[5] in order to "both know and show that they respect human rights in practice."[6] According to the UNGPs, such disclosure, along with the HRDD processes that underpin it, provides "a measure of transparency and accountability to individuals or groups who may be impacted and to other relevant stakeholders, including investors."[7]

As part of wider efforts to implement the UNGPs, one major initiative that specifically addresses Pillar II, in terms of its focus on corporate responsibility to respect, is the Business and Human Rights Reporting and Assurance Frameworks Initiative (RAFI) developed by Shift and the accounting firm Mazars.[8] The first phase of the RAFI project, the Reporting Framework,[9] was launched in 2015 and provides guidance to business enterprises regarding their responsibilities to manage human rights risks, to undertake due diligence, and to report effectively to stakeholders. In particular, the Reporting Framework stipulates that business enterprises should identify and report on salient human rights issues and how these issues have been determined and managed. The Reporting Framework requires business enterprises to implement processes for identifying risks (for example, through stakeholder engagement), tracking performance (for example, drawing on a range of data sources, relevant indicators, stakeholder surveys, and independent reports), and discharging accountability (through the disclosure of policies, processes, metrics, and indicators).

---

[3] UN Guiding Principles, 6.
[4] UN Guiding Principles, 16.
[5] UN Guiding Principles, 22.
[6] UN Guiding Principles, 16.
[7] UN Guiding Principles, 23–24.
[8] "Human Rights Reporting and Assurance Frameworks Initiative," Shift, 2014, accessed August 19, 2022, https://shiftproject.org/resource/human-rights-reporting-and-assurance-frameworks-initiative.
[9] Shift and Mazars LLP, *UN Guiding Principles Reporting Framework* (2015), https://shiftproject.org/resource/un-guiding-principles-reporting-framework.

The second phase of the RAFI project developed UNGP Assurance Guidance[10] for assurance practitioners who undertake either internal or external assurance assessments of the human rights performance or reporting of business enterprises. Published in 2017, the Guidance outlines the expected competencies of human rights assurance providers and develops a "comprehensive set of indicators of the appropriateness and effectiveness of a company's human rights-related policies and processes."[11] This set of indicators provides not only a detailed overview of core activities that assurance providers should consider but also insights into the extensive data management processes that business enterprises need to develop in order to meet assurance requirements.

Other initiatives seek to understand how business enterprises might better evaluate respect for human rights. For example, one of the six focus areas of Shift's "Valuing Respect" initiative[12] is concerned specifically with "Accounting for Respect" and asks whether respect for human rights "[has] a place on the balance sheet?".[13] This initiative seeks to "identify human rights issues that could be modelled in accounting terms."[14]

HUMAN RIGHTS INDICATORS

In addition to the UNGPs and the accounting and reporting initiatives associated with their implementation, a number of other efforts have sought to develop corporate reporting for human rights and human rights indicators. Most notably, there are a number of human rights indicators included under the social heading of the GRI. More specifically, these include:

"non-discrimination, freedom of association, child labor, forced labor, indigenous peoples, and complicity through the actions of security forces … [and] a more general standard on assessing human rights risks."[15]

---

[10] Shift and Mazars LLP, *Assurance of Human Rights Performance and Reporting* (2017), https://www.ungpreporting.org/wp-content/uploads/UNGPRF _AssuranceGuidance.pdf.

[11] Shift and Mazars LLP, *Assurance of Human Rights Performance and Reporting*, 15.

[12] "Valuing Respect," Shift, accessed August 19, 2022, https://shiftproject.org/ what-we-do/valuing-respect.

[13] Shift, "Valuing Respect."

[14] Shift, "Valuing Respect."

[15] David Hess, "The Transparency Trap: Non-Financial Disclosure and the Responsibility of Business to Respect Human Rights," *American Business Law Journal* 56, no. 1 (2019): 23.

While the GRI is considered the "de facto standard for sustainability report-ing,"[16] it is not without limitations. More specifically, corporate disclosure under the GRI framework is voluntary and corporations have discretion on their levels of disclosure. It has been noted that the human rights indicators under the GRI tend to be the least disclosed.[17] Further, de Felice draws atten-tion to how the construction of human rights indicators requires "simplifying and standardizing complex but partial data"[18] and how relying on such indica-tors can lead to a misleading picture of a business enterprise's human rights performance. In a specific example related to human rights performance in the GRI, de Felice observes:

> As a proxy measure of corporate human rights performance, GRI indicator G4-HR8 asks companies to "report the total number of identified incidents of violations involving rights of indigenous peoples." This indicator risks being an invalid measure of the adverse human rights impacts of corporations because it does not take into account numerous contextual factors that can affect the "score" of a company ... For instance, a reduction in the number of incidents could result from the previous (unjustified) arrest of all indigenous leaders ... a policy of intimidation can prevent local communities from protesting and registering complaints ... What appears as a good score on G4-HR8 would not derive from responsible behavior, but from a climate of repression.[19]

According to Hess, "The next most well-known set of voluntary standards" is produced by the Sustainability Accounting Standards Board (SASB).[20] Disclosures under SASB standards are aimed at providing information to investors about "environmental, social, and governance" (ESG) factors that are relevant to the financial performance of the reporting entity. For example,

---

[16] Dror Etzion and Fabrizio Ferraro, "The Role of Analogy in the Institutionalization of Sustainability Reporting," *Organization Science* 21, no. 5 (2010): 1092.

[17] Johannes Slacik and Dorothea Greiling, "Coverage of G4-Indicators in GRI-Sustainability Reports by Electric Utilities," *Journal of Public Budgeting, Accounting & Financial Management* 32, no. 3 (2020): 359.

[18] Damiano de Felice, "Business and Human Rights Indicators to Measure the Corporate Responsibility to Respect: Challenges and Opportunities," *Human Rights Quarterly* 37, no. 2 (2015): 513.

[19] De Felice, "Business and Human Rights Indicators," 540–541.

[20] Hess, "Transparency Trap," 24. From July 2022, the SASB is undertaking a planned consolidation into the International Sustainability Standards Board (ISSB). The ISSB was formed in 2021 and operates under the oversight of the International Financial Reporting Standards (IFRS) Foundation. The ISSB is a private-sector body that develops and approves IFRS Sustainability Disclosure Standards. See SASB, "SASB Standards Board Hosts Final Meeting in Preparation to Transition Standards to ISSB," press release, June 17, 2022 , https://www.sasb.org/wp-content/uploads/2022/06/2022_06-Standards-Board-Meeting-Outcomes-Final.pdf.

"corporations are expected to disclose the percentage of their suppliers that were audited ... for compliance with a labor code of conduct."[21] As with the GRI, it has been noted that the reliability of such indicators can be undermined by "structural features of the audit process – such as auditors' conflicts of interest or limited power ... Moreover, in highly corrupt environments, bribery can lead to the creation of false or misleading audit reports."[22]

Another influential development that has had an impact on human rights disclosure practice is the Corporate Human Rights Benchmark (CHRB). The CHRB (which operates under the auspices of the World Benchmarking Alliance) was established in 2013 as a multistakeholder initiative aimed at assessing and benchmarking corporate disclosure.[23] In developing a publicly available benchmark of corporate disclosure practice, the CHRB aims to improve corporate human rights performance. The CHRB methodology consists of specific human rights indicators across six measurement themes, which are grounded in the UNGPs and other international human rights standards.

While the CHRB have been successful in some respects, in terms of developing a set of indicators related to corporate human rights disclosures, stakeholders have raised concerns that the benchmark is overly focused on corporate policy and processes at the expense of considering impact and performance.[24]

CHALLENGES OF ACCOUNTING FOR HUMAN RIGHTS

As outlined in the above section, there are a number of challenges associated with accounting for human rights. In short, a degree of caution (or perhaps cautious optimism) is needed before concluding that accounting, reporting, and assurance can appropriately assess corporate respect for human rights. For example, when it comes to the role of accounting for human rights, an expert roundtable recently reported that:

> There was fairly broad agreement that financial accounts themselves are poorly placed to accommodate the value of respect for human rights. They suffer from the considerable disadvantages of being a historical snapshot in time, out-of-date at the

[21] Hess, "Transparency Trap," 25
[22] Hess, "Transparency Trap," 30.
[23] "Corporate Human Rights Benchmark," World Benchmarking Alliance, accessed August 19, 2022, https://www.worldbenchmarkingalliance.org/corporate-human-rights -benchmark.
[24] Corporate Human Rights Benchmark, *CHRB 2020–2021 Methodology Review: Second Public Consultation* (2021), https://assets.worldbenchmarkingalliance.org/app/ uploads/2021/05/Overview-of-the-CHRB-Methodology-Review-Process_2021.pdf.

point of publication, of very limited predictive value and narrowly focused in their purpose.[25]

While the group acknowledged that traditional accounting methods or traditional financial accounting statements might not be the most suitable vehicle for providing an account of a business enterprises human rights performance, they did acknowledge that other, alternative forms of reporting and disclosure might serve this purpose. However, to date, such alternative forms of accounting are either not very well developed or have inherent limitations. For example, de Felice highlights some of the difficulties related to "how to measure whether, and to what extent, corporations are meeting their responsibility to respect human rights."[26]

Similarly, concerns have been raised about the role of assurance services related to business and human rights. Numerous studies have highlighted instances of deception, fraud, and the falsification of records[27] and that audit and assurance services "rely on the superficial participation of workers."[28] As Ford and Nolan observe, "The failure of social auditing is perhaps most tragically exemplified by various high-profile disasters and scandals in the apparel sector" such as the fire at the Ali Enterprises garment factory in 2012 that killed almost 300 workers or the collapse of the Rana Plaza building in 2013 that killed over 1,134 workers. While social audits had been undertaken prior to both disasters, no violations or safety risks were identified or reported in either case.

TEACHING APPROACHES

Accounting, reporting, and assurance for human rights can be taught in a number of ways in different degree programs. Within an accounting degree program, business and human rights might be included as a discrete topic in course modules such as contemporary issues in accounting, social and envi-

---

[25] Shift, *Expert Roundtable on Business, Human Rights and Accounting: A Summary Report* (2019), https://shiftproject.org/wp-content/uploads/2019/09/VRP _Expert_Roundtable_Summary.pdf.

[26] De Felice, "Business and Human Rights Indicators," 513.

[27] Jason Judd and Sarosh Kuruvilla, "Why Apparel Brands' Efforts to Police Their Supply Chains Aren't Working," *The Conversation*, April 30, 2020, https://theconversation.com/why-apparel-brands-efforts-to-police-their-supply - chains-arent-working-136821.

[28] Chara De Lacey, "Who Audits the Auditor?: Shaping Legal Accountability Strategies to Redress Social Audit Failings," Business and Human Rights Resource Centre, March 30, 2021, https://www.business-humanrights.org/en/blog/who-audits -the-auditor-shaping-legal-accountability-strategies-to-redress-social-audit-failings.

ronmental accounting, or audit and assurance. In a business degree program, accounting, reporting, and assurance could form a substantive part of a course module on business and human rights or covered as a discrete topic, for example in a module on corporate reporting. In a law degree program or BHR course, accounting can be covered in conjunction with topics such as mandatory human rights due diligence legislation, mandatory human rights reporting, corporate governance, and corporate law.

Learning objectives for teaching accounting for human rights may include:

- Understanding the governance processes required in order for business enterprises to manage and account for their human rights impacts.
- Understanding how the management and accounting of human rights can be incorporated into different strands of accounting practice – for example, financial accounting and reporting, management accounting, audit and assurance.
- Understanding the challenges associated with accounting, reporting, and assuring human rights.
- Understanding different conceptualization of "materiality" and their relevance to accounting for human rights.

A useful approach is to situate discussion about the role of accounting, reporting, and assurance within the context of human rights due diligence and/ or mandatory human rights reporting. Teachers can ask students to consider what management and governance processes might be required for a business enterprise to adequately "know and show" their human rights impacts and how they are addressing them. The discussion provides an opportunity for students to reflect on what data might need to be collected, how it might be collected, how it might be processed for decision-making purposes, and how it might be reported to stakeholders. In doing so, students will quickly appreciate that to adequately "account" for human rights, business enterprises would need to establish sophisticated management information systems, underpinned by clear policy and guidelines, and concomitant processes for data collection involving, amongst other things, engagement with internal and external stakeholders (employees, suppliers, social auditors, non-governmental organizations, etc.).

EXERCISE 27.1

CORPORATE HUMAN RIGHTS REPORTS

The discussion above can be followed up with an exercise that requires students (organized into groups) to explore the human rights report of a business enterprise of their choice, addressing the following questions:

- What governance processes and policies have the business enterprise introduced in order to manage and account for their human rights impacts?
- What management systems have the business enterprise introduced in order to manage and account for their human rights impacts and what data informs?
- What human rights issues does the business enterprise report on and at which stakeholders is the report aimed?

EXERCISE 27.2

CASE STUDY: UNILEVER'S HUMAN RIGHTS REPORT

Rather than ask students to identify their own reporting business enterprise, an alternative approach would be to assign a specific corporate human rights report from a company that has performed well on the Corporate Human Rights Benchmark (for example, Unilever's Human Rights Report[29]), to form the basis of a case-based discussion. The advantage of taking this approach is that a high scoring CHRB report will generally be well developed, with a clear articulation of the governance mechanisms and policies that inform their approach as well as explicit discussion of the management processes they have implemented and the sources of data that underpin these processes. A case-based discussion related to a well-developed human rights report allows students to engage with best-practice and to appreciate the challenges involved and the scale of implementation. An interesting task to finish up this exercise is to ask students to search for case company on the Business and Human Rights Resource Centre website and identify one or two articles that report on human rights abuses associated with the com-

---

[29] Unilever, *Human Rights Report 2020*, https://assets.unilever.com/files/92ui5egz/production/0ead3d5a36007724459bb1acbf437a190cfc2e42.pdf/unilever-human-rights-report-2020.pdf.

pany. This task can encourage students to critically reflect on the limitations of accounting, reporting, and assurance mechanisms.

Another potential area for class discussion is around the concept of materiality and how it is framed in different reporting regimes – such as the Global Reporting Initiative (GRI), the Sustainability Accounting Standards Board (SASB), and EU non-financial disclosure Directive. The UNGPs call for the development of financial reporting standards that clarify, in some instances, that human rights impacts may be "material."[30] Classroom discussion could highlight how the concept of materiality differs according to the stakeholder group that is taken as the focus of the reporting regime. For example, for SASB "the level of materiality ascribed to an issue is entirely contingent on how much it influences decisions and assessments made by the providers of financial capital."[31] That is, for SASB, the primary target of reporting is investors – hence, materiality is framed around the financial relevance of ESG issues. In contrast, the GRI is orientated to a broader set of stakeholders and hence frames materiality more broadly around the impact of a company's activities to society, while the EU Directive employs the concept of "double materiality,"[32] which requires companies to report on material risks to company value as well as risks to people and the environment. Classroom discussion on the concept of materiality can draw attention to the different conceptualizations of the concept, the relative advantages and disadvantages of the different approaches, and the implications this has for how human rights issues are reported.

Audit and assurance is another topic that might form the basis of a lecture, either as part of a dedicated course module on business and human rights or perhaps as part of an auditing module for accounting and finance students. For business and law students, a useful approach would be to highlight the distinction between internal and external assurance and the role each plays in relation to human rights due diligence and reporting. Similarly, it might also be useful for students to be aware of the distinctions between traditional financial audit practice and social audit practice – in particular, drawing attention to the vastly different regulatory contexts of each.[33] Classroom discussion can draw

---

[30] UN Guiding Principles, 9.

[31] Mary Canning, Brendan O'Dwyer, and George Georgakopoulos, "Processes of Auditability in Sustainability Assurance: The Case of Materiality Construction," *Accounting and Business Research* 49, no. 1 (2019): 24.

[32] European Commission, "Questions and Answers: Corporate Sustainability Reporting Directive Proposal" (2021), accessed June 20, 2022, https://ec.europa.eu/commission/presscorner/detail/en/QANDA_21_1806.

[33] Larelle E. Chapple and Grace Mui, "Social Audit Failure: Legal Liability of External Auditors," in *Social Audit Regulation: CSR, Sustainability, Ethics and*

attention to the perceived limitations of audit and assurance practice related to human rights and how some of these limitations may be overcome. For law students, discussion might include a consideration of the regulation of social audit practice and the potential for legal liability in the event of social audit failure.

Finally, a course module on business and human rights could address the challenges associated with "accounting" for human rights in terms of the difficulties related to developing appropriate indicators and metrics and the potential moral issues related to the "measurement" of human rights.[34]

KEY QUESTIONS

General

- How is human rights reporting and measurement by business enterprises addressed in the UNGPs?
- What are the challenges related to the measurement and reporting of human rights issues by business enterprises?
- What are the challenges related to the assurance of human rights performance and reporting of business enterprises?
- How is measurement and reporting different from assurance?
- What are the relative advantages and disadvantages of voluntary and mandatory reporting regimes related to business and human rights?

For Business Students

- In what ways, if at all, can business and human rights issues be incorporated into traditional financial accounting statements?
- What management processes and governance mechanisms might a business enterprise need to implement in order to adequately report on human rights issues?
- How does the external assurance of business and human rights reporting differ from the external audit of financial statements?
- How do the roles of internal auditor and external assurance provider differ?

Governance, eds. Mia M. Rahim and Samuel O. Idowu (New York: Springer, 2015), 281–299.

[34] Galit A. Sarfaty, "Measuring Corporate Accountability through Global Indicators," in *The Quiet Power of Indicators: Measuring Governance, Corruption, and Rule of Law*, ed. Sally Engle Merry, Kevin E. Davis, and Benedict Kingsbury (Cambridge: Cambridge University Press, 2015), 103–132.

- What data is needed to measure and track corporate human rights performance?

For Law Students

- What is the potential for legal liability in relation to social audit failure?
- Are human rights impacts material under securities law for public companies?
- What are the key features of mandatory human rights reporting regulation?

For Policy Students

- What role does corporate reporting and disclosure play in promoting human rights protections?
- What alternative approaches to social auditing practice have been proposed to address the perceived limitations of social auditing?

TEACHING RESOURCES

Readings

Mandatory human rights reporting regulations

- EU Directive 2014/95/EU of the European Parliament and of the Council of 22 October 2014 amending Directive 2013/34/EU as regards disclosure of non-financial and diversity information by certain large undertakings and groups, OJ 2014 No. L 330 (entered into force December 6, 2014).
- French Corporate Duty of Vigilance Law. Unofficial English translation by Respect. https://respect.international/wp-content/uploads/2017/10/ngo-translation-french-corporate-duty-of-vigilance-law.pdf.
- The Dodd-Frank Wall Street Reform and Consumer Protection Act, Pub. L. No. 111-203, 124 Stat. 1376 (United States, 2010).
- United Kingdom, Modern Slavery Act 2015, 30, cl. 54. http://www.legislation.gov.uk/ukpga/2015/30/contents/enacted/data.htm.

Voluntary Human Rights Reporting Regimes

- Global Reporting Initiative (GRI) Standards. https://www.globalreporting.org/how-to-use-the-gri-standards/gri-standards-english-language.
- Sustainability Accounting Standards Board. SASB Standards. https://www.sasb.org/standards/download/?lang=en-us.

- World Benchmarking Alliance. Corporate Human Rights Benchmark. https://www.worldbenchmarkingalliance.org/corporate-human-rights-benchmark.

Commentary – Business

- Mehra, Amol and Sara Blackwell. "The Rise of Non-Financial Disclosure: Reporting on Respect for Human Rights." In *Business and Human Rights: From Principles to Practice*, edited by Dorothée Baumann-Pauly and Justine Nolan, 276–277. London: Routledge, 2016.
- Rees, Caroline. *Transforming How Business Impacts People: Unlocking the Collective Power of Five Distinct Narratives*. Cambridge, MA: Harvard Kennedy School, November 2020.
- Sinkovics, Noemi, Samia Ferdous Hoque, and Rudolf R. Sinkovics. "Rana Plaza Collapse Aftermath: Are CSR Compliance and Auditing Pressures Effective?" *Accounting, Auditing and Accountability Journal* 29, no. 4 (2016): 617–649.

Commentary – Legal

- Bengtsen, Peter. "Why Are Monitory Democracies Not Monitoring Supply Chain Slavery?" *GP Opinion* (blog). *Global Policy*, August 28, 2020. https://www.globalpolicyjournal.com/blog/28/08/2020/why-are-monitory-democracies-not-monitoring-supply-chain-slavery.
- Martin-Ortega, Olga and Johanna Hoekstra, "Reporting as a Means to Protect and Promote Human Rights? The EU Non-Financial Reporting Directive." *European Law Review* 44, no. 5 (2019): 622–645.
- Terwindt, Carolijn and Miriam Saage-Maass. *Liability of Social Auditors in the Textile Industry*. Friedrich-Ebert-Stiftung, 2016. https://www.ecchr.eu/fileadmin/Publikationen/Policy_Paper_Liability_of_Social_Auditors_in_the_Textile_Industry_FES_ECCHR_2016.pdf.

Websites

- Business and Human Rights Resource Centre. https://www.business-humanrights.org/en.
- Global Reporting Initiative. https://www.globalreporting.org.
- UN Guiding Principles Reporting Framework. https://www.ungpreporting.org.

28. Mega-sporting events and human rights[1]

Daniela Heerdt

OVERVIEW

Mega-sporting events (MSEs), such as the FIFA World Cup, the Summer and Winter Olympic and Paralympic Games (OPGs), the Commonwealth Games, the Pan-American Games, and the Jeux de la Francophonie, are more than just prestigious sporting competitions. Because of their scale and dimension, these events embody highly complex international business operations, and offer exceptional examples of the potential human rights impacts in our increasingly globalized and interconnected world. While many stakeholders benefit from MSEs,[2] it is well-known by now that MSEs can have negative human rights impacts. Reports highlighting the range of human rights that can be adversely impacted by staging these events have proliferated since the Beijing Summer Olympics in 2008.[3] The human rights issues highlighted in relation to the Beijing Games focused on forced evictions, exploitive and unsafe working conditions for those working on event-related infrastructure projects, and child labor.[4] During preparations for the World Cup and the Summer Olympic Games in Brazil between 2009 and 2015, more than 77,000 people living

---

[1] An earlier version of this chapter appeared online in Daniela Heerdt, "Teaching Note: Mega-Sporting Events and Human Rights," in *Teaching Business and Human Rights Handbook* (Teaching Business and Human Rights Forum, 2018), https://teachbhr.org/resources/teaching-bhr-handbook/teaching-notes/mega-sporting-events-and-human-rights-2.

[2] Megan Corrarino, "'Law Exclusion Zones': Mega-Events as Sites of Procedural and Substantive Human Rights Violations," *Yale Human Rights and Development Law Journal* 17, no. 1 (2014): 182, 189.

[3] Barbara Keys, "Reframing Human Rights," in *The Ideals of Global Sport: From Peace to Human Rights*, ed. Barbara Keys (Philadelphia, PA: University of Pennsylvania Press, 2019), 111.

[4] Minky Worden, *China's Great Leap: The Beijing Games and Olympian Human Rights Challenges* (New York: Seven Stories Press, 2008), 183–184.

in and around Rio de Janeiro were displaced or forcefully evicted.[5] In the run-up to the Sochi Winter Olympics in 2014, numerous cases of repression of political opposition became public.[6] Concerns for worker's rights abuses were raised in connection with the 2018 FIFA World Cup in Russia, as well as the 2018 Winter Games in Pyeongchang and the preparations for the 2022 FIFA World Cup in Qatar.[7] Child labor concerns linked to MSEs have been reported as common issue in an event's supply chain, for instance in connection with the production of Olympic logo goods, mascot toys, or other Olympic merchandise for the 2012 London OPGs.[8]

Studying and teaching the human rights impacts of MSEs illustrates many key business and human rights (BHR) issues, such as access to remedy, human rights due diligence, and supply chain management. At the same time, MSEs present a good case study to test findings and best practice guidance developed in the BHR field. Moreover, concrete cases of MSE-related human rights impacts, as well as human rights abuses in the broader sports industry, arise regularly, allowing for topical teaching approaches.

This chapter introduces the substance, outlines ideas for teaching approaches and study questions, and provides possible tools and resources for including the subject of human rights and MSEs in BHR teaching.

DIVERSE ACTORS

MSEs are jointly organized and staged by a range of diverse actors: international sports organizing bodies such as the International Olympic Committee (IOC), the Fédération Internationale de Football Association (FIFA), or Commonwealth Sport; national sport organizing bodies like national Olympic

---

[5] World Cup and Olympics Popular Committee, *Mega-Events and Human Rights Violations in Rio de Janeiro Dossier: Rio 2016 Olympics – The Exclusion Games* (November 2015), 20, http://www.childrenwin.org/wp-content/uploads/2015/12/DossieComiteRio2015_ENG_web_ok_low.pdf.

[6] Jules Boykoff, "The Sochi 2014 Winter Olympics Is a Political Tinderbox for Russia," *The Guardian*, January 2, 2013, https://www.theguardian.com/commentisfree/2013/jan/02/sochi-2014-winter-olympics-political-tinderbox.

[7] "Race to the Bottom: Exploitation of Migrant Workers Ahead of Russia's 2014 Winter Olympic Games in Sochi, " Human Rights Watch, February 6, 2013, https://www.hrw.org/report/2013/02/06/race-bottom/exploitation-migrant-workers -ahead-russias-2014-winter-olympic-games; "Qatar: Take Urgent Action to Protect Construction Workers," Human Rights Watch, September 27, 2017, https://www.hrw .org/news/2017/09/27/qatar-take-urgent-action-protect-construction-workers.

[8] Celia Brackenridge et al., *Child Exploitation and the FIFA World Cup: A Review of Risks and Protective Interventions* (2013), 14, https://resourcecentre.savethechildren .net/document/child-exploitation-and-fifa-world-cup-review-risks-and-protective -interventions.

Committees or national football federations; local organizing entities; local, regional, and central authorities of the host country; national and international companies; broadcasters; recruitment or other agencies; and sponsors.[9] MSEs typically rely heavily on the host country's public sector investments. Host governments see MSEs as an opportunity to attract tourism and investment. MSE-related construction projects and other operations create jobs, often leading to demand for foreign workers. The numerous corporate actors involved in MSEs generate revenue through the provision of goods and services, ticket sales, marketing, licensing, broadcasting, and numerous other commercial activities. Sponsors and broadcasting companies also provide financial support for the staging of MSEs. The economic benefits of MSEs extend across the borders of the respective hosting countries.

While similar collaborative projects exist in the investment and development field, such as large-scale infrastructure projects funded by international investors and organizations, executed by private national and multinational companies, and signed off by national governments, MSEs stand out as a unique case for two reasons: (1) the complex constellation of actors involved and (2) the range and scale of potential adverse human rights impacts connected to MSEs.

INTERNATIONAL VISIBILITY

MSEs are also unique because of the immense international attention they receive. This visibility brings opportunities for stakeholders to promote human rights and push for improved human rights protection in the respective hosting country and beyond. A recent example are the labor law reforms adopted in Qatar.[10] Since the 2022 World Cup was awarded to the country in 2010, the attention to the forced labor conditions under which migrant workers in Qatar are building the infrastructure related to the event has grown, and with it the pressure exercised on the country's government by other governments, human rights organizations, sponsors, and even FIFA. In 2020, the criticized "kafala system" was officially abolished.[11]

---

[9]   Jean-Loup Chappelet and Brenda Kübler-Mabbott, *The International Olympic Committee and the Olympic System: The Governance of World Sport* (Oxford: Routledge, 2008), 5–16.

[10]   ILO, "Landmark Labour Reforms Signal End of Kafala System in Qatar," press release, October 16, 2019, https://www.ilo.org/global/about-the-ilo/newsroom/news/WCMS_724052/lang--en/index.htm?shared_from=shr-tls.

[11]   The kafala system, also referred to as the "sponsorship system," has its roots in a time-honoured Bedouin tradition that originally regulated the treatment and protection of foreign guests and deepens the dependency of migrant workers on sponsors. The result is that employees cannot leave the country or switch employers without being provided with a permit by their employer.

ACCOUNTABILITY AND RESPONSIBILITY

Attempting to remedy MSE-related human rights violations highlights the accountability gap that surrounds these cases. This gap arises due to the multitude of actors involved in staging MSEs, as well as the complex and often non-transparent interaction between them. Most actions taken in the planning and preparatory stage of such events and during the events themselves are not carried out by one actor individually, but rather jointly by multiple actors. The requirements of sport bodies trigger hosting authorities and organizing committees to make certain decisions, issue permits, and engage contractors, subcontractors, and suppliers. The longer the chain of outsourcing, the higher the risk of human rights abuses.[12] This "problem of many hands"[13] blurs the lines of responsibility and accountability for human rights impacts and rightsholders may be unable to identify the actors responsible for the harm. Indemnification clauses in hosting contracts can help actors involved to evade their (legal) responsibility.[14]

The accountability problem presented by MSEs is not only a procedural one. On a substantive level, international human rights standards do not take effect the same way for each of the actors involved in MSEs. Non-state actors generally are not directly bound by regional or international human rights mechanisms. This does not mean that non-state actors involved in staging MSEs are free of human rights obligations. Host country governments implement their obligations under international human rights law by adopting policies and laws that non-state actors operating on their territory have to follow, for instance in the field of domestic labor law or criminal law. However, domestic laws differ from hosting country to hosting country. Therefore, the standard of human rights protection applicable to MSE actors can differ significantly. In addition, hosting countries often adopt new legislation in the run-up to the event, often at the expense of statutory human rights protection.[15]

---

[12]   Linde Bryk and Claudia Müller-Hoff, *Accountability for Forced Labor in a Globalized Economy* (Berlin: European Center for Constitutional and Human Rights, 2018), 12, https://www.ecchr.eu/fileadmin/Publikationen/ECCHR_QATAR.pdf.

[13]   Dennis F. Thompson, "Moral Responsibility of Public Officials: The Problem of Many Hands," *The American Political Science Review* 74, no. 4 (December 1980): 74, https://doi.org/10.2307/1954312.

[14]   International Olympic Committee (IOC), *Host City Contract Principles Games of the XXXIII Olympiad in 2024* (IOC, 2017), ¶ 37, https://stillmed.olympic.org/Documents/Host_city_elections/Host_City_Contract_Principles.pdf.

[15]   Mark James and Guy Osborn, "The Olympics, Transnational Law and Legal Transplants: The International Olympic Committee, Ambush Marketing and Ticket Touting," *Legal Studies* 36, no. 1 (March 2016): 93, https://doi.org/10.1111/lest.12095.

MSEs AND THE UNITED NATIONS GUIDING PRINCIPLES

Applying the United Nations Guiding Principles for Business and Human Rights (UNGPs) to MSEs can help to clarify human rights obligations and responsibilities of the various actors involved and to analyze what can be expected of MSEs with regard to their human rights impacts. (See The UN Guiding Principles on Business and Human Rights, Chapter 5.) The state duty to protect human rights under Pillar I of the UNGPs applies to the host governments. The corporate responsibility to respect human rights under Pillar II of the UNGPs applies to all private parties involved in delivering MSE, including international and national sports organizing bodies.[16] FIFA, for example, has publicly committed to the UNGPs in its human rights policy. The IOC started to refer to the UNGPs in their host city contracts for the 2024, 2026, and 2028 OPGs, as well as the Youth Olympic Games,[17] and publicly committed to the UNGPs in 2022.[18] Commonwealth Sport is committed to implementing the UNGPs in its activities and events.[19] This provides an interesting opportunity to investigate the nature of the other actors involved in delivering MSEs, such as organizing committees, sponsors, or broadcasters, and to what extent UNGPs would apply to them. Organizing committees are sometimes public and sometimes private bodies.

The UNGP's third pillar on remedy is also of relevance in the MSE context. In fact, it has been explicitly mentioned in the revised bidding guidelines for the 2026 FIFA World Cup and the Host City Contracts for the 2024 Olympic Games.[20] The latter include a reference to the provision of remedy mechanisms for any harmful consequences in terms of human rights violations of the bid

---

[16]   While not traditional commercial actors – FIFA and the IOC are established as non-profit associations under Swiss law – international sports governing bodies still fall within the scope of the UNGPs.

[17]   Fédération Internationale de Football Association, FIFA's Human Rights Policy, May 2017 ed., http://resources.fifa.com/mm/document/affederation/ footballgovernance/02/89/33/12/fifashumanrightspolicy_neutral.pdf; Zeid Ra'ad Al Hussein and Rachel Davis, Recommendations for an IOC Human Rights Strategy: Independent Expert Report by Prince Zeid Ra'ad (March 2020).

[18]   International Olympic Committee. Strategic Framework on Human Rights. IOC, 2022. (https://stillmed.olympics.com/media/Documents/Beyond-the-Games/Human -Rights/IOC-Strategic-Framework-on-Human-Rights.pdf).

[19]   Commonwealth Games Federation, *Commonwealth Games Federation Human Rights Policy Statement* (October 2017), https://thecgf.com/sites/default/files/2018-03/ CGF-Human-Rights-Policy-Statement-17-10-05_0.pdf.

[20]   Fédération Internationale de Football Association, *FIFA Regulations for the Selection of the Venue for the Final Competition of the 2026 FIFA World Cup* (2017), http://resources.fifa.com/mm/document/affederation/administration/02/91/60/99/bid dingregulationsandregistration_neutral.pdf.

for or organization of these events. However, relevant remedy mechanisms for MSE-related human rights abuses are often unavailable or ineffective.[21]

TEACHING APPROACHES

The key issues surrounding MSEs and human rights, such as their complex supply chains and non-transparent business relationships, the accountability gap among different actors, and their relationship with the UNGPs, provide interesting topics for business, law, and policy students studying BHR.

Representative **learning objectives** may include:

- Understanding the diverse actors involved in delivering MSEs and how they are connected.
- Explaining, with concrete examples, the human rights abuses that can occur within the context of delivering MSEs and how they occur.
- Explaining the difficulties in establishing responsibility and accountability for MSE-related human rights abuses.
- Analyzing the life-cycle of MSEs and evaluating the human rights risks attached to each stage of the MSE life-cycle.
- Interpreting and applying human rights clauses in MSE-related contracts and bidding requirements.
- Applying the UNGPs to MSE governance or individual actors involved in the MSEs.

The topic of MSEs and human rights can be covered as a single lecture or module within an existing business and human rights course, as a one- or two-day seminar, or via multiple modules if teachers would like to zoom in on the different stages of an MSE life-cycle. The topic can also be integrated in a BHR course as an example or case study when covering other topics, such as human rights due diligence, human rights impact assessment, or tools for corporate legal accountability and access to remedy. (See Exercise 9.2: Conducting a Human Rights Impact Assessment for a Mega-Sporting Event.)

For law students, it can be interesting to focus on the legal challenges and the different human rights responsibilities and obligations that are at stake when human rights abuses occur in the context of delivering MSEs. A key

---

[21] For many cases of human rights abuses related to sport and mega-sporting events, no adequate remedy mechanisms are available as those affected often do not have legal standing. Where they are available, they are often not effective. See Daniela Heerdt, "Mapping Accountability and Remedy Mechanisms for Sport," Centre for Sport and Human Rights, April 22, 2019, https://www.sporthumanrights.org/en/resources/mapping-accountability-and-remedy-mechanisms-for-sport.

issue to highlight is the difference between private and public actors. Examples of abuses can be provided linked to past and future events, and with reference to relevant human rights standards from international and regional human rights instruments.

Teachers can draw attention to how the delivery of MSEs impact children's or women's rights, as well as the relevance and application of standards like the UNGPs and the OECD Guidelines for MNEs[22] within the MSE context.

As an assignment or assessment, teachers can present a particular case in which human rights have been violated, such as through forced eviction, and ask students to write a legal memo on options for effective remedy. Law students can also prepare a case in groups, as claimants, defendants, and judges, and argue their case in a trial or mediation session. This approach works best if the teaching is spread out over different modules and if some of the relevant cases, most notably the cases brought against FIFA or corporate actors involved in the MSE business (see Teaching Resources below), have been covered in class.

For policy students, it can be interesting to look at the different actors involved in delivering MSEs, and consider the implications of establishing a public, private, or "hybrid" local organization committee. Policy courses can address the incentives and intentions of governments that bid for and host MSEs. They can also focus on the implementation of procurement processes. The life-cycle analysis of MSEs and their human rights risks can be a helpful tool for students to understand what is required and what the risks are. Case studies can focus on the engagement of local communities in the adoption of MSE-related policies and legislation. Teachers can also make policy students aware of existing multistakeholder initiatives that aim to make MSEs more sustainable and human rights-friendly.[23]

As an assessment or assignment, teachers can ask policy students to draft a human rights policy from the perspective of a local organizing committee, or as a human rights manager of one of the major international sports governing bodies, such as FIFA or the IOC. This can be done in groups, including presentations where students compare and evaluate each other, or on an individual basis as final assessment.

For business students, teachers can focus on the different corporate actors involved in delivering MSEs, and what human rights challenges they face. Teachers can zoom in on the different relationships, for instance how the

---

[22] Organisation for Economic Co-operation and Development, *OECD Guidelines for Multinational Enterprises* (Paris: OECD Publishing, 2011).
[23] See, for example, "About Us," Centre for Sport and Human Rights, accessed August 17, 2022, https://www.sporthumanrights.org/about-us.

business relationships for sponsors and broadcasters are different than for contractors or subcontractors. Teachers can then explore the complex and multiple supply chains of MSEs. Dividing students into groups to research and present on one of the supply chains is a good way to survey the distinct and common challenges from a human rights perspective. Another thematic hook is the sustainability of these events, from both financial and non-financial perspectives. Business students can study the particular economic challenges that developing countries face when hosting an MSE. Teachers can also address the impacts of corruption in the MSE business.

EXERCISE 28.1

MANAGING THE HUMAN RIGHTS IMPACTS OF

A MEGA-SPORTING EVENT BUSINESS

As assignment or assessment, teachers can ask business students to represent a fictitious company that is involved in the MSE business and explore that company's human rights challenges in that process.[24] This approach works best as an ongoing assignment, for the length of the course. Students can be divided into groups that each present one relevant department of that company, such as the marketing department, the public affairs department dealing with the host country's authorities, the communication department, the department responsible for procurement, or the business function responsible for hiring workers. The key question for each group is how to ensure that they contribute to the company's goal of delivering its targets related to the MSE project in a human rights-compliant manner. Teachers can ask each group to develop a human rights policy. Teachers may encourage students to communicate with each other throughout the semester, as a real company would; and provide each group with access to experts in the field.

---

[24] This approach has been developed and tested at the Institute for Business Ethics, University of St. Gallen (Switzerland), for example, by Florian Wettstein and Ron Popper. "Business and Human Rights Laboratory: The Case of Mega Sporting Events," course syllabus (spring 2017).

KEY QUESTIONS

General

- What are MSEs and how are they organized?
- Which actors are involved in the delivery of MSEs and what roles do they play?
- What is the MSE life-cycle?
- What human rights risks are linked to each stage of an MSE life-cycle?
- What are the potential positive human rights impacts of MSEs?

For Business Students

- What are the human rights challenges faced by the different kinds of companies involved in delivering MSEs?
- How are international sport associations similar to, and different from, private corporations?
- What human rights standards, tools, or guidelines exist to help companies and sponsors operate responsibly in the MSE business?
- Should there be the same standards for all different types of corporate actors involved in the MSE business? Or should, for example, sponsors have different human rights obligations than contractors and subcontractors?
- How do the UNGPs apply to corporate actors involved in delivering MSEs?
- How can human rights standards be implemented across MSE supply chains? How can companies implement human rights standards in a way that its subcontractors follow the same standards?
- Should companies establish operational-level grievance mechanisms especially for cases of human rights violations connected to their MSE operations? What would an effective remedy mechanism look like?

For Law Students

- Which international and national human rights standards are applicable to MSEs?
- What standards and guidelines are in place and applicable to cases of MSE-related human rights abuses? How can international law and international human rights law be used to address cases of MSE-related human rights abuses?
- What are the legal relationships between the different actors involved in organizing and staging MSEs?

- To what extent are the different actors involved bound by human rights obligations? What obligations do non-state actors have? How do these obligations relate to state actors?
- Can/should all actors be held accountable for MSE-related human rights violations?
- What are the shortcomings of international human rights law and national legal frameworks in holding the actors involved in MSE-related human rights abuses accountable?
- Should host governments bear primary responsibility for all MSE-related violations? If not, how could responsibility be shared among the various actors involved in MSE-related operations?
- What legal mechanisms are in place to provide remedies to victims of human rights abuse?
- What challenges do rightsholders face in claiming their rights?
- How can host countries incorporate human rights standards in MSE-related policies and legislation?
- How can MSE-related contracts incorporate internationally recognized human rights standards and how could these standards be enforced?

For Policy Students

- What roles do government actors play delivering MSEs and which tasks do they have?
- What is the relationship of government actors with other stakeholders involved in delivering MSEs?
- How can public authorities collaborate with civil society and local communicates to ensure a sustainable and responsible delivery of the event?
- Should host governments and organizing bodies adopt event-specific human rights policies and, if so, what should such a human rights policy contain? Which issues should it prioritize?
- How can local communities be engaged when governments adopt MSE-related policies and legislation?
- What is the potential of MSEs to bring human-rights-friendly policy changes to host countries?
- How can MSE-related procurement processes be made more human rights-friendly?
- What can host governments do to fight corruption and human rights issues related to corruption within the MSE business?
- What standards can host governments and the local organizing committee adopt to ensure that companies involved in the MSE business conduct their operations with respect for human rights?

TEACHING RESOURCES

Readings

International sports organizing bodies

- Commonwealth Sport. *Transformation 2022 Refresh.* https://thecgf.com/sites/default/files/2019-09/CGF_TRANSFORMATION_2022.pdf.
- Fédération Internationale de Football Association (FIFA). *Human Rights Policy.* May 2017 ed. https://img.fifa.com/image/upload/kr05dqyhwr1uhqy2lh6r.pdf.
- FIFA. *Regulations for the Selection of the Venue for the Final Competition of the 2026 FIFA World Cup.* 2017. https://img.fifa.com/image/upload/stwvxqphxp3o96jxwqor.pdf.
- International Olympic Committee. Host City Contract – Principles – Games of the XXXIII Olympiad in 2024. IOC, 2017. http://stillmed.olympic.org/media/Document%20Library/OlympicOrg/Documents/Host-City-Elections/XXXIII-Olympiad-2024/Host-City-Contract-2024-Principles.pdf.
- International Olympic Committee. Strategic Framework on Human Rights. IOC, 2022. https://stillmed.olympics.com/media/Documents/Beyond-the-Games/Human-Rights/IOC-Strategic-Framework-on-Human-Rights.pdf.

Books

- Gauthier, Ryan. *The International Olympic Committee, Law, and Accountability.* Oxford: Routledge, 2017.
- Heerdt, Daniela. *Blurred Lines of Responsibility and Accountability: Human Rights Abuses at Mega-Sporting Events.* Cambridge: Intersentia, 2021.
- Keys, Barbara, ed. *The Ideals of Global Sport: From Peace to Human Rights.* Philadelphia, PA: University of Pennsylvania Press, 2019.

Commentary

- Al Hussein, Prince Zeid Ra'ad and Rachel Davis. *Recommendations for an IOC Human Rights Strategy* (2020). https://stillmedab.olympic.org/media/Document%20Library/OlympicOrg/News/2020/12/Independent_Expert_Report_IOC_HumanRights.pdf.
- Amis, Lucy. "Mega-Sporting Events and Human Rights: A Time for More Teamwork?" *Business and Human Rights Journal* 2, no. 1 (2017): 135–141.

- Corrarino, Megan. "Law Exclusion Zones: Mega-Events as Sites of Procedural and Substantive Human Rights Violations." *Yale Human Rights and Development Law Journal* 17 (2014): 180–204.
- Ruggie, John G. *For the Game. For the World: FIFA and Human Rights* (2016). https://www.hks.harvard.edu/sites/default/files/centers/mrcbg/programs/cri/files/Ruggie_humanrightsFIFA_reportApril2016.pdf.

Non-governmental organization reports

- Amnesty International. *Reality Check: The State of Migrant Workers' Rights with Four Years to Go until the Qatar 2022 World Cup* (2019). https://www.amnesty.org/en/documents/mde22/3548/2016/en.
- Centre for Sport and Human Rights. *The Mega-Sporting Event Lifecycle: Embedding Human Rights from Vision to Legacy* (2018). https://www.sporthumanrights.org/library/the-mega-sporting-event-lifecycle-embedding-human-rights-from-vision-to-legacy.
- Centre on Housing Rights and Evictions (COHRE). *Fair Play for Housing Rights: Mega-Events, Olympic Games and Housing Rights: Opportunities for the Olympic Movement and Others* (2007). http://www.ruig-gian.org/ressources/Report%20Fair%20Play%20FINAL%20FINAL%20070531.pdf.
- Human Rights Watch. *Red Card: Exploitation of Construction Workers on World Cup Sites in Russia* (2017). https://www.hrw.org/sites/default/files/report_pdf/russiafifa0617_web_0.pdf.
- *Mega-Sporting Events Platform for Human Rights*. The Sporting Chance White Paper Series (2017). https://www.ihrb.org/megasportingevents/mse-news/sporting-chance-white-papers.

Cases

- *Handelsgericht des Kanton Zürich, Netherlands Trade Union Confederation (FNV) and Nadim Shariful Alam v. FIFA*. https://docplayer.net/44128350-Fnv-nadim-shariful-alam-versus-fifa-case-summary-1-introduction.html.
- OECD National Contact Point of Switzerland. "Initial Assessment: Specific Instance regarding the Fédération Internationale de Football Association (FIFA) submitted by Americans for Democracy and Human Rights in Bahrain (ADHRB)." August 17, 2016. https://www.oecdwatch.org/download/29341.
- *Sherpa v. Vinci Construction Grands Projects and Its Qatari subsidiary* (2015).

- *Sherpa, Comité contre l'Esclavage Moderne and six former Indian and Nepalese workers v. Vinci, Vinci Construction Grands Projets (VCGP), Its Qatar subsidiary, Qatari Diar Vinci Construction (QDVC)* (2018).

Videos

- Centre for Sport and Human Rights. "2018 Sporting Chance Forum: The Human Rights of Workers" January 24, 2019. YouTube video: 1:04:09. https://www.youtube.com/watch?v=1rmYrPctjSw.
- Children Win. "'I was playing marbles when the army guys shot me' – Police Violence in Complexo De Mare" October 14, 2014. YouTube video: 7:34. https://www.youtube.com/watch?v=iKYN6_DVI74.
- Children Win. Kell, Dara and Christopher Nizza, dirs. "The Fighter: The Rio Olympics are Tearing Naomy's Community Apart." Fireworks Media Film for Terre des Hommes. July 25, 2016. YouTube video: 25:38. https://www.youtube.com/watch?v=4vsjlt2xdqs.
- Journeyman Pictures. "The Hidden Brutality of Qatar's World Cup Preparations." June 8, 2015. YouTube Video: 22:54. https://www.youtube.com/watch?v=u6yoBcEXwmQ.
- Sobel, Adam, dir. *The Worker's Cup*. Documentary and Trailer. 2007. http://www.theworkerscupfilm.com.

Websites

- Centre for Sport and Human Rights. https://www.sporthumanrights.org/about-us/principles.
- EventRights. http://eventrights.net.

29. Trade and human rights

Margaret E. Roggensack and Eric R. Biel

OVERVIEW

At first glance, there would appear to be a clear symbiosis between trade and human rights that makes teaching about trade a logical, and perhaps not terribly challenging, part of a business and human rights (BHR) course curriculum. After all, the modern trade and modern human rights systems both grew out of the experiences of the 1930s and 1940s: the Great Depression, the rise of Fascism, World War II, and the efforts to put the international system back together again.

Indeed, a single pivotal year – 1948 – witnessed the adoption of the Universal Declaration of Human Rights and the Genocide Convention, linchpins of international human rights law, and the emergence of the norms that would govern global trade for the next half-century.[1] Those trade rules, however, only became enshrined as the infrastructure for global trade after the rejection of a bolder and more far-reaching agreement – the Havana Charter – that would have explicitly integrated human rights principles into the new trading system.

That development – and the marginalization of labor rights in trade agreements that followed for decades – is central to how we have tried to frame the discussion of international trade law and policy in our BHR course. Over our 13 years of teaching the course, we have expanded our effort to share this history with our students, particularly as labor rights finally have become more central to trade agreements. (See Labor Rights, Chapter 4.)

---

[1] January 1, 1948 was the official date for entry into force of the General Agreement on Tariffs and Trade (the GATT), even though the system came to be known as "GATT 1947." It was contemplated that the GATT rules then would be subsumed into a new International Trade Organization established by the Havana Charter, which was signed by 56 countries in March 1948. But when that failed to win U.S. support between 1948 and 1950 despite the efforts of the Truman Administration, the more modest GATT became the structure for advancing international cooperation on trade.

HISTORY OF INTERNATIONAL TRADE LAW

The traditional narrative of international trade law has ignored the fact that the General Agreement on Tariffs and Trade (GATT) only became the governing body of global trade due to a significant policy failure.[2] The demise of the proposed International Trade Organization (ITO) between 1948 and 1950, primarily due to the unwillingness of the United States Senate to ratify the Havana Charter in the face of strong business opposition, led to the more limited GATT structure carrying forward.

For many years, this story of the Havana Charter was largely missing from scholarship on the postwar trading system. That represents a huge historical omission because what was lost with the rejection of the ITO was nothing short of the opportunity to integrate labor rights and other provisions regarding business practices into that new trading system, fulfilling the vision of John Maynard Keynes and others. As Beth Baltzan has written, the U.S. Senate's opposition to enactment of the Havana Charter reflected an unwillingness to accept the notion not only of labor rights being integrated into global trade rules but also of a broader link between trade policy and business conduct.[3]

The recognition of this substantial effort decades ago to establish rules to address certain business practices is central to how we teach about trade law and policy in our BHR course.

HOW – AND WHY – DOES TRADE FIT IN THE BHR CURRICULUM?

Looking back, not focusing more on this historical narrative in the early years of teaching our BHR course complicated our efforts to explain the place of trade law and policy in our overall BHR syllabus and readings.

That challenge was magnified because, in getting our then novel BHR seminar at Georgetown Law approved with the title "Human Rights at the

---

[2]　GATT was succeeded by the World Trade Organization in 1994.

[3]　See, for example, Beth Baltzan, "The Old-School Answer to Global Trade", *Washington Monthly* (April/June 2019), https://washingtonmonthly.com/magazine/april-may-june-2019/the-old-school-answer-to-global-trade (53 countries signed the Havana Charter in 1948 and the Truman Administration supported it, but by 1950 the Administration had to abandon it in the wake of Senate opposition). See also Beth Baltzan, "It's Time to Rethink How We Regulate Global Trade," Open Society Foundations (November 2020), https://www.opensocietyfoundations.org/voices/its-time-to-rethink-how-we-regulate-global-trade; Trevor Sutton and Andy Green, "Adieu to Laissez-Faire Trade", *Democracy* (October 2020), https://democracyjournal.org/arguments/adieu-to-laissez-faire-trade.

Intersection of Trade and Corporate Responsibility," we expressly set ourselves up to try to explain the relationship among the pillars of trade, human rights, and business conduct. That title sounded good at the time, and we retained it for a decade before shifting to the less intriguing, but more accurate, "Business and Human Rights in the Global Economy" course title.

In the meantime, we had built a detailed and ever-evolving syllabus and reading list in which we were examining how human rights and corporate responsibility had come to interrelate over the previous two decades. And as former trade lawyers, we wanted to find a way to integrate the discussion of trade law and policy. So, we planned a session or two each semester on trade and human rights – looking forward to an interesting discussion based on our own work histories engaged in trade in private law practice, with a leading human rights organization, working in different multistakeholder initiatives, and in the legislative and executive branches of government.

But were we really finding a meaningful "intersection" between trade and corporate responsibility, as the longstanding course title suggested, that we could explain coherently to our students? And if so, how was it playing out within the broader and rapidly evolving world of business and human rights? Did our clever course title even make sense in that respect?

We clearly needed to go back to basics and ask why trade should be part of our BHR curriculum to begin with, and which trade issues merited scrutiny in the limited amount of time available during a seminar course. In exploring that question, we came to realize that teaching about trade in a BHR course has to be an historical inquiry – focusing on the arc of how labor rights came to be integrated, or in some important ways not, into trade negotiations, trade programs targeted at developing countries, and overall trade policy.

Our teaching on trade, human rights, and business had to be focused on the history of the previous decades, and the slow, uneven, but eventually substantial linkage between trade and labor rights – even as the WTO system remains largely devoid of labor coverage three quarters of a century after the ITO's rejection.

WHAT IS THE LINK BETWEEN TRADE AND BUSINESS CONDUCT?

While we were beginning to feel better about the trade leg of the stool and its relationship to human rights through the above historical framing, we faced another fundamental question: Where was the nexus between trade law and policy – largely the province of government – and business conduct? Put another way, where did trade fit with the broader discussion of corporate responsibility and efforts to hold business accountable for its human rights footprint? And how did trade advocacy directed at government officials, whether by business interests generally working to keep labor rights out of trade agreements or trade unions and civil society groups with exactly the opposite objective, tie in with discussions of corporate responsibility?

With our primary focus on the U.S. experience, we had plenty to work with in talking about worker rights provisions contained in trade agreements: moving forward from the North American Free Trade Agreement (NAFTA) in 1993 through a series of bilateral and regional agreements negotiated mainly by the George W. Bush Administration in the 2000s and then the decision at the beginning of the Trump Administration to abandon the Trans-Pacific Partnership (TPP)[4] – and framing much of it by going back to that missed opportunity of the Havana Charter in the aftermath of World War II. We were fully prepared to discuss the steadily increasing (though still far from adequate to labor rights advocates) efforts to "recapture" the lost trade-labor linkage in the course of different trade negotiations – and in the interactions between the executive and the legislative branch – both through more expansive coverage of labor rights and more enforceable provisions.

In addition, we had a great deal to convey regarding what are known as trade preference programs with developing countries, most notably the Generalized System of Preferences (GSP) but also regional ones such as the African Growth and Opportunity Act (AGOA), Caribbean Basin Initiative, and a series of measures tailored specifically to assist Haiti.[5] This discussion enabled us to explore the mix of "carrots and sticks" – trade incentives to foster improved labor rights (and other) performance and sanctions when program standards were not being met.

EXAMPLES OF A TRADE/LABOR/BUSINESS NEXUS

Where were the pieces of the trade and human rights discussion that involved direct linkages to business activities?

Fortunately, we did have a couple of modest examples to draw on. First, we could talk about the Haiti trade preference regime developed by the U.S. Government, which offers more liberal market access than under GSP, AGOA, or other programs. It includes (on a small scale, to be sure) for the first time a structure under with the U.S. Department of Labor's Bureau of International Labor Affairs (ILAB) is involved in monitoring labor rights conditions at

---

[4]   Congressional Research Service, "Worker Rights Provisions in Free Trade Agreements (FTAs)" (December 2020), https://fas.org/sgp/crs/misc/IF10046.pdf.

[5]   See AFL-CIO, *Raising Labor Standards Through Trade Preference Programs* (2020), https://aflcio.org/raising-labor-standards-through-trade-preference-programs.

specific factories exporting to the United States and conditioning access on compliance with applicable labor standards.[6]

This meant engagement between government and factory owners/suppliers (and the brands that sourced from them) concerning what measures those businesses needed to take in order to retain the trade benefits of program eligibility.

We also were able to discuss how the Clinton Administration in the late 1990s had developed an "incentive-based" program pursuant to a bilateral trade agreement under which greater market access was tied to Cambodian apparel factories meeting the core standards of the International Labor Organization.[7] This arrangement, which has been difficult to replicate since in the absence of a quota-based apparel trade structure, has prompted a fertile discussion of the relative merits of "positive" and "negative" methods – "carrots and sticks" in how trade is used to advance labor rights objectives.

That was a good start, but we still believed that we had not yet successfully found and advanced the nexus between trade, corporate responsibility/ accountability, and the foundational topic of business roles and responsibilities under Pillar II of the UN Guiding Principles on Business and Human Rights. (See The UN Guiding Principles on Business and Human Rights, Chapter 5.) We wanted to explore how trade policy decisions and business conduct might be more directly linked.

RECENT DEVELOPMENTS ESTABLISHING A STRONGER LINKAGE

Fortunately, in recent years, we have begun to be more successful in making our trade and human rights discussion more specifically relevant to the broader BHR framework and themes at the heart of our course.

Some of this has been due to our own greater recognition of how government-driven trade policy and private sector action (or inaction) can tie together. But more has been because government policymakers have decided to carry the expanding trade-labor linkages directly into the realm of corporate

---

[6] See Haitian Hemispheric Opportunity through Partnership Encouragement Act of 2008, 2018 USTR Annual Report on the Implementation of the Technical Assistance Improvement and Compliance Needs Assessment and Remediation (TAICNAR) Program and Assessment of Producer Eligibility, https://ustr.gov/sites/default/files/ 2018%20USTR%20Report%20Haiti%20HOPE%20II.PDF.

[7] See Sandra Polaski, "Combining Global and Local Forces: The Case of Labor Rights in Cambodia," World Development 34, no. 5 (May 2006), https:// carnegieendowment.org/2006/05/01/combining-global-and-local-forces-case-of-labor -rights-in-cambodia-pub-18544.

(mis)conduct through new approaches in trade negotiations and novel uses of expanded trade enforcement authority.

The three most notable developments with respect to U.S. trade policy have been:

(1)   The final negotiations of the U.S.-Mexico-Canada Trade Agreement (USMCA) and what has come to be known as the new "rapid response mechanism" targeting labor practices at particular factories;

(2)   The unleashing of Section 307 of the Tariff Act of 1930 in the wake of Congress' decision in 2015–16 to eliminate what was known as the "consumptive demand" exemption that had made the provision relatively toothless; and

(3)   The enactment of the Uyghur Forced Labor Protection Act of 2021, and its subsequent implementation by the Biden Administration.

Rapid Response Mechanism

The new rapid response mechanism enables petitions to be submitted with respect to certain labor conditions at a specific enterprise. From the U.S. side, the clear motivation for adding this novel provision was to enable actions to be targeted at factories in Mexico known to have persistent issues relating to freedom of association, inhibiting the ability of workers to freely organize.[8] This provision was a key difference maker in the passage of the USMCA with broad bipartisan support.

As of June 2022, there have been three petitions submitted under this mechanism. The first was brought by U.S. labor union and the second was "self-initiated" by the U.S. government.[9] Both cases resulted in responses from the Government of Mexico and redress for workers with respect to the core labor rights concerns raised – to the satisfaction of the key U.S. government agencies: the Office of the U.S. Trade Representative and the U.S. Department of Labor's ILAB.[10]

---

[8]   See, for example, Hogan Lovells, "USMCA's Rapid-Response Labor Mechanism" (February 2020), https://www.hoganlovells.com/~/media/hogan-lovells/pdf/2020-pdfs/2020_02_07_usmca_rapid_response_labor_mechanism.pdf?la=en.

[9]   See White & Case LLP, "USTR and US Labor Unions Initiate First Proceedings Targeting Mexican Facilities Under USMCA's 'Rapid Response' Mechanism" (May 2021), https://www.jdsupra.com/legalnews/ustr-and-us-labor-unions-initiate-first-4816417.

[10]   See the summaries of the two cases provided at U.S. Department of Labor, Bureau of International Labor Affairs, https://www.dol.gov/agencies/ilab/our-work/trade/labor-rights-usmca-cases.

The third, like the previous two, concerned practices in the automotive sector in Mexico, in this case at a Panasonic facility in the border city of Reynosa. After review of the petition, the U.S. government announced in mid-May 2022 that it was seeking Mexico's review of the alleged freedom of association and collective bargaining violations.[11]

Section 307

The "revitalized" Section 307 of the Tariff Act provides for import restrictions on products made with forced labor. It has been used by the U.S. government, following on active engagement by advocates long focused on efforts to eliminate forced labor and human trafficking,[12] to address a range of longstanding concerns about forced labor practices involved in the production of goods in different sectors.

However, since 2020 under both the Trump and Biden Administrations, it has focused primarily on the well-documented set of egregious human rights abuses in Xinjiang, western China.[13]

This has had major ramifications for a wide range of businesses sourcing (sometimes not knowingly) from that region, and reflects how the application of a provision tied to labor rights can have a direct impact on everything from companies' sourcing decisions to the level of due diligence they are prepared to perform concerning goods in their supply chains.[14]

Uyghur Forced Labor Protection Act

The Uyghur Forced Labor Prevention Act (UFLPA) was signed into law by President Biden on December 23, 2021. It reflects a broad bipartisan consensus

---

[11] See Office of the U.S. Trade Representative, https://ustr.gov/about-us/policy-offices/press-office/press-releases/2022/may/united-states-seeks-mexicos-review-alleged-freedom-association-and-collective-bargaining-violations (May 18, 2022).

[12] See Anasuya Syam and Meg Roggensack, "Importing Freedom: Using the U.S. Tariff Act to Combat Forced Labor in Supply Chains," The Human Trafficking Legal Center (2020), https://www.htlegalcenter.org/wp-content/uploads/Importing-Freedom-Using-the-U.S.-Tariff-Act-to-Combat-Forced-Labor-in-Supply-Chains_FINAL.pdf.

[13] Congressional Research Service, "Section 307 and Imports Produced by Forced Labor" (May 20, 2021), https://crsreports.congress.gov/product/pdf/IF/IF11360.

[14] See John Foote, "Can the U.S. End Supply Chain Links to Forced Uighur Labor?", LawFare (February 2, 2021), https://www.lawfareblog.com/can-us-end-supply-chain-links-forced-uighur-labor. U.S. Customs and Border Protection maintains a full list of Withhold Release Orders issued by the Commissioner and Findings published in the Federal Register, as organized by country, on its website at https://www.cbp.gov/trade/forced-labor/withhold-release-orders-and-findings.

concerning the need to further strengthen the tools available to combat imports from China made with forced labor.

At the core of the UFLPA is its establishment of a rebuttable presumption that the importation of any goods mined, produced, or manufactured wholly or in part in the Xinjiang region of China, or produced by certain entities, is prohibited by Section 307 of the Tariff Act of 1930 and that such goods are not entitled to entry into the United States. The presumption applies unless the Commissioner of U.S. Customs and Border Protection determines that the importer of record has complied with specified conditions and has demonstrated, by "clear and convincing evidence," that the goods were not produced using forced labor.

The UFLPA also requires an interagency Forced Labor Enforcement Task Force, chaired by the Secretary of Homeland Security, to develop and submit to Congress a strategy for supporting CBP's enforcement of Section 307 with respect to goods produced with forced labor in China.[15]

Beginning in 2020, our discussion of trade and human rights has focused heavily on Section 307 as applied to China and on the USMCA's rapid response mechanism. These have provided clear examples of the direct linkages between government trade policy mechanisms and business activities at the factory level and in global supply chains.

After years of working to establish a coherent linkage of trade to the rest of our BHR curriculum, we now have a clearer narrative that ties together trade, human rights, and business conduct/corporate responsibility.

TEACHING APPROACHES

Learning objectives for teaching trade and human rights may include:

- The history of labor rights provisions in trade agreements and trade preference programs – and their use to promote progress and to sanction non-compliance.
- How government trade policy decisions affect business decisions concerning the sourcing of products in sectors such as textiles/apparel and agriculture.

---

[15] There have been numerous legal and policy analyses of the UFLPA – many focusing on the Federal Register review process established after its enactment intended to clarify the "clear and convincing evidence" standard for overcoming the rebuttable presumption under the statute. See, for example, Verisk Maplecroft, "Everything You Need to Know about the Uyghur Forced Labour Prevention Act (UFLPA)" (May 2, 2022), https://www.maplecroft.com/insights/analysis/everything-you-need-to-know -about-the-uyghur-forced-labour-prevention-act-uflpa.

- Issues of enforcement of free trade and preference program labor rights provisions, such as the North American Agreement on Labor Cooperation of the NAFTA as compared with the USMCA Rapid Response Mechanism.

Teaching trade and human rights lends itself well to the use of guest speakers, given the specialized and technical nature of the subject matter and lack of accessible, integrative readings. We have relied heavily on guest speakers of three types: government officials, labor rights advocates, and those from academic institutes and clinics specializing in trade and labor rights. (See Teaching Resources below for relevant government agencies, worker rights organizations, and other stakeholders.) Class exercises can supplement lectures and guest speakers.

EXERCISE 29.1

FORCED LABOR IN XINJIANG

Ask students to assume the role of a lawyer advising an apparel brand client on how to comply with U.S. directives on forced labor in China's Xinjiang province and/or the threat of a Tariff Act Section 307 action. Students should consider the role of home governments in identifying and reporting on these risks, as well as the regulatory guidance available – or still missing. What elements of due diligence would be required, and what basic supply chain management issues should be addressed?

Other perspectives: assume the role of a civil society organization, or a company. What guidance should the U.S. Government provide to companies to ensure greater awareness of risks of forced labor in factories in China, including but not limited to Xinjiang? From the civil society or company perspective, what concerns would you have about government guidance and how would that inform your advocacy? Issues may include: parameters for corporate policy or benchmarks, whether to delineate requirements that if met would insulate companies from liability, such as self-certification or use of a third party to verify satisfaction of conditions or reporting requirements.

Further perspectives: assume the role of the enforcement agency and consider whether and when to order a ban on imports of goods, and how to address potential negative effects on workers as a result of the ban (for further guidance see the link to the Customs and Border Protection page in the Teaching Resources section).

EXERCISE 29.2

TRADE TOOLS TO ADDRESS LABOR RIGHTS ABUSES

Ask students to consider which of various trade tools might be available to address an ongoing and persistent pattern of labor rights abuse in a country – specifically, what would be the strengths and shortcomings of a Section 307 import ban, the withdrawal of preferential tariff benefits, or economic sanction? This question requires students to consider the impact on the workers as well as the level of home government leverage over the host country relative to other alternatives. An alternative approach is to ask students to consider this question from perspective of different agencies of the U.S. Government, such the Departments of Labor, State, and Commerce, and the Office of the U.S. Trade Representative.

EXERCISE 29.3

NEGOTIATING A TRADE AGREEMENT

Split students into two groups: one representing the U.S. Government and the other representing a country with a history of repressive working conditions. Provide the non-U.S. country team the more limited free trade agreement language[16] and give the U.S. Government team the most expansive version.[17] Ask students to negotiate a labor rights chapter for the trade agreement. This exercise can flesh out some of the differences in approaches and also the need for enforcement and related provisions.

KEY QUESTIONS

General

• What is the significance of the historical development of separate trade and labor frameworks to efforts to integrate both over recent decades?

---

[16] See, for example, pre-May 10, 2007 FTA agreement language: https://waysandmeans.house.gov/sites/democrats.waysandmeans.house.gov/files/documents/Concept%20Paper%20Final%205%2010%2007.pdf.

[17] See, for example, House Ways and Means Committee assessment of Trans-Pacific Partnership language (May 10 agreement): https://waysandmeans.house.gov/media-center/blog/tpp-focus-securing-rights-workers.

- How have trade mechanisms been used to address human rights? What are their limitations?
- What have been the impacts of trade negotiations and agreements on the structures of global supply chains?
- How can the greater integration of labor rights in trade agreements and preference programs affect decisions on sourcing and supply chains?

For Business Students

- How did business affect the development of the modern trade and labor rights frameworks?
- From a business perspective, what trade policymaking objectives are appropriate to identify and address labor and human rights issues?
- What trade remedy mechanisms are most/least effective from a business perspective in addressing labor issues in global supply chains?
- What role does business play in driving trade policies and what are the limits of business to address the human rights impacts of these policies?

For Law Students

- How have regional and bilateral trade agreements evolved to address human rights impacts?
- How have trade/labor-related remedies evolved in the context of free trade agreements, preference programs, and import restrictions such as Section 307 of the Tariff Act of 1930?
- What are the strengths and limitations of these approaches?
- What are the principal challenges to enforcement?

For Policy Students

- John Ruggie spoke of "horizontal policy coherence." What is its meaning and application in the context of trade and labor rights policy?
- What have been the principal challenges to enforcement of trade-related sanctions and remedies? Who are the principal external stakeholders affecting these considerations?
- What are the strengths and potential limitations of the USMCA approach – in particular the rapid response mechanism at the factory level – to strengthening labor rights protections?

TEACHING RESOURCES

Readings

- ILO. *Assessment of Labour Provisions in Trade and Investment Arrangements*. Geneva: ILO, 2016. https://www.ilo.org/wcmsp5/groups/public/---dgreports/---inst/documents/publication/wcms_498944.pdf.

U.S. Government resources

- Office of the U.S. Trade Representative. "Trade Agreements." https://ustr.gov/trade-agreements.
- Office of the U.S. Trade Representative. "Trade Enforcement: Issues, Remedies, and Roles." https://ustr.gov/sites/default/files/Trade-Enforcement_Issues-Remedies-and-Roles.pdf.
- Office of the U.S. Trade Representative. "US Trade Laws." https://ustr.gov/about-us/trade-toolbox/trade-laws.
- Office of the U.S. Trade Representative and ILAB. *Standing Up for Workers: Promoting Labor Rights through Trade to Promote Labor Rights through Trade Policy*. 2015. https://ustr.gov/sites/default/files/USTR%20DOL%20Trade%20-%20Labor%20Report%20-%20Final.pdf.
- U.S. Department of Homeland Security. "Customs and Border Protection Resource Page, including Existing Orders and Guidance." https://www.cbp.gov/trade/programs-administration/forced-labor.
- U.S. Department of Labor, Bureau of International Labor Affairs. "Trade Negotiation and Enforcement." https://www.dol.gov/agencies/ilab/our-work/trade.
- U.S. Department of State. "Guidance on Implementing the UN Guiding Principles for Transactions Linked to Foreign Government End Users for Products or Services with Surveillance Capabilities." https://www.state.gov/wp-content/uploads/2020/10/DRL-Industry-Guidance-Project-FINAL-1-pager-508-1.pdf.
- U.S. International Trade Administration. "Trade Preference Programs." https://www.trade.gov/trade-preference-programs.
- U.S.-Mexico-Canada Trade Agreement Labor Rights Report. https://www.dol.gov/sites/dolgov/files/ILAB/reports/FINAL-Labor-Rights-Report.pdf.

Non-governmental reports

- CSIS. *Addressing Forced Labor in the Xinjiang Uygur Autonomous Region.* https://csis-website-prod.s3.amazonaws.com/s3fs-public/publication/210203 _Lehr_Labor_XUAR.pdf.
- Human Trafficking Legal Center, *Practical Guide.* https://www .htlegalcenter.org/wp-content/uploads/Importing-Freedom-Using-the-U.S. -Tariff-Act-to-Combat-Forced-Labor-in-Supply-Chains_FINAL.pdf.
- International Corporate Accountability Roundtable. *Tools of Trade: US Sanctions Regimes and Accountability Strategies.* https://icar.ngo/wp -content/uploads/2021/04/SanctionsReport_Jun6-2018_WEBFINAL-1 .pdf.

Commentary

- Brewer, Elliot. "Closed Loophole: Investigating Forced Labor in Corporate Supply Chains Following the Repeal of the Consumptive Demand Exception." *Kansas Journal of Law & Public Policy* 28, no. 1 (2018): 87–112.
- Claussen, Kathleen. "Reimagining Trade-Plus Compliance: The Labour Story." *Journal of International Economic Law* 23, no. 1 (March 2020): 25.
- Harrison, James. "The Labour Rights Agenda in Free Trade Agreements." *The Journal of World Investment & Trade* 20 (2019): 705–725. 10.1163/22119000-12340153
- Posthuma, Anne and F. C. Ebert. "Labour Provisions in Trade Arrangements: Current Trends and Perspectives." *International Institute for Labour Studies* 1 (Discussion Paper 205, 2011), https://www.researchgate.net/publication/ 263734653_Labour_provisions_in_trade_arrangements_current_trends_and _perspectives.
- Vidigal, Geraldo. "Why Is There So Little Litigation under Free Trade Agreements? Retaliation and Adjudication in International Dispute Settlement." *Journal of International Economic Law* 20, no. 4 (December 2019): 927.

Websites

- AFL-CIO. "Trade." https://aflcio.org/issues/trade.
- Corporate Accountability Lab. https://corpaccountabilitylab.org.
- International Labor Rights Forum. "Trade Justice." https://laborrights.org/ strategies/trade-justice-0.
- ILO. "Better Work." https://www.ilo.org/global/programmes-and-projects/ WCMS_084616/lang--de/index.htm.

- ILO. "Free Trade Agreements and Labor Rights." https://www.ilo.org/global/standards/information-resources-and-publications/free-trade-agreements-and-labour-rights/lang--en/index.htm.
- ILO. "Labor Provisions in Trade Agreements Hub." https://www.ilo.org/LPhub.
- Public Citizen. "Globalization and Trade." https://www.citizen.org/topic/globalization-trade.
- Solidarity Center. "Workers and Human Rights." https://www.solidaritycenter.org/what-we-do/workers-human-rights/#.

30. Business and conflict
Salil Tripathi

OVERVIEW

Between 1995 and 2000, former United States Vice-President Dick Cheney was the chairman and chief executive officer of Halliburton Corp., the world's second-largest company servicing the oil industry. Halliburton operates in many parts of the world, including Africa, Asia, and the Middle East, and it is often in countries that are riven by conflict.

Extractive industries are often accused of benefiting from, or contributing to, conflict. The companies claim they have nothing to do with such conflict. Explaining the industry's rationale for being in fragile zones, Cheney had once said: "The Good Lord did not see it fit to put oil and gas only where there are democratically elected regimes."[1]

Cheney's point was that extractive companies must invest and do business wherever they find resources; they don't have the choice of investing only in countries that are at peace, or which are democratic, with rule of law and transparency. While it is true that resources can be extracted only where minerals are found, there is no fundamental reason why resources cannot be harnessed in ways that benefit the people without harming human rights.

This chapter outlines why a business and human rights (BHR) course should include a section on business and conflict. Even if companies are not engaged in industries that are intrinsic to conflict, such as arms manufacture and defense technology companies, their mere presence can exacerbate conflict, and their activities may prolong conflict. A company may also face reputational as well as legal challenges because of its presence in a conflict zone. Companies may also have to act and intervene in conflict situations to assist civilians. Increasingly, they are expected to take political positions with regard to conflict. The United Nations Working Group on Business and Human

---

[1] *The Wall Street Journal*, November 3, 2000 (citing speech delivered at the Cato Institute on June 23, 1998).

Rights expects companies to conduct "heightened due diligence" in situations of armed conflict.

THE EXTRACTIVE SECTOR AND HUMAN RIGHTS

Managing resources responsibly and realizing all human rights – civil, political, economic, social, and cultural – is the primary obligation of the state. At the same time, the academic literature[2] points out the pernicious effect of oil wealth on an economy. The so-called "resource curse" often leads to distorted investments, weakens transparency, entrenches oligarchies, leads to currency appreciation[3] that can undermine local manufacturing, and fuels conflict.[4] When the late John Ruggie began his study of existing BHR initiatives[5] to understand the adverse human rights impacts of business, he noted that of the nearly five dozen reports produced by human rights groups that focused on corporate impacts on human rights, nearly two-thirds dealt with the oil and mining sector.

Some of the prominent cases filed under the Alien Tort Statute against corporations in the United States had major extractive companies as defendants. (See The Alien Tort Statute, Chapter 13.) Aware that the industry has a problem, the extractive sector worked with governments and civil society groups to develop multistakeholder initiatives to promote responsible behavior. These initiatives include the Voluntary Principles for Security and Human Rights (2000)[6] that deal with the way the extractive sector should engage with private and public security forces. The Extractives Industries Transparency

---

    [2]   Jeffrey Frankel, "The Natural Resource Curse: A Survey of Diagnoses and Some Prescriptions" CID Working Paper #233, Harvard Kennedy School (2012), https://www.hks.harvard.edu/centers/cid/publications/faculty-working-papers/natural-resource-curse#:~:text=Countries%20with%20oil%2C%20mineral%20or,as%20the%20Natural%20Resource%20Curse. See also "The Resource Curse," *NRGI Reader* (March 2015), https://resourcegovernance.org/sites/default/files/nrgi_Resource-Curse.pdf; Jeffrey D. Sachs and Andrew M. Warner, "The Curse of Natural Resources" *European Economic Review*, 45 (2001): 827–838.
    [3]   Christine Ebrahimzadeh, "Dutch Disease: Wealth Managed Unwisely," *Finance and Development* (2020), https://www.imf.org/external/pubs/ft/fandd/basics/dutch.htm.
    [4]   Macartan Humphreys, "Natural Resources, Conflict, and Conflict Resolution: Uncovering the Mechanisms," *Journal of Conflict Resolution,* 49, no. 4 (August 2005): 508–537.
    [5]   John Ruggie, "Business and Human Rights: The Evolving International Agenda." *The American Journal of International Law* 101, no. 4 (2007): 819–840.
    [6]   "The Voluntary Principles," Voluntary Principles on Security and Human Rights, accessed August 31, 2022, https://www.voluntaryprinciples.org/the-principles.

Initiative (2003)[7] is intended to reduce corruption in the way royalties are shared and revenue is managed from extracting resources in host countries. The Kimberley Process Certification Scheme (2003)[8] was developed to eliminate trade in conflict diamonds from war-torn countries in Africa (in particular Angola, Sierra Leone, Liberia, and the Democratic Republic of Congo).

Human rights reports were written, lawsuits were filed, and these initiatives emerged because of the correlation between extractive sector, conflict, human rights abuses, and poor governance.

ADDRESSING POOR GOVERNANCE AND CONFLICT

The international community's response to poor governance and conflict has been mixed. Sanctioning the commodities in each instance is not an option, since many commodities are critical for the global economy to function and alternative supplies do not exist or are uneconomical to produce. In instances where a country is not strategically significant, the international community has tended to be more willing to impose sanctions or outlaw investments, as had been the case with the Sudan and Myanmar. In other countries that are crucial suppliers of critical resources, regardless of how odious the countries' human rights record may be, the international community has looked the other way and continued to do business. For example, Saudi Arabia has rarely faced similar scrutiny, despite its terrible human rights record or the conflict it is engaged with in Yemen. The Russian Federation has faced significant sanctions recently after it flouted international law and invaded Ukraine in February 2022.

Countries that impose sanctions often do so for reasons that have less to do with human rights and more with other strategic priorities. Relatively weaker and strategically less significant states are more likely to face hard sanctions than more powerful states. Countries that declare sanctions routinely apply double standards.

Even if sanctions are a necessary tool, they are not sufficient to bring about change. This is because sanctions are not applied uniformly, consistently, or evenly, and they are not applied universally. There is always an incentive for some country to bust sanctions to make lucrative gains. Despite the application of fairly rigorous sanctions following the Russian invasion of Ukraine in 2022, Russian oil continues to get traded; the Russian economy has not collapsed. The effectiveness of imposing sanctions to bring about meaningful change has been mixed, unless the enforcement is rigorous.

---

[7]   Extractives Industries Transparency Initiative, https://eiti.org.
[8]   Kimberley Process, https://www.kimberleyprocess.com.

South Africa became an apartheid state soon after the National Party came to power in 1948; India was an early country to apply sanctions on South Africa. In 1991, while the sanctions were still in place, this author found a wide range of Indian-made consumer goods easily available in Durban, South Africa.[9] Most other countries imposed sports and cultural boycotts, and consumer boycotts meant products visible in supermarkets, such as wines, were unavailable, but South African gold coins were traded easily, South African businesses were able to maintain bank accounts abroad, and South African businesses in industries not visible to consumers (such as defense equipment) continued to do business. Companies busted sanctions and it raised the cost of doing business. It took the end of the Soviet Union and diminishing importance of South Africa as a frontline state (as well as the unraveling of apartheid at home) for South Africa to initiate changes that led to its first non-racial election and the end of apartheid.

Compliance of sanctions regimes is often spotty and penalties are few. While the United States vigorously pursued companies that violated sanctions imposed on Iraq and Iran in the 1990s and later, the US has been less aggressive in charging companies that may violate trade norms with other countries in conflict.

Organizations calling for action to address business activity connected to conflict include campaigning groups, advocacy groups, ethical investors, and socially responsible investment funds. They target listed companies with high brand visibility. Their underlying assumption is that evidence-based campaigning to name and shame companies will force the companies to modify their conduct or to use their influence – overtly or covertly – over the concerned state that is violating human rights.

CORPORATE COMPLICITY IN STATE HUMAN RIGHTS ABUSES

Companies were alleged to have been complicit in the human rights abuses committed by the army, paramilitary forces, or other defense forces in Nigeria

---

[9]   See, for example, Salil Tripathi, "As Apartheid Crumbles, Indians Face Suspicion in South Africa," *India Today* June 15, 1992, https://www.indiatoday.in/magazine/international/story/19920615-as-apartheid-crumbles-indians-face-suspicion-in-south-africa-766456-2013-01-04.

(Shell),[10] Colombia (BP[11] and Occidental Petroleum),[12] Indonesia (Mobil Corp, now ExxonMobil),[13] Sudan (Talisman),[14] and Myanmar (Total[15] and Unocal[16]). In the 1990s, Shell and other oil companies in the Niger Delta were targeted for not doing enough to prevent the execution of Ken Saro-Wiwa and other Ogoni leaders.[17] In Colombia, BP was criticized[18] for its ties with paramilitary forces guarding the pipelines, and Occidental Petroleum was criticized for and accused of grabbing the land of minority groups in Colombia.[19] In Indonesia, Mobil was accused[20] of facilitating the security forces to commit abuses against pro-independence activists; in the Sudan,[21] Talisman Energy was accused of facilitating the conflict in the country's south (before its eventual secession); and in Myanmar, Total and Unocal[22] were accused of using forced labor provided by the army to build pipelines. Amnesty International and Human Rights Watch produced detailed reports investigating the abuses, and lawsuits were filed in the United States and Europe in each of these cases. To be fair, these were accusations, not proven, although in some instances

---

[10] Human Rights Watch, *The Price of Oil* (1999), https://www.hrw.org/reports/1999/nigeria; Amnesty International *Are Human Rights in the Pipeline?* (2004), https://www.amnesty.org/en/documents/afr44/020/2004/en.

[11] Amnesty International, *BP Risks Human Rights Conflict through Military Training* (1997), http://hrlibrary.umn.edu/links/aicolombia.html.

[12] Corporate Watch, "Occidental Petroleum to Leave U'wa Land" (2002), https://www.corpwatch.org/article/occidental-petroleum-leave-uwa-land.

[13] Michael Shari, "Indonesia: What Did Mobil Know?" *Businessweek*, December 28, 1998, https://www.bloomberg.com/news/articles/1998-12-27/indonesia-what-did-mobil-know#xj4y7vzkg.

[14] Amnesty International, "Talisman Energy Must Do More to Protect Human Rights" (2001), https://www.amnesty.org/en/documents/afr54/010/2001/en.

[15] "Total Settles Rights Case," *The New York Times*, November 29, 2005, https://www.nytimes.com/2005/11/29/business/worldbusiness/total-settles-rights-case.html.

[16] Earth Rights International, "Doe v Unocal" (2003), https://earthrights.org/case/doe-v-unocal/#:~:text=Unocal%20was%20forced%20to%20settle,in%20compensation%20for%20the%20survivors.&text=The%20plaintiffs%20were%20Burmese%20villagers,units%20securing%20the%20pipeline%20route.

[17] The 1995 executions continue to haunt Shell. See Ed Pilkington, "Shell Pays Out $15.5m over Saro-Wiwa Killing," *The Guardian*, June 8, 2009, https://www.theguardian.com/world/2009/jun/08/nigeria-usa; Amnesty International, "Nigeria: Shell Complicit in the Arbitrary Executions of Ogoni Nine as Writ Served in Dutch Court," (2017), https://www.amnesty.org/en/latest/press-release/2017/06/shell-complicit-arbitrary-executions-ogoni-nine-writ-dutch-court.

[18] *The Sunday Times,* https://asbarez.com/bp-accused-of-backing-arms-for-oil-coup-says-sunday-times.

[19] Corporate Watch, "Occidental Petroleum to Leave U'wa Land."

[20] See *Doe VIII v. Exxon Mobil Corp.*, 654 F. 3d. 57 (D.C. Cir., 2011).

[21] See *Presbyterian Church of Sudan v. Talisman Energy* (2nd Cir., 2009).

[22] See *Doe v. Unocal*, 395 F. 3d. 932 (9th Cir., 2002).

(as with Total and Unocal in Myanmar and Shell in Nigeria), the companies settled with victims without admitting wrongdoing.

In each of these instances, the entity committing the abuse – the state – was neither sued nor targeted by advocacy groups. Nor were companies that were contractors or suppliers, even if they were operating in the fragile zone, if they did not have a retail presence in the form of a gas station, for instance, or if they were not listed companies. Companies that were not from the developed world were also spared from allegations. For example, in Nigeria, the majority stake in oil concessions is typically owned by the Nigerian National Petroleum Company. In Colombia, the state-owned EcoPetrol was a partner of Occidental and had other business relationships with other companies. In Indonesia, the state oil company Pertamina was in partnership with international oil majors. In the Sudan, the Chinese National Petroleum Corp., Malaysia's Petronas, and India's ONGC Videsh were also invested in disputed territories. In Myanmar, the former Petroleum Authority of Thailand, now known as PTT, and the Myanmar Oil and Gas Enterprise (MOGE) have been partners of multinational firms, but have been largely spared from being targeted by campaigning groups. This dynamic has begun to change. As more companies from the developing world have begun raising capital from Western capital markets, increasingly investor groups have begun to focus on those companies, such as India's Adani group over its activities in Australia[23] and Myanmar.[24]

CORPORATE RESPONSES

One reason campaigning groups target companies is because companies are more likely to respond to criticism, by at least engaging in a conversation with civil society groups, unlike some governments, which ignore the campaigning groups. Human rights advocates in the Niger Delta have said that companies like Agip (now part of Eni), ExxonMobil, TotalEnergies, and Shell, which have all had operations there, would at least engage with Nigerian civil society groups over their concerns over pollution or human rights abuses, unlike the local and federal governments. While the companies do not admit any wrongdoing, they are willing to speak to civil society groups for three reasons:

(1) to learn about the local environment;
(2) to improve their reputation, burnish their public relations, and seek the social license to operate; and

---

[23] See, for example, "#StopAdani," https://www.stopadani.com.

[24] "India's Adani Faces Scrutiny over Port Deal in Myanmar," *The Wall Street Journal*, April 19, 2021, https://www.wsj.com/articles/indias-adani-faces-scrutiny-for -port-deal-in-myanmar-11618824601.

(3)   to figure out if there are practical steps they can take to bring about change.

Companies often defend their failure to meet the expectations of civil society by arguing: (1) that the state is the primary duty bearer for human rights; and (2) that the corporate responsibility to respect human rights under the UN Guiding Principles for Business and Human Rights (UNGPs)[25] does not create a legal obligation. But even where cases prosecuted against companies for criminal liability or complicity in a conflict zone are few, and the evidentiary threshold is high, there is growing understanding among companies that there may be liabilities in instances of potential violations of international crimes or international criminal law. But companies do face risks for their conduct during conflict, or their role in contexts of massive human rights abuses, and the web of liabilities is expanding.[26] Many companies say they do not initiate conflict, do not benefit from it, and nor do they prolong it. While many companies prefer operating in a society with a level playing field, where laws are clear and transparent and applied fairly, conflict produces war economies,[27] and there are other companies which benefit from such conflict, and/or seek to prolong conflict, interfering with peace processes.[28] These companies are often described as "predators" or "bottom feeders." The literature on war economies shows shadowy companies, headquartered in tax havens, with complicated ownership structures, which run the risk of being complicit in abuses because they trade with intermediary companies in conflict commodities, or provide

---

[25]   United Nations Human Rights Council, *Guiding Principles on Business and Human Rights: Implementing the United Nations "Protect, Respect and Remedy" Framework*, Report of the Special Representative of the Secretary-General on the issue of human rights and transnational corporations and other business enterprises, UN doc. A/HRC/17/31 (March 21, 2011) (UN Guiding Principles).

[26]   Robert Thompson, Anita Ramasastry, and Mark Taylor, "Translating *Unocal*: The Expanding Web of Liability for Business Entities Implicated in International Crimes," *George Washington International Law Review* 40, no. 4 (2009): 841–902; Jennifer Zerk, "Extraterritorial Jurisdiction: Lessons for the Business and Human Rights Sphere from Six Regulatory Areas" (Harvard Kennedy School, Working Paper 59, 2010), https://www.hks.harvard.edu/sites/default/files/centers/mrcbg/programs/cri/files/workingpaper_59_zerk.pdf; Office of the High Commissioner for Human Rights 'Accountability and Remedy Project' (2016), https://www.ohchr.org/en/business/ohchr-accountability-and-remedy-project/phase1-judicial-mechanisms; Red Flags Initiative (International Alert and Fafo, 2009), https://redflags.info.

[27]   Karen Ballentine and Jake Sherman, *The Political Economy of Armed Conflict: Beyond Greed and Grievance* (Boulder, CO: Lynne Rienner, 2003).

[28]   Heiko Nitschke and Kaysie Studdard, "The Legacies of War Economies: Challenges and Options for Peacemaking and Peacebuilding," *International Peacekeeping* 12 (2005): 222–239.

weapons, or pay illicit taxes to armed groups to continue operating, as cases from Liberia, Sierra Leone, and the Democratic Republic of Congo have shown.[29] The conduct of these companies may expose them to the risk of being complicit in international crimes. (See Complicity, Chapter 14.)

BUSINESS ACTIVITY IN ZONES OF CONFLICT

Many companies are law-abiding and yet they continue to operate in zones of conflict. Four lessons can be drawn from their conduct.

- **Companies providing essential services must consider the human rights impacts of exiting a conflict zone, as well as the risk of complicity in human rights abuses.** Some companies are providing services that are essential for human life and for the enjoyment of human rights. These include companies that provide food, water, electricity, pharmaceuticals, telecommunications, and other products that are considered necessary for human existence. These companies allow civilian life to continue even in cities being bombed, and their departure would either deprive the civilian population of essential goods and services, or drive up the prices, both of which would have adverse consequences for human rights, particularly of vulnerable, marginalized, and poor groups.

   However, as the experience of aid agencies in Ethiopia during its tragedies of famine and civil war have shown, sometimes actors providing essential services end up being exposed to the risk of being accused of complicity in the conflict, because their presence and activities enable the war economy to survive.[30] One of the risks is that sometimes the aid they intend to deliver may not reach civilians but gets appropriated by armed groups.

   A company that provides electricity to a city also supplies power to an ordnance factory. An oil company providing aviation fuel to aircraft which distributed famine relief (as in Sudan) was accused of providing the same

---

    [29]   Global Witness, "Wartime Timber Company DLH Penalized for Trading Illegal Liberian Private Use Permit Logs" (2015), https://www.globalwitness.org/en/archive/wartime-timber-company-dlh-penalized-trading-illegal-liberian-private-use-permit-logs-0.

    [30]   Gayle Smith, "Ethiopia and the Politics of Aid Relief," *MERIP* 145 (March 1987), https://merip.org/1987/03/ethiopia-and-the-politics-of-famine-relief. Politicization of aid has continued in the more recent conflict. Vanda Felibab-Brown, "Still Far From Peace in Ethiopia," Brookings Institution (February 1, 2022), https://www.brookings.edu/blog/order-from-chaos/2022/02/01/still-far-from-peace-in-ethiopia.

fuel to the Sudanese Air Force, which was bombing villages in the south, and later promised to make amends.[31]

- **Companies that remain in a conflict zone run the risk of being complicit in the conflict because of the payments they make to the warring party, be it the state or an armed opposition group.** Campaigning groups have often demanded that such companies should stop paying taxes to the government (or the armed group) that is abusing human rights, as such payments enable further abuses. A coalition of civil society groups called Business for Ukraine has, for example, called upon companies in Russia to leave the country or to stop paying taxes.[32] The demand has been more vociferous in Myanmar, where the military has arrested politicians including elected representatives and annulled elections after staging a coup in 2021. Companies operating in Myanmar are being urged to stop paying taxes.[33]

  But corporate lawyers have argued that companies do not have that choice. If companies unilaterally stop paying taxes, they run the risk of asset forfeiture, arrest of expatriate staff, and may face other penalties. Companies do not get the right to decide which tax to pay and which tax not to pay, unless the bilateral tax treaty between the countries permits such action, which is rarely the case. And even if that were the case, the matter can only be decided in a court of law or through arbitration. The case for a company to stop paying a specific tax to a government on moral grounds is legally problematic.

- **Companies in conflict zones must assess the human rights risks of their business relationships.** Companies face further complicity risks depending on who their partners and suppliers are, and how they treat their workers. If the company's local partners are associated with the government, or are government-owned companies, then the risk is heightened. Money being a fungible commodity, a company cannot control how the money it pays is used by the government. A company cannot say that the profits it shares, dividends it contributes, or fees it pays will only be used for specific purposes, or that they will not go toward paying for the conflict.

  This is where how a company chooses its partners becomes crucial. In many developing countries, foreign companies find it expedient and

---

[31] Terry Macalister, "Shell Tries to Block Bomber Fuel," *The Guardian*, May 18, 2001, https://www.theguardian.com/business/2001/may/18/internationalnews.

[32] See "Business for Ukraine," https://businessforukraine.info.

[33] Private conversation with the author.

opportune to tie up with well-connected local entrepreneurs with close ties to the government. While that may enable them to get their projects cleared quickly, it also exposes them to risks when the human rights situation worsens, since that is when the links with those entrepreneurs expose the companies to charges of being complicit.

- **Companies in conflict zones should be aware of the reputational risks of operating in such countries.** Companies that do not have a retail presence – in the supermarket, the mall, or at a gas station – are less likely to face pressure from consumers. If a business does not produce a product or offer a service that can be targeted, it is less likely to be the target of a boycott campaign. In such situations, companies may find it easier to continue operating in conflict zones. Suppliers of transformers, electrical equipment, diesel engines, critical components and machinery sold in business-to-business relationships often bypass consumer scrutiny, although they may prop up a war economy. Companies that are not listed on stock markets, or which rely on private equity, likewise are relatively immune from public criticism.

ADDRESSING HUMAN RIGHTS IMPACTS IN ZONES OF CONFLICT

Some companies choose to leave a conflict zone because of pressure from their domestic constituencies and markets. Companies headquartered in OECD countries – in particular, North America and Europe – are more likely to face consumer pressure than companies from Brazil, India, China, Russia, or South Africa. Products and services targeted at idealistic consumers, young people, and millennials are particularly vulnerable, and such companies are more likely to leave a conflict zone promptly, as can be seen in the speed with which companies like Coca-Cola and McDonald's left Russia after it invaded Ukraine.[34] Sometimes, such decisions are guided with a view to burnish the company's public image.

However, companies that leave without a proper plan, too, face human rights risks. For example, a company that leaves with inadequate preparation

---

[34] The Coca-Cola Company, "The Coca Cola Company Suspends Its Business in Russia," press release, March 8, 2022, https://www.coca-colacompany.com/media-center/press-releases/coca-cola-company-suspends-business-russia; McDonalds, "McDonalds to Exit from Russia," press release, May 16, 2022, https://corporate.mcdonalds.com/corpmcd/en-us/our-stories/article/ourstories.mcd-exit-russia.html#:~:text=CHICAGO%2C%20May%2016%2C%202022%20%E2%80%93,to%20sell%20its%20Russian%20business.

makes its local staff vulnerable to sudden loss of income as well as to pressure from the government, which may target the workers because the government can no longer punish the company. Companies also bear the responsibility to evacuate their own expatriate staff and dependents. International law does not require them to evacuate staff that includes local citizens from the country in which they are doing business, or third-country nationals, but they do have the responsibility to liaise with the embassies of third-country nationals for their safe passage, and with organizations such as the ICRC to protect their own staff drawn from local citizens.[35] Sometimes, the local staff is more vulnerable, particularly if they are from an ethnic minority and the conflict is on ethnic grounds, as was the case in Rwanda. What was the responsibility of a foreign company in Rwanda toward its Tutsi staff during the 1994 genocide in which Tutsis suffered disproportionate deaths? The company that leaves without a plan leaves its own staff and consumers in distress and makes it harder for it to return, should it ever wish to do so.

Companies need to note that their departure won't necessarily end abuses. Talisman's sale of its business did not end the war in the Sudan; Telenor's departure from Myanmar[36] does not mean that Myanmar won't have cellphone services anymore. As campaigning groups have argued, in fact, the absence of companies that claim to operate within the framework of the UNGPs (such as Telenor) could mean the entry of companies that have fewer scruples.

Companies face these dilemmas regarding their human rights impacts because there are no unambiguous rules about how they are expected to act in countries facing armed conflict. Except where there are clear sanctions that outlaw business with a particular country, companies are left to their own devices. That makes them susceptible to pressure from civil society groups, public opinion, investor expectations, and other factors that are often subjective.

None of this makes the task of a company that wishes to operate under the law and comply with international norms any simpler. Neither international criminal law nor international human rights law provides clear answers. While all companies are expected to conduct human rights due diligence in all contexts, the UN Working Group on Business and Human Rights has called

---

[35] Alex Irwin-Hunt, "Ukraine War: Are Foreign Firms Taking Care of Their Local Staff?' *FDI Intelligence* 11 (March 2022), https://www.fdiintelligence.com/content/feature/ukraine-war-are-foreign-firms-taking-care-of-their-local-staff-80776.

[36] Telenor, "Sale of Myanmar Telenor Approved by Myanmar Authorities," March 18, 2022, https://www.telenor.com/media/newsroom/press-releases/sale-of-telenor-myanmar-approved-by-myanmar-authorities.

for "heightened due diligence"[37] in cases where companies are operating in high-risk environments. This offers greater clarity for businesses about how it should approach the problem and how they must assess the impact of its decision to stay or to leave. As companies navigate this difficult path, they will need to be guided by two principles in conflict zones: (1) corporate actions should not contribute to grave abuses during armed conflict, which can expose them to potential complicity in violations of international law; and (2) businesses must ensure that a decision to leave a conflict zone does not worsen the human rights situation. Those are not easy calls and there is no solution that's fit for every purpose.

The recently published guidance by the UNDP and the UN Working Group for Business and Human Rights calls upon businesses in conflict-affected contexts to identify not only actual or potential adverse human rights impacts, but also actual or potential adverse impacts on conflict that the business may cause or contribute to due to its own activities, or those that may be directly linked to its operations, products, or services. The guidance states that while sanctions are a useful indicator, they are not a substitute for heightened due diligence. The context of a conflict varies from place to place, and is dynamic. In armed conflicts and other instances of widespread violence, businesses should carry out heightened due diligence on an ongoing basis and update assessments at regular intervals. The guidance also provides a framework to assess impact based on scale (how widespread is the conflict?), scope (how grave is the violence?), and irremediability (how practical is it and what are the limits of restoring the impacted people to the pre-conflict state?). The guidance calls upon companies to adopt a well-thought-out, proper exit strategy since a hasty exit can be as damaging as an exit that comes too late. Specifically, the guidance says companies should consider whether exiting or suspending could exacerbate tensions, and whether the potential harm to people outweighs benefits. The decision, ultimately, rests with the company; it is perhaps impossible for there to be guidance that applies in each case and every eventuality. But even the guidance offered by the UN Working Group provides a broad overview of questions to be answered, rather than the answers themselves.

---

[37] United Nations Development Programme and the UN Working Group on Business and Human Rights, *Heightened Human Rights Due Diligence for Business in Conflict-Affected Contexts: A Guide* (New York, 2022), https://www.undp.org/sites/g/files/zskgke326/files/2022-06/UNDP_Heightened_Human_Rights_Due_Diligence_for_Business_in_Conflict-Affected_Contexts_V2.pdf.

TEACHING APPROACHES

In courses on BHR that I curate or teach at two universities, I invite external faculty, including law school professors, practitioners, and corporate executives, to discuss both the theory and practice of corporate interface with conflict. The students are typically mid-career or early-career professionals, civil society groups, government officials (including from armed forces), or law firms. The classes that deal with conflict typically unpack a difficult situation and apply human rights standards to understand what the company could have done better. Where does the company get exposed to risk, what steps might it consider to mitigate harm, and what options should it consider to reduce liability? The framing lecture shows that the drivers for corporate action include not only the need to comply with the law but also reputational risks, besides the safety of staff and their families.

Learning objectives may include:

- Understanding the legal, financial, safety, and reputational risks of operating in a conflict zone.
- Understanding how the UNGPs treat issues of exposure to complicity and international crimes.
- Applying due diligence principles to specific situations and contexts.
- Examining how companies make their decisions and understanding the positive and adverse impacts of those decisions.

EXERCISE 30.1

SHOULD A COMPANY LEAVE A CONFLICT ZONE?

Among the real-life cases the experts and I teach in the course include the diamond industry in West Africa, oil in the Niger Delta and Colombia, and telecommunications in Myanmar. Current and former executives speak of their experiences in other contexts. In one case involving an oil company in a Latin American country riven by conflict, which I have taught for several years, the company has the option of drilling in a disused oil field because the oil price has risen to a point where drilling that region is economically viable again. Meanwhile, thousands of people have moved into the area, since industrial activity had ended a few years ago and it is safer to live there than in nearby areas where armed groups are in conflict with government forces. If the company were to begin operations, it would have to relocate the people. Is it possible to do it responsibly? What safeguards can be placed? What are the risks of operating? Or is it better not to drill at all?

I divide the class into three groups, with one representing the multinational company, one representing its local partner, and one representing civil society. Students examine specific questions about whether or not civilian population should be relocated because the company wants to initiate exploration, but moving the people in nearby areas may expose them to violent conflict.

Other cases which offer concrete examples include:

* Talisman Energy in the Sudan
* Shell in the Niger Delta
* BP in Colombia
* Lafarge Holcim in Syria
* TotalEnergies or Telenor in Myanmar
* De Beers and the international diamond sector in Sierra Leone/Liberia
* Facebook and the spread of hate speech in Myanmar

KEY QUESTIONS

General

* What are the elements of international law that apply to business in conflict contexts?
* How do the UNGPs apply in conflict contexts?
* How can companies assess the risks they pose and the risks they face?
* What elements should inform human rights due diligence in conflict contexts?

For Business Students

* What are the risks that a company faces during conflict, and what are the risks accompany poses during conflict?
* What steps should a company consider to mitigate harm?
* What functions within a company should be involved in decision-making?
* Which external stakeholders should the company consult?
* How should a company manage the decision it takes – to stay or to leave?
* What factors should companies that provide essential services consider, should they choose to stay or leave?

For Law Students

- How do legal definitions of responsibility apply to the state and non-state actors such as companies?
- How does the definition of aiding/abetting apply to companies?
- How does the definition of known/should have known apply to companies?
- What legal avenues do victims have to sue companies?
- What does the UNGP concept "cause, contribute, or directly linked" mean in the context of companies affected by conflict?

For Policy Students

- Are companies complicit in conflict when they pay taxes to the government? To an armed opposition group?
- What internal policy measures should companies have to reduce the likelihood of being exposed to conflict?
- What policy measures exist for states to guide corporate conduct during conflict?

TEACHING RESOURCES

Readings

- Ballentine, Karen and Jake Sherman, eds. *The Political Economy of Armed Conflict: Beyond Greed and Grievance* (Boulder, CO: Lynne Rienner, 2003).
- Office of the High Commissioner for Human Rights. "Accountability and Remedy Project" (2016). https://www.ohchr.org/en/business/ohchr -accountability-and-remedy-project/phase1-judicial-mechanisms.
- Thompson, Robert, Anita Ramasastry, and Mark Taylor. "Translating *Unocal*: The Expanding Web of Liability for Business Entities Implicated in International Crimes." *George Washington International Law Review*, 40 no. 4 (2009): 841–902.
- Van Ho, Tara. "Business and Human Rights in Transitional Justice: Challenges for Complex Environments." In *Research Handbook on Human Rights and Business*, eds. Surya Deva and David Birchall (Cheltenham: Edward Elgar Publishing, 2020), 379–401.
- Zerk, Jennifer. "Extraterritorial Jurisdiction: Lessons for the Business and Human Rights Sphere from Six Regulatory Areas." Harvard Kennedy School, Working Paper 59, 2010. https://www.hks.harvard.edu/sites/ default/files/centers/mrcbg/programs/cri/files/workingpaper_59_zerk.pdf.

Websites

- The Red Flags Initiative, International Alert and Fafo. https://redflags.info.

EXERCISE 30.2

OPINION WRITING AS A TEACHING TOOL

Christine Bader

During the multifaceted societal tumult that began in 2020 with the COVID-19 pandemic and relentlessly continued with the murder of George Floyd and subsequent racial justice protests, the U.S. presidential election and riot at the U.S. Capitol, and more, I began incorporating opinion writing into my teaching.[38] It seemed willfully ignorant, if not downright negligent, to continue delivering content about human rights without providing tools and space for students to express their opinions about how current events were affecting their lives.

No students were untouched by the pandemic: we were meeting virtually over Zoom, after all. Some of my students were working retail jobs, in which customers and managers were putting them at risk of contracting COVID-19. Many felt the racial justice movement of 2020 deeply, whether because they had experienced discrimination themselves, or had their privilege called out, or were called to participate in protests or become stronger allies. The U.S. presidential election created additional flashpoints and minefields.

I was already a practitioner and advocate for opinion writing, having taken a powerful seminar in 2007 with a social enterprise called The OpEd Project, whose mission is to change who writes history,[39] and penned dozens of op-eds in major publications since then. But before 2020 I had never seen the link to my teaching, and always had more than enough business and human rights content to pack into my syllabi.

Now I see opinion writing as a critical teaching tool, for four primary reasons:

Relationships and classroom dynamics shift when we open space for personal opinions. I taught a three-day intensive course in February 2021, when it was impossible not to acknowledge the massive social upheaval that was still underway. The ways in which business impacts human rights were not academic to my students: they were personal. Inviting their feel-

---

[38]   In February 2021 I taught a virtual three-day intensive course on business and society for Carthage College's Master of Science in Business program; in the spring of 2022 I taught a semester-long seminar, "The Evolving Role of Business and Work," for Linfield University's Master of Science in Business program.

[39]   TheOpEdProject.org.

ings into the open, rather than trying to mask them as dispassionate analysis, enabled us to look at tools like human rights due diligence as a way to structure and strengthen their opinions about business conduct instead of one more historical artifact to memorize.

Our students will need to advocate wherever they go. As an MBA student, I was taught to execute: strategies, financial models, ways to build effective teams. But in the career that followed, I had to advocate: often as a lone voice, to integrate human rights into company policies and practices. Opinion writing isn't just about publishing an op-ed in a newspaper: it's about formulating a timely and effective argument.

This isn't about giving students "voice" – it's about giving them a passcode. Students don't need our permission or supposed wisdom to develop opinions and voice; they need to know how to access the platforms that our generation designed to be exclusive. Yes, they can express their views on social media; but I for one know that my tweets do not reach the tens of millions of readers that my pieces in *The New York Times* and *The Atlantic* have reached – including the business leaders and policymakers who can implement the changes that I call for.

With my students, I share the data on underrepresentation (see below); I walk through a typical op-ed outline (timely news hook, main point, evidence, "to be sure" paragraph that anticipates and refutes counter-arguments, call to action); I have them submit a draft to a peer for feedback, then a final draft to me. These are the assignments where their personalities shine through, much more so than in their reports outlining recommendations to a company's board of directors.

The world needs more diverse voices in leadership and public discourse. In 2011, women wrote just 22 percent of opinion pieces in *The New York Times*, 19 percent in *The Wall Street Journal*, and 24 percent in *The Los Angeles Times*.[40] A 2012 analysis of *The Guardian*, *The Telegraph*, and *The Daily Mail* found that 26 percent of opinion pieces in those U.K. publications were penned by women.[41]

Opinion pages are scoured by television and radio producers looking for guests, book agents and publishers looking for authors, policymakers looking for ideas and public sentiment, and the general public looking for smart analysis. I can personally attest to the fact that opinion pieces can lead to book deals, TED talks, consulting and job opportunities, and eventually positions of real influence: elected offices, board seats, leadership

---

[40] "The Byline Survey Report 2012: Who Narrates the World?", The OpEd Project.
[41] Lisa Evans, Lynn Cherny, and J. Nathan Matias, "Women's Representation in Media: The Best Data on the Subject to Date," *The Guardian*, September 7, 2012.

positions in all sectors – where women and people of color are similarly underrepresented.

As Katie Orenstein, founder of The OpEd Project, says, "The stories we tell determine the world we live in: what wars we fight, what diseases we research." What are we missing when most of our stories are told by white men of privilege?

My students have written op-eds on a wide variety of topics, including arguing for gender pay equity for professional athletes; the right to employment for felons who have served out their sentences; the need for child-care to be considered an essential service; and improving and enforcing the National Football League's Rooney Rule promoting greater diversity in leadership.

To my knowledge, none of my students have yet been published in a major news outlet (though one experimented with sharing his thoughts in LinkedIn posts, receiving such great feedback that he is pursuing a book project). But that's not necessarily the point. After I took my very first seminar with The OpEd Project, I ran home, tapped out my op-ed, sent it off to *The New York Times*... and never heard back. It took a few years for me to publish my first op-ed in a major publication, and a few more years to get my first piece in the *Times*.

But for me the impact of learning opinion writing was much more profound: it was about understanding that my unique expertise matters to the world. My students ask about the risks of speaking up, which accrue unfairly to some more than others. As Orenstein says, "If you say things of consequence; there may be consequences. The alternative is to be inconsequential."

Bibliography

CHAPTER 1 – INTRODUCTION

Baumann-Pauly, Dorothée, and Justine Nolan, eds. *Business and Human Rights: From Principles to Practice*. London: Routledge, 2016.

Bernaz, Nadia. *Business and Human Rights. History, Law and Policy – Bridging the Accountability Gap*. London: Routledge, 2017.

Deva, Surya, and David Birchall, eds. *Research Handbook on Human Rights and Business*. Cheltenham: Edward Elgar Publishing, 2020.

Ewing, Anthony P. "Promoting Business and Human Rights Education: Lessons from Colombia, Ukraine, and Pakistan." *Business and Human Rights Journal* 6, no. 3 (2021): 607–615.

George, Erika, Jena Martin, and Tara Van Ho, "Reckoning: A Dialogue about Racism, AntiRacists, and Business and Human Rights," *Washington International Law Journal* 30 (2021): 171–253.

Orentlicher, Diane F., and Timothy A. Gelatt. "Public Law, Private Actors: The Impact of Human Rights on Business Investors in China." *Northwestern Journal of International Law & Business* 14 (1993–1994): 66–129.

Ramasastry, Anita. "Corporate Social Responsibility versus Business and Human Rights: Bridging the Gap between Responsibility and Accountability." *Journal of Human Rights* 14, no. 2 (2015): 237–259.

Ruggie, John Gerard, Caroline Rees, and Rachel Davis, "Ten Years After: From UN Guiding Principles to Multi-Fiduciary Obligations," *Business and Human Rights Journal* 6, no. 2 (2021): 179–197.

Santoro, Michael A. "Business and Human Rights in Historical Perspective." *Journal of Human Rights* 14, no. 2 (2015): 155–161.

CHAPTER 2 – CORPORATE RESPONSIBILITY

Bernaz, Nadia. *Business and Human Rights. History, Law and Policy – Bridging the Accountability Gap*. London: Routledge, 2017.

Bowen, Howard R. *The Social Responsibilities of the Businessman*. New York: Harper and Row, 1953.

Carroll, Archie B., ed. *Managing Corporate Social Responsibility*. New York: Little, Brown, 1977.

Clapham, Andrew. *Human Rights Obligations of Non-State Actors*. Oxford: Oxford University Press, 2006.

Coase, Ronald. "The Nature of the Firm." *Economica* 4, no. 16 (1937): 386–405.

Davis, Keith. "Can Business Afford to Ignore Corporate Social Responsibilities?" *California Management Review* 2 (1960): 70–76.

Donaldson, Thomas. *Corporations and Morality*. Hoboken, NJ: Prentice Hall, 1982.

Donaldson, Thomas, and Lee E. Preston. "The Stakeholder Theory of the Corporation: Concepts, Evidence, and Implications." *Academy of Management Review* 20, no. 1 (1995): 65–91.

Freeman, Edward. *Strategic Management: A Stakeholder Approach.* Boston, MA: Harper Collins, 1984.

French, Peter A. "The Corporation as a Moral Person." *American Philosophical Quarterly* 16, no. 3 (1979): 207–215.

Friedman, Milton. *Capitalism and Freedom.* Chicago, IL: University of Chicago Press, 1962.

Friedman, Milton. "The Social Responsibility of Business Is to Increase Its Profits." *The New York Times Magazine*, September 13, 1970.

Goodpaster, Kenneth E. "Business Ethics and Stakeholder Analysis." *Business Ethics Quarterly* 1, no. 1 (1991): 52–71.

Goodpaster, Kenneth E. *Conscience and Corporate Culture.* Oxford: Blackwell Publishing, 2007.

Handy, Charles. "What's a Business For?" *Harvard Business Review*, December (2002): 49–55.

Jensen, Michael, and William H. Meckling. "Theory of the Firm: Managerial Behavior, Agency Cost and Ownership Structure." *Journal of Financial Economics* 3, no. 4 (1976): 305–360.

Matten, Dirk, and Andrew Crane. "Corporate Citizenship: Toward an Extended Theoretical Conceptualization." *Academy of Management Review* 30, no. 1 (2005): 166–179.

Matten, Dirk, and Jeremy Moon. "'Implicit' and 'Explicit' CSR: A Conceptual Framework for a Comparative Understanding of Corporate Social Responsibility." *Academy of Management Review* 33, no. 2 (2008): 404–424.

Paine, Lynn S. "Does Ethics Pay?" *Business Ethics Quarterly* 10, no. 1 (2000): 319–330.

Phillips, Robert A., ed. *Stakeholder Theory: Impact and Prospects.* Cheltenham: Edward Elgar, 2011.

Ramasastry, Anita. "Corporate Social Responsibility versus Business and Human Rights: Bridging the Gap between Responsibility and Accountability." *Journal of Human Rights* 14, no. 2 (2015): 237–259.

Scherer, Andreas G., and Guido Palazzo. "Toward a Political Conception of Corporate Responsibility: Business and Society Seen from a Habermasian Perspective." *Academy of Management Review* 32, no. 4 (2007): 1096–1120.

Ulrich, Peter. *Integrative Economic Ethics. Foundations of a Civilized Market Economy.* Cambridge: Cambridge University Press, 2008.

Velasquez, Manuel. "Why Corporations Are Not Morally Responsible for Anything They Do." *Business & Professional Ethics Journal* 2, no. 3 (1983): 1–18.

Vogel, David. *The Market for Virtue. The Potential and Limits of Corporate Social Responsibility.* Washington, DC.: Brookings Institution Press, 2005.

Votaw, Dow. "The Politics of a Changing Corporate Society." *California Management Review* 3, no. 3 (1961): 105–118.

Waddock, Sandra, and Neil Smith. "Relationships: The Real Challenge of Corporate Global Citizenship." *Business and Society Review* 105, no. 1 (2002): 47–62.

Walsh, James P. "Book Review Essay: Taking Stock of Stakeholder Management." *Academy of Management Review* 30, no. 2 (2005): 426–438.

Wettstein, Florian. "CSR and the Debate on Business and Human Rights: Bridging the Great Divide." *Business Ethics Quarterly* 2, no. 4 (2012): 739–770.

Wettstein, Florian. "The History of 'Business and Human Rights' and Its Relationship with 'Corporate Social Responsibility'." In Surya Deva and David Birchall, eds. *Research Handbook on Human Rights and Business*. Cheltenham: Edward Elgar Publishing, 2020, 23–45.

CHAPTER 3 – HUMAN RIGHTS

Baumann-Pauly, Dorothée, and Justine Nolan, eds. *Business and Human Rights: From Principles to Practice*. London: Routledge, 2016.

Clapham, Andrew. *Human Rights Obligations of Non-State Actors*. Oxford: Oxford University Press, 2006.

Henkin, Louis. *The Age of Rights*. New York: Columbia University Press, 1990.

Henkin, Louis. "The Universal Declaration at 50 and the Challenge of Global Markets." *Brooklyn Journal of International Law*, 17–25 (April 1999): 25.

Henkin, Louis, Gerald L. Neuman, Diane F. Orentlicher, and David W. Leebron, eds. *Human Rights*. New York: Foundation Press, 1999.

International Council on Human Rights Policy. *Beyond Voluntarism: Human Rights and the Developing International Legal Obligations of Companies*. Geneva: International Council on Human Rights Policy, 2002.

Ramasastry, Anita. "Corporate Social Responsibility versus Business and Human Rights: Bridging the Gap between Responsibility and Accountability." *Journal of Human Rights* 14, no. 2 (2015): 237–259.

Scheffer, David, and Caroline Kaeb. "The Five Levels of CSR Compliance." *Berkeley Journal of International Law* 29, no. 1 (2019): 334–397.

Shue, Henry. *Basic Rights: Subsistence, Affluence and U.S. Foreign Policy*. Princeton, NJ: Princeton University Press, 1980.

CHAPTER 4 – LABOR RIGHTS

Albertson, Paula Church, and Lance Compa, "Labour Rights and Trade Agreements in the Americas." In Adelle Blackett and Anne Trebilcock, eds. *Research Handbook on Transnational Labour Law*. Northampton, MA: Edward Elgar Press, 2015, 474.

Atleson, James et al., eds. *International Labor Law: Cases and Materials on Workers' Rights in the Global Economy*. St. Paul, MN: Thomson/West, 2008.

Bauer, Joanne. "The Coalition of Immokalee Workers and the Campaign for Fair Food: The Evolution of a Business and Human Rights Campaign." In Dorothée Baumann-Pauly and Justine Nolan, eds. *Business and Human Rights: From Principles to Practice*. London: Routledge, 2016, 175–178.

Cornell, Angela B. "Inter-American Court Recognizes the Elevated Status of Trade Unions, Rejects Standing of Corporations." In *International Labor Rights Case Law*. Boston, MA: Brill, 2017, 29–44.

Cornell, Angela B., and Mark Barenberg, eds. *The Cambridge Handbook of Labor and Democracy*. New York: Cambridge University Press, 2022.

Craig, John D.R., and S. Michael Lynk, eds. *Globalization and the Future of Labour Law*. New York: Cambridge University Press, 2006.

Ebert, Franz Christian, and Martin Oelz. *Bridging the Gap between Labour Rights and Human Rights: The Role of ILO Law in Regional Human Rights Courts*. Geneva: ILO, 2012.

Fenwick, Colin, and Tonia Novitz, eds. *Human Rights at Work: Perspectives on Law and Regulation*. Portland, RI: Hart Publishing, 2010.

Gernignon, Bernard, Alberto Odero, and Horacio Guido. *ILO Principles Concerning the Right to Strike*. Geneva: ILO, 1998.

Gross, James A. ed. *Workers' Rights as Human Rights*. Ithaca, NY: Cornell University Press: 2003.

Hammer, Nikolaus. "International Framework Agreements in the Context of Global Production." In Konstantinos Papadakis, ed. *Cross-Border Social Dialogue and Agreements: An Emerging Global Industrial Relations Framework*. Geneva: International Institute for Labour Studies, 2008.

Locke, Richard M. "We Live in a World of Global Supply Chains," In Dorothée Baumann-Pauly and Justine Nolan, eds. *Business and Human Rights: From Principles to Practice*. London: Routledge, 2016, 299–316.

Ruggie, John Gerard. *Just Business: Multinational Corporations and Human Rights*. New York: W.W. Norton, 2013.

Sahan, Makbule. "The First International Standard on Violence and Harassment in the World of Work," *Business and Human Rights Journal* 5 (2020): 289–295.

CHAPTER 5 – THE UN GUIDING PRINCIPLES ON BUSINESS AND HUMAN RIGHTS

Bernaz, Nadia. *Business and Human Rights. History, Law and Policy – Bridging the Accountability Gap*. London: Routledge, 2017.

de Schutter, Olivier. "Toward a New Treaty on Business and Human Rights." *Business and Human Rights Journal* 1, no. 1 (2016): 41–67.

Deva, Surya, and David Bilchitz, eds. *Human Rights Obligations of Business: Beyond the Corporate Responsibility to Respect?* Cambridge: Cambridge University Press, 2013.

George, Erika. "Racism as a Human Rights Risk: Reconsidering the Corporate 'Responsibility to Respect' Rights." *Business and Human Rights Journal* 6, no. 3 (2021): 576–583.

Newton, Alex. *The Business of Human Rights: Best Practice and the UN Guiding Principles*. Abingdon: Routledge, 2019.

Pitts, Chip. "The United Nations 'Protect, Respect, Remedy' Framework and Guiding Principles." In Dorothée Baumann-Pauly and Justine Nolan, eds. *Business and Human Rights: From Principles to Practice*. London: Routledge, 2016, 51–63.

Ramasastry, Anita. "Advisors or Enablers? Bringing Professional Service Providers into the Guiding Principles Fold." *Business and Human Rights Journal* 6, no. 2 (2021): 293–311.

Rees, Caroline, and Rachel Davis. "Salient Human Rights Issues." In Dorothée Baumann-Pauly and Justine Nolan, eds. *Business and Human Rights: From Principles to Practice*. London: Routledge, 2016, 103–106.

Rodriguez-Garavito, César, ed. *Business and Human Rights: Beyond the End of the Beginning*. Cambridge: Cambridge University Press, 2017.

Ruggie, John Gerard. *Just Business: Multinational Corporations and Human Rights*. New York: W.W. Norton, 2013.

Ruggie, John Gerard. "The Social Construction of the UN Guiding Principles on Business and Human Rights." In Surya Deva and David Birchall, eds. *Research*

Handbook on Human Rights and Business. Cheltenham: Edward Elgar Publishing, 2020, 379–401.

Santoro, Michael A. "Why the United Nations Is Not the Ideal Forum for Business and Human Rights: The UNGPs and the Right to COVID-19 Vaccine Access in the Global South." *Business and Human Rights Journal* 6, no. 2 (2021): 326–335.

Sherman, III, John F. "The Corporate General Counsel Who Respects Human Rights." *Legal Ethics* (2021): 49–72.

Van Ho, Tara. "Business and Human Rights in Transitional Justice: Challenges for Complex Environments." In Surya Deva and David Birchall, eds. *Research Handbook on Human Rights and Business*. Cheltenham: Edward Elgar Publishing, 2020, 379–401.

CHAPTER 6 – RIGHT TO REMEDY

Antkowiak, Thomas M. "Remedial Approaches to Human Rights Violations: The Inter-American Court of Human Rights and Beyond." *Columbia Journal of Transnational Law* 46 (2008): 351–419.

Bhatt, Kinnari, and Erdem Türkelli, Gamze. "OECD National Contact Points as Sites of Effective Remedy: New Expressions of the Role and Rule of Law within Market Globalization?" *Business and Human Rights Journal* 6, no. 3 (July 2021): 423–448.

Bradlow, Daniel. "Private Complainants and International Organizations: A Comparative Study of the Independent Inspection Mechanisms in International Financial Institutions." *Georgetown Journal of International Law* 36 (2005).

Drimmer, Jonathan, and Laplante, Lisa. "The Third Pillar: Remedies, Reparations and the Ruggie Principles." In Jena Martin and Karen E. Bravo, eds. *The Business and Human Rights Landscape: Moving Forward, Looking Back*. Cambridge: Cambridge University Press, 2015.

George, Erika, and Laplante, Lisa. "Access to Remedy: Treaty Talks and the Terms of a New Accountability Accord." In Surya Deva and David Bilchitz, eds. *Building a Treaty on Business and Human Rights: Context and Contours*. Cambridge: Cambridge University Press, 2017, 377–407.

International Commission of Jurists (ICJ). *The Right to a Remedy and to Reparation for Gross Human Rights Violations: A Practitioners Guide*. Geneva: International Commission of Jurists, 2006.

International Federation for Human Rights. *Corporate Accountability for Human Rights Abuses: A Guide for Victims and NGOs on Recourse Mechanisms*. Paris: FIDH, 2016.

Laplante, Lisa J. "Bringing Effective Remedies Home: The Inter-American Human Rights System, Reparations, and the Duty of Prevention," *Netherlands Quarterly of Human Rights* 22, no. 3 (2004): 347–388.

Laplante, Lisa J. "Just Repair." *Cornell International Law Journal* 48 (2015): 513–578.

Laplante, Lisa J. "Human Torts." *Cardozo Law Review* 245 (2017): 251–258.

Lipsett, Lloyd, Daniel Berezowsky, and David Kovick. *Handling and Resolving Local-Level Concerns and Grievances*. London: ICCM, 2019.

McCracken, Kelly. "Commentary on the Basic Principles and Guidelines on the Right to a Remedy and Reparation for Victims of Gross Violations of International Human Rights Law and Serious Violations of International Humanitarian Law," *Revue International de Droit Penal* 76 (2005): 77–79.

McIntyre, Owen and Suresh Nanwani, eds. *The Practice of Independent Accountability Mechanisms: Towards Good Governance in Development Finance.* Boston, MA: Brill/Nijhoff, 2020.

Shelton, Dinah. *Remedies in International Human Rights Law.* London: Oxford University Press, 2006.

Shift Project. *Supporting Effective Factory-Level Grievance Mechanisms With the Better Work Programme.* 2013.

Shift Project. *Remediation, Grievance Mechanisms and the Corporate Responsibility to Respect Human Rights.* 2014.

Skinner, Gwynne. "Beyond Kiobel: Providing Access to Judicial Remedies for Violations of International Human Rights Norms by Transnational Business in a New (Post-Kiobel) World." *Columbia Human Rights Law Review* 46, no. 1 (2014): 158–265.

Wielga, Mark, and James Harrison. "Assessing the Effectiveness of Non-State-Based Grievance Mechanisms in Providing Access to Remedy for Rightsholders: A Case Study of the Roundtable on Sustainable Palm Oil." *Business and Human Rights Journal* 6, no. 1 (February 2021): 67–92.

Wilson, Emma and Blackmore, Emma. *Dispute or Dialogue? Community Perspectives on Company-Led Grievance Mechanisms.* London: Institute for Environment and Development, 2013.

Zerk, Jennifer. *Corporate Liability for Gross Human Rights Abuses: Towards a Fairer and More Effective System of Domestic Law Remedies. A Report Prepared for the Office of the UN High Commissioner for Human Rights.* New York: OHCHR, 2014.

CHAPTER 7 – CORPORATIONS

Bauer, Joanne, and Elizabeth Umlas. *Making Corporations Responsible: The Parallel Tracks of the B Corp Movement and the Business and Human Rights Movement.* Rochester, NY: SSRN, 2016.

Berle, Adolf A., and Gardiner C. Means. *The Modern Corporation and Private Property.* New York: Harcourt, Brace & World, 1932.

Chesters, Anna. "A Brief History of the Body Shop." *The Guardian*, 2011.

Coleman, Thomas S. *Corporate Social Responsibility: Friedman's View.* Chicago, IL: Becker Friedman Institute for Research in Economics, 2013.

Demsetz, Harold. "The Structure of Ownership and the Theory of the Firm," *Journal of Law & Economics* 26, no. 2 (June 1983).

Friedman, Milton. "The Social Responsibility of Business Is to Increase Its Profits." *The New York Times Magazine*, September 13, 1970.

Jarblum, William, and Bernard D. Bollinger, Jr. "Incorporation Issues: Why Delaware?" *American Bankruptcy Institute Journal* 18, no. 8 (October 1999): 6.

Martin, Jena. "Hiding in the Light: The Misuse of Disclosure for Business and Human Rights Issues." *Columbia Journal of Transnational Law* 56 (2018).

McMillan, Lori. "The Business Judgment Rule as an Immunity Doctrine." *William & Mary Business Law Review* 2, no. 2 (April 2013).

Stout, Lynn. *The Shareholder Value Myth: How Putting Shareholders First Harms Investors, Corporations, and the Public.* San Francisco, CA: Berrett-Koehler, 2012.

CHAPTER 8 – HUMAN RIGHTS DUE DILIGENCE

Bueno, Nicolas, and Claire Bright. "Implementing Human Rights Due Diligence Through Corporate Civil Liability." *International and Comparative Law Quarterly* 69 (2020): 789–818.

Martin-Ortega, Olga. "Human Rights Due Diligence for Corporations: From Voluntary Standards to Hard Law at Last?" *Netherlands Quarterly of Human Rights* 31 (2013): 44.

Smit, Lise et al. *Study on Due Diligence Requirements Through the Supply Chain.* Brussels: European Commission, 2020.

Taylor, Mark. "Human Rights Due Diligence in Theory and Practice." In Surya Deva and David Birchall, eds. *Research Handbook on Human Rights and Business.* Cheltenham: Edward Elgar Publishing, 2020, 88–107.

Tobalagba, Anaïs. "Corporate Human Rights Due Diligence and Assessing Risks of Sexual Violence in Large-Scale Mining Operations," *Australian Journal of Human Rights* 26 (2021): 1.

CHAPTER 9 – HUMAN RIGHTS IMPACT ASSESSMENT

Cordes, Kaitlin Y., Sam Szoke-Burke, and Tulika Bansal. "Collaborative and Participatory Approaches to HRIA: The Way Forward?" In Nora Götzmann, ed. *Handbook on Human Rights Impact Assessment.* Northampton, MA: Edward Elgar Publishing, 2019, 66–83.

Costa, Gino. *Comprehensive Review of Minera Yanacocha's Policies Based on the Voluntary Principles of Security and Human Rights.* Denver, CO: Newmont Mining, 2009.

DeWinter-Schmitt, Rebecca, and Kendyl Salcito. "The Need for a Multidisciplinary HRIA team: Learning and Collaboration across Fields of Impact Assessment." In Nora Götzmann, ed. *Handbook on Human Rights Impact Assessment.* Northampton, MA: Edward Elgar Publishing, 2019, 319–335.

Harrison, James. "Human Rights Measurement: Reflections on the Current Practice and Future Potential of Human Rights Impact Assessment.," *Journal of Human Rights Practice* 3, no. 2 (July 2011): 162–187.

Harrison, James. "Establishing a Meaningful Human Rights Due Diligence Process for Corporations: Learning from Experience of Human Rights Impact Assessment." *Impact Assessment and Project Appraisal* 31, no. 2 (June 2013): 107–117.

Hulme, David. "Impact Assessment Methodologies for Microfinance: Theory, Experience and Better Practice." *World Development* 28, no. 1 (2000): 79–98.

Gonzales, Alejandro, Tamar Aryrikyan, and Benjamin Cokelet. *Evaluating the Human Rights Impact of Investment Projects: Background, Best Practices, and Opportunities.* New York: Project Poder, 2014.

Götzmann, Nora. "Introduction to the Handbook on Human Rights Impact Assessment: Principles, Methods and Approaches." In Nora Götzmann, ed. *Handbook on Human Rights Impact Assessment.* Northampton, MA: Edward Elgar Publishing, 2019, 2–27.

Landman, Todd. "Measuring Human Rights: Principle, Practice and Policy." *Human Rights Quarterly* 26, no. 4 (2004): 906–931.

Lipsett, Lloyd, and Mark Wielga. "Kick-Starting Human Rights Due Diligence: The Role of Human Rights Impact Assessment." *Mineral Law Series: Rocky Mountain Mineral Law Foundation*, no. 2 (2016).

MacNaughton, Gilian, and P. Hunt. "Health Impact Assessment: The Contribution of the Right to the Highest Attainable Standard of Health," *Public Health* 123, no. 4 (April 2009): 302–305.

Ortolano, Leonard. *Environmental Regulation and Impact Assessment.* New York: Wiley, 1997.

Raworth, Kate. "Measuring Human Rights." *Ethics & International Affairs* 15, no. 1 (March 2001): 111–131.

Salcito, Kendyl et al. "Assessing Human Rights Impacts in Corporate Development Projects." *Environmental Impact Assessment Review* 42 (September 2013): 39–50.

Walker, Simon. *The Future of Human Rights Impact Assessments of Trade Agreements.* Cambridge: Intersentia, 2009.

CHAPTER 10 – NON-GOVERNMENTAL GRIEVANCE MECHANISMS

Harrison, James and Mark Wielga. "Grievance Mechanisms in Multi-Stakeholder Initiatives: Providing Effective Remedy for Human Rights Violations?" *Business and Human Rights Journal* (2023): 1–23.

Lukas, Karin et al. *Corporate Accountability: The Role and Impact of Non-Judicial Grievance Mechanisms.* Cheltenham: Edward Elgar, 2014.

Platzer, Hans-Wolfgang, and Stefan Rüb. *International Framework Agreements: An Instrument for Enforcing Human Rights.* Berlin: Friedrich-Ebert-Stiftung, 2014.

Wielga, Mark, and James Harrison. "Assessing the Effectiveness of Non-State-Based Grievance Mechanisms in Providing Access to Remedy for Rightsholders: A Case Study of the Roundtable on Sustainable Palm Oil." *Business and Human Rights Journal* 6, no. 1 (February 2021): 67–92.

CHAPTER 11 – MANDATORY HUMAN RIGHTS DUE DILIGENCE

Bueno, Nicolas. "The Swiss Popular Initiative on Responsible Business: From Responsibility to Liability." In Liesbeth Enneking et al., eds. *Accountability, International Business Operations, and the Law.* London: Routledge, 2019, 239–258.

Bueno, Nicolas, and Christine Kaufmann. "The Swiss Human Rights Due Diligence Legislation: Between Law and Politics." *Business and Human Rights Journal* 6, no. 3 (October 2021): 542–549.

Bueno, Nicolas, and Claire Bright. "Implementing Human Rights Due Diligence Through Corporate Civil Liability." *International and Comparative Law Quarterly* 69 (2020): 789–818.

Cossart, Sandra, Jérôme Chaplier, and Tiphaine Beau de Lomenie. "The French Law on Duty of Care: A Historic Step Towards Making Globalization Work for All." *Business and Human Rights Journal* 2, no. 2 (July 2017): 317–323.

Krajewski, Markus, Kristel Tonstad, and Franziska Wohltmann. "Mandatory Human Rights Due Diligence in Germany and Norway: Stepping, or Striding, in the Same Direction?" *Business and Human Rights Journal* 6, no. 2 (2021): 550–558.

Teaching business and human rights*

CHAPTER 12 – JUDICIAL REMEDY

Chambers, Rachel. "Parent Company Direct Liability for Overseas Human Rights Violations: Lessons from the UK Supreme Court." *University of Pennsylvania Journal of International Law* 42, no. 3 (2021): 519.
Chambers, Rachel, and Gerlinde Berger-Walliser. "The Future of International Corporate Human Rights Litigation: A Transatlantic Comparison." *American Journal of Business Law* 58 no. 3 (2021): 579.
Darcy, Shane. "The Potential Role of Criminal Law in a Business and Human Rights Treaty." In Surya Deva and David Bilchitz, eds. *Human Rights Obligations of Business: Beyond the Corporate Responsibility to Respect?* Cambridge: Cambridge University Press, 2013, 439–471.

CHAPTER 13 – THE ALIEN TORT STATUTE

Chambers, Rachel, and Jena Martin. "United States: Potential Paths Forward after the Demise of the Alien Tort Statute." In Ekaterina Aristova and Ugljesa Grusic, eds. *Civil Remedies and Human Rights in Flux: Key Legal Developments in Selected Jurisdictions*. London: Bloomsbury Publishing, 2022, 351–369.
Clapham, Andrew. "The Alien Tort Claims Act in the United States." In Andrew Clapham, ed. *Human Rights Obligations of Non-State Actors*. Oxford: Oxford University Press, 2006, 252–263.
Dodge, William S. "Business and Human Rights Litigation in US Courts Before and After *Kiobel*." *Business and Human Rights* (2016): 244–252.
Ruggie, John. "Kiobel and Corporate Social Responsibility," Harvard Kennedy School (September 4, 2012).
Scheffer, David J. "U.S. Supreme Court Assesses Corporate Complicity in Child Slavery." *Foreign Affairs* (December 9, 2020).
Sherman, III, John F. "*Jesner v. Arab Bank* and the UN Guiding Principles on Business and Human Rights." *The Clarion* 3, no. 1 (2017).
Skinner, Gwynne L. with Rachel Chambers and Sarah McGrath. *Transnational Corporations and Human Rights: Overcoming Barriers to Judicial Remedy*. Cambridge: Cambridge University Press, 2020.
Steinhardt, Ralph G. "Extraterritoriality Post-Kiobel: International and Comparative Legal Perspectives." *Maryland Journal of International Law* 28, no. 1 (2013).
Stephens, Beth. "The Curious History of the Alien Tort Statute." *Notre Dame Law Review* 89 (2014): 1467.
Stephens, Beth. "The Rise and Fall of the Alien Tort Statute." In Surya Deva and David Birchall, eds. *Research Handbook on Human Rights and Business*. Cheltenham: Edward Elgar Publishing, 2020, 46–62.

CHAPTER 14 – COMPLICITY

Bernaz, Nadia. *Business and Human Rights. History, Law and Policy – Bridging the Accountability Gap*. London: Routledge, 2017.
International Commission of Jurists. *Report of the ICJ Expert Legal Panel on Corporate Complicity in International Crimes*. Volumes I, II, III. Geneva: International Commission of Jurists, 2008.

MacKinnon, Rebecca. *Consent of the Networked*. New York: Basic Books, 2012.
Ruggie, John. *Business and Human Rights: Mapping International Standards of Responsibility and Accountability for Corporate Acts*, report of the Special Representative of the Secretary-General on the issue of human rights and transnational corporations and other business enterprises. UN doc. A/HRC/4/035 (February 9, 2007).
Shift Project. *Using Leverage in Business Relationships to Reduce Human Rights Risks*. November 2013.

CHAPTER 15 – THE OECD NATIONAL CONTACT POINT MECHANISM

Buhmann, Karin. "National Contact Points under OECD's Guidelines for Multinational Enterprises: Institutional Diversity Affecting Assessments of the Delivery of Access to Remedy." In Liesbeth Enneking et al., eds. *Accountability, International Business Operations and the Law: Providing Justice for Corporate Human Rights Violations in Global Value Chains*. London: Routledge, 2019.
Macchi, Chiara. "The Role of the OECD National Contact Points in Improving Access to Justice for Victims of Human Rights Violations in the EU Member States." In Maria del Carmen Márquez Carrasco and Inmaculada Vivas Tesón, eds. *La implementación de los Principios Rectores de las Naciones Unidas sobre empresas y los derechos humanos por la Unión Europea y sus Estados miembros*. Madrid: Aranzadi Thomson Reuters, 2017, 145–165.
Mokhiber, Craig. "Subject: The Issue of the Applicability of the Guiding Principles on Business and Human Rights to Minority Shareholders." United Nations Office of the High Commissioner for Human Rights. April 26, 2013.
Nieuwenkamp, Roel. "OECD's Human Rights Grievance Mechanism as a Competitive Advantage." Institute for Human Rights and Business, 4 November 2014.
Ochoa Sanchez, Juan Carlos. "The Roles and Powers of the OECD National Contact Points Regarding Complaints on an Alleged Breach of the OECD Guidelines for Multinational Enterprises by a Transnational Corporation." *Nordic Journal of International Law* 84, no. 1 (February 2015): 89–126.
Ruggie, John G., and Tamaryn Nelson. "Human Rights and the OECD Guidelines for Multinational Enterprises: Normative Innovations and Implementation Challenges." *Brown Journal of World Affairs* 22, no. 1 (2015): 99–127.

CHAPTER 16 – MULTISTAKEHOLDER HUMAN RIGHTS INITIATIVES

Arenas, Daniel, Laura Albareda, and Jennifer Goodman. "Contestation in Multi-Stakeholder Initiatives: Enhancing the Democratic Quality of Transnational Governance." *Business Ethics Quarterly* 30, no. 2 (2020): 169–199.
de Bakker, Frank G. A., Andreas Rasche, and Stefano Ponte. "Multi-Stakeholder Initiatives on Sustainability: A Cross-Disciplinary Review and Research Agenda for Business Ethics." *Business Ethics Quarterly* 29, no. 3 (2019): 343–383.
Bartley, Tim. "Institutional Emergence in an Era of Globalization: The Rise of Transnational Private Regulation of Labor and Environmental Conditions." *American Journal of Sociology* 113, no. 2 (2007): 297–351.

Bartley, Tim. "Transnational Governance as the Layering of Rules: Intersections of Public and Private Standards." *Theoretical Inquiries in Law* 12, no. 2 (2011): 517–542.

Baumann-Pauly, Dorothée, and Lilach Trabelsi. "Complementing Mandatory Human Rights Due Diligence: Using Multi-Stakeholder Initiatives to Define Human Rights Standards." NYU Stern School of Business, January 2021.

Baumann-Pauly, Dorothée, and Justine Nolan. "Mapping the Landscape of Multi-Stakeholder Initiatives – Few MSIs Are Equipped to Address Governance Gaps," NYU Stern Center for Business and Human Rights, July 5, 2017.

Baumann-Pauly, Dorothée, Justine Nolan, Auret Van Heerden, and Michael Samway. "Industry-Specific Multi-Stakeholder Initiatives that Govern Corporate Human Rights Standards: Legitimacy Assessments of the Fair Labor Association and the Global Network Initiative." *Journal of Business Ethics* 143, no. 4 (2017): 771–787.

Baumann-Pauly, Dorothée, Justine Nolan, Sarah Labowitz, and Auret van Heerden. "Setting and Enforcing Industry-Specific Standards for Human Rights: The Role of Multi-Stakeholder Initiatives in Regulating Corporate Conduct." In Dorothée Baumann-Pauly and Justine Nolan, eds. *Business and Human Rights: From Principles to Practice*. London: Routledge, 2016, 170–191.

Koenig-Archibugi, Mathias, and Kate Macdonald. "Accountability-by-Proxy in Transnational Non-State Governance." Governance 26, no. 3 (2013): 499–522.

Mena, Sébastien, and Guido Palazzo. "Input and Output Legitimacy of Multi-Stakeholder Initiatives." *Business Ethics Quarterly* (2012): 527–556.

Moog, Sandra, André Spicer, and Steffen Böhm. "The Politics of Multi-Stakeholder Initiatives: The Crisis of the Forest Stewardship Council." *Journal of Business Ethics* 128, no. 3 (2015): 469–493.

MSI Integrity. *Not Fit-for-Purpose: The Grand Experiment of Multi-Stakeholder Initiatives in Corporate Accountability, Human Rights and Global Governance*. Berkeley, CA: MSI Integrity, 2020.

Soundararajan, Vivek, and Jill A. Brown. "Voluntary Governance Mechanisms in Global Supply Chains: Beyond CSR to a Stakeholder Utility Perspective." *Journal of Business Ethics* 134, no. 1 (2016): 83–102.

Soundararajan, Vivek, Jill A. Brown, and Andrew C. Wicks. "Can Multi-Stakeholder Initiatives Improve Global Supply Chains? Improving Deliberative Capacity with a Stakeholder Orientation." *Business Ethics Quarterly* 29, no. 3 (2019): 385–412. doi:10.1017/beq.2018.38.

Utting, Peter. "Multistakeholder Regulation of Business: Assessing the Pros and Cons." In Rob Van Tulder, Alain Verbeke, and Roger Strange, eds. *International Business and Sustainable Development*. Bingley: Emerald Group Publishing Limited, 2014, 425–446.

CHAPTER 17 – BUSINESS AND HUMAN RIGHTS IN THE INTER-AMERICAN SYSTEM

Cantú Rivera, Humberto. "Towards a Global Framework on Business and Human Rights, Indigenous Peoples, and Their Right to Consultation and Free, Prior, and Informed Consent." In Claire Wright and Alexandra Tomaselli, eds. *The Prior Consultation of Indigenous Peoples in Latin America: Inside the Implementation Gap*. London: Routledge, 2018.

de Schutter, Olivier. *International Human Rights Law: Cases, Materials, Commentary*, 3rd ed. Cambridge: Cambridge University Press, 2019.

Rodarte Berbera, Hayde. "The Pro Personae Principle and Its Application by Mexican Courts." *Queen Mary Human Rights Law R*eview 4, no. 1 (2017): 1–27.

Rodríguez-Piñero, Luis. "The Inter-American System and the UN Declaration on the Rights of Indigenous Peoples: Mutual Reinforcement." In Stephen Allen and Alexandra Xanthaki, eds. *Reflections on the UN Declaration on the Rights of Indigenous Peoples*. Oxford: Hart, 2011.

Shelton, Dinah, and Gould, Ariel. "Positive and Negative Obligations." In Dinah Shelton, ed. *The Oxford Handbook of International Human Rights Law*. Oxford: Oxford University Press, 2013.

CHAPTER 18 – MODERN SLAVERY IN SUPPLY CHAINS

Bales, Kevin. *Understanding Global Slavery*. Berkeley, CA: University of California Press, 2005.

Choudhury, Barnali. "Social Disclosure." *Berkeley Business Law Journal* 13 (2016): 183.

Crane Andrew, Genevieve LeBaron, Jean Allain, and Laya Behbahani. "Governance Gaps in Eradicating Forced Labor: From Global to Domestic Supply Chains." *Regulation and Governance* 13, no. 1 (2019): 86–106.

Datta, Monti Narayan, and Bales, Kevin. "Slavery Is Bad for Business: Analyzing the Impact of Slavery on National Economies." *The Brown Journal of World Affairs* 19, no. 2 (Spring/Summer 2013): 205–223.

LeBaron, Genevieve. *Combatting Modern Slavery: Why Labour Governance Is Failing and What We Can Do About It*. Cambridge: Polity Press, 2020.

Locke, Richard M. *The Promise and Limits of Private Power: Promoting Labor Standards in a Global Economy*. Cambridge: Cambridge University Press, 2013.

Mares, Radu. "Corporate Transparency Laws: A 'Hollow Victory?" *Netherlands Quarterly of Human Rights* 36, no. 3 (July 2018): 189–213.

Nolan, Justine, and Martijn Boersma. *Addressing Modern Slavery*. Sydney: University of New South Wales Press, 2019.

CHAPTER 19 – HUMAN RIGHTS AND THE ENVIRONMENT

Atapattu, Sumudu, Carmen Gonzalez, and Sara L. Seck, eds. *Cambridge Handbook of Environmental Justice and Sustainable Development*. Cambridge: Cambridge University Press, 2021.

Boyd, David. *Rights of Nature: A Legal Revolution That Could Save the World*. Toronto: ECW Press, 2017.

Knox, John. "Policy Brief: Environmental Human Rights Defenders – A Global Crisis" (Universal Rights Group, February 2017).

Seck, Sara L. "Transnational Labour Law and the Environment: Beyond the Bounded Autonomous Worker." *Canadian Journal of Law and Society* 33, no. 2 (2018): 137–157.

Seck, Sara L. "A Relational Analysis of Enterprise Obligations and Carbon Majors for Climate Justice." *Oñati Socio-Legal Series: Climate Justice in the Anthropocene* 11, no. 1 (2021): 254–284.

Velenturf, Anne, and Phil Purnell. "What a Sustainable Circular Economy Would Look Like." *The Conversation*, May 6, 2020.

CHAPTER 20 – LAND RIGHTS

Behrman, Julia, Ruth Meinzen-Dick, and Agnes Quisumbing. *The Gender Implications of Large-Scale Land Deals.* International Food Policy Research Institute Discussion Paper. Washington, DC: International Food Policy Research Institute, 2011.

New Alliance and Grow Africa. *Analytical Framework for Land-Based Investments in African Agriculture.* Johannesburg: New Alliance and Grow Africa, 2015.

Nolte, Kerstin, Wytske Chamberlain, and Markus Giger. *International Land Deals for Agriculture. Fresh Insights from the Land Matrix: Analytical Report II.* Bern: Centre for Development and Environment, 2016.

Royal Institute of Chartered Surveyors and United Nations Global Compact. *Advancing Responsible Business Practices in Land, Construction, Real Estate Use, and Investment.* London: Royal Institute of Chartered Surveyors, 2015.

Vhugen, Darrly. "Responsible Governance of Tenure: A Technical Guide for Investors." *Governance of Tenure Technical Guide No. 7.* Rome: FAO, 2016.

CHAPTER 21 – RIGHTS OF INDIGENOUS PEOPLES

Adamson, Rebecca. *Investors and Indigenous Peoples: Trends in Sustainable and Responsible Investment and Free, Prior, and Informed Consent.* Fredericksburg, VA: First Peoples Worldwide, 2013.

Doyle, Cathal, and Jill Cariño, *Making Free, Prior and Informed Consent a Reality: Indigenous Peoples and the Extractive Sector.* London: Indigenous Peoples Links, Middlesex University and ECCR, 2013.

Kemp, Deanna, and John Owen. "Corporate Readiness and the Human Rights Risks of Applying FPIC in the Global Mining Industry." *Business and Human Rights Journal* 2, no. 1 (January 2017): 163–170.

Lehr, Amy, and Gare Smith. *Implementing a Corporate Free, Prior, and Informed Consent Policy: Benefits and Challenges.* Washington, DC: Foley Hoag, July 2010.

Mitchell, Terry, Courtney Arseneau, Darren Thomas, and Peggy Smith. "Towards an Indigenous-Informed Relational Approach to Free, Prior, and Informed Consent (FPIC)." *The International Indigenous Policy Journal* 10, no. 4 (October 2019).

Mullins, Dan, and Justus Wambayi. *Testing Community Consent.* Nairobi: Oxfam America, 2018.

Salcito, Kendyl. *Indigenous Peoples and the IFC: How Development Finance Can Better Safeguard Indigenous Rights.* Denver, CO: NomoGaia, October 2020.

Salcito, Kendyl. *Missing Peoples: IFC Projects that Did Not Apply PS7.* Denver, CO: NomoGaia May, 2021.

Stamatopoulou, Elsa ed. *Indigenous Peoples' Rights and Unreported Struggles: Conflict and Peace.* New York: Columbia University Institute for the Study of Human Rights, 2017.

CHAPTER 22 – THE RIGHT TO FOOD

Hamerschlag, Kari, Anna Lappé, and Stacy Malkan. *Spinning Food: How Food Industry Front Groups and Covert Communications Are Shaping the Story of Food.* London: Friends of the Earth, 2015.

CHAPTER 23 – THE RIGHT TO WATER

CEO Water Mandate. *Guidance for Companies on Respecting the Human Rights to Water and Sanitation: Bringing a Human Rights Lens to Corporate Water Stewardship.* January 2015.
Hoekstra, Arjen Y. "Water Scarcity Challenges to Business." *Nature Climate Change* 4 (May 2014): 318–320.
Human Rights Watch. *Toxic Tanneries: The Health Repercussions of Bangladesh's Hazaribagh Leather.* New York: Human Rights Watch, 2012.
Kishimoto, Satoko et al. eds., *Our Public Water Future: The Global Experience with Remunicipalisation.* Amsterdam: Transnational Institute, Public Services International Research Unit, Multinationals Observatory, Municipal Services Project, and the European Federation of Public Service Unions, 2015.
Witney, Heather. "Vietnam: Water Pollution and Mining in an Emerging Economy." *Asian-Pacific Law & Policy Journal* 15, no. 1 (2013).

CHAPTER 24 – TECHNOLOGY AND HUMAN RIGHTS

Donahoe, Eileen, and Megan MacDuffee Metzger. "Artificial Intelligence and Human Rights." *Journal of Democracy* 30, no. 2 (April 2019): 115–126.
Hope, Dunstan Allison, Faris Natour, and Farid Baddache. *Applying the Guiding Principles on Business and Human Rights to the ICT Industry.* BSR, September 2012.

CHAPTER 25 – ENGINEERING FOR HUMAN RIGHTS

Balakrishnan, Radhika, James Heintz, and Diane Elson. *Rethinking Economic Policy for Social Justice: The Radical Potential of Human Rights.* Abingdon: Routledge, 2016.
Bauer, Joanne. "Business and Human Rights: A New Approach to Advancing Environmental Justice in the United States." In Shareen Hertel and Kathryn Libal, eds. *Human Rights in the United States: Beyond Exceptionalism.* New York: Cambridge University Press, 2011, 175–196.
Berkey, Becca. "An In-Depth Look at the Coalition of Immokalee Workers." *Journal of Agriculture, Food Systems, and Community Development* 8, no. 1 (2018): 197–199.
Cech, Erin. "Great Problems of Grand Challenges: Problematizing Engineering's Understandings of Its Role in Society." *International Journal of Engineering, Social Justice, and Peace* 1, no. 2: 85–94.
Chacon Hurtado, Davis, Kazem Kazerounian, Shareen Hertel, Jonathan Mellor, Jack Barry, and Tulasi Ravindran. "Engineering for Human Rights: The Theory and Practice of a Human Rights-based Approach to Engineering." Storrs, CT: University of Connecticut, undated manuscript.

Deming, W. Edwards. *Out of the Crisis*. Cambridge, MA: Massachusetts Institute of Technology, Center for Advanced Engineering, 1986.

Goodhart, Michael. *Injustice: Political Theory for the Real World*. Oxford: Oxford University Press, 2018.

Herkert, Joseph R. "Future Directions in Engineering Ethics Research: Microethics, Macroethics and the Role of Professional Societies." *Science and Engineering Ethics* 7, no. 3: 403–414.

Hertel, Shareen. *Tethered Fates: Companies, Communities, and Rights at Stake*. Oxford: Oxford University Press, 2019.

Hertel, Shareen, and Allison MacKay. "Engineering and Human Rights: Teaching across the Divide." *Business and Human Rights Journal* 1, no. 1 (2016): 159–164.

Hoekstra, Arjen Y., and Thomas O. Wiedmann. "Humanity's Unsustainable Environmental Footprint." *Science*, June 6, 2014, issue 6188: 1114–1117.

Layton, Jr. Edwin T. *The Revolt of Engineers: Social Responsibility and the American Engineering Profession*. Baltimore, MD: The Johns Hopkins University Press, 1986.

Leydens, Jon A., and Juan C. Lucena. *Engineering Justice: Transforming Engineering Education and Practice*. 1st edition. Hoboken, NJ: Wiley-IEEE Press.

Melish, Tara J. "Putting 'Human Right' Back into the UN Guiding Principles on Business and Human Rights: Shifting Frames and Embedding Participation Rights". In César Rodríguez-Garavito, ed. *Business and Human Rights: Beyond the End of the Beginning*. New York: Cambridge University Press, 2017, 76–96.

O'Riordan, Timothy, and James Cameron. *Interpreting the Precautionary Principle*. London: Routledge, 2013.

Oosterlaken, E.T. "Taking a Capability Approach to Technology and Its Design: A Philosophical Exploration." Ph.D. diss., TU Delft, 2013.

Reinecke, Juliane, and Jimmy Donaghey. "Towards Worker-Driven Supply Chain Governance: Developing Decent Work Through Democratic Worker Participation." *Journal of Supply Chain Management* 57, no. 2: 14–28.

Sen, Amartya. *Development as Freedom*. Reprint edition. New York: Anchor, 2000.

Smith, Karl A., Sheri D. Sheppard, David W. Johnson, and Roger T. Johnson. "Pedagogies of Engagement: Classroom-Based Practices." *Journal of Engineering Education* 94, no. 1: 87–101.

CHAPTER 26 – FINANCE, INVESTORS, AND HUMAN RIGHTS

Behar, Andrew. *The Shareholder Action Guide: Unleash Your Hidden Powers to Hold Corporations Accountable*. Oakland, CA: Berrett-Koehler Publishers, 2016.

Eccles, Robert G., and Svetlana Klimenko. "The Investor Revolution: Shareholders Are Getting Serious about Sustainability." *Harvard Business Review*. June 2019.

George, Erika. *Incorporating Rights: Strategies to Advance Corporate Accountability*. Oxford: Oxford University Press, 2021.

Mandyck, John. "What if Banks Had to Disclose the Climate Impact of Their Investments?" *Harvard Business Review*. May 20, 2022.

Reinboth, Bettina, and Nikolaj Halkjaer Pedersen. *Why and How Investors Should Act on Human Rights*. London: UN Principles for Responsible Investing, 2020.

Robins, Nick. *The Corporation That Changed the World: How the East India Company Shaped the Modern Corporation*. London: Pluto Press, 2006.

CHAPTER 27 – ACCOUNTING FOR HUMAN RIGHTS

Canning, Mary, Brendan O'Dwyer, and George Georgakopoulos. "Processes of Auditability in Sustainability Assurance: The Case of Materiality Construction." *Accounting and Business Research*, 49, no. 1 (2019): 1–27.

Chapple, Larelle E., and Grace Mui. "Social Audit Failure: Legal Liability of External Auditors." In Mia M. Rahim and Samuel O. Idowu, eds. *Social Audit Regulation: CSR, Sustainability, Ethics and Governance*. New York: Springer, 2015, 281–299.

de Felice, Damiano. "Business and Human Rights Indicators to Measure the Corporate Responsibility to Respect: Challenges and Opportunities." *Human Rights Quarterly* 37 (2015): 511–555.

Etzion, Dror, and Fabrizio Ferraro. "The Role of Analogy in the Institutionalization of Sustainability Reporting." *Organization Science* 21, no. 5 (2010): 1092.

Ford, Jolyon, and Justine Nolan, J. "Regulating Transparency on Human Rights and Modern Slavery in Corporate Supply Chains: The Discrepancy between Human Rights Due Diligence and the Social Audit." *Australian Journal of Human Rights*, 26 (2020): 27–45.

Hess, David. "The Transparency Trap: Non-Financial Disclosure and the Responsibility of Business to Respect Human Rights." *American Business Law Journal* 56, no. 1 (2019): 23.

McPhail, Kenneth, and John Ferguson. "The Past, Present and Future of Accounting for Human Rights." *Accounting, Auditing and Accountability Journal*, 29, no. 4 (2016): 526–541.

Sarfaty, Galit A. "Measuring Corporate Accountability through Global Indicators." In Sally Engle Merry, Kevin E. Davis, and Benedict Kingsbury, eds. *The Quiet Power of Indicators: Measuring Governance, Corruption, and Rule of Law*. Cambridge: Cambridge University Press, 2015, 103–132.

Slacik, Johannes, and Dorothea Greiling. "Coverage of G4-Indicators in GRI-Sustainability Reports by Electric Utilities." *Journal of Public Budgeting, Accounting & Financial Management* 32, no. 3 (2020): 359–378.

CHAPTER 28 – MEGA-SPORTING EVENTS AND HUMAN RIGHTS

Brackenridge, Celia et al. *Child Exploitation and the FIFA World Cup: A Review of Risks and Protective Interventions*. London: Brunel University, 2013.

Chappelet, Jean-Loup, and Brenda Kübler-Mabbott. *The International Olympic Committee and the Olympic System: The Governance of World Sport*. Oxford: Routledge, 2008.

Corrarino, Megan. "'Law Exclusion Zones': Mega-Events as Sites of Procedural and Substantive Human Rights Violations." *Yale Human Rights and Development Law Journal* 17, no. 1 (2014): 182, 189.

Heerdt, Daniela. *Blurred Lines of Responsibility and Accountability: Human Rights Abuses at Mega-Sporting Events*. Cambridge: Intersentia, 2021.

James, Mark, and Guy Osborn. "The Olympics, Transnational Law and Legal Transplants: The International Olympic Committee, Ambush Marketing and Ticket Touting." *Legal Studies* 36, no. 1 (March 2016): 93–110.

Keys, Barbara. "Reframing Human Rights." In Barbara Keys, ed. *The Ideals of Global Sport: From Peace to Human Rights*. Philadelphia, PA: University of Pennsylvania Press, 2019, 109–135.

Ra'ad Al Hussein, Zeid, and Rachel Davis. *Recommendations for an IOC Human Rights Strategy*. Shift, 2020.

Thompson, Dennis F. "Moral Responsibility of Public Officials: The Problem of Many Hands." *The American Political Science Review* 74, no. 4 (December 1980): 905–916.

Worden, Minky. *China's Great Leap: The Beijing Games and Olympian Human Rights Challenges*. New York: Seven Stories Press, 2008.

CHAPTER 29 – TRADE AND HUMAN RIGHTS

AFL-CIO. *Raising Labor Standards Through Trade Preference Programs*. Washington, DC: AFL-CIO, 2020.

Baltzan, Beth. "The Old-School Answer to Global Trade." *Washington Monthly* (April/June 2019).

Baltzan, Beth. "It's Time to Rethink How We Regulate Global Trade." New York: Open Society Foundations, November 2020.

Polaski, Sandra. "Combining Global and Local Forces: The Case of Labor Rights in Cambodia." *World Development* 34, no. 5 (May 2006).

Sutton, Trevor, and Andy Green. "Adieu to Laissez-Faire Trade." *Democracy* (October 2020).

CHAPTER 30 – BUSINESS AND CONFLICT

Ballentine, Karen, and Jake Sherman. *The Political Economy of Armed Conflict: Beyond Greed and Grievance*. Boulder, CO: Lynne Rienner, 2003.

Humphreys, Macartan. "Natural Resources, Conflict, and Conflict Resolution: Uncovering the Mechanisms." *Journal of Conflict Resolution,* 49, no. 4 (August 2005): 508–537.

Nitschke, Heiko, and Kaysie Studdard. "The Legacies of War Economies: Challenges and Options for Peacemaking and Peacebuilding." *International Peacekeeping* 12 (2005): 222–239.

Ruggie, John. "Business and Human Rights: The Evolving International Agenda." *The American Journal of International Law*, 101 no. 4 (2007): 819–840.

Sachs, Jeffrey D., and Andrew M. Warner. "The Curse of Natural Resources." *European Economic Review*, 45 (2001): 827–838.

Thompson, Robert, Anita Ramasastry, and Mark Taylor. "Translating *Unocal*: The Expanding Web of Liability for Business Entities Implicated in International Crimes." *George Washington International Law Review* 40, no. 4 (2009): 841–902.

Zerk, Jennifer. "Extraterritorial Jurisdiction: Lessons for the Business and Human Rights Sphere from Six Regulatory Areas." Harvard Kennedy School, Working Paper 59, 2010.

Index

Voluntary Principles on Security and
    Human Rights (VPs) 133, 224,
    428
Votaw, Dow 17
vulnerable groups 29, 104, 322

war crimes 191

water *see* right to water
water privatization 332, 334, 335
WEF *see* World Economic Forum (WEF)
Wielga, Mark 7, 9
World Bank 132
World Economic Forum (WEF) 373, 374
World Health Organization 332